# BRITISH Motorcycles
## OF THE 1940s AND 1950s

# BRITISH Motorcycles
## OF THE 1940s AND 1950s

**Roy Bacon**

First Published in 1989 by Osprey Publishing,

British Library Catologuing in Publication Data.

Bacon, Roy
    British Motorcycles of the 1940s and 1950s : a
    comprehensive guide to 79 post war marques from
    Aberdale to Zenith.
    1. British motorcycles, to 1983
    1. Title
    629.2'275'0941

This edition published 1993 by The Promotional
Reprint Company Limited exculsively for Bookmart
Limited, Leicester, UK, Reed Editions in Australia,
and Chris Beckett Limited in New Zealand.

ISBN 1 85648 125 5

Reprinted 1993, 1995

Printed in Malaysia.

*Half-title page* **Typical prosaic model and background of a road test
of those times. The 1956 Panther 10/4 was powered by a 9E Villiers
engine.**

*Title page* **Prime Minister Harold Macmillan accompanies President
'Ike' Eisenhower along Fleet Street during his 1959 visit, flanked by
the inevitable Triumph outriders.**

# Contents

# Foreword

There are few people to whom we owe such a debt as we do to Roy Bacon, whom I count a friend since the days, alas, long ago, when we raced together in the early years of 50 cc racing in Britain. That he would rise to be a world authority on classic motorcycles and one of the most prolific – if not *the* most prolific – I had no way of knowing, and as an engineer in the aircraft industry, I doubt if Roy did either!

Roy was one of the first to write about what are now known as 'classics'. His many one-make histories in the Osprey Collector's Library series are an enormously valuable source of information and the books in his 'Restoration' series are invaluable, covering absolutely every aspect of the subject, even colour changes year by year.

This book neatly complements Roy's *British Motorcycles of the 1930s* and *British Motorcycles of the 1960s*. Nearly 80 makes are covered. Some of them are ephemeral and a few scarcely got beyond the proto-type stage. It is almost entirely thanks to Roy that their brief histories will be preserved.

Roy knows the 1950s, as the subtitle 'Austerity to boom' indicates, and he shows a rare understanding of economic forces that shaped – and eventually destroyed – the British industry. As ever, he has written an entertaining book, as well as an instructive one. Enjoy it.

Brian Woolley
TECHNICAL EDITOR
*The Classic Motor Cycle*

*Left* **Near the end of the decade, and a difficult choice between the Goldie the heart desires and the Leader the head and purse dictate**

*Right* **Post-war racing at Scarborough in late 1946, with Allan Jefferies on his Triumph ahead of Denis Parkinson and Roy Evans on Nortons**

# Austerity to boom

Peace came to Europe in May 1945, and by June there was a modest ration of two or three gallons of petrol per month for motorcyclists. Modest indeed, but after years without any private motoring, it was better than nothing, and in those days a restrained throttle hand could easily wring over 100 miles from a gallon of fuel.

Before then, in March, there had been news of the new Triumph range, hints as to the form of the big Vincent-HRD, and a patent for BSA relating to an ohv twin and its valve gear. Later came articles in the magazines on how to get the most from your fuel ration, and on how to persuade reluctant machinery back into life after the long period off the road.

The results of some backroom work appeared with a preview of the Wooler and its flat-four beam engine, but of rather more practical interest

was the announcement, in June, that AJS were about to return to civilian production. A week later the equivalent Matchless models were unveiled and, as the months rolled by, more and more firms introduced their wares.

Some machines were really new, such as the Vincent and Douglas twins, while others simply picked up the reins again after the six long years of war. The latter were either exactly the same as those from the 1939, or the aborted 1940, range, or were the same with the exception of a fresh coat of paint and the addition of the new telescopic front fork design. Rear suspension remained virtually unknown. For most of the industry, it was a case of restarting with black paint in the spray-guns instead of khaki.

Machine prices were high thanks, in part, to the imposition of purchase tax at $33\frac{1}{3}$ per cent. This was to prove the bane of the car and motorcycle industry, until it was replaced by VAT, as its rate was varied by the government to either stimulate or retard the economy as it thought fit. Early post-war writers thought that this tax was temporary, for it had been introduced in April 1940 as a wartime measure. On some goods it had risen to as much as 100 per cent in the darker days of war, and although, in time, it was reduced, it was never to drop to zero.

The early post-war years were a period of continued hardship in Britain; the people had been

drained by their six-year struggle for existence, but faced a battle for economic survival. Rationing of many items continued for some years, and everything was in short supply.

All manufacturers, regardless of product, were exhorted to produce more and more, the phrase 'export or die' being frequently quoted by politicians. The task was not made easy by the acute shortages of many materials and a plethora of wartime controls, which the bureaucrats were reluctant to relinquish.

For all these reasons, it was a time to concentrate on producing the goods, and most firms did this with as few changes as possible. In general, the new designs came from the smaller firms, many of which had been shifted from motorcycles to other work during the war. A considerable number of them never produced complete machines again, for they found that they had viable businesses which could switch to peacetime parts production with little trouble and minimal investment.

The major firms, which had been kept in production, were better placed to continue much as before but, under these conditions, kept innovation to a minimum. Most of their production went for export, and this was to continue for some years. Even in the early 1950s, certain new models were restricted to export markets when first introduced, and later only released at home in a trickle. In 1945 supply was even more restricted, and before being able to buy a new machine, the purchaser had to obtain a 'licence to acquire', which was only issued where an essential need could be shown.

This situation altered only gradually during the 1940s. Worldwide there were many changes as the old British Empire broke up, new nations were formed, and East-West attitudes hardened. Times were austere for most, and rationing and controls remained in Britain as a new socialist government sought to give fair shares to all, nationalize major industries, and to introduce substantial social reforms.

Motorcycling played its traditional role in that period as a means of getting to work, plus giving an occasional outing at the weekend. Despite the bombing, many workers, both office and manual, still lived close to where they worked, often only a few streets away. New towns, high-rise blocks, and longer journeys to work were still a decade away, so for many the daily round included a bus, tram, train or bicycle ride. Few aspired to cars,

and anyway these were restricted in their supply which, for a period, was hedged with covenants on resale.

The motorcycle became a means of easing longer journeys for many. Some had little option if their route did not coincide with public services, while others found it less costly and gradually came to prefer the freedom of their own road. Despite the rationing, which continued until 1950, and the shortages, it always seemed better to ride past the bus queue than stand in it, even in the rain.

Many machines were pre-war types, often repaired with guile and whatever came to hand, for there were few spares available. Exceptions soon became the ex-WD models, for many of these were auctioned off to the trade for resale. Most were given a quick, all-over respray in black, although a few of the avant-garde used maroon, but more likely because it was to hand than for aesthetic reasons.

It was a time for making do, and the reliance of the services on a few models, nearly all fitted with an Amal carburettor and Lucas electrics, was a great help. The same parts could be used on many pre-war models, and were just as effective for those riders lucky enough to obtain a new machine.

The magazines were full of hints and tips on how to repair, renovate, modify and make good, while, in the main, the machines would run with minimal service. Tyres were a major problem, as they were hard to find and none too good when obtained. Most riders learnt to ride on bald ones and to deal with the inevitable punctures.

In time, the situation improved, but the pre-war machine remained a common sight well into the 1950s, as did the ex-WD one. Before then, there were additions to the manufacturers' ranges, most major firms fielding a vertical twin before the end of the 1940s. These differed in many details, but all followed the same outline and all used many parts from the singles of the same marque.

So, whether with one or two cylinders, many models continued in much the same form as they had in the 1930s. The engine remained separate from the gearbox and had a vertically-split crankcase. The barrel was invariably iron, but a few of the more adventurous did turn to light-alloy cylinder heads. Valve gear was generally simple, but over the years the side-valve models were dropped, until only the services, and the AA and

Preparing Bob Ray's Ariel twin with puncture sealant for the 1951 ISDT, in which it was a member of the Trophy winning team

George Buck and Bob Ray about to set off on an ACU observed test through seven countries in seven days, late in 1953, to launch the new Huntmaster

RAC road patrols were using this type.

The electrics featured a magneto and dynamo, with a change to the alternator during the 1950s, but this was by no means universal. Lubrication was normally dry sump, with the oil tank under the saddle and twin pumps in the engine. The carburettor of larger machines was invariably an Amal, and most singles carried their exhaust system on the right.

The chassis was much the same as it was in 1939, with the addition of telescopic forks. Frames were still brazed, using forged lugs and pinned tubes, while rear suspension was slow to catch on. Where offered, it was often in plunger form, with little or no damping, other than that provided by the inherent friction of the system.

Larger machines had a four-speed gearbox, and virtually all used a positive-stop change mechanism. The gear pedal gave an up-for-down movement, in most cases, and it was on the right of the machine, together with the kickstarter. The primary and secondary drives were both on the

Far away in Japan, this Meguro twin followed the copy route, with its BSA lines, and remained in the Kawasaki list into the 1970s

left, as was the rear brake pedal; the first had a pressed-steel or cast-alloy case. Rear chain enclosure was rare.

Wheels had steel rims with wire spokes, and the 19 in. size was by far the most common, except for competition use, where a 21 in. front rim was fitted. A few models did use 20 in. wheels, but none 18 in. Tyres tended to be studded front and rear, except for sports models, which would have a ribbed front. Sections were invariably 3.25 in. front and the same, or 3.50 in., rear on the larger models, and 2.75 or 3.00 in. on the smaller ones. Brakes were offset, single-leading-shoe, drum types in most cases.

Supporting the traditional 350 and 500 cc singles, together with the newer 500 cc twins, were a line of similar, lighter 250 cc singles and many small two-strokes. The former were built on the same lines as the larger models, and some used common parts, but usually they were lighter and cheaper. The latter models were nearly all powered by Villiers engine and gearbox units, which were so numerous that they have a section of the book to themselves. The cycle parts were often minimal, but these models fulfilled their role of basic transport and, while the detail parts often gave trouble and caused annoyance, the machines normally completed their journeys.

By the beginning of the 1950s matters began to improve, with better petrol, fewer restrictions and more machines on the market. Many of the scars of war began to disappear as new buildings rose on bomb sites in the cities, and air-raid shelters in parks and suburbs were filled in or demolished.

Styles began to brighten, and the motorcycle followed suit with such models as the Golden Flash and Thunderbird, which broke away from the traditional black finish. Other colours were less successful, such as the blue used by Tandon but, in time, Barnetts became a pleasant green, James maroon and, of course, the Speed Twin was always in its Amaranth red.

Part of the reason for this was to suit the export market, and it was the American sector that sparked off the gradual increase in vertical-twin capacity. With vast stretches of straight roads, plus a performance and sports market on both coasts, the Americans needed more power, and the easy way to get it was with more 'cubes'. The big Vincent shone in this respect, as did the bigger twins from the major firms.

This process continued through the decade, together with a gradual refining process which, too often, was too slow. Detail changes only became the norm for each year's models, showing

**Typical 1959 scene at the dealers on a Saturday morning with decisions and deals to be made**

the complacency that lay behind the façade of prosperity.

There were new designs, but too few came from the home industry, while those that did were usually under-funded and never really got off the ground. Often, as with the Wooler, the designer tried to do too much at once, combining a new engine, transmission and cycle parts, so was unable to develop any one area completely.

The conservative nature of the buyer was no help, but too many had seen friends burn their fingers on the radical for them to risk their own money. Too often, final development was left to the riders of the initial production machines, and the word soon went round to let someone else buy the new design. Thus, too many would put off purchase for a year or two until the model was

sorted out, and the resultant low level of sales would hold the price too high.

While there may have been little that was innovative and which reached volume production, there were exceptions, such as the LE Velocette and Ariel Leader. Neither was fully sorted when launched, but both were closer than most and near enough to be successful. Thus, they ran on from slightly shaky starts to a reasonable lifespan.

The one really good feature the traditional singles and twins had going for them was that the steady improvements made them reliable. At the same time, the parts that wore out tended to remain the same, so spares were easy to stock and obtain, while problem areas became well known. At club and dealer level, the solutions to problems were passed around, and any modified detail parts could usually be bought or machined by a friend in industry.

**The ACU National Rally finished at Weymouth in 1958, where this mass of machines is parked**

Meanwhile, the world moved on, and other events affected motorcycling. The Korean war, early in the 1950s, caused a worldwide shortage of nickel, so chrome plating was restricted by government decree. Petrol-tank styles changed to suit, and some never went back to the older arrangement of chrome, painted panels and lining, for the new designs were often cheaper.

Later came the Suez crisis and, once more, there was petrol rationing, although it did not last for long and time spent building up stocks in advance proved to be wasted. Prior to the appearance of the coupons, there were queues at the pumps, which were repeated in the 1973 oil crisis, but the affair came and went with little long-term effect, except that petrol never cost under five shillings a gallon again.

At various times during the 1950s, there were booms in clip-on attachments, scooters, mopeds, and bubblecars, but few British firms had any significant investment in these. In the main, the industry kept to its solid, worthy models, which it produced in ever-increasing numbers up to 1959,

after which the numbers began to fall away. Total sales were to rise again in the 1970s, but these were nearly all imports, and sales figures fell again in the following decade.

That final year of the 1950s was a great one for motorcycling, as the sun shone, the economy was buoyant and even motorcycle dealers smiled. Motorcycles and scooters were in demand to beat the traffic jams and parking problems, while the appearance of the Mini and the Japanese had not yet made any impact. The former was to kill off the bubblecar and sidecar market, virtually at a stroke, while the latter were looking for expansion outside their home market to accommodate their enormous production rate.

Soon learners would be restricted to 250 cc machines, and later other measures would further limit the appeal of motorcycling, but that fine summer of 1959 was a good way to end the decade. John Surtees won every 350 and 500 classic, albeit on the Italian MV Agusta, the M1 opened, and the industry thought that good times had come to stay.

It was downhill from then on, but the legacy remained and was resurrected 30 years later with the classic revival.

# Aberdale

The Aberdale company of Edmonton, London, announced its autocycle to readers of *Motor Cycling* in March 1947, but failed to make the pages of its rival, *The Motor Cycle,* which that week produced three issues as one. This was due to the fuel crisis of the times, which closed some magazines and shut many factories, while others only worked a three- or four-day week. Lack of coal was the problem, but as the Aberdale was made at the Bown factory in Wales, this might have given them an edge in supplies.

The machine itself was a typical autocycle, being powered by a Villiers Junior de Luxe engine. This 98 cc, single-speed unit was hung from a simple tubular frame with dropped top tube and no rear suspension. At the front were basic blade girders. Both wheels had small drum brakes and heavy-duty bicycle rims and tyres.

The petrol tank held about $1\frac{1}{2}$ gallons of fuel (16:1 mixture) and fitted into the space formed by the top, down and seat tubes. Below the tank detachable side panels concealed the engine while, aft of these, there were guards for both the cycling and power chains. A toolbox was provided, together with a steel carrier over the rear mudguard. The pedalling gear revolved in the bottom bracket to the rear of the engine.

Equipment included lights, a bulb horn, and a speedometer driven from the front wheel. The controls were simple, with a throttle lever on the right, clutch on the left and inverted levers on each side for the brakes. There was also a catch to hold the clutch out and a decompressor.

All told, it was a smart example of the type and able to run up to around 30 mph, while fuel consumption could be almost 150 mpg, which gave a good range for working journeys. It continued in production as the Aberdale until 1949, but at the end of that year was revised in form and then sold as the Bown, under which name it is described further on page 47.

**The 1947 Aberdale autocycle with Villiers Junior de Luxe engine and very typical of the type**

# ABJ

This make was announced in July 1949, the correct company name being that of its chairman, A.B. Jackson. They were located in Pope Street, Birmingham. Pre-war, they had produced the Raynal autocycle, which was a production version of the 1937 Jones prototype, and they also made bicycles, so they were not strangers to two wheels. As with many other marques, their range was based around Villiers engines and was launched with two 98 cc models.

The machines were very similar in appearance, the first being the Autocycle, powered by a 2F engine, and the second, the Motorcycle, with the 1F. Both had more of a motorcycle than autocycle look, having a simple, rigid loop frame and telescopic front forks. The Autocycle frame had its

ABJ Autocycle of 1950 with 2F engine and pedals, but very similar to the two-speed Motorcycle from the same firm

pedal shaft fitted aft of the engine, and both had a low top tube and a single saddle on a pillar tube, which gave it height adjustment.

The forks had compression and rebound springs in each leg, with an arrangement of cones and split bushes to act as dampers. They were packed with grease and had seals to retain the lubricant. The upper tubes supported a deeply-valanced mudguard. The rear mudguard was a simple blade, but was hinged for easy wheel removal, while its stays acted as a luggage grid. A toolbox was attached to the left side on the Motorcycle, and a rear stand was provided for both.

The wheels had wire spokes and 2.25 × 26 in. tyres, while the hubs contained minute drum brakes, the rear one, at 4 in. diameter, being the larger. Fuel was carried in a $1\frac{1}{2}$ gallon tank mounted on four rubber blocks. The electrics of both models were powered by the flywheel magneto, but the Motorcycle had a rectifier and battery, so it was also equipped with an electric horn.

The controls were all on the bars for the Autocycle, both brakes being operated by inverted levers, but the Motorcycle had a foot pedal on the left for the rear brake. Both machines had a twistgrip and decompressor. They were finished in black with gold lining, although other colours were said to be available as options. These did not materialize and were not mentioned again,

**The ABJ Minor cyclemotor introduced in 1952 with friction drive to the bicycle front tyre**

but the two models continued to be offered up to 1952.

In July of that year they were joined by a cyclemotor, listed as the Auto Minor, and this drove the front wheel by means of a carborundum roller bearing on the tyre. The unit could either be supplied with a special front fork for fitting to any bicycle, or as a complete machine based on a single- or three-speed bicycle.

The two-stroke Auto Minor engine unit was pivoted to the fork so that the drive could be disengaged; its cylinder was on the left of the wheel and was inclined close to the horizontal. Its capacity was 49.9 cc. The iron barrel had an

alloy head, a downdraught Amal carburettor on top, and a drum-shaped silencer below. An over-hung crankshaft with needle-roller big-end was fitted, and the mainshaft extended through the drive roller to the Miller flywheel magneto on the right. This provided both lights and ignition. The petroil mixture was carried in a $\frac{1}{2}$ gallon tank clipped to the fork above the engine.

The cycle that ABJ supplied with this engine had hub brakes, heavy-gauge spokes and oversize tyres, which made it more suitable for its intended use.

At first, the two existing machines and the cyclemotor were listed for 1953, but before the year arrived the range had been reduced to the Auto Minor alone. This continued in production for that year, but then was dropped and the company reverted to making bicycles only.

# AJS & Matchless

As the 1930s moved to their close, the differences between AJS and Matchless models came closer to being limited to badge engineering. The process was delayed by the war, but accelerated after it, so for the purposes of this book the two are considered as one, as indeed they had become when joined together as Associated Motor Cycles, or AMC, in 1937.

It was well known that the machines were built on the same production line, largely with the same parts but, for all that, each marque had its adherents. The firm fostered this attitude with competition riders on both makes and separate advertising in the press, but at club level we all knew that only the badges and, up to 1951, the magneto position distinguished one from the other.

During the war the firm built little other than the 348 cc G3L Matchless model, and post-war continued with this, although the AJS models were announced first. There were two of them:

the 348 cc model 16M and 497 cc model 18, which were almost identical, except for the cylinder bore and, curiously, the run of the exhaust pipe. On the smaller machine it was above the right footrest, but on the larger it ran below.

The engines were typically British in design, with built-up crankshaft, vertically-split crankcase, and timing gear on the right. Both head and barrel were in iron, but the rocker box was in light alloy and had a side cover for tappet adjustment.

Tall pushrod tunnels ran from crankcase to head, and on the AJS the magneto was mounted on a platform ahead of the engine, where it was driven by chain from the exhaust camshaft. This, at least, allowed some access to the dynamo, which was fitted into the engine plates behind the engine and above the gearbox. It was chain driven from the left-hand end of the crankshaft, so its removal meant disturbing the primary chaincase, the seal of which was notorious for leaking. It enclosed the clutch and chain drive to the separate Burman four-speed gearbox with its foot-change.

The engine and gearbox went into a rigid cradle frame, and front suspension was by the Teledraulic forks developed, and used by the G3L, during the war. These had hydraulic damping and a long, smooth action, which gave the owner a comfortable ride. Both wheels had offset hubs with single-leading-shoe brakes and 19 in. rims.

The cycle parts were much as those which had been used by the military, with the oil tank on the right and battery on the left beneath the

First post-war G3L Matchless of 1946, which was based heavily on the wartime model

**Similar 1947 AJS ohv single with conventional construction and fine finish**

saddle. The toolbox was on the right above the upper chainstay, and the machine had Lucas lights and switches. Less usual was the provision of a prop-stand, in addition to the usual rear stand, although not all liked the way it sprang up when the machine's weight came off it.

The finish, which was to a very high standard indeed, was all black with gold lining and very little plating. For a while AMC had owned the Sunbeam firm and, before selling it to BSA, had learned how the famous Sunbeam finish was achieved. They continued to use the techniques for many years after the war, quickly gaining a reputation for producing one of the finest jobs in the industry.

A week after the AJS announcement, the equivalent two Matchless models appeared as the 348 cc G3L and 497 cc G80. They were known as Clubman models, as if to distinguish them from tourers. However, there were only the two of them, so the additional name had little real meaning, other than to remind owners that these were not the army versions.

As expected, the two machines were the same as the AJS models, except for the badges and the magneto position. On the Matchless this was behind the engine, where it took its drive from the inlet camshaft, and thus made the dynamo hopelessly inaccessible. The horn was ahead of the engine, but it was aft on the AJS, as it used the space vacated by the dynamo. The tank lining was silver with a red pin-stripe running through it.

Of interest to devotees of the two marques were two patents noted at the end of 1945. One concerned a system which ensured that the rear wheel would hold its alignment when moved to adjust the chain tension; the other applied to a pivot for a rear suspension fork. The firm had done some work on the latter aspect during the war, and the patent concerned how the fork pivot pin was first fixed to the machine and later lubricated with oil when in use.

In March 1946 the standard machines were joined by competition versions, which were built in small numbers. There were 50 of each marque, this number being split into 30 of the 348 cc size and 20 of the larger model. To identify them, a letter 'C' was added to the model number, for example the 498 cc AJS became the 18C. The actual changes, however, were minimal and based on the works models.

The front wheel gained a 21 in. rim, and the rear one a 4 in.–section tyre, while both had extra-heavy-gauge spokes. Competition tyres and alloy mudguards were fitted, and the silencer was canted upwards to deal with water splashes. The gearing was lowered, the lighting became optional, and the clutch and throttle cables were duplicated. Otherwise, it was all stock, with the unwanted frame lugs being removed to reduce the weight a little.

With production being the key issue, there were few changes to any model range in the 1940s, and AMC's was no exception. There were alterations and improvements to the engine for 1947, but only minor details changed on the cycle side. The most obvious of these on the 348 cc models was the exhaust pipe, which was run under the footrest. It was the same in the following year, although the brake size did increase a little. Another step towards rationalization took place during that year when the crankcase and crankshaft from the 497 cc engine were adopted by the smaller unit to make them common.

There was one new model for 1948, but this was for racing rather than the road. It was the 348 cc 7R with chain-driven overhead camshaft, and was intended for sale to private owners, as well as for use by the works team. The firm was already campaigning the Porcupine twin in the 500 cc class, and the addition of the smaller single allowed them to run in a second class.

The 7R followed the pattern set by the pre-war ohc models as far as the engine was concerned, although it was totally new. It followed the British layout, but its camshaft was driven from a half-speed timing gear by a chain with a Weller blade tensioner. The engine was all alloy with magnesium crankcase halves, and other parts were finished in a gold paint to protect them from corrosion.

The valve gear was fully enclosed, despite the hairpin valve springs, and the magneto was behind the barrel, where it was gear driven. There were twin-gear oil pumps in the timing chest for the dry-sump lubrication system, and the whole motor was very well made and oil-tight.

The gearbox was a close-ratio, racing Burman driven by an exposed chain and dry clutch. Together with the engine, it went into an all-welded duplex frame with pivoted-fork rear suspension controlled by AMC-designed-and-made spring-and-damper units. Teledraulics were used at the front, and at both ends the wheels had massive twin-leading-shoe drum brakes in conical hubs. These were in magnesium alloy and, curiously, spoked into high-tensile steel rims, although light-alloy ones were an option. Sizes were 21 in. front and 20 in. rear.

The fixtures and fittings were to suit road racing, so there was a large wrap-around oil tank with filler on the left. It looked nice, but suffered the snag that stones could be thrown over the tank by the rear tyre and often went down the bellmouth. A sponge block formed a cure.

The light-alloy fuel tank held nearly five gallons, and both tanks were rubber-mounted. There was a dualseat for the rider and passenger, which was

*Left* **A 1951 348 cc Matchless competition springer in action at a Normandy scramble**

*Right* **Fine, traditional Matchless springer in the form of a 1953 G80S with jampots at the rear and the comfortable dualseat**

an improvement over a saddle and pad, but it lacked any hump at the rear. The megaphone fitted at the end of the exhaust pipe was enormous and became a sore point for riders who tried to slipstream the AJS. The 7R was first called the Junior, but within weeks became the Boy Racer, which stuck to it, as did the type code.

The range expanded a good deal for 1949, with both spring frames and twin-cylinder engines making their debut on the road models. Unlike many of their contemporaries, AMC did not bother with the plunger frame at all, but went straight to the pivoted rear fork. Both rigid and sprung models used the same front frame half, the alternative rear sections being bolted in place. The rear end was controlled by the AMC spring-and-damper units, which became known as 'candlesticks'. They were never to be renowned for their stable damping or long life but, as they had clevis fork ends, it was not easy for the average owner to change to a proprietary unit.

The remainder of the rear end was altered to suit the rear suspension, the toolbox being in the rear subframe corner. A separate saddle and pillion pad remained, and the rear mudguard and its supports were amended to suit. There was a centre stand instead of the rear-mounted one,

and the models were identified by the addition of a letter 'S' to the existing codes. They came in both marques and engine sizes to produce the AJS 16MS and 18S, while the Matchless models were the G3LS and G80S.

The rigid models ran on in standard and competition forms, as did the racing 7R, and all the ohv engines had a new iron cylinder head with hairpin valve springs. At the same time the appearance was improved by moving the valve lifter to the rocker box. There were also other detail changes.

The remaining new models for 1949 were the 498 cc twins, which were coded 20 for AJS and G9 for Matchless. The engine used in both was a parallel twin made in the British mould, except for a third, central main bearing. The camshafts were fore and aft with a gear drive to both of them and the dynamo and magneto, which were mounted fore and aft respectively.

The iron barrels and alloy heads were separate, the rocker pedestals being cast integrally with the latter. The rockers were enclosed by alloy covers. Internally, there was a one-piece crankshaft, while twin-gear pumps in the timing case looked after the dry-sump lubrication system. The timing covers bore the marque logo and differed a little

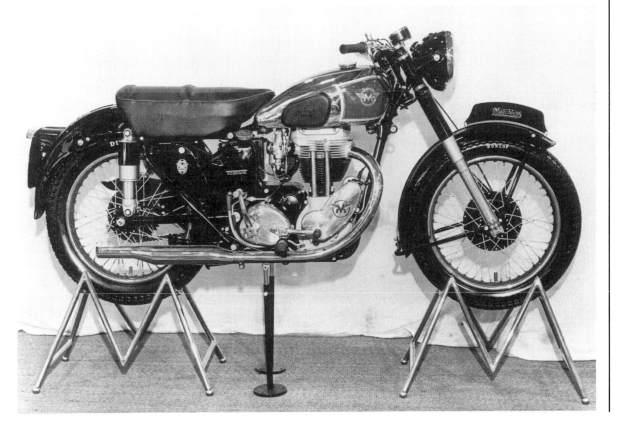

in shape, but otherwise the engines were identical.

The rest of the twin was based on the sprung single, so the gearbox, frame and forks were common, as was a large number of the detail fittings. There were minor differences between the two marques, and the most obvious were the seats and silencers. The Matchless had a dualseat and very neat megaphone-shaped silencers, but the AJS stuck to the saddle, pillion pad and tubular silencers, as on the other models. Both the sprung singles and the twins were produced for export only at first but, after a while, a few reached the home market. They were quickly snapped up and highly regarded as being some of the nicest motorcycles of their day.

There were few changes to the road models for 1950, but more to those on the competition side. For this field, the ohv engines went to an all-alloy top half, while the wheelbase was reduced, as was the tank size, to produce machines that looked much more like proper trials models, rather than converted roadsters. The 7R was given a number of detail engine improvements and a new Burman gearbox. The oil tank was slimmed down so it no longer grilled the rider's legs, and a shorter exhaust pipe with a smaller megaphone fitted.

There was a further expansion of the range for 1951, when competition springer singles appeared as the 16MCS and 18CS, or G3LCS and G80CS. Effectively, they comprised the all-alloy engine in the sprung frame, and were aimed more at scrambles use than trials. At the rear end were much fatter suspension units, which were immediately called 'jampots'. They were an improvement over the slimmer versions, as the internal pressure was lower, but they were still prone to variable damping as the temperature changed. The works riders had to use them, but everyone else changed to something better, and AMC still fitted them to all the sprung road models and the 7R. All the road singles were given an alloy head.

The whole road range ran on with little change until the end of 1955, for it was very much a case of annual detail improvements at AMC. There was a new Burman gearbox for 1952, when the Matchless single finally had its magneto moved ahead of the barrel like the AJS. The distinction between the marques was continued with the timing-case logo, while the shape of the case itself also differed. That year saw the underslung pilot lamp appear, but it was replaced by twin pilots, one on each side of the headlamp shell, for 1954.

Before then 1953 had brought detail alterations

only, plus a dualseat for sprung models, but 1954 saw a full-width front hub and auto-advance for the 497 cc road singles. The rigid competition singles were given an all-welded front frame that year, and the sprung ones a dualseat.

Nearly all models received Monobloc carburettors for 1955, together with another full-width front hub, the fins of which were in a barrel profile. There was a full-width rear hub to match it, a deeper headlamp shell to accommodate the speedometer, auto-advance for the 348 cc road singles, and many detail changes. The exception to the new Monobloc was the scrambles engine, which used the racing TT.

The 7R also progressed during this period, receiving a decrease in valve angle for 1953 and many detail improvements. The frame was new and narrower, while the forks were shorter, and 19 in. wheels were fitted. The front retained its twin-leading-shoe brake, but the rear became a single, which was all that was needed. Many of the cycle parts were also revised, either to suit the new frame or simply as improvements, and this process continued for the following two years.

For 1953 the 7R was joined by the Matchless G45, which was based on the 498 cc twin engine. The twins had previously run in the 1951 Clubman's event, and later that year a hybrid had come fourth in the Manx. This machine used a tuned twin engine in a 7R chassis, and the exercise was continued for 1952, when it won the Manx. This caused some controversy at the time, for works prototypes were not supposed to run in an amateur event, although it was not unheard of. AMC had made the mistake of winning, but all was forgiven when the firm announced that a batch of machines would be built for 1953.

The G45 was only ever built as a Matchless, just as the 7R was only an AJS, and its engine followed the G9 design closely. The camshafts and pistons were changed for racing parts, and alloy barrels were used. The covers were cast in a magnesium alloy, and triple valve springs fitted. On the outside were twin Amal GP carburettors, a racing magneto and a rev-counter. The cycle side was 7R with a minor alteration to suit the two exhaust pipes and megaphones, while the petrol tank carried the 'flying M' transfer.

There were detail alterations only for the next two years, and the machine soon took its place on the racing scene. It was never very successful, and no one seemed able to get the engine to run cleanly, but it filled a gap on the racing circuits.

Despite the packing, there is a Matchless G45 under there en route to Venezuela

It also enabled the AMC rider to run in the 350 and 500 cc classes using machines with common cycle parts, which was a great asset, as Manx owners already knew.

There were major changes to the range for 1956, when all the rigid models were dropped and the road models had a new frame. On the competition side, the trials machines were given a new frame with pivoted-fork rear suspension,

and the scrambles ones were given short-stroke, all-alloy engines.

The model codes continued unchanged, so the road singles were the 16MS and G3LS in 348 cc size, and 18S and G80S in 497 cc capacity. The new frame was still bolted together, much as before, but its appearance was improved with a long, slim oil tank on the right-hand side. This was matched by a combined toolbox and battery

A 1957 AJS model 16MC built for trials use only, hence the small saddle and raised silencer

The Matchless G9 twin in 1958 when it still had the lovely megaphone silencers, which set it off so well

carrier on the left, and there were further panels to tidy the machines up.

The twin had the same set of cycle parts and was joined by a larger version. This was of 593 cc, which gave it more power to meet the demands both at home and abroad, and was listed as the model 30 or G11. For export there had been a 550 cc G9B a year or two earlier, but this was produced as a temporary measure only.

The trials single was only built in 348 cc size and kept its 16MC or G3LC code, which was confusing, as it now had a pivoted-fork frame. This was of all-welded construction and had a shorter wheelbase to suit the model's use. The scrambles machines had new engines and were listed as the 348 cc 16MCS or G3LCS and the 497 cc 18CS or G80CS. Both had shorter strokes than before and integral pushrod tunnels, while the frame had extra bracing and stiffer suspension.

On the racing side, the 7R had revised engine dimensions, so its capacity came out at 349 cc. Together with the G45, it had various alterations to the cycle parts. Both tanks were altered, there were reverse–cone megaphones for the exhaust pipes, clip-on bars and other minor details. In fact, the machines were beginning to struggle a little to keep up, and the following year was to be the last for the G45. It was fitted with Girling rear units for that season, as was the 7R, which was to continue.

All road and competition models were fitted with the AMC gearbox from the middle of 1956, and this was based heavily on the pre-war Norton design, which had its roots in the Sturmey-Archer

*Right* **A special press test on a Matchless 248 cc G2 at Silverstone in 1958, when the model was set the task of covering 250 miles in the same number of minutes, but it took just five more**

box of the early 1930s. This came about because AMC had taken over Norton in 1953 and wished to use more of their own gear-cutting facility.

The gearbox also went into the Norton range, where it was to continue until 1977, and while the change mechanism was new, the gears were unchanged. It was a very good gearbox, but it worked better with its old Norton clutch than the AMC one it carried from then on.

The whole range went over to Girling rear units for 1957, but they remained unusual with clevis fork ends. Otherwise, the range ran on as it was, but there were plenty of changes for 1958. The most obvious of these appeared on the road singles, which went over to alternator electrics with the generator in a neat alloy chaincase. This was used on the twins as well, although they kept their magneto ignition. All road-equipped machines lost the twin pilot lights, which had never been too successful.

Two new 593 cc twins joined the range; both were more sporting, using the scrambles frame and an engine with raised compression ratio. One was the 30CS or G11CS which was, in effect, a street scrambler with siamezed pipes, small tank, fat tyres, alloy mudguards and quickly detachable lights. The second was the 30CSR or G11CSR, the first of the line quickly dubbed 'Coffee Shop Racer'. It used the CS engine, frame and exhaust

with the standard tank, but kept the shorter competition dualseat and special lights.

There was also a new road racing machine to replace the G45; the 496 cc G50. It was simply a bored-out 7R, and no one could understand why it had not been built back in 1948, for AJS had produced both 350 and 500 cc ohc singles in pre-war days. The prototype G50 ran in the 1958 TT, and production versions arrived later in the year. The 7R had a number of changes, which also applied to the G50, and most concerned the engine details. In addition, the racing version of the AMC gearbox was used and there were other minor chassis changes.

**Late AMC single in the form of the 1959 AJS, which used the same cycle parts for both models 16 and 18**

The 1959 Matchless G50, which was derived from the AJS 7R, and a model much to the fore in today's classic racing

During 1958 one more road single appeared to create the beginning of a lighter line. Although the new model, listed as the 248 cc 14 or G2, was always referred to as the lightweight single, this was simply to distinguish it from the other, heavyweight, models, and at 325 lb it hardly qualified.

The engine followed AMC practice in many respects, having a built-up crankshaft with roller big-end, iron barrel, alloy head, hairpin valve springs and access plate on the side of the rocker box. It differed in having the oil for the dry-sump lubrication system carried in a chamber within the vertically-split crankcase, and in having the gearbox strapped to the rear of the case. This gave the appearance of unit construction, but the box was housed in a drum-shaped casting which could be turned to adjust the primary chain. It contained four speeds with foot-change on the right, as usual, and its primary drive was enclosed by an alloy case, which also held the alternator.

The engine unit went in a built-up cradle frame with telescopic front and pivoted-fork rear suspension, the 17 in. wheels having full-width hubs with drum brakes. The mudguards, seat and side panels reflected a touring image or a machine for learners and riding to work.

The road singles had their type numbers changed, but little else for 1959. They became the 16, 18, G3 and G80, for the 'S' suffix was superfluous, as all had rear suspension. The trials models became the 16C and G3C, but with a new frame and small offset hubs to reduce weight, and the smaller scramblers became the 16CS and G3CS for what was to be their final year. The larger versions kept their existing codes and form.

The twins were changed, the 593 cc machines being replaced by 646 cc models, coded as the model 31 or G12. These, and the 498 cc machines, were listed in four versions; standard, de luxe, CS and CSR, with appropriate suffixes to the code. The first two were effectively the same machine with a variation only in finish and were little changed from the 1958 versions. The standard differed from the de luxe, and the others, in having an alternator and coil ignition, while the sports models followed the same format as before.

The 248 cc single ran on as it was for 1959 and was joined by a scrambles version, listed as the 14CS or G2CS. This had a tuned engine, heavier frame and forks, 19 in. wheels, and suitable fittings and fixtures, but it was not successful, as it was too heavy and too expensive.

On the racing front there were detail improvements for both the 7R and G50, which were no longer competitive in the classics. However, they continued to do their job well, giving the private owner reliability and no real troubles so that he could race consistently over the season.

That brought the decade to a close, with AMC ready to move to a duplex frame for 1960 and, later still, to an even closer amalgamation with the Norton name and component parts.

# AJW

Although always on the fringe of the industry, AJW kept going for a long time. The name came from the initials of the founder, Arthur John Wheaton, whose background was publishing. In pre-war days he used various bought-in engines and other parts to create his machines. In the 1930s this could mean anything from a 172 cc Villiers to a big 994 cc JAP or Anzani, and the range size varied from one to a dozen. By 1940 it was down to three.

After the war the firm changed hands, and it was late in 1948 before any more AJW motorcycles appeared. When they did, there were two models. One, the Speed Fox, was a speedway machine fitted with the usual 498 cc JAP engine running on dope and driving the rear wheel via two chains, a countershaft and a clutch. It was built in very small numbers indeed, and the records suggest that only a round dozen were made, some being produced in a grass-track form.

The other model for 1949 was in road trim and listed as the Grey Fox. It was powered by a 494 cc JAP vertical twin, which broke with that firm's tradition of building V-twins. The engine had been seen earlier in 1946 and was a very simple side-valve unit with one-piece alloy head and similar iron block. This last had well-splayed exhaust ports with the single inlet between them, so that the carburettor had to face forward and sat, well warmed, between the exhaust pipes.

The block was mounted on a vertically-split alloy crankcase, which extended downwards to include a sump for the oil. The crankshaft was originally in one piece, running in ball or roller races, and the connecting rods were forged in light alloy. In production, a built-up crankshaft was used. The camshaft ran across the front of the engine with tappets above and, at first, was driven by a chain, which also drove the front-mounted dynamo. This carried the ignition points at one end. Later, a separate duplex chain was used to drive the dynamo, and a vernier adjustment was added to the valve timing. Tappet adjustment remained by shims under the tappet-head caps. A simple cover enclosed the timing gear.

Lubrication was by the ancient dipper system. With this, the connecting-rod caps had hollow extensions which entered the oil near bottom dead centre so that it was forced up and into the plain big-ends. The timing gear was lubricated via pressure valves by the crankcase mist, and the oil simply drained back into the sump once it had done its work.

AJW fitted this very basic engine, together with a four-speed Burman gearbox, into a cradle, which

**The 1949 AJW Grey Fox with its 494 cc JAP vertical twin, side-valve engine**

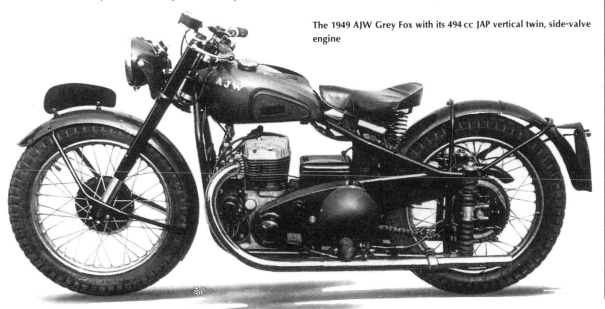

could be readily removed from the machine for maintenance. The main frame had a single top tube, but was duplex elsewhere and fitted with plunger rear suspension. This was undamped, with load and rebound springs to control the light-alloy fork ends, which were bronze bushed and greased to slide on the steel pins. There were gaiters top and bottom to keep the lubricant in and the outside clean.

At the front were Dowty Oleomatic telescopic forks, which relied on air as the suspension medium, backed up by oil to provide hydraulic damping. They were an offshoot of the firm's work in the aviation field, and were both good and bad

news. The good was their progressive action and rise in spring rate as the fork moved. The bad was the dependence on fine-tolerance parts; once wear began to take effect, repairs were difficult.

For the rest, the Grey Fox had a saddle, with the battery below, as there was no oil tank to share the space, a toolbox ahead of it above the gearbox, clean handlebars with inverted levers, and a centre stand. The two exhaust pipes ran to the rear of the machine without change of diameter, but incorporated absorption silencers. The petrol tank had a gutter to keep rainwater away from the rider's legs, a welcome pre-war AJW feature, and was finished in red and blue. Detail fittings were of the period.

In production, the finish was azure blue for the tank, mudguards, rim centres and rear suspension gaiters. The other painted parts were in black,

**AJW Fox Cub with 48 cc FBM engine unit, as imported and sold at the end of the decade**

AJW prototype built in 1952 with JAP 500 cc ohv engine. This was laid down with the gearbox above and mounted in a spine frame

while the wheel-rim edges and other usual items were chrome plated. Virtually all the initial production went for export, but the numbers were limited by the availability of the JAP twin engines. Manufacture continued into 1950, when the engine supply dried up, so there were no more Grey Foxes.

The firm continued with the Speed Fox and also a speedway sidecar outfit, which had its third wheel hinged like a castor, but spring-loaded. This was arranged so that under power, and when cornering, it turned out to run parallel with the front wheel, which would point the same way on the tracks' right-hand bends.

Around 1952 the firm built two prototypes with horizontal, single-cylinder engines fitted into spine frames with pivoted-fork rear and telescopic front suspension. The larger used a 500 cc JAP ohv engine with an Albion gearbox mounted above it. This forced the rear fork pivot to be higher than normal, and it had a bell-crank lever to connect to the suspension springs in monoshock style. The rear of the machine was enclosed by a tail-unit, which carried a pillion pad behind the saddle.

The second machine used a 125 cc JAP two-stroke engine, which was built in unit with its three-speed gearbox. It was of conventional construction with built-up crankshaft, roller big-end, iron barrel and alloy head. Less usual was a cast-iron piston, but the gearbox was straight from the Villiers of the same capacity, Wipac supplied the

ignition and generator unit, and Amal the carburettor.

As on the 500, the engine was positioned with the gearbox above it and in a spine frame with partial rear enclosure, but with just a short dual-seat. Brakes were drum with a 7 in. diameter at the front and 5 in. at the rear, both wheels being fitted with 2.75 × 19 in. tyres.

The 125 was listed as the Fox Cub for 1953, but the other models were to special order only. They included the Speed Fox speedway machine, the sidecar to go with it, and the Flying Fox. This last used a sports 500 cc JAP engine coupled to a four-speed Albion gearbox in a frame with pivoted-fork rear and telescopic front suspension.

Unfortunately for AJW, the supply of JAP engines, except for speedway, dried up, so their production of road models ceased. They left the market for a while, but returned in 1958 with another Fox Cub; this time a 48 cc light motorcycle.

In truth, it was an import with an FBM engine and three-speed gearbox hung from a pressed-steel spine frame with front and rear suspension. However, they continued to produce it into the next decade, when it was joined by others. The company remained in the motorcycle business until 1964.

# Ambassador

This concern was founded by Kaye Don, an ex-Brooklands rider and driver, who sought to expand his business, after the war, to include motorcycles. His company produced well-finished lightweights with Villiers engines and, from around 1954, also imported Zundapp mopeds, motorcycles and scooters.

One of Don's early prototypes, built in 1946, was very different and used the 494 cc vertical-twin JAP engine with side valves and coil ignition. This was fitted into a substantial cradle frame with girder forks at the front, but no rear suspension. The cycle parts were typical of the period, with drum brakes and saddle, but no more was heard of this machine.

The first production model appeared in 1947 and used the Villiers 5E 197 cc engine unit with twin exhausts, side inlet with long inlet tract, and three-speed gearbox. This went into a simple, rigid loop frame with pressed-steel blade girders at the front. There was a saddle, a petrol tank finished in silver with black and red lining and John Bull kneegrips, and Dunlop tyres. A bulb horn gave notice of approach, and the lighting was direct.

This first machine was listed as the Series I, becoming the Series II for 1948. Logically, it was the Series III for 1949, but of particular importance was a change to a 6E engine with single exhaust pipe. It continued for 1950, but with battery lighting, and was joined by two more models fitted with the 6E engine.

The first of the new machines was the Series IV, but this was better known as the Popular and was, in effect, the Series III from the previous year with its direct lighting. The second was the Series V, which differed from the others in being fitted with MP telescopic front forks in place of the girders. It became known as the Embassy in 1951, when the Series II became the Courier. Together with the Popular, they ran on much as before.

They were joined by the Supreme, still with the same 6E engine unit, but this had plunger rear suspension in addition to the telescopic forks and battery lighting, so it was the top model of the range. To enhance this, the finish was in grey for all painted parts plus the battery and footrest rubbers, while the petroil tank was chrome plated with lined grey panels.

There were only three models for 1952, as the Courier was dropped, but the range was expanded again for 1953. Of the existing models, the Supreme was fitted with larger 6 in. brakes and smaller 18 in. wheels, plus a deeper, valanced front mudguard. New was the Self Starter version, which was a Supreme with a Lucas starter motor tucked in under the front of the tank. The motor drove the engine by belt, so a large cover appeared on the right to enclose it, while two large batteries were hung in pannier boxes on each side of the rear wheel. The power needed to recharge them, and cope with all the extra weight, must have nearly exhausted the poor little engine.

If the Self Starter was tiring to the engine, the second new model put an almost impossible strain on it, for this was the Sidecar machine. For this, the firm hung a single-seat sports sidecar on to their Embassy machine, which was fitted with special Webb girders, and sold it as a complete outfit only. The gearing was lowered to suit, and the battery lighting retained, while the sidecar came complete with hood and screen.

During 1953 the range experienced a change in engine type, from the 6E to the very similar 8E. For the Supreme this was a short-lived alteration, as it was amended again for 1954, when it was fitted with the 224 cc 1H engine with its four-speed gearbox. At the same time, it was given a new frame with pivoted-fork rear suspension and dualseat. The Embassy took over its role, receiving the plunger frame, and the Popular was fitted with telescopic forks.

All the models continued for 1955, the Embassy being given the option of a four-speed gearbox, and there was one new machine. This was the Envoy, which continued with the 197 cc 8E engine and three-speed gearbox, but in the pivoted-fork frame with dualseat.

*Above right* **Ambassador prototype of 1946, with the 494 cc JAP vertical twin side-valve engine in rather dated cycle parts**

*Right* **A batch of early Ambassador models in 1947, when they still used the pre-war-style 5E Villiers engine**

*Right* **The Ambassador Sidecar model, with its girder forks, was only sold as a complete outfit and gave the 8E engine a hard time**

**Ambassador Supreme of 1953 with plunger frame and Villiers 8E engine**

The range was reduced to three models for 1956, the Envoy and Supreme being joined by a new version of the Popular. This used the 147 cc Villiers 30C engine with three-speed gearbox, which were fitted into the pivoted-fork frame. It was finished in a rather more basic manner than the other models, so some parts did not blend together very well, but it offered basic transport.

Effectively, there was a fourth model for 1956, as the Envoy was also offered with the 9E engine

and four-speed gearbox instead of the 8E. Of the range, it continued alone into 1957, when it was listed with only the 9E engine, but with a choice of three or four speeds. At the same time, the Popular switched to the 148 cc 31C engine, again with a choice as to the number of gears, and the Supreme to the 246 cc 2H engine. This had the word 'Single' added to its name.

The 1957 range was completed with the Supreme Twin model, which was fitted with the

249 cc Villiers 2T twin engine unit in place of the 2H. All the models had full-width, light-alloy hubs. These contained 6 in. drum brakes for all models, except the Popular, which had to manage with 5 in. versions.

The entire range ran on for 1958 with little change, the Popular and Envoy continuing to be offered with a choice of gearbox. The Supreme remained on offer as a Single or a Twin, but to this selection could be added the Statesman model. This used the 174 cc Villiers 2L engine, again with a choice of three or four speeds, so it slotted in between the other two singles.

This did not last for long as, for 1959, the 148 cc model was dropped and the 174 cc one took its name to become the Popular. The Envoy continued, but only for the first few months of the year, and the two Supreme models were also dropped. In their place came the Super S, which had the 249 cc 2T engine and a new, more enclosed, style. This was all the rage towards the end of the decade, and Ambassador followed the trend with a rear enclosure that ran from the seat nose to the rear number plate, but which kept the wheel in view. To go with it, there was a well-valanced front mudguard and 17 in. wheels with 7 in., full-width hubs.

In April 1959 the Envoy was replaced by the Three Star Special, which was similar to the Super S, but fitted with the 9E engine offering a choice of three or four speeds. The rear panels had a trio of stars to decorate each side, while the front mudguard enclosed even more of the wheel. The style was enhanced by a pressing over the bars and controls to conceal the cables, and there was a grab handle to the rear of the dualseat. An option of a rear chaincase was listed. The finish was in Tartan red and black.

All three models ran on for 1960, when the Super S was fitted with the front mudguard from the Three Star. However, in 1962, Kaye Don retired and the make was taken over by DMW, who continued to produce the marque for a few years only.

The Super S Ambassador of 1959 with its Villiers 2T twin engine, some rear enclosure and full-width hub

# Ariel

Ariel built one of their overhead-valve singles for the services during the war and, afterwards, simply continued with this in civilian guise. They added four more singles to expand the range and completed it with their unique Square Four model.

The wartime single became the 346 cc NG, which differed from the others in having the service frame with extra ground clearance, derived from the pre-war competition one. Except for this feature, and minor details such as mudguard valancing, the five singles were very similar. However, one, the 598 cc VB, had a side-valve engine.

Those with ohv were the NG already mentioned, plus the larger 499 cc VG, both of which were listed as de luxe models. The two capacities were then duplicated as the sporting Red Hunter models, coded NH and VH respectively. These had improved internals and a larger carburettor, so they were able to breathe more easily and produce more power. Their finish was also brighter, with red tank panels and wheel-rim centres, as in pre-war days.

The single-cylinder engine design dated from 1926, when Val Page had laid down its basic form. It replaced a truly elderly layout, and with the magneto being moved behind the cylinder in the following year, it assumed the shape it was to keep for over 30 years.

The engine was simple, sturdy and very tough indeed. It was laid out in traditional British form, with a built-up crankshaft, bearings to support it, and a vertically-split alloy crankcase. The timing gear was the simplest, with two spur pinions and followers to move the tappets or pushrods. The camshaft drove the mag-dyno and the oil pump for the dry-sump system, a cover being fitted to conceal both drive and pump.

Both head and barrel were cast in iron for side- and overhead-valve engines, with the former having a tappet chest with lid to enclose the valves. The ohv engine had stud fixings for the barrel and separate bolts to hold the head to it. The pushrod tubes ran up to the underside of the head from the crankcase, and each rocker had its own alloy box, which fitted on top of the head.

All the ohv models were said to be available with twin-port heads and either standard or upswept exhaust systems. It was also stated that a request for either, or both, features could delay delivery, so there can be few who asked for them at a time when new machines were in such demand. In all cases, the single-cylinder engine drove a four-speed Burman gearbox with foot-change. The primary drive was housed within a sleek, polished alloy chaincase, which had an outer space for the clutch. Consequently, this ran dry under its own domed cover.

The engine and gearbox went into a rigid frame with a duplex arrangement beneath them and single tubes for the main section. The front suspension remained as girders, although the firm was known to have a fully-developed telescopic fork. This was promised as soon as production would permit it.

The remainder of the cycle parts were pre-war in form and laid out in a traditional manner. Thus, the oil tank and battery were under the saddle, to right and left, while the toolbox was between the right-side chainstays. The mudguards varied, valanced, flared examples being provided for the de luxe VG and side-valve models, and more sporting ones for the smaller de luxe and Red Hunter machines.

In pre-war style, there was an instrument panel set in the top of the petrol tank, front and rear stands, and single-leading-shoe brakes in wheels with offset hubs and 19 or 20 in. rims. The headlamp was hung on the top of the fork girder and carried the light switch and ammeter, while the front number plate was in a style common to the Ariel marque.

The final machine in the range was the 995 cc Square Four, which was virtually unchanged from its 1939 form. It retained its then unique engine layout, but in other respects was much as the singles, having a rigid frame, girder forks and Burman four-speed gearbox. The one obvious change from pre-war days was the fitting of tubular silencers in place of the Brooklands cans, although this style was to be seen on the VB, possibly to use up stocks.

The four-cylinder engine had first appeared in its 1-litre, ohv form for 1937, but its origins could

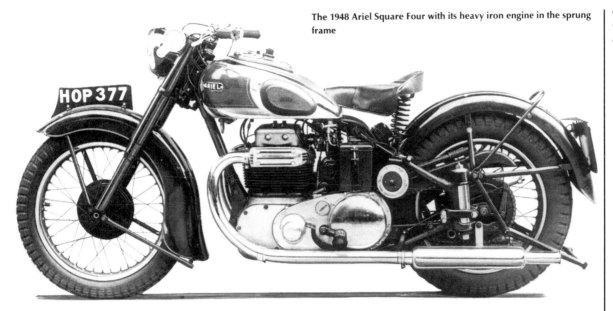

The 1948 Ariel Square Four with its heavy iron engine in the sprung frame

be traced back to 1931, when it was of 500 cc, but had an overhead camshaft. The larger engine was built much in the traditional British style with vertical crankcase joint, but inside it there were two crankshafts.

Each crankshaft was a one-piece forging, to which a central flywheel was bolted, and these were offset so that they could overlap, allowing the distance between the shaft centres to be kept to a minimum. The two crankshafts were coupled by large spur gears mounted on their left-hand ends within an alloy case, from the outside of which a chain took the drive to the gearbox. Connecting rods with split big-ends were used, and the four pistons moved in a very heavy, cast-iron block.

A one-piece, cast-iron head carried the valves in two vertical rows, and on top was an alloy rocker box. This was in the form of an open tray with a lid, the rockers being mounted in two lines. Incorporated into the box was the induction passage. This ran forward from a Solex carburettor to the centre of the box, from where it was directed down into the head and four inlet tracts. The exhaust ports ran out to the sides of the head casting, and to each was bolted a finned manifold, the pipe curling down from its forward end.

In the lower half of the engine, the camshaft was positioned high up in the crankcase, between the cylinders. It operated a line of tappets and pushrods, and was driven by chain from the crankshaft. This chain also drove the rear-mounted electrics and had a Weller tensioner to keep it under control. The twin-plunger oil pump

was driven from the camshaft nut. A special twin-spark magneto, which ran at engine speed, not only had the dynamo mounted on its back, but also drove a distributor via skew gears.

When this range was announced, in July 1945, there was mention of another multi, the telescopic front forks, and the unusual plunger-type rear suspension, which had been devised by Frank Anstey in 1939. The new model was a twin, which was to take some time to reach production, but the other items were soon in use.

In the middle of 1946 details of a patent relating to saddles were released. In the new design, the usual springs were dispensed with. They were replaced by a single, central, telescopic spring unit, which could include a hydraulic damper if required. The support this gave could be varied by changing either the spring or the top fixing position.

No more was heard of this, but two weeks later came news of the telescopic front forks. These were essentially simple with external springs between the seal holder and the bottom crown, while inside there was oil for the hydraulic damping. Initially, the new forks were used on the Square Four and the two Red Hunter models, and with them there was a new front hub with a knock-out spindle. The front brake was also revised with a wedge adjuster at the shoe fulcrum, as had been used at the rear wheel since pre-war times.

When the 1947 programme was announced, all the models had telescopic forks and the modified front wheel, and all, in theory, became available

33

with the special Ariel rear suspension. In practice, production was limited, so most examples went to the Four and the sports singles, export requirements taking priority.

The rear suspension was the same as in 1939, with plungers incorporated into the frame. Each had a very short, pivoted arm, which carried the wheel spindle at one end, was attached to the plunger slider in the middle, and was pivoted on a link at the front. This link was nearly vertical and ran down to a pivot on the frame's lower chainstay.

The effect of the linkage was that the wheel spindle moved in an arc about the gearbox sprocket, which kept the chain tension constant. It did this, however, at the expense of restricted wheel movement and the addition of several pivot points, all of which had to be kept well greased. If this was not done, they soon wore and put an even greater strain on the wheel spindle, as it alone kept the two sides working as one and the wheel itself upright. There was no damping, other than that provided by the friction of the pivots and sliders, so not all riders were totally convinced that the system was worth having at all.

At the time, many solo riders preferred a rigid frame, rather than undamped plunger suspension, for a good saddle gave just as comfortable a ride. Where a sidecar was attached, this applied to an even greater extent, and most outfits of the day had rigid frames and often girder forks as well. It was to be some time before the traditional sidecar driver was to consider any change in suspension systems as desirable, even though the option may have been taken from him.

One of the magazines ran a test with a Red Hunter and sidecar, using girders and telescopics. The result was a preference for the latter, although the fixed, solo trail did make the steering heavier. However, the traditional owner would have none of it and muttered about rigidity and feel.

The range had remained the same with six models, but the existence of the twin was now well known, a photograph appearing in the press late in 1946. It finally made its debut for 1948 and appeared as two models, the KG being the deluxe one and the KH the Red Hunter version. Both had a 499 cc vertical twin engine with overhead valves.

They were nearly identical, with many common parts, and the engines differed only in compression ratio, carburettor size and degree of polish to the cylinder head. Construction was conventional with vertically-split crankcase containing the one-piece, forged crankshaft with central bolted flywheel.

The mains were plain timing and roller drive, while the big-ends were plain shells in light-alloy rods. The camshafts ran high in the crankcase, to front and rear, and had a chain drive from the crankshaft. Each cam had a tappet above it, running in a guide. These, and the pushrods, were placed at the four corners of the cast-iron cylinder block.

Above the block was a cast-iron, one-piece head with integral rocker boxes, each pair of which had a single alloy cover held by one bolt. An Amal carburettor was bolted to the rear of the head, and twin pipes and silencers to the front. The inlet camshaft drove a long, vertical shaft, which ran down to the duplex-gear oil pump of the dry-sump lubrication system. Its drive sprocket had a gear fitted behind it, which drove a rear-mounted magneto. A similar arrangement on the exhaust camshaft drove the dynamo, which was clamped to the front of the crankcase.

For the rest, the twins were as the singles, having a four-speed gearbox driven by a dry clutch and a chain within a polished alloy case. The frame was amended a trifle to clear the dynamo, and the models were offered as rigid or with the rear-link suspension as an option. At the front there were telescopic forks and a 20 in. wheel for the Red Hunter, while the de luxe kept to the 19 in. size. The finish of both matched that of the singles.

These all continued with no significant change, as did the Square Four, and it was the latter that had the only real alterations for 1949. These were made in an attempt to reduce the very considerable weight, and this was done by switching to an all-alloy engine. While doing this, the manufacturers replaced the magneto by coil ignition with a special dynamo and skew-gear-driven points housing and distributor.

The result was considered by many to be the most handsome Squariel of all, with its chrome tank with red panels and matching wheel rims. The rear link suspension continued to be listed as an option, but few machines were built without it, and they continued to be supplied with a very comfortable saddle and pillion pad.

The suspension gave a very civilized ride, for the machine was fast for its era and accelerated well. The handling was adequate for most owners, although it would weave on rough roads if

Competition 1952 Ariel VCH model with an all-alloy engine in a rigid frame and with an odd exhaust-pipe run

pressed, but few who bought the model did this, preferring to use the acceleration to get back to their cruising speed.

For 1950 there was one new model in the form of the competition Hunter VCH, which could be supplied in trials or scrambles specification. Both presented the owner with a racing magneto and alloy mudguards, but no lights. The engine was all-alloy with the pushrod tunnels cast into the barrel. The internal specification, gearing and tyres were to suit the intended use, and the rigid frame was special with a shorter wheelbase. No rear suspension was offered, but there were telescopics at the front and standard hubs.

The rest of the range had detail alterations only, but the Square Four and the twins had their speedometers moved to the fork bridge where they were easier to read. All road models had a new top crown for 1951, which did this job, but the NG and VG models were no longer listed. The tank-top instrument panels were no more, although the Four and the twins still had an oil gauge set in the tank, and there were many detail changes.

The de luxe twin was no longer listed in 1952, but there was a new single in the form of the all-alloy VHA, which used the cycle parts from the other singles and either the rigid frame or the link

Ariel 499 cc vertical twin in 1950, when it was still built to KG or KH specification

Nice line of Ariel models at the 1950 New York motorcycle show, with the new, all-alloy Square Four at the front

suspension. There was also a new Burman gearbox for all models and an alloy head for the side-valve VB engine.

There were two more models for 1953, plus detail changes and a dualseat option for the ohv singles. One of the new machines was the KHA, which was an alloy-engine version of the twin with the dualseat option and a Wedgwood blue finish. The last was also used that year by the Four and Hunter singles and twins. The second model was another version of the Square Four, which became the Mark II, while the original continued as the Mark I.

The new model had a new cylinder head with four separate exhaust pipes, which became the main distinguishing feature. Inside, there was a gear-type oil pump and other improvements, but on the cycle side the two machines used common parts.

During the year, the firm tried Earles leading-link front forks on various models, with a view to putting them into production. They reached the catalogue, but then a combination of technical problems and the tragic death of Les Graham, who died in the TT when riding an MV with Earles forks, caused them to drop the idea. At the same time, their general manager also died. His successor, Ken Whistance, decided to keep to telescopics and to pursue other ideas.

The end of the 1953 season saw the Mark I Square Four, alloy KHA twin, alloy VHA single and competition VCH dropped from the range. This left the NH, VH and VB singles, the KH twin and

the Mark II 4G, to which another four models were added.

The smallest of these was a 198 cc ohv single, which revived a pre-war Ariel name, the Colt, and was listed as the LH. It owed a good deal to the BSA company, which had owned Ariel since 1944, and their Bantam and C11G designs. The result was a very simple engine, with alternator electrics and coil ignition, which drove a separate four-speed gearbox. The pressed-steel primary chain-case was a typical BSA design, having a row of small fixing screws, and the cycle parts showed their Small Heath lines as well.

There was telescopic front and plunger rear suspension, oil tank and battery beneath the dual-seat, and offset hubs with drum brakes, the rear brake being from a Bantam. It added up to a neat workaday machine, but was effectively a C11G reduced to fit in the 200 cc class.

At the other end of the scale was the 647 cc ohv twin FH, also known as the Huntmaster, which simply used the BSA Golden Flash engine with the minimum of changes to disguise the fact. No mention of the matter appeared in the press of the time. To help the model along, it had a new frame with pivoted-fork rear suspension.

This was also used by the smaller twin and ohv singles, and had duplex downtubes and single top and seat tubes to form a full cradle. Unlike others in the industry, the rear fork arms were built up from pressings welded together, which was an indication of the direction in which the Val Page design team was heading.

The Ariel all-alloy VHA was only built for 1953 and is seen here in the sprung frame

To suit the new frame there were new cycle parts and a dualseat fitted as standard. The finish became deep claret, as the blue had not been to the taste of many, but the Four and the VB went to black and the Colt to Brunswick green. The two black models also retained the link suspension, while it remained an option for the side-valve machine. The Four was given an SU carburettor in place of its earlier Solex instrument. As well as the new frame, the VH also gained an alloy cylinder head and an iron barrel with integral pushrod tunnels. The KH twin switched to an alloy head which, as on the all-alloy engine, had the rocker chambers formed differently. Each had its own cap.

The other two new models were both for competition, the HT having a rigid frame with saddle for trials, and the HS a pivoted-fork frame and dualseat for scrambles. Both had the all-alloy 499 cc engine, but with different internals, and cycle parts to suit their purpose.

After this major redesign, it was no surprise that little was altered for 1955 when the Monobloc carburettor was the most noticeable change. It went on to all the road singles and twins, plus the HT, but not the HS or 4G. The VB finally made it into the pivoted-fork frame, but the rigid one remained available for the diehards, who saw both the frame and side-valve engine as the only way to go.

The four-pipe Ariel Square Four, of 1953, hitched to a sporting sidecar to make a fast road outfit

There was a headlamp cowl for all road models in 1956, and full-width, light-alloy hubs front and rear for all singles and twins, except the Colt in either case, but only for the front of the Square Four. That model did receive the benefit of a much larger oil tank, which extended down behind the gearbox, so the toolbox had to be moved. It was mounted on the left, which can hardly have been helpful to sidecar owners, but at least they could pack their gear in the chair.

Of the singles, the NH finally received an alloy head and iron barrel to match the VH, and the VB was no longer listed with the rigid frame. The HS had its oil tank moved to the left to make way for a massive air filter, and also went over to a Monobloc. The HT was altered more drastically to a new frame with pivoted-fork rear suspension, but designed to retain the short trials wheelbase. In this form it became the HT5.

For 1957 it was joined by the smaller HT3 with an all-alloy, 346 cc engine, but otherwise this model was as the 499 cc one. The road models, except the Colt, were given a deeper valanced front mudguard, and there was a one-bolt tank for all except the Four. At the end of the season, the KH Ariel twin was dropped, for the firm were close to some major changes of direction.

There was no immediate sign of these when the 1958 range was announced with no alterations, but the firm had been working and planning for some time on a new future. They made

a major decision to design a new radical machine for the next decade, using modern production techniques to reduce costs and keep quality high. Initial market research indicated that a 250 cc twin two-stroke was the engine type to use, but not much else. Engineering sense dictated the use of pressings, mouldings and die-castings as much as possible, while the trend of the time lent towards enclosure.

So Val Page set to work, and the result was announced in July 1958 as the Ariel Leader. It was a sensation, for it not only used the suggested engine, but had a pressed-steel frame with full enclosure, legshields and windscreen, as for a scooter, but on motorcycle-size wire-spoke wheels.

The engine capacity was 247 cc and its two parallel cylinders were inclined well forward and cast in iron. Each had an alloy head with its plug inclined forward. The cylinders went into a single, massive, lower-half casting. This combined the crankcase, inner primary case and gearbox as one, but with space between the two major units.

The full-disc crankshafts went in from each side to be joined in the centre with a keyed taper joint, and the chambers were sealed with a door on each side. The alternator was on the right and the points, plus an external flywheel, were on the left, outboard of the primary drive. The gearbox was a four-speed Burman, and the final drive remained on the left within a chaincase.

*Left* **The Earles leading-link front forks tried out during 1953, but which never went into production and seen here on a KH twin**

*Right* **Basic Ariel single in the form of a 346 cc NH during a 1953 road test, when it demonstrated the tough nature of the type**

*Right* **The Ariel Colt, which owed much to the BSA C11G, but had a 198 cc engine**

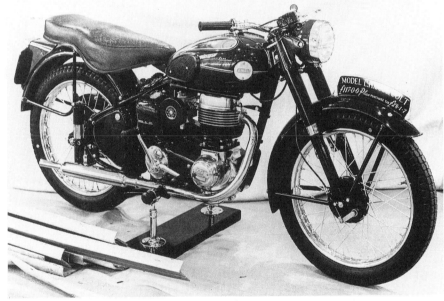

The engine unit was hung from the main frame beam, which was large enough to contain the box-shaped petroil tank. The beam was extended down behind the gearbox to support both the box and the rear fork, and swept up at the front for the headstock. The front suspension was by trailing links, the units and arms being concealed within the fork pressings. There was no top crown as such, so the handlebars were simply clamped to the top of the column. Both wheels had light-alloy, full-width hubs with 6 in. brakes, 16 in. rims and whitewall tyres.

The mechanics of the Leader were then hung with its clothes. A dummy tank, with parcel compartment, went on top of the main frame beam and extended back to form the seat base. The seat itself was hinged and beneath it were the tools and battery. The sides of the machine, beneath the dummy tank, were enclosed by panels and to the rear of these there was a hinged section to blend with the seat base.

At the front there were legshields, which blended into the side panels and continued up to form the base for the windscreen. There was an instrument panel behind it and a cowl for the headlight in front. The front wheel had its own well valanced mudguard, and there was an internal one at the back. A pressing on the bars concealed the pivots and cables.

The machine was conceived to have extras, which included panniers, indicators, clock and many more, rather in the scooter vein. They were available when the machine went on sale and combined with it to make the whole operation very successful. There were minor criticisms, but the machine ran well enough for 1958 and was received favourably by press and public.

Thus encouraged, Ariel decided on the major step of terminating their entire four-stroke range, which caused consternation among enthusiasts for the marque. The first to go was the venerable VB at the beginning of 1959, followed by the competition HT and HS models within a month or two. The remaining Colt, two Hunters, Huntmaster and Square Four went in August that year, although the 650 twin did survive into 1960 as the Cyclone for the USA.

This left the Leader, which was unchanged for 1959, but for 1960 it was joined by the Arrow. This was a sports version, which dispensed with

The scrambles HS model of 1954, on show at Earls Court and under close scrutiny

Traditional Ariel single, in pivoted-fork frame, having its finishing touches applied for the late 1954 show at Earls Court

The 1955 Ariel 598 cc VB hitched to a double-adult Watsonian Maxstoke sidecar, and thus carrying out its traditional role

Ariel Leader 247 cc twin-cylinder two-stroke with all its enclosure and forward-looking engineering

most of the enclosure, but kept the basic engine unit, frame beam and forks. To this was added a dummy tank, rear mudguard and revised seat and other details. The hubs were in cast iron, as the alloy ones had shown signs of cracking in a few cases. The machine was an instant success.

Later on, in the 1960s, were to come the Golden Arrow and the smaller 200 cc version, but in 1965 the parent group decided to stop production in a declining market. It was a tragic decision, for the formula could easily have been developed over many years, but it was not to be.

Val Page had other ideas for the Leader, including a 700 cc four-stroke tourer with in-line, four-cylinder engine laid down with the heads pointing to the left – just as the BMW K series of 1983. Sadly, the parent group did not share his vision and let it all fall apart.

# BAC

These were the initials of the Bond Aircraft and Engineering Company, which launched a three-wheeler and a light motorcycle in the late 1940s, both rather unusual in design and appearance. Manufacture was taken over by Ellis of Leeds at the end of 1950, and BAC moved on to a pair of lightweight motorcycles that owed nothing to the earlier design.

The BAC models were given the name Lilliput and really were machines in miniature, but in proportion. The engines used were either the 99 cc Villiers 1F with its two-speed gearbox, or the 125 cc JAP with three speeds.

The cycle parts were common and included a single-tube loop frame, which was rigid at the rear and had light telescopic front forks. The tyre size was 2.00 × 20 in., which matched the machine, and the rider was provided with a saddle. The lighting was direct, so the horn was a bulb type, although an electric one was listed as an option. The smaller model weighed in at 89 lb.

The 125 was only offered for 1951, partly because supplies of the JAP engine were not very reliable, but the smaller machine was built for 1952 as well. For that year, it was joined by a new model with rather odd styling. This was the Gazelle scooter with a 122 cc Villiers 10D engine.

The machine was laid out much as any other scooter, with twin frame tubes running down from the headstock and then back to the rear wheel. They were joined under the engine by a box that acted as a silencer, the gases being led out of the ends of the tubes which, thus, became tail pipes. The engine was mounted just ahead of the rear wheel with the saddle above it.

The petrol tank was behind the seat, immediately above the rear mudguard, and the oddest feature was the protective grille round the engine.

This comprised a number of wide steel bars, each of which ran across in front of the engine and back on each side. Their purpose was to keep the rider's clothing away from the hot cylinder without restricting the airflow to it, but they did little for the appearance.

There were telescopic forks at the front, 4.00 × 8 in. tyres on pressed-steel wheels, drum brakes and a typical scooter apron. The lighting was direct, and there was a bulb horn and a speedometer.

At the end of 1952, the 122 cc Gazelle was joined by a model powered by the 1F engine. Otherwise, it was the same, and both were given a triangular toolbox bolted to the rear of the apron and a new seat. This sat on four small springs and was based on a pillion pad with the addition of a little backrest for the rider.

In addition to the new model, BAC also offered a light sidecar, the body of which was fashioned in aluminium sheet. It used the same wheel as the motorcycle, so one spare could replace any in the event of a puncture. However, it seems unlikely that there were many customers who believed in 122 cc sidecar outfits.

The solos also failed to make much of an impact, and by May 1953 the Gazelle had been taken over by Projects and Developments of Blackburn. They moved the fuel tank forward under the seat, and over the hot engine, to leave room for a rear carrier or even a pillion seat. This was optimistically being suggested for the 99 cc version, but sanity must have returned, for no more was heard of the machines at all.

The BAC Gazelle scooter, for 1952, with its 10D Villiers engine and odd enclosing 'cage'

# Bantamoto

This was one of the many cycle attachments that came on to the market around 1949 or 1950 and stayed there for a few years until the true moped appeared. They were intended to take the effort out of cycling, which they did, and for a few years were a common sight. All could be attached, in some way, to a standard bicycle, so if all else failed, they could be pedalled home for repair.

The Bantamoto was produced by the Cyc-Auto firm in Acton, West London, and was attached to the cycle on the left side of the rear wheel, which it drove via a train of gears. The engine was a two-stroke with vertical cylinder and featured an alloy head and barrel, plus rotary-valve induction via a sleeve driven by the inboard end of the crankshaft.

Less modern was the deflector-top piston, while the crankshaft was pressed-up with bobweights and a roller big-end. A Wipac Bantamag rather appropriately went on the left-hand end of the crankshaft to provide ignition. The exhaust and silencer ran from the rear of the cylinder, with the Amal carburettor beneath it and feeding into a cast passage in the crankcase, which led to the rotary valve.

There were three stages of gear pairs from the crankshaft to the wheel to give an overall reduction of 26:1. The first two stages were by normal spur gears, but the third pinion drove an internally-toothed gear ring attached to the rear wheel.

The whole unit was mounted on a spindle which attached to the wheel spindle with a clip and to the lower chainstay with a rubber insulator. Clever design allowed the engine to slide out of mesh if necessary. Lubrication was by oil in the gear case and petroil in a small, separate tank.

It was a neat unit, and the positive drive was preferred by some to the more usual friction-roller on to a tyre. Controls were simply the throttle and decompressor. Running costs were minimal.

The unit came on to the market in 1951 and was offered for two years, but was dropped in favour of Cyc-Auto's more usual range.

**The Bantamoto cyclemotor unit, introduced for 1951, had a gear-train drive to the rear wheel and remote petroil tank**

# Bikotor

This was a short-lived cycle attachment that came and went in 1951. It was designed to drive the rear wheel by friction roller, and had a 47 cc two-stroke engine of all-alloy construction to keep the weight to a minimum.

The engine's cylinder was to the right of the wheel and upright, but inclined back a little. It was cast in one with the crankcase, having hard chrome plating on the bore and a simple alloy head to close it and carry the plug and decompressor. The overhung crankshaft was unusual in being a Meehanite iron casting that was fitted into a second casting. This, in turn, was spigoted into the crankcase. The connecting rod was in light alloy, as was the piston, although this was of the deflector type.

The drive roller went on the centre of the mainshaft, which had the flywheel magneto on the left-hand end. Above and ahead of the engine, a fuel tank was tucked in behind the cycle saddle and fed an automatic carburettor with a ported, cylindrical throttle and a mushroom control valve. Even the silencer was in light alloy and comprised three castings with a cylinder held between two detachable end caps, the top one of which had a flange for bolting to the exhaust port.

It was all very ingenious and well made, but it failed to catch on, so it was another of which no more was heard.

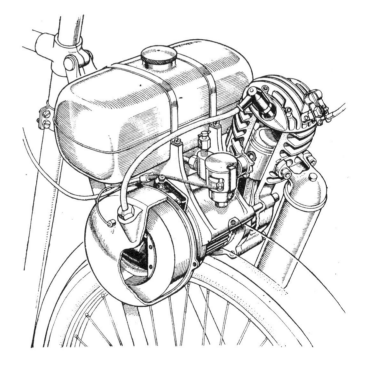

The Bikotor clip-on unit of 1951, which drove the rear wheel with a friction roller and was of all-alloy construction

# Bond

Lawrence Bond is best known for the small three-wheeled cars that carry his name, but for 1950 he introduced a motorcycle that was just as unusual.

The new machine was a lightweight using the 99 cc Villiers 1F engine with two-speed gearbox and weighing in at 90 lb, thanks to its unusual all-alloy frame. This was based on a large, tapered, oval-section tube, which ran back from the headstock. It was rolled from sheet and lap riveted on its underside. At the rear, it was cut away for the wheel, but stiffened by a massive rear mudguard that enclosed more than half the wheel

The engine was hung from the main beam and flanked by footboards with deep legshields. The fuel tank went into the beam, which was closed at the front by an aluminium casting with a plain-bearing steering head. The forks on the prototype were steel strips, but these were replaced by tubes for the initial production run. The front mudguard was as large as the rear, so it also concealed much of the wheel.

There was no springing front or rear, so comfort was provided by the saddle and the 4.00 × 16 in. balloon tyres, which were fitted on split rims. The alloy hubs had 4 in. drum brakes, the rear one being heel operated. The lighting was direct, and there was a bulb horn and a rear carrier.

By July 1950 the forks had become telescopic, and for 1951 the machine was joined by a de luxe version powered by a 125 cc JAP engine with three-speed gearbox. The prototype of this had been seen a year earlier, but no doubt supply problems had kept it back.

Previously, the machines had been built by the Bond Aircraft and Engineering Company in Lancashire, but for 1951 manufacture was taken over by Ellis of Leeds, while the original firm produced another small range under the BAC label (see page 42). The new firm incorporated some minor frame changes, but the models continued with their unique frames and a light-blue polychromatic paint finish.

Both machines ran on in this form for a year or two, but early in 1953 the smaller was dropped and production of the 125 ceased later that year. However, it was not the end of the name, for the three-wheeler continued in production, and the company moved to a new factory in Preston, Lancashire, returning to two wheels in 1958.

The new machine was a scooter listed as the P1 and powered by a fan-cooled, 148 cc Villiers 31C engine with three-speed gearbox and Siba electric start. This sat ahead of the rear wheel and acted as a frame member, with twin tubes running over it and back to support rider, fuel tank and rear fork pivot. At the front, these tubes joined the main frame tube, which ran down from the headstock and back to the engine plates.

**The Bond motorcycle with its monocoque main beam and well enclosed wheels in 1951**

*Above* **First of the P-series Bond scooters at the start of the 1959 Isle of Man rally, with a TWN behind it**

*Below* **Bond P4 of 1960 with 197 cc 9E Villiers engine and improved lines at the front**

At the front there was a single, pivoted leading arm to carry the wheel on a stub axle. The same was used at the rear, with a single suspension unit to control each. The wheels had split rims and carried 4.00 × 10 in. tyres, and rear chain tension was set with an eccentric at the pivot point.

On to this framework went a plastic body in scooter style, with apron, footboard and rear enclosure with detachable side panels. There was a dualseat on top of the body, which was hinged to give access to the top of the engine and the

fuel tank. This last was also moulded in plastic and incorporated the rear mudguard mounting.

At the front there was a good sized mudguard, which turned with the wheel and had a flat nose for a bumper bar. The headlamp was mounted in the apron, which had a fascia panel moulded to its top with a lockable container below and to the rear.

Styling was provided by a two-tone finish and the side panels, which were extended back to form small fins in the American car style. Two small portholes on each side highlighted this aspect.

In the middle of the year the P1 was joined by the P2, which used the 197 cc Villiers 9E engine, still with fan cooling and Siba electric start, but with a four-speed gearbox. Otherwise, it was the same, and both continued for 1959.

They were replaced by the P3 and P4, which retained the same engines, but had them set lower in the frame. The bodywork was amended by dispensing with the rear panels and hinging the entire rear section from the tail. When raised, it gave exceptional access to the mechanics; it was held down by a single knurled nut.

At the front the mudguard became part of the apron moulding and assumed a lighter and more graceful line. Behind the apron, the fascia and stowage compartment remained and, despite the changes, the lines were really much as before, including the twin fins and portholes. The two models continued in production until 1962, after which the firm concentrated on its three-wheelers only.

# Bown

This name from the 1920s was revived in 1950 and used by the firm for its autocycle, which replaced the Aberdale they had built previously (see page 13). The machine itself was revised to use the single-speed, 99 cc Villiers 2F engine, rather than the earlier Junior de Luxe, and the frame was modified to suit its mountings.

The new frame was of the cradle type with duplex downtubes, but otherwise the model was cast in the normal autocycle mould. The petroil tank was fitted between the upper and lower downtubes, there was extensive panelling beneath the tank to shield the engine, and pedals were fitted.

Pressed-steel blade girder front forks were provided for the rigid frame, and there was a saddle, rear carrier and rear stand. The lighting was direct and the finish in maroon with gold lining, which gave the machine a smart appearance. It was listed as the Auto Roadster.

For 1951 the autocycle was joined by a small motorcycle, powered by the Villiers 1F engine with two-speed gearbox. This went into a neat cradle frame with duplex downtubes and tubular forks, which retained girder links, spring and movement. There was a saddle, a tubular toolbox

The tank may say Aberdale, but this is the model which became the 1950 Bown autocycle with the 2F Villiers engine

Bown 99 cc motorcycle with the two-speed 1F engine in a nice duplex frame, but still with girder forks

clipped to the seat tube, and the same maroon finish. Two versions were offered, either with direct lighting as standard or with a battery in the de luxe form.

In the middle of 1952 a further model was added to the range as the Tourist Trophy, which used the 122 cc Villiers 10D engine with three-speed gearbox. The cycle parts were much as for the smaller model, but telescopic front forks were fitted and the toolbox was repositioned to clear the carburettor. The finish remained maroon, but with blue-grey tank panels. The model continued the Welsh firm's reputation for well made, sturdy machines.

All four models continued as they were for 1953 and 1954, but in the latter year production ceased. Two years later the firm returned to the market with a moped powered by a 47.6 cc Sachs engine with two-speed gearbox. This went into a pressed-steel and tubular rigid frame with trailing-link front forks and moped styling. The next year it was given plunger rear suspension, but then faded from the scene.

# Bradshaw

The name of Granville Bradshaw runs like a thread through the history of the British motorcycle industry, from as far back as 1913 when he designed a flat-twin for ABC. However, he became better known for the machine that appeared just after World War 1. This had a transverse flat-twin engine, unit four-speed gearbox and leaf springs for front and rear suspension.

It was highly innovative, but also very costly to produce, so its price soon cut the extensive waiting lists. Then the early models showed some weaknesses. These were mainly in the valve gear, but by the time they were eradicated, the firm building them was running down motorcycle production and returning to its aviation roots.

Bradshaw's name was next involved with the idea of oil-cooled engines, and his 350 cc single was used by the Dot company in the mid-1920s. From there, he went to P & M to design the 250 cc V-twin Panthette with its unit construction and forged-steel frame backbone. This, too, was not a success, due to a combination of high price and some technical problems.

In 1939 another Bradshaw design exercise appeared in the form of rear suspension for the big Panther models. As on the ABC, and for the Panthette valve gear, he used leaf springs rather than coils, a pair on each side supporting a vertical tube to which the wheel was attached. All was fine until a spring broke on test, making the machine nearly uncontrollable. As a result of this, together with the complicated design, the cost and the outbreak of war, it was dropped.

Around the same time, he also designed an in-line twin with overhead valves and a complex primary drive. Because the crankshafts ran across the machine, the original used a chain wrapped around the sprockets so that they ran in opposite directions. This proved weak and was replaced by helical gears, which were noisy and consumed power, so the project was dropped.

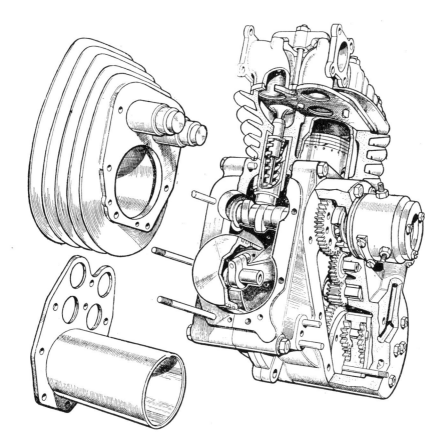

**The Bradshaw Bumble-bee 100 cc V-twin engine schemed out for 1946 and very compact**

After the war another Bradshaw engine appeared in the form of a 100 cc V-twin with side valves. What might have been prosaic to others, except for the small size, was less so to Granville. The engine was very compact, the valve gear being fully enclosed, and inside were some ingenious features.

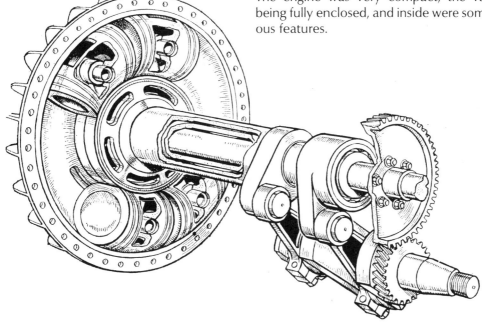

Bradshaw Omega engine of 1955 with its oscillating and double-ended pistons, toroidal cylinder and shaft links

One was the liner for each alloy cylinder, which had a flat plate brazed to it that included the valve seats. The liner was only a push fit in its finned muff, which was partly machined away in the bore to allow oil to circulate and assist the cooling. The oil pump was a gear type, driven from the gear train that drove the single, central camshaft. This, in turn, drove an unusual contact breaker and distributor with auto-advance for the coil ignition, but with rollers and contacts in place of the usual points.

Finally, late in 1955, came the Omega engine, which was of a rotary form, ingenious and most unusual. It was difficult to see how it worked at all, but the design was intended to reduce the inertial loadings of the conventional layout.

The design was based on an annular cylinder, formed from two light-alloy castings bolted together. Within these was formed a toroidal chamber, which can be likened to an inner tube or an O-ring, being a ring with a round cross-section.

For the Omega, the working surface was hard chrome plated and within it were four double-ended pistons with rings at each end and a shape to match the toroid. Each opposing pair was joined by a cross-link, and each of these was bolted to one of two concentric shafts. These each had a short arm at the other end, with a connecting rod to join that to a 180-degree, two-throw crankshaft.

As this turned, the links caused the pistons to move some 30 degrees back and forth, so the space between the opposing crowns varied. If this was not enough, the entire cylinder also rotated at half crankshaft speed and was driven from this by helical gears. In its sides were cut inlet and exhaust ports, and the single sparking plug was screwed into the side. Lubrication was by petroil, with a separate system for the crankshaft, and cooling was by fins on the toroid and enclosure to guide the air.

The Omega was the final fling of a man whose ideas were always clever and innovative, but who sadly failed to understand the commercial needs of the business. His designs were novel, but invariably costly and seldom trouble-free, so his long involvement with the industry made news and kept everyone intrigued, rather than producing machines for riding. Without such men, the world would be the poorer.

# Britax

This accessory firm moved into the motorcycle field late in 1949 with a 48 cc Ducati Cucciolo engine unit with two-speed gearbox, which they imported. As in its Italian homeland, the engine, the name of which meant 'little pup', was sold as a bicycle attachment, and it was very successful with over a quarter million sold worldwide.

The engine unit was unusual in a number of ways; for a start it was a four-stroke in a two-stroke class. Next were the overhead valves, which were opened by pull-rods moved by rockers at the camshaft. Then there was the two-speed gearbox, which had a preselector control and an all-metal clutch.

Engine construction was actually simple, the crankcase being a major part of the engine and gearbox; the left side formed a lid. Oil for all bearings was carried in the sump. The head and barrel were cast as one in alloy, with inserts for the valves and a sleeve for the piston.

The crankshaft drove the camshaft, which was combined with the input gear shaft. The output shaft carried a gear on the right-hand end, outside the case, and this meshed with an internal gear attached to the right-hand pedal crank. A small sprocket took the drive to the rear wheel, and the whole assembly was clamped to the cycle bottom bracket. The left-hand pedal was also special and acted as the gearchange lever to give either gear or neutral after being positioned appropriately, and the clutch worked.

Britax simply sold the engine unit at first, and owners soon realised that, if they had a three-speed rear hub, they were blessed with a total of six ratios. In addition, the cycle freewheel allowed the engine to tick over on descents, although this meant that there was no engine braking.

In the middle of 1953 the firm moved on to a complete machine, using Royal Enfield bicycle and motorcycle parts. The main frame had a dropped top tube and was constructed of heavy-

gauge tubing in bicycle style. However, the front forks were blade girders with rubber-band suspension and came from the 125 cc motorcycle. The wheels were cycle size, but had 4 in. drum brakes, and the mudguards were heavier than usual. A saddle, rear carrier and fuel tank completed the package, which had direct lighting and a bulb horn. The model was given the name Monarch, but this was soon dispensed with and it became known as the Britax or Cucciolo.

It ran on without change and was joined for 1955 by two further models, one a scooter and the other a road racer. Both had 20 in. wheels and retained the Ducati engine unit, rigid frame and girder forks.

The Scooterette was enclosed with mainly flat panels and had a vast front mudguard, none of which did anything for its looks. Legshields were incorporated, but not a screen, so the rider still became wet in the rain. However, the performance in town was adequate for the time but, despite this and a competitive price, there were very few takers.

The racer was given the name Hurricane and was notable for its aluminium full fairing. This 'dustbin', as all such were called in the 1950s, was joined by further extensive panelling, which

*The Britax Hurricane road racer, which had a 48 cc ohv Ducati engine under all the panelling. It had a short life in 50 cc racing*

enclosed the tank and ran back to form a seat base and rear mudguard to shield half the rear wheel.

Under all this was the same Ducati engine fitted with stronger valve springs and a megaphone exhaust system. The racing of 50 cc machines was in an embryonic stage in 1955, so the sight of a number of Hurricanes at a Blandford race meeting looked good, even if they failed to win.

There were improvements to the road models for 1956, with enclosure for the valve gear, normal gearchanging with handlebar control and reduced gear whine. The Hurricane was given telescopic front forks and a reverse-cone megaphone, but this would seem to have been for style rather than power. By the end of the season, the Itom had taken over on the race tracks and the Hurricane was dropped.

With it went the other models, for Ducati were moving on to other matters and Britax went back to accessories. Over two decades later they imported a 50 cc Italian fold-up machine for a while, but this was simply as an accessory to a car, caravan, boat or light aircraft.

# BSA

Even before their post-war range was announced, BSA were in the news, thanks to a patent for a twin-cylinder engine with overhead valves. This set out how a single camshaft, placed at the rear of the crankcase, could control the valves which were set at an included angle by the use of different length pushrods and rocker arms. The arrangement was to appear in the A7 twin late in 1946.

The patent was announced in March 1945, and three months later was joined by another, which concerned a telescopic centre stand. The idea for this was Edward Turner's, for his name, along with BSA, appeared in the original application, which had been made in 1943 when Turner was technical director at the Small Heath firm.

The stand comprised a tube which slid up into the frame's seat tube and a transverse foot to support the machine at ground level. Inside the tube was a spring to hold it up, and on the outside there was a pawl and ratchet to lock the stand down. Thus, the rider was required to push the stand foot down, where the pawl would hold it, but to raise either wheel from the ground required him to lift the machine while still holding the stand down. Not an easy task with a machine of any real weight.

The pawl had a lever for disengagement, when the stand would spring up and the machine fall over if the rider was not prepared for it. The possibilities of interference by small boys, or the consequences of a spring failure when riding, were best not mulled over.

It was not until August 1945 that BSA announced their post-war range, which comprised just four models. However, these covered the learner, commuter, tourer and sidecar markets quite well, and within a few years the BSA range was to be the largest in the country.

The range offered for those first austere months comprised the 249 cc side-valve C10, the C11 of the same capacity (but with ohv), the side-valve 496 cc M20 and, the only new model, the 348 cc ohv B31. Even this last was not totally new, for it was based on the 1940 B29 and wartime WB30 with a strong bottom half, but it was the one model with telescopic front forks.

The two C-range machines shared cycle parts and many engine details, although the C11 did have 20 in. wheels, unlike the C10, which used

**Post-war 1945 BSA C10 249 cc side-valve model for getting to work and still with pre-war girder forks**

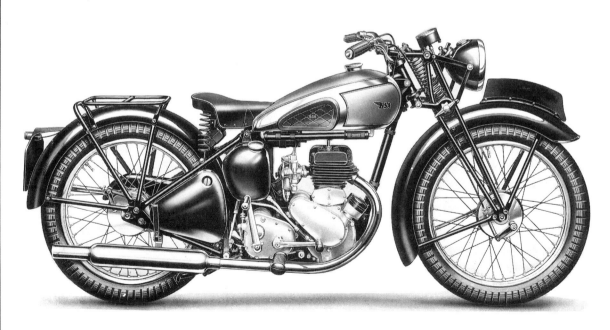

Matching BSA C11 with ohv for the slightly more sporting rider, but little different from the side-valve model

the 19 in. size. The engines were traditionally British with vertically-split crankcase, built-up crankshaft and dry-sump lubrication. The timing gear was of the simplest, with cam followers and then either tappets or pushrods.

In the C11, the pushrods crossed over on their way to the cylinder head, as the rockers lay across the engine, so they and the pushrods had to sit at the valves' included angle. An alloy cover enclosed the top end, but both head and barrel were in iron, as they were for the C10.

The bottom half was completed with a timing cover, which carried the skew-gear-driven points in their external housing. Outboard of this was a chain drive to the dynamo, which was clamped to the rear of the crankcase with an outer cover to enclose it. The oil pump sat low down in the crankcase, where it was driven from the crankshaft.

Both engines drove a three-speed, foot-change gearbox with the primary drive and clutch in a pressed-steel chaincase. The mechanics went into a rigid frame, which had girder front forks that carried the headlamp and speedometer. The oil tank was tucked under the saddle on the right, with the battery to match it on the left, while the toolbox went between the right-hand chainstays. A rear carrier was provided, and a pillion pad and rests were available. The tank was finished in chrome with silver panels, but the rest of the machine was in black for both models.

The M20 was really the same machine that BSA had supplied in large numbers to the army for some six years, and by simply painting the tank silver and the rest of the machine black, another civilian model was available. The sturdy frame and girder foks were ideal for sidecar work, as was the heavy-duty gearbox, while the layout of the detail parts was as for the C-range. A plodder it may have been, but a reliable plodder, for which spares were easily obtained and one that plenty of men were now well acquainted with. At a time when cars were both few in number and expensive to run, machines such as the M20, with the addition of a sidecar, enabled many a family to get out and about without relying on buses or trains.

While the C and M models were all pre-war in design and style, the new B31 represented the early post-war period very well. Its roots lay in the past, but with the new forks and a sprightly performance it blew a breath of fresh air into the range. The machine itself was to seem prosaic enough in later years, but in 1945 it was bright, shining and a rapid means of travel on the twisting roads of the day.

The B31 engine was a combination of light and heavy builds of the past, which gave it a good strong bottom end with less weight than before. In layout and construction, it was very conventional, with an all-iron top half, mag-dyno and all the expected BSA construction methods. About the only uncommon feature was the design of the head studs, which were attached to the crankcase and threaded into the underside of the cylinder head. By this means there were no bolt holes running through the head casting, decreasing the fin area, and no need for spanner access and deep counterbores.

For the rest, the engine drove a four-speed gearbox, similar to that of the M20, with a steel primary chaincase to enclose the chain and clutch. The engine and gearbox went into a rigid diamond frame, so there were no frame tubes under the crankcase. At the front were the new telescopic forks, which had hydraulic damping and supported the headlamp on lugs welded to the upper shrouds.

Both wheels had offset hubs with 7 in. single-leading-shoe brakes and 19 in. rims. Long mudguards kept the weather at bay, and the rest of the equipment was arranged in much the same way as for the other models. One variation occurred with the speedometer, which went in the top of the tank next to the filler cap and well out of the rider's line of sight.

The four models formed the basis of much of the BSA single range for the next decade or so, and before the end of the year were joined by one more machine. This was the M21, which was simply the M20 fitted with a 591 cc engine to provide more grunt for hauling even larger sidecars, packed with ever bigger families.

Within a month the five had become six, with the appearance of the B32 competition version of the B31. This was aimed at both the trials and scrambles rider, despite the lack of rear suspension, and most of it was pure B31. The differences were mainly external, although the gearing was lowered, and a magneto and battery lighting set could be substituted for the usual mag-dyno if the purchaser wished.

In other areas, there was a 21 in. front wheel, 4 in.-section rear tyre and abbreviated, chrome-plated mudguards. The exhaust system was swept up to waist level, and competition tyres fitted, together with a crankcase shield. There was more plating than usual and the result was a cobby mount that allowed many a trials rider a chance to compete at weekends.

In April 1946 the C-range machines received hydraulically-damped, telescopic front forks. At the same time, the speedometer was moved into the tank top, so these models copied the B-range in both these aspects. The headrace adjustment of these forks was by a patented method that the firm was to use for many a year.

In May 1946 a further patent was granted, and this related to the wheel hub. It became known as the 'crinkle' hub, due to the shape of the outer tubular part, which was formed in a 'pie-crust' style to allow the use of straight spokes. The outer tube was riveted to the inner one, which housed the bearings and carried the drive splines to the brake drum and sprocket. These rivets were the only weak point in the design, for they could work loose under heavy sidecar loads and if all failed, so did the drive to the wheel rim.

The new hub made its first appearance on a new twin-cylinder model announced in September 1946. This was the A7, from which an extensive range was to come over the years. The engine was a 360-degree vertical twin, of mainly conventional construction, with an iron head and barrel. The layout utilized the single rear camshaft for all four valves, as patented earlier, and this was gear driven with the train extending on to the rear-mounted magneto. The dynamo was clamped to the front of the engine and had a chain drive, while the oil pump went in the timing case with a worm drive from the crankshaft.

This last part alone was unusual, for it featured a built-up construction that allowed the use of one-piece connecting rods. Each crankpin was forged in one with its outer web and mainshaft, so the rod could be assembled and the pin fitted to the central flywheel. The two outers were held in place by a single through-bolt, with a double thread which, thus, slowly, but powerfully, pulled the parts together. The whole assembly then ran in a bush and a ball race.

The bottom half carried a one-piece, cast-iron block, while the cylinder heads were also in one and in iron. They were fed by a single carburettor via a separate manifold. The valve gear was completed by two rocker boxes, which were in alloy and bolted in place. Each carried a pair of rockers, access to their ends being via caps.

The four-speed gearbox was a separate assembly that bolted to the rear of the crankcase, which was formed to suit. The effect was the same as unit construction, and the appearance was enhanced by a handsome, cast, light-alloy chaincase, which enclosed the primary drive and included a tensioner for the chain.

The engine unit went into a loop frame with duplex downtubes that ran back under the engine to the rear wheel. There was no rear suspension, but the standard telescopic forks, as used by the B model, were fitted at the front. The remaining cycle parts were much as for the B31, but adapted to the twin frame, so the oil tank, saddle and toolbox were placed as expected.

The patented stand also appeared on the twin, but failed to inspire much confidence, for the

For more serious work, BSA offered this 499 cc B33 in 1947, and it continued right up to 1960 with its solid and reliable performance

*Below* The early BSA 495 cc vertical twin, as in 1947, in a rigid frame and with a saddle

*Below* The 1948 BSA M33 model produced by fitting the 499 cc ohv B33 engine into the heavy-duty cycle parts shared by the M20 and M21 side-valve models result seemed unstable. The speedometer went into the top of the tank, which was chrome plated with black or Devon red panels. The rest of the machine was finished in one of those two colours, and was matched by the rims, which were also plated with painted centres.

The rest of the range continued as it was for 1947, and right at the beginning of the year was joined by yet another new model, the B33. This was a 499 cc version of the B31 and was virtually identical, with the exception of an enlarged cylinder bore, higher gearing, greater power and a fatter rear tyre.

By April of that year, it had been joined by a competition version, listed as the B34. This, again, duplicated the smaller model. For 1948 one further single was added by slotting the 499 cc ohv B33 engine into the M20 frame and forks to make the M33. This had a brighter finish as standard and a little more pep for the sidecar driver, for whom it was intended.

There was a de luxe edition of the C11 for 1948 with a nice blue finish and more chrome, while the B-range had their speedometers moved from the tank to the fork top, and the competition versions were given a folding kickstart. The twin copied the B-range with its speedometer also moving, and most models had some detail changes, although production remained paramount in those austere days.

In June 1948 one of the best known of all BSA models made its debut as the 123 cc Bantam. This simple two-stroke was to become their most popular model, and it sold round the world in large numbers. The engine unit had been announced three months before and, in fact, the design was a mirror-image copy of the pre-war DKW RT125.

The engine was built in unit with its three-speed gearbox and was based on a vertically-split crankcase. In this ran the pressed-up crankshaft with roller big-end on three ball races, a steel rod and domed piston. The barrel was cast in iron and the head in alloy, with the plug laid back at an angle. Both parts were secured by nuts on long through-studs.

The Wipac flywheel magneto and generator for the direct lights went on the left, with the contact points outboard and easily accessible. On the right was the primary drive to the very sturdy, three-plate clutch, which drove the cross-over gearbox. The gear pedal and kickstart went on the right on concentric shafts, and the design enabled the machine to be kicked over when in gear, a rare feature in Britain at that time.

The complete unit went into a rigid loop frame with light telescopic front forks. There was a petroil tank, saddle, rear carrier and toolbox, 5 in. drum brakes, and a flat silencer that had a nice

An M33 doing its duty attached to a single-seat sidecar, which it would haul along with little trouble

The first post-war Gold Star was this 1949 B32GS, which set the style for the machine from then on

line to it. The front mudguard was sprung and deeply valanced, the bulb horn worked through the steering column, and the headlamp switch was cable operated from a handlebar lever.

The M-range was also in the news that month, for all three models were fitted with the telescopic front forks used by the A and B models.

By now the BSA empire was really getting into its post-war stride, and 1949 brought more new models and improved features for the existing ones. Foremost among the latter was the option of plunger rear suspension for the twin and the B-range singles. The suspension was undamped, but had load and rebound springs. The gearbox of the heavier models was revised and became common to the B- and M-ranges, and also for the twin, except for the special shell needed to mate it with the engine. Of rather less note was the appearance of an alloy head on the C10 during the year.

The most exciting news for 1949 was the launch of the Gold Star at the show held late in 1948. This revived a name the firm had first used in 1938 for a sporting 500 cc model and which was associated with the gold star awarded for a lap of the Brooklands track at over 100 mph during a race. It was never an easy award to win, but in June 1937 Wal Handley managed a lap at over 107 mph, riding a tuned Empire Star running on alcohol fuel.

The resulting production model was listed for two years, but not 1940, and the new one moved into a new class with a 348 cc engine. It was built in a super-sports style, but based on the B-range

with an all-alloy engine. This had the usual gearbox and was mounted in the plunger frame as standard with mainly stock parts, which included the chrome-plated mudguards from the competition machines.

There was a large range of options listed to suit road use, trials, scrambles or racing, and with the last BSA had their eye on the TT Clubman's races. For this there was an extension pipe to go with an open exhaust – then allowed – provision for a rev-counter, and a racing pad to go with the saddle. During the year the Gold Star, listed as the B32GS, was joined by a larger 499 cc version, which was built to the same specification and with the same options.

The final new model for 1949 was the A7 Star Twin, which was a sports version of the original. It was given a second carburettor and raised compression ratio to perk up the engine, the revised gearbox and the plunger frame being standard. It also had a brighter finish for its tank and wheel rims, making it a very handsome motorcycle.

There were two more models, various options and some detail changes for 1950, the most important being the 646 cc A10 Golden Flash twin. On the surface this was an enlarged A7 but, in fact, the engine had been revised, using the original basic design simply as a starting point. Few parts remained common, and the most obvious change lay in the cylinder head, where the rocker box became a one-piece part and the inlet manifold was cast as part of the head.

That aside, the new engine looked very much like the old one, although there were many internal changes. The gearbox continued as before, being bolted to the back of the crankcase, and there was still the polished alloy chaincase on the left. Both rigid and plunger models were offered, and much of the cycle side was unchanged, although the model did have the benefit of an 8 in. front brake from the start. The finish was new, being golden beige for all painted parts. This gave the machine its name. There was an all-black finish as well, which tended to be used for home-market machines at first, but in time the beige became the norm and was generally preferred.

At the other end of the scale, a competition version of the Bantam appeared. This had a raised saddle, fatter rear tyre, tilted silencer, blade mud-guards and a decompressor. It proved a handy tool, for its light weight made it easy to paddle through sections if things went wrong, which was better than stopping.

There were options that year for the all-alloy or Gold Star engines in the B-range machines, although it is unlikely that these were taken up. Otherwise, changes were minor, the Bantam leading the way with a revised Wipac magneto, and the options of plunger rear suspension for road or competition models, and a Lucas alter-nator and battery lighting system. Either or both options could be taken, although most road models with the Lucas equipment would also have the plunger frame. The Gold Star models were given the 8 in. front brake, except when built for trials or scrambles, while the rest of the range stayed as it was.

The A7 and Star Twin were revised in line with the A10 for 1951, so many components became common to both engine sizes. The capacity of the new version was 497 cc. Both had a single Amal carburettor and, as before, the A7 was in a rigid frame with the plunger version being an option, but standard for the Star Twin.

There were changes for the more prosaic models that year, with options of plunger rear suspension and a four-speed gearbox for the C10 and C11 machines. The plunger option was also made available for the M-range, in which the side-valve models were given light-alloy cylinder heads.

The rigid-frame versions of the A7 and A10 were not continued into 1952, when the only noticeable change was the option of a dualseat for the A-, B- and M-ranges. More happened for 1953 on the home market, with a headlamp cowl for the larger models, a dualseat option for the Bantam and C-ranges, and an 8 in. front brake for the B33.

The Gold Star machines went over to a frame with pivoted-fork, rear suspension, and in this form were known as the BB models, the earlier ones being designated ZB. These letters were to be found as the prefix of the engine number, which also included the letter GS if the motor was genuine.

On the export market there was more news, for the first of the hotter twins appeared as the Super Flash. This used the A10 engine, with its power output raised, and retained the plunger frame, but with sports mudguards and a brighter finish. The power was really too much for the frame, which weaved even in standard A10 form, but on long, straight American roads it was fine.

**First of the sports twins was this 1949 Star Twin, which had two carburettors and was supplied in the plunger frame as standard**

During 1953 BSA joined the cyclemotor market, which had sprung up a few years before. They made bicycles anyway, so it was a logical move. Their solution was the Winged Wheel, which was fitted in place of the standard rear wheel. The only other part was the fuel tank, which was made as a flat carrier to fit above the wheel.

A simple two-stroke engine with clutch and gears was housed in the hub, its capacity being 35 cc. The horizontal cylinder was on the left and was fed by a small Amal, the mixture being ignited by a flywheel magneto. The gears took the power via the clutch to the hub, which was formed as a full-width type with brake-drum surface.

There were major changes to most of the range for 1954, when the pivoted-fork frame came into more general use. The original user, the BB Gold Star, was joined by the CB model, which had a revised engine with much deeper finning and a swept-back exhaust pipe.

The B31 and B33 followed suit with the frame, although the rigid and plunger models stayed in the range until the ends of 1954 and 1955 respectively. With the new frames came a dual-seat as standard, a one-bolt fixing for the petrol tank, and a slim oil tank tucked into the corner of the subframe on the right side. It was matched on the left by a cover for the toolbox and battery.

The competition B32 and B34 went over to a new rigid frame with duplex downtubes and had the all-alloy engine as standard. They were also listed with the pivoted-fork frame as an option, when they became very similar to the ZB Gold Star.

The new frame and all its matching features was also used by the twins, although the four plunger-frame models continued. The A7, A7ST and A10SF were dropped at the end of the year, but the A10 ran on until 1957 to keep the sidecar buyer happy. The touring twins in the new frame remained the A7 and A10, but the engine and gearbox became separate units, although the internals stayed the same.

The sports models were the A7 Shooting Star and A10 Road Rocket, which had many common parts between them and the tourers, but had light-alloy cylinder heads. They kept to the single carburettor, but differed from the tourers in respect of their finish.

Among the smaller models, the Bantams with Lucas electrics were phased out, but the D1 was still available in rigid or plunger frames, with direct or battery lighting, and in road or competition

Looking over a Bantam in 1955 to see if it would meet their needs if a pillion seat was added

form. It was joined by the 148 cc D3, which was produced by simply boring out the engine, but it also had heavier front forks and a larger front brake. The road model had the plunger frame as standard, but either electric system, while the competition version had the choice of frames.

The C-range, too, was altered from 1954 with a change to alternator electrics. The side-valve model became the C10L, using some Bantam cycle parts, and only came with three speeds and a plunger frame. The ohv machine was the C11G. The rigid-frame version of this came with three speeds, but the plunger one with three or four. In other respects, they carried on as they had from 1945 to provide cheap, reliable transport.

Following all these changes, there was little alteration for 1955, except a change to Monobloc carburettors for most models. There were no competition Bantams in plunger frames, and the C11G gained a 7 in. front brake, but was no longer built in rigid form. The BB and CB versions of the Gold Star continued to be built, but were joined by a DB, which was very similar to the CB.

At the end of the year there was a major reduction in the number of models, along with

news of some new ones, and this simplified the range. Right at the bottom end of the scale, the Winged Wheel was dropped, despite having been offered as a complete machine, for the day of the clip-on was past and the moped was taking over.

Next, out went the rigid and competition Bantams, to leave the D1 in the plunger frame available with direct or battery lighting. These were the forms that buyers liked, and the models continued to run errands for them for the rest of the decade, and a little beyond. For the Bantam purchaser seeking a little more power and comfort, BSA fitted the D3 engine unit into a new frame with pivoted-fork rear suspension. This, too, had the choice of lighting system.

In the 250 class, the C10L acquired a four-speed gearbox and continued with the plunger frame, while the C11G was replaced by the C12. This used the same ohv engine with a four-speed gearbox in a pivoted-fork frame. Both wheels had full-width hubs. The one odd feature was the position of the light switch, on a panel behind the oil tank on the right.

The B31 and B33 also changed to full-width hubs in light alloy with 7 in. brakes that came from the Ariel range, but the plunger-frame versions were no more. It was the same with the rigid competition models, and the B32 and B34 were only listed with the pivoted-fork frame, in which their oil tank was now centrally mounted.

The Gold Star line-up was also simplified, being reduced to the two DB versions, which were joined by the DBD in the 499 cc size only. This

*Above* **The Beeza scooter shown late in 1955 at Earls Court, but not put into production**

*Below* **Assembly line of BSA Dandy machines in the Small Heath works around 1957**

The 1956 BSA B31 which retained its 1945 engine with little change, but now had a new frame, tank, seat and wheels

was very similar to the others, except for a tapered front section for the silencer. All three had the option of the 190 mm, full-width front hub and a five-gallon alloy tank added to the list. The Gold Stars were only built in road, scrambles, road-racing and Clubman's forms that year, the first being phased out that season.

The side-valve range lost the M20 and the M33 in rigid form, but the M21 with either frame and the plunger M33 were given the 8 in. front brake. The twins alone stayed much as they were, except for the brakes, which became the full-width type, as used on the road B models.

Two new models were shown at the end of 1955, one being a 70 cc scooterette and the other a 200 cc scooter. The former was called the Dandy and had a moped-style, pressed-steel beam frame with short, leading-link front forks, legshields, a small fuel tank under the saddle, and a pivoted fork for the rear wheel. The engine and gearbox were built as part of this rear fork, and it was this area that was both the clever part and the flaw in the design.

The engine was a two-stroke with overhung crankshaft and arranged so the axis of this lay close to the fork pivot, the cylinder being laid back as part of the right-hand fork leg. The end of this leg was bolted to the cylinder head, while the crankcase extended across to the left, ahead of the wheel.

Along its length were first the flywheel magneto and then the clutch, followed by a two-speed gearbox. From this, a chain on the left drove the

rear wheel. Within this area lay the problems, for the points could only be inspected by taking the engine out of the frame, and the trade knew only too well that this was the second item to check after the plug. The other snag lay in the gear-change, which was a preselector arrangement controlled from the handlebars and much more trouble than the type by then common on con-tinental mopeds.

The scooter was called the Beeza and had a side-valve engine laid across the frame, with the cylinder laying flat and pointing to the left, while the crankshaft was in line with the machine. The mechanics were built as one unit, so the engine drove back to the clutch and then to the all-indirect, four-speed gearbox, all on the right-hand side. A short shaft ran back from the box to the spiral bevel gears and the rear hub.

All this was contained in a series of alloy cast-ings, which were bolted together and pivoted to act as a rear swinging arm. A spring unit controlled it, and the construction allowed for a stub axle at the rear for the 12 in., pressed-steel wheel. At the front were short, leading-link forks, while the works were enclosed in scooter style, but with a noticeable tunnel to conceal them and the frame. Electric starting was standard, and the machine appeared to have potential, but by then the market was used to light, zippy Italian scooters with two-stroke engines, so a side-valve plodder was unlikely to find much favour.

BSA decided not to proceed with the Beeza and put the Dandy on ice for another year, so it

*Left* **The C10L was the final form of the 249 cc BSA side-valve model**

*Below* **By 1958 the A10 Golden Flash was only built in pivoted-fork-frame form, even for sidecar use, but it still made a nice outfit**

*Left* **The first 172 cc Bantam was the 1958 D5, and this example is being made to work for its living by the full load of AA gear it carries**

The DBD34 was the final form of the 499 cc Gold Star and is seen here in its 1958 Clubman build

*Below* The BSA C15 was based on the Triumph Cub and was to sire a whole range of models in the next decade

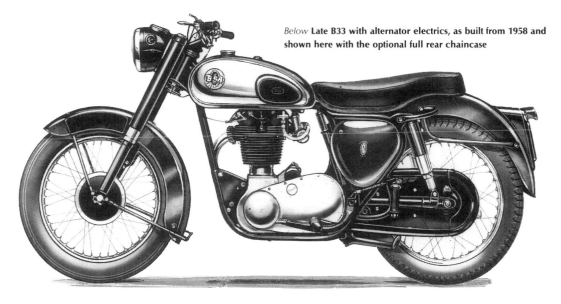

*Below* Late B33 with alternator electrics, as built from 1958 and shown here with the optional full rear chaincase

did not appear until 1957. It was the only new machine that year, which was a period when the firm was nearing the end of an era and approaching some major changes. This was highlighted at the end of the season by the disappearance of a number of old favourites from the range.

Out went the C10L, for a new 250 cc range was in development, and out went the M33 and plunger A10, to leave only the M21 for the sidecar man. This old stager was now mainly sold to the AA and the services, for there were few private owners left for such machines. The competition B32 and B34 singles were dropped, for the trend was to smaller and lighter machines for trials or scrambles. Out went the DB Gold Stars, so only the DBD remained, and solely in scrambles and Clubman's form as a 500.

The D3 and A10 Road Rocket were replaced by new versions for 1958, and the smaller was enlarged to 172 cc, becoming the D5. As with the D1, which continued, the D5 was listed with a choice of direct or battery lighting. The sports A10 became the Super Rocket and was given new full-width hubs and a nacelle for the headlamp, as well as detail improvements.

The other three twins continued, also with the new hubs and nacelle, and were joined by the 646 cc Rocket Scrambler, which was built in street scrambles form for the USA with open, waist-level exhaust pipes, no lights and off-road cycle parts. Among the singles, the C12 continued as it was, but the M21 lost its headlamp cowl without gaining the nacelle, so it reverted to its earlier style.

The Dandy ran on with some detail changes, while for that year the Gold Star came in DBD form only. Finally, the B31 and B33 went over to alternator electrics and coil ignition, plus the new full-width hubs and headlamp nacelle.

In September 1958 BSA launched the first of a new series of unit-construction singles, which were to run on to the end of the company. The machine was the 247 cc C15, and while presented as new, it was, in truth, a stretched Tiger Cub. It repeated the features of this model, with plain big-end for the pressed-up crankshaft, simple timing gear for the overhead valves, and skew-gear drive to a points housing behind the iron cylinder. The head was in alloy with a separate rocker box, and the pushrods moved in a chrome-plated tube running from the crankcase to the head. An alternator provided the current and was

mounted on the left-hand end of the crankshaft, from where a chain drove the four-speed gearbox. This was the same as in the Cub. A polished alloy cover enclosed the left-hand side.

The engine unit went into a simple loop frame with twin tubes under the engine, and telescopic front and pivoted-fork rear suspension. Full-width drum brakes, similar to the others of the range, were fitted, along with a headlamp nacelle and dualseat. The oil tank and toolbox were blended into one by a central panel, which carried the ignition switch, while the lighting switch went into the headlamp.

With the advent of the C15, the C12 was dropped, and for 1959 the D5 gave way to the D7. This used the same engine unit with an extra cover to streamline the generator, but in a new frame with pivoted rear suspension and new forks. These were based on those used by the Tiger Cub and fitted with the headlamp nacelle.

The two B models continued, although their days were numbered, the B31 leaving the lists at the end of 1959, and the B33 following suit a year later. The M21 was available to special order and only listed in the plunger frame, although some rigid ones were built from stocks for that year alone. The 348 cc DB Gold Star reappeared, but was listed as the 500 cc version fitted with the smaller engine. The larger model was only built in DBD form, and as Clubman's or scrambles models, the latter having a central oil tank.

The twins in A7 and A10 forms continued, as did the Dandy, which was joined by a trio of scooters, but these were sold under the Sunbeam label (see page 168). Once the road C15 was underway, it was joined in the New Year by two competition versions, listed as the C15S for scrambles and C15T for trials. These had minor changes inside the engine, raised exhaust systems and competition wheels and tyres, but retained much from the standard model.

In this form, the BSA range entered the 1960s. The company was flush with success and sure it was set for a long period of prosperity. For this, they revamped the twins in 1962, while introducing the much favoured Rocket Gold Star, expanded the unit-single range, and kept the Bantam, at least in 172 cc form, for many years. It was, however, the beginning of a decline but, regardless of what was to come, BSA could look back on many years of producing some of the best motorcycles for all classes of user.

# Cairn                                                    # Commander

This machine was built by a Mr Farrow, of Reading, in the Corgi mould (see page 67), but with full enclosure. It was based around a 99 cc Villiers 2F engine, hung from a brazed, steel-tube frame.

There was no suspension front or rear, although this was promised for the future, and disc wheels with 4.00 × 16 in. tyres were used. The entire frame and engine were hidden by panels, which had louvres to assist cooling. Both the handlebars and saddle were adjustable for height, and there was a rear carrier, luggage grid and twin tail lights as part of the direct lighting system.

The machine performed as well as the Corgi, but had more positive steering. It made a reasonable runabout, but Mr Farrow soon found that, while a one-off is difficult to build, repeating the exercise brings many more problems. No more was heard of the Cairn, which remained an interesting solo endeavour.

This make made a dramatic appearance in the press in October 1952, and certainly existed, for one was given a brief run on the road and they were exhibited at Earls Court. There were three models in the range, all powered by small Villiers engines, but the styling was in total contrast to the pedestrian looks offered by the rest of the industry.

The machines were made by the General Steel Group of Hayes, in Middlesex, and all used the same set of cycle parts. The frame was all-welded, from square-section steel tubing, and of the beam type with pivoted-fork rear suspension. The main part ran from the headstock as two pairs of tubes, one on each side, and these swept back, down and back again as each pair came together near the rear wheel.

From this beam, a loop hung down to carry the engine and also helped to support the rear fork

**The Cairn built by Mr Farrow around a Villiers 2F engine in 1950**

The Commander range on show at Earls Court in late 1952, when the machine's strange styling created great interest

pivot. A subframe ran up for the seat to complete the frame and had cross-members to brace it. The rear fork was also made from square-section tubing, the legs running forward to a cross panel and then down to the pivot. The panel had a compression spring bolted to it, which reacted against a matching frame panel ahead of it to provide the undamped suspension. At the front were short, leading-link forks, for which the suspension medium was a rubber band on each side, working on suitably arranged bobbins and links.

On to this basic structure went the bodywork, which was quite unprecedented for a British model and more relevant to a prototype for the Paris show. As a start, the frame beam was panelled in and its front section housed the petroil tank with a flush fitting cap. The beam line ran to its end and was continued in a stay that ran to the tail of the rear enclosure and number plate.

The enclosure rose from the middle of the beam and ran along under the single seat, or optional dualseat, until it reached the end of the machine. The tail light was at the top of the rear panel, which dropped to the stay, curled forward on the line of the tyre, and then down to the rear wheel centre.

Below and ahead of the beam, the line was continued in the form of a chrome-plated grille, which enclosed the entire engine unit. The lines of this tied in with the upper part, and only the foot controls lay outside it. The theme was continued with the sprung front mudguard, which extended up into a cowl for the headstock, a cover for the handlebars, and a shaped glass for the headlight.

The finish was ivory for the beam and fork top, with the front mudguard, rear enclosure and grille framework in light blue, dark blue or maroon, depending on model. There was a good deal of chrome plating, and the Commander name was emblazoned on each side of the tail.

Rather sadly, all that was under this exciting styling were the very prosaic Villiers 2F, 1F and 10D engines, in 99 and 122 cc sizes. The models became the Commanders I, II and III, with the same numbers of transmission speeds. The enterprise really deserved something a little better.

Whether this was the reason or not, the make left the market as quickly as it arrived, and no more was heard of it. Traditional riders were pleased at its demise, but it showed an imagination much needed in the industry, the lack of which was to cut the firms down in the years to come.

# Corgi

The notion of a small motorcycle that can be folded up for easy transit when not in use has been around for a long time, and the Corgi was such a machine. It was developed from the wartime Welbike, which was built for parachute drops and used a 98 cc Villiers engine to propel its very basic chassis.

The Welbike was made by Excelsior and proved useful in both its original role for the paratroops, and for short-distance duties on camps and airfields around the globe. After the war the design was made more suitable for the civilian market, and the results often confused with the Welbike. The Corgi, as the post-war model was called, used a 98 cc Excelsior Spryt engine, but was made by Brockhouse Engineering of Southport, who also built the engine under licence.

The first news of the machine came in 1946, although it was 1948 before supplies reached the

public. The engine was a two-stroke with horizontal cylinder and was virtually a carbon copy of the Villiers Junior de Luxe, having minor alterations to the barrel. It drove a countershaft with clutch contained in an extension of the crankcase and thence to the rear wheel.

The engine unit went into a duplex cradle frame, the tubes of which ran back from the headstock, turned, came back under the engine and then up to the steering head again. On top went the petroil tank, while the saddle was on a pillar so it could be raised for riding and lowered again for storage.

At the front were rigid forks with handlebars that rose up to match the saddle, but could be swung down when necessary. The wheels had small drum brakes and were originally spoked, but were soon changed to discs. The tyre size was 2.25 × 12.5 in., so the Dunlop tyres were special. The lighting was direct with a small headlamp at the front, and there was no kickstarter, for the rider was expected to push the machine to start the engine.

It was crude, but it was transport, which was all that mattered in those days, so they sold quite

**The Corgi, which was developed from the wartime Welbike, but had an Excelsior 98 cc Spryt engine**

Corgi with sidecar, which enabled parcels and the shopping to be carried, so it was a useful tool for the time

well for shopping and trips to work. By the middle of 1948, the starting was improved with a kickstart lever, plus a dog-clutch, which disengaged the drive by the output sprocket to provide a neutral. Rather ingeniously, this was linked to the right-hand footrest, so raising this, as was required to give the kickstart lever clearance, put the machine into neutral.

As a further asset, a sidecar platform became available with a steel box and canvas top. This proved very handy for taking parcels to the post or when collecting the shopping.

The original machine was known as the Mark I, and with the dog clutch as the Mark II. In the middle of 1949 both became available with two major options, one a two-speed gearbox and the other telescopic front forks. The box was an Albion with a kickstarter and foot control, while the forks were basic, but included hydraulic damping.

During 1950 an enclosed bodywork was offered for the Corgi by the Jack Olding company, which handled the sales of the marque. This turned it into a miniature scooter, but removed its ability to be folded up, so did not catch on. There was also a banking sidecar for this version, which was intended for carrying loads and not a person.

The enclosure and sidecar continued to be available for 1951, when the machine itself ran on unchanged. It became the Mark IV for 1952, but this was simply the older type fitted with the two-speed gearbox and telescopic forks as standard. A weathershield was added and the headlamp moved to its top, while a luggage grid appeared on the tank top. The Mark II continued to be offered, although it had really been overtaken by time, and in October of that year it was dropped.

The Corgi continued in Mark IV form for 1953 and 1954 without any major change, but the advent of the moped and improvements in standards caused it to come to an end late that year. It had been a useful method of transport, but its day had run.

# Cotton

This Gloucester-based firm was best known between the wars for its fully triangulated frame, which gave exceptional handling for its day. Stanley Woods won his first TT on a Cotton in 1923, and for two decades the company built ranges of machines using proprietary engines.

They returned to motorcycles during 1954 with a simple lightweight called the Vulcan. This used the 197 cc Villiers 8E engine in a rigid frame, built on the triangulated principles of the past. At the front were light MP telescopic forks, and both wheels had 19 in. rims and 6 in. drum brakes. There was a dualseat, battery lighting and electric horn to complete a neat, if conventional, machine.

For 1955 the Vulcan was joined by the Cotanza, which used the 242 cc British Anzani engine in a new frame with pivoted-fork rear suspension. The engine was a twin-cylinder two-stroke and unusual in having a horizontally-split crankcase with a plain centre bearing, in which was incorporated a rotary inlet valve. This gave the incoming mixture a rather convoluted path, which

one two-stroke specialist described as strangling it at birth.

The rest of the engine was conventional, with one carburettor, an iron cylinder block and one-piece alloy head. The four-speed gearbox was bolted to the rear of the crankcase, and the primary drive was enclosed by an alloy cover.

The cycle side was conventional, and during 1955 was also used for another version of the Vulcan, but this time fitted with the 9E engine with three-speed gearbox. For 1956 it was also offered with four speeds, and the Cotanza with the 322 cc Anzani twin engine. This was similar to the smaller unit, except that it combined piston-controlled inlet ports with the rotary valve.

One further model for 1956 was the Trials, which used the 9E engine, four-speed gearbox and pivoted-fork frame. The cycle parts were altered to suit its job, with competition tyres, no lights and a saddle.

During 1956 the original Vulcan, with 8E engine and rigid frame, was dropped, and for 1957 the whole range continued with one addition. This was the Villiers Twin model, which had the 2T engine in the Cotanza cycle parts. The complete range then continued for 1958. The one significant change for that year applied to the Vulcan only and comprised the fitting of Armstrong leading-link front forks.

The whole range had these forks for 1959, when it remained unchanged, except for the Villiers Twin. This was renamed the Herald and given a rather crude design of rear enclosure to follow the trend of the times. It emphasized the limited

The 242 cc British Anzani twin engine, with rotary valve, installed in a Cotton Cotanza and fitted with a siamezed exhaust system

Cotton trials model based on an 8E engine, the pivoted-fork frame and leading-link forks. In production, in 1956, the 9E was used

The 1959 Cotton Herald with the 249 cc Villiers 2T engine and rather crude rear enclosure

resources of the small company and their need to produce such parts with the minimum of costly tooling.

They did add another model to the list that year, in the form of the Messenger, which was powered by the 324 cc Villiers 3T twin-cylinder engine. The cycle parts were mainly the same as for the Herald, except that the front rim was of 21 in. diameter and both wheels had 7 in., full-width drum brakes. The rear enclosure of the smaller twin was fitted.

The appearance of the Villiers twin-powered models made the Anzani ones redundant, so for 1960 the Cotanzas were only listed to special order. The other models continued as they were and were joined by a Scrambler, powered by a 246 cc Villiers 33A engine.

From then on, the Cotton range expanded greatly, a sports 249 cc twin – the Double Gloucester – arriving in March 1960, and all manner of road, trials, scrambles and road-racing models during the 1960s.

# Cyc-Auto

This machine was the ancestor of the autocycle and, thus, in a way, of the clip-on and moped, which were all aimed at providing transport at minimal cost. It was announced in 1934 and, at first, used its own engine, but later switched to Villiers. Just before the war, it was sold to the Scott concern, who redesigned the power unit, and in post-war years, this alone was used. Its production remained in Yorkshire, although the machine itself was built in Acton, London.

The engine was unusual in that the crankshaft lay along the machine. For the rest, it was a conventional, 98 cc two-stroke with upright iron cylinder which, at first, had an integral head but, from July 1947, had a detachable alloy one.

The carburettor sat in front of the cylinder on an inlet stub, and the flywheel magneto on the front of the crankshaft. This ran straight back to the clutch, and the drive continued on to a worm under the machine's bottom bracket. This contained the worm wheel which, in turn, drove the rear wheel by chain. A shaft ran through the worm wheel centre for the cycle pedals and chain, which complemented the engine. The silencer was bolted straight on to the rear of the barrel and comprised a large, cast alloy box above and around the clutch housing.

The engine went into an open frame, typical of autocycle practice, except for the worm wheel housing at the bottom bracket. There were pressed-steel blade girders at the front, and a cylindrical petroil tank behind the saddle.

The Cyc-Auto continued in this form, and for 1949 was joined by the Carrier model, which was aimed at the delivery market. To this end, it was fitted with strutted forks, which lacked suspension, and a large butcher's-boy-type carrier over the front wheel. The engine was modified for both models for 1950, the carburettor being behind the barrel, which was given twin front exhaust ports, each connected to a long pipe and tubular silencer.

**The Cyc-Auto in its 1940 form, which was continued in the early post-war years**

Otherwise, the Carrier model continued as it was, but the other became the Superior. This had the petroil tank moved to between the upper and lower frame tubes. It continued with the blade girders, while the Carrier kept its rigid, strutted fork, Both retained their saddle and rear carrier. For 1952 the Carrier was fitted with the blade girders, but from then on the two models continued as they were. They were no longer listed by 1955, but continued in a small way for another three years.

There was one attempt to produce a small motorcycle using the Cyc-Auto mechanics, and this was shown at Earls Court late in 1953. The engine remained as it was, but behind the clutch was a two-speed gearbox installed in unit with the engine. From this, a shaft drove to the rear wheel.

A simple loop frame carried the engine and had plunger rear suspension and telescopics at the front. Motorcycle-size 19 in. wheels with small drum brakes were used, and the equipment included lights, electric horn, saddle, rear carrier and toolbox. The machine was listed as the Scott model, but no more was heard of it.

# Cyclaid

This was one of a number of cycle attachments that sat over the rear wheel, but differed in that the drive to it was by V-belt. The unit was made by British Salmson at Raynes Park, London, and first appeared during 1950.

The engine was an all-alloy two-stroke of 31 cc with horizontal barrel. All the major parts were die-cast. The cylinder was lined and fed by a small Amal, while the exhaust was to the rear of the assembly. Inside was a built-up crankshaft, with roller big-end, running on ball races. This carried a Wipac flywheel magneto on the right.

A countershaft was fitted above the crankshaft and driven by helical gears, also on the right and inboard of the magneto. The V-belt pulley was on the left to give the second stage in the reduction ratio to the rear wheel.

A petroil tank went above the engine, and at the rear was extended downwards to form the number-plate mounting. Suitable brackets supported the unit, a spring-loaded arrangement being provided to allow the belt to be adjusted and then to keep it in tension. Controls were a twistgrip throttle and lever decompressor, with the choke mounted on the carburettor.

The engine worked well, so the Cyclaid remained in production until 1955, which was as long as most. By then, the day of the clip-on was really past, and riders were moving on to the moped, so the unit was taken out of production.

**The Cyclaid cyclemotor unit fitted above the rear wheel, which it drove by belt**

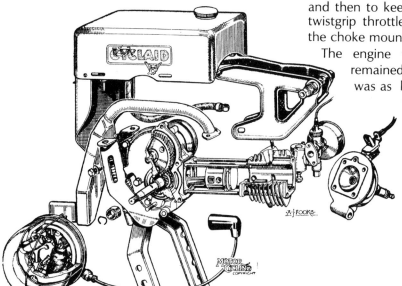

# Cyclemaster

This cycle attachment came as a complete rear wheel, so hardly qualified as a clip-on, although it served the same purpose. It was first seen at the 1950 Utrecht fair, and some of its parts were also used in the Berini unit, which was mounted over the front wheel with friction-roller drive.

The Cyclemaster unit was formally introduced in Britain two months after the fair and was to be made by the giant EMI concern at Hayes, in Middlesex. That same company bought the Rudge firm in the 1930s, so were not unacquainted with two-wheelers, although they stopped production at the end of 1939, as they needed the space. Later, they sold the name to Raleigh.

The Cyclemaster wheel replaced the standard bicycle one and was built with heavier-gauge rim and spokes. These were connected to a large drum, and most of the mechanism was contained within its 13 in. diameter, which was vented to assist engine cooling. The engine was a two-stroke of 25.7 cc with inclined iron barrel, alloy head and vertically-split crankcase. The crankshaft was pressed up with caged needle rollers for the big-end and ball races for the mains.

Induction was controlled by a disc valve, driven by the right-hand end of the crankshaft, and the mixture was fed from a small Amal at the rear of the crankcase through a passage to the valve. A Wipac flywheel magneto was on the left, and inboard of this was the first stage of the chain drive. This ran back to a countershaft, on which the clutch was mounted. This shaft then drove the second-stage chain. This was connected to a sprocket that was riveted to the inside of the drum to complete both the reduction ratio and the drive.

The upper part of the drum was filled by a small petroil tank, while the exhaust pipe ran down to a silencer tucked under the magneto. Suitable covers concealed much of the mechanism, and the complete wheel weighed in at 33 lb. Controls

were the clutch and throttle, with a tap to turn the fuel on and a choke built into the air filter attached to the carburettor.

The unit sold well, and for 1952 was bored out to raise the capacity to 32.6 cc, which gave it a little more power. At the same time, lighting coils were added to the flywheel magneto and the paint finish changed from black to grey. By then, at least one bicycle maker, Mercury, was producing a machine especially for the Cyclemaster. This was sturdier than usual and sold without a rear wheel!

This trend continued, and by the middle of 1953, Cyclemaster themselves were offering complete machines. In addition to the Mercury, there was the Pillion which, optimistically, was fitted with a pad and rests for a second person, and the Roundsman. The last made more sense and was built as a delivery bicycle with small front wheel and large carrier. It was ideal for a tradesman to use for local deliveries, especially if the roads were hilly or the wind inclined to blow hard.

The next move came for 1955, when the Cyclemate was created. This was more in the moped image. For this the engine was moved ahead of the bottom bracket and went into a frame built

**The Cyclemaster unit, which replaced the bicycle rear wheel, had a disc-valve engine of 25.7 cc at first**

for Cyclemaster by the Norman company. It was open, as a woman's cycle, and retained the rigid forks, but did have drum brakes. The petroil tank was fixed to the lower downtube.

It was a good attempt at producing something with minimal tooling costs, but lacked the style of the mopeds then beginning to arrive in Britain.

This was highlighted when the firm revived the Berini connection and began to import their moped for 1956, as this Dutch machine showed how far the trend and styling had moved on.

Despite this, the firm continued to build the Cyclemate and the rear wheel unit, the latter remaining in production until 1958, and the former until 1960. However, by then both were well out of date.

Before that the firm tried another tack with a small scooter of unorthodox construction. It was called the Piatti, after its Italian designer, and the prototype was shown at the 1952 Brussels show. Two years later negotiations were concluded for the rights to build the machine in Britain, and in mid-1956 the model was launched on that market.

In appearance, the machine was low and small, having a monocoque body built up from four steel pressings, which were welded together. This produced an inverted bath-like form, under which went the mechanics and the wheels, while on top was a dualseat mounted on a single saddle pillar. The steering column also rose above the main body, and ahead of it there was an apron, the lower edges of which ran into footboards.

There were two small access panels, but for anything else the machine was simply laid on its side. The body was rigid enough to act as the frame, and the engine unit, complete with transmission and rear wheel, was pivoted to it. A tension spring acted as the suspension medium

*Above* **Cyclemaster taking the hard work out of riding a bicycle against the wind and on hills, whether carrying a load or not**

**The Cyclemate, which appeared in 1955 to combine the Cyclemaster engine with a Norman cycle built for it**

**A Piatti scooter, as built under licence by Cyclemaster from 1956, but only until 1958**

and had three settings to provide a load adjustment. Front suspension was by a leading arm. Thus, both wheels with their 7 in. split rims were quickly detachable.

A wide centre stand went under the body, and this was lowered by pulling a knob beneath the instrument panel, which shrouded the handlebars. The knob was connected by cable to the stand. Once the stand was lowered the machine would readily roll back on to it.

The engine unit assembly pivoted at a point just below the base of the horizontal cylinder. Capacity was 124 cc, and the two-stroke had an iron barrel and alloy head. The carburettor was on the left, and the rectangular silencer on the right, so both items moved with the engine as the suspension worked.

The crankcase was cast in two parts, which made up the case, plus a beam to run back on the right to carry the wheel and the suspension spring attachment. At the front of the case was the crankshaft. This had an overhung big-end and

a mainshaft that extended to the right to the clutch and then the flywheel magneto.

A chain took the drive from the clutch to the three-speed gearbox, which was housed so that one of its shafts also acted as the wheel stub axle. A jockey sprocket dealt with chain adjustment, while the gearbox was controlled by a handlebar twistgrip.

As supplied, the machine came with dualseat, spare wheel and front carrier, while there was an optional windscreen. It was a trifle odd in looks, due to its small size and the vertical louvres in the front of the body, but adequate transport for town use.

For 1958 the original machine became the De Luxe and was joined by a Standard model. This came without the spare wheel, carrier and dualseat, having a saddle in place of the last, and at a reduced price. The missing items were available as options, so could be added when funds allowed.

In this form, the two models continued for another year, but late in 1958 production came to an end. This left the Cyclemate, which was to trickle on, well out of date, until 1960.

# Cymota

This 1950 clip-on had a conventional, 45 cc two-stroke engine, which drove the front wheel with a friction-roller. The unit sat above the wheel, ahead of the steering column, and was nicely styled with a cowling, in which a small headlamp was fitted.

The engine was not very sophisticated, even by the standards of that time, for it had a deflector piston, overhung crankshaft and plain bronze bush big-end bearing. The mains were ball races, but crankcase compression was low, due to a nut on the crankpin to keep the rod in place and a bobweight flywheel, which was keyed and bolted to the crankshaft.

A Miller flywheel magneto and generator was on the left-hand end of this, and the friction roller in the middle. The head was alloy and the barrel cast iron. A small Amal supplied the mixture, and there was a drum-shaped silencer on the end of the exhaust pipe.

The engine was mounted on a backplate, with a small petroil tank above it, and could be moved by a lever to bring the drive roller into contact with the tyre. Springs provided a degree of tension, and the arrangement allowed the machine to be used as a bicycle if desired. The cowling completely enclosed the whole unit and was louvred to assist cooling.

The Cymota came and went in two short years, for even by 1951 the clip-on era was beginning to show signs of age. It was very much an early post-war trend and, although it persisted well into the 1950s, buyers were always aware of its shortcomings. As soon as they could, they moved on to something a little better, and the Cymota, along with the rest, was replaced.

The sole concessionaires had been Blue Star Garages, and this, too, must have been a factor in its demise. The profit margins were slim, for the unit sold at 18 guineas, and they must have soon found that their normal car business was more rewarding.

The Cymota clip-on went over the front wheel and had a bonnet that carried a headlight powered by the engine magneto

# Dayton

On their fiftieth anniversary as a bicycle maker, in 1955, this firm entered the scooter market with a luxury model they called the Albatross. It was powered by the 224 cc Villiers 1H engine and was larger and heavier than the popular Italian models, so it was also more expensive.

The engine unit, with its four-speed gearbox, was installed in a tubular-steel frame with pivoted-fork rear suspension. At the front were Earles leading-link forks, and both ends were controlled by Girling or Woodhead-Monroe spring units. The wheels had split rims and were shod with 4.00 × 12 in. tyres, while the alloy hubs contained 6 in. brakes with steel liners bonded in place.

The bodywork comprised the usual apron, floor and rear section, with both hinged and detachable panels for access. The dualseat was hinged at the rear to give access to the petroil tank over the engine, and the tail section could also be swung up to let the rear wheel roll out. The body was cut away for the sides of the engine, which also allowed the controls to emerge, and footboards ran along most of the body length.

The tunnel behind the apron was very deep to assist airflow and ran into a shroud enclosing the steering column. At the top of this was a small panel for the instruments and switches, while the headlamp was built into the apron. The front mudguard was separate and well valanced. It turned with the steering, but did not enclose the

**Dayton Albatross in 1955 with Villiers 224 cc 1H engine unit**

The Albatross for 1956, but still with rather unfortunate front end. The name did nothing to help, either

fork tubes. A screen and luggage grid were listed as options.

The Albatross continued with minor alterations for two years, and early in 1957 was joined by the Albatross Twin. This used the same set of cycle parts, but was fitted with the 249 cc Villiers 2T twin engine, which gave the machine a little more zip.

Both were to continue unchanged for 1958, except for a new front mudguard, which enclosed the fork tubing and improved the looks. However, in March, the twin became the Empire and was joined by the restyled Continental Twin, while the Albatross became the Single. Both continued to bear the Albatross name as a prefix, and this practice remained with the firm, resulting in rather clumsy nomenclature.

The Single was fitted with the 246 cc 2H engine, which derived from the 1H and preceded the better known A-series. It went into a machine with some revised bodywork, which was also used by the new twin. The major change was to the apron. This now included a glove compartment, and there were other changes to the dashboard, footboards and dualseat, all of which enhanced the luxury specification.

Within two months, there were some name changes and the Empire became available to special order only, remaining so until withdrawn in the middle of 1959. The Single became the Continental Single, while the new twin stayed as it was, but both still retained the Albatross prefix.

The two models continued for 1959, when they were joined by a third, called the Albatross Flamenco. This was lighter in style and concept, having a 174 cc Villiers 2L engine with fan cooling, electric start and three-speed gearbox. The frame and bodywork were new, but were shared with Panther and Sun (see pages 140 and 165) to reduce costs. Each firm tricked out the parts to look a little different.

The frame was still tubular and the forks of the Earles type, but with the suspension units outside the mudguard valance. The bodywork had no tunnel, so the floor was flat behind the apron, which had twin compartments in it and the dashboard panel just above these. The seat remained hinged to the rear body, but a single panel gave access under each side of this. Wheel size was down to 10 in., but they still had split rims.

The Flamenco was far more in the style of the scooter world than the original Albatross, despite a rather heavy appearance to the front mudguard. It continued for 1960, along with the Twin, but the Single became available to special order only. This only lasted to the end of that season, when the make went out of production.

# DKR

This scooter was built in Wolverhampton and launched in July 1957 as the Dove. It had a rather heavy appearance, but had to make do with a 147 cc Villiers 30C engine with fan cooling and a three-speed gearbox.

The engine went into a frame comprising a single, large-diameter tube running from the headstock to the pivot for the rear fork. There were long leading-links at the front, 10 in. split-rim wheels, and drum brakes of 5 in. diameter at the front and 6 in. at the rear.

Much of the heavy appearance came from the petroil tank's location in front of the headstock, above the front wheel. It was enclosed by a massive pressing that extended down to form the mudguard and up into the headlamp nacelle. The pressing swept back to the apron, and its top ran back to form an instrument panel on top of a large glove compartment at the back of the apron.

From then on, the looks lightened, with a small tunnel in the floor and a rear body with detachable side panels. The dualseat was hinged, and the various sections of the body could be removed quite easily for maintenance. A neat, oval-section silencer went under the gearbox and could be readily dismantled for cleaning.

The Dove went forward into 1958 as it was, and in February was joined by two more models. Both used the same frame and body, and both had electric starting and a fan-cooled engine. The first was the Pegasus with a 148 cc Villiers 31C engine. This copied the Dove in having a three-speed gearbox. The second was the Defiant, which used the 197 cc 9E unit, but with a four-speed gearbox.

All three went forward for 1959, when they were joined by the Manx, which was powered by the 249 cc Villiers 2T engine. As with the Defiant, it had four speeds, fan cooling and electric start, but also a 70 mph potential. However, it still retained the same size brakes as the other models, which indicated the tight financial constraints under which the firm worked.

At the end of the season, the Dove was replaced by the Dove II, which used the 31C engine, but with kickstart. Early in 1960 the Pegasus was replaced by the Pegasus II with 174 cc 2L engine, while the Defiant and Manx ran on as they were.

The last two continued for another year, but the two smaller models were dropped at the end of 1960, when the firm launched a new model. This was the Capella, which had lighter looks and took the firm on to their end in 1966.

**DKR Dove in 1957 with heavy front end due to the forward mounting of the fuel tank**

# DMW

This firm was briefly associated with the Calthorpe name just after the war, when a small prototype was built, using a twin-port, 122 cc Villiers engine. This went into a rigid loop frame with telescopic forks. Its most noticeable feature was a saddle mounted on a single post, bicycle style, which, thus, was adjustable for height.

It was April 1950 before any more was heard of the Sedgely firm, but then came news of a small range of lightweights. The machines were available with Villiers 1F, 10D or 6E engines, and the two larger with rigid frames or plunger rear suspension. All had MP telescopic forks, which the firm themselves had developed and were to sell to other companies for many years.

The machines retained the post saddle mounting and could have direct or battery lighting, the power source for the latter being housed in a box on the left. This could also act as a toolbox and was matched by another on the right. The machines were nicely finished in turquoise blue.

The range was revised for 1951, when the smallest model with the 1F engine only stayed in the line-up for a few months. The others became the Standard or De Luxe, depending on whether they were rigid or had plungers, and had direct or battery lighting respectively, although the latter was an option for the Standard models.

Two further De Luxe models were added in 122 and 197 cc capacities, and these had plunger frames constructed from square-section tubing. This was all-welded and gave a weight saving, thanks to the reduction of lugs. The machine was fitted with a dualseat, and the toolbox was formed by a pressing between the seat nose and the frame. Access to the box was by removing the seat, which was held by two wing nuts.

The De Luxe models with round-tube frames were dropped for 1952, to leave four road machines, comprising Standard and De Luxe with 10D or 6E engines. These were joined by competition models using the same engines, again in rigid or plunger frames. In effect, they were the road models with trials tyres and without lights, which remained an option.

During the year, the frame was amended to allow a 4 in. rear tyre to be fitted to the competition models, and for 1953 these were only listed in plunger form. The rigid versions remained as options for a few months, while the 197 cc

**The 1952 competition DMW with square-tube frame, plunger rear suspension and Villiers engine**

DMW fitted with the French 170 cc ohv AMC four-stroke engine unit and offered for 1954

model became referred to as the 4S. The four road models continued, the 197 cc De Luxe being fitted with a headlamp cowl to match the style of the times. The 122 cc rigid model became the Coronation to mark the event that took place that year. Later in the year, it was tried with some short leading-link front forks, not seen elsewhere.

There was a considerable change to the model line-up for 1954, as DMW established a link with the French AMC engine company. This was Ateliers de Mécanique du Centre, nothing to do with the Plumstead group, who produced a nice line of single-cylinder, four-stroke engines. The largest of these was of 249 cc and had a chain-driven, single overhead camshaft, hairpin valve springs, gear primary drive and unit construction of its four-speed gearbox. The other two engines, of 125 and 170 cc capacity, had overhead valves. All three were well finned and nicely styled.

There was also a new frame, which became known as the P-type. This had the top and downtubes in square-section, but the rear half comprised a series of pressings welded together. Rear

suspension was by pivoted fork, which was located on a movable pivot at the front to provide rear chain adjustment. The pressings were continued to the rear to form the mudguard and number plate, while there were compartments formed in it for the battery and tools. Access to these was by raising the dualseat, which was hinged at the rear.

This frame was used by the Dolomite model, which had the 249 cc AMC engine, the 175P with the 170 cc AMC, and three using Villiers power. Of these, the Cortina had the 224 cc 1H, and the De Luxe the 197 cc 8E, while the Moto Cross used the similar-sized 7E. The plunger frame remained for another 197 De Luxe and the competition 4S. These followed suit and changed to the 8E and 7E engines.

The model with the 125 cc AMC engine failed to get off the ground, but there were two more with French engines that did. One made only a brief appearance during 1954 and used the 170 cc engine in the P-type motocross frame, fitted with Earles front forks. It was an export-only model with a short life.

The other model was a show surprise at Earls Court, late in 1953, and was built purely for road racing in the ultra-lightweight class. It had a twin-overhead-camshaft engine based on the pushrod job, so the bottom half looked much as that of the 170. The camshaft drive was by bevels and vertical shaft, with a train of spur gears in the cambox. Lubrication was much improved to suit, and a well finned oil filter and cooler unit went in the return line from the cambox. The engine unit went into the P-frame with Earles forks and was called the Hornet.

All these models continued for 1955, when they offered the option of the Earles forks in place of the usual telescopics. There was one new machine, which replaced the earlier 125 cc model, and this used the 147 cc Villiers 29C engine in the P-type frame. It was called the Leda and was one of the few to run on into 1956, when all the AMC engines were dropped. As a result, the firm used only Villiers engines.

Also out was the road plunger model, but the competition one continued as the 5S. The other models with the P-frame were given Mark numbers, the 197 cc De Luxe becoming the 200P Mk I. The Moto Cross with the 7E had Mk V added to its name and was joined by a Mk VI, which used the 9E engine. In matching style, there was

a 7E-powered MK VII Trials and, for the road, the 200P Mk IX with a 9E engine. The Cortina simply continued, as did the Earles forks option, except for the Leda and Moto Cross models, which had these as standard.

The Leda, 5S and Mk V were all dropped for 1957, but the Mk I, VI, VII, and IX all continued, as did the Cortina. There were five new models, including two more Mk IXs as the 150P and 175P. These used the usual P-type frame and telescopic front forks, but were fitted with the 148 cc 31C and 174 cc 2L engines respectively. The same cycle parts were also used by the Dolomite II, which was powered by the 249 cc Villiers 2T twin two-stroke. However, the 200 Mk VIII was simpler, having an 8E engine in a tubular loop frame with telescopics, 5 in. brakes and a utility specification.

The final new model was totally different, for it was a scooter that used the 99 cc Villiers 4F engine with two-speed gearbox. It was called the Bambi. The prototype had been seen a year or more earlier at Earls Court, but now the machine was ready for production. The frame was a mono-coque, built up from steel pressings that were welded together in scooter style, with apron, tunnel and rear body. The front forks were of the Earles pattern, but with a stirrup linking the fork arms to a helical spring concealed within the steering column. A well valanced mudguard con-cealed most of the supporting members.

At the rear, the wheel was carried in a pivoted fork constructed from two major pressings. These

The DMW Bambi scooter launched in
1957 and fitted with a Villiers 4F engine
with two-speed gearbox

also supported the engine unit between them, so
the whole became a major assembly that was
readily detached from the main frame. Both
wheels were of the disc type with 2.50 × 15 in.
tyres, so they were larger, but narrower, than the
norm for a scooter. Together with the body shape,
single seat pad and windscreen, they gave the
machine a rather unusual line. Access panels and

a hinged seat enabled routine servicing to be
carried out.

The range was well thinned out for 1958, only
four models remaining, although there was a newcomer. Those left were the Bambi scooter, 200 Mk
VIII, 200P Mk IX and Dolomite II, so little of the
past remained. New was the Mk X, which was
built as either a trials or scrambles machine, fitted

*Left* **The basic DMW 200 Mk VIII
with Villiers 8E engine in
tubular frame, as listed for 1957**

*Below* **The Dolomite II with 249 cc 2T engine in the DMW P-type
frame with pressed-steel rear section**

**Trials version of the Mk X with 2T engine, Earles forks and increased ground clearance**

with, of all things, the 2T engine. The frame members were cut short to increase ground clearance, and high-level pipes, suitable tyres, and wide or close gear ratios to suit the intended competition were fitted.

The Mk VIII did not continue into 1959, but the other models did, and in the middle of the year the Dolomite IIA was produced by fitting the 324 cc 3T twin engine in the Dolomite II frame. Late that year, a competition Mk XII appeared, which was much as the Mk X, but fitted with a 246 cc 32A engine for trials, or a 33A for scrambles.

These two were revised a little with alloy hubs and Girling brakes, and for 1960 were joined by two more with 9E engines. Otherwise, the range was as before and was to continue with a variety of road and competition models until 1967. These included the unique Deemster, which was part scooter and part motorcycle.

# Dot

Dot were mainly a competition company, and one of the oldest in the business, for they began building their machines in 1903 – the founder, Harry Reed, won a TT in 1908. They continued with motorcycles until 1932, but from then on only built a tradesman's three-wheeler until 1949.

They then decided to return to motorcycles, and initial plans were for 125 and 200 cc road models, but only the larger machine was built. It used the Villiers 6E engine in a rigid loop frame with blade girder forks. Equipment included a battery, saddle and centre stand, making a neat machine.

For 1950 two versions were offered with direct or battery lighting, and for 1951 these were fitted with telescopic front forks. They were joined by the Scrambler model, which had alloy mudguards, trials tyres and a waist-level exhaust system. It was supplied with lights, which could be easily removed, and a silencer.

During 1951 the firm introduced a road-going 250, which used the 248 cc Brockhouse side-valve engine in the road cycle parts. The engine was made by the Lancashire firm because they had an involvement with the American Indian company, as well as making the Corgi (see page 67). It was of unit construction with a three-speed gearbox, an iron barrel and alloy head. Its oil was carried in the sump. To suit the USA, the gear pedal and kickstart were on the left, which put the final drive on the right, but Dot fitted it into their cycle parts without much trouble.

The range began to take the shape it was to keep for the rest of the decade in 1952 with a variety of models, which used the same basic

Dot Mancunian with 9E engine, which was one of the few road models built by this competition-oriented firm

85

A Dot 246 cc scrambler of 1960 with the inevitable Villiers A-series engine

parts. From these, a series of competition machines was introduced by varying the basic specification. The two road models remained, as did the Scrambler, which became the S and had road equipment, but no lights. With direct lighting added, it became the SD, while stripped for action it was the SC. In a similar manner, the trials machines were the T and TD, with direct lighting only fitted to the latter.

They all continued for 1953, when they were joined by a range with a new frame with pivoted-fork rear suspension. These models had the letter H added to their type, so the two road machines became the DH and RH. The three scrambles and two trials models followed suit, and the latter were joined by two more. These were the THX and TDHX, which had a further change to a 21 in. front wheel.

This massive range was much reduced for 1954 by deleting the road models, including the 250, and the rigid-framed scramblers. All that remained went over to the 8E engine, with the option of the four-speed gearbox, while all models had telescopics as standard. An Earles-type leading-link fork was offered as an option.

The T and TD remained alone with the rigid frame and were accompanied by the sprung trials models with 21 in. front wheel, but not the TH or

TDH. The scramblers were in the three forms as before, with or without lights and stripped for racing.

The rigid trials machines were dropped for 1955, when the TH and TDH returned, so there remained three scrambles and four trials models in the range. They were dropped again for 1956, as all trials riders wanted the larger-diameter wheel, so there were five competition machines. Their front fork option became short leading links controlled by long external units. The range was joined by a road model once more, which used the Villiers 9E engine and the leading-link forks. It was called the Mancunian and displayed an attempt to cowl the headlamp and enclose the area beneath the dualseat nose. Colours were British Racing green or Continental red.

For 1957 there was talk of offering the 31C and 2L engines to special order, as the 10D had been in the past. Nothing came of this, but the range was given a new engine in the form of the 9E. The five competition models were joined by one more called the Works Replica Trials Special, which had detail changes to improve its trials capability. All models were fitted with the leading-link forks as standard.

Early in 1957 the firm began to import the Italian Vivi machines, produced by Viberti of Turin. All those brought in were of 50 cc with a two-stroke engine and two-speed gearbox. They were built as moped, racer and scooterette and helped to augment the company's cash flow.

The whole range continued as it was for 1958, at the end of which the Mancunian was withdrawn. The other models ran on, and the range was extended by offering all of them with a 246 cc Villiers A-series engine in place of the 9E. Otherwise, the machines were the same, and for scrambles were fitted with the 31A, or for trials the 32A.

There were also three new models with twin-cylinder engines, two being built for scrambles and the third for the road. The first competition model used the 249 cc Villiers 2T and was much as the single-cylinder version, except for the twin open pipes. These had no expansion box and were simply cut-off short. The machine was listed as the SCH Twin.

The second scrambles model had the same name, but differed in having a 349 cc RCA engine. This unit was of advanced construction, with horizontally-split crankcase and full flywheels, twin Amals and a four-speed gearbox. The block was in iron, with side exhausts feeding alloy adaptors to the pipes, while separate alloy heads were fitted. The cycle parts were as for the Villiers twin model.

The third twin was a road machine, named the Sportsman's Roadster. It also used the RCA engine and had leading-link front and pivoted-fork rear suspension. Its specification included dual 6 in. front brakes and polished aluminium mudguards and petroil tank.

The range still included the Vivi machines, and the firm continued with these for 1960, along with some motorcycles from the Guazzoni range. Otherwise, the 1960 range was as 1959, except that the 2T-engined scrambler was dropped. This happened to nearly all the Dot range at the end of that year, and from then on they offered a much reduced selection of models until 1968, after which they were forced to use foreign engine units.

# Douglas

Douglas were building flat-twins before World War 1 and continued to do so throughout their commercial life. There were other models along the way, but they were few in number, and while the company went through many financial ups and downs, they remained true to that original concept.

So it was no surprise to learn that their post-war model had a flat-twin engine when it was first described in September 1945. What was nearly new was that it was mounted transversely, as they had only done that once in pre-war days, while the 348 cc capacity and overhead valves had not been seen on a Douglas since 1932.

The machine was totally new, with unit construction of the engine and gearbox, but with chain final drive. The engine dimensions were near square, and the crankshaft built up with roller big-end bearings. There were twin camshafts beneath the crankshaft, and the valve gear was totally enclosed.

Both heads and barrels were in cast iron, but the rockers were concealed by a polished alloy cover, and there was an Amal for each side. The exhaust pipes curled under the cylinder, and both ran to a cast alloy silencer box under the gearbox. The timing gears were at the front of the engine, under a large polished cover, and the drive was extended up to a Lucas mag-dyno mounted on top of the alloy crankcase. This item was extended downwards to form the sump for the oil system.

The drive was taken via a single-plate, dry clutch with Ferodo linings to the four-speed gearbox. This was controlled by a pedal on the right, while its output shaft drove a bevel-gear pair. This, in turn, passed the drive to the rear wheel by chain. The kickstart lever was also on the right and swung in line with the machine, so a further pair of bevels was used to enable it to turn the layshaft and, thus, the engine.

*Left* **The post-war 348 cc flat-twin Douglas T35, as first seen in 1946 with its leading-link forks and torsion-bar rear suspension**

*Right* **The T350, or Mk III, road tested during 1948, when the superb suspension was greatly and rightly praised**

The engine and gearbox unit was mounted in a duplex frame with pivoted-fork rear suspension and short leading links at the front. Both were unusual in that the suspension medium was torsion bars, and the rear ones ran along inside the lower frame tubes. The front end was locked with an arm splined to the bars, while a lever at the rear connected to the fork with a short link.

The front suspension in the original design used torsion bars running up the main fork tubes and secured at their upper ends. At the bottom were the short leading links, which were connected to the bars to provide the suspension. For production, this arrangement was altered to what Douglas called their Radiadraulic fork, which kept the short leading links, but connected these to compression springs within the fork legs. The springs were taper ground to give a variable-rate action over a total 6 in. of movement, and hydraulic damping was incorporated in the fork legs.

Both wheels had 19 in. rims and 7 in. drum brakes in offset hubs. A deep rear mudguard was supported by a subframe, and the machine came with full electrical equipment, a saddle and a centre stand. A large toolbox was tucked under the saddle in the frame bend. In this form, the machine was known as the T35, or Mk I, and eventually reached production in 1947.

For 1948 the cylinder head was revamped by Freddie Dixon and the frame improved, as there had been breakages. The engine work improved the performance, and the manner in which it was achieved, and in this form the machine was called the Mk III. In the middle of the year it was joined by a second model, listed as the Sports, and this was styled to suit, with upswept exhaust pipes and a tubular Burgess silencer on each side. The mudguards were slimmer, and a small toolbox appeared above each silencer, which left the original space over the gearbox available for an air filter if the owner wished.

The two models continued in Mk III form for 1949, but the range was expanded for 1950 with three new machines, while the existing ones were modified to a Mk IV form. For this, they had the subframe altered to carry a large triangular toolbox on each side and to provide support for the pillion footrests, which had previously been mounted on the pivoted fork.

The front mudguard was no longer sprung, so followed the wheel more closely, which meant that it had to be attached to the brake backplate on one side and the hub spindle on the other. The result was rather messy and not carried out particularly well. The exhaust system of the standard model varied, with either the silencer box of the early machines being used or separate low-

level pipes and tubular silencers, which were raised by an upward kink in the pipes.

Of greater interest to the enthusiast were the 80 Plus and 90 Plus models, which were built as sports machines, although the second could be obtained in Clubman's form, stripped for racing. The engines had deeper finning and were well worked on inside to raise the power output. They were bench tested and anything over 25 bhp

became a 90 Plus, while the failures were used for the 80 Plus.

On the cycle side, both models were much as the Mk IV, except that the exhausts ran straight back to the silencers, the front brake was a massive 9 in. diameter, and its hub was spoked into a 21 in. rim. The finish was maroon for the 80 Plus and gold for the 90 Plus, which made them stand out.

The 1948 Sports model Douglas introduced during that year

When supplied for competition, the 90 Plus came with racing magneto and tyres, close-ratio gears, rev-counter, alloy guards and a dualseat of most uncomfortable appearance. A further option was the fitting of alloy heads and barrels, but their only advantage was weight reduction. Cooling was no problem once the big finned exhaust nuts were removed from the air flow, but the different expansion rate of the steel hold-down studs could pull them out of the crankcase. The Douglas solution was slack head nuts when the engine was cold, but this caused leaks, so the all-alloy engine was soon abandoned.

The final new 1950 machine was the Competition model, which was built for trials use. The engine and gearbox were standard items, but the frame was new and rigid. Its ground clearance was increased and an undershield added to protect the crankcase, but the forks were stock and a 21 in. front wheel was used. At the rear was a 4.00 in.-section tyre, and the gearing was lowered to suit the intended use. The exhaust pipes were swept up, the left one crossing over above the gearbox to a single silencer high on the right. A raised saddle and light-alloy mudguards were fitted, the front one being sprung and well clear of the tyre. An air cleaner went above the gearbox, and the machine had the option of lights, dualseat and alloy cylinder heads. It was a nice machine, but the engine width soon became a major problem, both in and between sections, while a small twin was not the easiest to ride in the trials of the day.

The standard and Sports models became a single model for 1951, listed as the Mk V, which was very much as the year before, except for the Plus-type exhaust pipes and a ribbed front mudguard. The early box silencer remained available as an option, along with crash bars, a dualseat and a steering damper. The Plus models continued much as before, but with alloy heads, while the Competition model could still have the all-alloy engine.

Of equal importance to the firm was the launch of the Douglas Vespa scooter for 1951, following an earlier showing at Earls Court. At that time, scooters were viewed disparagingly by the British industry in general, but Douglas had the good sense to see which way the tide was running. They came to an arrangement with the Italian Piaggio firm of Genoa to make the Vespa under licence, and the official launch took place in March 1951.

The design was brilliant, the concept of a monocoque frame with a compact engine and gearbox unit running on for many years. There was no frame in the accepted sense, for the Vespa followed car practice and combined this with the body panels to save weight, while retaining rigidity. Thus, the apron and floor were one pressing, to which a bracing section was welded and which carried the rear suspension arm with its single right leg. A rear body was welded to the main section to form the seat mounting, enclose the petroil tank and act as a rear mudguard. Large blister cowlings on each side gave a balanced appearance; the right-hand one enclosed the engine, while that on the left was used to conceal the battery and tools. The fuel cap was set in the top between the saddle and the rear carrier, which could have a mounting for a spare wheel added to it. The cables and wiring harness were all located within the body shell, which made replacement awkward.

The front suspension was by a single trailing arm, pivoted at the lower end of the steering column, which was cranked round the wheel. A compression spring provided the suspension medium, as it did at the rear, where there was a hydraulic damper, a fitting the front end lacked. The front muguard was mounted on the steering column, so it was sprung and turned with the

*Left* **First signs of the Vespa came at the late 1949 Earls Court show, where this early model with mudguard-mounted headlamp was shown**

*Right* **The production Vespa differed in the headlamp location and is seen here in 1951, outside Victoria bus station in London**

bars. In Italy it had the headlight mounted on top of it, as on the 1945 Piaggio original, but this was too low for the British height regulations, so it was moved up and on to the apron. Below it went the electric horn, the fitting of which doubled as an access hole when dealing with the cables.

Both wheels were of the split-rim type with small 3.50 × 8 in. tyres, and they were interchangeable, so the spare was a real asset. There were drum brakes in the hubs and studs for the wheel mounting.

The engine and gearbox were built as a very compact unit, which was mounted to the rear pivoted arm. Thus, it was very easy to detach the wiring, controls and rear unit, pull out the arm's pivot bolt and wheel the whole assembly to the bench for maintenance.

The engine was a simple 125 cc two-stroke with alloy head and horizontal iron barrel. A deflector piston was used, along with a built-up crankshaft with roller big-end and bobweight flywheels. The flywheel magneto, with its lighting coils and cooling fan, went on the right, to the outside, and the clutch on the left. This drove back to the all-indirect, three-speed gearbox, which was carried within the extended crankcase castings.

The gearbox had all three input gears locked as one on their shaft and selected by engaging the output gears to their shaft with a drawbar device. This was controlled by rotating the left handlebar twistgrip, complete with clutch lever, and the connection between them was by rods. Thus, the model is referred to as the 'rod type' more often than by its formal 2L2 designation. The output shaft extended from the gearbox to the rear wheel, so the drive was very direct. It was supported by two ball races, which were housed in an extension of the left-hand crankcase casting, as this, in turn, was clamped into the end of the cast alloy rear pivot arm.

Thanks to the compact design and need for a minimum number of bearings and seals, the Vespa was always a lively performer, which usually had the edge over the rival Italian Lambretta. The snag was that, as many parts had more than one job to do, once they wore, the effect could be dramatic. For all that, the machines proved very popular and, in their green finish, were soon selling well. As they were made in the Douglas Bristol works, they featured British components from Amal, BTH, Lucas and others. There were plenty of options to catch the scooterist's fancy. The machine had a centre stand that was easy to use, and the offset engine weight did not seem to worry riders.

The Douglas Competition model was dropped at the end of 1951, to leave the three flat twins and the Vespa with little change. At the show, there was a 489 cc prototype that was based on the existing design, but had the mag-dyno enclosed by a finned cover, which extended back to include the air cleaner. It went into a frame with sidecar lugs and was exhibited with a chair attached.

The production twins had an external Vokes oil filter added for 1953, at the end of which the 80 Plus was dropped. The other two twins continued for 1954 without change, but the Vespa became the model G, the gearchange being controlled by twin cables instead of the complicated rod system.

It was all change for 1955, as a new flat-twin replaced the earlier models and the Vespa had a revamped engine. The twin was first called the Dart, but in production became the Dragonfly. It represented a major update of the original design, especially with regard to the frame and suspension.

The engine was basically as before, but most components were revised in some way or other. The crankcase and crankshaft were stiffer, the iron barrels recessed deeper, but the heads remained iron and the timing gear unchanged. The magneto was replaced by a points and distributor unit under a cover, and the dynamo by a Miller alternator on the crankshaft nose. There was only one Amal carburettor, which fed an inlet tract cast into the clutch housing. This emerged on each side, where a curved and plated tube took the mixture to the cylinder. The exhaust ran down and back to a silencer on each side. The transmission was as before, with four speeds and chain final drive.

The frame was duplex with a single top tube and conventional, pivoted rear fork controlled by Girling hydraulically-damped suspension units. At the front were Earles-type leading-link forks with more Girlings, while both wheels had 19 in. rims and 7 in. drum brakes. The mudguards were deeply valanced, and the model had a dualseat fitted as standard with a large toolbox under its nose. This could accommodate the optional air filter, if required, but not the battery, which was low down on the left, just behind the cylinder. The most distinctive feature of the model was the headlamp mounting, which was flared back to the fuel tank, so the lamp did not turn with the bars. The tank itself held over five gallons of petrol, so the model was a true tourer in that respect.

The Vespa became the GL2 with revised engine

*Right* **A Douglas Vespa on tour in Glencoe, Scotland, and highlighting something of what two-wheeled transport is about**

*Below* **The Douglas Dragonfly, which kept the essence of the past in a new frame and forks with an unusual fuel tank**

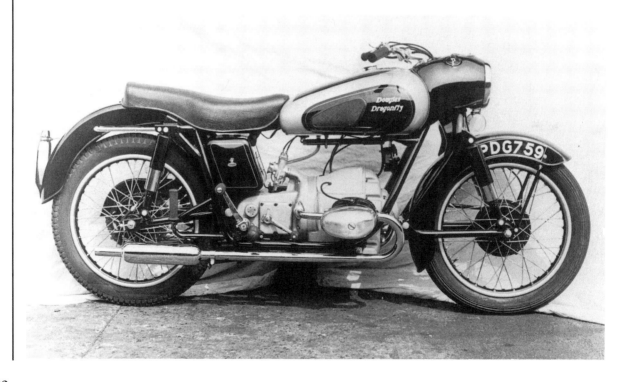

dimensions, full flywheels and a new head and barrel. The last now had two transfers. Outside the engine were other alterations to the cycle parts, including the option of a dualseat. The model had a very short life, for early in 1955 it was replaced by the 42L2 and joined by the 145 cc GS. The 42L2 differed from its predecessor in having the headlamp mounted on the handlebars, instead of the apron, where it was joined by the speedometer, which had also been apron-mounted up to then. The front suspension gained a hydraulic damper, and the engine blister was cleaned up with louvres in place of a cut-away section for cooling.

The GS, or Gran Sport, had a four-speed gearbox, as well as the extra capacity, and was an import built entirely in Italy. It continued with the 42L2 and the Dragonfly for 1956 without change, and on into 1957. For that year, the 42L2 became the Vespa Standard and was joined by the Magna and Ultra models, which had different levels of equipment.

Unfortunately, time ran out for Douglas and they were unable to develop the Dragonfly, which had become known as being too slow for sports riding and too noisy and fussy for touring. Sales were poor, and late in 1956 the company was taken over by Westinghouse Brake and Signal. By March 1957 production at Bristol had ceased and the flat-twins were no more. The Vespa continued as an import, of course, but to devotees of the marque, it was the end. Only the old sales slogan remained: 'A twin is best, and Douglas is the best twin'.

# Dunelt

# Dunkley

This company had first appeared in 1919 and became best known between the wars for a two-stroke engine design with a double-diameter piston. They continued with proprietary engines until 1935 and then left the industry.

Dunelt returned for the briefest of spells in 1957, when the name was revived for a 50 cc moped. This had a two-stroke engine with two-speed gearbox and twistgrip change. The frame had front and rear suspension by telescopic and pivoted forks respectively, the wheels had small drum brakes in full-width hubs, and there was direct lighting.

It came and went in months, with virtually no record nor any impact on the market. At that time, there were scores of continental mopeds of all styles, so there was little call for yet another marque.

This make came and went in three short years, leaving barely a mark on the industry but, for all that, represented a good attempt to break into the market. The models often had continental lines, but were mainly made at Hounslow on the outskirts of West London.

They came on to the market early in 1957 with the Whippet 60 Scooterette, which had a 61 cc ohv engine with inclined alloy barrel and parallel valves in an alloy head. These were arranged across the engine, so the carburettor was mounted to an inlet tract on the right, and the exhaust emerged from the left. The camshaft lay behind the cylinder, where it was gear driven, lubrication was wet sump, and ignition was provided by a Wipac flywheel magneto. A two-speed gearbox was built in unit with the engine and controlled by a left-hand twistgrip.

**The Dunelt 50 cc moped, which made the briefest of appearances on the market in 1957**

The engine unit went into a spine frame with telescopic front and pivoted rear suspension. There were 4 in. drum brakes in wheels with 23 in. rims, a short dualseat and direct lighting.

Later in the year, the Scooterette was joined by the Super Sports 65. This had an engine with a slightly longer stroke, to increase the capacity to 64 cc, and a raised compression ratio. The two-speed gearbox remained, but the frame took on a very continental look and was made from two pressings in spine form. The suspension systems were as before, as were the full-width hubs. The dualseat, as well as the rear legs, came from Italy.

For 1958 these two models were joined by the S65 Scooter, which retained the 64 cc engine in a new set of cycle parts. The frame had a single, large tube which ran from the headstock, under the engine, to a vertical member. This supported the fuel tank, the bodywork and the pivot for the rear suspension fork.

The body, including the apron, was a single assembly, which was hinged from the top of the apron to give access to the engine and rear wheel. A deep mudguard enveloped the front wheel, while both had 15 in. rims with the same full-width hubs and 4 in. drum brakes as the other models. The front suspension differed from these, being by short leading links. The scooter came with a dualseat and footboards on each side of the deep engine tunnel.

For 1959 the Super Sports 65 became the Whippet Sports and the other two models ran on with two new ones. These were very similar and listed as the 49.6 cc Popular Scooter and 64 cc Popular Major Scooter. They had a common rigid frame with telescopic front forks and the 15 in. wheels. The engine was set well back and was fan-cooled so that the apron could lead to a flat floor ahead of the rear bodywork. This simply enclosed the engine unit, with a further rear mudguard enclosure extending to the number plate. There was a simple saddle. The result was somewhat stark, but functional.

The two models used similar engines, the larger being the same as that used by the other models, and the smaller having reduced bore and stroke. The larger-capacity machine had some additional trim to enable it to carry a de luxe tag, but otherwise they were the same.

At the end of 1959 the firm dropped the entire range, and the marque vanished as quickly as it had come. Maybe they had a premonition about the next decade.

# EMC

Josef Ehrlich came to Britain in 1937, and by 1939 had an engine of his own manufacture installed in an old Francis-Barnett for road and track testing. He was Austrian, so it was hardly surprising that his interest lay in two-strokes and that these were of the split-single type, favoured by Puch and the German DKW.

The 1939 engine was of this type, with two 44 mm bore cylinders sharing a common 79 mm stroke to give 240 cc capacity. The cylinders sat one behind the other, with a side inlet and rear exhaust for the back one, while the transfer port was in the front one. The two were joined at the top under the single combustion chamber. The connecting rod was of Y-shape and joined to both pistons, having a slotted small-end for one of them to compensate for the movement of the parts.

After the war, Ehrlich set up in business to produce his EMC machines, which were launched in 1947. The engine had grown to 345 cc, but otherwise was laid out as before. However, it had a master connecting rod and a slave rod. Its appearance was odd, and this was accentuated by the fins on the cast-iron block, for they were rectangular in outline and alternated in depth. Due to this, a casual glance suggested few fins, widely spaced.

The head was in alloy, as was the crankcase. Lubrication was by petroil for the model T tourer and by a Pilgrim oil pump, driven from the magneto sprocket, for the sports model S. This item sat behind the engine and above the Burman four-speed gearbox, the drive of which was enclosed by a cast alloy case.

The engine and gearbox went into a rigid duplex frame with a forged bronze backbone and steering head. This had twin tubes formed into loops bolted to it at each end, and these completed the structure. The front forks were Dowty oleo-pneumatics, which combined air suspension with

The machine Joe Ehrlich was showing to the press in 1939 with its 240 cc split-single engine

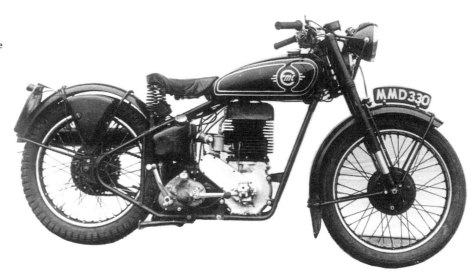

The post-war 345 cc EMC split-single engine installed in a rigid frame with Dowty Oleomatic forks

The EMC exhibited at the 1952 show with a 125 cc JAP engine, spine frame and downtube suspension unit

hydraulic damping. Both wheels had 7 in. drum brakes, but the front had one on each side, its hub being fitted into a 20 in. rim.

The machine was highly geared, and Ehrlich claimed over 100 mpg in advertising, which was an important point in those days of petrol rationing. Owners, however, found it difficult to achieve half that figure and spoke of vibration at the

70 mph top speed. It was also expensive, so most buyers opted for AMC, Ariel or BSA, which they knew and understood.

For 1948 there was talk of a second model in a plunger frame, which came to nothing, but the backbone forging was changed to a light alloy. The oil pump was modified so its output could be varied by a cable connected to the throttle, and conical hubs with 7 in. brakes were adopted for both wheels.

There was also mention of a road-racing model, which had a phasing piston, despite the ban on supercharging. Ehrlich held that it would become admissible and that the engine was all his, but it looked remarkably like the pre-war blown DKW. It was installed with a Burman gearbox in a frame with Dowty suspension front and rear, and a 250 cc version won the Hutchinson 100 race late in 1947. This was not Ehrlich's first involvement in post-war racing, for he had been in a dispute at the 1946 Manx with claims regarding patents and demands for the two DKWs entered to be run as EMCs. Once the daily paper correspondents had filed their stories, with suitably sensational headlines, no more was heard of the matter.

In the early 1950s Ehrlich became linked with the Puch firm, and one outcome was a neat 125 cc racing model. This used the split-single Puch engine with its unit-construction, four-speed gearbox, twin carburettors and twin exhaust pipes and megaphones. The engine went into a simple loop frame with telescopic forks and a Puch rear fork constructed from pressings welded together. They performed quite well and were on offer for two or three years.

A 500 cc split-single was also spoken of, and a 125 cc road model with a JAP engine. The latter was shown at Earls Court and had an unusual frame. It looked conventional at first, but was of the spine type with pivoted rear fork. This fork also extended ahead of its pivot and carried the engine and three-speed gearbox unit in one. What looked like a normal downtube was, in fact, a lengthy suspension unit, and the pivoted fork tubes also doubled as exhaust pipes. The weight of the unsprung parts was thus considerable, and only the prototype was seen.

There was a move to sell the Puch 250 cc road model with EMC badges, but this did not last for long, for the firm was wound up in 1953. Puch later set up their own organization, while Joe Ehrlich went on to fresh pastures, but remained with motorcycle racing for a good few years.

# Excelsior

This company dates back to before the dawn of the industry, for they began with penny-farthing bicycles in 1874 and took to power in 1896. They had their ups and downs and built just about anything, from TT winners to utility models.

The 1939 range reflected this, with models from 98 to 496 cc, and with two-stroke, ohv and ohc engines. During the war, they built the Welbike, from which the Corgi sprang (see page 67), but after that, restricted themselves to lightweight models.

There were just two of these for 1946; one was the Autobyk with a 98 cc Villiers Junior De Luxe engine, and the other the Universal model O with a 122 cc 9D unit and three-speed gearbox. The latter was a neat machine with rigid loop frame and blade girder forks, but its oddest feature was the hand gearchange. This worked in a gate set in the top of the petroil tank, which had a slot in it for the linkage to pass down to the box.

It continued in this form until the end of 1948, while for 1947 the Autobyke became the model VI. It was joined by the Super Autobyk G2, which was fitted with an Excelsior 98 cc Goblin engine with two-speed gearbox. This was not unlike the Villiers JDL and retained the near horizontal inclination for the iron barrel with its alloy head. An overhung crankshaft was used, with the flywheel magneto on the right, outboard of the chain drive to the clutch and simple gearbox, which had the output sprocket on the left.

This engine unit went into the same simple autocycle frame as before, with light blade girders, petroil tank between the frame tubes, engine covers, saddle and rear carrier. Before the year began, however, the forks were altered to tubular girders and their suspension medium from a compression spring to rubber bands working on crossbars.

Within a few months, it was joined by the Autobyk de luxe model S1, which used the single-

The 1949 M1 Excelsior Minor with 98 cc Goblin engine, two-speed gearbox and miniature proportions

speed, 98 cc Excelsior Spryt engine. This was much as the Goblin, but with a single shaft for the clutch and output sprocket in place of the two speeds. All three autocycles continued with the model O for 1948.

There were changes for 1949, but not to the autocycles. The Universal became the model LO and was fitted with the 122 cc Villiers 10D engine with three-speed gearbox. During the year, it gained telescopic front forks to become the U1, which had direct lighting, and was joined by the U2, which had a battery and rectifier. With these two machines came the R1 and R2 Roadmaster models, which were the same, except for a 197 cc Villiers 6E engine. Two further machines were added to the list, both with the name Minor, and coded M1 and M2. They were miniature

motorcycles with loop frame and blade girders, but with a wedge-shaped tank hung beneath the top tube. Both models had Excelsior engines, the M1 using the 98 cc Goblin, and the M2 a bored-out, 123 cc version. Both kept the two-speed gearbox.

This design only lasted for the year, and when the two models were dropped, the V1 Autobyk with the JDL engine went with them. This left the S1 and G2 autocycles and the Universal and Roadmaster models, which were all given plunger rear suspension for 1950. There was one further model introduced that year, and this was, perhaps, the best known post-war Excelsior – the Talisman Twin.

For this, the firm built their own 243 cc, twin-cylinder two-stroke engine. It was of conventional

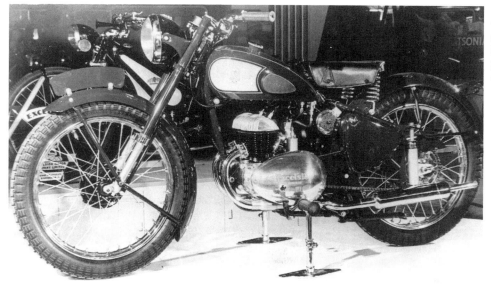

**Early Talisman Twin with its 243 cc two-stroke engine and Excelsior form of plunger rear suspension**

One of the two Excelsior autocycles in 1951, both of which had their own make of 98 cc engine with one or two speeds

The 1957 Excelsior Consort F4 with 99 cc engine, two speeds and girder forks to provide minimal transport

The Excelsior Skutabyk, as it appeared in 1957 based on a Consort with enclosure panels

form, the crankcase being divided vertically into three sections, and the two crankshafts keyed together and held by a nut on one mainshaft. The cast-iron cylinders were separate with alloy heads, and an alloy manifold carried the single Amal that supplied the mixture. A flywheel magneto went on the right and the primary drive to the four-speed Albion gearbox on the left.

This engine unit went into the same loop frame, with plunger rear suspension and telescopic front forks, as used by the other motorcycles. The fittings were either common or similar, and there was a saddle. However, there were two toolboxes instead of only one on the left, and there was a battery in front of the right one. The twin exhaust pipes were connected to a single silencer on the left, and the machine had full lighting and an electric horn.

The whole range went forward unchanged for 1951 and 1952, when it was joined by a Sports version of the twin. This was listed as the STT1, which had twin Amal carburettors and a strange dualseat with side pads below the rider's part to act as kneegrips for the passenger.

The 1953 range showed some change, for the Universal models became export-only machines, being replaced on the home market by the C2 Courier. This had a 147 cc Excelsior engine, which was very much in the Villiers mould, other than the Wipac generator and Amal carburettor. One further difference was that it was mated to a Burman three-speed gearbox, rather than the usual Albion. The cycle parts were as before, and as still used by the Roadmaster models, while the Courier had battery lighting and a rectifier as standard.

The two Autobyks were still going strong, so with the twins made a useful range. It was expanded in April 1953 with the F4 Consort, which was a small motorcycle fitted with the 99 cc Villiers 4F engine with two-speed gearbox. This went into a simple, rigid loop frame with light girder forks, 19 in. wheels and small drum brakes. The equipment included a saddle and cylindrical toolbox beneath it, bulb horn and direct lighting.

The whole range continued for 1954, with a change to the 8E engine for the Roadmaster models and a direct-lighting C1 version of the Courier. There were also five new machines, four in a new frame with pivoted-fork rear suspension. With this came a dualseat. The first two models were the R3 and R4 Roadmaster with the 8E engine and direct or battery lighting respectively. The

other two were twins, the TT2 being the Talisman and the STT2 the Sports version.

The final new model was the D12 Condor, which was effectively the Consort fitted with a 122 cc Villiers 13D engine, but still with the rigid frame and girder forks. It was only built for 1954 and was dropped at the end of the year, along with the plunger-framed C1 and C2 Courier, R1 and R2 Roadmaster, TT1 and STT1 twins, and U1 and U2 Universal, which were no longer even available for export.

The direct-lighting R3 was also phased out, but the R4 continued, as did the Consort and two twins, this line-up being joined by five new models in a new frame for 1955. The smallest of these was the C3 Courier with a 147 cc Excelsior engine and three-speed gearbox, while its frame was simpler than before, having a single tube loop under the engine unit.

The same frame was used for the R5 and R6 Roadmaster models, which had direct or battery lighting, and for two more twins. One was listed as the Popular Talisman, or TT3, and was distinguished by oval toolboxes, as well as the new frame. The second was the Special Equipment Sports Talisman Twin, or SE-STT2, which had full-width alloy hubs.

There were more revisions and new models for 1956, when the Consort changed to the 6F engine and was joined by the F4S Consort, which was much the same, but with plunger rear suspension. Of the Roadmaster models, only the R6 continued, but it was joined by the A9 Autocrat, which was powered by the 9E Villiers engine with four-speed gearbox. Also new was the C1 Condex with 147 cc Villiers 30C engine and three-speed gearbox, which used the Consort spring frame with telescopic front forks.

Among the twins, the Special was dropped, along with the TT2, to leave the TT3 and the Sports model in STT4 form with twin pipes and silencers. That year, the firm also moved into the scooter and moped market by importing the Heinkel products, which served them for a few years.

The C3 Courier was joined by the C4 Convoy in April 1956 and, like the C3, this used the 147 cc Excelsior engine. It was very similar, but had had a few economies made to reduce the price. It replaced the C3 for 1957, when there were finally no Autobyks as both went, along with the R6, C1 and A9, although the last did remain for export only for a short while.

The Excelsior scooter, which was launched in 1959 in two forms, both powered by the firm's 147 cc engine. It shared body pressings with DKR

The two Consort models continued for 1957, but with the sprung one listed as the F6S, along with the TT3 and the Sports Twin, which became the STT5 with deeper fins and revised porting. New was the Skutabyk which, in a sense, replaced the Autobyk. It was based on an F6S Consort, but to this was added extensive exclosure panels, which ran on each side from the downtube to the rear plunger. At the front, legshields were formed and footboards ran back from these to the rear of the machine. The panels had louvres to assist cooling and access holes, while the machine was finished with a dualseat with a suggestion of the pillion kneegrips of the past.

The Consorts, as such, were dropped at the end of the year, although the Skutabyk continued and a new Consort CA8 joined it. This had a pivoted-fork frame with telescopic forks, in which to accommodate the 6F engine, while the rider was provided with a dualseat. A new Universal model, coded UB and fitted with a 147 cc Villiers 30C engine, replaced the Convoy and had a similar specification. The Talisman became the TT4 and the Sports version the STT6, but of more

Excelsior Roadmaster R10, of 1959, with Villiers 9E engine in conventional cycle parts

interest to enthusiasts of the marque was the appearance of the larger 328 cc S8 Super Talisman. This was much as the Sports Twin, with twin carburettors and the same set of cycle parts, including 6 in. brakes in full-width hubs.

The S8 engine had been developed to suit the light three-wheelers then on the market, and late that year this idea was taken one step further. The result was a 491 cc, three-cylinder engine with Siba electric start and suitable Albion gearbox.

Most of the range continued for 1959 with minor changes. The Consort became the CA9, and the Universal the U9 and UR9 with battery and rectifier. The Skutabyk, Talisman and Super Talisman also ran on, but not the Sports Twin model. In its place, there was a new Special Talisman, the S9, but this used the 328 cc engine, with twin carburettors, and was distinguished by full enclosure of the rear end down to wheel-spindle level. It was also unusual in having a tool compartment set in the tank top, the filler neck being inside this with its cap part of the toolbox lid.

The early form of the Consort reappeared in April 1959 as the F4F, complete with rigid frame and girder forks, as in the past. The 6F engine with foot-change was used, but otherwise the fixtures and fittings were as before.

A week later, the firm announced a two-model scooter range, achieving this by dint of using the DKR cycle and body parts (see page 79) fitted with their own 147 cc engine. The models were given the name Monarch, and were designated KS with kickstarter, and EL with an electric one. The body kept the large front section of the DKR, because the fuel tank remained in place ahead of the headstock and above the front wheel, so it was hard to tell the two makes apart, except by the badges fitted to them.

The scooters became the MK1 and ME1 for 1960, when the Roadmaster model returned as the R10 with 9E engine and four-speed gearbox. It used a frame based on that of the twins, of which the Talisman became the TT6, the S9 ran on as it was and the S8 was dropped. Among the smaller models, the Skutabyk was no longer listed, while the Consorts became the C10 and the utility F10. The Universal had its engine changed to the 148 cc Villiers 31C to become the U10.

In this way, the long established firm entered the 1960s, but soon began to flag. After 1962 the range was down to just two models, and the last of these went in 1965 to remove one more famous name from the role of British manufacturers.

# FLM

This was Frank Leach Manufacturing of Leeds, who entered the lightweight market in 1951 with a machine that looked like many others, but differed a good deal. Unlike most, they used the 125 cc JAP engine with three-speed gearbox, installing it in a frame with pivoted-fork rear suspension.

The frame differed further from the norm in being constructed from channel-section steel, while control of the rear fork was by four springs located beneath the engine unit. These were linked to the fork and allowed it some 5 in. of undamped wheel movement.

At the front were telescopic forks, and both 19 in. wheels had 5 in. drum brakes and well valanced mudguards. The machine had a dualseat and was called the Glideride, while a Utility model with rigid frame was also spoken of, but not seen. Only the Glideride was offered for 1952, but during the year a second machine was seen in prototype form.

This was larger with a 197 cc Villiers 6E engine installed in a neat tubular loop frame, which retained the unusual rear suspension of the 125. It failed to reach production, so there was still just the one model for 1953, although it was then offered with a choice of colour schemes and either direct or battery lighting.

Production of this model was totally dependent on supplies of the JAP engine, and as these began to dry up the firm decided to stop production. Perhaps they could have continued with a Villiers engine, but FLM preferred to leave the market.

# Francis-Barnett

A famous firm, best known for its lightweight models and a between-the-wars frame built from lengths of straight tube bolted together. The first machine produced by Gordon Francis and Arthur Barnett appeared in 1920, and soon they had a good range. After the war, they returned to the market with just two models for 1946, one being an autocycle and the other a light motorcycle.

The former was the model 50 Powerbike, which was built much as others of that type, with a 98 cc Villiers JDL engine. This went into a drop frame with blade girder forks, saddle, rear carrier and the usual extensive side-shields around the engine. The other was the model 51 Merlin with 122 cc Villiers 9D engine and three-speed hand-change gearbox. The frame was a simple rigid loop with tubular girder forks, and both wheels had 19 in. rims and 5 in. drum brakes. The machine came with a saddle and rear carrier, while the toolbox between the right-hand chainstays was matched by an oil tank on the left. This had a tap and the fuel tank cap a measure, so mixing the petroil was an easy task.

In 1947 the firm became part of the AMC group, but it was some time before this had any great effect. Meanwhile, the two models continued, the Powerbike changing to tubular girders with rubber-band springing for 1948. These were further braced for 1949, when the original Merlin was replaced by two models with a 10D engine and joined by two more with the 197 cc 6E engine and the name Falcon.

All four new models used the same rigid frame, which was much as before, but with telescopic front forks. The saddle, carrier and oil tank continued, as did the wheels. The Merlin models were the 52 with direct lighting, and the 53 with a battery on the right, under the saddle. The equivalent Falcons were the 54 and 55, all four having a quickly detachable rear number plate to assist wheel removal.

During 1949 a new version of the Powerbike appeared as the model 56, which used the 99 cc Villiers 2F engine in a new loop frame. The front forks continued to be tubular girders with rubber-band suspension, while the remainder of the machine stayed in the autocycle style with saddle, carrier and engine enclosure. These five models continued for the next two years with no real alteration, except that for 1951 the motorcycles were offered in an azure blue finish as an option. Quite a change for a utility range.

At the end of 1951 the Powerbike was dropped, and for 1952 the four motorcycles were joined by four more. Two of these had a new frame with pivoted-fork rear suspension, using a system of rubber bushes as the pivot point. The hydraulically-damped rear units were made by the firm, and there was a rubber rebound stop on the frame beneath the fork.

To suit the new frame, there was a centre stand, rather than one at the rear, and a single toolbox on the left with battery and electric horn on the right. The facility of an easily-removed rear number plate remained, as did the saddle. With the 10D engine, the machine was the Merlin 57, and with the 6E, it became the Falcon 58.

The same names and engines were used by the models 59 and 60, but these had rigid frames and were built for competition use with the cycle parts suitably altered. These two were replaced by four more purpose-built models for 1953, the Merlin 61 and Falcon 62 being for trials and the Merlin 63 and Falcon 64 for scrambles. The two types no longer used the same cycle parts, for the trials models kept the rigid frame, but the scramblers went into the pivoted-fork version.

The Merlins used the competition 10D engine, but the Falcon 62 and 64 changed to the 7E unit to match the 54, 55 and 58, which went over to the 8E. Otherwise, the four rigid and two pivoted-fork models ran on, still with the optional blue finish, and were joined by one further machine.

This was the Overseas Falcon 65, which fell between the road and trials models and was effectively a trail bike. Thus, it had the 8E engine in the pivoted-fork frame, but with narrow sprung mudguards — the front one with massive clearance — stiffer forks and a 21 in. front wheel.

The rigid road models did not continue for 1954, and neither did any of the Merlins. The Falcon 58 became the 67, much as before, and the models 62, 64 and 65 continued as they were. New was the Kestrel 66, which had the 122 cc

A 1951 Francis-Barnett 55 with 197 cc 6E engine in rigid frame

The 1953 pivoted-fork-frame Francis-Barnett, which was built as the model 57 with 10D engine, and as the 58 with the 6E

The export Falcon 65 Francis-Barnett with 8E engine, an early trail machine

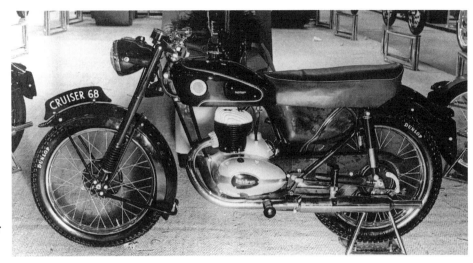

The Francis-Barnett Cruiser 68 with 224 cc Villiers 1H engine in a built-up frame

Villiers 13D engine with three-speed gearbox fitted into a simple loop frame. This had plunger rear suspension and telescopic forks. The equipment included a saddle and direct lighting, while the finish was in azure blue. The machine offered low-cost transport to the commuter.

Shortly after the main range was announced, Francis-Barnett reintroduced a pre-war name for another new model. This was the Cruiser 68, which used the 224 cc Villiers 1H engine with its four-speed gearbox. The machine's frame was built up from a massive, tapered down-member, to which were bolted tube loops with a fabricated pressing in the area beneath the dualseat that extended down to form the rear engine plates. This then formed a stowage space for the battery, rectifier and tools, and gave the model a very neat appearance. Telescopic front and pivoted-fork rear suspensions were used, along with 19 in. wheels and 6 in. drum brakes. The mudguards were deeply valanced, and the finish was in a very nice dark green, set off with gold tank lining.

There were only five models for 1955, all of them having a new front fork with hydraulic damping. The road Falcon was also given a new pivoted-fork frame to become the model 70, while the Cruiser became the 71 with full-width hubs, and the scrambles model the 72. The last, and the trials 62, now had four-speed gearboxes with suitable ratios as standard, while the 62 still kept to its rigid frame.

The one new model was the Kestrel 69, which replaced the 66, had full-width hubs and the new forks, but kept the plunger frame. Into this went a 147 cc Villiers 30C engine with three-speed gearbox to give cheapest model of the range

a touch more power.

All the models had their numbers changed for 1956, the smallest becoming the Plover 73. It retained the 30C engine, but this went into a new frame with tubular front, but pressed-steel rear sections. The pressing supported the pivoted rear fork, concealed its rear suspension units, and housed the tools, battery and electrics, with a single seat for the rider. There were oil-damped telescopics at the front, full-width hubs and a cast alloy expansion box beneath the gearbox with twin outlet pipes.

The other road models became the Falcon 74, with 18 in. wheels, and the Cruiser 75, which had this change for the front only. On the competition front, the trials model became the Falcon 76, and the scrambles machine the Falcon 77. Both had a new frame and a specification to suit their intended use.

The only model to have its number changed for 1957 was the Plover, which became the 78 and gained a dualseat. It also had its silencing arrangements altered, the expansion box becoming a pressed-steel, welded assembly with a single outlet, to which a further silencer was attached. The range was joined by the Cruiser 80, which was the first Francis-Barnett to be fitted with the unhappy AMC two-stroke engine.

The 80 used the 249 cc version, which was the first to appear and presented a smooth shape to the world. Smooth would also seem to apply to the Italian designer, who accepted his brief and fee, but departed for home before his work was either developed or fully tested.

The engine was laid out much as the Villiers 1H, with the four-speed gearbox being bolted to the rear of the crankcase, the castings blended together and full-length covers on each side. The right-hand one concealed a Wipac generator and had a points cover set in it, while the Amal carburettor was enclosed by a further cover. The main odd feature of the engine was the head, barrel and piston assembly, for there were no transfer ports, only depressions in the cylinder walls. To guide the mixture, the long piston had ports in its skirt and a tall crown shaped to match the head. This was different from most in having sunburst radial fins and internal downward projections to match the piston.

In use, this design was to prove poor in operation and reliability, while weak gear-selector parts and poor electrics did nothing to enhance its reputation. In keeping with their traditions, AMC never took the obvious way out with a new top half, but persevered with their troublesome design well into the 1960s, until their empire collapsed from this and other similar ailments.

For the Cruiser 80, this engine was fitted into the 75 frame, with minor alterations, which included Girling rear units. The rear wheel size came down to match the front, at 18 in., and the wiring and switches were amended to suit the Wipac circuits. The filler cap was set flush with the tank top and was hinged to swing up in use.

Early Francis-Barnett scrambler with the 249 cc AMC single engine, which led to the model 82, but no real success

Cut-away show model of the Francis-Barnett Cruiser 84, of 1959, with 249 cc AMC engine and normally fully enclosed with panels

The older Cruiser was dropped for 1958, to leave the AMC-engined 80, which continued with the Plover 78. For the 200 cc class, the Falcon became the 81 with the more streamlined, 197 cc Villiers 10E engine, but with three-speed gearbox, while the cycle side remained as it was. The trials and scrambles Falcons were both dropped, for AMC had fully committed themselves to their new engine, but it was April before a new competition machine appeared.

This was the Scrambler 82, which used a tuned version of the 249 cc AMC engine in a very nice frame with Norton front forks. There were Girlings to control the rear end, and the whole package was very neat, except for the engine. The heart of the problem was the strange piston design and its poor ring sealing, but this was aggravated by the Wipac energy-transfer ignition system.

A month after the Scrambler, the second road model appeared with the AMC engine. This was the 171 cc Light Cruiser 79. The engine was simply a smaller edition of the 249 cc version and the cycle side was similar to the Cruiser. The centre-section enclosure was even larger, extending forward to the carburettor and along the subframe down to footrest level.

All the models continued for 1959, when the Trials 83 with the 249 cc AMC engine joined them. This used the same frame and forks as the Scrambler, but had a long silencer tucked inside the right-hand subframe tube and rear unit. Also new was the Cruiser 84, which created great interest due to its extensive enclosure and legshields fitted as standard. It was based on the 80, so had the 249 cc AMC engine, but was fully enclosed from the cylinder to the rear number plate, and down well below wheel spindle height. It made an impressive machine.

The two Cruiser models ran on for 1960, along with the Light Cruiser and the two competition machines, of which the Trials version became the 85. The last two machines with Villiers engines were changed to AMC units to make the Plover 86 and Falcon 87, but in later years the company had to eat its words and ask Villiers for both engines and technical assistance.

As it was, the 1960 range ran on into the new decade, minus the model 79, and, with later changes, on to the company's end in 1966. It was a sad fate for a firm that had lived through some hard times by building good reliable machines, and from them gaining a reputation of producing some of the better utility motorcycles.

# Greeves

Bert Greeves came into the motorcycle industry because his cousin, Derry Preston Cobb, was paralysed from birth. Bert made him more mobile by fitting a small engine to his wheelchair, and this led to the foundation of Invacar to build powered invalid carriages.

Derry joined in this enterprise as salesman and buyer for the Southend-based firm and, despite his handicap, often travelled about the country, either selling or attending sports meetings once the Greeves name was established. At a later date, his invalid car was powered by a hot Starmaker engine, which must have surprised a few people.

Invacar built up a good business after the war, serving the needs of the disabled, and in 1951 began their move into motorcycles. Unlike most of the industry, they set out on a development programme, which was long enough to sort out most of the problems. Part of this work was done by running a machine in scrambles, which also helped, as the public became used to the machine and its odd appearance and specification.

This centred on the suspension system, which used rubber bushes in torsion as the springing medium. The design was taken from the invalid carriage, so they had experience of it, but it did make for an odd machine. This was especially so at the front, where trailing links were used with the bushes located at the pivot point. The links were joined by a tube that ran round in front of the wheel, while a brake torque stay ran down from the fork leg to the backplate.

At the back there was a conventional pivoted fork, but the rubber bushes were sited above this and at the rear end of the top tube. Each had a short lever arm which was connected to the fork ends by a link on each side. There were no dampers at either end.

For the rest, there was a tubular loop frame with duplex downtubes, a 197 cc Villiers engine tuned for scrambles, offset hubs with drum brakes, and a dualseat. Development work continued on this and other models until late 1953, when the marque was finally launched on to the market.

There were four machines at first, and all used the 197 cc Villiers 8E engine. If this was a feature common to most British lightweights, the Greeves frame and forks were unique. The frame was part tubular, but included a cast alloy beam that ran down from the headstock to the front of the engine. The casting was poured round the welded tubular section which, consequently, was totally locked to it for all time.

Further deep alloy sections ran under the engine unit and were bolted to the main beam and to the rear end of the top tube. The frame loops carried the lugs for the rear fork pivot and the housings for the rubber torsion bushes, which had friction dampers incorporated into them. At the front, there was a leading-link fork which, again, used the rubber bushes at the pivots and had the dampers incorporated with them. The links were joined by a tubular loop behind the wheel, so they did not have to rely on the wheel spindle for their rigidity.

The road models were the 20R with three speeds and the de luxe 20D with four. Both had battery lighting and an electric horn, which sat just ahead of a cylindrical toolbox beneath the dualseat. The headlamp was held by four thin stays, and the entire rear mudguard and seat assembly was easily removed to give access to the rear wheel. Both wheels had 6 in. drum brakes in offset hubs and 19 in. rims.

The competition models were the 20T trials and 20S scrambles, which had special hubs with plain bearings that had proved successful during development. The trials model alone had a 21 in. front wheel, while the cycle parts of both models were altered, or dispensed with, to suit the machine's purpose.

A further model was added to the range for 1954 and differed from the others in using the 242 cc British Anzani twin two-stroke engine with four-speed gearbox. It was listed as the 25D Fleetwing and used the same cycle parts as the Villiers-powered road models with an exhaust system on each side.

For 1955 it was joined by the 25R Standard Twin, which used the same engine in a tubular frame. For this there was a front section, comprising top and downtubes, which were well supported in the headstock, the downtube being extended under the engine unit and up to the rear fork pivot. In this way, it was a direct replacement for the composite tube and alloy frame, was cheaper and nearly as strong. Unlike the earlier models, it used normal rear suspension units, rather than the rubber ones, and these went on to the scrambler as well.

The tubular frame with rear suspension units was also used by the 20R3 and 20R4 Standard models with three- or four-speed gearboxes, which replaced the 20R, but retained the 8E engine. Both had 5 in. brakes in both wheels, unlike the other models. The 20D ran on as it was, as did the two competition models, except that

they now had wheel hubs with ball race bearings in place of the previous year's plain ones.

One new model joined the range that year as the 32D Fleetmaster Twin, which used the 322 cc British Anzani engine in the cast alloy frame. It differed from the smaller twin in having dual 6 in. brakes at the front and a 7 in. one at the rear, but was otherwise very similar. Neither twin was very speedy, and contemporary tests recorded 61 and 73 mph for the two sizes, at a time when the 197 cc model was good for 60 mph.

Perhaps that was why the 25D was not listed for 1956, although the other two twins remained. All models now had hydraulically-damped rear suspension units, so the original linkage was seen

**The 1957 Greeves Fleetmaster with 322 cc British Anzani twin engine in standard frame with revised forks**

no more, although the friction dampers remained at the front. Of the singles, the 20R3 continued with its 8E engine, but the 20R4 was dropped and the 20D, 20S and 20T had their engines changed for the 9E unit, all with the four-speed gearbox.

For all road models, the cylindrical toolbox was replaced by a tray under the left rear of the dualseat, but it remained for the trials model with its saddle. The change did little for the line of the road machines, which always seemed ungainly to some extent, in sharp contrast to the competition machines. These had a very purposeful air to them

*Left* **Greeves 20D road model, from 1955, with 8E engine and four-speed gearbox in original frame with rubber suspension at both ends**

*Below* **Greeves trials model 20T with 9E engine, as in 1957, with saddle and tilted silencer**

**Fleetwing 25D Greeves with 2T Villiers twin engine, as in 1958**

and always looked the business – which they were.

The whole range ran on for 1957 with one addition in the form of the 25D. This was a new Fleetwing, powered by a 249 cc Villiers 2T twin engine with four-speed gearbox, which went into the cast alloy frame. It had the dual 6 in. front brakes, but a 6 in. brake at the rear, not the 7 in. version. The Fleetwing retained the rubber bushes at the front, but their movement was damped by a slim Girling unit concealed in each fork leg. The same fork also went on the 32D and the two competition models.

During the year, the 20R4 reappeared, but with a 7E engine and four-speed gearbox in the 20R3 cycle parts. Both models were dropped at the end of the season, along with most of the rest of the range, other than the 20D and 25D. There were four other models for 1958, all for competition, and the 197 cc ones were updates of the previous machines. They continued with the 9E engine and four speeds as the 20TA Scottish Trials and 20SA Hawkstone Scrambler models. Their frame was new, but retained the cast alloy beam, and there were a number of detail changes to improve both models to suit their function.

The other new models were the 25TA Scottish Trials 25 and 25SA Hawkstone 25, which used the Villiers 2T engine unit, suitably modified for the intended use. Both were to special order only and used the cycle parts from the appropriate 197 cc machine. They were dropped at the end of the year, as riders knew as well as Greeves did that the single-cylinder engines were best.

The 20TA continued as it was for 1959, but otherwise there were changes and additions on the competition front. The basic trials model was joined by the 20TAS Scottish Trials Special, which had a 9E engine with a special, extra-heavy flywheel to aid low-speed pulling. The scrambler became the 20SAS Hawkstone Special, and two further models were created by fitting the 246 cc Villiers 31A engine in place of the 9E to give the 24TAS and 24SAS. For road use, the model with the 2T engine became the 25DB and was joined by the 24DB, which had the 31A engine in the same set of cycle parts.

For 1960 there was little change for the trials models, which became the 20TC, 20TCS and 24TCS, but the last had its engine changed to the 32A unit. The scramblers were given a new frame, so the two competition types no longer shared, having become more specialized. The coding changed to 20SCS and 24SCS, with a 33A engine for the latter, while the two road models ran on. The single also had its engine changed to a 32A. During the year, the 25DB was joined by the 32DB, which used the 324 cc Villiers 3T engine in the same set of cycle parts.

With this range, Greeves ran into the 1960s to more success, road racing and their own engine.

# GYS

This was another of the cyclemotor attachments that gave one of the cheapest means of powered transport. It was mounted over the front wheel, which it drove by roller with a 50 cc two-stroke engine, and was made in Bournemouth.

The engine was nearly all alloy, with the crankcase cast in one with the cylinder. The head was separate and the sides of the crankcase were closed with circular doors, the left-hand one of which was extended to carry the main bearings and housed the drive roller. The crankshaft had an overhung roller big-end and a Wipac flywheel magneto on its left-hand end. The silencer was bolted directly to the barrel and was cast in alloy, as was the petroil tank. Carburation was by a small Amal, and its lever control was linked to the decompressor for simplicity. The whole unit was mounted so that the roller was held in spring-loaded contact with the tyre, or could be raised clear of it.

The unit was first sold as the GYS in June 1949, and by the end of the year a firm in Lancashire was making them under licence. Distribution was by the Cairns Cycle firm, who sold bicycles complete with the GYS attachment.

In 1951 a kit became available from Cobli, a London firm, which mounted the engine below the saddle to drive the rear wheel. The kit replaced the normal rear seat stays, so the roller could be engaged or held clear of the tyre. The unit remained offset to the right of the wheel.

The GYS became the Motomite for 1951, but then changed its name again to become the Mocyc for 1952. It kept this name until 1955, when it was withdrawn from the market.

**The 1949 GYS clip-on with all-alloy engine, silencer and fuel tank, which was later sold as the Mocyc**

# Harper

Some makes never really got off the ground, and this was one of them. The intention was to build an all-British scooter at the Harper Aircraft works at Exeter Airport, and the prototype was first seen in March 1954. It had low, wide lines, so both rider and passenger sat in the bodywork, rather than on the machine, and this style was accentuated by the twin headlamps used.

The basis of the scooter was a rather hefty frame that ran low down along each side, behind the rear wheel and up to the headstock at the front. Further tubes ran from the rear, over the engine area, to take the rider's weight, and were braced by more tubing. This also provided a pivot for the rear suspension fork, which was controlled by a torsion bar.

At the front the headstock was bolted to the frame so it could be easily removed, together with the telescopic forks. Both wheels were 12 in. with drum brakes, and the power unit proposed was either a 122 or 197 cc Villiers with three-speed gearbox. This was fan-cooled, so it had a cowling over it. A starter motor was mounted ahead of the engine and drove the flywheel magneto with a V-belt. The engine was installed just ahead of the rear wheel, and the petroil tank went behind it, over the wheel.

**The Harper scooter, of 1954, with its futuristic lines, which enclosed the inevitable Villiers engine and was a good try**

It was the bodywork that set the Harper apart. This was in fibreglass, the front section being formed rather like a full racing fairing to enclose most of the front wheel and extend back to the rider's legs. In it were set the two headlights, with a nose between them and the number plate below, which resulted in an odd facial look.

The top of the apron was formed as a fascia behind a deep, curved windscreen and then ran down to the footboards and a good sized tunnel. The body widened out behind the passenger's legs to match the width of the front section, so it did not conform to the normal scooter style. It then ran back to the number plate with provision for two rear lamps, reflectors and turn signals, the last being a rarity then. The style was of the period, but without the excesses of fin seen on some American cars of the time.

Development continued during 1954 after the initial press coverage, and the machine was shown at Earls Court that year, although with only the 197 cc engine. A year later, work was still in progress, so for 1956 there were various alterations, but very few machines indeed.

Then, in 1957, the name began to be used by a Surrey-based firm making a well-styled invalid carriage, and that was the end of the Harper scooter.

# Hercules

This was an all-British moped, built by one of the largest bicycle firms in the country and launched at the Earls Court show late in 1955. It was a true moped, with pedals and a 49 cc, two-stroke engine, and was sold as the Grey Wolf. Its finish matched its name.

The engine was made by the JAP company and, like the Cyc-Auto, had its crankshaft set along the machine. The crankshaft was pressed up with bobweights and a roller big-end. It carried a Miller flywheel magneto at its front end and a drive tongue at the rear. The top half was conventional, with iron barrel, alloy head, small Amal to the rear, and long exhaust pipe to a good sized silencer on the left. An extension casting was bolted to the rear of the crankcase, and behind this was a further housing for the clutch and two-speed gearbox, which were driven by a shaft mated to the crankshaft tongue. The rear casting also housed a bevel-gear pair and the output shaft, which connected the drive to the rear wheel by chain.

This unit was hung by lugs in the rear casting from a spine frame, the main member of which was a pair of D-section tubes. These ran down from the headstock, over the engine, and then divided to form the chain stays. A bracket pro-

**The Her-cu-motor, as sold for 1957 and fitted with a small in-line JAP engine with two-speed gearbox**

The Hercules Corvette in 1960, but really an
imported French Lavalette given new tank
transfers

vided the engine mountings and carried the pedalling gear, while another supported the seat tube,
which had a toolbox clamped between it and the
rear mudguard.

At the rear, there was no suspension, other
than the saddle, but the front forks had short
leading links. These used rubber in shear as the
suspension medium, the units being housed in
small drums. Both wheels had small drum brakes
and 2 × 23 in. tyres with an offset front hub. At
the rear, a ribbed alloy cover gave a full-width
effect.

The fuel tank was pear-shaped and mounted
above the frame tube, just behind the headstock,
while a rear carrier, centre stand and electric horn
were provided. Control was easy, with a throttle
on the right bar and twistgrip gearchange, which
incorporated the clutch lever, on the left. The
gearchange was connected by cable and pulled

the selector into first against a spring, which
returned it to neutral and then second.

The Grey Wolf name was soon dropped, and
the machine became the Her-cu-motor. It ran well
and was best cruised at 25 mph, as the exhaust
intruded a little at 30. The main problems were
electrical, a contemporary report mentioning a
faint horn note and a number of short circuits.

The model was listed as a Mk II for 1958, but
around that time production came to a halt when
the JAP engine supply dried up. The firm
continued, however, and in 1960 introduced
another moped as the Corvette, but it used a
49 cc French Lavalette engine. This had a V-belt
primary drive and automatic clutch for its single
speed, and went into a simple rigid moped frame
with telescopic forks. Its appearance was similar
to the earlier machine, but it was short-lived, for
it was withdrawn at the end of 1961.

# HJH

H. J. Hulsman gave his initials to this small Welsh firm, which was based at Neath, in Glamorgan. There, in 1954, he began production of a conventional lightweight, which was called the Dragon, for all its prosaic Villiers 8E engine and three speeds.

The frame, at least, was individual, to the point of using square-section tubing, but was otherwise a loop type with plunger rear and telescopic front suspension. Equipment included a dualseat and twin toolboxes, while the machine was nicely finished in maroon and silver with chrome-plated tank and mudguards.

For 1955 the Dragon was joined by four other models to create a range of engine sizes and suspension systems. Thus, the Super Dragon kept the 8E engine and plunger frame, but had Earles leading-link forks. The Dragon Major used the 224 cc Villiers 1H engine with four speeds, but in a frame with pivoted-fork rear suspension and the Earles front forks, while the Dragonette had the 147 cc 30C engine, a rigid frame and telescopic forks. The fourth new model was the Trials, which had a 7E engine, rigid frame and Earles forks. It had four speeds as standard and a small light tank, so was well thought out and constructed.

There were changes and more new models for 1956, but not the Super Dragon, which was dropped. The Dragon went into a rigid frame and was joined by the Sports Dragon with three-speed 8E, telescopic front and pivoted rear forks. This model was also offered in Super Sports form with the Earles forks, and in a de luxe version of this with four speeds and rectified lighting.

The Dragon Major and Dragonette continued as they were, the latter being joined by a sports version with pivoted-fork frame. The Trials model was also given this type of rear suspension and was joined by a Scrambles model, which was much the same, but had its 7E engine tuned and close gears in its four-speed box.

This extensive programme was altogether too much for a small firm, and financial problems arose during 1956. Some were to do with the purchase tax, which was then levied on sales and for which the firm had to account. There were other difficulties of lack of capital and obtaining local skilled labour, so by June, production had ceased, and in October, Henry William James John Granville Hulsman admitted a deficit of £5800 at a bankruptcy hearing. The HJH era was over.

# Indian

This was an American make which had a number of different links with British firms in the postwar era. These included Royal Enfield, AMC and Velocette at different times, but the first on the scene were Brockhouse.

This Southport, Lancashire, firm was already producing the Corgi (see page 67) when it became involved with Indian in the early post-war years. Between them, they decided they needed a model to fit between the tiny Corgi and the heavy V-twins, and the outcome was the 248 cc Indian Brave.

The machine was built on British lines as far as the cycle parts went, but this was less true of the engine. For a start, this was in unit with the three-speed Albion gearbox and employed wet-sump lubrication, the oil being carried in the base chamber formed in the crankcase castings.

The engine was a side-valve type with a cast-iron barrel set vertically on the crankcase. It was closed with an alloy head, and the valves went in a chest on the right with a cover to enclose them. The timing gear comprised one crankshaft gear, two cam wheels which meshed with it, and tappets and adjusters.

The primary drive went outboard of the timing gear in its own chamber with chain drive to a three-plate clutch. The gearbox was typically British, so the final drive sprocket remained inboard of the clutch, but on the right-hand side of the machine. The gear pedal and kickstart lever were on concentric spindles, but on the left to suit the American market. The gearchange mechanism was also on the left in its own compartment and separate from the Lucas alternator, which was ahead of it on the left-hand end of the crankshaft. The contact breaker went outboard of it, with access via a small cover in the main one, and coil ignition was used. Carburation was by Amal, equipped with an air filter, and the oil was circulated by a submerged pump driven from the timing gears.

The engine unit went into a simple rigid loop frame with undamped telescopic front forks. The wheels had 18 in. rims and offset hubs with 5 in. drum brakes, and were protected by ample mudguards. There was a saddle for the rider, a toolbox under it on the right, and a battery beside this. Only a prop-stand was provided for parking and, thus, there was no means of holding the machine up to deal with a puncture.

**Indian Brave in rigid form with its left-hand-side pedals, wet sump, and side-valve engine**

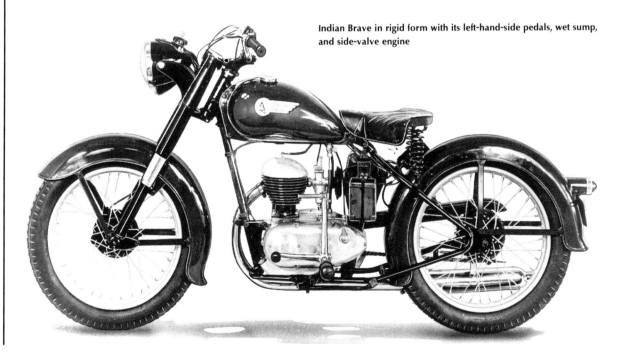

The later model S Indian Brave with spring frame, but otherwise little altered

In some ways, the machine had an advanced specification for 1950, the year it was first seen. It was built for export only, with a price of 345 dollars and a finish in red, blue, green, yellow or black. In later years, it was looked on as slow, but the 56 mph recorded by both British magazines in 1950 was not unusual for the times. It was about par for lightweights with a 197 cc Villiers engine and the LE Velocette, while its direct competitor, the BSA C10, recorded the same 56 mph in 1953, a little down on its 1938 performance.

The real problem for the Brave was poor assembly and a lack of reliability. It failed to make any real impact in the USA, and by 1952 became available in the sterling area, although still not in its home country.

This situation finally changed in 1954, when a second model was introduced with rear suspension. The engine unit remained the same, but the frame gained a pivoted rear fork with tapered bronze bushes, which were adjusted with lock nuts. The rear fork ends hooked into place, where they were held by shouldered nuts. The design failed to impress much, even in 1954.

The springer model S was also given 6 in. brakes, a centre stand and a dualseat, but its other details were as for the rigid model R, which continued. Only red or black colours were available for the home market for either model. The two British magazines managed to squeeze 58 or 59 mph from the springer.

The price of the rigid model was reduced for 1955, when both models had the handlebars cleaned up with fixed pivot blocks, but this did nothing to enliven sales. At the end of the year, production ceased, and within two years Indian were selling Royal Enfields with their name on the tank.

The Brave slipped out of sight, but the Indian name kept reappearing until the 1970s.

# James

In later years, this make became part of the AMC group, and the amalgamation brought them ever closer to Francis-Barnett. This led to badge engineering, which began in the mid-1950s, but in the early post-war years the Greet factory followed its own path. It had done this since its first motorcycle in 1902, and at one time was well known for its pleasing machines with V-twin engines. However, from the mid-1930s, the company concentrated on the utility market and stuck with this from then on.

During the war, they had built large numbers of their Military Lightweight, or ML, model, which used a 9D Villiers engine in a simple rigid frame with girder forks. It was intended for paratroops, so was light enough to lift over obstacles, and was known as the Clockwork Mouse. Post-war, it

formed one half of their programme as the ML, which had a maroon and silver tank finish and the addition of a rear carrier.

The ML was joined by the Superlux autocycle, which used the Villiers JDL engine in a typical machine of the type with pedals, engine shields, girder forks, saddle and carrier. It was a minimal range, but met the urgent needs of the times for transport of any sort. Both machines continued in production until the end of 1948.

The autocycle ran on into 1949, but the ML was replaced by a small range of machines in three capacities. Smallest was the Comet, built in standard or de luxe form, the latter being fitted with a battery and rectifier. Both used the new 99 cc Villiers 1F engine with two-speed gearbox controlled by a handlebar lever, and this went into a simple rigid loop frame. At the front were girder forks with single tubes on each side to give the appearance, at least, of telescopics, and both wheels had small drum brakes. There was a saddle for the rider and a cylindrical toolbox beneath this on the standard model, but the battery was in this position on the de luxe, with a toolbox between the right-hand-side chainstays.

Next in size were standard and de luxe Cadet models, which used the 122 cc Villiers 10D engine in similar cycle parts. The electrical variation between the two models was as for the Comet,

*Left* **James Superlux autocycle of 1948 powered by the Villiers 98 cc JDL engine installed in typical frame with girder forks**

*Right* **The 1951 James Cadet with 122 cc Villiers 10D engine in a rigid frame with light telescopic forks**

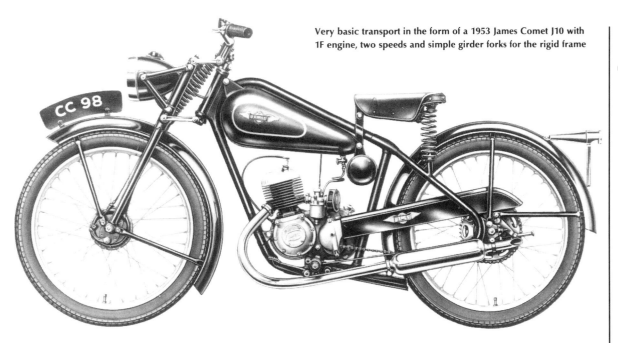

Very basic transport in the form of a 1953 James Comet J10 with 1F engine, two speeds and simple girder forks for the rigid frame

but the larger machines had a rear carrier and the battery and toolbox as on the smaller de luxe machine.

Finally, for the road, there was the de luxe Captain with 197 cc Villiers 6E engine in the Cadet cycle parts, and with battery lighting as standard. Unlisted, but built in small numbers, were competition models using either the 10D or 6E engine with suitably modified frame, forks and wheels.

During March 1949 the autocycle was redesigned to use the 99 cc Villiers 2F single-speed engine unit, but retained its Superlux name. The same month saw telescopic front forks appearing for the 122 and 197 cc road models. These used Dunlop rubber cushions as the suspension medium.

In general, the range continued as it was for 1950, with the autocycle, two each of the Comet and Cadet, plus the Captain, which took the listing

J8. In time, all the James models would have a similar code, but this did not become general practice until 1953. A second version of the J8 was listed with plunger rear suspension, which became an option for the 122 cc competition model. The 197 cc size of this machine was listed in rigid (/D suffix) and plunger (/RS suffix) forms for riders to make their own choice. All models, other than the autocycle, now had the telescopic front forks.

There was little change for 1951, but the rigid J8 became the Captain standard J7 and there was one new model. This was the 99 cc Commodore, which was really a Comet, with 1F engine and enclosure panels. These ran from the downtube to the rear axle, and up from the footrest to the cylinder head, with legshields at the front. The whole range continued for 1952, the 197 cc competition machines being replaced by a single model with rigid frame as the Colonel Competition.

Things changed more for 1953, although the autocycle continued as before as the Superlux, but with a code of J1. The Commodore became the J4, and the standard Comet the Mark II or J10, while the de luxe version became the J3 and was fitted with the 4F engine.

In the 122 cc class, the standard Cadet and competition models were dropped and the de luxe Cadet became the J6. It was joined by the J5, which used the 13D engine with three speeds in a new frame with plunger rear suspension. The J7 and J8 models remained, but with coil spring forks, also used on the 122 cc models, and the competition version became the J9 Commando. This kept the rigid frame, but had a 7E engine and telescopic forks with two-way hydraulic damping.

During 1953 a telescopic fork conversion kit was made available for all the older Comet models. These forks were fitted as standard to the J11, which took over for 1954. This Comet used the 4F engine and a frame with plunger rear suspension and was the only 99 cc model left in the range, except the J1 autocycle. Only one 122 cc model continued, as the J5, while the J9 was joined by a new 197 cc Captain, the K7 with an 8E engine in a pivoted-fork frame. This model had a dualseat with neat toolboxes under its nose, so was much more modern in its appearance.

Similar cycle parts were also used by the K12 Colonel, which was powered by the 224 cc Villiers 1H engine. This had four speeds, and the machine larger brakes, but otherwise the style was the same. Finally, there was the K7C Cotswold scrambler with 7E engine, four speeds, pivoted-fork frame and suitable wheels and tyres.

The autocycle was dropped during the year, but most of the range ran on for 1955. New was the J15 Cadet, which replaced the J5 and had a 147 cc Villiers 30C engine in place of the 13D. The plunger frame remained, along with the saddle, but there were full-width hubs for all models that year.

The Cadet had a major change for 1956, when it became the L15. It kept the 30C engine, but this went into a completely new frame with pressed-steel rear section and pivoted rear fork. This was controlled by coil springs, set far enough forward to be concealed by the very deep valance of the rear guard, which was formed as part of the pressing. Light telescopic forks went at the front, and there was a short dualseat for just one person.

Also new was the L1 Comet, which used the new Cadet frame and forks to house the 4F engine, and the K7T Commando, which replaced the J9. This kept the 7E engine, but it was housed in the pivoted-fork frame from the K7C, which continued. Both the K7 and K12 ran on with 18 in. wheels in place of the earlier 19 in. ones.

The range continued as it was for 1957 with two additions. One was simply the option of the 6F engine in the L1 Comet, in place of the 4F, which remained available. The model kept its single seat, but a dualseat became an option for the Cadet. The second model was a more major addition and was the 249 cc Commodore with AMC engine.

This machine, coded the L25, was the first to use the engine, which was the same as that used by Francis-Barnett (see page 103). It followed the Cadet in the design of its frame. Thus, the front section was tubular, but the centre section was built up from pressings. It carried the pivoted fork and housed the electrics, while the deep rear mudguard, the same part as used by the Comet and Cadet, was bolted to it. The machine had stylish side covers, a deeply valanced front mudguard and a dualseat.

The firm switched more to the AMC engines for 1958, when the Commodore was joined by the 171 cc Cavalier L17. This was much in the manner of the Comet and Cadet, which both continued, as did the Captain, although that was fitted with a 10E engine in place of the older 8E. There were no competition models listed at all at first, but the K7T made a brief reappearance during

*Above* **Despite the lights and silencer, this is a James K7C Cotswold scrambler fitted with a 7E engine. It was sold in this form for 1954, but in a more suitable style for the next year**

*Below* **James Commodore, fitted with the 249 cc AMC engine, during a 1958 road test**

the year, when it, too, was fitted with a 10E engine. Otherwise, it was much as before, with pivoted-fork frame and suitable equipment for trials use. It was only listed for a few months.

For 1959 the Comet, Cadet, Cavalier, Captain and Commodore ran on and were joined by two new competition models. Both were powered by the 249 cc AMC engine, modified to suit the intended use. The pivoted-fork frame was common to both, but the L25T trials model used James forks, whereas the L25S scrambler had AMC Teledraulic forks. The fixtures and fittings were to suit each machine's respective role.

During that last year of the decade, James made even greater use of the AMC engine by fitting it in the Flying Cadet L15A model, which used the 149 cc version in the L15 cycle parts. For 1960 only the Comet kept to Villiers power, now with the 6F as standard, and the other models were dropped. This left the roadster and two competition models, with the 249 cc AMC engine, and the Flying Cadet, but not the Cavalier, which had also gone. For the 200 cc class, there was a new Captain L20 with the 199 cc AMC engine in cycle parts that followed the style of the Commodore. On this note, James entered the new decade. That year, they added a scooter to their list, and later came twins and a return to Villiers power for other models, after the trials and tribulations of the AMC units.

# Lohmann

This was a German make of clip-on engine, but is included because it was handled in the United Kingdom by Britax and because of its sheer novelty. It was a mere 18 cc in capacity, but even more unusual was the fact that it was a compression-ignition two-stroke with variable compression ratio.

The engine, therefore, was much like a large-scale model aircraft unit, but designed to clamp under the bottom bracket of a standard bicycle. Consequently, it was very narrow, as it had to fit between the pedal cranks. It had a horizontal cylinder with the fins extending above and below it to some extent, but not to the sides to any degree. The cylinder head contained a twistgrip-controlled moving sleeve, which varied both the ratio and some of the port timings, while the mixture was supplied by a simple carburettor. This avoided the complications of the fuel-injection system of a true diesel.

Due to the small engine size, the crankshaft was geared to a countershaft, which carried a drive roller. This had a means of engaging and releasing it from contact with the tyre, as was usual with the clip-on engine type.

The engine was first seen in 1949, but it was late 1952 before it reached the Britax lists. It proved able to generate enough power to push a cycle along at 15 mph on the flat and to deal well with steep hills. However, it was rather late in the day for a new clip-on and buyers looked for a little more performance, preferring an engine type they understood better, even if it brought them a flywheel magneto to struggle with.

Thus, the Lohmann disappeared from the lists as quickly as it had arrived, and no more was heard of it.

The tiny Lohmann diesel engine fitted to a cycle in 1950, before it was imported into the UK by Britax

# Mercury

This firm of bicycle makers decided to enter the powered two-wheeler world in 1956, and for this offered two models. Both were a little unusual, for one was a moped, but with an ohv engine, while the other was a small scooter with motorcycle-size wheels.

The moped was the Mercette, which carried its four-stroke engine ahead of the frame bottom bracket, with the cylinder inclined to match the downtube. It was of 48 cc, built in unit with a two-speed gearbox, and had the ports on the sides of the cylinder head, with consequent effect on the inlet and exhaust pipes. The frame was rigid with light telescopic forks, small drum brakes and a fuel tank perched on the top tube, which ran from the headstock to the rear wheel spindle. The machine had direct lighting and, as standard, was fitted with a pillion seat and rests.

The scooter was called the Hermes and used a 49 cc ILO two-stroke engine with two-speed gearbox to propel it. The engine was fan-cooled with a hand-pull starter and went into a rigid frame with telescopic front forks. The wheels were 20 in. diameter, with small drum brakes, and the rear chain was fully enclosed.

The scooter bodywork suggested that the machine had rear suspension, for the deeply valanced rear mudguard was painted a contrasting grey to the general maroon. This colour applied to the main apron panel, which ran back as the floor and rear cover for the engine unit.

These two models were joined by three more for 1957, two of which used 99 cc Villiers engines with two-speed gearboxes. One was the Grey Streak motorcycle, which used the 6F unit with foot-change in a simple frame. This had telescopic front and pivoted-fork rear suspension, full-width hubs and a dualseat. The other was the Dolphin scooter with 4F engine, and this followed the lines of the Hermes. The third newcomer was the Whippet 60, which was an enlarged version of the Mercette with the same features.

The Mercette and Grey Streak continued alone for 1958, but the two scooters were replaced by one new one, the Pippin, which continued to use the 4F engine. The frame was still rigid, but the wheelbase was shorter and 15 in. wheels were fitted. The body, especially at the rear, was more conventional, and the rear section was easily lifted clear as one part. It carried a dualseat. On test, the machine proved to have an adequate performance.

Despite this, the firm found limited demand for its products, and during the year ceased production of its powered models.

# Mini-Motor

This was perhaps the best known of the British clip-on engines and, although of Italian origin, when it appeared in 1949, it was built in Croydon. There was nothing exceptional about the unit, but it was well made and available at a time when anything was better than nothing.

The engine sat above the bicycle rear wheel, which it drove with a friction-roller on the left-hand end of the crankshaft. On the right, there was a Wipac flywheel magneto, and between this and the roller, a crankcase with bobweight flywheels and a horizontal iron barrel. An alloy head closed this, and the capacity was 49.9 cc for the conventional two-stroke unit. The petroil tank went over the engine, with the number plate at its rear. A means of lifting the roller clear of the tyre was provided.

The unit could drive a bicycle at 30 mph, which was as fast as most wished to go on a rigid machine with narrow tyres. Thousands found them ideal for short trips, whether to station, office or shops, and they were soon seen about in large numbers. Some were even fitted to tandems, where they proved equal to the task of hauling two people along at 20 mph.

There were minor improvements for 1951, and during that year, a decompressor was added to the cylinder head to aid both starting and stopping. In this form, the unit ran on until 1955, but by then the moped was taking over and the Mini-Motor was no more.

**Mini-Motor at the end of the 1953 National Rally at Weston-super-Mare – a long ride for owner D. J. Anderson**

# New Hudson

This firm built motorcycles for 30 years from 1903 but, during the 1930s, turned to the manufacture of Girling brakes. Early in 1940 they returned to two wheels with an autocycle, and it was this that they first produced after the war. By then, they were part of the BSA group.

Their 1946 model was the same as the one built six years before, with 98 cc Villiers JDL engine in a typical autocycle frame, having pedals and a rigid front fork. At that time, there were no engine shields, but a rear carrier and centre stand were provided, along with direct lighting.

For 1948 the machine was fitted with pressed-steel blade girder forks, plus engine shields and other detail improvements. It received a new frame and engine for 1949, when the JDL unit was replaced by a 99 cc 2F, which required a major frame change to carry it. The appearance remained much as before, however, as the alterations were concealed by the engine shields. The rest of the cycle parts continued unchanged. In this form, the machine ran on for some years, the centre stand being strengthened for 1952, but otherwise there was little change.

It was May 1956 when the machine was revamped, and on this occasion only the 2F engine remained as before. The frame was amended to make it easier for the rider to mount, and the forks became tubular, although they kept the girder action. The tank shape, and that of the side panels, was new and much more modern, while the chains were well enclosed. Both leg-shields and a windscreen were available as options, while the saddle, centre stand and rear carrier remained as of old.

It was a good attempt to update an old design, but by then the moped was taking over from the autocycle, offering similar performance for a lower running cost and better styling. The machine continued to be listed until 1958, but that year saw the end of the 2F engine, so the New Hudson also left the market.

**The 1950 New Hudson autocycle with Villiers 2F single-speed engine unit in rigid frame with blade girder forks**

# Norman

This company was based in Ashford, Kent, and for 1946 picked up their pre-war models more or less where they had left off. Then, they had built for both themselves and the Rudge company, but post-war simply offered an Autocycle and a Motorcycle.

The former used the 98 cc Villiers JDL engine in a rigid frame with fixtures and fittings that were typical of the type. The latter was equally simple, but used the 122 cc 9D engine with three-speed gearbox, although still in an austere rigid frame.

These two models comprised the Norman range until late 1948, when they were replaced by more modern machines. The Autocycle became the model C with a 99 cc 2F single-speed engine unit. This was mounted in a frame to suit and had the usual engine enclosure panels that were common to the type. The frame remained rigid and had light girder forks at the front, while the lighting was direct and the finish in maroon.

The other models were the B1 and B2 in standard and de luxe forms, the latter with rectifier and battery lighting. Engines were the 122 cc 10D and 197 cc 6E respectively, and the cycle parts were common, with rigid frame and telescopic forks. The whole range was little altered for 1950, when it was joined by the model D, which mirrored the others, having standard or de luxe forms, but used the 99 cc two-speed 1F engine unit. The frame for these models stayed rigid, but the forks were tubular girders, which were changed to telescopics for 1951.

Otherwise, the range ran on, as it did for 1952, but in February of that year, a pivoted-fork rear suspension system was announced. This differed from most in that the spring units were positioned as upper chainstays, so were laid well down, while the rear subframe was formed to run around them.

It was not until late in the year that the new frame reached production and was offered on the B1S and B2S, again in standard and de luxe forms. The larger machine kept to the 6E engine, but the smaller one used the 13D, while the existing B1 models were replaced by the E models. These

Norman model C autocycle with 2F Villiers 99 cc engine enclosed by rather bulbous shields

were economy jobs, but kept the 10D engine in a very simple set of cycle parts, albeit still in standard or de luxe forms with direct or battery lighting.

At the lower end of the scale, the C and D models continued for 1953, as did the two B2 models, while a competition model was added as the B2C. This used a 197 cc engine, altered to suit trials work, in a rigid frame with telescopic forks, 21 in. front wheel and 4 in.-section rear tyre. These latter features were nearly unheard of on a lightweight at that time, but helped the small company achieve some good results.

Although the model numbers stayed as before, there were a good few changes for 1954. Alone, the autocycle ran on as it was, but the model D machines were given the 4F engine. The B1S machines continued, but the model E was dropped early in the year. The 197 cc road models all switched to the 8E engine, and the B2C to the 7E with the option of a four-speed gearbox. The rigid B2 models were dropped during the year, while the sprung B2S machines had their frame revised to use normal, upright Armstrong units.

There were more changes for 1955, the engine of the B1S models becoming the 147 cc 30C unit. The range lost the B2 models, but gained a twin

Norman B1S with 122 cc 10D engine unit and their laid-down rear units, as still used on this 1954 example

in the form of the TS model, which used the 242 cc British Anzani engine. This model and the B2S were both fitted with Armstrong leading-link front forks, which were an option for the competition B2C. The 99 cc models were little changed, and at the end of the year the model D was dropped.

The autocycle continued for 1956, along with the B1, now with the leading-link forks, the B2 with a further version fitted with a 9E engine, and the TS. The competition model became the B2CS with a spring frame and leading-link forks, while its engine could be the 7E with three speeds, or 9E with four.

New was a moped named the Nippy, which was based on a continental design and powered by a 47.6 cc Sachs engine with two-speed gearbox. This unit went into a pressed-steel beam frame, rigid at the rear and with leading-link forks at the front. It was a smart machine, and the firm intended to gradually increase their own production of parts in place of buying them in.

The autocycle entered its last year in 1957, when the two 147 cc B1 models were joined by another de luxe one, fitted with the 148 cc 31C engine unit. The three B2 machines ran on, two with 8E engines and one with the 9E, as did the TS and the B2CS. All but the first and last had a degree of rear enclosure, which had been developed from prototype designs seen two years earlier. It incorporated toolboxes and mountings

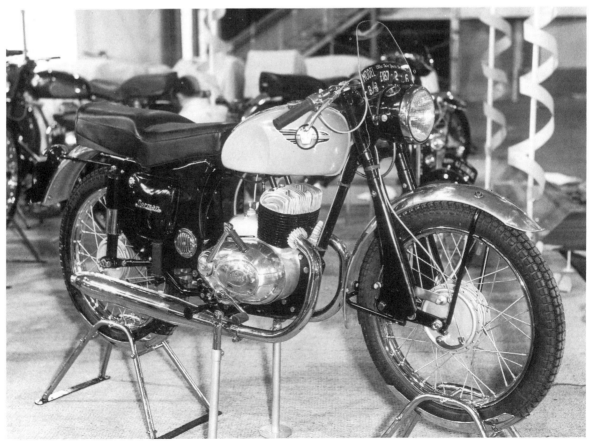

*Left* **Showtime late in 1955 at Earls Court for the Norman model TS fitted with the 242 cc British Anzani twin engine**

*Right* **Norman Lido moped of 1959 fitted with the Villiers 3K engine unit with styled enclosure**

*Below left* **The B3 Sports Norman with 2T engine, leading-link forks, low bars and small screen**

for the electrical equipment, so tidied the machine up nicely. The Nippy continued, but in a plunger frame.

There was no autocycle for 1958, as the moped had taken over its duties and the 2F engine was no longer available. The B1 and B2 models continued with their variety of engines, as did the competition model, which now only used the 9E engine unit. The TS remained in the list when the models were announced, but early in the year it was replaced by the B3, which used the 249 cc Villiers 2T engine.

For 1959 this model was joined by the B3 Sports, which had dropped bars, alloy mudguards, plastic flyscreen and knee recesses in the fuel tank. The same cycle parts were used by the B2S Sports with 9E engine, which also joined the range, while the 8E units were dropped to leave a single 197 cc roadster. The three B1 models remained, along with the competition model, and the Nippy was joined by two more mopeds.

Both had a 49.9 cc Villiers 3K engine with two-speed gearbox, and the Nippy II used the same

cycle parts as the Sachs-powered model. The Lido differed in having pivoted-fork suspension and styled enclosure for the engine unit, which extended back to the rear wheel.

That brought the small firm to the end of the decade, when they dropped their B1 models, but continued with the B2S, B3 and B2CS into the 1960s. All the mopeds were altered and the Nippy IV was alone in keeping the 3K engine, but this now went into a frame with pivoted-fork rear suspension and leading links at the front. The Nippy III looked similar, but had a 47.6 cc, single-speed, Italian Mi-Val engine in a frame that looked like it had suspension, but was, in fact, rigid. The remaining moped was the Super Lido, which kept to the Sachs engine, but in cycle parts based on the earlier Lido model.

The next year, the firm was taken over by Raleigh, so the motorcycles were soon dropped, while the mopeds went no further. Thus, another firm disappeared after some good years and nice, well finished machines.

# Norton

On the face of it, all Norton had to do to produce civilian machines after the war was to change the paint colour in their spray guns from khaki to black. In practice, they did rather more to both engine and frame of the 490 cc, side-valve 16H model and added the same size overhead-valve model 18.

Both machines were based on the firm's 1939 engine, so the 16H had enclosed valves unlike the service model, which was based on the 1937 unit. Up to the crankcase mouth, both engines were essentially the same and had a distinctive Norton line that ran back closely to 1931, and could be traced even to the first 1907 single.

Construction was traditionally British and very conservative, for the firm seldom changed much without very good cause. Thus, the crankshaft was built up with a roller big-end, ran in ball and roller mains in a vertically-split crankcase, and had its simple timing gears on the right. One drove the mag-dyno by chain, and a crankshaft worm meshed with the duplex-gear oil pump of the dry-sump system.

Followers above the cams were formed to suit the valve gear, with tappets for the 16H and long pushrods for the 18. The former had a simple cast-iron barrel with valve chest, plus cover. The head was also in iron, as were the head and barrel of the 18, which had an alloy rocker box with side access cover.

The rest of both machines was the same, except for the gearing, where the ohv model had two more teeth on the engine sprocket. The primary drive was enclosed within the Norton pressed-steel case, which remained oil-tight until the single fixing nut was over-tightened. Within it, the very good Norton clutch drove a four-speed Norton gearbox. All of these parts had their origins in pre-war times. The gearbox was one of the best, even though the gear pedal was not positioned very well and had an excessive movement. The only

concession to the post-war period was a new outer cover that enclosed the clutch worm and its cable.

The engine and gearbox went into a rigid cradle frame, rather than the pre-war open type, and kept the Norton girders with their check springs at the front. Both wheels had offset hubs with good 7 in. drum brakes, and were quickly detachable. They could also be interchanged. For the rest, the oil tank was under the saddle on the right, with the battery matching it on the left, the toolbox went between the right chainstays, and there was no tank-top instrument panel, as pre-war. The finish was black, the petrol and oil tanks and wheel rims being chrome plated before painting and lining.

The two models were announced in August 1945 and continued as they were through most of the following year. During 1946 a few road-racing machines were built and supplied in time for the Manx Grand Prix. These were in full racing form and based on the pre-war models. They were the first to carry the simple Manx Norton name and were listed as the 348 cc model 40M and 498 cc model 30M.

Both had single-overhead-camshaft engines, in the familiar Carroll mould, with shaft-and-bevel drive up to the cambox. The design dated from 1930, and the format was altered little in over 30 years, so the post-war engines looked like the pre-war ones. A massive alloy head with separate cambox went on top of the alloy barrel, but the piston gave a rather low ratio in deference to the pool petrol then in use. Compression plates allowed for some variation should anything better come to hand.

The bottom half continued with the massive, well-ribbed crankcase cast in magnesium alloy, and the camshaft drive and oil pump side by side on the right, the racing magneto being chain driven from the latter. The usual oil pipe ran up from the crankcase to the cambox, and the valves were closed by hairpin springs. Carburation was by a remote-needle Amal, and the exhaust terminated in an open megaphone.

An open primary chain and dry clutch connected the engine to the four-speed, close-ratio gearbox, which naturally dispensed with a kickstarter. Both units went into a cradle frame with plunger rear suspension, much as pre-war, but it was fitted with the famous Norton Roadholder telescopic front forks. The frame became known as the 'garden gate', but the forks had hydraulic damping, so were an improvement on the pre-war works type.

Both wheels had conical hubs, the front one containing an 8 in. brake with an air scoop on its alloy backplate. The wheels were 21 in. front and 20 in. rear, fitted with racing rubber and shielded by short guards. The petrol tank was massive and still of the bolt-through type, while the oil tank carried a full imperial gallon of lubricant.

The machines came with a full set of racing details, so had saddle, rear pad, racing plates, flyscreen, chin pad, rev-counter and quick-action filler caps on both tanks. Their finish remained traditional, the tanks being in silver with red and black lining, while the rest of the machine was in black.

The rest of the range for 1947 was announced soon after the Manx had been run, and was expanded a good deal from the two basic 1945 models. They were still there, but with the Road-holder front forks and the speedometer mounted in the fork bridge. They were joined by two similar road models, the first of which was the Big 4 fitted with a 634 cc side-valve engine. This, again, was a pre-war model revived for the sidecar market and much as the 16H, with rigid cradle frame and the new front forks. The second machine was the ES2, which was as the 18 with the 490 cc ohv engine, but with plunger rear suspension, as on the ohc models.

There were two more of these, the models 40 and 30 International, which had all-iron engines with the single overhead camshaft in 348 and 490 cc sizes. The cams were designed to run best on an open pipe, which was to be allowed in the 1947 Clubman TT. The cycle parts were as the ES2 with the plunger frame and Roadholder telescopic forks, but the tanks were larger with wing-nut filler caps.

To complete the range, there were 350 and 500 Trials models, but these were really based on the wartime 16H frame fitted with either capacity ohv engines, telescopic forks and raised exhaust, but full lighting equipment. Competition tyres were provided, but the model was totally unsuitable, even for the events of the time. Some owners changed to girder forks to reduce the wheelbase, and discarded as many heavy items as possible, but it was still a lump for trials work.

The 490 cc side- and overhead-valve engines were modified for 1948, having a new timing case and direct-action tappets in place of the followers. The side-valve engine was given an alloy head and an alloy casting to enclose the valves, while the ohv unit gained a one-piece rocker box. The Big 4 followed the 16H in respect of the engine changes, but also had the bore and stroke revised and the capacity reduced to 597 cc. The ohc models continued as they were, while the Trials ones were dropped, but there was news of their replacement early in the year.

This was listed for 1949 as the 500T and was much lighter, thanks to an all-alloy engine, a short-ened version of the diamond 16H frame and other measures. Special fork yokes helped to reduce the wheelbase, and various means were used to lower the weight. A nice slim petrol tank was fitted, along with alloy mudguards and high-tensile steel rims, while the lighting was optional. The result worked well for many private owners.

Nice 'Garden Gate' Norton with the ohc engine and all the racing goodies of the late 1940s

The major news from Nortons for 1949 was the launch of their model 7 Dominator twin, the engine of which was designed by Bert Hopwood. It was a conventional vertical twin with overhead valves and both head and barrel in iron. The camshaft ran across the front of the crankcase, where it was driven by chain and gear, with a further gear drive on to the dynamo. The magneto went behind the crankcase and was chain driven with auto-advance.

The valve gear was laid out within the integral rocker box to splay the exhaust ports well out for better cooling. The tappets ran in the block, and the crankshaft was built up with a cast-iron flywheel. It ran in ball and roller mains, in a vertically-split alloy crankcase, and drove a typical duplex-gear Norton oil pump.

This engine went into the ES2 cycle parts with plunger frame and telescopic forks, but the gearbox had to be modified to suit the shape of the new engine. In effect, the positive-stop mechanism was moved from above the box to ahead of it, to place the pedal in a much better position and reduce its travel. The box became known as the laid-down type, but the internals were very much as before, although the shell mountings were improved.

The rest of the range ran on with little alteration that year, except that the Manx models supplied to riders in the TT had twin overhead camshafts and alloy tanks and wheel rims. For 1950 all the side- and overhead-valve road models changed to the laid-down gearbox, but not the 500T, the short frame of which could not accommodate it. The ohc machines for both road and track stayed as they were.

Norton fortunes had taken a real upturn in 1950, thanks to the advent of the famous Featherbed frame for the works racers, coupled with the skills of Geoff Duke and Artie Bell. The frame was the result of eight years of work by Rex McCandless and was deceptively simple, with its duplex tubular loops welded to the headstock with a cross-over arrangement. The subframe was bolted in place, and the petrol tank sat on the top rails with a strap to retain it. It was a design that was to accommodate both Norton and many other makes of engine over the years.

For 1951 the production Manx Norton was built with the Featherbed frame and was also given the laid-down gearbox and 19 in. wheels. It was an immediate success. The other singles and the twin stayed as they were, except for a cast alloy front brake backplate, which had been used by the 500T from the beginning.

The singles and model 7 remained the same for 1952, but the twin was joined by the machine many riders had been asking for since the Featherbed frame had first appeared. It was a marriage of the new frame and the twin engine, and for 1952 it became available, but for export only, as the model 88 Dominator.

The twin engine sat easily in the frame with its usual gearbox, and the model used short Roadholder forks and the road wheels and brakes. A deeply valanced, sprung front mudguard was fitted that first year, along with a strap-held fuel tank, dualseat and long, pear-shaped silencers. The finish was grey for all painted parts, and the result a very smart, fast and well handling motorcycle.

Another new frame appeared for 1953 and, like the Featherbed, this had a pivoted rear fork, but was based on the cradle frame. This was modified to provide the fork pivot and a subframe to support the dualseat, which took over from the saddle. The frame was used by both the model 7 Dominator and the ES2, and both models also adopted the pear-shaped silencer.

The model 88 ran on with just a change to a neater, unsprung front mudguard, while the two side-valve machines and the 18 were given a dualseat, despite remaining in rigid frames. There were, in fact, some side-valve models built with the plunger frame, but these were made in small numbers only.

The Manx was unaltered for 1953, but the Internationals received their last real changes. The engines became all-alloy and went into the Featherbed frame with the laid-down gearbox and pear-shaped silencer. They had become, in effect, a model 88 with an ohc engine. The one difference lay with the front brake, which was increased to 8 in. for the Inter.

The bigger brake was adopted by the rest of the range for 1954, except for the 500T, which kept the 7 in. version. Otherwise, the road singles and both twins remained as they were, while the Manx underwent more extensive engine changes. The strokes of both were shortened and there were a good number of detail alterations, plus a welded subframe for the chassis and a twin-leading-shoe front brake to stop the machine.

At the end of the year, the two side-valve machines, the model 18 and the 500T were dropped, but in their place appeared two new

One of the nicest trials models of the period was the Norton 500T introduced in 1949 and built for just five years

First of the many Norton twins was this 1949 model 7, which had a plunger frame and new laid-down gearbox

A rather special Manx Norton with Featherbed frame, for this is Geoff Duke's 1951 Junior TT winner

The ES2 Norton in its new pivoted-fork frame for 1953. Note the pear-shaped silencer

The Norton model 88 Featherbed twin, as it was in 1957 and one of the best machines of the decade

The 1958 Norton Nomad 99, which used the larger twin engine in off-road cycle parts to make an export model

singles with 597 cc ohv engines. These were the 19R in a rigid frame, and 19S in a pivoted-fork frame, so really they were simply enlarged versions of the 18 and ES2. The engine had an alloy head, which also went on the ES2, along with a Monobloc carburettor and various detail improvements. The twins were also given an alloy head and the Monobloc, while the 88 received the welded subframe, introduced on the Manx the year before, and full-width hubs. These two features also went on the International, but the Manx itself continued as it was.

The model 7 went at the end of the year, along with the rigid-frame 19R, but the ES2 and the 19S ran on for 1956 with another similar single. This was the 348 cc model 50, which was as the others, except in capacity, so was stuck with the weight penalty all such machines have to suffer. These three models were fitted with full-width hubs and had many detail changes, but otherwise remained rather prosaic singles with adequate, but unexciting, performance.

Not that the International models offered much more when fitted with the standard, restrictive silencer; these were now only produced in small numbers and to special order. The Manx models had numerous minor changes, but were really very close to the limit of their development and proving the point of diminishing returns.

The 88 had its battery enclosed for 1956 and lost its fork-top instrument panel, as the contents were transferred to a deeper headlamp shell. It was joined by a larger 596 cc version, which used the same cycle parts and was listed as the model 99. The same engine was used for a further model for 1957, this being the 77, which was intended for sidecar work and had the frame from the later model 7.

This model 77, along with all the road machines, changed to a revised gearbox in May 1956, the new type being known as the AMC. It was much as before within the shell, but had a new, more compact change mechanism and revised clutch-lift mechanism. It was also used on AJS and Matchless machines, and continued in service for over 20 years.

The twins, Manx and Inters were little altered for 1957, but the three ohv engines had new cylinder heads with integral pushrod tunnels and many detail changes. There were more changes for 1958, when the twins went over to alternator electrics, except for the 77, had twin carburettors listed for them during the year, and were joined

by the 99 Nomad. This was an export enduro model, which used the 596 cc engine, model 77 frame, an alternator, magneto and off-road cycle parts. Its finish was bright red and chrome, and it had twin carburettors for performance.

The singles had few changes for 1958, and at the end of the year, the International models and the 19S were dropped. For 1959 the ES2 and 50 were considerably revised, with alternator electrics and the Featherbed frame. This was to prove a great blessing to Triton builders, as in later years, more often than not, the donor frame was to come from the underpowered model 50.

The Manx engines had the bevel drive modified, so they lost the lower bevel housing, and this was really the final form for the Carroll engine. Further changes were to play little part in its development, and the better engines became the ones assembled with care by such Manx experts as Bill Lacey or Ray Petty. The twins had no real alteration, but the 77 was dropped, so only the 88, 99 and 99 Nomad continued. They were, however, joined by a new model, which was to sire a further small group.

The new twin was the 249 cc Jubilee, which differed in concept from the Dominator series in most areas. Again, the engine was from Bert Hopwood and originally had each head and barrel cast as one in alloy, but the firm did not allow him to keep this radical feature.

The end result was a conventional, parallel twin engine, built in unit with its four-speed gearbox. It had a short stroke, nodular iron crankshaft, separate iron barrels and alloy heads. Two gear-driven camshafts were employed, with tappets and short pushrods in front of and behind the barrels, the rockers being concealed by domed covers. The points went on the end of the inlet camshaft, and the oil pump in the timing cover.

Complete with gearbox, it made a compact unit and was installed in a frame built up from tubes and pressings. This was similar to a Francis-Barnett design and had a pivoted rear fork and telescopics from the AMC lightweight range. Both wheels had full-width hubs with 6 in. brakes and 18 in. rims, the front one being shielded by a deeply valanced mudguard. The enclosure was more extensive at the rear, with a deep tail unit, which combined with massive side panels that ran forward to conceal the single Monobloc carburettor.

The Jubilee style of rear enclosure was adopted by the larger twins for 1960, and in this form they

*Above* **Norton 99 de luxe for 1960 with slimline frame and rear enclosure, but little change to engine or gearbox**

*Right* **The 249 cc Norton Jubilee twin in 1959 with its extensive enclosure and AMC detail parts**

became the 88 and 99 de luxe models. To suit the panels, the frame was modified by pulling in the top rails, which also enabled riders to tuck in their knees more easily. In its new form, the frame soon became known as the slimline, so, inevitably, the earlier type became the wideline.

The new frame was also used by the twins without rear enclosure, and these became the standard 88 and 99. The Jubilee ran on as it was, while the 99 Nomad was joined by a 497 cc

version. For the singles, the new decade brought numerous detail changes for the Manx racers, but little alteration to the road models.

On this note, the firm continued into the 1960s with much more to happen to it. There was to be a move from the traditional Bracebridge Street to London, the end of the Manx, bigger twins and finally the Commando range. Then, with the late 1980s, came a revival of the marque with a rotary engine.

# OEC

In pre-war days, the Osborne Engineering Company, of Portsmouth, were well known for their strange motorcycles, which often had a novel duplex steering system and, in some cases a very low, feet-forward riding position. Despite these odd adventures, they survived until 1940, but when they started in business again, in 1949, their machines were totally conventional.

The new models were lightweights, much like other manufacturers', for they used 10D and 6E Villiers engines in rigid frames with telescopic forks. The two machines listed were both called Atlanta, and this name was to continue to apply to all the firm's two-strokes. Model codes were S1 for the smaller, and S2 for the larger, both being supplied as standard with battery lighting.

These two road models were joined by the D1 and D2 for 1950, and these duplicated the first pair, except in having direct lighting. At the same time, C1 and C2 competition machines were introduced, but these differed little from the road ones. They were given the benefit of competition tyres, with a slightly fatter rear one, together with lower gearing, but otherwise remained with the

**Press test OEC model ST2 with 6E Villiers engine leaving watering hole for rider in 1953**

The OEC Apollo with Brockhouse 248 cc side-valve engine in rigid frame form in 1953

stock cycle parts. The exhaust was raised to waist level on the left and protected at the front by an added plate.

The range continued for 1951 with the addition of further models with pivoted-fork rear suspension. They were available in both sizes and with either lighting system, so this action brought in four new model codes; SS1, SD1, SS2 and SD2. This brought the list up to ten machines, which stayed as they were for 1952, when they were joined by one further model.

This was listed at first as both the Atlanta and the Apollo, but the latter name became normal within a short time. The machine itself hardly lived up to its name, for it was powered by the same 248 cc, side-valve Brockhouse engine unit as the Indian. It retained the wet sump, coil ignition and three-speed gearbox with the change on the left, and was no great performer. For that first year, it went into the rigid frame, but for 1953 it was also available in a pivoted-fork one.

All the other road models ran on, but the competition pair was replaced by a single 197 cc machine. This was the ST3, which had a pivoted-fork frame and an unusual two-stage final drive.

For this, there was a sleeve, which ran on the rear fork pivot centre, with a sprocket at each end. That on the left was driven by a short chain from the gearbox, while the right-hand one drove the rear wheel. All this was in aid of constant chain tension, but the effect was to lengthen the wheelbase, which was not helpful for trials work.

There was a changeover of models during the early part of 1953, with new ones taking over from the old. Thus, all, except the S2 and D2, were dropped, but in their place came the D55 and ST2. The first was little altered from the D1 and retained the rigid frame, while the second was as the SS2 with rear suspension and battery lighting. During the year, they were joined by the D55RS, which had rear suspension.

For 1954 the two 122 cc models continued, along with the ST2 and ST3. These had their engines changed to the 8E and 7E respectively, while the rigid- and sprung-frame Apollo models stayed as they were. In this manner, the range ran to late 1954, when motorcycle production ceased.

# Oscar

This all-British scooter was sprung on an unsuspecting motorcycle world late in 1953, with full descriptions in the press and exhibits at shows in Frankfurt and London. Not a lot more happened, but the prototypes did exist, and one, at least, continued running for several years doing development work for the Siba importers based in Surrey.

The scooter presented bulbous lines with its two-section bodywork, which was fabricated in fibreglass, so the manufacturers in Blackburn were in the vanguard of the use of this material. The front section comprised mudguard, apron and footboards, while the rear enclosed the engine unit and was hinged for access.

Underneath the skin went a duplex tubular frame with pivoted-fork rear suspension. This differed from most in that the fork legs were malleable castings, clamped and pinned to the spindle. The suspension medium was a Spencer-Moulton Flexitor bonded-rubber unit, and the preload could be adjusted. There was also a rubber loop on each leg, which assisted when a passenger was carried. The front suspension was formed as leading links in a similar manner, using the same construction and medium. The wheels were pressed-steel discs shod with 12 in. tyres and mounted on hubs with 5 in. brakes. They were both quickly detachable and interchangeable.

The power units were rather less exciting, being either the 122 or 197 cc Villiers with fan cooling and a three-speed gearbox. Less usual was the engine mounting, which used rubber to insulate any vibration, the unit being able to pivot a little on its rear mounting, but restrained by rubber blocks in shear.

The machine was finished off with a dualseat and could have a spare wheel, but following the first announcement all went quiet. Aside from acknowledging its use by Siba five years later, no more was heard of this make.

**The Oscar scooter launched late in 1953 with bonded-rubber suspension units and basic Villiers engine**

# Panther

Panthers were built at Cleckheaton, in Yorkshire, and had their roots in the dawn of motorcycling. They became famous for manufacturing very sturdy machines, including the extremely cheap Red Panther of the 1930s, and for their use of the engine as the frame downtube.

During the war, they made aircraft parts, but late in 1945 came news of their simple post-war range. This ignored the excursions into upright engines and spring frames that had been scheduled for 1940, and kept to their well tried, inclined engine formula. There were three models, listed as the 60, 70 and 100, all with ohv, but with capacities of 249, 348 and 594 cc. They kept their proven oil system with the lubricant carried in a separate chamber cast within the sump.

The engines differed in their method of ignition, for the two smaller machines had a coil with the points set in the timing cover, while the 100 kept to a magneto. On this model, an auto-advance was incorporated into the drive and, as in the past, this extended on to the separate dynamo. Transmissions also varied, the 60 having three speeds and the two larger models four, but in other respects, the 60 and 70 were the same.

All models had rigid frames and girder forks, the smaller ones having a downtube. The 100 alone had a twin-port cylinder head and, thus, two exhaust systems, while it also had a good roll-on rear stand. The other two used centre stands.

It was a good, solid range for the times, so Panther stuck to it for a while, but with a change to telescopic front forks for 1947. These were Dowty Oleomatic, which relied on air for suspension and oil for damping and lubrication. Dowty had extensive experience of such designs in the aircraft industry, and with its progressive rise in effective spring rate, it offered an improvement over conventional springs. Of course, it also offered disaster if the seals failed, and both Panther

and Dowty were to find out that using aircraft-quality components, serviced to commercial standards, could give problems.

One useful feature of the new forks was that the wheel spindle axis was offset from the fork leg. Thus, they were able to arrange that the leg could be used either way round, thanks to common mudguard lugs, giving solo or sidecar trail according to position. This was an asset for the owner, and for Panther, with most model 100s hauling sidecars, as they only needed the one assembly for either condition.

The range was continued for 1948, and during the year, the firm began to compete in trials, using one each of the smaller models. These differed from the road machines in that the cylinder was set vertically, but were otherwise little altered in their essentials. Naturally, there were alloy guards, a 21 in. front wheel, competition tyres and a high-level exhaust, but the main parts were based on the road model.

The use of an engine with vertical cylinder spread to the two smaller road models for 1949, and these took the numbers 65 and 75 to replace the older ones. Both were much in the mould of the past using the same engine dimensions – which made the 250 a real long-stroke – the enclosed ohv arrangement and the separate crankcase sump for the oil. Both had a Lucas dynamo clamped to the front of the crankcase, but differed in ignition. The 75 had a rear-mounted magneto, but the 65 kept to a coil with a points housing, incorporating an auto-advance, in the same mounting position.

Otherwise, the models seemed as before, although the frame was new and the 75 had the roll-on rear stand. The model 100 simply stayed as it was. The works competition models led to a further pair of machines which were based on them and listed as the Stroud in either capacity. They were much as the works machines, but came complete with full lighting equipment and no great weight reduction.

For 1950 a 65 de luxe was added. This had a four-speed gearbox and improved finish, but was otherwise as the standard machine. There was little other alteration, except to manual ignition control for the 100. All six models ran on for 1951, with many detail changes. For the Strouds, this included a low-level exhaust pipe with tilted silencer. It was the same again for 1952, but at the end of that year the 65 was dropped and there were some more major changes.

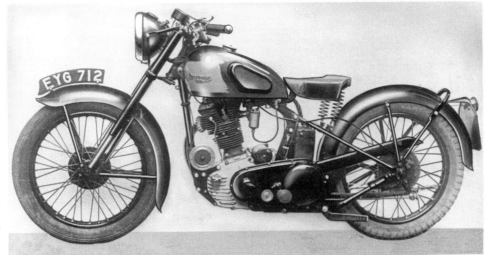

Early post-war Panther single 60 or 70 from the 1947–8 period, when the inclined engine was used with the Dowty forks

This Panther 100 ran in the 1949 ISDT, but retired on the fifth day with sidecar chassis trouble

Panther Stroud 348 cc model from 1952 with vertical cylinder and odd exhaust-pipe run

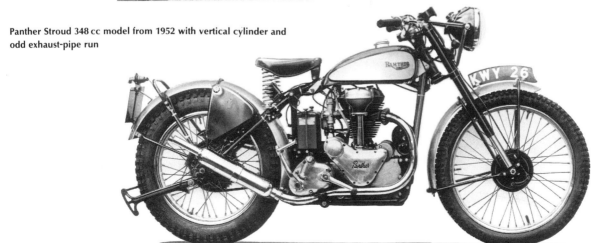

The 1958 model 75 Panther in pivoted-fork frame

Foremost were those to the suspension, for a frame with pivoted-fork rear suspension appeared for the 65 and 75, and with it a new telescopic fork with springs. The Dowtys continued on the rigid models, and the competition Stroud engines were given a light alloy head and barrel. There was also the option of magneto ignition for the 65 de luxe.

At the end of the season, the Stroud models were withdrawn, but the others ran on for 1954, when they were joined by a version of the 100 in a pivoted-fork frame. This, too, used the Panther telescopic forks with springs, which became standard wear, and all models had the option of a dualseat.

The rigid 75 was dropped at the end of the year, so for 1955 there were three sprung models and only two rigid ones, these being the 65 de luxe and 100. The 75 had full-width hubs fitted as standard, these being an option for either 65, and all models had a new headlamp with the speedometer, ammeter and light switch set in it.

*Right* **The Panther Princess scooter of 1960 with 174 cc Villiers 2L engine under the body panels it shared with Dayton and Sun**

Panther twin model 45 from 1959 with 324 cc 3T engine and Earles leading-link forks

The 65 de luxe was dropped that year, so only the 100 remained in its rigid frame to suit the die-hard sidecar man.

The three sprung models continued with it for 1956, when full-width hubs appeared on the model 100 and were offered as an option for the rigid version. Two entirely new machines were also added to the range, both having 197 cc Villiers engines.

These new lightweights were the models 10/3 with three-speed 8E unit, and the 10/4 with four-speed 9E engine. Otherwise, they were the same and had a loop frame, pivoted-fork rear suspension and Earles leading links at the front. The last were well disguised to appear as telescopics at a casual inspection. The front mudguard was unsprung. Both models had a dualseat, and the area below this was enclosed by panels with spaces for the tools, battery and electrics.

The range was extended for 1957 with further two-stroke models, while the four-strokes kept going with one addition. There was a further 197 cc machine in the form of the 10/3A, which had the 9E engine and three-speed gearbox. The

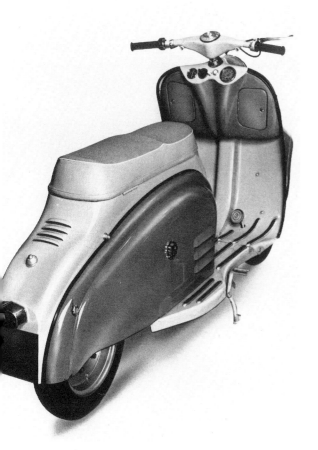

cycle parts were unchanged and were also used by the model 25, which had a 246 cc 2H Villiers single, and the model 35 with a 249 cc 2T twin. The first was never a successful engine unit and was short lived, as was the Panther 25.

The new four-stroke was a de luxe version of the sprung 100, which kept the full-width hubs, while the original became the Standard 100 without them. The final addition to the Panther line-up was a 125 cc Terrot scooter, which failed to match the Vespa or Lambretta in style or much else.

As well as the 25, the rigid 100 was finally dropped at the end of the year, but all the others continued for 1958. They were joined by a 35 Sports model, which had a tuned engine and revised finish to distinguish it from the basic 35. It retained the same cycle parts, and this policy ran on into 1959, when two more twins were added as the models 45 and 50 Sports, using the larger 3T Villiers engine.

The four-strokes also had a new model in the form of the 120, which was a 645 cc version of the big single. It shared cycle parts with the de luxe 100, and both models still used the archaic twin-port head, unlike the standard 100. The Terrot scooter activity continued, but there was news, late in the year, of a Panther scooter, although it was not to reach the market until 1960.

This it did, along with the rest of the range, which continued much as before, although the lightweight twins were fitted with telescopic forks. The scooter was called the Princess and powered by the 174 cc 2L engine in kickstart or electric-start forms. Both had fan cooling and went into a conventional scooter frame with pivoted-arm suspension at front and rear. This made wheel changing much easier. The wheels themselves were 10 in. split-rim types on alloy hubs. The bodywork had a better line than that of the Terrot and was produced in conjunction with Dayton and Sun (see pages 77 and 165) to reduce costs. It was built up from panels in the usual manner, those at the sides being detachable for access.

On this note, Panther entered the 1960s, but times were soon to become harder for them, and few models survived more than three years. A couple did for a while longer, but with a receiver at the company's helm and built from the stock bins.

Many survivors still demonstrate how tough they built them in Yorkshire.

# Phillips

This famous cycle firm moved into powered two-wheelers in 1954, when they exhibited a clip-on model at the Earls Court show as a complete machine. For this, they took a conventional cycle, but shaped the rear end of the top tube so that it curved down to lower the seat, and added bracing struts to the front forks. The front wheel was given a drum brake, and the rear one a coaster hub, so in this area, the machine had an edge on basic clip-on cycles.

The engine was a 49.2 cc two-stroke with alloy head and barrel, and had a clutch built into the assembly. It was mounted above the bottom bracket and drove the rear wheel by chain on the left, while the standard cycle pedals and chain remained as usual. A silencer ran parallel to the downtube, and the engine provided direct lighting.

For 1956 the machine was given telescopic front forks and was joined by the P39 Gadabout. This was much more in the moped image and used a 49.6 cc Rex engine with two-speed gearbox hung from a rigid spine frame with telescopic forks. The result was much as any other mid-1950s moped and the performance adequate. This meant 35 mph if you could stand the ride and vibration, and 25 mph as the practical speed over any distance.

The original model continued until late 1957, and the P39 into 1959, but for that year it was joined by others. The first to appear was the P40 Panda, which had a single-speed, 49.2 cc Rex engine, which went into a simple frame similar to that used for a woman's bicycle. The engine had a light-alloy head and barrel, while the cycle side was basic with no suspension, other than the saddle.

A little later, the P39 was joined by the P50 Gadabout de luxe, which was similar to the cheaper machine, but with three speeds. A month later, the P45 Gadabout was added. This was as the P50, except that the power unit was a 49.9 cc Villiers 3K unit with the two-speed gearbox.

By the end of 1959 the P39 had gone, but the other three models continued and were joined during 1960 by the P49 Panda Plus. This was much as the P40, but had telescopic forks and well valanced mudguards, although it retained the single-speed Rex engine.

During 1960 the P40 was dropped, but the other three mopeds ran into the new decade and were joined by others, before the name, which was one of the Raleigh group of companies, was dropped. By late 1964 the models were no more.

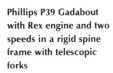

**Phillips P39 Gadabout with Rex engine and two speeds in a rigid spine frame with telescopic forks**

# Phoenix

Ernie Barrett went racing in the 1950s by building a trio of frames and fitting various sizes of JAP engine into them, so when he turned to scooters, it was not surprising that he adopted the same principle. He used the name of the mythical bird that arose from its ashes for his products, which were built in Tottenham, London.

All models used Villiers engines, and the prototype of 1956 had a 147 cc 30C. When the production model was launched later that year, it kept the same engine, which was fitted into a typical tubular scooter frame. This had pivoted-fork front and rear suspension with an 8 in. wheel size. The frame carried a scooter form of body, although this lacked any great style.

A year later, the range was expanded for 1958 with Standard and De Luxe versions of the 147 cc model, which had been tidied up a little by extending the fixed front mudguard cowl upwards to carry the headlamp. This improved the front end, although it remained rather large and heavy in appearance, but the rear body kept its single-curvature forward panel and an enormous fretwork-type Phoenix badge.

In May 1958 the style improved further, as four new models launched had a fibreglass moulding for the rear enclosure. It was held in place by three car-bonnet catches of the period, so was easy to remove for major work. For refuelling, the dualseat swung upwards, which also gave access to the plug.

The new models included two in the 150 class, but with different engines. The 150 Super de Luxe kept to the 30C with kickstart, but the S150 used the 148 cc 31C engine with electric start. Both were fan-cooled, as were the other two models, which used the 197 cc 9E engine for the S200, and the 249 cc 2T twin for the T250. Both had electric start, and the last also had 10 in. wheels.

The range grew further for 1959, although the De Luxe model with the 30C was dropped, but this still left three machines for that class. The two larger ones were listed in solo and sidecar form,

**The Phoenix 150 model with 31C Villiers engine under a body shared with the whole range**

**Phoenix T250 scooter with stowage compartment in rear of apron and fascia above**

while the extra model was the T325, which used the larger 3T twin engine. It, too, had fan-cooling and electric start, and was available for solo or sidecar use. It was fitted with the 10 in. wheels, which became an option for all models.

For 1960 the 150 Super de Luxe was fitted with the 31C engine, and a Standard 200 model

appeared with kickstart. Two further new models were the Standard 175 and S175. These had the 174 cc 2L engine and specifications as for the 200. The Standard machines were alone in fitting the 8 in. wheels, but the 10 in. ones remained an option for them and a standard fit for the rest.

Thus, the Phoenix range continued into the 1960s, now with far more style, but only until 1964, when production ceased. Once more, the declining market took its toll.

# Power Pak

This was one of the many clip-on units on the market around 1950, which functioned by driving the bicycle tyre with a crankshaft-mounted roller. In this case, the rear wheel was used, the unit being mounted above it with the cylinder of its two-stroke engine inverted and on the right-hand side of the machine.

This arrangement allowed the fuel tank to sit neatly over the crankcase, which extended across the machine, with the flywheel magneto on the left. Inside, there was a deflector piston and over-hung crankshaft, while outside were hung the carburettor and a tubular silencer. The unit was clamped to the cycle saddle stays with a strut on the right, and a lever was provided to bring the drive roller into contact with the tyre.

Control was by a single lever, which activated the decompressor when moved one way, and the throttle when moved in the other. In a year or two, this was altered, as the engine had gained a clutch and a twistgrip, which disengaged it when turned to its stop. Thus, opening the throttle first allowed the clutch to engage and then lifted the carburettor slide.

The unit remained on the market until 1956, but by then the world had moved on to mopeds, so the firm endeavoured to follow suit. The result was rather odd, for they retained the friction-roller drive to the rear tyre, but positioned the engine unit beneath the model's bottom bracket.

The frame was much as for a woman's cycle, but the downtubes were replaced by a beam, which also acted as a fuel tank. At the front were light blade girder forks, by then very dated, but on top of the handlebars went a fascia panel. This carried a speedometer, ignition key and switches for both lights and direction indicators, the last being a rare feature on two wheels then. Leather panniers were fitted on each side of the rear wheel.

Nothing further was heard of this design, and it is likely that the firm had a good look at an NSU Quickly and realized they would be wasting their time. Of course, they should have done this before building their prototype.

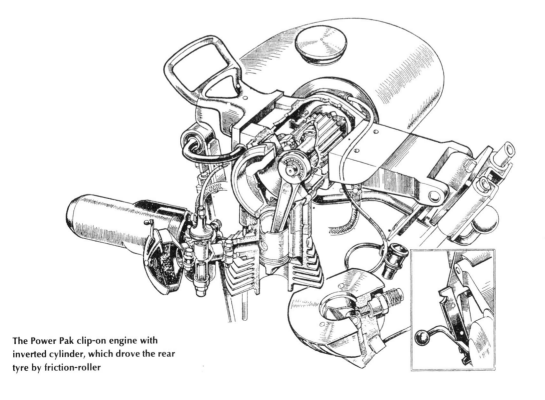

The Power Pak clip-on engine with inverted cylinder, which drove the rear tyre by friction-roller

# Powerwheel

Cyril Pullin won the 1914 Senior TT and after World War I produced some interesting motorcycle designs in the form of the Pullin Groom and Ascot Pullin. Both were advanced and innovative, but neither sold in any numbers.

Late in 1951 his name appeared once more as the designer of the Powerwheel, which was to be made and marketed by Tube Investments. It was aimed at the clip-on market but, like the Cyclemaster and Winged Wheel, sought to build the motive power into a wheel, which could be exchanged for the normal cycle one. This was usually the rear wheel, although the front was equally feasible, as was one at each end.

The engine was a 40 cc two-stroke, but what made it nearly unique was that it was a rotary. Thus, the crankshaft stayed still and the internal workings forced the cylinder and crankcase to rotate about it, along with the piston and connecting rod. Detail arrangements were made to achieve balance, while the intake was along the hollow crankshaft mainshaft, which had the carburettor attached to its outer end. A disc valve between the flywheels controlled the ingoing mixture, which then passed through twin transfers in the iron barrel.

The exhaust was by two opposed ports, each with an alloy silencer, which discharged into an

The complex Powerwheel, which appeared in 1951 as a prototype, but never made it into production. This exploded diagram shows the many parts involved, from the carburettor on the left to the magneto on the right

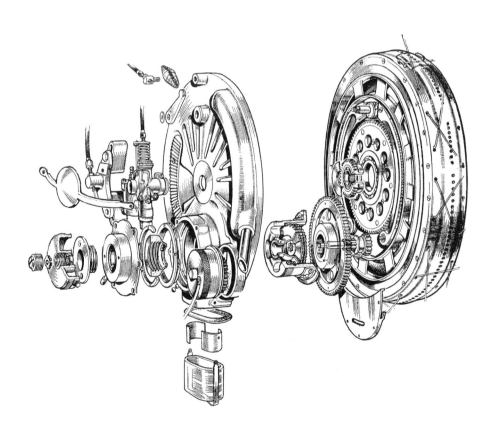

annulus and then to an external chamber. Ignition was by flywheel magneto, the points of which were opened by a face cam, and the compression-release valve was held open by a light spring, until centrifugal force shut it as the engine spun.

In addition to this ingenuity and complication, there was also a transmission with a gear train to give the necessary reduction to the wheel itself. Into this was built a clutch and also a drive to a small dynamo for the lights. The whole was housed within the wheel hub, which also contained a 7 in. drum brake with link operation of the shoes from the single cam.

All told, it was very clever and worked well enough in prototype form on the road. However, although it ran smoothly, thanks to its rotating inertia, it was a complex solution to a simple problem. Most likely this is why no more was heard of it.

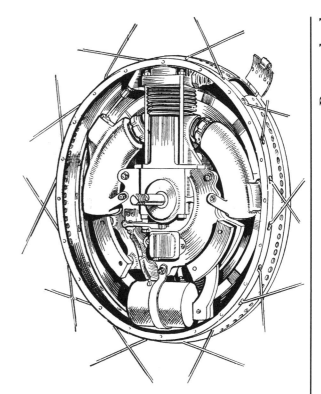

*Above* **The assembled Powerwheel with the cylinder balanced by the magneto armature. The door in the hub shell gave access to the sparking plug, although a special spanner was needed to extract it**

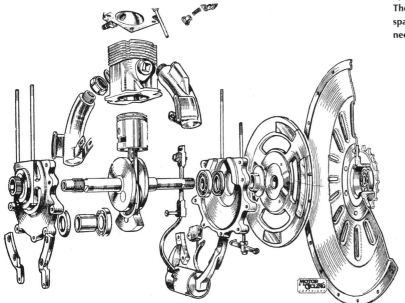

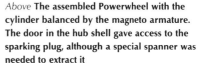

# Progress

# Pullin

This was the name of an imported German scooter that appeared in 1956, which was joined for 1957 by models with Villiers engines. There were three of these, all of which used the same chassis with fibreglass bodywork. This sat on a welded tubular frame with pivoted-fork front and rear suspension, while the wheels with 16 in. rims were larger than usual for a scooter.

For the Anglian model, the engine was the 147 cc 30C, while the Briton had the 197 cc 8E, both being fan-cooled. The Britannia also had a 197 cc engine, but this was a 9E with four speeds and electric start.

Sadly, the machines lacked the style and line of the Teutonic models, and by late 1958 had been discontinued. They were never seen again.

After the Powerwheel exercise (see page 148), Cyril Pullin turned his attentions to the scooter field, and in 1955 offered a design and prototype to any manufacturer willing to produce it. The machine was planned to need minimal and inexpensive tooling, while much that was under the skin came straight off the shelf.

The engine unit was a 197 cc Villiers with fan-cooling and Siba electric start, which went into a monocoque type of chassis. The rear body was formed from sheet alloy with cross-members and was bolted to the front section. Both wheels were suspended on pivoted arms with 8 in. rims and 6 in. brakes, the front one being enclosed by the combined apron, mudguard and headlamp housing.

The appearance was acceptable and the model was shown fitted out with windscreen, dualseat, spare wheel and rear carrier, so offered the right menu to the scooter rider. However, this failed to suit the taste of any manufacturer, so only the prototype was ever built.

This was a pity because it worked well and could have had possibilities.

**Progress scooter at the 1956 Earls Court show with its larger-than-usual wheels**

# Radco

This make of machine was produced by the Birmingham firm of E. A. Radnall from just before World War I. Their range was on the market for most of the 1920s, but tailed off in the next decade, with production coming to a halt in 1933.

For the next 20 years, they stuck to making components for the industry, but in 1954 returned to the fray with a single model called the Ace. In truth, there was little enough to distinguish it from many other utility mounts, for its motive power came from a 99 cc 4F engine with two speeds.

This went into a simple rigid loop frame, but a novel note was struck by the front suspension. This was by short leading links with external spring units and was supplied by Metal Profiles. For the rest, the equipment included a saddle with a cylindrical toolbox beneath it, a centre stand and direct lighting.

As happened with others in the 1950s, there was an announcement, a prototype, maybe a buyer's guide listing, and then silence. No more was heard of the model, and the firm went back to making components. They did have one more go in 1966 with a basic mini-bike, but this, too, failed to catch on and met with the same fate.

*Above* **The Radco Ace, which appeared in 1954 with its Villiers 4F engine and short leading-link forks, but it failed to reach production**

*Right* **The Pullin scooter prototype shown and offered for manufacture in 1955, with monocoque body over its Villiers engine**

# Rainbow

# Raleigh

This machine was built as a prototype in 1950 by a gentleman of the same name who wanted to create a link between cycle and motorcycle. In some respects, it was likened to an autocycle but, once an allowance was made for the restricted facilities of the builder, it could be seen more as a step-through.

This was reinforced by the design parameters Rainbow set himself; low centre of gravity, enclosed engine, easy mounting of the machine by the rider, and legshields, all of which can be found in current step-through models. For the 1950 designer, there was little option, other than to use a 99 cc Villiers 1F engine unit with its two speeds, but the rest of the machine was less usual.

The frame had twin tubes, which ran down from the headstock, under the engine and then up and back to the rear wheel. Vertical tubes supported the saddle and rear carrier, while the cylindrical fuel tank was mounted behind the headstock. There were legshields and, in addition, there was a cover that enclosed most of the engine unit. Part of the machine's neat appearance came from the use of a circular, drum silencer, which went on the left of the crankcase to match the flywheel magneto on the right.

Front suspension was by single tube girders with rubber-band suspension, and the forks carried a 26 in. wheel, much as a heavy bicycle or autocycle. This pattern was not repeated at the rear, where a 20 in. wheel was installed, its use allowing a low seat height. It would have been easy enough in production to have amended the front end to accommodate a smaller wheel, and this could have given the project a more balanced line.

Unfortunately, this was not to be and the Rainbow stayed as a prototype only, in recognition of the ingenuity of its designer. There was no production and, thus, no further mention of the machine.

Raleigh are best known for their bicycles, but have dabbled with power from Victorian times. This involved motorcycles, three-wheelers and the sale of engines and gearboxes to others in pre-war times, but from 1935 they concentrated on their first love – the bicycle.

In 1958 they returned to powered machines in a modest way and produced a moped late in the year, which was typed the RM1. It had a 49.5 cc Sturmey-Archer two-stroke engine with V-belt drive to a countershaft, and chain to the rear wheel. Inside the engine, there was an overhung crankshaft with a Lucas flywheel magneto on its end, outboard of the V-belt pulley.

The engine was made for Raleigh by BSA, but they kept the cycle parts to themselves and used

**The Sturmey-Archer engine used by the Raleigh moped when launched in 1958 as the RM1**

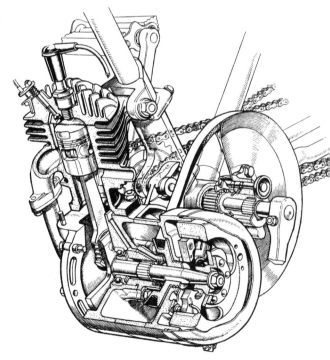

a woman's model as the basis for the frame, which lacked rear suspension and had rigid bicycle front forks. The wheels were of the normal 26 in. cycle size, but did have drum brakes in the hubs, while the rear wheel had a sprocket on each side.

The fuel tank went between the twin down-tubes, and there was a saddle, rear carrier and toolbag. The engine was clamped to the down-tubes, with the pedal shaft running though the countershaft, and there was a means by which the rider could simply pedal the device home if the engine failed or the fuel supply ran out. There were guards over the chains and belt drive, a centre stand, and a single twistgrip control, which operated both throttle and decompressor.

Accessories such as screen and legshields were offered, and during 1959 the original model was joined by the RM1C, which had a clutch. Both were replaced for 1960 by the RM2C, which had a larger fuel tank with a fairing over it, among other detail improvements.

At the end of 1960 this, too, was dropped, for Raleigh changed course to use imported engines and designs for the rest of that decade.

# Raynal

This company led the way to the autocycle in pre-war days by building a production version of the Jones prototype in 1937. The Jones had been made in conjunction with Villiers, and the original engine had provision for the pedal shaft to run through the middle of the clutch shaft.

The arrangement was fine, until the machine toppled over, or was even parked, bicycle fashion, with one pedal on the kerb. Then, sooner or later, the shafts would bend and bind, giving trouble. For production, this was avoided by relocating the pedals to a normal bottom bracket and moving the engine forward a little.

The power unit became the Villiers Junior, and the machine the archetype of the autocycle. The frame was an open bicycle type with a simple sprung fork, while both wheels had drum brakes. In 1939 it was joined by a model with rigid forks.

Post-war, the JDL engine was used to produce the Popular, which was much as the pre-war model, but with girder forks. After a season, it was renamed the De Luxe for 1947, with no real change, and in this form ran on until late 1950.

**A suffering Raynal autocycle struggling with too much of a load for its 98 cc JDL engine in 1948 – actually a 1938 machine**

# RCA

This was an engine, rather than a machine, which first appeared in 1957. The name came from R. Christoforides and Associates, but the design was that of Peter Hogan. He, and brother John, had been at the forefront of British 125 cc racing in the early 1950s with a pair of Bantams, John winning many events.

Peter's first twin was built by coupling two Bantam engines, and with the experience gained from this venture he laid out the 349 cc RCA twin. It was modern in concept, with a horizontally-split crankcase, full flywheels and twin Amal carburettors, following bench tests with a single Zenith. Electric starting was provided by a Siba unit, and the one unusual feature was the location of the exhaust ports. These were in each side of the iron block, alloy adaptors being bolted to this and then connected to the exhaust pipes. The cylinder heads were separate and in alloy, as the Hogans had made and sold these for Bantams at one time.

The engine drove an Albion gearbox, and an alloy chaincase, carrying the RCA badge, enclosed the drive. The complete assembly was first tried in a Greeves, which was altered to suit where necessary, and in this form was the subject of a road test. The report gave a top speed of 75 mph, which was about par for stock models that year, although sports machines, such as the Velocette Viper, were good for 90. The RCA did, however, pull well, which mattered when only four speeds were to be had.

The RCA engine was tried by Dot for two models in 1959, one for scrambles and the other a road machine. This exercise only lasted for two

Greeves with 349 cc RCA twin engine on test in 1958

years, for the power curve was unsuited to the off-road task and engine supplies were limited anyway. There was a brief attempt at road racing, for which the engines had the exhaust adaptors reversed to point to the rear, where they were fitted with short open pipes.

These machines failed to provide any impact on the racing scene, although that same year a race-kitted Yamaha twin made an appearance on some British circuits. For one make it was to be oblivion, and for the other further development and years of success.

# Reynolds

# Royal Enfield

Reynolds Tubes were much involved with the motorcycle industry and, as well as producing the raw material, often helped with the development of frames, forks and complete machines for both road and competition use. From all this background activity, one exercise was shown at the 1955 London show and in the following year during TT week.

It was a prototype moped, built to show what could be done, but without any intention of Reynolds themselves becoming involved in selling a complete machine. The design followed European practice in most respects, and the engine unit was a two-speed German Victoria.

This went into a beam frame with pivoted-fork rear suspension, while at the front there were leading links for the show, but telescopics at the TT. For the rest, there was a tank, saddle and rear carrier, so the model conformed to the accepted standards of the day.

It was an interesting project, but no-one stepped forward to take it further, and Reynolds wisely stuck to their main business of making tubing, so nothing further was heard of it.

Royal Enfield were masters of the technique of using a small number of major assemblies in various ways to create a model range to cover most requirements. They did this before the war, and even during it to some extent, and were to use the trick throughout most of their post-war years.

This was not too apparent when their 1946 range was announced with just three models, although two, at least, had common cycle parts and nearly identical engines. These were the 346 cc ohv model G and 499 cc J, which were based largely on earlier Enfield practice.

The engines differed in bore only to obtain the two sizes, so the stroke was common and really only the head and barrel varied. Both of these were in iron, which was normal then, but much else of the design was less so, although common to the Redditch firm.

Thus, the connecting rod was forged in light alloy with a plain big-end bearing. The crankshaft was built up conventionally and ran in a crankcase that was split on the centre line, but which also had a compartment for the oil of the dry-sump lubrication system. The timing gear was by a train of gears, the mag-dyno being sited behind the cylinder, and the valve gear was fully enclosed. The timing cover shape was typical for the marque, for it also encompassed the twin oil pumps, their drive and an oil filter chamber.

The engine drove a four-speed Albion gearbox, which had an extra external pedal. This allowed the rider to select neutral from any gear, except first, and was to remain an Enfield feature for a long time. These two assemblies went into a rigid cradle frame, which had twin tubes that ran under the massive crankcase to protect it. At the front were telescopic forks, and both wheels had 19 in. rims and 6 in. brakes in offset hubs. There was a deeply valanced sprung mudguard at the front and a two-part guard at the rear. Most of this was easily removed, which made dealing with punctures a little less of a problem.

Both the G and J were fitted with the usual Amal carburettor, Lucas electrics, saddle, toolboxes, and speedometer, although the last was always listed as an extra, rather like purchase tax. Both were not always wanted, but were compulsory in Britain.

In addition to these two models, the firm carried out factory rebuilds of its wartime C and CO models. These were both of 346 cc, but with side or overhead valves respectively, and while the cycle parts were much as for the G and J, the wartime girder forks were retained. The CO used the same engine as the G, but the C had a side-valve head and barrel.

These models were reworked to meet the intense demand for transport in the immediate post-war years, at a time when there were great shortages. Most new machines went for export, and ex-army models filled the gap. Many were simply sold off by the services, but Enfield had this involvement for a couple of years.

The third 1946 model was in complete contrast and effectively new on its home market, although it had first been seen in 1939 and was quite familiar to many service users. It was the 125 cc two-stroke model RE, which was known to the forces as the Flying Flea and based on the pre-war 98 cc DKW model RT.

This last had been handled in Holland by a Jewish-owned firm in the 1930s, but in 1938 the concession was abruptly removed. Undeterred, the firm looked to Britain and arranged for Enfield to build them a copy, right down to the finish, but with a 125 cc engine. It was to be called the Royal Baby, or RB, not too far from the German RT.

By April 1939 prototypes were in Holland, and a few machines were sold just before war broke out. While that closed one door firmly, it left Enfield with a fully-developed lightweight, ready tooled up, and the army was soon a customer. Around 55,000 were built, some being supplied in a parachute crate for airborne use. They proved invaluable in action and for general duties. After the war, Enfield simply changed to black paint in the spray shop, added a touch of chrome, and continued to build them.

The RE engine was built in unit with its three-

**Royal Enfield 125 cc model RE based on the wartime Flying Flea, as it was in 1950 when it had gained telescopic forks prior to a redesign in the following year**

speed hand-change gearbox and had conventional construction. Inside, there was a flat-top piston and bobweight flywheels with a pressed-up crankshaft, while the head was in alloy and the barrel in iron. A Miller unit on the right looked after the lights and ignition, and a pressed-steel cover on the left enclosed the primary drive.

The engine unit went into a simple rigid frame, which picked up on lugs at each end. Front suspension was by girders with rubber bands as the medium, and the wheels had 19 in. rims and small drum brakes, 4 in. at the front and 5 in. rear. The fixtures and fittings were simple and included a saddle, cylindrical toolbox, centre stand and rear carrier.

With production so important, there were no real changes for two years, and for 1948 it was the RE that had a little amendment. This was to the exhaust pipe, which was given a distinct bulge as it curved down from the exhaust port, but other changes were minimal. This continued for 1949, when the 500 single became the J2 model, thanks to a change to a twin-port head and the addition of a second exhaust system for the left side of the machine.

The real Enfield news for 1949 was the introduction of two new models, one reviving a prewar single name and the other a vertical twin. The single was the Bullet, the name of which went back to 1933 and which had always been associated with sporting models. During 1948 the postwar prototype had been seen in action in various trials and had already raised eyebrows by using rear suspension, then unheard of for such events.

The model was released in three forms for road, trials or scrambles use, but the essentials were the same for all. The engine followed many Enfield principles, but these were amended to suit, so the oil compartment was moved to the rear of the crankcase to move the engine's weight forward. The length was then held to a minimum by bolting the gearbox to the rear of the crankcase and driving it with a duplex chain. This was tensioned with a slipper and enclosed in a cast alloy case with single fixing for the outer, so the resulting assembly was much as unit construction.

The engine itself followed Enfield practice in most areas, but had the iron cylinder deeply spigoted into a much taller crankcase. On top went an alloy head with separate rocker housings, so this, too, differed from the touring engines. Internally, things were less altered in design or layout, but were improved in detail and materials.

The engine and gearbox assembly went into an open frame with pivoted-fork rear suspension and telescopics at the front. The wheel and brake sizes were as for the tourers, but blade mudguards were used, along with generally more modern features, except for the saddle. The result was a smart motorcycle that stood out during a drab period, its silver-grey finish being topped off by a chrome-plated tank with frosted silver panels.

For trials, the machine was fitted with a Lucas racing magneto, wide gear ratios, raised exhaust and more suitable wheels and tyres. Both lights and a mag-dyno were available, for it was an era when most competitors rode their machines to and from events, as well as in them. The scrambler received a similar treatment, but without the options, and had close gears and an open exhaust.

The second new model was the 500 Twin, which never had any other name, but annoyed Triumph by being listed as the 5T. It had a brand-new, 495 cc ohv vertical twin engine with separate heads and barrels in alloy and iron respectively. The crankshaft was a single alloy-iron casting with plain big-ends and ball and roller mains. There were two camshafts, which were driven by chain, with a further chain from the inlet camshaft to the dynamo. This ran at engine speed with a skew-gear-driven points housing and distributor for the coil ignition system built into it.

Lubrication was by the normal Enfield pumps, and the oil was kept in a crankcase sump, as on the Bullet. Like that model, the gearbox was bolted to the rear of the case, and from then on, the Twin followed the lines of the road Bullet, except for details, such as an ignition and lights switch, plus ammeter set in a box beneath the saddle. Only the sprung front mudguard spoilt the machine's fine lines.

Despite launching two new models, Enfield kept at it, and for 1950 the RE was fitted with telescopic front forks, which picked up on the girder mountings. There were other details, but it was only the cast alloy fork top cover for the Bullet and Twin which was notable.

The smallest model received a major redesign for 1951, when its engine unit became more streamlined and went into a new frame. Internally, the engine was much as before, but the works were housed in a new set of alloy castings of much neater style. Changes were to an external ignition coil, crankshaft-mounted clutch and footchange for the gearbox.

**Prosaic model J2 Royal Enfield from 1952 with its iron engine, separate gearbox and rigid frame**

The new frame gave more support to the engine, as it had a full loop. It was still rigid, but the telescopics at the front were revised to normal yokes, the top one carrying the speedometer and handlebars. These had been cleaned up with welded-on pivot blocks, alloy levers and axial cables for throttle and decompressor. The front brake size was increased to 5 in. to match the rear, but the cycle parts remained much as before. Thus, the RE2, as it was called, stayed true to its roots as a light, handy machine.

The other models ran on with little change for 1951 and 1952, although for that year, the trials Bullet gained a sleeved alloy barrel, and the Twin had its switches moved around and was given the option of a dualseat. The G and J models continued as they were, with no real alteration. The former was dropped in 1954, and the latter a year later.

There were more additions for 1953, with new models at both ends of the range. Smallest newcomer was the Ensign, which had a 148 cc version of the RE2 engine. This was installed in a frame that appeared to have plunger rear suspension with exposed springs, although it was, in fact, a pivoted fork. The springs were simply held in the same manner as for a plunger frame and, thus, copied a pre-war European style. Otherwise, the Ensign was very much as the RE2, which continued

unchanged to the end of the year and was then dropped.

The 346 cc Bullet had some internal changes and was joined by a 499 cc version. This duplicated the smaller model on most points, but it was fitted with a larger rear brake and sidecar lugs. In addition, the forks were available with extended wheel lugs to give sidecar trail. These, along with a steering damper, were also available for some other models.

The Twin had some new parts, but more important was the appearance of a larger version, the 693 cc Meteor. This was much as the smaller model, but it had dual 6 in. front brakes, the 7 in. rear brake and a larger fuel tank. Despite the fact that the machine was their new top model, a dualseat remained an option.

More new models and changes were introduced for 1954, the Bullets and both twins being fitted with a styling cowl at the top of the forks. This carried a small pilot lamp at each top corner, plus the headlamp, enclosed the top of the forks, and provided a mounting for the instruments and switches. Enfield called it a casquette, and it was to be a styling feature for many years.

The Bullet range was extended by introducing a road-racing version, but this looked far from competitive when compared to the well developed BSA Gold Star. The same options were also offered for the larger Bullet, but few took them up. For the Twin, there was a mag-dyno option, which was a curious move at a time when

The Bullet was listed in trials and scrambles form, and this is the latter around 1953, but it lacks conviction

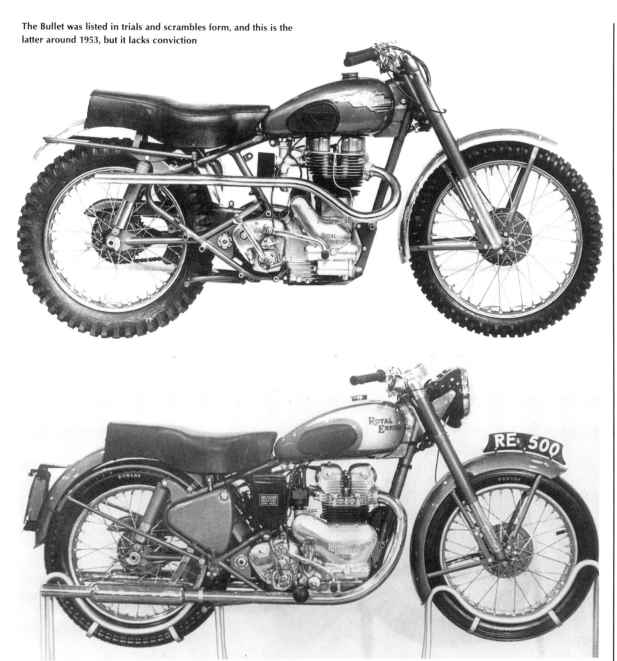

First of the Royal Enfield twins was the 495 cc model listed as the 500 Twin and shown here in 1953 form

the industry was turning to alternators. It involved alterations to the drive to achieve the correct magneto speed.

The final new models were for the 250 class, which the firm had ignored in post-war years. To deal with this, they built a 248 cc version of the model G engine and produced the model S by fitting this in an open-diamond, rigid frame with a light, four-speed Albion gearbox. At the front

were telescopic forks, and the cycle parts were as for the G model. Unlike the other models, it had coil ignition and a Miller alternator on the left-hand end of the crankshaft.

The model S was only built for the one year, but the Clipper, which was launched with it, ran on for a little longer. This used the same engine and gearbox in a pivoted-fork frame with telescopics, so was a cross between the Bullet and G models.

The Clipper was fitted with a casquette without pilot lights for 1955, while the road Bullets were given a dualseat and dual front brakes. These items appeared on the Twin, too, where the mag-dyno became standard. This also went on the Meteor. All the larger models had the gearbox amended so that the pedals were on concentric spindles, and the Ensign continued with covers to hide its rear springs.

The range of Bullets was modified for 1956, and the two road versions changed to an alternator for charging, although they kept the magneto for ignition. This led to an enlarged chaincase, while the models also had a new frame and many detail alterations. All the competition machines were dropped, to be replaced by a Moto-Cross Bullet in each size for that year only.

The utility 250 Clipper was joined by a similar 350 model, which retained the same separate engine and gearbox format. It kept to a saddle, so was cheaper than the Bullet, and appeared to follow the typical Enfield trick of clearing the stores of excess stocks by building a model to use them.

At the bottom of the scale, the two-stroke became the Ensign II with some detail changes and a dualseat, which gave it a much more solid look. For the twins, the smaller stayed as it was and the larger was renamed the Super Meteor. In

this form, it produced more power and had an alternator for charging, while retaining the magneto. The engine unit went into a new frame, and the result was a fast, beefy motorcycle.

A new model was introduced for 1957 as the 248 cc Crusader, which was to lead to many versions and be a mainstay of the firm well into the next decade. It featured unit construction, but otherwise followed Enfield methods in most respects, if not all.

The engine had a short stroke and iron top half. Inside, there was a one-piece, cast-iron crankshaft with plain big-end and alloy rod. A single alloy cover enclosed the rockers, but the location of the camshaft on the left was not usual. It was driven by a chain outboard of the primary and, in turn, drove the oil pump, which had a cross-shaft to the points on the right. The alternator was also on the right, and the oil for the dry-sump system in a chamber in the crankcase, as usual.

The complete unit went into an open frame with telescopic front and pivoted-fork rear suspension. The wheels were 17 in. with full-width hubs and 6 in. brakes, while the rear was driven by a fully-enclosed chain. There was a dualseat and a centre section with a lid on each side to carry the electrics and tools.

Alongside the new Crusader, the two Clippers continued for 1957 only, as did the two road Bullets, Ensign II and both twins, although the smaller of these did gain an alternator and coil ignition. A Clipper II appeared for 1958 as a low-cost version of the Crusader, and an Ensign III ran alongside the II with a higher specification level. The two Bullets continued much as before and were joined by another 346 cc Clipper, which was based on the Bullet engine with iron top half, alternator electrics and Crusader-type cycle parts, but with 19 in. wheels.

The Crusader itself was little altered, but became available with a factory fairing during the year. Earlier, in 1956, the firm had co-operated with *The Motor Cycle* to build a full fairing for a Bullet, so had learnt much from this project, which was known as the Dreamliner. That had been a complete front and rear enclosure with dual headlights, but the 1958 design was simpler, being a basic dolphin type plus a deeply valanced front mudguard. It was called the Airflow, and within two years was offered for all the road models as a factory fitment.

Thus, it appeared for the 250 and 350 Clippers in 1958, as well as for the twins, which had other

**A 1956 Royal Enfield 693 cc Super Meteor on test, where its power and low-speed pulling came in for praise**

additions and alterations. The Super Meteor alone had little change and did not get its Airflow until 1959, but the 500 Twin was replaced early in the year by a new model. In addition, the larger twin was joined by a high-performance version.

The new small twin was the Meteor Minor, which was listed in Standard and De Luxe forms. It followed the lines of the earlier machine, but had a short-stroke, 496 cc, ohv engine and a number of detail amendments. The cycle parts were much as for the Crusader and, thus, in a style which had become a standard for the firm. An Airflow version of both models was offered from the start.

The performance 700 was the Constellation, which had yet more power, a TT carburettor, magneto and siamezed exhaust system. The cycle side was much as for the Super Meteor, but more sporting with chrome-plated mudguards.

Even the Ensign III was given an Airflow for 1959, when it was joined by the Prince model, which used the same engine. It did, however, finally receive full-circle flywheels and went into a pivoted-fork frame with extensive chaincase and side covers, much as the larger models. An Airflow version was offered, as it was for the two road Bullets, which had other changes, including 17 in. wheels for the 346 cc model only.

The Crusader was given an alloy head and joined by a Sports version, while the two sizes of Clipper model continued, all with the Airflow option. All the twins ran on, with just a change

*Above* **The Royal Enfield Dreamliner on the Isle of Man in 1957 where it drew the crowds as always, despite its basic Bullet engine**

**The later small twin was the Meteor Minor, shown here in 1958 standard guise with saddle rather than dualseat**

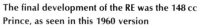

The final development of the RE was the 148 cc
Prince, as seen in this 1960 version

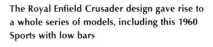

The Royal Enfield Crusader design gave rise to
a whole series of models, including this 1960
Sports with low bars

to siamezed pipes for the Super Meteor, but the
Standard Meteor Minor was dropped at the end
of the year.

The one new machine for 1959 was the 346 cc
Works Replica Trials model, which was the final
version of this long-running type. It had the all-
alloy engine with heavy flywheels and a well-
tucked-in exhaust system, but really came along
too late, for the two-stroke engine was taking
over in trials.

The range ran into 1960 and the new decade
with limited changes. The Ensign was dropped, to
leave the Prince, while the standard and Sports

Crusaders continued, as did the Bullets, the trials
model and the Clipper II. The larger Clipper was
revised with an alloy head and 17 in. wheels, so it
became a cheap version of the Bullet.

For the twins, there were changes for the Super
Meteor and twin carburettors for the Constellation. The Meteor Minor ran on as one model
only with a new silencer, but was joined by a
Meteor Minor Sports with increased power and
more sporting fittings.

It made a good range, typical of the marque,
for the future, and they carried it on for quite a
while.

# Scott

The Scott is perhaps the strangest of production motorcycles, and it kept its unique layout from its earliest days. There may have been odder machines built as prototypes, or in short runs, but only the Scott could lay claim to a more or less constant build for some 60 years. Certainly, it was an acquired taste for any enthusiast and, while the company had its best days in the 1920s, they kept going through the bad times as well.

They returned to motorcycles in 1946 with a Flying Squirrel, little altered from that of the late pre-war days. There was the same 598 cc, twin-cylinder two-stroke engine with its water-cooling, single Amal and two-into-one exhaust pipe. The block was inclined, as it had always been, and the central primary chain drove a three-speed gearbox.

A duplex rigid frame carried the engine and gearbox, along with the traditional Scott radiator and fuel tank. At the front were Brampton or Webb girder forks, which carried the one new post-war feature, a dual front brake in a full-width hub. The rear hub was also full-width, and the model was promised with a roll-on centre stand in place of the older rear one.

Few machines were built with girder forks before these were replaced by Dowty telescopics, using air as the suspension medium and oil for damping and lubrication. These were similar to those also used by Panther and Velocette; all depended totally on the air seals to keep the model on an even keel.

In this form, the Scott continued until 1949, when a change was made to coil ignition with a distributor on the right. This was driven by skew gears from the Pilgrim oil-pump drive, while a pancake dynamo went on the left. The changes and removal of the magneto drive chain allowed for a separate oil tank, which went on the right, below the saddle. The roll-on centre stand now made its appearance, and in this form the Flying Squirrel continued for 1950.

Unfortunately, the Scott had become a rather expensive anachronism, with a price tag well above most four-stroke twins and on a par with an Inter Norton. It also failed to offer a comparable performance, and the few sales to enthusiasts were not enough to prevent the firm going into voluntary liquidation.

The result of this was the sale of the old Saltaire works, while manufacture was transferred to the Aerco Jig and Tool Company in Birmingham, a firm owned by Matt Holder, who was a keen Scott enthusiast. They announced that the 1951 model would continue as before, but it was some time before new machines were made, and for a while only those which had been part of the purchase as stock were available.

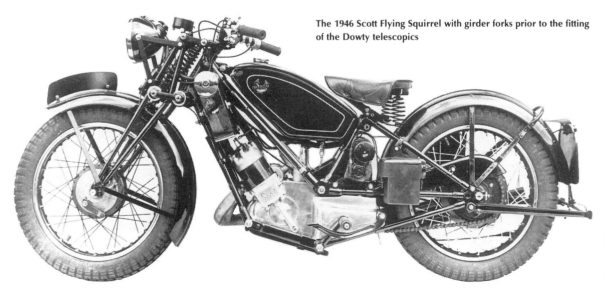

**The 1946 Scott Flying Squirrel with girder forks prior to the fitting of the Dowty telescopics**

**The Scott Swift of 1958 with the smaller 493 cc engine, but which failed to go into production**

It was 1954 before there was any further news, and a further two years before machines were available again. The new model was much as the old one in the engine department, but was available in 497 and 598 cc sizes. Rigid and pivoted-fork frames were made available, both being new and of the duplex type. At the front were telescopic forks, and there was a Lycett dualseat for the rider. The fuel tank lost its traditional, sharp-edged style, which had always been so very distinctive, and the line seemed to suffer from this.

Thus, the Scott continued in small numbers, and for 1958 was fitted with an alternator in place of the dynamo. This called for a rectifier, rather than a regulator, and that year the speedometer was mounted in an extended headlamp shell.

During 1958 a new model, the Swift, was seen. This had a revised 493 cc engine with flat-top pistons. Six prototypes were built, but the model did not go into production. At the end of the year, the rigid models were dropped and the smaller-capacity model was to special order only.

In this way, the Scott ran to the end of the decade and on for another. For those who understood the machine, there was no other way, and for the rest – well, they did not know what they were missing.

# Sun

As with so many others in the motorcycle industry, this firm had its roots in Birmingham and the cycle trade. In 1911 they built their first powered two-wheeler and continued with them, apart from a break during the war years, until 1933. They then dropped their line, but continued to make parts and machines for others until 1940, when they reappeared with an autocycle.

This machine was offered in three versions, and it was one of these that was their first post-war model in 1946. It used the 98 cc Junior de Luxe Villiers engine in a rigid frame with blade girder forks to provide the most basic motorized transport.

The Autocycle was listed with the JDL engine up to 1948, but for the next year was revised to use the 2F unit. At the same time, it was joined by the Motor Cycle, which had the two-speed 1F engine in a rigid frame, also with girder forks, and was equally basic. These two machines continued for 1950, at the end of which, the Autocycle was dropped and the Motor Cycle revised and joined by two more models.

Its main change was to tubular girders in place of the blades, while it retained its saddle and rear carrier, but gained a nice maroon finish. The other two models shared cycle parts and had a loop frame with plunger rear suspension and telescopics at the front. The specification was intended to be better than standard, hence the rear springing, and, thus, also included battery lighting and an electric horn.

The power units were the 122 cc 10D or 197 cc 6E Villiers engines with three-speed gearbox, and the models were called the 122 de luxe and the Challenger de luxe. Both had 19 in. wheels with 5 in. brakes, adjustable footrests, and a good saddle.

The three models continued for 1952 with detail improvements, and in March a 197 cc Competition machine was announced, although it did not reach the market until 1953. It was listed as the Competition Challenger and was first seen with a plunger frame. However, it became rigid for production, but was a full loop type with the saddle raised on its own little subframe. The telescopic forks carried a 21 in. front wheel, while the rear stayed at 19 in., and there were alloy

The 1953 Sun Challenger with 6E Villiers engine in rigid frame with telescopic forks

mudguards and wide-ratio gears with options of a tuned engine and close gears.

The road models also had changes for 1953, the smallest having the 4F engine unit, and the 122 cc version the 12D. The largest model became available in a rigid frame, while a dualseat was offered as an option.

For 1954 the 122 and 197 cc Challenger road models went into a new pivoted-fork frame and kept their battery lighting. Despite the frame change, a saddle was still the standard fit, although a dualseat was listed as an option. The engine of the larger machine became the 8E, which allowed the model to be offered in three- or four-speed forms.

The competition model stayed in its rigid frame, but was now offered in three forms, all powered by the 8E engine. The basic model was listed as the C1, but with a tuned engine, it became the C3, and with this engine plus a four-speed box, the C4.

The range was completed by the 99 cc model, which was unchanged, and extended by the addition of the Cyclone, which used the 224 cc Villiers 1H engine unit. This went into a new pivoted-fork frame with telescopic forks. The machine also had battery lighting and a dualseat.

The Cyclone continued with little alteration for 1955, as did the 99 cc model, which had a new tank and a new name – Hornet. The smaller Challenger had a change of engine to a 147 cc 30C unit, becoming the Mk 1A, while the larger became the Mk IV. On the competition side, just two models were listed, one of which, the Trials, was much as the C4, but the other, the Scrambler, was new. This last had a pivoted-fork frame and Earles leading-link forks with a standard or tuned engine and three or four speeds.

The road range of Hornet, Challenger 1A and Cyclone continued as they were for 1956, while the larger Challenger became the Mk V. It was joined by the Wasp, which used the 9E engine in a pivoted-fork frame with Armstrong leading-link forks and a degree of rear enclosure. The same engine and forks were also used for the Wasp Competition model, which replaced the Trials and Scrambles machines and had a raised saddle and alloy mudguards to suit its intended trials use.

There were more changes and additions for 1957, the Hornet becoming Saxe blue in colour and the smaller Challenger becoming the Mk IV with a 148 cc 31C engine unit. The 197 cc version stayed as it was with its 8E engine, as did the

Wasp with the 9E, but there was also a new machine of the same capacity. This was the Century, which used the 8E engine with three speeds in a pivoted-fork frame with telescopic front forks and a degree of rear enclosure. The Wasp Competition continued, as did the Cyclone, and a second new model was the Wasp Twin with the 249 cc 2T Villiers twin engine. The cycle parts were much as for the Wasp, so included the Armstrong leading-link forks, and the name was soon changed to the Overlander.

One further model was proposed for 1957, which was the Geni scooter with a 99 cc 4F engine unit. It differed from most scooters in having a distinct tunnel behind the apron, but this allowed the engine to sit well forward. In addition, it had 15 in. wire-spoked wheels, which added to the stability. The frame had pivoted-fork rear and leading-link front suspension, and the rear was enclosed by a body that extended up to the dualseat.

When the Geni reached production, it was fitted with the 6F engine with foot-change and incorporated other detail alterations. In this form, it went forward for 1958 as part of a much reduced range. At the start of the year, this totalled four machines, including the Geni, but the Hornet was soon dropped, as were both Challengers, the Century, the Cyclone and the Wasp Competition. Left were just the Wasp and Overlander, which continued with the same cycle parts.

In June 1958 the Geni became the Mk II, thanks to some improvements, and went forward with the Wasp and Overlander for 1959. The last two had their rear enclosure improved to give a smoother line, but both were dropped during the year. This left the Geni, but during 1959 it was joined by another scooter called the Sunwasp. This shared its bodywork with Dayton and Panther (see pages 77 and 140), while under the skin went a tubular frame and a 174 cc 2L fan-cooled Villiers engine with three-speed gearbox and Siba electric start. The suspension was by leading links at the front and pivoted fork at the rear, while the wheels were 10 in. pressed steel with 6 in. brakes.

The Geni and Sunwasp both continued for 1960, but there were no longer any Sun motorcycles. The smaller model went at the end of that year, while the other continued, but only for one more year. The family that had run the concern from Victorian times retired and sold out to Raleigh, who soon removed the name from the cycle and scooter market.

The Wasp Twin, which soon had its name changed to the Overlander, but kept its Villiers 249 cc 2T engine and leading-link forks

The Sun Geni scooter, which was powered by a 99 cc 6F Villiers engine and had a style similar to that of the DMW Bambi

The larger Sunwasp scooter, which shared body panels with Dayton and Panther and was driven by a 174 cc 2L engine

# Sunbeam

The Sunbeam originated in Wolverhampton, where John Marston, a Victorian in manner and outlook, demanded the highest standards of work from himself and his employees. Their cycles and motorcycles reflected this, and for many years the Little Oil Bath Chain Case and the phrase 'The gentleman's motorcycle' meant Sunbeam.

In 1928 they became part of ICI and soon felt the dull hand of accountancy upon them, as well as the chill wind of the depression. Neither suited a firm which specialized in quality work, so profits fell and the business passed to AMC in 1937, and then to BSA in 1943. There were to be no more Marston Sunbeams, but post-war the firm did produce one of the few really new British models, although the parent group failed to support it as well as they might have.

The new machine was first described in the press early in 1946 and offered a great deal that was new on the British market. Features of particular note were the in-line vertical twin engine, its overhead camshaft, unit construction, shaft drive, plunger rear suspension, fat 16 in. tyres and a variety of interesting details.

The short-stroke engine, another innovation for the time, had a capacity of 489 cc and was an all-alloy unit. The cylinders had sleeves with a lip at the top, and the block and crankcase were cast as one down to the alloy sump plate. Above went the alloy head, with a single camshaft, which had the distributor at its rear, and the valves in an angled row. The rockers were supported by pillars, and a cover enclosed the entire mechanism.

The camshaft was driven at the rear by a pair of timing gears and a short chain with a Weller tensioner. The gear also drove down to the single oil pump of the wet-sump system. The one-piece, cast-iron crankshaft carried a pancake dynamo on its nose. The connecting rods were forged alloy and had shell big-end bearings.

The whole engine made a very neat unit, for there were no external pipes. On the left went the two sparking plugs, and on the right a single Amal carburettor, flanked by the two exhaust pipes. These swept down into one and then on to the silencer.

The engine had the gearbox and clutch housing bolted directly to it, with the clutch on the back of the crankshaft. The gearbox had four speeds and was of the indirect type, which allowed the drive to step over for the final shaft. Despite the in-line nature of the layout, both gear and kickstart pedals were on the right and moved in the normally accepted planes. An open shaft took the drive to the rear wheel. It had a rubber-coupling universal joint at the front end and a Hardy-Spicer at the rear. The drive to the wheel was by an underslung worm, rather than the more usual bevels, and the rear brake was incorporated into the housing.

The engine unit was housed in a duplex frame with plunger rear suspension and telescopic front forks. The latter were a little unusual in that a single spring was housed between a bridge bolted to the sliders, with its upper end attached to the top crown. A small rebound spring was included, but there was no damping in the fork legs, only a little oil for lubrication.

The wheels were interchangeable and had 16 in. rims carrying special 4.75 in. section Dunlop tyres. The brakes were 8 in. offset drums, the cable and lever of the front one being hidden inside the backplate. Massive mudguards protected each wheel, while rider comfort was looked after by a pan saddle. This had rubber mountings and a long spring housed in the frame top tube and linked to provide support.

Beneath the saddle were two boxes that housed the battery, on the left, and the coil, regulator and cut-out on the right. The latter box also carried the ammeter and lights, plus ignition switch, in its cover, while tools were stored in another box mounted low down on the left, beside the gearbox. A roll-on centre stand was provided with a ratchet to lock it, and the machine was topped off with a handsome fuel tank with twin taps and kneegrips.

That was 1946, and during the year there was also news of a sports model, which had a revised cylinder head. This gave a crossflow layout, so the carburettor moved over to the left. The extra power pushed the maximum speed up.

Unfortunately, all was not well, for the machine suffered from bad vibration, a peaky power

*Above* **The S7 Sunbeam twin with its fat tyres and in-line engine with shaft drive to the rear wheel**

*Left* **A sectioned Sunbeam twin engine on display**

output, torque reaction geared to throttle movement and rapid wear of the worm wheel. The solutions chosen were to restrict the engine speed and power, which removed the torque and wear troubles, although it did leave the model underpowered. In this form, a batch was made with improved forks, as there had been dangerous breakages, and sent to South Africa, only to be returned as unrideable.

The original designer, Erling Poppe, had by now left the company, so BSA personnel had to deal with the problems and endeavour to tame what was meant to be a group flagship. They decided the answer was to mount the engine on rubber, which was done with two mountings and two sets of snubbers. This entailed the addition of a flexible section of pipe between the exhaust and silencer, plus flexible petrol lines. As the engine no longer contributed to the frame's stiffness, a small cross-bar was added ahead of the engine. A 4.50 in. ribbed front tyre was also fitted.

Finally, in 1947, the model went into production as the S7 and, in the meantime, had acquired a cast alloy cover over the sparking plugs. There was also one for the carburettor, and the exhaust pipes had elbows between them and the head.

The performance was hardly vivacious, for the weight was over 400 lb, and the meagre power gave a top speed of only 72 or 75 mph in contemporary road tests. Even allowing for the pool petrol of the time, this was not the expected performance of a 500 cc twin, for the docile 3T Triumph was as fast. In addition, the ride induced by the combination of the fat tyres, long saddle spring and undamped suspension was lively and the machine snaked in fast bends. It was also an expensive machine to produce, for there was nothing about it in common with other BSA products to help keep the price down.

The result of these problems was a revision, plus a second model for 1949. The original became the S7 de luxe, and the new machine the S8 with narrower tyres and a lighter line. Both kept the same engine unit, rear drive and frame, but the forks became standard BSA for the S8 and stock legs in special yokes for the S7. The S8 also used a 7 in. BSA brake at the front, where a 19 in. rim with a 3.25 in. section tyre was fitted. At the rear, that model used a 4.00 × 18 in. tyre.

The S8 had a different cast alloy silencer and a conventional saddle. The mudguards were reduced in width to suit the tyres, and the handle-bars had stock controls, not the inverted ones with hidden cables used by the S7. A new air cleaner and cover appeared, as did a prop-stand, while the S8 took the black finish previously used by the S7, which now was painted mist green. There was also an option of silver grey for the S8.

From then on, the two models continued to be built in small numbers, the S8 being the more popular, but neither sold well, for the market demanded more for its money. There were detail improvements, but also problems that remained. One was the engine's habit of cutting out when the machine was braked a trifle hard for traffic lights. The cause was the float chamber being ahead of the mixing chamber, which could be starved of sufficient fuel to allow this.

As the 1950s rolled by, the two Sunbeams continued without change, year by year, but fewer and fewer buyers came forward. BSA made no real attempt to improve it, although a variant known as the S10 was built. This had the power-sapping worm replaced with bevels, while a crossflow head moved the performance up to a level comparable with its rivals. However, it was not proceeded with.

The models were announced for 1957, but production ceased before then, although new machines were stuck in showrooms for another year or two. It was not, however, the end of the name, because BSA found another use for it.

To the horror of Sunbeam enthusiasts, it appeared on a scooter. When the group finally did get round to this fast-selling type of transport, they chose to produce both BSA and Triumph

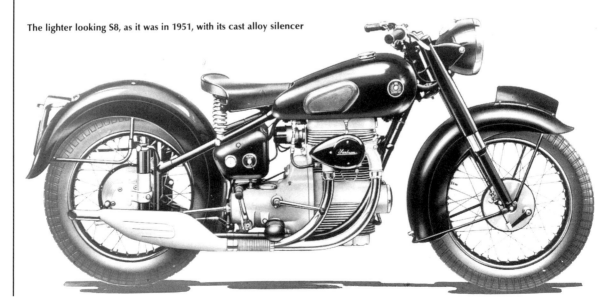

**The lighter looking S8, as it was in 1951, with its cast alloy silencer**

machines, by changes of colour and badges, and labelled the first a Sunbeam.

For both marques, there were two models, one with a 172 cc two-stroke engine and the other with a 249 cc ohv twin, offered with electric or kick starting. Both were launched in 1958 after a long development period, but it was 1959 before the twin reached the shops, and nearly 1960 before the single joined it.

The two engines differed totally, but otherwise the machines were nearly the same, with common transmission and chassis, except for minor details. The single was based on the D7 Bantam, although there were few common parts, as the barrel differed, the flywheels were smaller and the mainshafts longer. A flywheel magneto went on the right, with a fan to assist the cooling, and the clutch was on the left.

*Right* **An S7 serving with the police in Wellington, New Zealand, in 1952. It has a white finish and is fitted with radio**

*Below* **Sunbeam S7 pictured in 1973, but still much as it was when it left the factory**

**The Sunbeam scooter built with single or twin engine and in these or Triumph colours, here with matching sidecar**

The twin engine sat across the frame with a gear-driven camshaft to the rear. It was an all-alloy unit with one-piece forged crankshaft, generator on the right, points and oil-pump drive on opposite ends of the camshaft, and a Zenith carburettor to provide the mixture.

From then on, both twin and single drove back from the clutch by gears to a four-speed gearbox based on that used by the C15 and the Cub. The positive-stop change was retained, with control by a single rocking pedal, and final drive was by a duplex chain. This was enclosed in alloy castings, which also acted as the rear suspension pivoted arm to carry the 10 in. pressed-steel wheel and its 5 in. drum brake.

The chassis was in scooter style, but with duplex front tubes, to which the headstock tube was bolted. The front fork was telescopic, but with a single leg on the left, which had two tubes, one each for the spring and damper. The front wheel and brake were as for the rear. The bodywork was built up from pressings, but access to the mechanics was limited by the small panels provided. The dualseat was hinged to allow refuelling, and the one or two batteries were carried in boxes on the back of the apron.

All Sunbeam models were given a polychromatic green finish and listed as the B1, B2 and B2S to distinguish single, twin and electric-start versions. There was a long list of accessories in typical scooter style, which were essential for the dealer, who could do good business with them.

The machines continued with little change until the mid-1960s, but were never able to challenge the chic Italian models in the mass market, or the sophisticated German ones at the top end. As time moved on, the market shrank, so BSA went in other directions.

Sunbeam motorcycles were no more.

# Swallow

This company was best known for its sidecars, but in the early post-war years it also built an elementary scooter which they called the Gadabout. Details were first released late in 1946, the model taking the form that the Italians were to make so popular a few years later.

The Gadabout lacked the performance produced by the foreign models, as it was heavier than them and its 122 cc Villiers 9D engine was a pre-war design. This unit, with its three-speed gearbox, was just ahead of the rear wheel in a rigid duplex frame with unsprung forks. Suspension was the province of the 4.00 × 8 in. tyres on their split rims, which were attached to hubs with 5 in. brakes.

The rider was given a slab seat, which was hinged for access to the engine, while the fuel tank went behind the seat, over the wheel. This was protected by a simple mudguard, which kept the worst of the dirt at bay and, in addition, there

was a complete rear body. Ahead of this was a flat floor, which rose to form an apron with a string holdall on its rear face.

The front section of the body was held by four quick-release Oddie fasteners, so it was very easy to remove. The remainder could also be detached quite easily. A rear stand and prop-stand were provided, and among the novel details was the use of the frame side tubes as silencers, so each had a tailpipe. Direct lighting and a bulb horn took care of those areas, and the controls were much as a motorcycle, but with a hand-change in the form of a long lever on the right of the body.

Thus, the Gadabout went its rather slow way in 1947, but was able to keep up with the traffic of those days. It was available with a box sidecar for commercial use, and for this had its gearing lowered, along with its performance.

For 1950 it became the Mk II with a 10D engine, fan cooling and foot-change, as well as a little more power. Rider comfort was improved by a change to leading-link forks with bonded rubber in torsion as the suspension medium, but the seat and tyres stayed as they were. The body was revised so that the rear section could be lifted up, and battery lighting was fitted.

The Gadabout continued in this style, but was now becoming upstaged by the Vespa and Lambretta, which had much sleeker lines. The days when anything with power and wheels would sell were sliding away, and buyers were starting to demand rather more than a crude scooter.

It continued for 1951, when it was joined by the Major model, which had a 197 cc 6E engine and was intended to go with the sidecar. There were a number of changes that appeared with this machine, while the smaller one ran on as it was, but at the end of the year, both were dropped. From then on, the firm concentrated on its sidecars.

**The Swallow Gadabout with the box sidecar available for commercial use**

# Tailwind

# Tandon

This was an enterprising clip-on design, which featured a disc valve and two speeds, that was seen in 1952 and built by a Mr Latta of Berkhamsted. The engine was a 49 cc two-stroke positioned above the front wheel, and the disc was driven by a peg on the overhung crankshaft.

At the other end of the shaft was a flywheel magneto, and between it and the crankcase a two-diameter roller. The entire assembly could be moved from side to side by a left-hand twistgrip, and the rollers were spring-loaded into contact with the tyre. A conical section between the two diameters ensured a smooth transition, and the whole unit functioned well.

As so many have found before and since, building one prototype may not be easy, but production is another and far more difficult matter altogether. In addition, the clip-on boom was close to becoming a moped boom, so no more was heard of this interesting device.

This firm was set up by Indian-born Devdutt Tandon to build cheap lightweights for both home and export markets, their first model appeared in 1948. Initially, it was known as the Special, but later as the Milemaster, and had a generally simple specification.

The power unit was a 122 cc Villiers twin-port 9D with three-speed, hand-change gearbox, which went into a duplex loop frame. There was no rear suspension, but at the front were telescopics with compression and rebound springs, plus a preload adjustment. The wheels had 19 in. rims and 4 in. brakes, while a pillar-mounted saddle and angular fuel tank did nothing to update the elderly lines of the engine. This had the usual twin pipes running down to a cylindrical silencer, from which one pipe ran up and back to the rear. There was a rear carrier, a prop-stand and direct lighting. The petrol tank was a little unusual in that it had a channel in its top surface for the

**The two-speed Tailwind clip-on, which drove the bicycle front wheel with one of two roller diameters**

frame's twin top tubes and was hung from them. In addition, the cavity was used as a toolbox with a chrome-plated lid secured by knurled nuts.

This simple model continued with few changes for some years and was joined for 1950 by another of the same capacity, but with a very different appearance. The new machine was called the Supaglide and powered by the 10D engine with its three-speed foot-change gearbox. This went into a new loop frame, which had pivoted-fork rear suspension controlled by a rubber cartridge mounted beneath the engine.

Telescopic forks were at the front, and the tank continued to have a recess in the top for the tools, but was of a much nicer shape with conventional rounded lines. The machine now had rectified lighting with the battery mounted beneath the saddle. There was a single exhaust pipe and silencer, a centre stand and a blue paint finish. The rear brake size was increased to 5 in.

For 1951 the two 122 cc models were joined by the Supaglide Supreme, which had a 197 cc 6E engine in place of the 10D, but was otherwise the same, except for a 5 in. front brake. During the year, a further 125 appeared as the competition Kangaroo, which differed from standard in gearing, a 21 in. front wheel, tyres, the 5 in. front brake and alloy mudguards. In addition, the saddle was raised and the headlight quickly detachable.

All four models continued for 1952, at the end of which the Milemaster was replaced by the Imp, which used the 10D engine in a rigid frame with telescopic forks and wheels with 5 in. brakes. The two Supaglide models continued, with just a change to the 5 in. front brake for the smaller one, but the Kangaroo had rather more alteration.

It went into a new frame, the rear fork being controlled by conventional spring units and the saddle replaced by a trials seat. In other respects, it was as before and was joined by the Kangaroo Supreme, which had the 6E engine. The same frame type was also used with road cycle parts to create the Imp Supreme.

This was one of only two models to continue for 1954, but with an engine change to an 8E. The other was the Imp, which had a similar alteration to a 12D. The Supaglide and Kangaroo models were dropped.

To make the range up, there were four other models, the Imp Supreme De Luxe being much as the basic model, but with four speeds, a dualseat and extra equipment. It kept to the 8E engine, which was also used for the Scrambler. This had Earles-type leading-link front suspension, an open exhaust, no lights and a racing seat.

The remaining models were larger in capacity and used the best of the Imp cycle parts with a choice of engines. For the Monarch, which was

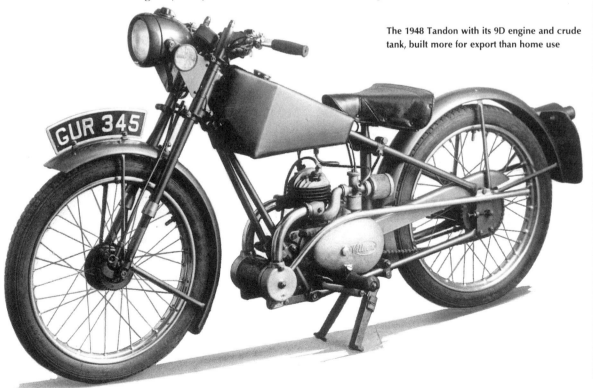

The 1948 Tandon with its 9D engine and crude tank, built more for export than home use

*Above* **The competition Tandon Kangaroo with 10D engine and rubber-block rear suspension, as built for 1951–2**

*Below* **Tandon Imp introduced for 1953, still with the 10D engine, but in a rigid frame**

initially called the Sprite, it was the 224 cc Villiers 1H unit, but the Twin Supreme had the 242 cc British Anzani twin with its rotary inlet valve.

Both had the frame improved for 1955, when it was also used by a new model, listed as the Viscount and fitted with the 322 cc British Anzani twin engine. All three were given full-width hubs front and rear with much needed 6 in. brakes and short leading-link forks, which also went on the Imp Supreme De Luxe. The other Imps continued, but the smaller one had an engine change to the 147 cc 30C unit. They were joined by the Imp Supreme Special, which had the 8E engine, three speeds, short leading links, rear suspension and direct lighting to reduce costs. For competition, the Scrambler continued, but with a 7E engine, and was joined by a 250 Scrambler, which used the British Anzani twin unit fitted with stub pipes.

However, time and finance were running out for the Tandon, and late in 1955 there was an order to wind them up. They had always operated on a knife edge, so it did not take much to push them over. This was not the end of the name, however, for they were back by the middle of 1956 with a simple two-model range.

This comprised the Imp Supreme Special and the Monarch, the former being fitted with the 8E engine with three speeds. The pivoted-fork frame had the short leading-link forks, a dualseat, wheels with 5 in. brakes and direct lighting. Four speeds and battery lighting were options, but standard on the Monarch with its 1H engine. Otherwise, this was similar, except for the use of the full-width hubs with the 6 in. brakes.

These models remained in the lists until 1959, when production finally ceased for good.

# Teagle

# Triumph

This was a clip-on engine made in Cornwall and first seen late in 1952. It was derived from one designed for garden power tools, so it was light and simple, and the company saw the powered bicycle as a method of expanding their market.

The 50 cc two-stroke engine was largely a single alloy casting, which formed the cylinder and crankcase, with an iron liner and separate head. An overhung crankshaft with forged alloy rod were used, the one running on the other for the big-end. The crankcase was open on both sides, with a bearing housing on one side and a simple door on the other. A drive roller went on the mainshaft, as did the Wipac flywheel magneto, which incorporated cooling fans.

The engine sat over the rear wheel, the cylinder being laid back close to the horizontal, and had its fuel tank mounted above it. The whole unit was pivoted, so it could be lifted clear of the tyre, and was spring-loaded to it when in contact.

It was 1954 before there was any more news of the Teagle and it remained on the market for some two years before the moped overtook it and all its brothers.

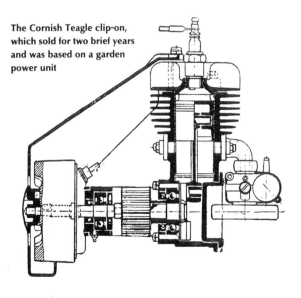

**The Cornish Teagle clip-on, which sold for two brief years and was based on a garden power unit**

Triumph were the first firm to announce their post-war range, and the news came in March 1945, well before the end of the war. Not only were they first off the mark but, unlike many others, their machines were not the wartime ones with a new civilian finish.

One reason for this was the vertical twin range, which they had introduced in the late 1930s and which set a style that the major firms were all to copy. However, Triumph had a ten-year start over the opposition, which they exploited to the full in their advertisements.

There were five models in the range, as announced, one single and four twins, the latter being sports and touring versions in two sizes, but only three models were to go into production. The single was one of the pair not destined to reach the public, although at first sight, it should have been the obvious choice, as it was the wartime model with a new paint finish.

As the army machine, it had been the 343 cc 3HW, based firmly on the pre-war 3H with ohv engine, four-speed gearbox, rigid frame and girder forks. In army service, it gained a one-piece head and rocker box cast in iron, and it was intended to keep this for the post-war model. After the announcement, it was realized that it made more sense for the firm to concentrate on the more profitable twins and leave 350 cc singles to other marques, so the 3H never reached production.

The two 499 cc twins were the Speed Twin and Tiger 100, and were much as they had been in 1939. There were changes, however, and the major one for the cycle parts was the adoption of telescopic front forks of a neat, slim style. These were based on a wartime design and had hydraulic damping, while the front wheel diameter was reduced to 19 in. to match the rear.

The engine was the trend-setting Edward Turner design, which had contrived to look like a twin-port single at its launch. It was compact, light and went well, so had few post-war changes. The design was based on a built-up crankshaft, the two shaft forgings being bolted to a central flywheel and the assembly supported by a ball race on each side.

The aluminium crankcase was split on the vertical centre line and carried the two camshafts high up, the exhaust being ahead of, and the inlet behind, the crankshaft line. They were gear driven via an intermediate gear, with a train in the timing chest on the right. This extended to the rear to drive the magneto. Unlike the pre-war design, which had a mag-dyno, the post-war version had a separate dynamo clamped to the front of the crankcase, where it was gear driven from the exhaust camshaft.

An iron block was bolted to the crankcase, with the two light-alloy pistons moving in unison in it, and to this was bolted the one-piece, iron cylinder head. The rocker box was in two parts, each an alloy casting, with access caps to the valve adjusters in the outer rocker ends. The pushrods ran up within tubes placed on the engine centre line and forward and aft of the block. Unlike the pre-war engine, the rockers were lubricated from the oil return line. This oil drained down through drillings and the pushrod tubes, which no longer had external drain pipes running to them.

The Tiger 100 engine had a higher compression ratio than the Speed Twin, and its internals were

polished, but otherwise the two were the same. On the outside, the sports model had a slightly larger carburettor, but its exhaust was no longer special, being the same set of parts as used by the tourer, including the tubular silencers.

Virtually all the transmission and cycle side were common to both models, only the finish and the petrol and oil tanks differing. The transmission was by the very typical Triumph four-speed gearbox with a foot-change that operated in the reverse manner to most others of that time. The multi-plate clutch continued to stick first thing in the morning and was housed, together with the primary drive, in a handsome alloy chaincase.

A rigid frame with telescopic front forks was used with wheels incorporating offset hubs and single-leading-shoe drum brakes. The oil tank went on the right, under the saddle, and the Tiger 100 had a wing-nut cap, as did some early post-war Speed Twins. The battery was on the left to match the tank, and the toolbox between the frame chainstays, on the right.

Although the speedometer was mounted on the top of the forks, the other instruments, plus the light switch, went into a tank-top panel, as in pre-war days. The tank itself was chrome plated with lined, painted panels. The machine's finish was the famous Amaranth red for the Speed Twin, and black with silver mudguards and tank panels for the Tiger 100.

These two models were to be matched by two smaller ones with 349 cc engines, to be known as the 3T and Tiger 85. On the face of it, they would

**Nice 1947 Triumph Tiger 100 on test with sprung hub to enliven the ride**

Smallest of the twins was the 3T, and this was the 1948 version

have been virtually the same models with revised engine dimensions but, in fact, the differences went much deeper.

The 349 cc engine used a wartime crankshaft design, in which the two halves were clamped into a central flywheel and, thanks to this, one-piece connecting rods could be used. They retained their plain big-ends, and the crank assembly still turned in a drive-side ball race, but there was a bush for the timing side.

Most of the rest of the lower half, and the valve gear, was as for the larger engine, but both head and block differed. Their fixing was by long through-studs with top bolts, which could be seen quite easily from either side of the engine. At the top, the head and rocker boxes were cast in one with alloy covers for each pair of valves and rocker adjusters. This also was easy enough to spot.

There were other differences, too, with a smaller carburettor and changes to both exhaust pipes and silencers. The gearbox remained the same, as did the forks and a number of the detail fitments, but the frame itself was smaller and lighter, which affected some of the parts that were bolted to it.

In the event, only the 3T went into production, having the same finish as the Speed Twin, but in black. The Tiger 85 would have mirrored the larger sports model in black and silver, but it made sense, at that time of acute shortages, for the firm to concentrate on the larger models.

With the Government screaming for production and exports, there were few changes over the next few years, but for 1947 there came the

famous sprung hub. This was listed as an option, for it replaced the standard rear wheel and, at first sight, appeared to be a rather large, full-width hub.

This it was, but inside was a slider box, which allowed the wheel to move in a curve, centred on the gearbox sprocket, with a total of 2 in. of movement. Also within the hub were the compression and rebound springs, under considerable stress and preload, while to each side were caged ball races and their inner and outer cups. Due to the size of the hub, the rear brake was increased to an 8 in. drum, and it was necessary to take the speedometer drive from the gearbox instead of the rear wheel.

Otherwise, the range ran on with its three models, although during 1948 the 3T had the fixing of its head and block changed to that used by the larger engine. Rather more exciting for that year was the news that Triumph were to produce a real racing motorcycle in limited numbers. This was based on the machine used by Ernie Lyons to win the 1946 Manx Grand Prix and had a Tiger 100 engine with alloy head and block. It was called the Grand Prix.

The alloy top half came from a wartime generator unit and, due to this origin, was of a square format. This was to suit the enclosing cowl of the generator, and the castings retained the small bosses for its fixing screws. The layout also dic-

**The Triumph Grand Prix, as introduced in 1948 with alloy top half and external oil filter in front of the gearbox**

tated that both inlet and exhaust ports were parallel to each other, but despite this, twin Amal carburettors were crammed in and fed by a remotely-mounted float chamber.

Otherwise, the engine looked stock, but it had racing camshafts and magneto, a blanked off dynamo drive and a raised compression ratio. The standard gearbox was given close ratios and, in the style of the times, the primary drive was fully exposed, having a light top guard only. The cycle

parts were essentially standard and included the sprung hub, but the front brake size was increased to 8 in. There were alloy mudguards and wheel rims, a bigger oil tank and megaphone exhausts, but a saddle and rear pad remained.

On the circuits, the Grand Prix proved fast, but fragile, so it was competitive with the Manx Norton of the day while it kept going. The handling was not so good, the hub often being more of a hindrance than an asset, so as soon as the Norton

**The sporting TR5 Triumph Trophy with the die-cast head and barrel used from 1951 in the short-wheelbase, rigid frame**

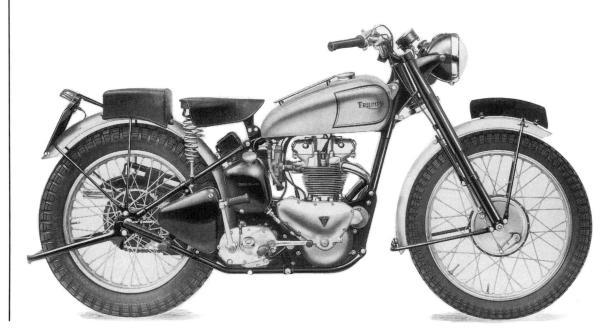

Nice line of early 1950s Triumph twins

gained its Featherbed frame, there was no contest. In addition, engine technology moved on, pool petrol disappeared, and within two or three years, the GP was no longer able to stay with the front runners. By the end of 1950 production ceased and the firm concentrated on what it did best, building good road motorcycles.

Prior to that, it was 1949 before there was any real change to these, and then it was mainly cosmetic with the appearance of the famous nacelle for the front forks. This enclosed the upper part and extended forward to carry the headlight unit, while its upper surface accommodated the instruments and switches. This removed the need for the tank-top instrument panel, so its place was taken by an optional parcel grid.

That same year saw another model join the range as the TR5 Trophy, which was aimed at the sporting off-road and trials rider. The design was based on the machines used by the firm for the ISDT, hence the model name, but both engine and cycle parts were special to some degree.

The engine was mainly Speed Twin, but above the crankcase were the alloy head and block used by the Grand Prix, but with much lower-ratio pistons within. There were also softer cams, only a single carburettor and a lovely siamezed exhaust system, which curled round to a waist-level silencer on the left.

This unit went into a special frame with boxed-in front engine plates, and the wheelbase was reduced, so parts were a tight fit. The four-speed gearbox was used and the sprung hub was an option. The mudguards were short and sporting.

A 20 in. front wheel and 4 in. section rear tyre were fitted, along with quickly-detachable lights, so there was no nacelle. A saddle and pillion pad looked after the seating, and the finish was in chrome, silver and black to produce a very smart, dual-purpose machine.

The range had a revised gearbox for 1950, when the tank styling was altered to four horizontal bars, and an additional, larger model appeared as the 649 cc 6T Thunderbird. This took the Turner twin on to its next logical step, the increase in capacity coming mainly from a larger bore, although the stroke went up a little as well. The general details were as for the 5T, and both engines had the external oil drain pipes, as in pre-war days. For the rest, it was the same gearbox, frame, forks and cycle parts.

Changes for 1951 were limited to the sports models, as little altered on the three sizes of tourer. For the T100 and TR5, there was a new die-cast head and barrel in light alloy with close-pitched fins. The exhaust ports were splayed out, as they always had been for the T100, but this change meant a new exhaust pipe was needed for the TR5. The T100 also had a dualseat fitted as standard, it having been an option the year before, and all models had new filler caps and the parcel grid fitted as standard.

The Grand Prix was not continued for 1951, but in its place was an official racing kit for the T100. This included high-ratio pistons and better camshafts, along with twin carburettors, all the associ-

ated pipes and controls, megaphones and a big oil tank. It did the job well and allowed the firm to concentrate on production of their road models.

The 3T was quietly dropped at the end of the year, for it was never popular nor very profitable to the firm. The other four models and the race kit continued for 1952, with an SU carburettor for the 6T and little other alteration. It was much the same for the twins in 1953, although the 5T was fitted with an alternator and the race kit was replaced by a complete model in the form of the T100c. This was effectively the same thing, but was supplied with silencers and full electrics, as well as the tuned internals.

There was a second new model for 1953 and it was to lead to many versions, including a whole range for BSA. The newcomer was the 149 cc Terrier, which was aimed at the lightweight market, then the province of the Bantam, Enfield and a hoard of machines using the small Villiers engines.

The Terrier had an ohv unit-construction engine with four-speed gearbox. The iron cylinder was inclined forward and topped by an alloy head with integral rocker box, while the timing gear was of the simplest, with two gears, a camshaft, tappets and pushrods. The crankcase was a little unusual in that its vertical split line was on the left, so the pressed-up crankshaft went in from that side, while the drive main went into a casting

that acted as a door and the chaincase inner.

The crankcase also contained the gearbox, with a single cover on the right for both gears and timing side, plus an outer cover to conceal the gearchange mechanism. An alternator went on the left-hand end of the crankshaft in the primary chaincase, and the points for the coil ignition were in a housing behind the barrel. Their cam was skew-gear driven from the crankshaft, and the same shaft drove the twin-plunger pump for the dry-sump oil system. An Amal supplied the mixture, and the exhaust system ran low down on the right.

This engine unit went into a loop frame with plunger rear and telescopic front suspension, neither of which had any damping. Construction was simple, but the front end looks mirrored those of the twins with a nacelle. The wheels had offset hubs and 19 in. rims, while the rider had a saddle. The oil tank was beneath this, on the right in true British style, with the battery housing on the left to match it.

For 1954 the Terrier was joined by the larger 199 cc Cub, which had an upswept exhaust system as standard and a shell blue finish for the tank and mudguards in place of the overall Amaranth red of the Terrier. Both models were given a mechanical gear indicator and had common cycle parts, while the Cub had a dual-seat as standard.

*Left* **The Triumph Terrier single, at its launch at Earls Court late in 1952, with its typical marque line and plunger frame**

*Right* **Checking over a 1956 6T Thunderbird for fork and headrace wear. Front brake also needs attention with that cam-lever angle**

Other changes that year were to the 6T, which switched to alternator electrics, and to the T100. The latter was joined by a larger 649 cc version, listed as the Tiger 110, and both went into a pivoted-fork frame with dualseat and an 8 in. front brake to arrest progress. The other models stayed as they were, except for the T100c, which was dropped, but for 1955 all the twins went into the pivoted-fork frame and several had internal changes. For the singles, the Cub had the low-level exhaust system fitted as standard.

For 1956 the T110 was fitted with an alloy cylinder head and joined by the TR6, which used the same 649 cc engine in the TR5 cycle parts. Both now had higher-performance engines, so the old power style that suited the TR5 both on and off road so well had gone. The singles also had changes, the most noticeable being to the Cub, which went to 16 in. wheels.

The Cub continued alone for 1957, for the Terrier was dropped, but in a pivoted-fork frame with damped front forks. It was joined by the T20C competition model, which used the same frame, but had an upswept exhaust and came with trials tyres and a crankcase shield, although it retained the lights and headlamp nacelle.

There was also a new tank badge for the Cub models, and this was fitted on all the twins as well. In addition, the 5T, 6T and TR5 had a full-width front hub, and the TR6 an 8 in. front brake. They

were joined by one new model, which was the first of the unit-construction twins and listed as the model 21 or 3TA.

The new machine had a twin-cylinder, 349 cc engine, much as its predecessors, with a bolted-on flywheel, twin gear-driven camshafts, plain big-ends and separate rocker boxes. Ignition was by coil, with the points and distributor in a housing behind the iron block and driven by skew gears from the inlet camshaft, which also drove the oil pump.

The crankcase extended rearwards to carry the four-speed gearbox, while an Amal supplied the mixture and an alternator went on the left-hand end of the crankshaft. This drove the clutch with a duplex chain within a polished alloy case, and much of the transmission was stock conventional Triumph.

The engine unit went into a simple loop frame with pivoted-fork rear and telescopic front suspension. The fixtures and fittings followed Triumph practice in the main, with a nacelle for the headlamp and the new badge on the sides of the tank. The wheels had 17 in. rims and 7 in. brakes, the front one in a full-width hub, but the real feature of the model was its rear enclosure. This was extensive and, thanks to its shape, quickly became known as the 'bathtub', a name it was to keep through the years.

With this new model, the firm began to plan a

Triumph Tiger Cub in its 1958 form, before it was given a rear skirt

*Below* **A 1959 Triumph Tigress TW2 scooter enjoying cobbles in the rain, but better than queueing for a bus**

new range, so there were few changes for the pre-unit models in 1958. All the twins were given the slickshift gearchange, where the clutch was withdrawn by the gear pedal movement, but this was never very popular with riders. The two Tiger models were given full-width front hubs for their 8 in. brakes, the same hub being fitted to the TR6.

The two Cubs ran on with detail changes, which included a move to Zenith carburettors during the year.

At the end of 1958 the 5T and TR5 were dropped, the former being replaced by the 5TA. This was simply a bored-out version of the 3TA, finished in the traditional Amaranth red, and it kept the Speed Twin name. Of the older models, the T100, T110, 6T and TR6 ran on much as before, but were joined by one of the most exciting Triumphs of all time, the T120 Bonneville.

This was, in essence, a twin-carburettor T110 with the optional splayed-port head fitted as standard and was the final development of the original twin for Edward Turner. He maintained that 650 cc and 6500 rpm were as much as one could expect from the layout without excessive vibration problems. The Bonneville soon became a legend.

However, the Bonneville and the 5TA were not the only new models for 1959, as there were more, plus changes to the Cubs. Many of the latter were detail changes only, but for the road model, there was also some partial enclosure with rear skirts, which followed the lines of the unit twins, but not to the same extent. For the single, the rear wheel was left more exposed and there were cut-outs for the oil tank and toolbox.

The final new models were scooters and replicas of those in the Sunbeam range (see page 168),

First of the new breed of unit-construction twins was the 3TA, seen here in 1960 form, but still with bathtub

Flagship of the Triumph line was the T120 Bonneville, which lost the nacelle for 1960 when it gained a new frame and an alternator

except for colour and badges. They were called Tigress with the Triumph badge, the single being listed as the TS1 and the twins as the TW2 and electric-start TW2S. All were in a shell blue colour. The single did not reach the lists until 1960.

For the new decade, Triumph kept nearly all their models from the previous year, but the T100 and T20C were both replaced. The first became the T100A and had a higher-powered version of the unit-construction engine with energy-transfer ignition. It used the same set of cycle parts, but in a black and ivory finish.

The T20S also had energy-transfer ignition, as well as direct lighting, no battery and a small, off-road-style headlamp. The front forks were heavy-duty and based on those of the 3TA with gaiters, while there were other detail improvements. The Cub changed to 17 in. wheels, and during the year, both models had a major engine change.

This concerned the crankcase split line, which moved to the cylinder centre-line, while the internals stayed as they were.

The scooters continued as they were, as did the 3TA and 5TA, while all the 649 cc models had a new duplex frame. The first version of this had problems, but these were soon overcome, and all four models also had revised forks. The 6T and T110 were both fitted with the 'bathtub' rear enclosure and its associated deep front mudguard, while the T120 lost its nacelle in favour of a separate headlamp shell. The T110, T120 and TR6 all retained their magnetos, but went over to an alternator to charge the battery.

Thus Triumph entered the new decade with a strong range, which became fully unit-construction in 1963. Later came the trauma of the Meriden sit-in, the co-operative and the difficult times of the 1980s.

# Turner

This machine was one of the eccentricities of the motorcycle world and made its brief appearance in Brussels in April 1946. Its full name was the Turner Byvan, but there seems to be no record as to whether or not Turner was the builder, nor are there any details of his background.

The machine was an oddity because it had front-wheel-drive. The engine unit was a 125 cc Royal Enfield Flying Flea, but turned round so that the gearbox was at the front. The cylinder was special, having the carburettor on the right and the exhaust at the front, while the whole assembly ran in reverse to its normal direction.

This only called for the retiming of the Miller flywheel magneto. The gearbox sprocket drove the wheel by chain. A small petroil tank sat above the engine, which was started by a hand-operated recoil mechanism attached in place of the kick-start lever. The gear lever remained hand-operated in a gate and was positioned close to the twistgrip.

Special pressed-steel front forks carried the complete motor package, which had a small headlight in front of it. The whole of the remainder of the machine, from headstock to rear number plate, was fully enclosed to form a large parcel holder. There was a saddle on the top for the rider and a lid for access, but otherwise it simply acted as a carrier and held the rear wheel.

The machine had motorcycle-style spoked wheels, but with fairly fat tyres and was equipped with twin prop-stands. The finish was in bright red and the machine was run on the day it was shown, performing well enough on steepish Belgium slopes and cobbles.

It was far too radical, even for Europe, which was to have its share of show oddities over the years, so no more was heard of it.

The strange front-wheel-drive Turner Byvan, of 1946, being tried out in a Brussels street

# Velocette

After the war, Velocette continued with their tradition of black and gold singles of high performance with ohv or ohc engines, and the range was little different from 1939. Missing were the KTS and, at first, the racing KTT, while the GTP only appeared briefly as an export batch of machines. Present and correct were the three sizes of M-range ohv models and the KSS.

The GTP had been in the range since 1930 and had a 249 cc two-stroke engine with throttle-controlled pump lubrication. The small post-war batch differed from its predecessors in having magneto ignition rather than coil, but the cycle side remained as it was, with a rigid frame and girder forks.

The ohv models were the 248 cc MOV, 349 cc MAC and 495 cc MSS. All had their roots in the 1930s, the first appearing in 1933 and the others following at the rate of one per year. All were similar in engine layout, with the camshaft set high up in the timing side, where it was driven by helical gears, which also drove the magneto.

The crankcase was typically Velocette, being narrow with the mains close in to the flywheels, and with the primary chain equally near the bearings. From this layout came the need for the gearbox sprocket to be outboard of the clutch, and for the clutch to have its own special design with a lift mechanism that few ever got to understand.

The very stiff crankcase carried an equally stiff crankshaft assembly within its walls, the cylinder and head being held to it by long bolts. The valve gear was fully enclosed, and engine lubrication was by dry sump, the gear oil pump being driven from the crankshaft. An Amal carburettor supplied the mixture, while a Miller dynamo was clamped to the front of the crankcase and was belt driven to provide the volts.

The four-speed gearbox had foot-change and a none-too-helpful kickstart ratio. The mechanics were housed in a cradle frame, which was improved from the pre-war one by the use of wartime developments for the army. The MSS had a heavier frame than the other two, and it also had a vertical seat tube, which made it easy to spot.

The frame was rigid, and at the front were Webb girder forks with friction shock absorbers and a steering damper. Both wheels had offset hubs and all used 19 in. rims. Tyre sizes were 3.25 in. front and rear for the MOV and MAC, but 3.50 front and 4.00 in. rear for the MSS. The brake sizes also differed, with 6 in. drums for the two smaller models and 7 in. versions for the largest.

The cycle parts were very much as British tradition required, with a saddle, oil tank beneath it on the right, and battery on the left to match it. The toolbox went above the right upper chainstay, and a pillion pad and footrests were included in the standard specification.

The KSS used the MSS cycle parts with its own 348 cc overhead-camshaft engine. This dated back to the 1920s, so by 1946 it was a very well developed assembly in a classic mould. Its design was based on the narrow crankcase common to the marque, and the iron barrel carried an alloy head with integral cambox. Thus, the camshaft rockers were fully enclosed, with access covers to the valves and their coil springs. The cam drive was by shaft and bevels, using a hunting tooth to spread the loads, and the right mainshaft also drove the oil pump and, via a chain, the rear-mounted magneto.

The engine was the major item to distinguish the KSS from its ohv brothers, but the wheels also differed, with 3.00 × 21 in. front and 3.25 × 20 in. rear tyres being used. The need for a high level of skill to set the engine up was reflected in the model's price, which was the highest of the road machines. It would only be exceeded by its racing cousin, the KTT, for 1947.

For that year, the other four models ran on, while the KTT reappeared, very much in its 1939 form, as the Mk VIII. Its overhead-camshaft engine had both head and barrel in alloy with massive finning. The valves were held shut by hairpin springs, but the head casting was extended to enclose them, while the rockers had return springs. They were mounted on eccentric pins for setting the gaps and were well lubricated.

The KTT bottom half was similar to the KSS and the others with a narrow crankcase, but with the parts designed for road racing. The four-speed gearbox had close ratios and some resemblance

187

to the road units, but the frame was very different. It retained the cradle loop, but at the rear was pivoted-fork suspension controlled by oleo-pneumatic units. As in pre-war days, these used air for suspension and oil for damping, but were never easy to set correctly. At the front were Webb girders, and both wheels had high-tensile steel rims and conical alloy hubs with 7 in. brakes. There was a saddle and rear pad for the rider, a large oil tank and a rev-counter driven from the magneto sprocket.

There was no change to the range for 1948, but all the road models had to dispense with the girder forks, as they were no longer to be had from Webb. In their place, Velocette fitted Dowty Oleomatic telescopics, which used the same principles as the rear legs on the KTT. This model kept its girders, while the others had minor changes to suit the new forks. The two smaller M models also had their front brake size increased to 7 in.

At the end of the year, Velocette dropped the expensive KSS with its assembly problems, along with the MOV and MSS. The MAC continued as the most popular of the ohv singles, along with a limited number of KTT racers, but the sensation of the range for 1949 was the totally new LE.

This really broke with the firm's tradition, for it had a 149 cc, side-valve, horizontally-opposed, twin-cylinder engine with water cooling among its many radical features. It also had shaft drive, hand-lever starting, a monocoque frame and good weather protection. It was a very quiet-running machine.

The LE was aimed at the mass market and incorporated a host of ideas and ideals which, it was said, would ensure success in this fickle area of sales. Other firms had been along this path in the past and found that there were many obstacles. It was not until the scooter came along that there was much of a breakthrough, and it took the Honda Cub scooterette to reach a true world-wide market.

The Velocette came close, but was rather expensive, partly because the firm insisted on doing the job properly, as was their way. This led to looks without style, handling that the mass market would never appreciate, and too much of the mechanics on view. The social scene was no help either, for it was to be well into the 1950s before the scooter became accepted, and the LE was always too much of a motorcycle to fit the image.

The machine, one of the few really new post-war models to go into long-term production, had a side-valve engine to keep the width down, which seems odd in comparison with modern flat-twin BMW or Honda Gold Wing motors. However, in 1949 motorcycles were slim, so the LE had a small side-valve engine.

It was designed as one with the rest of the mechanics, so engine, gearbox, drive shaft and rear bevel box were effectively a unit, which was mounted to the frame. The engine had a built-up crankshaft, which went into the barrel crankcase from the front. There were iron barrels and alloy heads with tiny 10 mm sparking plugs, and the camshaft sat above the crankshaft with tappets to operate the valves.

A combined generator and ignition unit went on the front of the crankshaft, and just behind it a worm drove the pump of the wet-sump oil system. The camshaft was driven by gears at the rear of the crankcase, and there was no water pump, as the system relied on the thermo-syphon principle.

A special multi-jet Amal carburettor, with tiny jets, supplied the mixture to a long induction pipe, while the two exhaust pipes ran round to a common silencer box under the engine. It was very efficient, and the low noise level of the machine was one of its most outstanding features.

Unlike most flat-twins, the LE did not have its clutch hung on the back of the crankshaft, but drove this via helical reduction gears. These also moved the drive-line centre up and over, ready for the three-speed, all indirect gearbox. This was controlled by a hand lever working in a gate on the right, in car fashion, so neutral could be selected directly from top gear.

The hand-start lever lay below the gear lever and was connected to an internal quadrant via levers and shafts. The quadrant meshed with a gear in front of the clutch to give primary starting, and the lever was linked to the centre stand to retract this should the rider have left it down inadvertently. From the gearbox, the drive shaft ran down the left leg of the pivoted rear fork, having a universal joint at the front end. At the rear was a bevel box, to which the brake shoes were mounted.

The engine unit was hung from a frame made from sheet steel, the main part being a beam of inverted U-section, to which a massive rear mudguard was welded. At the front, the head-stock was bolted in place, with the toolbox set just aft of it and welded into the top of the main pressing. Behind it, the petrol tank was bolted into place under the pressing and then came the battery chamber. This was open at the top, with the saddle above it and arranged to tip forward to give access.

The rear body had mountings for the suspension units, but in place of the usual bolt or stud, there was a slot on each side. This allowed the units to be laid down or made more upright to vary the stiffness of the suspension. The remainder of the frame comprised a tubular assembly at the front, which carried the radiator, two footboards that were bolted to it, and a steel pressing bolted to the back of the gearbox. This supported the rear ends of the footboards and provided the mounting for the rear fork pivot bearings.

The front suspension was provided by undamped telescopic forks, but these turned in taper-roller head races, a rare find in a small-capacity machine at that time. They carried a massive front mudguard, which partly enclosed them, and both wheels had 19 in. rims and offset hubs with 5 in. brakes.

This then was the revolutionary LE Velocette, which sold well, but not quite well enough to allow the firm to get the price down. They also had problems with it at the factory, for it needed a new production line and techniques far removed from those that had coped with the singles. It really was an extraordinary achievement by the Goodman family, who always were Velocette, with their limited resources, and if they had had a BSA or Triumph purse they might have succeeded with it.

There were no changes for 1950, which was the last year for the KTT, and only the LE and MAC went forward for 1951. Both had changes, the first becoming the Mk II with its capacity raised to 192 cc, along with a good number of internal engine improvements. For the MAC, there was a change of front fork to a Velocette design using springs and damping oil in a conventional manner.

In June 1951 the MAC was further modified with a new alloy cylinder and head, and a cleaner timing cover. The new head included full valve-gear enclosure with a deep well in its top, into which the rocker assembly was bolted with a simple lid to complete the job. The barrel was of the Alfin type with the alloy fins cast on to the iron liner.

The two machines continued in this form for 1952, but for 1953 there was another MAC introduced with a sprung frame. This was similar to the rigid one, but with the chainstays formed as a loop to the rear. From each rose an ear made from pressings, and these were slotted for the attachment of the rear spring units. Thus, as on the LE, the suspension could be made hard or soft by altering the unit angle.

The rear fork was built up, each of the two legs being clamped to a spindle, which turned in bushes in a frame lug. Thus, the fork had to be aligned on assembly, but the arrangement worked

**The Velocette MAC for 1951 when it gained marque forks and changed to an alloy top half**

The MSS Velocette in 1954 with adjustable rear suspension and odd dualseat

well, as long as it was greased regularly. To go with the new frame, the gearbox had its end cover cleaned up and the change mechanism improved. The cycle parts were amended to suit the new frame and included a two-level dualseat. There was an alloy centre stand and a prop-stand, and both petrol and oil tanks were altered.

The rigid MAC and the LE continued, the former being unchanged and the second altered with an external oil filter. This was bolted to the right-hand cylinder head, while on the chassis side, the start

lever was no longer linked to the centre stand.

For 1954 the two MAC models and the LE ran on much as they were, but were joined by a new version of the old MSS model. The newcomer's appearance was much as that of the sprung MAC, for similar cycle parts were used and the engine was on the same lines. Unlike the old one, it had an equal bore and stroke, and alloy head and barrel, so was a much sharper performer than in the past. The top end differed from the MAC in that the valves were closed by hairpin springs and

the head was machined off just above their wells. The rocker box was separate, with the rockers held in split housings, but the valve lifter remained in the crankcase.

There was another 499 cc model for 1955 in the form of the Scrambler, which used a tuned MSS engine with a TT carburettor and open exhaust pipe. The frame and forks had minor changes to suit, plus alloy mudguards, an undershield, competition tyres and a smaller fuel tank. The other singles also had minor changes, while the LE gained an induction-pipe heater, using the cooling water, and an option of a two-level dualseat. During the year, the twin switched to a die-cast alloy rear fork, which replaced the original arrangement.

There were more new models for 1956, but the LE carried on as it was for most of the year before its wheels were changed to 18 in. rims and full-width hubs, while the carburettor became an Amal Monobloc. The rigid MAC was dropped, and the sprung one and the MSS ran on as they were, as did the Scrambler. An Endurance model appeared, which was based on the Scrambler, but was fitted with lights and was street legal. However, the best news for Velocette single enthusiasts was the appearance of the Viper and Venom models.

These were high-performance sports models with 349 or 499 cc engines, $7\frac{1}{2}$ in. front brakes, full-width hubs, and a deep headlamp shell that carried the instruments in its top surface. The Viper engine differed from the MAC in that it had a shorter stroke and copied the design of the MSS unit, on which the Venom was based. Both sports models used the normal pivoted-fork frame, forks and 7 in. rear brake.

All the singles changed to a Monobloc carburettor and single-level dualseat, while the dynamo was driven by a V-belt in place of the older flat one. Early in the year, a second Scrambler appeared with the Viper engine in the same cycle parts as the 500, and later in the year, the deep headlamp shell went on to the MAC and MSS.

The range continued as it was for 1957 and was joined by the 192 cc Valiant. This had an engine based on the LE, but with air-cooling, overhead valves and twin carburettors. It was coupled to a four-speed gearbox with foot-change, and the whole unit was mounted in a duplex tubular loop frame. The forks and wheels came from the LE, and the engine unit was enclosed by a bonnet, which left the top halves out in the breeze. There was a dualseat for the rider and a good range of fitments, but the machine came to the market at a high price for a 200 and without the performance of a 250. Many felt that a revamp of

Left **The 192 cc LE Velocette on test early in 1955 when its water cooling was hardly needed**

Right **Velocette Venom, as tested in 1958, although the number appears on another Venom test in 1956 – naughty**

the MOV would have been much better and more suited to the impending capacity restriction for learners.

The whole range continued much as it was for 1958, with one addition. This was a Mk III version of the LE, which had the four-speed gearbox from the Valiant with foot-change and kickstart. In addition, the speedometer, ammeter, and light switch were moved from the top of the legshield into a deeper headlamp shell, which was shrouded with a cowl to the forks. The Mk II continued in production for that year, but then was dropped.

For 1959 the Valiant was joined by the Veeline, which had a neat dolphin fairing with a good sized screen as standard. The LE continued in Mk III form only, and the four single-cylinder road models were fitted with an enclosure around their lower engine half and gearbox. This was made in fibreglass and cleaned up the lines of the machine, while allowing the firm to omit the polishing of timing and gearbox covers. The two scrambles models were given a revised frame, and there was a Willow green colour option for the road machines and two-tone for the Viper and Venom.

For the new decade, there were two more models, listed as the Viper and Venom Clubman. Both came without the lower enclosure, but with a selection of extras from the options list to suit the needs of the sporting rider. The rest of the range ran on as it was and would do so for another decade, with even more variations on both the flat-twin and sporting singles.

The nadir was shared by the Viceroy and Vogue, but the zenith was the fabulous Thruxton.

Sporting S501 Steib sidecar hitched to a 1958 Venom during a road test

The 1959 Velocette Valiant Veeline with air-cooled, flat-twin engine based on the LE unit

The MSS and other models gained extensive side covers for 1959, but kept their own line – again, a 1956 number on a later model

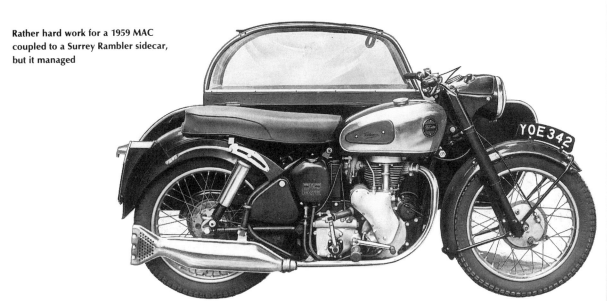

Rather hard work for a 1959 MAC coupled to a Surrey Rambler sidecar, but it managed

The 1960 Velocette scrambler model was offered in both engine sizes, this one being the larger

# Velosolex

This was a French design of power-cycle, which sold in enormous numbers in its own country and, for a while, was built under licence in Britain. It always came as a complete machine, although the design was effectively a clip-on, which drove the front tyre by roller.

The engine was a 45 cc two-stroke with upright iron cylinder and alloy head incorporating a decompressor, and the unit straddled the front wheel. The crankshaft had an overhung big-end and carried the drive roller in the middle, and the flywheel magneto on its left-hand end. Both inlet and exhaust ports were at the rear of the cylinder, with the transfer at the front, and the exhaust was piped to a small drum silencer.

The petroil tank was also drum-shaped and went to the right of the crankcase to match the magneto. Both were used to carry the registration number. A membrane fuel pump was used to raise the fuel to the carburettor and was activated by the pressure pulses in the crankcase. The carburettor, mounted behind the cylinder, was unusual in not having a float chamber. Instead, there was, in effect, a weir return to the tank and a simple main jet feed for the engine.

The engine unit was carried in plates so that it could be spring-loaded to drive the tyre or held free from it. The rest of the machine was pure bicycle, but in a French style, for it had an open frame with a single curved tube that ran down from the headstock, curved round above the bottom bracket and rose to the saddle. Smaller tubes supported the bracket and formed the chainstays, while the fittings were pure cycle.

There was only one control, which was a trigger connected to the throttle with a link to the decompressor. To suit the nature of the model type and its home country, it was spring-loaded to fully open, as Gallic logic dictated that it would spend all of its time in that position. It made the machine extremely easy to ride. There was no fuel tap, only a choke for brief use when starting from cold.

The Velosolex appeared in France in 1946 and was an immediate success. Two years later, a few reached Britain, and gradually British components were phased in, production being carried out by Solex in North London. This was well underway by 1949, and there were detail changes in 1951 and 1956. Otherwise, the model continued to be offered until 1957, when British production ceased.

It never enjoyed the sheer volume of demand as in its home country, where it continued for many a year to carry people from all walks of life around the French countryside and towns.

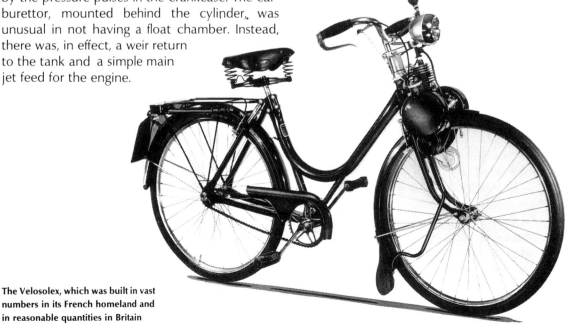

**The Velosolex, which was built in vast numbers in its French homeland and in reasonable quantities in Britain**

# Villiers

The Villiers engine had been part of the British motorcyle scene from before World War I and served many marques, both at home and abroad. The latter market began to decline after the 1940s, but at home a great number of firms continued to rely on the Wolverhampton units right through the post-war era.

Villiers produced an enormous range of engines, of which the motorcycle versions were just a part. Even these were highly diverse, and for years a great company strength was the ability of their basic designs to be varied to suit the customer. Thus, the same engine may crop up in these pages at many different points, but sometimes with three speeds and at others with four. It may have an electric starter and fan-cooling for a scooter in one version, or have a mildly-tuned cylinder for a competition model in another.

The engines ranged in size from a 50 cc moped unit to a 324 cc twin, and the gearboxes from single to four speeds. All, bar a pair of scrambles units, had a Villiers carburettor, and most relied on the Villiers flywheel magneto for ignition and lights.

Smallest of the range was the 50 cc 3K engine unit with its two-speed gearbox, which differed from most Villiers models in having true unit construction. Otherwise, it followed normal practice, with iron barrel, alloy head and bobweights, but the clutch was on the right-hand end of the crankshaft, while the flywheel magneto was on the left.

At what was normally viewed as the bottom of the range were the 100 cc engines, and post-war, up to 1948, there was just one unit listed as the Junior de Luxe or JDL. It was of 98 cc with a horizontal cylinder incorporating four transfer ports and twin exhausts, one on each side. Below it was a substantial cast alloy silencer box, which was connected to the ports by a cast elbow on each side. A further alloy casting carried the carburettor on the left. The cylinder head was in light alloy with an 18 mm sparking plug and a decompressor. The crankpin was overhung, with alternate steel and bronze rollers in the big-end, and turned in twin races in the crankcase. The main part of this extended back to house a chain-driven clutch, which drove the rear wheel.

For 1949 the JDL was replaced by two new engines, both of 99 cc, with their cylinders only

**One of the few unit-construction Villiers engines was the 50 cc 3K used by this 1959 Norman Lido**

*Above* **The two 99 cc F-series engines, with one or two speeds, used for light motorcycles and autocycles**

*Below* **The 1950 Villiers 10D of 122 cc, which was built along with the very similar 197 cc 6E; plug position indicates which is which**

inclined a little from the vertical. The construction of both was similar, the 2F having the single speed and countershaft clutch of the JDL. The 1F featured a two-speed gearbox with hand-lever selection and a clutch. The flywheel magneto was moved to the right for both engines, which had a full crankshaft in place of the overhung type. Both engines were designed to fit into a frame, rather than hang from it, as in the past.

The 2F remained in use without any real change until it was dropped in 1958, but the two-speed model was replaced by the 4F for 1953. This was a more modern design, with the flywheel magneto enclosed and the ignition points remote from it on the left-hand side. The result was a streamlined appearance, more in keeping with the times, but inside there were still only two speeds. In 1956 they were given foot-change to become the 6F, and this last version ran on into the 1960s, while the 4F was dropped in 1958.

The next Villiers capacity was of 122 cc, and the immediate post-war model was the 9D, which had a three-speed, hand-change gearbox. It followed pre-war lines, for it dated from 1937, but was of true unit construction with a vertical split line for the main castings. Within them went a built-up crankshaft with roller big-end, and

outside was the flywheel magneto on the right and the primary drive on the left.

The top half was distinctively pre-war, the iron barrel having an exhaust-port elbow, cast in alloy, bolted to each side. Both had a short pipe to lead to a cylindrical silencer, mounted ahead of the crankcase, and below the left one was bolted a curved, cast alloy, inlet pipe. The cylinder head was also in alloy with sparking plug and decompressor.

This simple engine was replaced by the 10D for 1949, and this design reverted to a separate gearbox, which was bolted to the rear of the crankcase. This was a step to give the firm the freedom to ring the changes, while another was to make both halves of the primary chaincase separate from the crankcase. The flywheel magneto continued on the right under a polished, spun-aluminium cover, and the crankshaft continued to be built up. The cylinder was vertical and more up to date, with single inlet and exhaust ports at the rear and front, while the head continued in light alloy, but without the decompressor.

From this simple beginning came a range of builds with options of electric starting, fan-cooling, a reverse gear, wide or close gear ratios and a competition specification. This last was listed as the 11D for 1954, while the basic model became the 12D for that year, both with the option of three or four speeds. For 1953 the 13D was built as a utility model, using the 12D crankcase and the 10D head and barrel. In all these cases, however, the differences were minimal, and the engine size was dropped during 1954.

It was replaced by the 147 cc 30C, which was a bored-out 12D, but also with new crankcase castings to allow this. With it came the competition 29C, and both engines were closely modelled on the 122 cc versions. The 29C ran to 1956 and the 30C to 1959, but they were effectively replaced for 1956 by the 31C. This had both bore and stroke revised to give it a 148 cc capacity and kept the older construction form, but was modified to give a streamlined appearance. Most of this came from enclosing the magneto and gearbox end with a single cover, and recessing the carburettor into the top of both crankcase and gearbox castings. The result was the appearance of unit construction, while retaining the flexibility of build that the firm found so useful.

The same layout, and many common parts, were used for the 174 cc 2L engine, introduced for 1957 and soon joined by the fan-cooled 3L for scooters. As with the 148 cc model, there were options of three or four speeds, and the two engines were interchangeable.

The Villiers 197 cc engine was possibly their most popular of the 1950s, and it served thousands of owners on their regular ride to work each

**A 1957 DKR Dove with 147 cc Villiers 30C engine, which was based on the D-series**

day. In the immediate post-war period, they did offer the 5E, which was as the smaller 9D with twin exhaust ports, although it did have foot-change for its three speeds. Ambassador seem to have been the sole British firm to have used this engine, as others of those times stuck with the 9D.

Like that model, the 5E was replaced for 1949 by a new design, the 6E, which was a larger version of the 10D and one destined to follow the same route. It repeated the separate gearbox arrangement and three speeds with larger crankcase castings and many common parts. It was replaced by the 8E for 1954, and this was joined by the competition 7E, both being offered with four speeds, as well as the three. The list of options was as for the 122 cc engine, but the 7E was dropped in 1956, while the 8E continued to 1958. However, this was only in three-speed form.

Both were joined by the 9E for 1955, and this repeated the streamlined design of the 31C, while retaining all the options available for the others. It was to continue as the firm's mainstay for the 200 cc class and was joined by two other versions.

One was the 10E, which had the cylinder mounted vertically instead of inclined forward a little, and the other was the 11E for scooters, with electric start and fan-cooling. Both the 9E and 10E were also listed in competition form, and the former for scooter use. All ran on into the 1960s.

The next capacity class Villiers used was an intermediate one of 224 cc for their 1H, which appeared for 1954. It was the first to have the streamlined construction, as befitted what was then the top of their motorcycle range, and this extended to enclosing the carburettor as well. It was only built with a four-speed gearbox.

The engine had full flywheels, but retained the separate gearbox, as with the smaller models. The major castings were formed to flow together to maintain the unit looks, which they did very well, and were assisted in this by the use of a smaller flywheel magneto. This fed an external coil, which was an improvement, and the points were under an access plate on the right-hand cover, which also carried an ignition switch. For the rest, the construction followed Villiers practice.

The 1H was joined by the 246 cc 2H in 1957, but this was little used, although it remained in the range until the end of the decade. For most firms, its place was taken by the 246 cc A-series

**The final development of the E-series was the 9E, used here by a 1956 Panther 10/4**

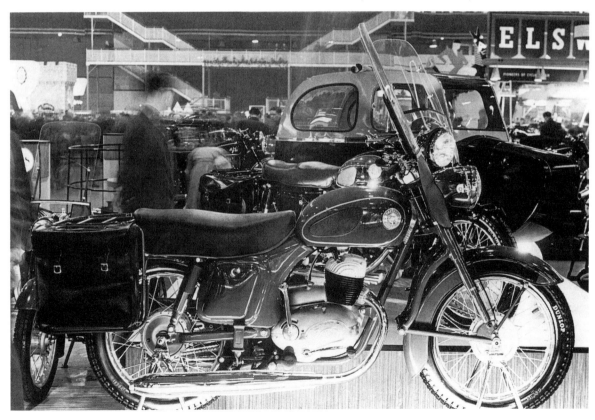

engines, which were built from 1958 on. In essence, they were the 9E, which had been bored out and fitted with a different rod to produce a whole range with many parts in common with the 197 cc units.

First to appear were the 31A and 33A, the former for road models and the latter for scrambles. All were to have four-speed gearboxes, but there was a great range of specification builds, some duplicated by the 9E and others special to the A-series. The 31A saw Villiers into the 1960s on the road, but for that year, the 33A was replaced by the 34A and joined by the 32A, which was built to trials specification. The two scrambles engines were among the few Villiers units to use an Amal carburettor.

The final Villiers engines were the twins, beginning with the 249 cc 2T of 1956. This followed the lines of the 1H and retained the separate four-speed gearbox, flywheel magneto on the right and ignition key in the cover. The twin-cylinder crankshaft was built up and had a centre web with bearing and oil seal so it could be bolted in between the two case halves. The alloy heads and iron barrels were separate, while a manifold was fed by a single carburettor. There were two sets of points under the access plate.

**Another Panther, but with a 324 cc 3T Villiers twin engine, rather than the more usual 249 cc 2T**

The 2T was joined by the 324 cc 3T, which became available for motorcycle use from 1958. Both twins could also be had with electric start, fan-cooling and reverse-running options in various packages to suit scooter and bubblecar use. The reverse was obtained by running the engine backwards, thanks to special wiring and controls, but its operation was tedious for a three-point turn.

Square barrel conversions should also be mentioned in connection with Villiers engines. The phrase refers to kits which came on the market in the late 1950s for both the E- and A-series engines. Their purpose was to improve the performance by changing both head and barrel, the latter invariably being cast in alloy with well-spaced, square-outline fins, hence the name. Marcelle and Parkinson were the best known, and some of these conversions enlarged the smaller engine to 246 cc. In the 1960s the kits progressed further to be used by a number of firms for their new models. They were also joined by an improved crankshaft and, later still, an entire bottom half.

# Vincent-HRD

Monolever rear suspension, shaft drive, stub axle wheel mounting, hub centre steering, hydraulic clutch operation, enclosure and direct attachment of the suspension members to the engine and gearbox unit could all be features of a very modern motorcycle, but were all ideas propounded by Philip Vincent in 1943. His was a fertile mind, and while few of his ideas were to come to fruition in the hard practical daylight of the post-war years, they go a long way to show the man's advanced thinking.

The Vincent-HRD was a name to conjure with anyway, the pre-war 998 cc Rapide being a very different kettle of fish from the usual V-twins of the times with their side valves and sidecar calling. The Rapide was a grand tourer with plenty of power and high gearing for effortless riding at all speeds, which was how Vincent saw high-class motorcycling.

During the war years, he worked with his chief engineer, Phil Irving, to design a better and lighter Rapide, which would do the same job as the pre-war edition, but in an improved manner. The aim was to learn from the past and produce a very high-speed tourer with a host of rider features. They came pretty close to succeeding, too.

The pre-war model looked a mess, with pipes, plates, carbs, links and levers in a glorious disarray with no harmony at all. Post-war, all this was to change, with a shorter wheelbase, unit construction of engine and gearbox, the extensive use of light alloys, and a very clean appearance.

All this and a host of detail improvements were promised in a March 1945 announcement, for both Vincent and Irving had been hard at work on the new design, much of which was described by Irving in a talk given in June. This really whetted the appetite, but it was December before full details of the post-war Rapide were released.

The impact was tremendous, for the machine was as compact as a 500 single and incorporated many new features. The major part was the engine, which had the gearbox built in unit with it to provide a single, rigid structure. It was so rigid, in fact, that there was little frame at all, the rear fork being the major part, and even this was attached to the rear of the engine structure.

The rest of the frame comprised a beam over the engine, which had the headstock at its front end and also doubled as the oil tank. To its rear were fixed the rear spring and damper, which controlled the rear fork structure, while the tube itself was bolted to both cylinder heads. At the front were Brampton girders, as the two Phils considered telescopic forks to be inadequate for solo riding and totally unsuitable for sidecar work.

The engine was the heart of the machine and was a 50-degree V-twin with overhead valves and alloy heads and barrels. These were fitted to a massive crankcase casting, which was split vertically on the centre line between the two cylinders. These were offset to one another. Within the cases turned a large, built-up crankshaft, the mainshafts being pressed into the flywheels, which were drilled for balance.

The two big-ends each comprised three rows of uncaged rollers, running on a single crankpin, so the connecting rods sat side by side. Nuts pulled the pin into place, and the complete assembly was supported by two roller races on the timing side, and one roller and one ball race on the drive side.

The timing side on the right used a train of gears, with a large, central, intermediate gear meshing with each camshaft gear. The front one of these drove an idler, which meshed with the auto-advance magneto mounted ahead of the crankcase, under a protective alloy shield. Each camshaft looked after one cylinder, with cam followers and widely splayed pushrods running up to the unusual rockers and valve gear.

The pushrods, and the tubes in which they moved, had to be laid out to match the arrangement of the rockers, which lay across the engine, so the valve angle dictated the pushrod position. Each rocker was mounted in a pivot block, which was clamped into the head casting. Access to this, and the adjuster at the outer rocker end, was via a screwed cap carrying the firm's logo. There were further caps above the valves, which differed from normal practice in that the rockers engaged with them around the mid-point of their length, while the springs were above this.

The arrangement was as for the pre-war Rapide,

The Series B Rapide, as introduced in 1946, this one being photographed in Seattle, in the USA, in 1948

except that duplex coil springs were used in place of the earlier hairpins. This allowed the valve gear to be fully enclosed, while retaining the very short pushrod length and isolating the springs from engine heat. In some ways, it was a curious line to follow, for the engine was never meant to reach high speeds, hence the crowded roller big-end, and thus, had little need for ultra-light valve gear.

A single cover enclosed the timing side, an access plate being provided for the magneto gear. Under this was the oil pump, which was driven directly from the crankshaft. An oil filter went in a chamber in the lower front portion of the crankcases while the breather was driven by a timing gear.

Both cylinder heads had the exhaust port at the front, and the two pipes swept down to a single tubular silencer on the right. Thus, two Amal carburettors had to be used, each with its own float chamber, and these were fed by two petrol taps. The heads were cast with integral rocker chambers and fitted on long studs in the crankcase with mounting plates above them. These, in turn, were attached to the top frame beam-cum-oil tank, the details being designed to compensate for any differences in thermal expansion between the steel beam and alloy engine.

The primary transmission was by triplex chain within a large, polished alloy case, and this chain

also drove the Miller dynamo, which sat above the gearbox section of the crankcase. The clutch was rather special to cope with the tremendous engine torque, which had proved too much for the Burman unit used pre-war. The new design was often thought to be operated by centrifugal force, but this was not the case all.

It was, in fact, two clutches in one, with most of the power being transmitted via a drum and shoes, not unlike a brake. This clutch was engaged by a simple plate type and, thanks to its servo action, it was able to transmit all the power, while remaining very light in action. So light were the original springs that excessive cable friction could prevent the clutch engaging fully, so they had to be strengthened.

The gearbox was of a very compact, four-speed, cross-over design, so the rear chain went on the right. The change mechanism was on the right of the engine case, under an outer cover, and was linked by shaft and bevel gears to the selector camplate, which was mounted above the two gear shafts. These were arranged with the mainshaft at the rear to place it as close to the rear fork pivot as possible. The kickstarter was on the right, along with the gear pedal, and had a long, curved lever, which ran under the footrest to give the rider the best chance of a long swinging kick when starting.

The complete engine and gearbox unit, with its minimal frame, rode on spoked wheels, each with two single-leading-shoe brakes. Twin drums for the wheels dated from the pre-war models, and the rear ones each carried a sprocket. Thanks to some good detail design, the wheel could be very quickly taken out and turned round to provide an easy change to sidecar gearing.

Sporting alloy mudguards were used and there was a dualseat, rather than a saddle and pillion pad. The seat was supported at the rear by struts from the rear fork structure, so it rose and fell a little as the suspension worked. The rear fork carried a rear stand, which was held up by a small T-bar screw, and at the front of the crankcase there was a prop-stand on each side. By means of a minor adjustment, these could be used as one to become a front stand.

The stands made it very easy to work on the machine, and it was a simple task to remove either the whole of the front end, plus the frame top beam, or the rear fork complete with wheel. In both cases, this left the engine unit ready and accessible for working on. This philosophy of making it easy for the owner to maintain the machine was continued throughout its design, while long-term appearance was enhanced by the use of stainless steel for many parts.

The result of all this work was a motorcycle with a shattering performance, despite the low-octane pool petrol the engine had to suffer in its early days. The weight came out at around 450 lb, and the 45 bhp produced by the relaxed and stress-free V-twin was sufficient to propel it quite fast enough for the road conditions of the times, when few were straight and most were excessively bumpy.

Inevitably, there were problems in getting the new design into production, and it was May 1946 before the very first machine was fired up and taken out on to the Great North Road by Phil Vincent, minus hat, gloves or goggles. Phil Irving was next and then Arthur Bourne of *The Motor Cycle*, with cap and goggles, followed by Graham Walker of *Motor Cycling*. The two editors were very impressed, while the factory personnel must have been thankful it had all worked out so well.

Thus was the post-war Vincent-HRD Rapide born, and it was soon, correctly, advertised as 'the world's fastest standard motorcycle – this is a fact, not a slogan'. It was September before the first production machine was built, and it went to Argentina. More followed, many for export, while

the firm struggled with the shortages of materials and parts then so common.

Because the pre-war twin had been the model A, the post-war version became the Series B. It proved to be a real grand tourer, with the maximum speed in top simply 'not obtained' during one 1947 road test. Another managed 112 mph, and this with a low compression ratio, pool petrol, a riding coat and an engine with a docile tick-over for town use.

Early in 1948 the Rapide was joined by a faster version! This was the Black Shadow, which had larger carburettors and a small rise in compression ratio to produce a top speed beyond the 120 mph mark with little loss of docility or easy town riding. To match the name, the engine was finished in black, and the result looked wonderful. In addition to the engine improvements, the brakes were given ribbed drums and, best of all, a large 5 in. speedometer, reading up to 150 mph, appeared and sat boldly at the top of the forks.

Never ones to rest on their laurels, the two Phils, Vincent and Irving, had more new offerings for 1949 to expand the range and provide even better motorcycles for the discerning rider. The two Series B models continued, but were joined by the Series C, which had totally new front forks, called Girdraulics, and a damper for the rear suspension. The series C Rapide and Black Shadow were listed in the same form as the Series B, except for the suspension, and were joined by two singles and a racing model called the Black Lightning.

The singles were the Series B Meteor and Series C Comet, which had the same suspension variation and a good deal in common with the V-twins. They reversed the events of pre-war days, when Phil Irving created the Rapide by mounting two single top halves on a common crankcase. For 1949 he simply replaced the rear cylinder with a cast alloy frame member and added some gearbox plates so that he could use a separate four-speed Burman gearbox. The crankcase was modified to suit the needs of the single and, thus, the front cylinder and general line remained, but the dynamo was driven from the timing gear train. On the cycle side, the singles followed the twins with minor alterations, so the two looked much the same, the Meteor differing from the others in having a saddle and no pillion rests.

The Black Lightning was built for road racing, so its engine was tuned with TT carburettors and straight-through exhaust pipes. It had a rev-counter, but no kickstart, lighting equipment or

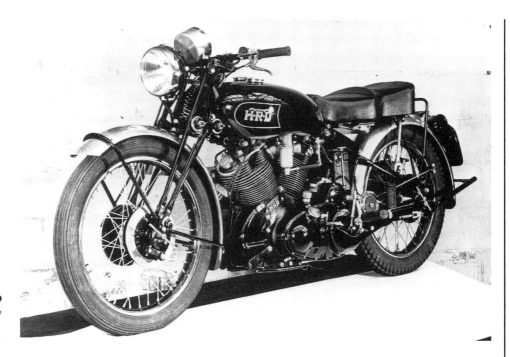

The 1948 Vincent–HRD
Series B Black Shadow
with its big, upright
150 mph speedometer

The Vincent–HRD was also built as a
500 single, and this is a 1949 Series
C Comet with the Girdraulic forks

Series C Black Shadow with 120 + mph
potential on pool petrol

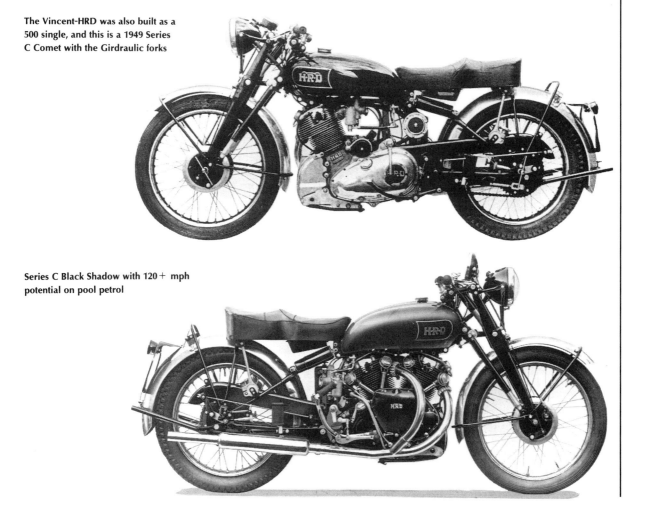

stands. Both wheels had alloy rims and alloy brake backplates, while the tyre sizes were 3.00 × 21 in. front and 3.50 × 20 in. rear. There were short alloy mudguards and a racing seat, which used the standard mountings.

The new forks used for the Series C models were still of the girder type, as the two Phils continued to consider telescopics poor for solos and useless when a sidecar was hitched to a machine. Their design was based on a pair of forged alloy blades linked to the headstock by forged links, the top one alloy and the lower one steel. As these were in one piece, they did not twist relative to one another, as separate links were prone to do, and the blades were further braced by a plate bolted to their front faces, just below the bottom link pivot.

This point had a further ingenious arrangement, for the link moved on an eccentric bush fixed to the spindle. As this bush was turned, it moved the pivot point and, thus, effectively altered the link position which, in turn, changed the trail. The dimensions were arranged so that the positions available gave solo or sidecar trail, and the change-over could be carried out in a few minutes.

Each eccentric bush also carried the top mounting for a long, slim spring unit, which ran down to the lower end of the fork blade. This allowed long, low-rated springs to be used to give a comfortable ride, while damping was dealt with by a separate hydraulic unit mounted between the fork links in the normal girder fork spring position. One final touch was to place the spring mountings on the eccentrics so that their loading was increased in the sidecar setting.

For 1950 the range continued with one more single in the form of the racing Grey Flash. This was a Comet built on the lines of the Lightning, with tuned engine, no road equipment and the racing fitments. It was listed in three forms, one of which was the basic road racer. Another was a road machine, effectively a Comet with a tuned engine, and the third was the same, but came with a kit of parts to convert it to the racer.

The Series B was dropped during 1950, so only the Series C continued for 1951, together with the three V-twins, the Comet and the three versions of the Grey Flash. The last was dropped for 1952, while the Lightning was built to special order only. However, the two road twins and single continued to offer the same high-speed touring as always.

It was the same for 1953, with minor improve-ments, but during the year, the firm tried a totally different line with a clip-on engine unit. This was, in truth, developed and launched by the Miller company, who supplied Vincent with electrical parts, and was first seen early in 1952. The engine was designed to fit under a cycle's bottom bracket, to keep the weight low and to drive the rear tyre with its friction-roller.

The 48 cc, two-stroke engine had a horizontal cylinder and was made as narrow as possible to fit between the pedals, in the same manner as the German Lohmann. The engine was conventional, having an iron barrel, alloy head and pressed-up crankshaft with conical expanders for the crank-pin and roller big-end. A flywheel magneto was on the right with an external ignition coil, while a gear on the left drove a countershaft carrying a large-diameter roller. The engine was held so that it could drive or be free, and its mixture was supplied by a small Amal, while a silencer box went under the barrel. The petroil tank was mounted on the frame downtube, and the ignition coil housed in a recess in its base.

In the middle of 1953 it was announced that Vincent had taken over both production and sales of this unit, which became known as the Firefly. It was soon offered with a Sun bicycle that had been specially designed for it. This had a semi-open frame that was able to deal with the added weight, power and vibration. It had drum brakes front and rear, plus a widened bottom bracket to ensure that the cranks cleared the engine.

To the deep chagrin of members of the Vincent Owners' Club, the Firefly unit was listed alongside the three twins and the Comet for 1954. The Lightning was given caged roller big-ends, and there were a number of minor changes to the motorcycles, which otherwise ran on as before.

To augment their range, Vincent did a deal with the German NSU company, and for a year imported the Quickly moped, which pointed the way to the future and killed off the clip-on engines. In addition to the moped, there was a range of small motorcycles listed as NSU-Vincent. These had German engine units, frames and forks, but British wheels, tyres, tank, carburettor and other equipment. This arrangement side-stepped the tariff rules applicable at the time.

Four models were to be available. All had unit construction of the engine and four-speed gearbox, a spine frame, leading-link front forks and pivoted rear fork, which was controlled in much the same way as the big Vincents. The

A modified 1950 Black Shadow with many stainless-steel parts and other detail improvements

larger machines had hydraulic damping at both ends, but the smaller ones had to make do with friction units.

The smallest model was the 98 cc Fox, which had an ohv engine and was offered in standard or de luxe forms. The former had direct lighting and a saddle, while the latter was given a battery and dualseat, which was supported as on the Vincent, but with spring-loaded struts at the rear.

Next, came the 123 cc Fox, which had a two-stroke engine and similar specification, but neither Fox model was made in any numbers to speak of.

The larger models were the 199 cc Lux two-stroke and 247 cc Max, with overhead camshaft driven by eccentrics and connecting blades. This system worked well, and the German Max had a fine reputation, enhanced by the racing successes of the Rennmax model. For the venture with Vincent, both machines proved too expensive for the market, and neither went into production.

The exercise continued for 1955, but was then dropped, for Vincent had something far more

The Vincent Firefly taken over from Millers and never discussed by the Owners' Club

exciting to offer that year in the shape of the fully-enclosed Series D range. This was a remarkable development for the time and was to lead the firm into grave problems, but the object, as always, was to provide the discerning rider with a high-speed tourer; a two-wheeled Bentley, as Phil Vincent put it.

The enclosure began with a large and deeply valanced front mudguard, which ran outside the fork blades. Above it was a cowl, which carried the headlamp, extended outwards to protect the hands, and had a fascia for the instruments, and a windscreen to keep rain off the rider.

The rear of the machine was enclosed by a single moulding mounted on a subframe and carrying the seat. It enclosed the rear wheel to below the spindle and was hinged to give access to the rear end once two bolts had been slackened. A normal petrol tank was used, but below it was a panel on each side. These ran forward to form legshields, each topped by a forward-facing beak.

Under the mouldings went the familiar engine, frame and forks, but with a number of alterations. Both carburettors were on the right and became Monoblocs; ignition was by coil, with the points in the old magneto position; and the oil tank was fitted in the rear body, which simplified the frame's top beam. The rear suspension was controlled by a single Armstrong hydraulic spring unit, and the tyres were changed to 3.50 × 19 in. front and 4.00 × 18 in. rear. Only one brake was used in the rear wheel, although two remained at the front. The tommy bars on the spindles disappeared and the stands were revised. The prop-stands were no longer fitted and, in place of the rear stand, there

was a central stand operated by a long hand lever, much as on a pre-war Rudge.

With their new clothes, the models were given new names; the Rapide became the Black Knight, the Shadow the Black Prince, and the Comet the Victor, but only one of these was built. The models created a sensation at the show that year, but production problems arose with the mouldings, which Phil Vincent insisted should be to his usual high standards.

As a stop-gap, he decided to build Series D models without enclosure to Rapide and Black Shadow specifications. There was also one Comet, but this was later fitted with enclosure for a show. The open Series D V-twins had a tubular subframe to support the dualseat, but retained all the other new features. The mudguards reverted to the usual Series C type, and a toolbox appeared on the left of the subframe.

The machines kept the factory going, but the new seat and subframe lacked the lithe lines of the earlier models, and the company was, by now, once more in financial trouble. At the bottom end of the scale, the Firefly was offered as a complete machine, but in September 1955, at an Owners' Club dinner in Cambridge, Phil Vincent announced that the motorcycles would no longer be produced.

They had to build another hundred or so machines to fulfil outstanding orders, but in December the last official machine, a Black Prince, was completed. The Firefly continued for 1956 as a machine, and for two more years as a clip-on attachment, while the firm moved to other industrial uses for its engines.

*Left* **Open Series D Black Shadow built as a stop-gap with tubular subframe, but minus the lovely lines of the earlier models**

**The Series D Vincent Black Prince with Shadow engine under the full enclosure**

**The Series D created a sensation at Earls Court, and there was a queue to sit on one for most of the show**

**The NSU–Vincent Max with 247 cc ohc engine seen at Earls Court, but never put into production**

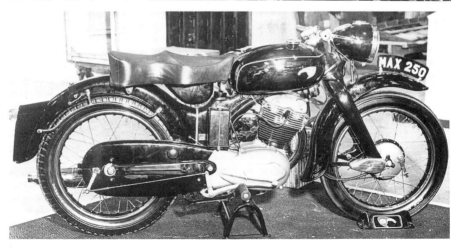

# Wabo

This was a Dutch make of scooter, but one which used Villiers power for the models imported into Britain. These were two in number and, except for the engine units and forks, they were identical.

Engines were the 99 cc 4F, with two speeds, or the 147 cc 30C, with three, and both went into a rigid duplex frame with light or heavy telescopic front forks. The wheels had 16 in. rims and wire spokes, so were larger than usual for a scooter, and the bodywork was extensive. It followed normal scooter lines, but included a very deep tunnel, which ran from near the top of the leg-shields to the rear body and had footboards on each side.

The front mudguard turned with the wheel. The fuel tank was at the rear with an access panel for filling, while the rear body could be quickly released, thanks to car-bonnet-type fasteners. In continental style, it carried a saddle each for both rider and passenger.

The models were fully equipped and had a certain style, but the enterprise was short-lived, for the make both came and went in 1957, having but a brief life on the British scene.

The Dutch Wabo scooter with Villiers engine under the extensive bodywork, which came and went in 1957

# Watsonian

This sidecar firm built a prototype machine in 1950 to haul its products and, for a first attempt, it turned out rather well. For power, they chose a 996 cc V-twin JAP engine, which had side valves, but alloy heads and barrels, so was lighter than usual.

The engine was coupled to a four-speed Burman gearbox by a chain in an oil-bath case, and both went into a duplex loop frame. This had plunger suspension at the rear and Dunlop telescopic forks, which used rubber for the springs, at the front. Massive alloy hubs with 9 in. twin-leading-shoe brakes were used front and rear, so this was one outfit that defied convention and could stop quickly and easily.

The engine had coil ignition and an alternator housed in its timing cover, the distributor being fitted into the rear of this. A large battery went behind the rear cylinder and beneath the dualseat, and further back, between the right-hand chainstays, was the oil tank. This was made in alloy from a casting and sheet, its outer surface being ribbed. A large petrol tank of over five gallons capacity was fitted, and the whole machine was finished in pale green.

It made an excellent sidecar machine, but by 1950 the market for a rather thirsty V-twin of modest performance was vanishing. The low-down pull was tremendous and much appreciated when the going was bad, but in the showrooms the new 650 twins looked far more attractive. To settle the matter, JAP proved less than interested in supplying engines for a project with limited appeal, so the idea came to a halt. The machine itself existed at the time of writing and has modern lines, compared with pre-war haulers, so it was a good, but unsuccessful try.

**Watsonian prototype, as built in 1950 and seen here some 35 years later, with its distinctive engine, oil tank and forks**

# Wooler

The Wooler was always one of the strange machines that make motorcycles so interesting. The industry is peppered with individuals who saw their way as being correct and often refused to deviate a fraction from their chosen path. They seldom built many machines, and those they did produce were frequently troublesome, but we all gained by the excitement they generated.

The Wooler was one such machine, and the first model, built in 1911, had a horizontal two-stroke engine with double-ended piston to avoid the need for crankcase compression. It also had plunger rear suspension and a similar arrangement on the front forks, while the fuel tank was extended round and in front of the headstock.

This tank style was to continue, and in the 1920s the firm built machines with flat-twin, four-stroke engines of rather more conventional form, although the plunger suspension for both wheels continued. They were entered for a couple of TT races, for which they retained the tank form, but were painted in a bright yellow, so were quickly named 'flying bananas'.

Other models were tried, the sole 1926 machine having a 500 cc ohc engine with the cams on the top end of the vertical shaft. Horizontal tappets and rockers took the movement to the valves, and the engine had twin exhaust ports. The machine had a more conventional rigid frame and girder forks, but even these had the Wooler touch. The frame differed from normal in having a series of flat plates to join the headstock to the duplex downtubes, while the fork springs, which were enclosed, were three in number and could be adjusted while riding.

It was back to the flat twin for 1927, but soon after that motorcycle production ceased, and all was quiet until 1945. When news of a new Wooler design and prototype came in May of that year, it was expected that the machine would be unusual. Press and public alike were not disappointed, for

it was unique in engine, frame, suspension and details.

The engine was the feature of greatest interest and was laid out as a transverse-four, the cylinders on each side being one above the other. This alone was far from normal, but really unique was the way in which they were connected to the crankshaft, for this was based on the beam engine. Capacity was 500 cc, and overhead valves were used.

The crankshaft ran along the machine, below all the cylinders, and was of a single-throw design. In fact, for the prototype, a modified assembly from a 150 cc New Imperial was used. Above the crankshaft was a T-shaped beam, which was pivoted at the junction of the leg and arms, this axis also lying along the machine. A master connecting rod joined the end of the T-leg to the crankshaft, so as this rotated, the beam oscillated. The arm of the T was set vertically, and each end was attached to two connecting rods, which pointed in opposite directions and ran out to the pistons. Thus, these moved in pairs, and the two pairs moved in opposition.

Engine construction was fairly simple, despite the complex linkage within, and a single alloy casting formed the block for all four cylinders, which had liners pressed in for the bores. It also included the section between the cylinders and extended down as the upper part of the crankcase. One alloy cylinder head went on each side and had vertical valves in a row. The rocker box was fixed to the head and had a lid held by three bolts.

**Arrangement of pistons, rods, T-beam, master rod and crankshaft for the Wooler beam engine**

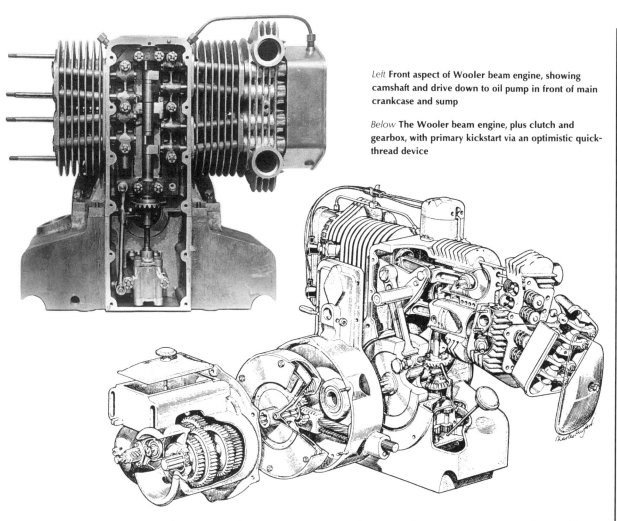

*Left* **Front aspect of Wooler beam engine, showing camshaft and drive down to oil pump in front of main crankcase and sump**

*Below* **The Wooler beam engine, plus clutch and gearbox, with primary kickstart via an optimistic quick-thread device**

A massive sump-cum-lower crankcase was bolted to the base of the block, with cover plates to front and rear. The plate at the front concealed the camshaft, which ran up the front of the engine and was driven by a bevel gear on the crankcase nose. Thus, it was able to operate the valves via pushrods and also drove the oil pump from its lower end and a distributor at the top. The front cover also provided a mounting for a pancake dynamo, which was driven by a further bevel gear from the camshaft gear.

It was suggested that a supercharger could be substituted for the dynamo, in which case, a single carburettor would feed it and long pipes would take the mixture to the inlet side. However, for normal use, twin carburettors, one on each side, were to be used. The exhaust pipes from each side swept down to join and then connect to the frame, which acted as the silencing system.

This extremely interesting engine was not the end of the matter, for bolted to its rear was to be either a four-speed gearbox or an infinitely-variable gear. This was to take the place of both clutch and gearbox, be purely mechanical in operation, and controlled by a twistgrip with a lock-up for the highest ratio. After all this, it was positively prosaic that the output should be stepped over by a pair of spur gears and then taken by shaft to the rear wheel. The shaft had a universal joint at the rear and a rubber coupling at the front, while spiral bevels were used to turn the drive.

The frame was constructed from tubes brazed into lugs that, in the main, were formed in welded steel, with a single top tube and widely splayed down tubes. These ran down to a large cross-tube, from which the bottom tubes led straight back to the rear plungers. Further tubes linked the tops of the plungers to the seat, with bracing tubes from there to the bottom tubes.

The front cross-tube had an aluminium manifold at each end, to which the exhaust pipes were connected, and the gases passed right along the bottom tubes to fishtail exhausts at the end. Quite what one did when the system eventually cor-

roded away was never discussed, and there was no mention of any provision against condensation.

Rear suspension was by twin plunger boxes on each side with the wheel spindle between them. Each box enclosed compression and rebound springs, but no damping, other than friction. At the front, the same arrangement was used at the bottom end of the forks, which gave them an odd appearance, but allowed the wheels to be interchangeable. The front fork had a massive lower crown only, with just a headrace adjustment and handlebar clamp above the headstock. The crown had a main tube running straight down to the rear plunger on each side, with a light one to the front. Again, there was no damping.

Both wheels had offset hubs with drum brakes, so they were very ordinary by Wooler standards, as were the mudguards that protected them. The saddle itself was normal, but not its springs, which were concealed in the two saddle tubes. The petrol tank followed the style of the past, stretching out ahead of the forks and bars, with the headlamp set in its nose. It certainly gave the machine an unusual line, but there were many other interesting details. The combined toolbox and air filter formed in the top of the gearbox was one, and the stand another, as it had two separate legs, the angle of which could be readily altered to create a prop-stand. Only three spanner sizes dealt with the entire machine, including the ignition, and there were no fixings with screwdriver slots. Access and servicing were all good

and easy, some operations requiring no tools at all since they could be done by hand alone.

The Wooler created great interest and gained much publicity, for it differed so much from the usual machines of the day. It also proved difficult to put into production, and it was late in 1946 before even a complete prototype was seen, although the engine had run some time earlier. Finally, in May 1947, this machine was shown to the trade, and an indication of the ease of servicing was provided by demonstration.

Once again, production was talked of as 'commencing next year', and it was much the same in 1948, although the firm did exhibit at the Earls Court show late in the year. Then, all went quiet, and it was late in 1952 before there was any further news of Wooler.

What was announced then was more new than old, for the engine had become a much more conventional 499 cc flat-four with air-cooling and overhead valves. The crankshaft ran along the frame and, for the best balance, the rods had normal and forked big-ends. They were forged in alloy with plain shells; the mains were also plain bearings.

The alloy cylinders were cast in blocks, as were the heads, which had separate rocker boxes. There were two camshafts, driven by one chain, and it was intended that one model would have alternator electrics, while a faster, sports machine would have a magneto. Wet-sump lubrication was specified, the oil pump being driven by the left-hand camshaft.

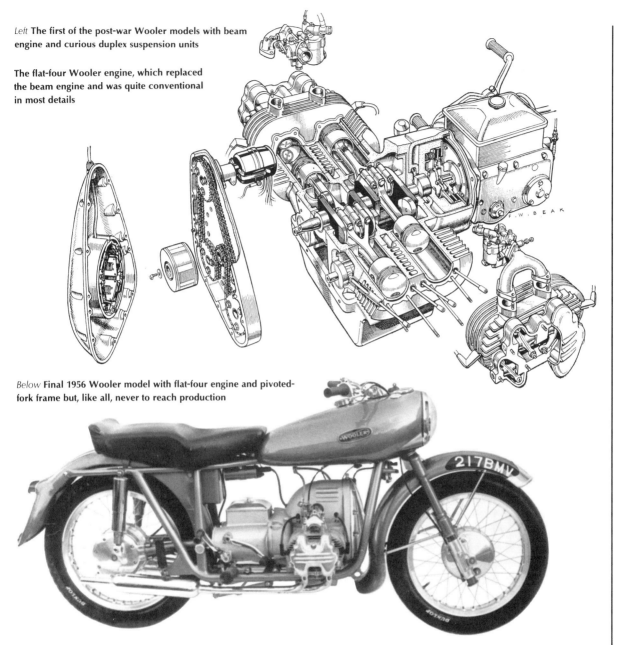

*Left* **The first of the post-war Wooler models with beam engine and curious duplex suspension units**

**The flat-four Wooler engine, which replaced the beam engine and was quite conventional in most details**

*Below* **Final 1956 Wooler model with flat-four engine and pivoted-fork frame but, like all, never to reach production**

One Amal supplied each pair of cylinders, and the exhaust pipes on each side joined and fed into a single silencer. The original four-speed gearbox was retained and bolted to the engine, while the shaft drive and rear bevel box also came from the 1945 model.

The frame was much as before, but the rear plungers only had one spring box on each side. At the front. the forks were similar, the plunger units being fitted at the ends of the fork tubes, which had the appearance of telescopics. The large lower crown still supported them, and the tank still extended forward to include the headlamp. Both wheels had full-width alloy hubs with 7 in. brakes and could be interchanged, although the tyres were ribbed front and studded rear, so the practice was not recommended.

The next year, the Wooler was described, once more, as being close to production, and the press reported favourably on their rides of the proto-type during development. It was the same thing late in 1954, when even extras were listed, in the form of a dualseat and crash bar, but for 1956 there was a revised frame. This had pivoted-fork rear suspension and a dualseat, but that was the end of the line for the Wooler, which never did make it into production, despite a decade of development.

# Zenith

It is hard to believe that this firm ever returned to the market after the war. Their best days had been in the 1920s and prior to World War 1, but by the late 1930s, the range had dwindled to six models, all with JAP power.

After the war, only one appeared, and that was little altered from the 1939 version. It was the 750, powered by a 747 cc, side-valve JAP engine, which had its mag-dyno mounted on the side of the timing case, where it was bevel-gear driven. Total-loss lubrication was provided by a Pilgrim pump, and a single Amal carburettor was mounted between the cylinders.

Separate exhaust pipes ran back to twin silencers on the right, and the electric wiring from the engine was taken up under the tank via a vertical plated pipe. The engine drove a four-speed Burman gearbox, and both went into a duplex cradle frame, which was rigid at the rear and had Druid girder forks at the front. Later, these were changed for Dowty Oleomatics and, in either case, carried a 19 in. wheel, while at the rear the size was 18 in.

The appearance was, inevitably, pre-war, with a well valanced front mudguard, saddle, small oil tank and a three-gallon fuel tank. The last was finished in the traditional Zenith style of chrome and black with a red panel on each side.

The machine did not come on to the market until 1947, and production ended in 1950 after, it is said, some 250 examples had been built. Very few were ever seen, so most may have been exported, although one or two did survive at home.

**The 1947 Zenith 750 with JAP side-valve engine in pre-war-style cycle parts and mainly for export**

# Model charts

These supplement the text to show how the model ranges varied through the years. Thus, each list gives the range for each year, and this includes models introduced during the year. Normally, the model year ran from October of the previous calender year, but in the 1960s this practice was to fall by the wayside.

The charts show the models and their capacity and engine type. The capacity is calculated from the bore and stroke, which is also given for many makes. Where a Villiers engine was used, its type number is given instead, and for some mopeds, just the name of the engine manufacturer is shown. The model number, or name, is given under each year it was produced, with abbreviations where necessary. These are listed under each make.

The charts are arranged to run from the smallest to largest model by capacity groups; thus, sequences of a particular size of machine can be traced through the years. Singles are dealt with first, followed by twins, and then, in Ariel's case, the four. Reference to the main text should help clarify any doubtful points.

## ABERDALE

| | Engine | 47 | 48 | 49 |
|---|---|---|---|---|
| 98 ts Au-Autocycle | JDL | Au | Au | Au |

## ABJ

| | Engine | 49 | 50 | 51 | 52 | 53 |
|---|---|---|---|---|---|---|
| 49.9 ts | 42 × 36 | | | | A M | A M |
| 99 ts | 2F | Au | Au | Au | Au | |
| 99 ts | 1F | M/C | M/C | M/C | M/C | |

A M – Auto Minor    M/C – Motor Cycle
Au – Autocycle

## AJW

| | Engine | 49 | 50 | 51 | 52 | 53 | 54 | 55 | 56 | 57 |
|---|---|---|---|---|---|---|---|---|---|---|
| 125 ts | JAP | | | | | FC | | | | |
| 494 sv tw | JAP | GF | GF | | | | | | | |
| 498 ohv | JAP | SF | SF | SF | SF | SF | ·SF | SF | SF | SF |
| 500 ohv | JAP | | | | | FF | | | | |

| | Engine | 58 | 59 | 60 |
|---|---|---|---|---|
| 48 ts | FBM | FC | FC | FC |

FC – Fox Cub    GF – Grey Fox
FF – Flying Fox    SF – Speed Fox

215

## AMBASSADOR

| | Engine | 47 | 48 | 49 | 50 | 51 | 52 | 53 | 54 | 55 |
|---|---|---|---|---|---|---|---|---|---|---|
| 197 ts | 5E | I | II | | | | | | | |
| 197 ts | 6E | | | III | III | Cou | | | | |
| 197 ts | 6E | | | | Pop | Pop | Pop | Pop | | |
| 197 ts | 6E | | | | V | Emb | Emb | Emb | | |
| 197 ts | 6E | | | | | Sup | Sup | Sup | | |
| 197 ts | 6E | | | | | | | S/C | | |
| 197 ts | 6E | | | | | | | SS | | |
| 197 ts | 8E | | | | | | | Pop | Pop | Pop |
| 197 ts | 8E | | | | | | | Emb | Emb | Emb |
| 197 ts | 8E | | | | | | | Sup | | |
| 197 ts | 8E | | | | | | | S/C | S/C | S/C |
| 197 ts | 8E | | | | | | | SS | SS | SS |

| | Engine | 54 | 55 | 56 | 57 | 58 | 59 | 60 |
|---|---|---|---|---|---|---|---|---|
| 147 ts | 30C | | | Pop | | | | |
| 148 ts | 31C | | | | Pop | Pop | | |
| 174 ts | 2L | | | | | Stat | | |
| 174 ts | 2L | | | | | | Pop | Pop |
| 197 ts | 8E | | En | En | | | | |
| 197 ts | 9E | | | En | En | En | En | |
| 197 ts | 9E | | | | | | Star | Star |
| 224 ts | 1H | Sup | Sup | Sup | | | | |
| 246 ts | 2H | | | | Sup | Sup | | |
| 249 ts tw | 2T | | | | Sup | Sup | | |
| 249 ts tw | 2T | | | | | | Super | Super |

Cou – Courier    SS – self starter
Emb – Embassy    Star – 3 Star Special
En – Envoy    Stat – Statesman
Pop – Popular    Sup – Supreme
S/C – sidecar    Super – Super S

## AMC – AJS

| | b × s | 45 | 46 | 47 | 48 | 49 | 50 | 51 | 52 |
|---|---|---|---|---|---|---|---|---|---|---|
| 348 ohv | 69 × 93 | 16M | 16M | 16M | 16M | 16M | 16M | 16M | 16M |
| 348 ohv | 69 × 93 | | 16MC | 16MC | 16MC | 16MC | 16MC | 16MC | 16MC |
| 348 ohv | 69 × 93 | | | | | 16MS | 16MS | 16MS | 16MS |
| 348 ohv | 69 × 93 | | | | | | | 16MCS | 16MCS |
| 348 ohc | 74 × 81 | | | | 7R | 7R | 7R | 7R | 7R |
| 497 ohv | 82.5 × 93 | 18 | 18 | 18 | 18 | 18 | 18 | 18 | 18 |
| 497 ohv | 82.5 × 93 | | 18C | 18C | 18C | 18C | 18C | 18C | 18C |
| 497 ohv | 82.5 × 93 | | | | | 18S | 18S | 18S | 18S |
| 497 ohv | 82.5 × 93 | | | | | | | 18CS | 18CS |
| 498 ohv tw | 66 × 72.8 | | | | | 20 | 20 | 20 | 20 |

| | b × s | 53 | 54 | 55 | 56 | 57 | 58 | 59 | 60 |
|---|---|---|---|---|---|---|---|---|---|
| 248 ohv | 70 × 65 | | | | | | 14 | 14 | 14 |
| 248 ohv | 70 × 65 | | | | | | | 14CS | 14CS |
| 348 ohv | 69 × 93 | 16M | 16M | 16M | | | | | |
| 348 ohv | 69 × 93 | 16MC | 16MC | 16MC | 16MC | 16MC | 16MC | 16C | 16C |
| 348 ohv | 69 × 93 | 16MS | 16MS | 16MS | 16MS | 16MS | 16MS | 16 | 16 |
| 348 ohv | 69 × 93 | 16MCS | 16MCS | 16MCS | | | | | |
| 348 ohv | 72 × 85.5 | | | | 16MCS | 16MCS | 16MCS | 16CS | |
| 348 ohc | 74 × 81 | 7R | 7R | 7R | | | | | |
| 349 ohc | 75.5 × 78 | | | | 7R | 7R | 7R | 7R | 7R |
| 497 ohv | 82.5 × 93 | 18 | 18 | 18 | | | | | |
| 497 ohv | 82.5 × 93 | 18C | 18C | 18C | | | | | |
| 497 ohv | 82.5 × 93 | 18S | 18S | 18S | 18S | 18S | 18S | 18 | 18 |
| 497 ohv | 82.5 × 93 | 18CS | 18CS | 18CS | | | | | |
| 497 ohv | 86 × 85.5 | | | | 18CS | 18CS | 18CS | 18CS | 18CS |
| 498 ohv tw | 66 × 72.8 | 20 | 20 | 20 | 20 | 20 | 20 | 20dl | |
| 498 ohv tw | 66 × 72.8 | | | | | | | 20std | 20std |
| 498 ohv tw | 66 × 72.8 | | | | | | | 20CS | |
| 498 ohv tw | 66 × 72.8 | | | | | | | 20CSR | |
| 593 ohv tw | 72 × 72.8 | | | | 30 | 30 | 30 | | |
| 593 ohv tw | 72 × 72.8 | | | | | | 30CS | | |
| 593 ohv tw | 72 × 72.8 | | | | | | 30CSR | | |
| 646 ohv tw | 72 × 79.3 | | | | | | | 31 | 31 |
| 646 ohv tw | 72 × 79.3 | | | | | | | 31dl | 31dl |
| 646 ohv tw | 72 × 79.3 | | | | | | | 31CS | 31CS |
| 646 ohv tw | 72 × 79.3 | | | | | | | 31CSR | 31CSR |

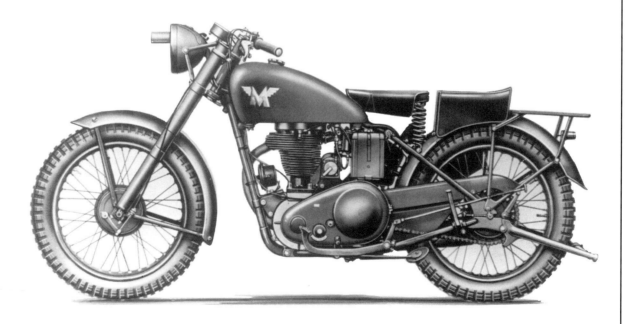

The wartime Matchless G3L, on which the post-war range was based and which was sold off with many others to provide early post-war transport

## AMC – Matchless

| | b × s | 45 | 46 | 47 | 48 | 49 | 50 | 51 | 52 |
|---|---|---|---|---|---|---|---|---|---|
| 348 ohv | 69 × 93 | G3L | G3L | G3L | G3L | G3L | G3L | G3L | G3L |
| 348 ohv | 69 × 93 | | G3LC | G3LC | G3LC | G3LC | G3LC | G3LC | G3LC |
| 348 ohv | 69 × 93 | | | | | G3LS | G3LS | G3LS | G3LS |
| 348 ohv | 69 × 93 | | | | | | | G3LCS | G3LCS |
| 497 ohv | 82.5 × 93 | G80 | G80 | G80 | G80 | G80 | G80 | G80 | G80 |
| 497 ohv | 82.5 × 93 | | G80C | G80C | G80C | G80C | G80C | G80C | G80C |
| 497 ohv | 82.5 × 93 | | | | | G80S | G80S | G80S | G80S |
| 497 ohv | 82.5 × 93 | | | | | | | G80CS | G80CS |
| 498 ohv tw | 66 × 72.8 | | | | | G9 | G9 | G9 | G9 |

| | b × s | 53 | 54 | 55 | 56 | 57 | 58 | 59 | 60 |
|---|---|---|---|---|---|---|---|---|---|
| 248 ohv | 70 × 65 | | | | | | G2 | G2 | G2 |
| 248 ohv | 70 × 65 | | | | | | | G2CS | G2CS |
| 348 ohv | 69 × 93 | G3L | G3L | G3L | | | | | |
| 348 ohv | 69 × 93 | G3LC | G3LC | G3LC | G3LC | G3LC | G3LC | G3C | G3C |
| 348 ohv | 69 × 93 | G3LS | G3LS | G3LS | G3LS | G3LS | G3LS | G3 | G3 |
| 348 ohv | 69 × 93 | G3LCS | G3LCS | G3LCS | | | | | |
| 348 ohv | 72 × 85.5 | | | | G3LCS | G3LCS | G3LCS | G3CS | |
| 496 ohc | 90 × 78 | | | | | | G50 | G50 | G50 |
| 497 ohv | 82.5 × 93 | G80 | G80 | G80 | | | | | |
| 497 ohv | 82.5 × 93 | G80C | G80C | G80C | | | | | |
| 497 ohv | 82.5 × 93 | G80S | G80S | G80S | G80S | G80S | G80S | G80 | G80 |
| 497 ohv | 82.5 × 93 | G80CS | G80CS | G80CS | | | | | |
| 497 ohv | 86 × 85.5 | | | | G80CS | G80CS | G80CS | G80CS | G80CS |
| 498 ohv tw | 66 × 72.8 | G45 | G45 | G45 | G45 | G45 | | | |
| 498 ohv tw | 66 × 72.8 | G9 | G9 | G9 | G9 | G9 | G9 | G9dl | |
| 498 ohv tw | 66 × 72.8 | | | | | | | G9std | G9std |
| 498 ohv tw | 66 × 72.8 | | | | | | | G9CS | |
| 498 ohv tw | 66 × 72.8 | | | | | | | G9CSR | |
| 593 ohv tw | 72 × 72.8 | | | | G11 | G11 | G11 | | |
| 593 ohv tw | 72 × 72.8 | | | | | | G11CS | | |
| 593 ohv tw | 72 × 72.8 | | | | | | G11CSR | | |
| 646 ohv tw | 72 × 79.3 | | | | | | | G12 | G12 |
| 646 ohv tw | 72 × 79.3 | | | | | | | G12dl | G12dl |
| 646 ohv tw | 72 × 79.3 | | | | | | | G12CS | G12CS |
| 646 ohv tw | 72 × 79.3 | | | | | | | G12CSR | G12CSR |

## ARIEL

| b × s | | 45 | 46 | 47 | 48 | 49 | 50 | 51 | 52 |
|---|---|---|---|---|---|---|---|---|---|
| 346 ohv | 72 × 85 | NG | NG | NG | NG | NG | NG | | |
| 346 ohv | 72 × 85 | NH | NH | NH | NH | NH | NH | NH | NH |
| 499 ohv | 81.8 × 95 | VG | VG | VG | VG | VG | VG | | |
| 499 ohv | 81.8 × 95 | VH | VH | VH | VH | VH | VH | VH | VH |
| 499 ohv | 81.8 × 95 | | | | | | | | VHA |
| 499 ohv | 81.8 × 95 | | | | | | VCH | VCH | VCH |
| 598 sv | 86.4 × 102 | VB | VB | VB | VB | VB | VB | VB | VB |
| 499 ohv tw | 63 × 80 | | | | KG | KG | KG | KG | |
| 499 ohv tw | 63 × 80 | | | | KH | KH | KH | KH | KH |
| 995 ohv 4 | 65 × 75 | 4G | 4G | 4G | 4G | 4G | 4G | 4G | 4G |

| b × s | | 53 | 54 | 55 | 56 | 57 | 58 | 59 | 60 |
|---|---|---|---|---|---|---|---|---|---|
| 198 ohv | 60 × 70 | | LH | LH | LH | LH | LH | LH | |
| 346 ohv | 72 × 85 | NH | NH | NH | NH | NH | NH | NH | |
| 346 ohv | 72 × 85 | | | | | HT3 | HT3 | HT3 | |
| 499 ohv | 81.8 × 95 | VH | VH | VH | VH | VH | VH | VH | |
| 499 ohv | 81.8 × 95 | VHA | | | | | | | |
| 499 ohv | 81.8 × 95 | VCH | | | | | | | |
| 499 ohv | 81.8 × 95 | | HT | HT | HT5 | HT5 | HT5 | HT5 | |
| 499 ohv | 81.8 × 95 | | HS | HS | HS | HS | HS | HS | |
| 598 sv | 86.4 × 102 | VB | VB | VB | VB | VB | VB | | |
| 247 ts tw | 54 × 54 | | | | | | Le | Le | Le |
| 247 ts tw | 54 × 54 | | | | | | | | Ar |
| 499 ohv tw | 63 × 80 | KH | KH | KH | KH | KH | | | |
| 499 ohv tw | 63 × 80 | KHA | | | | | | | |
| 647 ohv tw | 70 × 84 | | FH | FH | FH | FH | FH | FH | FH |
| 995 ohv 4 | 65 × 75 | 4G | | | | | | | |
| 995 ohv 4 | 65 × 75 | 4GII | 4GII | 4GII | 4GII | 4GII | 4GII | 4GII | |

Ar – Arrow    Le – Leader

## BAC

| | Engine | 51 | 52 | 53 |
|---|---|---|---|---|
| 99 ts | 1F | Li | Li | |
| 99 ts | 1F | | | Ga |
| 122 ts | 10D | | Ga | Ga |
| 125 ts | JAP | Li | | |

Ga – Gazelle
Li – Lilliput

## BANTAMOTO

| | b × s | 51 | 52 |
|---|---|---|---|
| 38.5 ts | 38 × 34 | Ba | Ba |

## BOND

| | Engine | 50 | 51 | 52 | 53 |
|---|---|---|---|---|---|
| 99 ts | 1F | Mi | Mi | Mi | |
| 125 ts | JAP | | Mi | Mi | Mi |

| | Engine | 58 | 59 | 60 |
|---|---|---|---|---|
| 148 ts | 31C | P1 | P1 | P3 |
| 197 ts | 9E | P2 | P2 | P4 |

Mi – Minibyke

## BOWN

| | Engine | 50 | 51 | 52 | 53 | 54 | 55 | 56 | 57 |
|---|---|---|---|---|---|---|---|---|---|
| 47.6 ts | Sachs | | | | | | | 50 | 50 |
| 99 ts | 2F | AR | AR | AR | AR | AR | | | |
| 99 ts | 1F | | MC | MC | MC | MC | | | |
| 122 ts | 10D | | | TT | TT | TT | | | |

AR – Auto Roadster    TT – Tourist Trophy    MC – motor cycle    50 – Bown 50 moped

## BRITAX

| | b × s | 49 | 50 | 51 | 52 | 53 | 54 | 55 | 56 |
|---|---|---|---|---|---|---|---|---|---|
| 48 ohv | 39 × 40 | En | En | En | En | | | | |
| 48 ohv | 39 × 40 | | | | | Br | Br | Br | |
| 48 ohv | 39 × 40 | | | | | | | Sc | Sc |
| 48 ohv | 39 × 40 | | | | | | | Hu | Hu |

Br – Britax    Hu – Hurricane    En – engine unit    Sc – Scooterette

## BSA

| | b × s | 45 | 46 | 47 | 48 | 49 | 50 | 51 | 52 |
|---|---|---|---|---|---|---|---|---|---|
| 123 ts | 52 × 58 | | | | D1 | D1 | D1 | D1 | D1 |
| 123 ts | 52 × 58 | | | | | | D1cp | D1cp | D1cp |
| 249 sv | 63 × 80 | C10 | C10 | C10 | C10 | C10 | C10 | C10 | C10 |
| 249 ohv | 63 × 80 | C11 | C11 | C11 | C11 | C11 | C11 | C11 | C11 |
| 348 ohv | 71 × 88 | B31 | B31 | B31 | B31 | B31 | B31 | B31 | B31 |
| 348 ohv | 71 × 88 | | B32 | B32 | B32 | B32 | B32 | B32 | B32 |
| 348 ohv | 71 × 88 | | | | | B32GS | B32GS | B32GS | B32GS |
| 496 sv | 82 × 94 | M20 | M20 | M20 | M20 | M20 | M20 | M20 | M20 |
| 499 ohv | 85 × 88 | | | B33 | B33 | B33 | B33 | B33 | B33 |
| 499 ohv | 85 × 88 | | | B34 | B34 | B34 | B34 | B34 | B34 |
| 499 ohv | 85 × 88 | | | | | B34GS | B34GS | B34GS | B34GS |
| 499 ohv | 85 × 88 | | | | M33 | M33 | M33 | M33 | M33 |
| 591 sv | 82 × 112 | | M21 | M21 | M21 | M21 | M21 | M21 | M21 |
| 495 ohv tw | 62 × 82 | | | A7 | A7 | A7 | A7 | | |
| 495 ohv tw | 62 × 82 | | | | | A7ST | A7ST | | |
| 497 ohv tw | 66 × 72.6 | | | | | | | A7 | A7 |
| 497 ohv tw | 66 × 72.6 | | | | | | | A7ST | A7ST |
| 646 ohv tw | 70 × 84 | | | | | | A10 | A10 | A10 |

# BSA

| | b × s | 53 | 54 | 55 | 56 | 57 | 58 | 59 | 60 |
|---|---|---|---|---|---|---|---|---|---|
| 34.6 ts | 36 × 34 | WW | WW | WW | | | | | |
| 70 ts | 45 × 44 | | | | | Dandy | Dandy | Dandy | Dandy |
| 123 ts | 52 × 58 | D1 | D1 | D1 | D1 | D1 | D1 | D1 | D1 |
| 123 ts | 52 × 58 | D1cp | D1cp | D1cp | | | | | |
| 148 ts | 57 × 58 | | D3 | D3 | D3 | D3 | | | |
| 172 ts | 61.5 × 58 | | | | | | D5 | D7 | D7 |
| 249 sv | 63 × 80 | C10 | C10L | C10L | C10L | C10L | | | |
| 249 ohv | 63 × 80 | C11 | C11G | C11G | C12 | C12 | C12 | | |
| 247 ohv | 67 × 70 | | | | | | C15 | C15 | C15 |
| 247 ohv | 67 × 70 | | | | | | | C15S | C15S |
| 247 ohv | 67 × 70 | | | | | | | C15T | C15T |
| 348 ohv | 71 × 88 | B31 | B31 | B31 | B31 | B31 | B31 | B31 | |
| 348 ohv | 71 × 88 | B32 | B32 | B32 | B32 | B32 | | | |
| 348 ohv | 71 × 88 | B32GS | B32GS | B32GS | B32GS | B32GS | | B32GS | B32GS |
| 496 sv | 82 × 94 | M20 | M20 | M20 | | | | | |
| 499 ohv | 85 × 88 | B33 | B33 | B33 | B33 | B33 | B33 | B33 | B33 |
| 499 ohv | 85 × 88 | B34 | B34 | B34 | B34 | B34 | | | |
| 499 ohv | 85 × 88 | B34GS | B34GS | B34GS | B34GS | B34GS | B34GS | B34GS | B34GS |
| 499 ohv | 85 × 88 | M33 | M33 | M33 | M33 | M33 | | | |
| 591 sv | 82 × 112 | M21 | M21 | M21 | M21 | M21 | M21 | M21 | M21 |
| 497 ohv tw | 66 × 72.6 | A7 | A7 | A7 | A7 | A7 | A7 | A7 | A7 |
| 497 ohv tw | 66 × 72.6 | A7ST | A7ST | | | | | | |
| 497 ohv tw | 66 × 72.6 | | A7SS | A7SS | A7SS | A7SS | A7SS | A7SS | A7SS |
| 646 ohv tw | 70 × 84 | A10 | A10 | A10 | A10 | A10 | A10 | A10 | A10 |
| 646 ohv tw | 70 × 84 | A10SF | A10SF | | | | | | |
| 646 ohv tw | 70 × 84 | | A10RR | A10RR | A10RR | A10RR | A10SR | A10SR | A10SR |
| 646 ohv tw | 70 × 84 | | | | | | A10Sp | A10Sp | A10Sp |

D1cp – D1 competition    Sp – Spitfire    St – Star Twin
RR – Road Rocket    SR – Super Rocket    WW – Winged Wheel
SF – Super Flash    SS – Shooting Star

**Another route was the scooterette, but the BSA Dandy was not to be the best example**

## COMMANDER

|         | Engine | 53  |
|---------|--------|-----|
| 99 ts   | 2F     | I   |
| 99 ts   | 1F     | II  |
| 122 ts  | 10D    | III |

## CORGI

|        | b × s    | 48 | 49 | 50 | 51 | 52 | 53 | 54 |
|--------|----------|----|----|----|----|----|----|----|
| 98 ts  | 50 × 50  | I  |    |    |    |    |    |    |
| 98 ts  | 50 × 50  | II | II | II | II | II |    |    |
| 98 ts  | 50 × 50  |    |    |    |    | IV | IV | IV |

## COTTON

|            | Engine | 54 | 55  | 56  | 57  | 58  | 59  | 60  |
|------------|--------|----|-----|-----|-----|-----|-----|-----|
| 197 ts     | 8E     | Vu | Vu  | Vu  |     |     |     |     |
| 197 ts     | 9E     |    | Vu  | Vu  | Vu  | Vu  | Vu  | Vu  |
| 197 ts     | 9E     |    |     | Tr  | Tr  | Tr  | Tr  | Tr  |
| 246 ts     | 33A    |    |     |     |     |     |     | Sc  |
| 242 ts tw  | Anz    |    | Cot | Cot | Cot | Cot | Cot |     |
| 249 ts tw  | 2T     |    |     |     | VT  | VT  | He  | He  |
| 249 ts tw  | 2T     |    |     |     |     |     |     | DG  |
| 322 ts tw  | Anz    |    |     | Cot | Cot | Cot | Cot |     |
| 324 ts tw  | 3T     |    |     |     |     |     | Mes | Mes |

Cot – Cotanza    He – Herald    Sc – Scrambler    VT – Villiers Twin
DG – Double Gloucester    Mes – Messenger    Tr – Trials    Vu – Vulcan

## CYC-AUTO

|        | b × s    | 46 | 47 | 48 | 49 | 50 | 51 | 52 |
|--------|----------|----|----|----|----|----|----|----|
| 98 ts  | 50 × 50  | Au | Au | Au | Au | Su | Su | Su |
| 98 ts  | 50 × 50  |    |    |    | Ca | Ca | Ca | Ca |

|        | b × s    | 53 | 54 | 55 | 56 | 57 | 58 |
|--------|----------|----|----|----|----|----|----|
| 98 ts  | 50 × 50  | Su | Su | Su | Su | Su | Su |
| 98 ts  | 50 × 50  | Ca | Ca | Ca | Ca | Ca | Ca |

Au – Autocycle    Su – Superior
Ca – Carrier

## CYCLAID

|        | b × s    | 50 | 51 | 52 | 53 | 54 | 55 |
|--------|----------|----|----|----|----|----|----|
| 31 ts  | 35 × 32  | Cy | Cy | Cy | Cy | Cy | Cy |

## CYCLEMASTER

| | b × s | 50 | 51 | 52 | 53 | 54 | 55 |
|---|---|---|---|---|---|---|---|
| 25.7 ts | 32 × 32 | Cy | Cy | | | | |
| 32.6 ts | 36 × 32 | | | Cy | Cy | Cy | Cy |
| 32.6 ts | 36 × 32 | | | Me | Me | Me | Cym |
| 32.6 ts | 36 × 32 | | | | Pi | Pi | |
| 32.6 ts | 36 × 32 | | | | Ro | Ro | |

| | b × s | 56 | 57 | 58 | 59 | 60 |
|---|---|---|---|---|---|---|
| 32.6 ts | 36 × 32 | Cy | Cy | Cy | | |
| 32.6 ts | 36 × 32 | Cym | Cym | Cym | Cym | Cym |
| 124 ts | 51 × 61 | Pia | Pia | Pia | | |

Cy – Cyclemaster     Pi – Pillion     Pia – Piatti
Cym – Cyclemate      Me – Mercury     Ro – Roundsman

## CYMOTA

| | b × s | 50 | 51 |
|---|---|---|---|
| 45 ts | 38 × 40 | Cy | Cy |

Cy – Cymota

## DAYTON

| | Engine | 55 | 56 | 57 | 58 | 59 | 60 |
|---|---|---|---|---|---|---|---|
| 174 ts | 2L | | | | | AF | AF |
| 224 ts | 1H | Al | Al | Al | Al | | |
| 246 ts | 2H | | | | AS | | |
| 246 ts | 2H | | | | ACS | ACS | ACS |
| 249 ts tw | 2T | | | AT | AT | | |
| 249 ts tw | 2T | | | | AC | AC | AC |
| 249 ts tw | 2T | | | | AE | AE | |

AC – Albatross Continental           Al – Albatross
ACS – Albatross Continental Single   AS – Albatross Single
AE – Albatross Empire                AT – Albatross Twin
AF – Albatross Flamenco

## DKR

| | Engine | 57 | 58 | 59 | 60 |
|---|---|---|---|---|---|
| 147 ts | 30C | Dove | Dove | Dove | |
| 148 ts | 31C | | Peg | Peg | Peg |
| 148 ts | 31C | | | | Dove II |
| 174 ts | 2L | | | | Peg II |
| 197 ts | 9E | | Def | Def | Def |
| 249 ts tw | 2T | | | Manx | Manx |

Def – Defiant     Peg – Pegasus

## DMW

| | Engine | 50 | 51 | 52 | 53 | 54 | 55 | 56 | 57 |
|---|---|---|---|---|---|---|---|---|---|
| 99 ts | 1F | 100 | 100 | | | | | | |
| 99 ts | 4F | | | | | | | | Bambi |
| 122 ts | 10D | 125 | 125 | 125 | 125 | | | | |
| 125 ohv | AMC | | | | 125 | | | | |
| 125 dohc | AMC | | | | | Hor | Hor | | |
| 147 ts | 29C | | | | | | Leda | Leda | |
| 148 ts | 31C | | | | | | | | 150P |
| 170 ohv | AMC | | | | 175 | 175 | 175 | | |
| 170 ohv | AMC | | | | | MX | | | |
| 174 ts | 2L | | | | | | | | 175P |
| 197 ts | 6E | 200 | 200 | 200 | 200 | | | | |
| 197 ts | 6E | | | Comp | Comp | | | | |
| 197 ts | 8E | | | | | 200 | 200 | 200 | 200 |
| 197 ts | 7E | | | | | Comp | Comp | Comp | . |
| 197 ts | 9E | | | | | | | VI | VI |
| 197 ts | 7E | | | | | | | VII | VII |
| 197 ts | 8E | | | | | | | | VIII |
| 197 ts | 9E | | | | | | | IX | IX |
| 224 ts | 1H | | | | | Cor | Cor | Cor | Cor |
| 249 ohc | AMC | | | | | Dol | Dol | | |
| 249 ts tw | 2T | | | | | | | | Dol |

| | Engine | 57 | 58 | 59 | 60 |
|---|---|---|---|---|---|
| 99 ts | 4F | Bambi | Bambi | Bambi | Bambi |
| 197 ts | 8E | VIII | VIII | | |
| 197 ts | 9E | IX | IX | IX | IX |
| 197 ts | 9E | | | | Mk 12 |
| 246 ts | 32A | | | Mk 12 | Mk 12 |
| 246 ts | 33A | | | Mk 12 | Mk 12 |
| 249 ts tw | 2T | Dol | Dol | Dol | Dol |
| 249 ts tw | 2T | | Mk X | Mk X | Mk X |
| 324 ts tw | 3T | | | Dol | Dol |

Cor – Cortina     Hor – Hornet
Dol – Dolomite     MX – Moto Cross

## DOT

| | Engine | 49 | 50 | 51 | 52 | 53 | 54 |
|---|---|---|---|---|---|---|---|
| 197 ts | 6E | 200 | DS | DST | DST | D | |
| 197 ts | 6E | | RS | RST | RST | R | |
| 197 ts | 6E | | | S | S | S | |
| 197 ts | 6E | | | | SC | SC | |
| 197 ts | 6E | | | | SD | SD | |
| 197 ts | 6E | | | | T | T | T |
| 197 ts | 6E | | | | TD | TD | TD |
| 197 ts | 6E | | | | | DH | |
| 197 ts | 6E | | | | | RH | |

# DOT

| 197 and 246 ts | Engine | 53 | 54 | 55 | 56 | 57 | 58 | 59 | 60 |
|---|---|---|---|---|---|---|---|---|---|
| 197 and 246 ts | | SH | SH | SH | SH | SH | SH | SH | SH |
| 197 and 246 ts | | SCH | SCH | SCH | SCH | SCH | SCH | SCH | SCH |
| 197 and 246 ts | | SDH | SDH | | SDH | SDH | SDH | SDH | SDH |
| 197 and 246 ts | | TH | | TH | | | | | |
| 197 and 246 ts | | THX | THX | THX | THX | THX | THX | THX | THX |
| 197 and 246 ts | | TDH | | TDH | | | | | |
| 197 and 246 ts | | TDHX | TDHX | TDHX | TDHX | TDHX | TDHX | TDHX | TDHX |
| 197 and 246 ts | | | | | | WR | WR | WR | WR |

Note that the above models were all fitted with 6E engines up to 1953, with 8E for 1954–6 and 9E from 1957. From 1959 they were also available with 246 cc engines, the 31A being fitted for motocross, and the 32A for trials.

| | Engine | 51 | 52 | 53 |
|---|---|---|---|---|
| 248 sv | Bro | 250 | 250 | 250 |

| | Engine | 56 | 57 | 58 | 59 | 60 |
|---|---|---|---|---|---|---|
| 48 ts | Vivi | | Mo | Mo | Mo | Mo |
| 48 ts | Vivi | | Ra | Ra | Ra | Ra |
| 48 ts | Vivi | | Sc | Sc | Sc | Sc |
| 48 ts | Vivi | | | | | Gu |
| 197 ts | 9E | Man | Man | Man | | |
| 249 ts tw | 2T | | | | SCH | |
| 349 ts tw | RCA | | | | SCH | SCH |
| 349 ts tw | RCA | | | | SR | SR |

Bro – Brockhouse    Ra – racer    Man – Mancunian    SR – Sportsmans Roadster
Gu – Guazzoni    Sc – scooterette    Mo – moped

# DOUGLAS

| | b × s | 47 | 48 | 49 | 50 | 51 |
|---|---|---|---|---|---|---|
| 348 ohv tw | 60.8 × 60 | T35 | III | III | | |
| 348 ohv tw | 60.8 × 60 | | Sp | Sp | Comp | Comp |
| 348 ohv tw | 60.8 × 60 | | | IV | | |
| 348 ohv tw | 60.8 × 60 | | | IV Sp | | |

# DOUGLAS

| | b × s | 50 | 51 | 52 | 53 | 54 | 55 | 56 | 57 |
|---|---|---|---|---|---|---|---|---|---|
| 125 ts | 56.5 × 49 | | | 2L2 | 2L2 | 2L2 | G | | |
| 124 ts | 54 × 54 | | | | | | GL2 | | |
| 124 ts | 54 × 54 | | | | | | 42L2 | 42L2 | Std |
| 124 ts | 54 × 54 | | | | | | | | Magna |
| 124 ts | 54 × 54 | | | | | | | | Ultra |
| 145 ts | 57 × 57 | | | | | | GS | GS | GS |
| 348 ohv tw | 60.8 × 60 | 80 | 80 | 80 | 80 | | | | |
| 348 ohv tw | 60.8 × 60 | 90 | 90 | 90 | 90 | 90 | | | |
| 348 ohv tw | 60.8 × 60 | | V | V | V | V | DF | DF | DF |

Comp – Competition    Sp - Sports
DF – Dragonfly    Std – Standard

## DUNKLEY

| | b × s | 57 | 58 | 59 |
|---|---|---|---|---|
| 49.6 ohv | 39 × 41.5 | | Pop | Pop |
| 61 ohv | 44 × 40 | Whi | Whi | Whi |
| 64 ohv | 44 × 42 | SS | SS | |
| 64 ohv | 44 × 42 | | WS | WS |
| 64 ohv | 44 × 42 | | Sc | Sc |
| 64 ohv | 44 × 42 | | PM | |

PM – Popular Major scooter    Sc – S65 scooter    Whi – Whippet scooterette
Pop – Popular scooter    SS – Super Sports 65    WS – Whippet Sports

## EMC

| | Engine | 47 | 48 | 49 | 50 | 51 | 52 | 53 |
|---|---|---|---|---|---|---|---|---|
| 125 ts | JAP | | | | | | 125 | 125 |
| 125 ts | Puch | | | | | racer | racer | racer |
| 345 ts split single | | 350 | 350 | 350 | 350 | 350 | 350 | 350 |

## EXCELSIOR

| | Engine | 46 | 47 | 48 | 49 | 50 | 51 | 52 |
|---|---|---|---|---|---|---|---|---|
| 98 ts | JDL | Au | V1 | V1 | V1 | | | |
| 98 ts | Goblin | | G2 | G2 | G2 | G2 | G2 | G2 |
| 98 ts | Spryt | | S1 | S1 | S1 | S1 | S1 | S1 |
| 98 ts | Goblin | | | | M1 | | | |
| 122 ts | 9D | 0 | 0 | 0 | | | | |
| 122 ts | 10D | | | | U1/U2 | U1/U2 | U1/U2 | U1/U2 |
| 123 ts | Goblin | | | | M2 | | | |
| 197 ts | 6E | | | | R1/R2 | R1/R2 | R1/R2 | R1/R2 |
| 243 ts tw | Tal | | | | | TT1 | TT1 | TT1 |
| 243 ts tw | Tal | | | | | | | STT1 |

| | Engine | 53 | 54 | 55 | 56 | 57 | 58 | 59 | 60 |
|---|---|---|---|---|---|---|---|---|---|
| 98 ts | Goblin | G2 | G2 | G2 | G2 | | | | |
| 98 ts | Spryt | S1 | S1 | S1 | S1 | | | | |
| 99 ts | 4F | F4 | F4 | F4 | F4 | | | | |
| 99 ts | 4F | | | F4S | F4S | | | | |
| 99 ts | 6F | | | | F4 | F4 | | F4F | F10 |
| 99 ts | 6F | | | | F4S | F6S | CA8 | CA9 | C10 |
| 99 ts | 6F | | | | | SB1 | SB1 | SB1 | |
| 122 ts | 13D | | D12 | | | | | | |
| 147 ts | Excel | C2 | C1/C2 | C3 | C3/C4 | C4 | | | |
| 147 ts | Excel | | | | | | | KS | MK1 |
| 147 ts | Excel | | | | | | | EL | ME1 |
| 147 ts | 30C | | | | C1 | | U8 | U9 | |
| 148 ts | 31C | | | | | | | | U10 |
| 197 ts | 6E | R1/R2 | | | | | | | |
| 197 ts | 8E | | R1/R2 | | | | | | |
| 197 ts | 8E | | R3/R4 | R4 | | | | | |
| 197 ts | 8E | | | R5/R6 | R6 | | | | |

# EXCELSIOR

| | Engine | 53 | 54 | 55 | 56 | 57 | 58 | 59 | 60 |
|---|---|---|---|---|---|---|---|---|---|
| 197 ts | 9E | | | | A9 | | | | R10 |
| 243 ts tw | Tal | TT1 | TT1 | TT3 | | | | | |
| 243 ts tw | Tal | STT1 | STT1 | | SESTT2 | | | | |
| 243 ts tw | Tal | | TT2 | TT2 | TT3 | TT3 | TT4 | TT4 | TT6 |
| 243 ts tw | Tal | | STT2 | STT2 | STT4 | STT5 | STT6 | | |
| 328 ts tw | Tal | | | | | | S8 | S8 | |
| 328 ts tw | Tal | | | | | | | S9 | S9 |

Au – Autobyk          Excel – Excelsior          Tal – Talisman

# FLM

| | Engine | 51 | 52 | 53 |
|---|---|---|---|---|
| 125 ts | JAP | Gl | Gl | Gl |

Gl – Glideride

# FRANCIS-BARNETT

| | Engine | 46 | 47 | 48 | 49 | 50 | 51 | 52 | 53 |
|---|---|---|---|---|---|---|---|---|---|
| 98 ts | JDL | 50 | 50 | 50 | 50 | | | | |
| 99 ts | 2F | | | | 56 | 56 | 56 | | |
| 122 ts | 9D | 51 | 51 | 51 | | | | | |
| 122 ts | 10D | | | | 52 | 52 | 52 | 52 | 52 |
| 122 ts | 10D | | | | 53 | 53 | 53 | 53 | 53 |
| 122 ts | 10D | | | | | | | 57 | 57 |
| 122 ts | 10D | | | | | | | 59 | 61 |
| 122 ts | 10D | | | | | | | | 63 |
| 197 ts | 6E | | | | 54 | 54 | 54 | 54 | |
| 197 ts | 8E | | | | | | | | 54 |
| 197 ts | 6E | | | | 55 | 55 | 55 | 55 | |
| 197 ts | 8E | | | | | | | | 55 |
| 197 ts | 6E | | | | | | | 58 | |
| 197 ts | 6E | | | | | | | 60 | |

| | Engine | 53 | 54 | 55 | 56 | 57 | 58 | 59 | 60 |
|---|---|---|---|---|---|---|---|---|---|
| 122 ts | 13D | | 66 | | | | | | |
| 147 ts | 30C | | | 69 | 73 | 78 | 78 | 78 | |
| 149 ts | AMC | | | | | | | | 86 |
| 171 ts | AMC | | | | | | 79 | 79 | 79 |
| 197 ts | 8E | 58 | 67 | 70 | 74 | 74 | | | |
| 197 ts | 7E | 62 | 62 | 62 | 76 | 76 | | | |
| 197 ts | 7E | 64 | 64 | 72 | 77 | 77 | | | |
| 197 ts | 8E | 65 | 65 | | | | | | |
| 197 ts | 10E | | | | | | 81 | 81 | |
| 199 ts | AMC | | | | | | | 87 | |
| 224 ts | 1H | | 68 | 71 | 75 | 75 | | | |
| 249 ts | AMC | | | | | 80 | 80 | 80 | 80 |
| 249 ts | AMC | | | | | | 82 | 82 | 82 |
| 249 ts | AMC | | | | | | | 83 | 85 |
| 249 ts | AMC | | | | | | | 84 | 84 |

## GREEVES

| | Engine | 54 | 55 | 56 | 57 | 58 | 59 | 60 |
|---|---|---|---|---|---|---|---|---|
| 197 ts | 8E | 20R | 20R | 20R | 20R | | | |
| 197 ts | 8E | 20D | 20D | | | | | |
| 197 ts | 8E | 20S | 20S | | | | | |
| 197 ts | 8E | 20T | 20T | | | | | |
| 197 ts | 7E | | | | 20R4 | | | |
| 197 ts | 9E | | | 20D | 20D | 20D | | |
| 197 ts | 9E | | | 20S | 20S | 20SA | 20SAS | 20SCS |
| 197 ts | 9E | | | 20T | 20T | 20TA | 20TA | 20TC |
| 197 ts | 9E | | | | | | 20TAS | 20TCS |
| 246 ts | 31A | | | | | | 24DB | |
| 246 ts | 32A | | | | | | | 24DB |
| 246 ts | 31A | | | | | | 24TAS | |
| 246 ts | 31A | | | | | | 24SAS | |
| 246 ts | 32A | | | | | | | 24TCS |
| 246 ts | 33A | | | | | | | 24SAS |
| 246 ts | 33A | | | | | | | 24SCS |
| 242 ts tw | Anz | 25D | 25D | | | | | |
| 242 ts tw | Anz | | 25R | 25R | 25R | | | |
| 249 ts tw | 2T | | | | 25D | 25D | 25DB | 25DB |
| 249 ts tw | 2T | | | | | 25TA | | |
| 249 ts tw | 2T | | | | | 25SA | | |
| 322 ts tw | Anz | | 32D | 32D | 32D | | | |
| 324 ts tw | 3T | | | | | | | 32DB |

## GYS

| | b × s | 49 | 50 | 51 | 52 | 53 | 54 | 55 |
|---|---|---|---|---|---|---|---|---|
| 50 ts | 40 × 40 | GYS | GYS | Mot | Moc | Moc | Moc | Moc |

Mot – Motomite
Moc – Mocyc

## HERCULES

| | Engine | 56 | 57 | 58 | 59 | 60 |
|---|---|---|---|---|---|---|
| 49 ts | JAP | HCM | HCM | HCM | | |
| 49 ts | Lav | | | | Cor | |

Cor – Corvette
HCM – Her-Cu-Motor
Lav - Lavelette

## HJH

| | Engine | 54 | 55 | 56 |
|---|---|---|---|---|
| 147 ts | 30C | | Dn | Dn |
| 147 ts | 30C | | | SpDn |
| 197 ts | 7E | | Tr | Tr |
| 197 ts | 7E | | | Sc |
| 197 ts | 8E | D | D | D |
| 197 ts | 8E | | SD | |
| 197 ts | 8E | | | SpD |
| 197 ts | 8E | | | SSD |
| 224 ts | 1H | | DM | DM |

D – Dragon
DM – Dragon Major
Dn – Dragonette
Sc – Scrambler
SD Super Dragon
SpD – Sports Dragon
SpDn – Sports Dragonette
SSD – Super Sports Dragon
Tr – Trials

# INDIAN

| | Engine | 50 | 51 | 52 | 53 | 54 | 55 |
|---|---|---|---|---|---|---|---|
| 248 sv | Brock | R | R | R | R | R | R |
| 248 sv | Brock | | | | | S | S |

Brock – Brockhouse

# JAMES

| | Engine | 46 | 47 | 48 | 49 | 50 | 51 | 52 | 53 |
|---|---|---|---|---|---|---|---|---|---|
| 98 ts | JDL | Su | Su | Su | Su | | | | |
| 99 ts | 2F | | | | | Su | Su | Su | J1 |
| 99 ts | 1F | | | | Co | Co | Co | Co | J10 |
| 99 ts | 1F | | | | | | Com | Com | J4 |
| 122 ts | 9D | ML | ML | ML | | | | | |
| 122 ts | 10D | | | | Ca | Ca | Ca | Ca | J6 |
| 122 ts | 10D | | | | comp | comp | comp | comp | |
| 197 ts | 6E | | | | Cap | J8 | J8 | J8 | J8 |
| 197 ts | 6E | | | | | | J7 | J7 | J7 |
| 197 ts | 6E | | | | | | | Col | |
| 197 ts | 6E | | | | comp | comp | comp | | |

| | Engine | 53 | 54 | 55 | 56 | 57 | 58 | 59 | 60 |
|---|---|---|---|---|---|---|---|---|---|
| 99 ts | 2F | J1 | J1 | | | | | | |
| 99 ts | 4F | J3 | J11 | J11 | L1 | L1 | | | |
| 99 ts | 6F | | | | | L1 | L1 | L1 | L1 |
| 122 ts | 13D | J5 | J5 | | | | | | |
| 147 ts | 30C | | | J15 | L15 | L15 | L15 | L15 | |
| 149 ts | AMC | | | | | | | L15A | L15A |
| 171 ts | AMC | | | | | | L17 | L17 | |
| 197 ts | 7E | J9 | J9 | J9 | K7T | K7T | | | |
| 197 ts | 10E | | | | | | K7T | | |
| 197 ts | 10E | | | | | | K7 | K7 | |
| 197 ts | 8E | | K7 | K7 | K7 | K7 | | | |
| 197 ts | 7E | | K7C | K7C | K7C | K7C | | | |
| 199 ts | AMC | | | | | | | | L20 |
| 224 ts | 1H | | K12 | K12 | K12 | K12 | | | |
| 249 ts | AMC | | | | | L25 | L25 | L25 | L25 |
| 249 ts | AMC | | | | | | | L25T | L25T |
| 249 ts | AMC | | | | | | | L25S | L25S |

Ca – Cadet
Cap – Captain
Co – Comet
Col – Colonel
Com – Commodore
comp – competition
SU – Superlux

## MERCURY

| | Engine | 56 | 57 | 58 | | | |
|---|---|---|---|---|---|---|---|
| 48 ohv | | Mer | Mer | Mer | | | |
| 49 ts | Ilo | Her | Her | | | Do – Dolphin | Mer – Mercette |
| 60 ohv | | | Wh | | | GS – Grey Streak | Pi – Pippin |
| 99 ts | 4F | | Do | Pi | | Her – Hermes | Wh – Whippet |
| 99 ts | 6F | | GS | GS | | | |

## MINI-MOTOR

| | b × s | 49 | 50 | 51 | 52 | 53 | 54 | 55 |
|---|---|---|---|---|---|---|---|---|
| 49.9 ts | 38 × 44 | unit | unit | unit | unit | unit | unit | unit |

## NEW HUDSON

| | Engine | 46 | 47 | 48 | 49 | 50 | 51 | 52 |
|---|---|---|---|---|---|---|---|---|
| 98 ts | JDL | Au | Au | Au | | | | |
| 99 ts | 2F | | | | Au | Au | Au | Au |

| | Engine | 53 | 54 | 55 | 56 | 57 | 58 | |
|---|---|---|---|---|---|---|---|---|
| 99 ts | 2F | Au | Au | Au | Au | Au | Au | Au – Autocycle |

## NORMAN

| | Engine | 46 | 47 | 48 | 49 | 50 | 51 | 52 | 53 |
|---|---|---|---|---|---|---|---|---|---|
| 98 ts | JDL | Au | Au | Au | | | | | |
| 99 ts | 2F | | | | C | C | C | C | C |
| 99 ts | 1F | | | | | D | D | D | D |
| 122 ts | 9D | MC | MC | MC | | | | | |
| 122 ts | 10D | | | | B1 | B1 | B1 | B1 | E |
| 122 ts | 13D | | | | | | | | B1S |
| 197 ts | 6E | | | | B2 | B2 | B2 | B2 | B2 |
| 197 ts | 6E | | | | | | | | B2S |
| 197 ts | 6E | | | | | | | | B2C |

| | Engine | 53 | 54 | 55 | 56 | 57 | 58 | 59 | 60 |
|---|---|---|---|---|---|---|---|---|---|
| 47.6 ts | Sachs | | | | Ni | Ni | Ni | Ni | SL |
| 47.6 ts | Mi-Val | | | | | | | | Nilll |
| 49.9 ts | 3K | | | | | | Nill | | |
| 49.9 ts | 3K | | | | | | | Lido | NilV |
| 99 ts | 2F | C | C | C | C | C | | | |
| 99 ts | 4F | | D | D | | | | | |
| 122 ts | 10D | E | E | | | | | | |
| 147 ts | 30C | | | B1S | B1S | B1S | B1S | B1S | |
| 148 ts | 31C | | | | B1S | B1S | B1S | | |
| 197 ts | 8E | | B2 | | | | | | |
| 197 ts | 8E | | B2S | B2S | B2S | B2S | B2S | | |
| 197 ts | 9E | | | | B2S | B2S | B2S | B2S | B2S |
| 197 ts | 7E | | B2C | B2C | | | | | |

# NORMAN

| | Engine | 53 | 54 | 55 | 56 | 57 | 58 | 59 | 60 |
|---|---|---|---|---|---|---|---|---|---|
| 197 ts | 9E | | | | B2C/S | B2C/S | B2C/S | B2C/S | B2C/S |
| 197 ts | 9E | | | | | | | | B4C |
| 246 ts | 32A | | | | | | | | B4C |
| 242 ts tw | Anz | | | TS | TS | TS | | | |
| 249 ts tw | 2T | | | | | | B3 | B3 | B3 |

Au – Autocycle    MC – Motorcycle    SL – Super Lido
Anz – Anzani    Ni – Nippy

---

# NORTON

| | b × s | 45 | 46 | 47 | 48 | 49 | 50 | 51 | 52 | 53 |
|---|---|---|---|---|---|---|---|---|---|---|
| 348 ohv | 71 × 88 | | | Tr | | | | | | |
| 348 ohc | 71 × 88 | | | 40 | 40 | 40 | 40 | 40 | 40 | 40 |
| 348 ohc | 71 × 88 | | | 40M | 40M | 40M | 40M | 40M | 40M | 40M |
| 490 sv | 79 × 100 | 16H | 16H | 16H | 16H | 16H | 16H | 16H | 16H | 16H |
| 490 ohv | 79 × 100 | 18 | 18 | 18 | 18 | 18 | 18 | 18 | 18 | 18 |
| 490 ohv | 79 × 100 | | | Tr | | 500T | 500T | 500T | 500T | 500T |
| 490 ohv | 79 × 100 | | | ES2 | ES2 | ES2 | ES2 | ES2 | ES2 | ES2 |
| 490 ohc | 79 × 100 | | | 30 | 30 | 30 | 30 | 30 | 30 | 30 |
| 498 ohc | 79.62 × 100 | | | 30M | 30M | 30M | 30M | 30M | 30M | 30M |
| 634 sv | 82 × 120 | | | Big 4 | | | | | | |
| 597 sv | 82 × 113 | | | | Big 4 | Big 4 | Big 4 | Big 4 | Big 4 | Big 4 |
| 497 ohv tw | 66 × 72.6 | | | | | 7 | 7 | 7 | 7 | 7 |
| 497 ohv tw | 66 × 72.6 | | | | | | | | 88 | 88 |

| | b × s | 54 | 55 | 56 | 57 | 58 | 59 | 60 |
|---|---|---|---|---|---|---|---|---|
| 249 ohv tw | 60 × 44 | | | | | | Jub | Jub |
| 348 ohc | 71 × 88 | 40 | 40 | 40 | 40 | 40 | | |
| 348 ohv | 71 × 88 | | | 50 | 50 | 50 | 50 | 50 |
| 349 dohc | 76 × 76.85 | 40M | 40M | 40M | 40M | | | |
| 348 dohc | 76 × 76.7 | | | | | 40M | 40M | 40M |
| 490 sv | 79 × 100 | 16H | | | | | | |
| 490 ohv | 79 × 100 | 18 | | | | | | |
| 490 ohv | 79 × 100 | 500T | | | | | | |
| 490 ohv | 79 × 100 | ES2 | ES2 | ES2 | ES2 | ES2 | ES2 | ES2 |
| 490 ohc | 79 × 100 | 30 | 30 | 30 | 30 | 30 | | |
| 498 dohc | 86 × 85.8 | 30M | 30M | 30M | 30M | | | |
| 497 dohc | 86 × 85.62 | | | | | 30M | 30M | 30M |
| 597 sv | 82 × 113 | Big 4 | | | | | | |
| 597 ohv | 82 × 113 | | 19R | | | | | |
| 597 ohv | 82 × 113 | | 19S | 19S | 19S | 19S | | |
| 497 ohv tw | 66 × 72.6 | 7 | 7 | | | | | |
| 497 ohv tw | 66 × 72.6 | 88 | 88 | 88 | 88 | 88 | 88 | 88 |
| 497 ohv tw | 66 × 72.6 | | | | | | | 88dl |
| 497 ohv tw | 66 × 72.6 | | | | | | | Nom |
| 596 ohv tw | 68 × 82 | | | | 77 | 77 | | |
| 596 ohv tw | 68 × 82 | | 99 | 99 | 99 | 99 | 99 | 99 |
| 596 ohv tw | 68 × 82 | | | | | | | 99dl |
| 596 ohv tw | 68 × 82 | | | | | Nom | Nom | Nom |

Jub – Jubilee    Nom – Nomad    Tr – Trials

## OEC

|         | Engine | 49 | 50 | 51  | 52  | 53    | 54    |
|---------|--------|----|----|-----|-----|-------|-------|
| 122 ts  | 10D    | S1 | S1 | S1  | S1  | S1    |       |
| 122 ts  | 10D    |    | D1 | D1  | D1  | D1    |       |
| 122 ts  | 10D    |    | C1 | C1  | C1  |       |       |
| 122 ts  | 10D    |    |    | SS1 | SS1 | SS1   |       |
| 122 ts  | 10D    |    |    | SD1 | SD1 |       |       |
| 122 ts  | 10D    |    |    |     |     | D55   | D55   |
| 122 ts  | 10D    |    |    |     |     | D55RS | D55RS |
| 197 ts  | 6E     | S2 | S2 | S2  | S2  | S2    |       |
| 197 ts  | 6E     |    | D2 | D2  | D2  | D2    |       |
| 197 ts  | 6E     |    | C2 | C2  | C2  |       |       |
| 197 ts  | 6E     |    |    | SS2 | SS2 | SS2   |       |
| 197 ts  | 6E     |    |    | SD2 | SD2 | SD2   |       |
| 197 ts  | 6E     |    |    |     |     | ST2   |       |
| 197 ts  | 8E     |    |    |     |     |       | ST2   |
| 197 ts  | 6E     |    |    |     |     | ST3   |       |
| 197 ts  | 7E     |    |    |     |     |       | ST3   |
| 248 sv  | Bro    |    |    |     | Ap  | Ap    | Ap    |

Ap – Apollo          Bro – Brockhouse

## PANTHER

|          | b × s    | 46  | 47  | 48  | 49   | 50   | 51   | 52   | 53   |
|----------|----------|-----|-----|-----|------|------|------|------|------|
| 249 ohv  | 60 × 88  | 60  | 60  | 60  | 65   | 65   | 65   | 65   | 65   |
| 249 ohv  | 60 × 88  |     |     |     | 65St | 65St | 65St | 65St | 65St |
| 348 ohv  | 71 × 88  | 70  | 70  | 70  | 75   | 75   | 75   | 75   | 75   |
| 348 ohv  | 71 × 88  |     |     |     | 75St | 75St | 75St | 75St | 75St |
| 594 ohv  | 87 × 100 | 100 | 100 | 100 | 100  | 100  | 100  | 100  | 100  |

|          | b × s    | 53   | 54  | 55  | 56  | 57  | 58  | 59  | 60  |
|----------|----------|------|-----|-----|-----|-----|-----|-----|-----|
| 249 ohv  | 60 × 88  | 65   | 65  | 65  | 65  | 65  | 65  | 65  | 65  |
| 249 ohv  | 60 × 88  | 65St |     |     |     |     |     |     |     |
| 348 ohv  | 71 × 88  | 75   | 75  | 75  | 75  | 75  | 75  | 75  | 75  |
| 348 ohv  | 71 × 88  | 75St |     |     |     |     |     |     |     |
| 594 ohv  | 87 × 100 | 100  | 100 | 100 | 100 | 100 | 100 | 100 | 100 |
| 645 ohv  | 88 × 106 |      |     |     |     |     |     | 120 | 120 |

|           | Engine | 56   | 57   | 58   | 59   | 60    |
|-----------|--------|------|------|------|------|-------|
| 174 ts    | 2L     |      |      |      |      | Pr    |
| 197 ts    | 8E     | 10/3 | 10/3 | 10/3 | 10/3 | 10/3  |
| 197 ts    | 9E     |      | 10/3A| 10/3A| 10/3A| 10/3A |
| 197 ts    | 9E     | 10/4 | 10/4 | 10/4 | 10/4 | 10/4  |
| 246 ts    | 2H     |      | 25   |      |      |       |
| 249 ts tw | 2T     |      | 35   | 35   | 35   | 35    |
| 324 ts tw | 3T     |      |      |      | 45   | 45    |
| 324 ts tw | 3T     |      |      |      | 50   | 50    |

Pr – Princess
St – Stroud

# PHILLIPS

| | Engine | 54 | 55 | 56 | 57 | 58 | 59 | 60 |
|---|---|---|---|---|---|---|---|---|
| 49.2 ts | | P36 | P36 | P36 | P36 | | | |
| 49.2 ts | Rex | | | | | | P40 | P40 |
| 49.2 ts | Rex | | | | | | | P49 |
| 49.6 ts | Rex | | | P39 | P39 | P39 | P39 | |
| 49.6 ts | Rex | | | | | | P50 | P50 |
| 49.9 ts | 3K | | | | | | P45 | P45 |

# PHOENIX

| | Engine | 56 | 57 | 58 | 59 | 60 |
|---|---|---|---|---|---|---|
| 147 ts | 30C | pro | pro | | | |
| 147 ts | 30C | | | 19S | 19S | 19S |
| 147 ts | 30C | | | 19D | | |
| 147 ts | 30C | | | 150dl | 150dl | |
| 148 ts | 31C | | | S150 | S150 | S150 |
| 148 ts | 31C | | | | | 150dl |
| 174 ts | 2L | | | | | S175 |
| 174 ts | 2L | | | | | 175std |
| 197 ts | 9E | | | S200 | S200 | S200 |
| 197 ts | 9E | | | | | 200 std |
| 249 ts tw | 2T | | | T250 | T250 | T250 |
| 324 ts tw | 3T | | | | T325 | T325 |

pro – prototype

# POWER PAK

| | b × s | 50 | 51 | 52 | 53 | 54 | 55 | 56 |
|---|---|---|---|---|---|---|---|---|
| 49 ts | 39 × 41 | unit | unit | unit | unit | unit | unit | unit |

# PROGRESS

| | Engine | 57 | 58 |
|---|---|---|---|
| 147 ts | 30C | An | An |
| 197 ts | 8E | Br | Br |
| 197 ts | 9E | Bri | Bri |

An – Anglian
Br – Briton
Bri – Britannia

# RALEIGH

| | Engine | 58 | 59 | 60 |
|---|---|---|---|---|
| 49.9 ts | S/A | RM1 | RM1 | |
| 49.9 ts | S/A | | RM1C | RM2C |

S/A – Sturmey-Archer

# RAYNAL

| | Engine | 46 | 47 | 48 | 49 | 50 |
|---|---|---|---|---|---|---|
| 98 ts | JDL | Pop | DL | DL | DL | DL |

DL – De Luxe
Pop – Popular

## ROYAL ENFIELD

| | b × s | 46 | 47 | 48 | 49 | 50 | 51 | 52 | 53 |
|---|---|---|---|---|---|---|---|---|---|
| 126 ts | 54 × 55 | RE | RE | RE | RE | RE | RE2 | RE2 | RE2 |
| 148 ts | 56 × 60 | | | | | | | | En |
| 346 sv | 70 × 90 | C | C | | | | | | |
| 346 ohv | 70 × 90 | CO | CO | | | | | | |
| 346 ohv | 70 × 90 | G | G | G | G | G | G | G | G |
| 346 ohv | 70 × 90 | | | | G2 | G2 | G2 | G2 | G2 |
| 346 ohv | 70 × 90 | | | | Tr | Tr | Tr | Tr | Tr |
| 346 ohv | 70 × 90 | | | | Sc | Sc | Sc | Sc | Sc |
| 499 ohv | 84 × 90 | J | J | J | J2 | J2 | J2 | J2 | J2 |
| 499 ohv | 84 × 90 | | | | | | | | JS |
| 495 ohv tw | 64 × 77 | | | | Tw | Tw | Tw | Tw | Tw |
| 693 ohv tw | 70 × 90 | | | | | | | | M |

| | b × s | 53 | 54 | 55 | 56 | 57 | 58 | 59 | 60 |
|---|---|---|---|---|---|---|---|---|---|
| 126 ts | 54 × 55 | RE2 | | | | | | | |
| 148 ts | 56 × 60 | En | En | En | EnII | EnII | EnII | Pr | Pr |
| 148 ts | 56 × 60 | | | | | | EnIII | EnIII | |
| 248 ohv | 64 × 77 | | Cl | Cl | Cl | Cl | | | |
| 248 ohv | 64 × 77 | | S | | | | | | |
| 248 ohv | 70 × 64.5 | | | | | Cr | Cr | Cr | Cr |
| 248 ohv | 70 × 64.5 | | | | | | Cl II | Cl II | Cl II |
| 248 ohv | 70 × 64.5 | | | | | | | CrS | CrS |
| 346 ohv | 70 × 90 | | | | Cl | Cl | Cl | Cl | Cl |
| 346 ohv | 70 × 90 | G | G | | | | | | |
| 346 ohv | 70 × 90 | G2 | G2 | G2 | G2 | G2 | G2 | G2 | G2 |
| 346 ohv | 70 × 90 | Tr | Tr | Tr | | | | WRT | WRT |
| 346 ohv | 70 × 90 | Sc | Sc | Sc | MX | | | | |
| 346 ohv | 70 × 90 | | Ra | Ra | | | | | |
| 499 ohv | 84 × 90 | J2 | J2 | J2 | | | | | |
| 499 ohv | 84 × 90 | JS | JS | JS | JS | JS | JS | JS | JS |
| 499 ohv | 84 × 90 | | Tr | Tr | | | | | |
| 499 ohv | 84 × 90 | | Sc | Sc | MX | | | | |
| 499 ohv | 84 × 90 | | Ra | Ra | | | | | |
| 495 ohv tw | 64 × 77 | Tw | Tw | Tw | Tw | Tw | Tw | | |
| 496 ohv tw | 70 × 64.5 | | | | | | MM | MM | MM |
| 496 ohv tw | 70 × 64.5 | | | | | | | | MMS |
| 693 ohv tw | 70 × 90 | M | M | M | SM | SM | SM | SM | SM |
| 693 ohv tw | 70 × 90 | | | | | | Con | Con | Con |

Cl – Clipper
Con – Constellation
Cr – Crusader
CrS – Crusader Sports
En – Ensign
M – Meteor
MM – Meteor Minor
MMS – Meteor Minor Sports
MX – Moto Cross
Pr – Prince
Ra – Racer
Sc – Scrambler
SM – Super Meteor
Tr – Trials
WRT – Works Replica Trials
Tw – Twin

## SCOTT

| | b × s | 46 | 47 | 48 | 49 | 50 | 51 | 52 |
|---|---|---|---|---|---|---|---|---|
| 598 ts tw | 73 × 71.4 | FS | FS | FS | FS | FS | FS | FS |

| | b × s | 56 | 57 | 58 | 59 | 60 |
|---|---|---|---|---|---|---|
| 497 ts tw | 66.6 × 71.4 | FS | FS | FS | FS | FS |
| 598 ts tw | 73 × 71.4 | FS | FS | FS | FS | FS |

# SUN

| Engine | | 46 | 47 | 48 | 49 | 50 | 51 | 52 | 53 |
|--------|------|----|----|----|----|----|----|----|----|
| 98 ts  | JDL  | Au | Au | Au |    |    |    |    |    |
| 99 ts  | 2F   |    |    |    | Au | Au |    |    |    |
| 99 ts  | 1F   |    |    |    | MC | MC | MC | MC |    |
| 122 ts | 10D  |    |    |    |    |    | DL | DL |    |
| 197 ts | 6E   |    |    |    |    |    | Ch | Ch | Ch |

| Engine | | 53 | 54 | 55 | 56 | 57 | 58 | 59 | 60 |
|--------|------|------|------|------|------|------|------|------|------|
| 99 ts   | 4F   | MC   | MC   | Hor  | Hor  | Hor  |      |      |      |
| 99 ts   | 6F   |      |      |      |      | Geni | Geni | Geni | Geni |
| 122 ts  | 12D  | DL   | DL   |      |      |      |      |      |      |
| 147 ts  | 30C  |      |      | Ch   | Ch   |      |      |      |      |
| 148 ts  | 31C  |      |      |      |      | Ch   |      |      |      |
| 174 ts  | 2L   |      |      |      |      |      |      | SW   | SW   |
| 197 ts  | 8E   |      | Ch   | Ch   | Ch   | Ch   |      |      |      |
| 197 ts  | 6E   | Comp |      |      |      |      |      |      |      |
| 197 ts  | 8E   |      | C1   |      |      | Cen  |      |      |      |
| 197 ts  | 8E   |      | C3/C4 | Tr  |      |      |      |      |      |
| 197 ts  | 7E   |      |      | Sc   |      |      |      |      |      |
| 197 ts  | 9E   |      |      |      | Wasp | Wasp | Wasp | Wasp |      |
| 197 ts  | 9E   |      |      |      | WC   | WC   |      |      |      |
| 224 ts  | 1H   |      | Cyc  | Cyc  | Cyc  | Cyc  |      |      |      |
| 249 ts tw | 2T |      |      |      |      | Ov   | Ov   | Ov   |      |

Au – Autocycle
Cen – Century
Ch – Challenger
Comp – Competition
Cyc – Cyclone

DL – De Luxe
Hor – Hornet
MC – Motor Cycle
Ov – Overlander

Sc – Scrambler
SW – Sunwasp
Tr – Trials
WC – Wasp comp

# SUNBEAM

| b × s | | 47 | 48 | 49 | 50 | 51 | 52 | 53 | 54 |
|-------|---------|----|----|----|----|----|----|----|----|
| 489 ohc tw | 70 × 63.5 | S7 | S7 | S7 | S7 | S7 | S7 | S7 | S7 |
| 489 ohc tw | 70 × 63.5 |    |    | S8 | S8 | S8 | S8 | S8 | S8 |

| b × s | | 55 | 56 | 57 | 58 | 59 | 60 |
|-------|---------|----|----|----|----|----|----|
| 172 ts     | 61.5 × 58   |    |    |    |    |     | B1  |
| 249 ohv tw | 56 × 50.6   |    |    |    |    | B2  | B2  |
| 249 ohv tw | 56 × 50.6   |    |    |    |    | B2S | B2S |
| 489 ohc tw | 70 × 63.5   | S7 | S7 | S7 | S7 |     |     |
| 489 ohc tw | 70 × 63.5   | S8 | S8 | S8 | S8 |     |     |

# SWALLOW

| Engine | | 47 | 48 | 49 | 50 | 51 |
|--------|------|-----|-----|-----|-----|-------|
| 122 ts | 9D   | Gad | Gad | Gad |     |       |
| 122 ts | 10D  |     |     |     | Gad | Gad   |
| 197 ts | 6E   |     |     |     |     | Major |

Gad – Gadabout

## TANDON

| Engine | 48 | 49 | 50 | 51 | 52 | 53 | 54 | 55 |
|---|---|---|---|---|---|---|---|---|
| 122 ts | 9D | Mk1 | Mk1 | Mk1 | Mk1 | Mk1 | | | |
| 122 ts | 10D | | | S | S | S | S | | |
| 122 ts | 10D | | | | K | K | K | | |
| 122 ts | 10D | | | | | | Imp | | |
| 122 ts | 12D | | | | | | | Imp | |
| 147 ts | 30C | | | | | | | | Imp |
| 197 ts | 6E | | | | SS | SS | SS | | |
| 197 ts | 6E | | | | | | KS | | |
| 197 ts | 6E | | | | | | IS | | |
| 197 ts | 8E | | | | | | | IS | IS |
| 197 ts | 8E | | | | | | | Sc | ISS |
| 197 ts | 7E | | | | | | | | Sc |
| 224 ts | 1H | | | | | | | Mon | Mon |
| 242 ts tw | Anz | | | | | | | TS | TS |
| 242 ts tw | Anz | | | | | | | | Sc |
| 322 ts tw | Anz | | | | | | | | Vis |

| Engine | 56 | 57 | 58 | 59 |
|---|---|---|---|---|
| 197 ts | 8E | ISS | ISS | ISS | ISS |
| 224 ts | 1H | Mon | Mon | Mon | Mon |

Anz – Anzani  
K – Kangaroo  
KS – Kangaroo Supreme  
IS – Imp Supreme  

ISS – Imp Supreme Special  
Mon – Monarch  
S – Supaglide  
Sc – Scrambler  

SS – Supaglide Supreme  
TS – Twin Supreme  
Vis – Viscount  

## TEAGLE

| b × s | 54 | 55 | 56 |
|---|---|---|---|
| 50 ts | | unit | unit | unit |

## TRIUMPH

| b × s | 45 | 46 | 47 | 48 | 49 | 50 | 51 | 52 | 53 |
|---|---|---|---|---|---|---|---|---|---|
| 149 ohv | 57 × 58.5 | | | | | | | | | T15 |
| 349 ohv tw | 55 × 73.4 | 3T | 3T | 3T | 3T | 3T | 3T | 3T | | |
| 499 ohv tw | 63 × 80 | 5T | 5T | 5T | 5T | 5T | 5T | 5T | 5T | 5T |
| 499 ohv tw | 63 × 80 | T100 | T100 | T100 | T100 | T100 | T100 | T100 | T100 | T100 |
| 499 ohv tw | 63 × 80 | | | | GP | GP | GP | | | |
| 499 ohv tw | 63 × 80 | | | | | TR5 | TR5 | TR5 | TR5 | TR5 |
| 649 ohv tw | 71 × 82 | | | | | | 6T | 6T | 6T | 6T |

# TRIUMPH

| 149 ohv | b × s | 53 | 54 | 55 | 56 | 57 | 58 | 59 | 60 |
|---|---|---|---|---|---|---|---|---|---|
| 149 ohv | 57 × 58.5 | | T15 | T15 | T15 | | | | |
| 172 ts | 61.5 × 58 | | | | | | | | TS1 |
| 199 ohv | 63 × 64 | | T20 | T20 | T20 | T20 | T20 | T20 | T20 |
| 199 ohv | 63 × 64 | | | | | T20C | T20C | T20C | T20S |
| 249 ohv tw | 56 × 50.6 | | | | | | | TW2 | TW2 |
| 249 ohv tw | 56 × 50.6 | | | | | | | TW2S | TW2S |
| 349 ohv tw | 58.25 × 65.5 | | | | | 3TA | 3TA | 3TA | 3TA |
| 499 ohv tw | 63 × 80 | | 5T | 5T | 5T | 5T | 5T | | |
| 499 ohv tw | 63 × 80 | | T100 | T100 | T100 | T100 | T100 | T100 | |
| 499 ohv tw | 63 × 80 | T100c | | | | | | | |
| 499 ohv tw | 63 × 80 | | TR5 | TR5 | TR5 | TR5 | TR5 | | |
| 490 ohv tw | 69 × 65.5 | | | | | | | 5TA | 5TA |
| 490 ohv tw | 69 × 65.5 | | | | | | | | T100A |
| 649 ohv tw | 71 × 82 | | 6T | 6T | 6T | 6T | 6T | 6T | 6T |
| 649 ohv tw | 71 × 82 | | T110 | T110 | T110 | T110 | T110 | T110 | T110 |
| 649 ohv tw | 71 × 82 | | | | TR6 | TR6 | TR6 | TR6 | TR6 |
| 649 ohv tw | 71 × 82 | | | | | | | T120 | T120 |

# TURNER

| | Engine | 46 |
|---|---|---|
| 126 ts | RE | Byvan |

# VELOCETTE

| | b × s | 46 | 47 | 48 | 49 | 50 | 51 | 52 | 53 |
|---|---|---|---|---|---|---|---|---|---|
| 149 sv tw | 44 × 49 | | | | LE | LE | | | |
| 192 sv tw | 50 × 49 | | | | | | LE | LE | LE |
| 248 ohv | 68 × 68.25 | MOV | MOV | MOV | | | | | |
| 249 ts | 63 × 80 | GTP | | | | | | | |
| 348 ohc | 74 × 81 | KSS | KSS | KSS | | | | | |
| 348 ohc | 74 × 81 | | KTT | KTT | KTT | KTT | | | |
| 349 ohv | 68 × 96 | MAC | MAC | MAC | MAC | MAC | MAC | MAC | MAC |
| 495 ohv | 81 × 96 | MSS | MSS | MSS | | | | | |

| | b × s | 54 | 55 | 56 | 57 | 58 | 59 | 60 |
|---|---|---|---|---|---|---|---|---|
| 192 sv tw | 50 × 49 | LE | LE | LE | LE | LE | | |
| 192 sv tw | 50 × 49 | | | | | LE3 | LE3 | LE3 |
| 192 ohv tw | 50 × 49 | | | | V200 | V200 | V200 | V200 |
| 192 ohv tw | 50 × 49 | | | | | | VL | VL |
| 349 ohv | 68 × 96 | MAC | MAC | MAC | MAC | MAC | MAC | MAC |
| 349 ohv | 72 × 86 | | | Vi | Vi | Vi | Vi | Vi |
| 349 ohv | 72 × 86 | | | Sc | Sc | Sc | Sc | Sc |
| 349 ohv | 72 × 86 | | | | | | | ViC |
| 499 ohv | 86 × 86 | MSS | MSS | MSS | MSS | MSS | MSS | MSS |
| 499 ohv | 86 × 86 | | Sc | Sc | Sc | Sc | Sc | Sc |
| 499 ohv | 86 × 86 | | | En | En | En | En | En |
| 499 ohv | 86 × 86 | | | Ve | Ve | Ve | Ve | Ve |
| 499 ohv | 86 × 86 | | | | | | | VeC |

En – Endurance    Ve – Venom    Vi – Viper    VL – Veeline
Sc – Scrambler    VeC – Venom Clubman    ViC – Viper Clubman

## VELOSOLEX

| | b × s | 48 | 49 | 50 | 51 | 52 | 53 |
|---|---|---|---|---|---|---|---|
| 45 ts | 38 × 40 | VS | VS | VS | VS | VS | VS |

| | b × s | 54 | 55 | 56 | 57 |
|---|---|---|---|---|---|
| 45 ts | 38 × 40 | VS | VS | VS | VS |

## VILLIERS

| | b × s | 45 | 46 | 47 | 48 | 49 | 50 | 51 | 52 | 53 |
|---|---|---|---|---|---|---|---|---|---|---|
| 98 | 50 × 50 | JDL | JDL | JDL | JDL | | | | | |
| 99 | 47 × 57 | | | | | 2F | 2F | 2F | 2F | 2F |
| 99 | 47 × 57 | | | | | 1F | 1F | 1F | 1F | 1F |
| 122 | 50 × 62 | 9D | 9D | 9D | 9D | 10D | 10D | 10D | 10D | 10D |
| 122 | 50 × 62 | | | | | | | | | 13D |
| 197 | 59 × 72 | | 5E | 5E | 5E | 6E | 6E | 6E | 6E | 6E |

| | b × s | 54 | 55 | 56 | 57 | 58 | 59 | 60 |
|---|---|---|---|---|---|---|---|---|
| 99 | 47 × 57 | 2F | 2F | 2F | 2F | 2F | | |
| 99 | 47 × 57 | 4F | 4F | 4F | 4F | 4F | | |
| 99 | 47 × 57 | | | 6F | 6F | 6F | 6F | 6F |
| 122 | 50 × 62 | 12D | | | | | | |
| 122 | 50 × 62 | 11D | | | | | | |
| 147 | 55 × 62 | 30C | 30C | 30C | 30C | 30C | 30C | |
| 147 | 55 × 62 | 29C | 29C | 29C | | | | |
| 148 | 57 × 58 | | 31C | 31C | 31C | 31C | 31C | |
| 174 | 59 × 63.5 | | | | 2L | 2L | 2L | 2L |
| 174 | 59 × 63.5 | | | | 3L | 3L | 3L | 3L |
| 197 | 59 × 72 | 8E | 8E | 8E | 8E | 8E | | |
| 197 | 59 × 72 | 7E | 7E | 7E | | 10E | 10E | |
| 197 | 59 × 72 | 9E | 9E | 9E | 9E | 9E | 9E | 9E |
| 224 | 63 × 72 | 1H | 1H | 1H | 1H | | | |
| 246 | 66 × 72 | | | | 2H | 2H | 2H | 2H |
| 246 | 66 × 72 | | | | | 31A | 31A | 31A |
| 246 | 66 × 72 | | | | | 33A | 33A | 32A |
| 246 | 66 × 72 | | | | | | | 34A |
| 249 tw | 50 × 63.5 | | | 2T | 2T | 2T | 2T | 2T |
| 324 tw | 57 × 63.5 | | | | | 3T | 3T | 3T |

## VINCENT–HRD

| | b × s | 47 | 48 | 49 | 50 | 51 | 52 | 53 |
|---|---|---|---|---|---|---|---|---|
| 499 ohv | 84 × 90 | | | BM | BM | | | |
| 499 ohv | 84 × 90 | | | CC | CC | CC | CC | CC |
| 499 ohv | 84 × 90 | | | | CGF | CGF | | |
| 998 ohv tw | 84 × 90 | BR | BR | BR | BR | | | |
| 998 ohv tw | 84 × 90 | | BBS | BBS | BBS | | | |
| 998 ohv tw | 84 × 90 | | | CR | CR | CR | CR | CR |
| 998 ohv tw | 84 × 90 | | | CBS | CBS | CBS | CBS | CBS |
| 998 ohv tw | 84 × 90 | | | CBL | CBL | CBL | CBL | CBL |

## VINCENT–HRD

| | b × s | 53 | 54 | 55 | 56 | 57 | 58 |
|---|---|---|---|---|---|---|---|
| 48 ts | 38 × 42 | F | F | F | F | F | F |
| 98 ohv | NSU | | Fox | Fox | | | |
| 123 ts | NSU | | Fox | Fox | | | |
| 199 ts | NSU | | Lux | | | | |
| 247 ohc | NSU | | Max | | | | |
| 499 ohv | 84 × 90 | | | DV | | | |
| 499 ohv | 84 × 90 | CC | CC | DC | | | |
| 998 ohv tw | 84 × 90 | CR | CR | DR | | | |
| 998 ohv tw | 84 × 90 | CBS | CBS | DBS | | | |
| 998 ohv tw | 84 × 90 | CBL | CBL | CBL | | | |
| 998 ohv tw | 84 × 90 | | | DBP | | | |
| 998 ohv tw | 84 × 90 | | | DBK | | | |

BBS – B Black Shadow  CC – C Comet  DBS – D Black Shadow
BM – B Meteor  CGF – C Grey Flash  DC – D Comet
BR – B Rapide  CR – C Rapide  DR – D Rapide
CBL – C Black Lightning  DBK – D Black Knight  DV – D Victor
CBS – C Black Shadow  DBP – D Black Prince  F – Firefly

## WABO

| | Engine | 57 |
|---|---|---|
| 99 ts | 4F | Scooter |
| 147 ts | 30C | Scooter |

## ZENITH

| | Engine | 47 | 48 | 49 | 50 |
|---|---|---|---|---|---|
| 747 sv tw | JAP | MC | MC | MC | MC |

MC – motorcycle

**Typical mount for the enthusiast of the 1950s was this 1956 Triumph Tiger 110, then one of the fastest available**

# Acknowledgements

This book completes the trio which covers British motorcycles from 1930 to 1970 and represents the period during which I did much of my riding and racing. Most of the machines discussed were outside the range of my pocket at the time, but many were sampled by one means or another, and all were seen or studied at Earls Court or close to hand at the local club.

Club riding was a disciplined pastime in the 1950s, well apart from the café racers, who could be seen grouped around the coffee stall outside the local railway station. Partly, this came from a strong road-racing section in the club, who actually went on to the circuits, so the café crowd were viewed as pseudo racers. Club members supported the racers at meetings and also ran local trials, the training scheme and rode discreetly in town, such social behaviour being encouraged to enhance the motorcyclist's image where possible.

The main help with this book concerned the pictures and, once more, I am indebted to the EMAP archives, which hold the old *Motor Cycle Weekly* files, and Malcolm Gough, of *Motor Cycle News*, from whence they came.

My thanks also go to old friend and fellow writer and racer Brian Woolley for kindly writing a foreword for this book.

A number of the pictures used would have carried the imprint of a professional and, normally, they would have been listed, as is the practice of both myself and the publishing house, but this is no longer possible due to the way in which the prints now reach us. However, our thanks, as always, go to those who drove their cameras in the past, when correct exposure owed more to the man behind the lens, than the electronics in front of it.

Finally, to both editors – Tony Thacker who commissioned this one, and Ian Penberthy who had to take it over in mid-sail – my thanks for support during its production. And, of course, to the staff at Osprey who, as always, did a great job, despite the change of editor and a move to a new office with all the trauma that brings.

Roy Bacon
Niton, Isle of Wight
December 1988

# THE FOUNTAINS
# OF FLORENTINE SCULPTORS

LONDON: HUMPHREY MILFORD

OXFORD UNIVERSITY PRESS

FOUNTAIN IN THE COURT, PALAZZO VECCHIO, FLORENCE

SCULPTURE BY VERROCCHIO; BASIN BY FRANCESCO DEL TADDA

# THE FOUNTAINS OF
# FLORENTINE SCULPTORS AND
# THEIR FOLLOWERS FROM
# DONATELLO TO BERNINI

BY

BERTHA HARRIS WILES

CAMBRIDGE · MASSACHUSETTS
HARVARD UNIVERSITY PRESS
1933

PRINTED AT THE HARVARD UNIVERSITY PRESS

CAMBRIDGE, MASSACHUSETTS

UNITED STATES OF AMERICA

*To*

MY MOTHER

# PREFACE

WRITERS on Florentine sculpture have tended to concentrate upon the religious and civic monuments, slighting the host of figures in lighter vein that abound in the gardens and villas. This neglect has resulted in a somewhat distorted picture of the art of the Renaissance. Especially is this true in the Cinquecento, when garden sculpture provided one of the most characteristic mediums of expression for Florentine masters, reflecting the essentially pagan character of the age more truly than the tombs and ecclesiastical works to which intensive study has hitherto been confined, and enlisting the services of highly skilled sculptors in the solution of new technical problems. The present study of Florentine fountains is intended as a contribution toward a more complete understanding of the sculpture of this fertile, many-sided period.

Except for the opening chapters on the fountains of the Quattrocento and the general characteristics of Florentine fountains, the following pages are devoted entirely to works of the late Renaissance and early Baroque periods. In successive chapters I define the most common types, and trace the development of each through the Cinquecento and early Seicento. Here the reader may follow, step by step, the transition to the baroque; for the germs of that exuberant style flourished in the free air of the villas and gardens long before they invaded the architectonic world of the churches and palaces. The closing chapter deals with the culmination of the Florentine development in the baroque fountains of the Roman sculptor Bernini, presenting evidence of Florentine prototypes, not only for Bernini's fountain figures, but also for the very rustic and naturalistic types which have hitherto been considered his peculiar contribution to the development of the fountain.

As the works of many of the Cinquecento sculptors are imperfectly known, I have provided complete illustrations of the extant fountains and fountain figures, and have been careful to indicate the source of each illustration wherever possible, even in the numerous cases in which photographs were taken expressly for this work.

My examination of the fountains themselves has been supplemented by an exhaustive study of the references to fountains in contemporary literature. I have drawn upon the numerous biographies of artists, travellers' journals, guide-books, and collections of letters, as well as the wealth of unpublished material in the Medici account books in the State Archives at Florence. This documentary evidence is so voluminous that I find it impossible to indicate the sources of all of my statements by footnotes, in the usual scholarly fashion. I have therefore included in the footnotes to the text only such matters as seem to me of interest to the general reader; but the serious student will find in Appendix A very complete references to the sources consulted and to the bibliography of the subject, as well as discussions of minor controversial points. Limitations of space have made it necessary to abbreviate the titles of authorities cited repeatedly, both in the footnotes and in the appendices. The key to these abbreviations which I have provided will serve as a working bibliography.

Although an astonishing number of fountains and fountains figures have come down to us, many works described by contemporary writers have disappeared. In a section entitled "Lost Fountains" (Appendix B), these descriptions are quoted, in the hope that they may lead to the identification of works which have strayed to collections in distant lands.

As an authoritative history of Florentine sculpture in the Cinquecento has yet to appear, the attribution of undocumented statues has been particularly difficult. In the text I have given my own ascriptions, often without much discussion of the alternatives. In such cases variant attributions and reasons for and against their acceptance will be found in Appendix A.

Of the many difficulties that I have encountered in the preparation of this book, the greatest have been those of wording. How often I have longed for an English equivalent of the German "Wasserkunst," or sighed for the Italian wealth of fountain terminology! I ask the reader to bear with me in the unavoidable repetition of terms and in the cumbersome and wordy phrasing of ideas which I might have expressed more simply and forcefully, had I been writing in the language of a country richer in the lore of the fountain.

B. H. W.

CAMBRIDGE, MASSACHUSETTS
    November 15, 1933

# ACKNOWLEDGMENTS

M Y GREATEST debt I owe to my friend and teacher, Professor Chandler Rathfon Post of Harvard University, who first suggested to me the study of Italian fountains. His brilliant lectures and writings on sculpture have inspired much that appears in these pages; and it was through his staunch support that this work, in troublous times, found a publisher.

I am deeply grateful to the Carnegie Corporation for fellowships which made possible the research on which this work is based. To the American Council of Learned Societies I owe double thanks, for the grant which enabled me to complete that research, and for their subvention for the publication of this book.

Among the many European scholars to whom I am indebted, I have drawn most freely upon the special knowledge and advice of the following: in Florence, Dr. Giovanni Poggi, the omniscient head of the Reale Soprintendenza all' Arte, Dr. Odoardo H. Giglioli, curator of the Uffizi's great collection of prints and drawings, and Dr. Ulrich Middeldorf, in charge of the unique collection of photographs of sculpture in the Kunsthistorisches Institut; in Germany, Dr. Friedrich Kriegbaum of the University of Berlin, unquestionably the foremost authority on Florentine sculpture of the Cinquecento; in Vienna, those encyclopedic scholars, Dr. Leo Planiscig and Dr. Ernst Kris, both of the Kunsthistorisches Museum; in London, the busy director of the Victoria and Albert Museum, Sir Eric Maclagan, and his learned and gracious assistant in the Department of Architecture and Sculpture, Miss Margaret Longhurst.

In America I wish to thank particularly Professor Paul J. Sachs, Associate Director of the Fogg Art Museum, for letters of introduction which opened many doors in my search for Florentine fountains; Professor Clarence Kennedy of Smith College, for helpful discussions of sculpture of the Florentine Quattrocento; my colleague, Dr. Catharine W. Pierce of Radcliffe College, for her critical reading of my manuscript; Mr. Leonard

Opdycke of Harvard University for valuable suggestions in the bibliography of the Baroque period; Miss Ethelwyn Manning, head of the Frick Art Reference Library in New York, for generous assistance of various kinds; and Miss Louise Lucas, Librarian of the Fogg Art Museum, for her sound advice in the many technical problems that arise in the making of a book.

More specific debts are, I trust, duly indicated in the following pages.

# CONTENTS

# THE FOUNTAINS
# OF FLORENTINE SCULPTORS

*Photo Brogi*

FIGURE 1. MEDIEVAL FOUNTAIN
PIAZZA DI PIANOSCARANO, VITERBO

*Photo Alinari*

FIGURE 2. NICCOLÒ PISANO AND OTHERS, FONTANA MAGGIORE, PERUGIA

# INTRODUCTION

DURING the Middle Ages, Italian fountains were chiefly civic structures, erected in town squares to supply the communes with water. The state provided for their maintenance, and punished any pollution of their precious contents by death. Their lines, in harmony with those of the surrounding palaces, were compact and severe. Decorative sculpture was usually confined to the coats of arms of the town and its dignitaries, carved in low relief upon the sides of the polygonal receiving basin, and conventionalized masks or monsters, grouped round the central shaft to spout forth the water, as in the Fontana di Piano Scarano at Viterbo (Fig. 1). When figure sculpture was used, as in the Fonte Maggiore at Perugia (Fig. 2), it was kept subordinate to the architectonic lines of the basins and shaft, and its subject matter was chiefly religious or civic, as, again, in the great fountain at Perugia, where the richness of the iconography rivals that of medieval cathedral façades.

With the Renaissance, all this changed. As the private palace in the city and the villa in the country developed in luxury and display, pleasure fountains increased in number. In the new interest in classical mythology, the old repertoire of heraldry and of religious and civic allegory was forgotten. Pagan statues of Venus and amorini, of river gods and nymphs, replaced the allegorical figures that had decorated the medieval fountains; for the influence of classical antiquity — always a factor in Renaissance art — was nowhere more potent than in the sculptured fountains. It is apparent in the changed iconography, in the use of the nude, in the classicizing style of both figures and basins; and it is proved by references to ancient precedent in contemporary literature.

Above all, the pagan delight of the Renaissance sculptor in the representation of the human form, stimulated by the newly formed collections of ancient statuary, led to a reversal of the decorative principle that had governed the medieval fountain. The figure sculpture now burst its architectural bonds, dominating the structural portions of the fountain (that is, the basins and shaft), as in the Great Fountain at Castello (Fig. 3).

It was this predominance of the figure sculpture over the structural elements that distinguished the Florentine fountains of the Renaissance from the architectonic types developed at Rome. As the sixteenth century advanced, the centrifugal lines and excited poses of the figures designed by the Florentine Mannerists for the decoration of fountains approached the complete freedom of the baroque, as in Taddeo Landini's bronze youths on the famous Fountain of the Tortoises (Fig. 4).

The present work follows this triumphal progress of the figure sculpture from its beginning, in the Florentine fountains of the Quattrocento, to its culmination in the Seicento, in the baroque creations of the Roman Bernini.

FIGURE 3.  NICCOLÒ TRIBOLO AND OTHERS, DETAIL OF THE
GREAT FOUNTAIN

ROYAL VILLA, CASTELLO

*Photo D. Anderson, Rome*

FIGURE 4.  GIACOMO DELLA PORTA AND TADDEO LANDINI, FOUNTAIN OF THE TORTOISES

PIAZZA MATTEI, ROME

FIGURE 5.  WALL FOUNTAIN

BANCA DEL MONTE DEI PASCHI, FLORENCE

# CHAPTER I

## THE FOUNTAINS OF FLORENTINE SCULPTORS
## IN THE QUATTROCENTO

TRUE fountains, intended for the continuous display of water, cannot have been common at Florence during the Quattrocento, since the scanty water supply available in that period was drawn chiefly from wells and springs. Consequently, examples from this period are extremely rare. Less than a dozen fountain figures, a pair of marble basins, and one wall fountain are all that have come down to us. Nevertheless, with the aid of the numerous representations of fountains in contemporary art, we have sufficient evidence to distinguish two broad classes of fountains known in the fifteenth century — the freestanding or "isolated" type, designed for the center of a piazza, court, or garden, and the "engaged" or wall fountain, addorsed against a wall at the end of a square or courtyard.

The wall fountains are soon disposed of, as the only extant example from this period in Florence is the handsome structure of *pietra serena* in the court of the Palazzo Orlandini, now the property of the Banca del Monte dei Paschi (Fig. 5). This consists of a single niche, crowned by an arch and framed by classical pilasters, the water falling from an ornamental spout within the recess into a basin placed at its foot. The simplicity and restraint of the Corinthian pilasters and sculptured frieze suggest a date in the early Quattrocento, but the naturalistic style of the lion's head spout above the fluted basin seems more characteristic of the latter part of the century. The *rocaille* which decorates the niche was probably added at a much later period.

Structures of similar form, known as lavabos, abound in Florentine churches and monasteries. These, although supplied with running water, are not true fountains; for the water, controlled by a tap, is turned on only when needed, not utilized for continuous display. The lavabo was a lavatory at which the celebrant washed his hands before consecrating the host. Consequently the basin was placed much higher than in the true wall fountain. Figure 6 illustrates an attractive example of enamelled terracotta by Giovanni della Robbia, erected in the sacristy of Santa Maria Novella in 1497. The figures of the Madonna and angels which decorate the tympanum are in keeping with the ecclesiastical character of the structure; but the nude, garland-bearing putti and classicizing arabesques which cover the pilasters and frieze seem more suited to a secular fountain. This work is reminiscent of the altars and wall tombs of earlier sculptors; was the river scene on the tympanum within the niche drawn from the landscape background of some contemporary painting? The marble slabs and cherubs' heads below date from the eighteenth century, probably replacing an original decoration in Della Robbia tiles. The oval, footed marble basin recalls the form of contemporary freestanding fountains and holy water basins.

The lavabo had its secular counterpart in the *acquaio* or lavatory of the private palace, illustrated by a large and elaborate example of *pietra serena* in the Victoria and Albert Museum (Fig. 7). Here the niche is unusually deep. The water issued from graceful urns of classical form, topped by drinking birds; and side jets fell from the roguish pair of *putti pissatori* carved in the splayed sides of the recess. Rich, classicizing arabesques in very low relief cover the pilasters, frieze, and spandrels of the arch, while the tympanum within is carved to simulate a fluted shell. The style of the classicizing bas-reliefs and the resemblance of the putti to those of Antonio Rossellino place this work either in the closing years of the Quattrocento or the opening years of the Cinquecento.

Isolated fountains of the fifteenth century have rarely been preserved intact; but museums and private collections contain scattered basins and figures in the style of the Florentine Quattrocento, pierced for the passage of water. From these, with the help of contemporary Italian engravings, paintings, and drawings in which fountains are represented, we can reconstruct the most common forms. From the small size of both statues and basins it is evident that they were intended for private courts or gardens.

The Florentine fountain figures that have come down to us are almost without exception variations on the popular theme of the putto; but representations of fountains in contemporary Italian art indicate that a wide range of subjects, generally based upon classical prototypes, was known in the Quattrocento. Indeed, most of the *motifs* current in the following cen-

FIGURE 7. ACQUAIO

VICTORIA AND ALBERT MUSEUM, LONDON

FIGURE 6. GIOVANNI DELLA ROBBIA, LAVABO

S. MARIA NOVELLA, FLORENCE

*Photo Alinari*

FIGURE 8. SCHOOL OF MANTEGNA, DRAWING OF
A FOUNTAIN

GABINETTO DEI DISEGNI, THE UFFIZI, FLORENCE

*Courtesy of British Museum*

FIGURE 9. ZOAN ANDREA, ENGRAVING OF
A FOUNTAIN

BRITISH MUSEUM, LONDON

From *The Catalogue of Early Italian Engravings in the British
Museum*, by Arthur M. Hind

FIGURE 10. WOODCUT OF A FOUNTAIN
From Francesco Colonna's *Hypnerotomachia Polifili*

tury appear. The jet of water was usually connected in some way with the statue. At times it fell from some accessory held by the figure, trickling from an urn (Figs. 8 and 9) or spouting from a fish or dolphin (Figs. 13 to 15); often it issued directly from the human figure, as in the case of the three Graces (Fig. 10) or the *putto pissatore* (Figs. 11 and 12) [1] — both *motifs* scarcely acceptable to modern taste, but very popular in the Renaissance.

In the wall fountains and lavabos, the sculptors had merely adapted to their purpose the forms of contemporary altarpieces and wall tombs. In the isolated fountains, however, they had to face new problems. Chief of these was the necessity for a plurifacial treatment in freestanding figures. In most of the sculpture produced in the Quattrocento this problem did not arise, since freestanding figures of that period were usually given an architectural background, or set within a niche, where a frontal treatment sufficed. But a statue decorating the summit of an isolated fountain, in the center of a court or garden, was naturally approached from various angles, and called for a more complex handling which would make it interesting from many points of view.[2]

Naturally this difficult technical problem was not solved at a single stroke. The earliest of the series of putti from Florentine fountains, the bronze cupid with a fish in the Victoria and Albert Museum, although probably planned for a freestanding fountain, is really satisfactory from the front view alone (Fig. 13). The small size of this statuette (it is about fifteen inches in height) indicates that it originally decorated a chamber or table fountain. Whether by Donatello himself or by some member of his workshop, it obviously dates from the early period (*c.* 1430–1440), when his work was closest to its classical prototypes. Not only is the putto based upon the Hellenistic fountain *motif* of the boy with a dolphin;[3] its very pose recalls the classical formula for the standing figure.

Among the extant fountain figures are three which seem to have been designed for the decoration of gardens. Their composition suggests that

1. Other marble *putti pissatori*, of the school of Donatello, are to be found in the Louvre (No. 709) and the Musée Jacquemart André (No. 863).

2. On the necessity and difficulty of giving a freestanding figure several "sides" or profiles Benvenuto Cellini has written at some length: *Varchi*, p. 147, and *Cellini*, III, 212–213.

In these footnotes, authorities printed in italic are given in full in the Key to Abbreviations (p. 140); initials refer to the work cited.

3. An ancient example of this fountain *motif*, from some garden at Pompeii, is preserved in the Naples Museum: No. 111701.

they stood at the head of small pools or basins, where they would be seen chiefly from the front. Such are the two *putti pissatori* illustrated in Figures 11 and 12: the mischievous marble figure in the Museo Bardini ascribed to some follower of Donatello, and the statuette of enamelled terracotta of a little boy standing over a clump of iris, in the Kaiser Friedrich Museum, from the atelier of Andrea della Robbia. Both of these figures date from the second half of the Quattrocento.

Andrea della Robbia's glazed terracotta boy with a dolphin, in the collection of Mrs. Edwin C. Hoyt in New York (Fig. 14), must be placed toward the end of the century, for the broader and softer treatment of the child's chubby body implies a knowledge of Verrocchio's putti.[1] The facial type of course recalls Andrea's *bambini* on the façade of the Ospedale degli Innocenti. Our earlier putti were represented in static poses; here, the child is caught in a momentary attitude, head turned, lips parted, legs spread. The suggestion of potential motion is enhanced by the curving line of the dolphin's tail. Still, the figure is kept within one frontal plane.

Verrocchio's famous bronze boy with a dolphin, now in the court of the Palazzo Vecchio (Fig. 15), is one of the most successful examples of the plurifacial treatment of a freestanding figure in all art. From whatever aspect it is viewed, it presents a clear profile. Yet there is none of the violent torsion to which sculptors of the following century resorted in order to make their statues interesting in the round. Only the head of the putto is turned, the torso remains frontal; from it extend in radiating lines the wings, extended leg, and the dolphin's head and tail. The perfect balance of these parts, in a sort of chiastic *contrapposto*, about the torso as a center results in a miraculous effect of poise within motion.

This figure was originally designed for a fountain at the Villa Careggi, the precise form of which is unknown. The porphyry basin by Francesco del Tadda (Frontispiece) dates from about 1555, when the figure was moved to its present site. The three marble lions' heads which decorate the baluster-shaped shaft are part of the original fountain; for an inventory of 1496 lists with the putto four lions' mouths of marble and three heads of bronze. The exact date of the figure is unknown, although its

---

1. Figs. 12 and 14 show no evidence of having been actually used as fountain figures, but their *motifs* undoubtedly reflect those of actual fountain figures in other mediums.

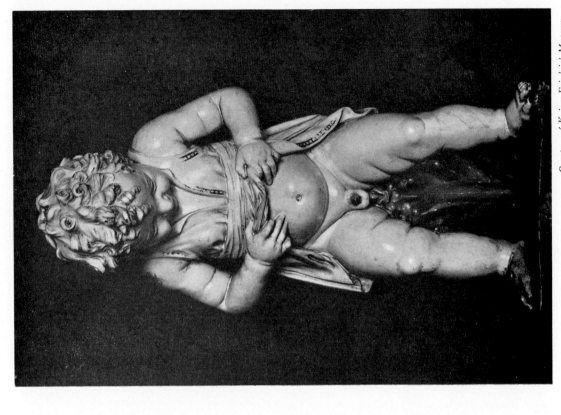

FIGURE 12. WORKSHOP OF ANDREA DELLA ROBBIA, PUTTO PISSATORE

KAISER FRIEDRICH MUSEUM, BERLIN

FIGURE 11. SCHOOL OF DONATELLO, PUTTO PISSATORE

MUSEO BARDINI, FLORENCE

FIGURE 14. ANDREA DELLA ROBBIA,
BOY WITH A DOLPHIN
COLLECTION OF MRS. EDWIN C. HOYT,
NEW YORK

FIGURE 15. VERROCCHIO, BOY WITH A DOLPHIN
DETAIL OF THE FOUNTAIN IN THE PALAZZO VECCHIO,
FLORENCE

FIGURE 13. SCHOOL OF DONATELLO, CUPID WITH A FISH
VICTORIA AND ALBERT MUSEUM, LONDON

commission for Careggi, under Lorenzo dei Medici, places it after 1469. According to a German traveller, who saw the bronze figure in its present site in the late Cinquecento, the putto then revolved on its axis, driven by the force of the water. Was this part of the original conception for the fountain at Careggi? Verrocchio is known to have made another putto operated by mechanical means, described by Vasari as striking the clock of the Palazzo Vecchio with a hammer.

The fascinating clay putto from the Dreyfus Collection, a younger brother to the winged sprite from Careggi (Fig. 16), generally accepted as the work of Verrocchio, is believed to be a model for a bronze fountain figure; for his puffed out cheeks, which can be explained only by the action of blowing, are thought to indicate that the figure was designed to blow water through a trumpet held in the raised hand — a *motif* actually found in certain German fountains. The mouth would, then, have been pierced for the jet of water when the casting of the bronze was completed. A *motif* more in accord with the position of the hand is suggested by Vasari's description of the bronze "Mercury" modelled by Rustici in 1515, now in the collection of Mr. Henry Harris in London (Fig. 17). According to Vasari, this figure originally held a "butterfly," or toy with revolving blades, caused to turn by the water blown from the Mercury's mouth. A comparison of the two figures reveals the same puffed out cheeks and a similar concentration upward.[1] Rustici, being a pupil of Verrocchio, would have been in a position to know the *motif* of the clay putto, and carry it to completion in a figure of his own; for apparently Verrocchio's model was never cast in bronze. This fact probably indicates a date shortly before the sculptor's death in 1488.

In this statue (Fig. 16) the endearing awkwardness of infancy is paradoxically combined with a perfect balance of parts. Again the torso remains comparatively frontal, while arms and legs penetrate backward and forward in space. This figure, too, is equally attractive from different points of view, as Professor Clarence Kennedy has shown in his exquisite photographs for the catalogue of the sculpture from the Dreyfus Collection.

Verrocchio's putti were undoubtedly planned as the crowning orna-

1. I am told that Miss Elizabeth Wilder, in studying the works of Verrocchio, has independently arrived at the same conclusion concerning the *motif* of this figure. For a fuller discussion of Rustici's statue, see pp. 83–84. For lost fountain figures by Verrocchio, see p. 139.

ments of small freestanding fountains of a form which I call the "cylix" type, because the footed, bowl-shaped basin which forms its nucleus resembles both in shape and in proportions the classical cylix or drinking cup.[1] So far as I know, only two basins of this type in the style of the Florentine Quattrocento have been preserved — the marble fountain which originally adorned the garden of the Pazzi Palace, now in New York in the collection of Mr. George Blumenthal, to whom I am indebted for the photograph reproduced in Figure 21; and the example, also in marble, bearing the insignia of the Medici, now in the vestibule of the Pitti Palace (Fig. 23). The attempt to determine the general characteristics of the cylix type is complicated by the fact that neither of these examples has remained intact. The Pazzi basin has lost a portion of its pedestal, while the figure and upper basin in the Medici fountain appear to be additions of the sixteenth century.[2] Representations of similar fountains in contemporary paintings, medals, and drawings (Figs. 18 a to d) help us to reconstruct the norm. These indicate that the cylix was usually surmounted by a shaft, in the shape of a short column or baluster. This often attained a considerable height (Fig. 18d), and sometimes received elaborate decoration (Fig. 18c). This portion, although lacking in the Pazzi cylix, is still preserved in the Medici fountain (Fig. 23). The primary function of the shaft was the elevation of the water, which issued from spouts near its summit, falling into the cylix below (Fig. 18b). There it gathered until it brimmed over the rim into an inconspicuous receiving basin, commonly of circular form, which served as the outlet (Figs. 21, 23, and 18d). The shaft was frequently surmounted by a statue, usually poised upon a globe, as in the contemporary Italian representations of fountains illustrated in Figures 18a, b, and d.

The numerous paintings, drawings, and engravings of the Quattrocento in which cylix fountains appear prove that this type was well known in the early Renaissance, in spite of the dearth of extant basins from secular

1. "Cylix" seems to me an apt term for this type of basin, with its bowl and low stem and foot, in spite of the fact that it lacks the handles usually found in the painted vase of that name. Of course I do not imply that the Quattrocento basin was derived from the painted Greek cylix. Ancient fountains of this form were known both in Greece and Rome. Professor George Henry Chase has called my attention to an example reproduced on a Corinthian flask by Timonidas, which dates from the seventh century B.C.! See Buschor's Greek Vase Painting, fig. 44.

2. The later style of this basin and its terminal figure was first remarked by *Reymond*, S. F., IV, 144, n. 2. On the statue see also pp. 84, 130 of the present work.

*Photo Boecker. Courtesy of Duveen Brothers*

Figure 16. VERROCCHIO, MODEL FOR A FOUNTAIN FIGURE

*Courtesy of Mr. Henry Harris*

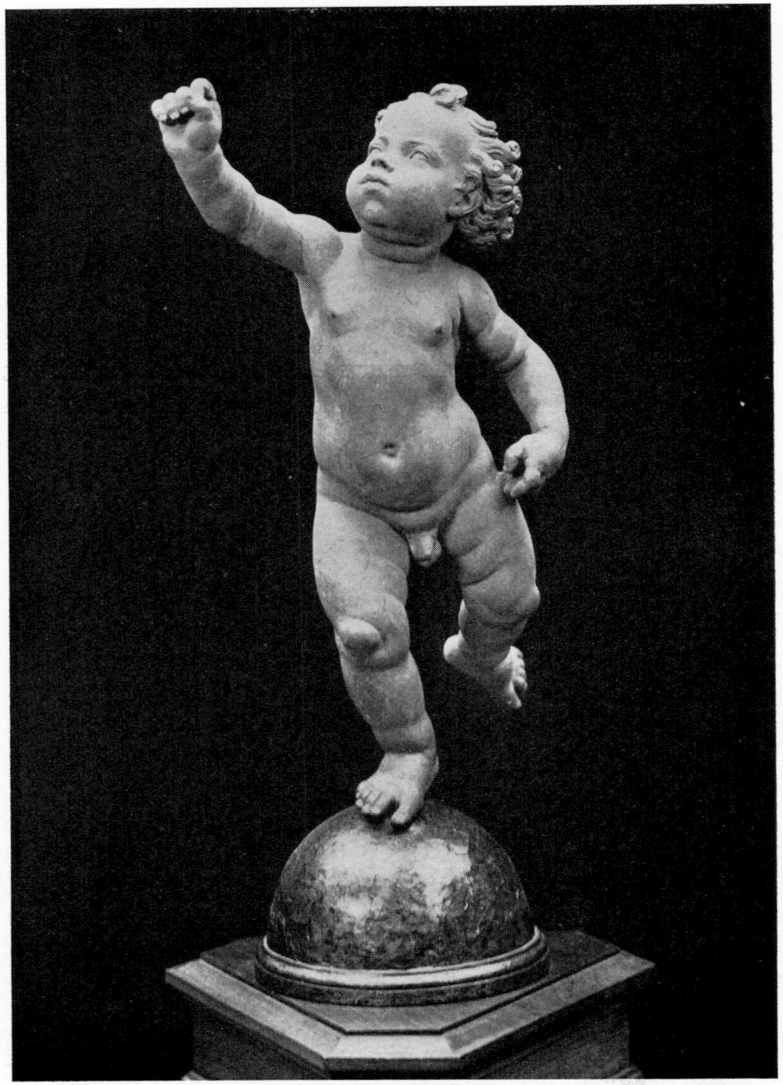

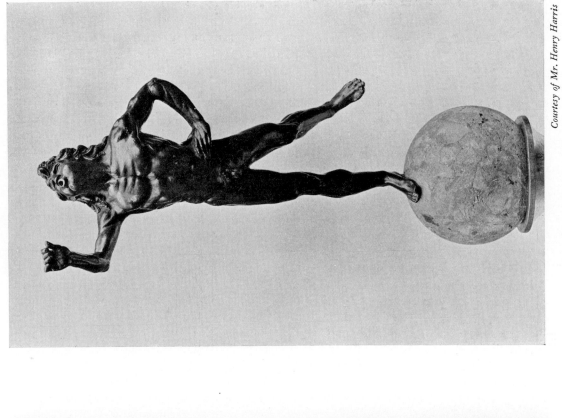

Figure 17. RUSTICI, FOUNTAIN FIGURE
Collection of Henry Harris, London

*Photo Alinari*

FIGURE 18a.  GIROLAMO DA CREMONA (?),
FRESCO WITH A FOUNTAIN

PALAZZO VENEZIA, ROME

*Courtesy of Mr. Fiske Kimball and the Walters Collection*

FIGURE 18b.  DETAIL FROM AN ARCHITECTURAL
PANEL BY LUCIANO LAURANA

WALTERS COLLECTION, BALTIMORE

*Photo Alinari*

FIGURE 18c.  DETAIL FROM A PAINTING
BY JACOPO DEL SELLAIO

THE UFFIZI, FLORENCE

*Courtesy of British Museum*

FIGURE 18d.  REVERSE OF A MEDAL BY
MATTEO DEI PASTI

From G. F. Hill's *Corpus of Italian Medals of the
Renaissance before Cellini*

FIGURE 20.  MATTEO CIVITALI, HOLY WATER BASIN

CATHEDRAL, LUCCA

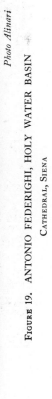

FIGURE 19.  ANTONIO FEDERIGHI, HOLY WATER BASIN

CATHEDRAL, SIENA

FIGURE 21.  DONATELLO OR HIS WORKSHOP (?), THE PAZZI FOUNTAIN
COLLECTION OF GEORGE BLUMENTHAL, NEW YORK

fountains. Holy water basins of similar form, however, abound in the churches, their pagan decoration often contrasting strangely with their Christian setting, as in the richly decorated pair by the Sienese sculptor Antonio Federighi, in the Cathedral at Siena, one of which is illustrated in Figure 19. As these are not supplied with running water, they must be distinguished from the true fountains, intended for the display of a continuous jet, which they resemble both in their classicizing form and rich ornament. The height of the pedestal is increased to make the holy water easily accessible to the worshipper. Such basins were clearly inspired by ancient prototypes; it may be that the earliest examples of the Renaissance were modelled upon the Roman vases of marble which often served as fonts and holy water basins in Italian churches during the Middle Ages. Sometimes the Tuscan *acquasantiere* bore figures like their secular counterparts, as in the example illustrated in Figure 20, one of a pair carved by Matteo Civitali for the Cathedral at Lucca (*c*. 1490). The tiny figure of the infant Christ which surmounts the basin might easily be mistaken for a putto.

The rarity of true cylix fountains known to date from the Quattrocento makes the handsome marble basin from the garden of the Pazzi Palace (Fig. 21) of exceptional interest, quite apart from the beauty of its contour and carving, and its traditional ascription to so great an artist as Donatello. Here, as in the holy water basins, the decoration is based upon classical *motifs* drawn from ancient urns, altars, and pilasters, applied with the lavish feeling for all-over ornament characteristic of the Florentine Quattrocento, when sculptors were invariably trained as goldsmiths. Coats of arms bearing the Pazzi dolphins decorate each corner of the upper surface of the triangular base. The missing shaft, said to have been shaped like a baluster or vase, probably resembled that of the *acquasantiera* at Lucca (Fig. 20), although it was undoubtedly shorter, supplying the needed transition between the triangular pedestal and the bowl above, and somewhat increasing the height of the basin. Presumably the basin originally contained an ornamental central shaft, through which the water issued; but this too has been lost.

This fountain was long ascribed to Donatello on the authority of Vasari and certain anonymous writers of the early Cinquecento, who saw it still *in situ*. Recently, however, it has been attributed by Bode to Antonio

Rossellino because of a somewhat obscure statement in Albertini's *Memoriale*: "In the garden of the Medici are some ancient things come from Rome; and in that of the Pazzi; and the fountain is by the hand of Rossello, except for the Hercules of ancient bronze." Although Albertini's reference in 1510 is the earliest mention of this fountain, I see no more reason for accepting it than for following his ascription to Rossellino of the lavabo in San Lorenzo, now generally rejected on stylistic grounds. Certainly the delicate tendrils and cupids on the triangular base (Fig. 21) have no parallel in Rossellino's known work, while they are somewhat similar to the *rinceaux* and putti upon the bronze console that supports Donatello's outdoor pulpit at Prato (1433). I am therefore inclined to assign this basin to Donatello or his workshop.[1]

According to Vasari and the *Anonimi*, a similar fountain by Donatello, carved of granite and decorated with ornaments of marble, adorned the garden of the Medici Palace. This lost basin was almost certainly the one crowned by Donatello's bronze group of Judith and Holofernes before it was seized by the state in 1495 and transferred to the *ringhiera* of the Palazzo Vecchio; for four openings at the corners of the cushion on which the body of Holofernes rests (Fig. 22) prove that this group was designed for the decoration of a fountain. As the most elaborate and monumental example of Florentine fountain sculpture from the entire century, this work merits special study. Although Donatello chose a Biblical subject, he made use of a classical fountain *motif*; the water spurted from the openings in the corners of the cushion below the drunken Holofernes, as from Hellenistic figures of tipsy satyrs on wineskins.[2] The theme of intoxication was continued in the bronze reliefs of the triangular pedestal in three Bacchic scenes representing the vintage, the wine press, and a drunken revel — all enacted by the inevitable putti. A potential water spout appears in the center of each side of the pedestal, as in the Gorgon's head on the great crater in the Bacchanal (Fig. 22); but these "mouths," although obviously designed for jets of water, were never pierced.

1. In later editions of his Florentiner Bildhauer der Renaissance, Bode himself returned to the older attribution.

2. A well known Hellenistic example of this *motif* in bronze is preserved in the Naples Museum: No. 5628. Some authors even interpret the cushion under Holofernes as a wineskin. Schubring believes that the water spurting from the corners of the cushion represents the blood of Holofernes; *Schubring*, D., p. li.

FIGURE 22.   DONATELLO, JUDITH AND HOLOFERNES
PALAZZO VECCHIO, FLORENCE

FIGURE 23.   THE MEDICI FOUNTAIN IN THE GROTTO
ROYAL VILLA, CASTELLO

Conscious of the need of plurifacial treatment in a freestanding group, Donatello designed the Judith and Holofernes as a pyramid which presents three distinct profiles, each corresponding to a side of the pedestal below. The triangular plan of this pedestal undoubtedly repeats the broader triangle of the base of the lost cylix (compare Figures 21 and 23); and the granite of which that basin was carved recurs in the balusters that frame the reliefs. Few works of art have suffered as much as this group when removed from their original setting. The broad base supplied by the cylix undoubtedly tended to stabilize the statue, now perched precariously upon a slender column which certainly has no connection with the original fountain.

The group of Judith and Holofernes was probably executed about 1455, after the artist's return from Padua; the relaxed head of the Holofernes is similar to that of the Christ in his Crucifix in Sant' Antonio. The complicated drapery of the Judith and the intensity and confusion of the bas-reliefs are also in his later vein. Moreover, the fountain was almost certainly designed for the Medici Palace, which was not commenced till 1444, after his departure for Padua.

Some writers assume that Donatello's bronze David, which originally stood in the courtyard of the Medici Palace, was also a fountain figure, Dr. Paul Schubring exalting it in a long passage as "the first fountain figure of the Renaissance." [1] Naturally I should be only too happy to swell the scanty number of fifteenth century fountain figures by the addition of so distinguished an example; but I can find no evidence that this statue was either intended or used as the decoration of a fountain. Certainly the head of the Goliath shows no signs of having been pierced for a jet of water.

Figure 23 shows the Medici cylix as it stood in the grotto at Castello, before it was moved to its present site; but as this grotto cannot have been constructed before 1538, when Tribolo commenced the work at Castello, and was probably considerably later,[2] it may originally have been designed for another Medicean villa or palace. Its triangular base is adorned on two sides with the diamond ring and the motto "*Semper*," and at the corners

1. *Schubring*, D., pp. xxviii–xxix; *Bode*, K. F. R., p. 26, and Semrau, in *Thieme-Becker*, IX, 422.
   2. See p. 75.

of its upper surface with shields containing six Medici balls. As the number of *palle* upon the Medici coat of arms was first reduced to six during the reign of Lorenzo il Magnifico (1469–1492), the basin cannot be earlier than 1469. The cryptic legend on one side of the pedestal: "Lest you be a prey to your own thoughts, the golden god of the godless in his waters turns men into birds or into adamant," [1] probably refers to a lost fountain figure, which may have surmounted the shaft before the addition of the present basin and putto in the style of the Cinquecento.

This fountain has been variously ascribed. Milanesi in his annotations to Vasari's Lives assigned it first to Donatello, attempting to identify it with that master's granite fountain made for the garden of the Medici Palace, and later to Antonio Rossellino, who, according to Vasari, constructed a marble fountain for the same palace, with figures of putti squeezing dolphins. The *terminus post quem* of 1469, however, precludes the first attribution; and the second is often questioned on stylistic grounds. The name of Francesco di Simone Ferrucci has also been proposed in recent years, on what grounds I have been unable to discover. Whoever the artist may be, he has obviously drawn upon the decorative works of Donatello and his school for many of the *motifs* used. For example, the dolphins and shells on the rim of the basin occur in the singing gallery at San Lorenzo; and the decoration of the vase-like shaft recalls that of the balusters round the base of the Marzocco.

A charming fountain of a more complex type is depicted in Pinturicchio's mural of the legend of Susanna, in the Borgia Apartments of the Vatican (Fig. 24). A richly carved cylix resembling the basin of the Medici fountain is set over a polygonal receiving basin raised upon steps, and surmounted by a secondary basin, decorated with three bronze putti, bearing dolphins or cornucopias. Still more elaborate fountains, with additional basins and a central shaft lavishly decorated with figure sculpture, appear in the fascinating sketchbooks attributed to Jacopo Bellini, in the Louvre and the British Museum. The one illustrated in Figure 26 is almost as pretentious as the Great Fountain which Tribolo constructed at

---

1. I am indebted to Professor Edward Kennard Rand for this translation of the ambiguous inscription:

"Ne sis preda tuis atheon deus aurea unda
In volucres vertit vel adamanta viros."

Figure 25.  AGOSTINO DI DUCCIO, PUTTI DANCING ROUND A FOUNTAIN

S. Francesco, Rimini

Figure 24.  PINTURICCHIO, SUSANNA AND THE ELDERS BY A FOUNTAIN

Borgia Apartments, Vatican, Rome

FIGURE 26.  JACOPO BELLINI, DETAIL OF A DRAWING WITH A FOUNTAIN
THE LOUVRE, PARIS

Castello in the following century (Fig. 39). Another instance of this type occurs in a bas-relief by the Florentine sculptor Agostino di Duccio, in the Tempio Malatestiano at Rimini (Fig. 25). Were such complicated fountains actually constructed in Italy in the Quattrocento, or are these representations merely creations of the artist's fancy? So far as I can determine, no actual fountains with the rich use of figure sculpture seen in these pictured ones have been preserved from the fifteenth century.

The dearth of monumental public fountains in Florence and its environs during the Quattrocento was due chiefly to the inadequate water supply. Their place was undoubtedly taken by ornamental well-heads, like the handsome examples by Bernardo Rossellino still preserved at Pienza. However, public fountains were frequently included in ideal projects for piazzas, as in a panel from a Florentine *cassone* in the Schlossmuseum, Berlin, dated in the last years of the century, from which a detail is reproduced (Fig. 27). Within a severe polygonal receiving basin rises a richly carved shaft in the shape of a great classicizing vase, crowned by a statue of Abundance. Slender streams of water spurt from the vase into the great basin below, and the ubiquitous putti appear on the edge of the receiving basin. This vase-form occurs in an actual Tuscan example, believed to date from the Quattrocento — the monumental public fountain at Asciano, in which the decorative sculpture is probably by a Florentine hand (Fig. 28).

In the Quattrocento well-heads, lavabos, and holy water basins undoubtedly far outnumbered the true fountains. For this there were several reasons. First, the water supply of Florence was extremely limited in the fifteenth century, being chiefly supplied by wells and springs.[1] Vasari tells us that the fountains which Michelozzo devised for the Palazzo Vecchio played only on special occasions, and had to be supplied either by water raised from wells, or by rain water collected in reservoirs which he had constructed at the top of the palace.[2] Even in Vasari's day, fountains seldom played continuously; when, on a special occasion in 1536, the fountain in the Palazzo Medici played all day long, he deemed it worthy of special comment.[3] Apparently it was not till late in the reign of Cosimo I that a

1. According to Guido Carocci, in the Illustratore Fiorentino (1906), p. 43, the water supply of Florence in the Quattrocento was drawn chiefly from wells.
2. *Vasari*, II, 436–437.
3. *Vasari*, VII, 260.

supply of running water sufficient to permit the luxury of continuously playing fountains was brought to the city.[1]

Second, private commissions for sculpture in the Quattrocento were still largely for ecclesiastical structures, such as tombs, pulpits, altars, fonts, and lavabos. The great field for the secular fountain — the private villa — was still almost undeveloped. The grounds of the early Tuscan villas consisted chiefly of flower beds of geometrical design, surrounded by elaborate topiary work, and occasionally accented by a simple fountain.[2] Toward the end of the century more ambitious plans were made throughout Italy, for gardens with elaborate sculptural decoration and numerous fountains; but these were seldom carried to completion — often because of the inadequate water supply. The realization of the Florentine sculptor's dream of reproducing the magnificence of the ancient Roman fountains came only in the Cinquecento, with the phenomenal development of the Tuscan villa in that period.

To this generalization there was one monumental exception — the Villa of Poggio Reale at Naples, commenced in 1487 by the Florentine architect and sculptor, Giuliano da Maiano, and famous for the number and richness of its fountains. We read of one so large that it could furnish all Naples with water! Fountains with figure sculpture are mentioned, and the reservoirs with representations of aquatic animals anticipate similar Florentine types in the sixteenth century. Evidently most of the forms known to the Cinquecento — fishponds, isolated fountains, grottoes, and canals or brooks — were represented. Unfortunately, this villa was later destroyed, and of all its grandeur nothing remains except vague references in the literature. Its destruction leaves a wide *lacuna* in the history of the Florentine fountain; for Poggio Reale undoubtedly contained the prototypes of the fountains erected in the Tuscan villas of the Cinquecento.

1. Cosimo I's addition to the water supply of Florence is commemorated upon a medal, dated 1567, cast by Pietro Paolo Galeotti. The reverse is decorated by an aqueduct and a fountain; *Vasari*, III, 27, and VII, 542, and Supino, Il Medagliere Mediceo nel Museo Nazionale, nos. 384–385 and p. 134.

2. See Luigi Dami, "Il Giardino Italiano nel Quattrocento," in Dedalo (1920), p. 368 ff.

FIGURE 28.  PUBLIC FOUNTAIN

ASCIANO

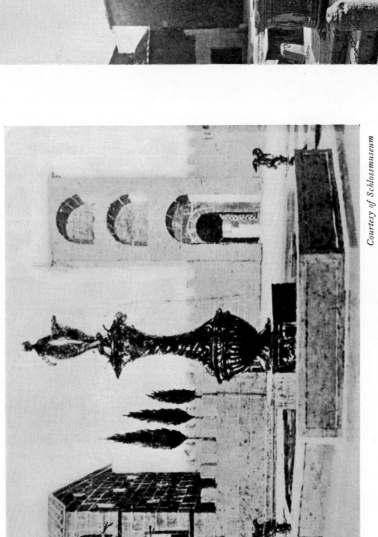

FIGURE 27.  DETAIL OF A CASSONE PAINTING

SCHLOSSMUSEUM, BERLIN

FIGURE 30.  FOUNTAIN OF THE DRAGONS

VILLA D'ESTE, TIVOLI

FIGURE 29.  VENTURINI, ETCHING OF THE AXIS OF THE
VILLA D'ESTE, TIVOLI

From Falda's *Fontane di Roma*

# CHAPTER II

## THE CHARACTERISTICS OF FLORENTINE FOUNTAINS
## IN THE CINQUECENTO

IN ORDER to appreciate the peculiarly Florentine characteristics of the fountains constructed in the villas during the Cinquecento, one must first consider the part that fountains played in the design of Tuscan gardens. This stands out in particularly sharp relief when contrasted with their divergent rôle in contemporary Roman villas.

In the latter, wall fountains were generally used in preference to the freestanding types; for, placed on axis on successive terraces, they lent themselves to the grandiose effects of perspective which are the essence of the Roman garden style. The wall fountains which mark the central axis of the Villa d'Este at Tivoli (Fig. 29) and line the crossing, horizontal avenues (Fig. 34) are but recurring *motifs* of rising and falling water in a great symphony; the individual fountain loses its importance in contributing to the effect of the whole. Even when fountains of elliptical ground plan were used, they were combined with some architectural feature, losing the individual character of the centrally composed fountain. Thus the Fountain of Arethusa at the same villa was incorporated into an exedra (Fig. 31), while in the great Fountain of the Dragons (Fig. 32) the oval basin was set before one of the wall fountains which mark the longitudinal axis of the villa, and surrounded by circular steps.

The copious supply of water made available by the restoration of ancient aqueducts in Rome and its environs [1] led to the particular study of water effects, which were treated with a new grandeur and freedom. Majestic cascades fall from great heights into calm pools below (Fig. 33); a veritable geyser gushes upward from the Fountain of the Dragons (Fig. 30);

1. Apparently the first instance of the new grandiose treatment of the water appears at the Villa d'Este, commenced in 1550, where an unlimited supply of water was available, diverted from the falls of the River Aniene. In Rome itself, the partial restoration of the aqueducts in the last quarter of the sixteenth century under Gregory XIII and Sixtus V provided a surplus of water which made possible the elaborate effects for which the fountains of that city are famous.

and along the bypaths, a myriad minor jets toss their cooling spray into the air (Fig. 34). Roman fountains, above all others, seem primarily designed for the display of water; when temporarily deprived of the liquid element, they present a most unnatural appearance. The pathetic effect of one that remains permanently dry can be described only by the Italian phrase "una fontana morta."

The sculpture which decorated the Roman fountains, however, received little attention. This was due in part to the plethora of ancient statuary which could be reused, and the dearth of contemporary sculptors at Rome. The great second court of the Vigna di Papa Giulio and the grounds of the Villa Montalto were once alive with classical figures; while at the Villa d'Este there was originally a wealth of ancient statuary, much of which is now in the Vatican Museum. The late Thomas Ashby, in his study of the classical sculpture from this villa, remarked upon the inferior character and cheap material of the contemporary decorative sculpture which here and there eked out the supply of ancient marbles. But the chief cause for this indifference to the sculpture lay in the fact that the men who designed the fountains were primarily interested in the water and in architectural effects. In a word, the fountains of the Roman villas are architects' fountains.[1]

At the Florentine villas, where the design of fountains remained the function of sculptors, there was a marked predilection for the freestanding types, doubtless because of the opportunity which they afforded for sculpture in the round, a consuming interest in the Florentine school of the Cinquecento. Three large isolated fountains dominate the grounds of the Boboli Garden as depicted in 1599 on a lunette preserved in the Museo Topografico, Florence (Figs. 35 and 35a);[2] and two monumental examples mark the central axis of the lunette of the Villa at Castello (Figs. 36 and 36a), in contrast to the predominance of wall fountains in the gardens of

1. Their design was entrusted to the great papal architects from the time of Bramante to that of Maderna.

2. This lunette, painted in tempera, is one of a series of fourteen depicting Medicean villas preserved in the Museo Topografico at S. Marco. Two others are reproduced in the present work in Figs. 36 and 204. I owe my knowledge of the origin, author, and date of these paintings to the courtesy of Dr. Giovanni Poggi, who has discovered a document recording payment to a certain Giusto Utens for painting them in a room at the Villa Artimino in 1598–1599. They formed an important part of the section entitled "Ville Medicee" in the fascinating Exhibition of the Italian Garden held in the Palazzo Vecchio in 1931.

FIGURE 31. ETCHING OF THE FOUNTAIN OF ARETHUSA, VILLA D'ESTE, TIVOLI

From Percier and Fontaine's *Les Plus Celèbres Maisons de Plaisance de Rome*

FIGURE 32. ETCHING OF THE FOUNTAIN OF THE DRAGONS, VILLA D'ESTE, TIVOLI

From Falda's *Fontane di Roma*

FIGURE 33. WATER ORGAN AND CASCADES, VILLA D'ESTE, TIVOLI

FIGURE 34. THE HUNDRED FOUNTAINS, VILLA D'ESTE, TIVOLI

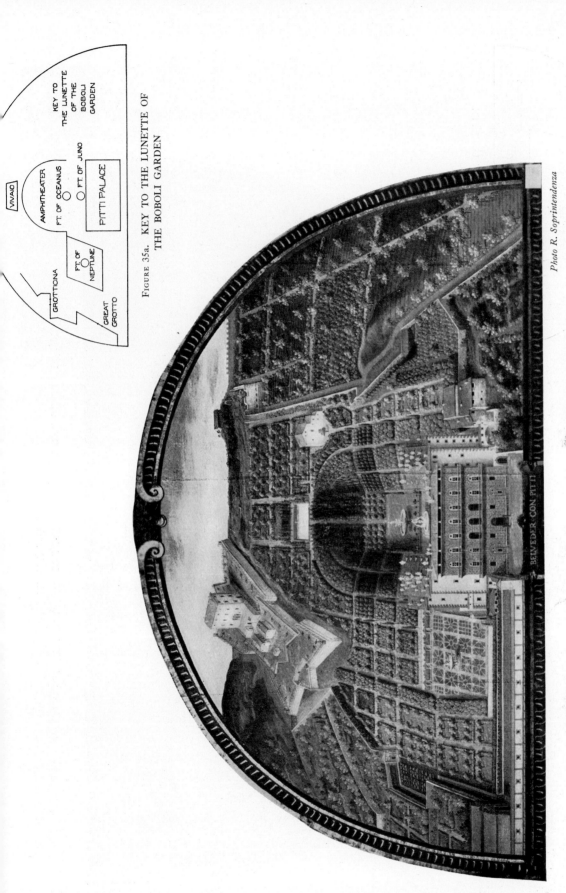

FIGURE 35a. KEY TO THE LUNETTE OF
THE BOBOLI GARDEN

KEY TO
THE LUNETTE OF
THE BOBOLI GARDEN

VIVAIO

AMPHITHEATER

FT. OF OCEANUS

FT. OF JUNO

GROTTICINA

FT. OF
NEPTUNE

GREAT
GROTTO

PITTI PALACE

BELVEDER CON PITTI

*Photo R. Soprintendenza*

FIGURE 35. GIUSTO UTENS, THE PITTI PALACE AND BOBOLI GARDEN IN 1599

MUSEO TOPOGRAFICO FLORENCE

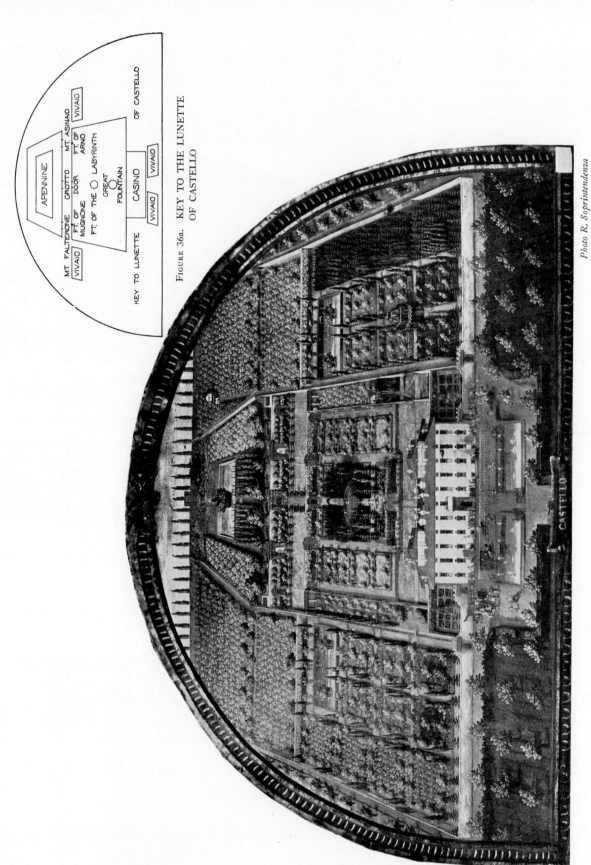

KEY TO LUNETTE

FIGURE 36a.  KEY TO THE LUNETTE
OF CASTELLO

| MT. FALTERONE | APENNINE | MT. ASINAIO | |
| VIVAIO | GROTTO | FT. OF ARNO | VIVAIO |
| | FT. OF MUGNONE | DOOR | |
| | FT. OF THE ○ LABYRINTH | | |
| | GREAT ○ FOUNTAIN | | |
| VIVAIO | CASINO | VIVAIO | |
| | OF CASTELLO | | |

CASTELLO

FIGURE 36.  GIUSTO UTENS, THE MEDICEAN VILLA OF CASTELLO IN 1599

Museo Topografico, Florence

the Villa d'Este (Fig. 29). Now the isolated fountain, when placed in the center of a square or garden, does not lend itself to larger unities, but retains its separate entity. Thus the Great Fountain at Castello (Fig. 39), though undoubtedly planned to mark the central axis of the gardens, actually obstructs the continuity of the perspective, and completely dominates its surroundings, telling as the focal point of the square garden in which it stands. The resulting effect, as seen in the lunette (Fig. 36), is one of coördination of equal parts about a central point, rather than the subordination of many parts to a vast plan, as at the Villa d'Este (Fig. 29).

The Roman fountains seem designed primarily for the display of water; the Florentine fountains exist rather for the display of sculpture. Certainly their outstanding characteristic in the Cinquecento is the tendency of the figure sculpture to dominate the structural portions of basins and shaft, as in the overpowering nudes upon Giovanni Bologna's Fountain of Oceanus in the Boboli Garden (Fig. 37), or the riot of sculpture which covers Ammannati's great Fountain of Neptune in the Piazza della Signoria (Fig. 38). In the design of Florentine fountains, the water plays only a minor part, seldom receiving a monumental treatment. This fact was due partly to the artists' primary interest in the sculpture, partly to the limited supply of water in Florence and its environs, which confined the sculptor to the effects possible with slender jets. The linking of the stream of water with the statue, which we have already observed in the Quattrocento,[1] was well adapted to this limitation; and the designers of fountains rang the changes on the water *motifs* evolved in the preceding century, adding others, such as the wringing out of the water from the hair or beard. Thus in Tribolo's charming Fountain of the Labyrinth, at the Villa of Petraia (Fig. 40),[2] a slender stream falls from the locks of the terminal figure. Such effects seem to us, with our knowledge of the naturalistic and massive handling of the water in the later Roman fountains, petty and artificial; but the Florentines of the Renaissance delighted in their ingenuity. Even when a considerable supply of water was available, as in the Great Fountain at Castello (Fig. 39), for which Tribolo united all the streams from the fountains on higher levels, there was a tendency to

1. See p. 7.
2. See p. 22, n. 2.

weaken the effect by subdivision into numerous petty jets. The water of the Tuscan fountain trickled rather than gushed. Today, after the wholesale deforestation of the Tuscan countryside in the nineteenth century, the water supply of Florence and its environs is more limited than ever, so that one frequently sees dry fountains. Yet the effect of the whole is seldom greatly impaired by the lack of the water, so slight is the part which it plays in the design, so great the emphasis upon the sculpture.

The isolated Tuscan fountains were constructed chiefly of white marble, although one or more figures of bronze might be added for the sake of contrast. The dazzling white of the stone stands out in sharp relief against the dark foliage of the Tuscan cypresses in the villas (Fig. 39) or the gray-brown walls of the city palaces (Fig. 38). Color was usually confined to the receiving basins, which might be made of granite or of one of the several kinds of variegated marbles known as "*breccia*" or "*marmi misti*," [1] while the basin of the fountain made by Francesco del Tadda for Verrocchio's Boy with a Dolphin (Frontispiece) was carved from a block of precious porphyry. For the wall fountains, a grayish sandstone known as "*pietra bigia*" or "*macigno*" was commonly used.

At Florence, since there was no surplus of classical sculpture to be reused, sculptors of the first rank sought the commissions for fountains. Indeed, a list of the Florentine artists who designed fountains in the Cinquecento reads like a roll call of contemporary sculptors. The chief patrons were the Medici, and the great centers of development their three villas — Castello, Boboli, and Pratolino. The development begins, properly speaking, in 1538, soon after Cosimo the First succeeded Alessandro dei Medici. Now secure in his position, he turned at once to the embellishment of his villa at Castello.

An aqueduct to supply water to the villa had already been commenced by Piero da San Casciano; but a man of greater originality was needed to design the elaborate fountains and gardens which Cosimo had in mind. The commission was finally given to the sculptor Niccolò Tribolo.[2] His elaborate plans for the grounds of this villa, as described by Vasari, already

---

1. Many of the basins made of these variegated marbles had their origin in the particularly rich vein discovered at Pietrasanta in 1563: *Maclehose*, ¶ 99.
2. Also known as Niccolò dei Pericoli.

*Photo Alinari*

FIGURE 37.  GIOVANNI BOLOGNA, FOUNTAIN OF OCEANUS

BOBOLI GARDEN, FLORENCE

*Photo Alinari*

FIGURE 38.  AMMANNATI, FOUNTAIN OF NEPTUNE

PIAZZA DELLA SIGNORIA, FLORENCE

FIGURE 39.  TRIBOLO, THE GREAT FOUNTAIN
ROYAL VILLA, CASTELLO

included most of the types developed in the Cinquecento: the freestanding fountain with superimposed basins, the cylix, the wall fountain with a single niche, the *vivaio*, and the canal, of the formal sort; and in addition such rustic forms as the grotto and the island. Examples of several of these types can be made out on the lunette of the grounds of Castello in the Museo Topografico (Figs. 36 and 36a).

# CHAPTER III

## THE CANDELABRUM TYPE

THE most striking of the fountains which Tribolo designed for the Villa of Castello were undoubtedly the two freestanding examples with superimposed basins whose water effects we have already noted in the preceding chapter (Figs. 39 and 40), which appear upon the lunette of Castello (Figs. 36 and 36a). In a frescoed *tondo* in the Palazzo Vecchio which depicts Cosimo I surrounded by the chief artists in his employ, Tribolo sits at the right of the duke, proudly displaying the models for these fountains (Fig. 51). In them he has continued the tendency toward greater elaboration of the freestanding type which we have already noted in Quattrocento drawings and reliefs of fountains (Figs. 24 to 26), multiplying the number of basins and covering the shaft with figure sculpture.

Because of its rich sculptured ornament and tall shaft in several stages I have christened this elaborate form the "candelabrum type." [1] Tribolo's Fountain of the Labyrinth, now at the Villa Petraia (Fig. 40),[2] is a classic example. Sculptured groups on different levels, represented in an ingenious variety of poses, support successive basins, which decrease in size as they ascend; the whole is terminated at the apex by a dominant statue or group, from which the central stream of water issues. The subordinate figures, however free their postures may be, are as a rule so closely affixed to the shaft, or so overshadowed by the projecting basins, that they serve chiefly to carry the eye upward. As a result, the culminating figure or group, rising independently above the fountain, and commonly given centrifugal lines, seems to burst forth from the comparatively formal lines of the structure like the jet of water itself.

1. Lomazzo, writing in 1585, also noted the resemblance of this type to classical candelabra: "Dalla forma de' candelieri sopradetti ne sono cavate le fontane, tonde, ovate, e quadre, in fondo di cui si fa il vaso che riceve l'acqua che da di sopra esce fuori da bocche di maschere, o di altre simili cose, ed in cima si fa qualche Dio Marino" (*Lomazzo*, bk. 6, chap. XLIX). The nucleus of this type was of course known in the Middle Ages: a large polygonal basin to receive the water, and a central shaft in the form of a column bearing a minor basin surmounted by a statue.

2. This fountain, originally erected at Castello, and moved to Petraia only in the time of Pietro Leopoldo, takes its name from the Garden of the Labyrinth at Castello; see Figs. 36, 36a.

FIGURE 40. TRIBOLO, FOUNTAIN OF THE LABYRINTH
ROYAL VILLA, PETRAIA

FIGURE 42. TRIBOLO, FOUNTAIN OF THE LABYRINTH

ROYAL VILLA, PETRAIA

GAILLON

FONS MARMOREVS
SITVS IN AREA

LA·FONTAINE·DE
MARBRE·DANS·LACOVRT

FIGURE 41. DU CERCEAU, ENGRAVING OF THE GREAT FOUNTAIN
AT GAILLON

From Les Plus Excellents Bâtiments de France

It is interesting to compare the two fountains at Castello (Figs. 39 and 40) with the earliest extant example of this type that I have discovered, made in 1506 by a group of Genoese sculptors working under the direction of Agostino Solario, for the château of the Cardinal d'Amboise at Gaillon. Although this fountain was destroyed in the seventeenth century, its design is preserved in an engraving by du Cerceau, reproduced in Figure 41. The comparison reveals striking similarities, not only in the general contour but in the detail as well. The tiny satyrs decorating the shaft in the engraving are practically identical with those on Tribolo's Fountain of the Labyrinth (Fig. 42). Only in the lower or receiving basin at Castello is there a marked advance. Instead of the high basin shown in the engraving, a low, vase-like form is used, so that the water is visible even from a distance. The profile of the basin, too, shows changes. During the Middle Ages and the Quattrocento the ground plans of basins had usually been confined to such simple geometrical figures as the circle, square, or polygon; and their sides were either merely curved (as in the bowl-shaped upper basins) or perpendicular (as in the receiving basins). In the Cinquecento receiving basins became more elaborate; mistilinear [1] effects (that is, combinations of straight and curving lines), were introduced both in ground plan and in elevation. Generally speaking, the tendency appeared first in the elevation; the severe perpendicular lines of the earlier receiving basins were replaced by more varied profiles, recalling the forms of classical mouldings. So far as I know, the basins at Castello are the first instances of the new form. [2]

In the exquisite Fountain of the Labyrinth (Fig. 40), with its just proportions, its subtle transitions from stage to stage, and its delicate bas-reliefs, the fine decorative tradition of the Quattrocento lives on. Save for the crowning figure, it is entirely of marble. According to Vasari, Tribolo himself carved the tritons which support the second basin, that basin, with its frieze of dancing putti bearing garlands, and the smaller bowl above, decorated with spouting masks and putti (Fig. 43). Pierino da Vinci made the shaft after Tribolo's model, carving the satyrs in very low relief,

1. I have formed this word after the Italian *mistilineo*, meaning "composed of straight and curving lines."
2. This development is paralleled in the profiles of contemporary well-heads.

the projecting putti, masks, and garlands, and even adding a few touches of his own devising. For the graceful bronze figure of Florence, wringing out her hair (Fig. 44), Tribolo had also made a model; but the present statue was executed by Giovanni Bologna. It is one of his loveliest figures, recalling his small bronzes of bathing women.

As usual, the Florentine sculptor has made the most of a meager jet of water. The *motif* of the terminal figure is of course based upon the classical type of Venus Anadyomene. The slender stream that drops from the locks of this statue (Fig. 40) falls into the rim of the basin at the summit of the fountain, trickles through the mask-like spouts on its under side, and gathers in the larger bowl below, until at length it brims over the bevelled edge into the receiving basin. The form of this fountain expresses perfectly the function of the candelabrum type: the vertical shaft parallels the upward movement of the jet, while the graduation and spacing of the basins correspond to the rhythm of the descending stream of water.

The Great Fountain, constructed in the adjoining garden at Castello (Figs. 39, 36, and 36a), was much larger and more imposing than its neighbor. For it Tribolo gathered an unprecedented volume of water by joining all the conduits from the fountains on higher levels. The central jet gushes upward from the mouth of the strangled Antaeus in the bronze terminal group like a geyser,[1] rising with force to a great height (Figs. 45 and 39). Such a spectacular display of water is unusual in the Florentine fountain, where slender streams are the rule. Yet even here, where the water supply is comparatively unstinted, it is subdivided into a number of small jets, so that the effect, though elaborate, is on the whole petty. The various minor outlets for the falling water are: the dolphins on which the four putti below the main group ride (Figs. 45 and 46); the capricorns, insignia of Cosimo I, which serve as gargoyles on the basin below (Fig. 46); and the beaks of the geese held by the boys round the shaft (Fig. 47).

According to Vasari, the commission for the execution of the terminal group, designed by Tribolo (Fig. 45), was given first to Montorsoli and then to Vincenzo Danti; but the present bronze group was finally executed by Bartolommeo Ammannati, in the years 1559 and 1560, as payments for

1. Representing the breath of Antaeus, forced from his body — surely one of the most bizarre of the water *motifs* evolved in the Cinquecento!

FIGURE 44. DETAIL OF THE FOUNTAIN OF THE LABYRINTH

ROYAL VILLA, PETRAIA. BRONZE FIGURE OF FLORENCE BY GIOVANNI BOLOGNA

Photo Alinari

FIGURE 43. DETAIL OF THE FOUNTAIN OF THE LABYRINTH

ROYAL VILLA, PETRAIA. SHAFT CARVED BY PIERINO DA VINCI

FIGURE 46. TRIBOLO AND OTHERS, SHAFT OF THE GREAT FOUNTAIN

ROYAL VILLA, CASTELLO

FIGURE 45. AMMANNATI, HERCULES AND ANTAEUS

TERMINAL GROUP OF THE GREAT FOUNTAIN, ROYAL VILLA, CASTELLO

the casting of the two figures recorded in the Medici account books show. These massive forms have none of the wiry energy of Pollaiuolo's group of Hercules and Antaeus; rather they recall the ancient marble group in the courtyard of the Pitti Palace, or engravings of this scene by masters of Mantegna's school. However, the contrast of the heavy, downward tendency felt in every line of the figure of Hercules with the lighter body and centrifugal pose of his victim is Ammannati's own. The affinity between the lines of Antaeus' body, struggling upward and outward, and the explosive character of the jet is obvious.

From the heavy, classicizing character of the Hercules and Antaeus one turns with relief to the lively naturalism of the putti who sit upon the pedestal of the fountain, clamber over the edge of the basin above, dance round the shaft, or perch with dangling legs just below the great bronze group (Figs. 48, 47, and 46). These are no decorative cupids drawn from the repertoire of classical mythology; they are real children, represented at varying ages and in an ingenious variety of poses. In one field at least — the treatment of the child form — the sculpture of the Cinquecento cannot be dismissed as cold and academic.

Unfortunately, Vasari is not so specific as we could wish as to the sculptors of these little figures, stating only that the four bronze urchins who play on the edge of one of the basins (Figs. 47 and 49) were modelled by Pierino da Vinci and cast in bronze by Zanobi Lastricati, and that four of the marble putti were carved by Antonio Lorenzi. Records in the Medici account books prove that the latter sculptor worked upon this fountain for several years after Tribolo's death in 1550, at times assisted by his brother, Stoldo Lorenzi; but unfortunately the payments are marked simply "For working on the marbles of the Great Fountain in the garden at Castello," and only once specifically "For work on the statue of Esculapius *and on the shaft of the great fountain* in the garden at Castello." This, coupled with Vasari's statement, may indicate that Antonio Lorenzi executed the four putti at the top of the shaft. According to Borghini, the eight putti round the base, four of which appear in Figure 48, were by Tribolo's own hand. Dr. Ulrich Middeldorf's assumption that the boys playing with the geese round the center of the shaft (Figs. 47 and 49) are by Pierino da Vinci is not supported by any statement by Vasari; for the shaft of the Fountain of the Labyrinth, which Vasari definitely gives to this sculptor, is not to be confused with the shaft of this fountain. He is right, however, in pointing out the strong stylistic affinities of these figures, particularly in the quivering modelling of the flesh, with other works attributed to this artist. To sum up a complicated situation: the design is Tribolo's and the execution partly his, partly that of his pupils, Pierino da Vinci and Antonio Lorenzi; and the latter carried the whole to completion, with some assistance from his brother Stoldo.

In this fountain the sculpture is no longer confined to low and high reliefs, carved from the shaft, as in the Fountain of the Labyrinth, but consists of figures in the round, projecting boldly beyond the architectural lines of shaft and basins (Figs. 3 and 49). This tendency of the human form to break through the architectural lines is a symptom of the approaching baroque [1] found even earlier in paintings and drawings of fountains, which undoubtedly influenced the design of actual fountains. Thus the figures climbing over the edge of the basin are paralleled in the frescoed fountains attributed to Girolamo da Cremona in the frieze of the Sala dei Paramenti in the Palazzo Venezia at Rome, one of which is reproduced in Figure 18a.[2] Both Mantegna and Correggio made similar use of putti in their ceiling paintings.

Another symptom of the baroque is the addiction to momentary poses. The children on the fountain — from the boys round the base, who once bore garlands, through the bronze bathers on the edge of the bowl and the twisting dancers round the shaft, to the little rogues dangling their legs at the top — are represented in the most elaborate and varied *contrapposto*. In the figures on the rim of the basin and those of the boys with the geese, the body is turned sharply on its axis. Although executed by several hands, these figures are unquestionably based on models by Tribolo, and show him deeply interested in the representation of form in strongly moved and involved poses, as might be expected in a sculptor who had worked under

1. I use the word "baroque" in its established stylistic sense, not as a blanket term for all art of the seventeenth century. The exuberant emotion and expression and the centrifugal composition of baroque art are diametrically opposed to the repose, restraint, and closed composition of classic art (using "classic" in its stylistic sense, not as a blanket term for all Greek and Roman art). Furthermore, the full-blown baroque is generally characterized by a love of the grandiose.

2. On these paintings see Mario Salmi's article in the Bollettino d'Arte for April, 1923, pp. 467 ff.

Photo Brogi

FIGURE 47. DETAIL OF THE GREAT FOUNTAIN, CASTELLO

BRONZE PUTTI BY PIERINO DA VINCI

Photo Brogi

FIGURE 48. PUTTI BELOW THE FIRST BASIN OF THE GREAT FOUNTAIN, CASTELLO

FIGURE 49. DETAIL OF THE GREAT FOUNTAIN, CASTELLO

BRONZE PUTTO BY PIERINO DA VINCI

Michelangelo in the Medici Chapel. Tribolo's preoccupation with the problems of motion and of the human figure in torsion undoubtedly influenced his successor in fountain sculpture, Giovanni Bologna.

Tribolo must have designed both of these fountains shortly after 1538, when the new work at Castello commenced. The sculpture of the Fountain of the Labyrinth was probably completed before his death in 1550, since the documents after that date speak of setting up both fountains and installing the water, but specify actual sculptors' work for the marbles of the Great Fountain only. This is in perfect accord with Vasari's statements concerning the sculpture of the two fountains. As for the terminal statues, we have seen that Ammannati's bronze group of Hercules and Antaeus was completed about 1560; and Giovanni Bologna's "Florence" can scarcely have been added earlier, for he was not employed by the Medici until the year 1559. Indeed, its free conception in the round and the comparative maturity of its style suggest an even later date.

The Fountain of Orion, erected in the Piazza del Duomo at Messina between the years 1547 and 1553 by Giovanni Angelo Montorsoli,[1] is the most elaborate example of the candelabrum type in the entire century (Fig. 50). Now the vertical lines and ornate decoration of this type are best suited to the villa, where the form apparently originated; the strong contrasts of the white and variegated marbles and the profusion of fantastic sea creatures seem out of place in the center of a city piazza. Montorsoli perhaps felt this, for he added to the type as we have known it in the villa a series of steps to serve as a transition between the piazza and the fountain proper. He also used a higher receiving basin, so that the water can be seen only at close range.

We are struck at once by the more complicated ground plan (Fig. 52). Hitherto, this had been comparatively simple: square, circular, or octagonal, as in the two fountains at Castello. Here, the steps are twelve-sided,

1. Stefano Bottari [(L'Arte XXXI (September–December, 1928), 235 ff.] quotes a portion of a document of 1547 in the Archives at Messina, which speaks of a model made for this fountain by the local Domenico Vanelli, who was to obtain a sculptor to execute his design; but the model was probably of the most general sort, leaving much to the initiative of Montorsoli. Certainly in the dedicatory inscription of 1553 he signs himself "architect" as well as sculptor, while no mention of Vanelli is made there. The whole fountain seems to me to bear the imprint of the Florentine master. He was assisted in this work by several sculptors: Martino Montanini, Giuseppe Bottone, Battista and Gian Domenico Mazzolo, Domenico and Andrea Calamec. Several of these remained at Messina to spread the Florentine style of the Cinquecento through Sicily.

and opposite four of these sides the great basin is indented to admit a small oval one, which catches the water from an urn held by a huge, recumbent river god, stretched out on the edge of the basin above — a *motif* hitherto confined to wall fountains.[1] In addition to the minor basins below the river gods, still smaller ones are set before the curious monsters which serve to carry the eye inward to the indented portions of the basin.

These recumbent figures undoubtedly reflect the influence of the ancient river gods — the Nile, Tigris, and Tiber — set up over fountains in the garden of the Belvedere in the Vatican,[2] which Montorsoli had seen when employed by Clement VII in 1523 to 1524 to restore the Laocoon; but the limbs are thrown into more restless poses, recalling those of the reclining figures of Michelangelo in the Medici Chapel, where Montorsoli had worked in 1533; note the sprawling legs of the figure at the left of Figure 53. The streams personified are the Nile, Tiber, Hiberus (symbolical of the countries over which Charles V ruled), and the local Cumano, from which the water of the fountain was derived. This allegory was probably suggested by the four fountains made for the temporary decoration of the Ponte Santa Trinità at Florence in the year 1536, on the occasion of the Emperor's triumphal entry into Florence — a colossal figure of the Arno, modelled by Montorsoli, and smaller ones of the Rhine, Bagradas, and Hiberus by Tribolo and Raffaello da Montelupo.

The elaborate shaft of this fountain depicts the triumph of Orion. The effect of motion and excitement that pervades this fountain increases as the eye travels inward and upward (Fig. 50). First we note the sea monsters, cast in rigid poses; then the recumbent river gods, who seem a bit restive; next, the tritons that support the first basin. Their nether limbs are spread, their tails wave, their arms are raised; yet their figures still conform to the compact lines of the shaft. The naiads above, riding dolphins, fling their legs and arms upward in wild abandon; and the putti on dolphins upon the next stage, while managing their unruly steeds with one hand, wave the other hilariously in the air. The excitement culminates at the summit in the triumphant figure of Orion, the fabled founder of Messina.

On the Great Fountain at Castello the richness of the sculptural decora-

1. See pp. 32–35.                    2. See p. 32.

Figure 50.  MONTORSOLI, FOUNTAIN OF ORION, MESSINA

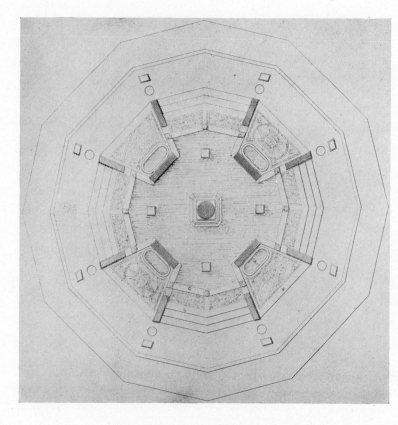

FIGURE 52. GROUND PLAN OF MONTORSOLI'S FOUNTAIN OF ORION
AT MESSINA

From Hittorff and Zanth's *Architecture Moderne de la Sicile*

*Photo Brogi*

FIGURE 51. DUKE COSIMO I AND HIS ARTISTS, WITH TRIBOLO
AND HIS MODELS FOR CASTELLO AT THE RIGHT

FRESCO BY VASARI IN THE PALAZZO VECCHIO, FLORENCE

tion was relieved by the simplicity of the basins and by the architectural portions of the shaft. Here, the shaft is completely concealed by the swarm of moving creatures who with their upraised arms reinforce the vertical lines of the shaft. In addition to these figures there is an unbelievable wealth of decorative sculpture. Each of the twenty faces of the main basin bears a bas-relief with a story drawn from the mythology of the waters: Narcissus turned into a fountain, Diana and Actaeon, Icarus falling into the sea, the story of Arethusa, et cetera (Fig. 53). The angles are marked by grotesque terms, and the remaining surfaces of the basin decorated with fruits of the sea. Even the inner basins are not left unadorned; fluting, shells, masks cover every available inch of surface. There is no reminiscence of the delicacy of the Quattrocento here; rather we have the hard, classicizing style generally associated with the Cinquecento, with a hint of the baroque in the tendency to agitated movement.

Nowhere in the sculpture of the sixteenth century can this tendency be studied to better advantage than in the fountains. Evidently the sculptors felt an affinity between the intense motion and centrifugal poses of their figures and the rush of the waters. A notable illustration of this effect is seen in the four bronze youths upon the Fountain of the Tortoises in the Piazza Mattei at Rome (later works by the Florentine sculptor Taddeo Landini), whose pose is strikingly similar to that of the four naiads on the Messina fountain (Figs. 4 and 50).

The abundant water supply for this fountain was divided among many jets, which issued from the mouths of the dolphins under the putti and naiads, from hideous masks carved on their basins, from four fish placed within the great basins, through the urns of the river gods, and from the eight masks set under the sea monsters, into the little outer receptacles.

The receiving basin, mistilinear in profile, differs from that of the Great Fountain at Castello not only in its greater size and height, which precludes a view of the water within except at close range, but also in the exaggerated contrast of the straight and curved lines which lends a baroque character to its profile. No subtle transitions here!

In a small fountain of the candelabrum type to the left of the loggia of the Palazzo Doria at Genoa (Fig. 54) the swollen profile of the receiving basin, the use of conventionalized figures at regular intervals round its sides, and the tritons with raised arms bearing the first inner basin recall Montorsoli's fountain at Messina. On the other hand, the two inner, fluted basins, decorated by spouting masks, are strikingly similar to one of the basins on the earlier Genoese fountain at Gaillon, which would suggest a local origin and a date early in the sixteenth century. The resemblance of the putti with dolphins who dance round the shaft to the boys with geese round the shaft of the Great Fountain at Castello, however, indicates a date at least as late as the forties. This accords with the rather baroque profile of the basin and with the known date of the garden works at the Palazzo Doria, of which Montorsoli had charge shortly before his departure for Messina in 1547. This fountain has been variously attributed (to Montorsoli, to Perino del Vaga, and to Silvio Cosini); but the weight of the evidence seems to me to indicate that it was designed by Montorsoli, although probably executed by another hand. It would then be dated about 1547.

The complex ornament, elaborate water *motifs*, and vertical lines of the candelabrum type made a particular appeal to German taste; for fountains of this sort abound in German paintings and engravings of the early sixteenth century. One of the best known examples appears in Altdorfer's painting of the Rest on the Flight into Egypt, in the Kaiser Friedrich Museum (Fig. 55), signed and dated 1510. The Italianate character of both the ornament and the figure *motifs* is obvious. Actual fountains of this sort, dating from the second half of the century, are also preserved in Germany, some of them close to their Italian prototypes, others betraying in their sculpture an intermediary Flemish influence. As the type was assimilated to German taste, there was a tendency to suppress the basins and stress the central shaft, so that the result is often close to that of the native "Stockbrunnen," a fountain in which the shaft resembles a column. Thus, in Benedikt Wurzelbauer's Tugendbrunnen beside the Lorenz Kirche in Nuremberg (Fig. 56) (1585–1589), the upper basins are little more than ledges on which the statues stand, while the shaft has assumed very sturdy proportions. The nude figures of the Italian fountains are here replaced by draped allegorical statues, but the pagan fountain *motifs* remain; the water issues from the bare breasts of the Virtues![1]

1. For Italian examples of this *motif* see Figs. 10, 26, and 80.

FIGURE 53.   DETAIL FROM MONTORSOLI'S FOUNTAIN OF ORION  MESSINA

FIGURE 54.   MONTORSOLI (?), FOUNTAIN IN THE GARDEN OF THE PALAZZO DORIA, GENOA

*Photo Franz Hanfstaengl, Munich*

FIGURE 55. ALBRECHT ALTDORFER, REST ON THE FLIGHT INTO EGYPT

KAISER FRIEDRICH MUSEUM

*Photo Liebermann and Co.*

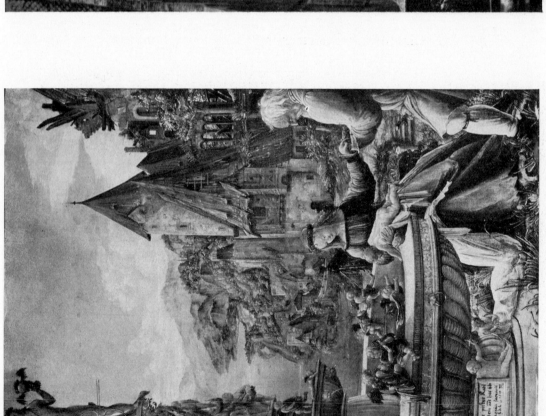

FIGURE 56. BENEDIKT WURZELBAUER, TUGENDBRUNNEN

NUREMBERG

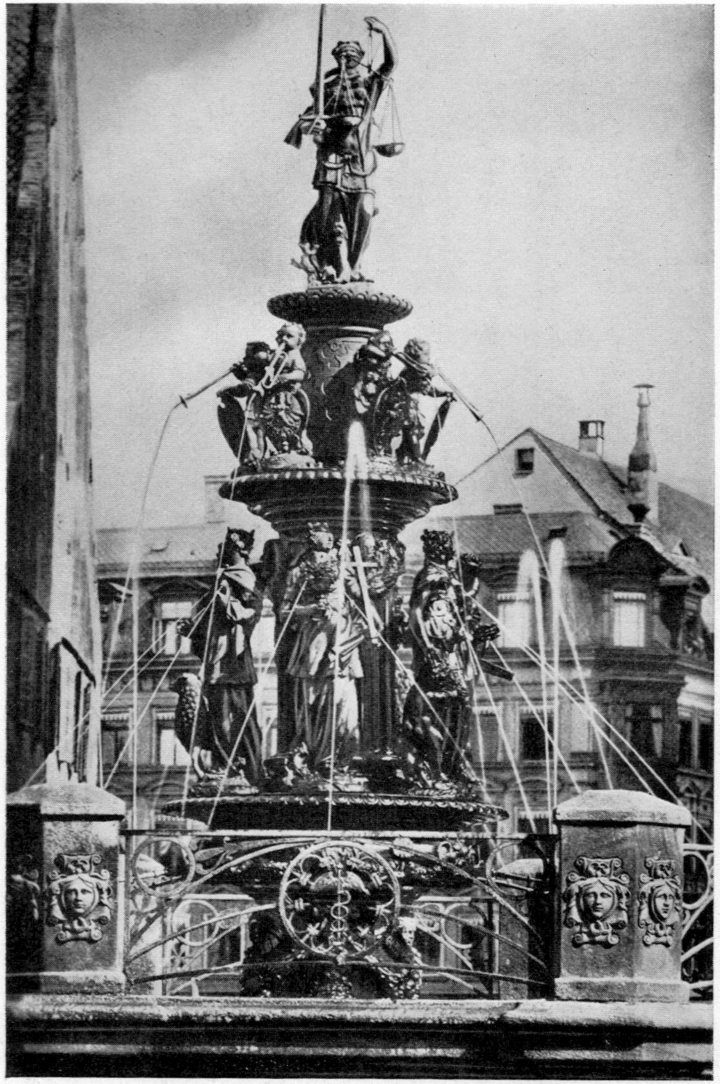

*Photo D. Anderson, Rome*

FIGURE 57. MAZO, THE FOUNTAIN OF THE TRITONS AT ARANJUEZ
THE PRADO, MADRID

*Photo Laurent*

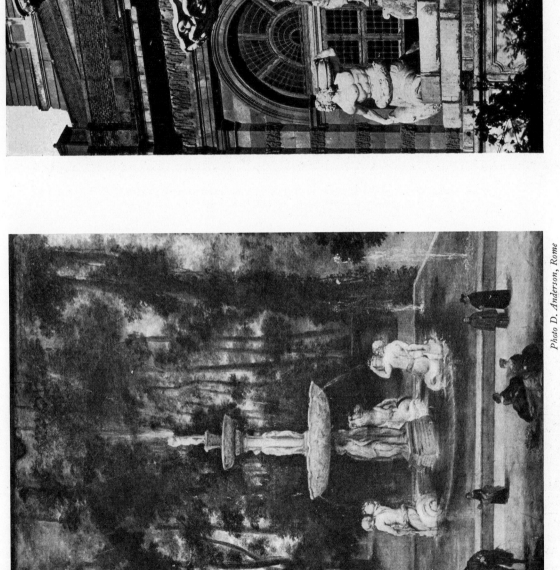

FIGURE 58. COSIMO LOTTI (?), FOUNTAIN OF THE TRITONS
ROYAL PALACE, MADRID

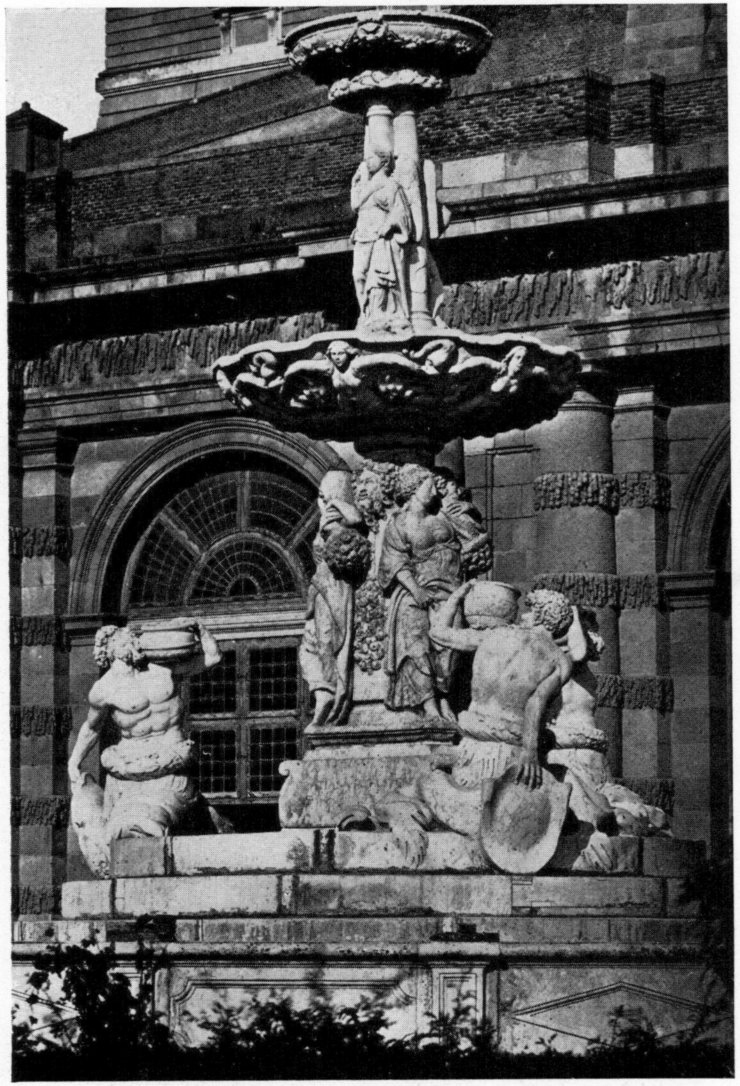

FIGURE 59.   FRANCESCO SUSINI, FOUNTAIN OF THE ARTICHOKES

TERRACE OF THE PITTI PALACE, FLORENCE

FIGURE 60.   BAROQUE FOUNTAIN WITH BASIN BY TRIBOLO

VILLA CORSINI, CASTELLO

Although the candelabrum type could scarcely develop beyond Montorsoli's Fountain of Orion either in size or in elaborate decoration, fountains of this sort were constructed by Florentine sculptors well into the seventeenth century. It was probably Cosimo Lotti, who in 1628 carried the Florentine garden style into Spain, who designed the Fountain of the Tritons at Aranjuez, which a painting in the Prado by Mazo, long attributed to Velasquez, reproduces in its original site (Fig. 57). This fountain is now situated in the Campo del Moro in the garden of the former royal palace at Madrid (Fig. 58). The contorted and fantastic figures of the tritons are in the more robust style of the baroque. Jets of water were originally contrived to fall from the four tall trees at the corner of the rectangle in which the fountain was placed, into the urns held by the four tritons![1]

A particularly attractive example of this type is the Fountain of the Artichokes, erected on the terrace above the courtyard of the Pitti Palace between 1639 and 1641, on the design of Francesco Susini. Placed on the axis of both the court and the amphitheater of the Boboli Garden, this fountain forms the central accent in a magnificent vista (Fig. 59). The naturalistic cascade which falls from a series of graduated basins on the side toward the court shows the influence of Roman water effects. The vertical effect usually sought for in the candelabrum type is here rejected in favor of more horizontal lines, in accord with the heavy, rusticated architecture of the palace (Fig. 61). In spite of the charm and naturalism of the putti and other figures, the artist has subordinated the sculpture to the lines of the structural portions and to the water effects to an extent unprecedented in a Florentine fountain. But, while the lines of the fountain proper are kept severely simple, broken only by the playful forms of the children placed at the corner of the octagonal basin, in the rich curves of the steps below, the spreading artichoke leaves which give the fountain its name, and the shell-like outer basin, a new decorative spirit appears, anticipating the effects of the rococo.

1. These streams can be seen in the actual painting, although they are not clear in the photograph reproduced in Fig. 57.

# CHAPTER IV

## WALL FOUNTAINS

### I. The River God and the Type with a Single Niche

URING the High Renaissance, the type of wall fountain with a single niche remained popular in Italy, but the delicate carving in low relief which the Quattrocento masters had lavished upon the architectural members was forgotten in the new interest in sculpture in the round. The enframement was now left almost severely plain, while the sculptors concentrated upon the classicizing figure, carved completely in the round, within the recess. The basin was usually of an oblong, trough-like shape reminiscent of ancient sarcophagi or of the great bathtubs from Roman thermae. A drawing of a fountain by some follower of Mantegna preserved in the Uffizi indicates that this type was already known in Italy in the late fifteenth century (Fig. 8); but its full development belongs to the Cinquecento.

Such wall fountains flourished particularly at Rome, where the inexhaustible supply of antique marbles could be utilized for their decoration. All that was needed was a niche, an ancient river god, and a sarcophagus to serve as a basin. The famous garden of the Belvedere in the Vatican, rich in classical sculpture, set the example for such *pastiches* to all Italy. Four ancient statues were there incorporated into fountains — three river gods, the Nile, Tiber, and Tigris, and the recumbent female figure then known as "Cleopatra." These fountains have long since been dismantled, and their marbles deposited in museums; but a drawing by Martin van Heemskerck preserves the form of the fountain of the Tigris, designed by Michelangelo at the request of Clement VII, and therefore to be dated during the years of his pontificate, 1523 to 1534 (Fig. 62).

At first glance, one is struck by the apparent formality of the single niche fountain reproduced in the sketch. The architectural enframement was apparently quite innocent of ornament, so that attention was focussed chiefly upon the recumbent river god and the richly carved sarcophagus.

FIGURE 61. FRANCESCO SUSINI, FOUNTAIN OF THE ARTICHOKES

TERRACE OF THE PITTI PALACE, FLORENCE

FIGURE 62. DRAWING OF THE FOUNTAIN OF THE TIGRIS IN THE VATICAN BELVEDERE

From Hülsen's *Römischen Skizzenbücher von Martin van Heemskerck*

A closer study of the drawing, however, reveals the naturalism of the setting devised by Michelangelo. The niche is conceived as a rocky cave which, according to Vasari, was carved from the pale greenish, stratified marble known as "cippollaccio." The treatment of the water is particularly interesting. It does not issue in a formal, single jet from the urn of the river god, but trickles from his rocky bed in irregular rivulets into the sarcophagus, from which it overflows into a small basin in the form of a fluted shell. This undoubtedly fed the outlet of the fountain, a shallow, rocky pool beneath the sarcophagus, from which crawl two lifelike turtles, which incidentally serve as supports at the corners of the sarcophagus.

At Florence, too, the reclining river god proved a popular subject for the decoration of the recess of the single niche wall fountain, to which its horizontal lines were well adapted. Since there was no supply of ancient statuary as at Rome, the sculptors carved their own figures, copying the classical style and recumbent pose of the Roman examples, but adding attributes appropriate to the local streams. The earliest examples recorded at Florence were modelled for the colossal temporary fountains constructed by Montorsoli, Tribolo, and Raffaello da Montelupo on the occasion of Charles the Fifth's visit to Florence, representing the local Arno and the Rhine, Danube, Bagradas, and Hiberus, the four latter symbolical of the emperor's far-reaching dominions. From Vasari's description of the attributes and recumbent position of these lost river gods it is clear that they followed the ancient types; but he does not mention their setting.

Fortunately we have more complete information concerning the twin fountains of the Arno and Mugnone, which Tribolo erected at the Villa of Castello between the years 1538 and 1547. These fountains, long since destroyed, can be dimly discerned on the lunette of Castello, on either side of the door in the wall at the end of the Garden of the Labyrinth (Figs. 36 and 36a). The indications of their form upon the lunette are too small and too sketchy to reproduce clearly, but a careful study of the lunette *in situ* reveals two wall fountains of the single niche type, each arched niche being crowned by a pediment and adorned with a reclining figure which pours water from an urn into an elaborate, oblong basin below. The representations upon the lunette are supplemented by the detailed description of Vasari, who tells us that Tribolo himself carved the statues of the two river gods and a relief of Fiesole which decorated the niche of the Mugnone. The river gods were of heroic size, each measuring four *braccia* in length (almost eight feet!), and were carved from a grayish sandstone ("pietra bigia"). His description of the poses of these statues is of special interest. The Mugnone reclined, bearing his urn on one shoulder, resting the other arm upon the ground, and crossing his left leg over his right; while the companion figure of the Arno rested his urn upon his thigh, leaning his arm upon the Florentine lion holding a lily.

The recumbent position of these statues was of course based on that of the classical river gods of the Belvedere; but a more involved treatment of the limbs seems implied by the phrase which Vasari uses of the Mugnone, "Raccolta in bellissima attitudine." This is borne out by the representation on the lunette of the Arno, the only one of the two figures to appear at all clearly. This complication of the calm classical pose is undoubtedly due to the influence of Michelangelo's reclining figures in the Medici Chapel, of which Tribolo had made small copies in clay only a few years before.[1] The discovery in the Boboli Garden of a portion of the relief which once decorated the arched recess of the Fountain of the Mugnone (Fig. 63) tends to corroborate this hypothesis concerning the Michelangelesque style of the statues; for the robust form, involved pose, and elaborate *contrapposto* of the figure personifying the city of Fiesole, arising from the rocks with the moon beneath her arm, clearly betray the influence of Tribolo's great master.

In many ways these wall fountains, with their reclining figures, oblong basins, and architectural framework, follow the type designed by Michelangelo for the Fountain of the Tigris in the Belvedere (Fig. 62); but in the latter, the naturalistic effect of a rocky cave was confined to the interior of the niche, leaving the architectural enframement severely plain. In the two fountains at Castello, on the other hand, not only were the slabs of grayish sandstone which formed the backgrounds of the niches carved to simulate stalactites, as in the fragmentary block of the Fiesole (Fig. 63), but the entire enframement of the niche was covered with actual stalactites of the type used in contemporary rustic fountains,[2] as may be seen on

1. Three of these are now preserved in the Museo Nazionale at Florence.
2. See p. 74 and Figure 145 for the type of natural stalactite used in the grotto at Castello.

the lunette (Fig. 36). This is undoubtedly the "Tuscan work covered with stalactites," of which Vasari speaks in a passage on fountains in the introduction to the *Lives*; for in the same section, discussing the types of natural stalactites used in rustic fountains, he specifically mentions the variety used by Duke Cosimo in his garden at Castello "in the rustic ornaments of the fountains made by Tribolo the sculptor."

Before each fountain extended an oblong basin, sustained by two capricorns, festooned with garlands and masks. The water, falling from the urn of the river god, overflowed through the indentations at the ends of the basin, issuing through the mouths of the goats. With the help of the scholar and poet, Benedetto Varchi, Tribolo had devised an elaborate allegory to link these fountains with the adjoining ones, with which their conduits were connected. The water for the Arno and Mugnone came from two fountains in the wall of the garden just behind that of the Labyrinth, where Tribolo had planned to set up figures personifying the nearby mountains Asinaio and Falterone, in which the respective rivers had their sources. The Asinaio was to have been represented as wringing out his beard into the basin below — a novel, if somewhat bizarre, fountain *motif*! Unfortunately these statues were never completed; in the lunette of 1599, the tall niches covered with stalactites which appear in the rear garden, on either side of the entrance to the grotto (Figs. 36 and 36a), remain empty, save for a simple water spout and basin.

During the years that Tribolo was working in the Medicean gardens at Castello, he made for the adjoining villa of Cristofano Rinieri a third river god of the same gray sandstone, for a fountain of the single niche type which stood at the end of a pool. The water fell from his urn into a huge stone basin decorated with lions' heads. This statue has survived in its original site, now the Villa Corsini (Fig. 64); but today it stands in a niche of another period and has been separated from its basin, which forms part of a baroque fountain. Again we feel the influence of Michelangelo; the dynamic pose of the river god recalls certain Ignudi of the Sistine ceiling. The almost Scopasian expressiveness of the head was probably inspired by the ancient Roman statue known as "Pasquino," but has certainly been heightened by long exposure to the elements. The water fell from the urn set between the legs of the figure into the great basin, with its curving lip and rather baroque profile (Fig. 60), which probably reflects the form of those designed for the fountains of the Arno and Mugnone. The background of the original niche (if not its entire surface) must have been composed of stalactites like those which still adhere to legs and urn.

This statue adds to the iconography of the Renaissance fountain a new *motif* — the seated river god. Previously these deities of the streams had been represented in the recumbent position of their classical prototypes; indeed, this rather static pose remained the usual formula throughout the sixteenth century. Since Tribolo carved this figure during the time that he was employed at the Medicean villa of Castello, it must be dated between the year 1538, when the work on the gardens of Castello was commenced under Cosimo I, and 1550, the year of Tribolo's death, and probably falls within the early forties. It thus antedates the seated river gods on Giovanni Bologna's Fountain of Oceanus in the Boboli Garden, which was constructed between the years 1567 and 1576 (Figs. 114 to 116), and was probably their prototype; the young Fleming, who made the terminal figure for Tribolo's Fountain of the Labyrinth at Castello, as well as the bronze birds in the grotto of that villa, must have known this figure at the adjoining Villa Rinieri.

Tribolo probably adopted the sitting posture partly because of its adaptability to a narrow niche, partly because of his desire to work out in the round the agitated pose suggested by one of Michelangelo's frescoed Ignudi. In doing so he set the precedent for a new conception of the river god, which typifies the turbulence rather than the fluid character of the stream. Giovanni Bologna transferred this *motif* from the wall fountain to the freestanding type (Fig. 114), copying the position of the urn, but giving his figures downward lines rather than the upward and outward lines of the earlier statue. Professor Antonio Muñoz, in considering the Boboli figures as possible prototypes for Bernini's famous river gods on the fountain in the Piazza Navona, Rome, has contrasted their comparative calm, characteristic of the usual Cinquecento treatment of the river god, with the agitation that pervades the baroque statues. Yet the Corsini river god, in spite of its early date, anticipates to an astonishing degree the excitation of the baroque.

For the figures of the Tiber and the Arno in his companion fountains in

*Photo Alinari. Courtesy of Prince Andrea Corsini*

FIGURE 64. TRIBOLO, RIVER GOD

VILLA CORSINI, CASTELLO

*Photo Brogi*

FIGURE 63. TRIBOLO, FIESOLE RISING FROM THE ROCKS

BOBOLI GARDEN, FLORENCE

FIGURE 66. AMMANNATI, THE ARNO

VILLA GIULIA, ROME

FIGURE 65. AMMANNATI, THE TIBER

VILLA GIULIA, ROME

the "loggia" or second court of the Villa Giulia at Rome (1550–1555), Bartolommeo Ammannati chose the more static recumbent pose, well adapted to the horizontal lines of these wide rectangular niches, and more attractive to his classic temperament (Figs. 65 and 66). These river gods, carved of *peperino*, recline against a stucco background of rocks and vegetation. The Tiber is attended by the Roman wolf; the Arno, with the usual Florentine lion, holds a cornucopia symbolizing plenty. The water issued from their urns into the trough-like marble basins of classical design, decorated at the angles with harpies. Both the figure *motifs* and the iconography of the Arno recall Vasari's description of Tribolo's Arno and Mugnone; indeed, the treatment of the entire court, with its many niches decorated with ancient sculpture (Fig. 76), is reminiscent of the latter's design for the garden of the Labyrinth at Castello. The free treatment of the form possible in the plastic *peperino* is particularly expressive of the fluid character of the streams, and suggests that the sculptor was influenced by the more pictorial figure of Marforio (Fig. 70), rather than by the usual hard, academic type of ancient river god.

It is unusual to find a wall fountain of the Cinquecento preserved intact, with figure, niche, enframement, and basin in good condition, as in the example in the great courtyard of the Palazzo Nonfinito in Florence (Fig. 67).[1] Relieved against a tall arched niche of *pietra serena* stands a marble Perseus of heroic size, represented in the act of slaying the dragon. No attempt is made at a naturalistic setting; the group is raised upon a formal pedestal of *pietra serena* above an oval marble basin into which water once flowed from slender metal tubes in the mouth of the monster. The rather baroque character of the consoles ornamenting the pilasters which frame the niche, the profile and grotesques of the basin, and the brackets upon the pedestal; the mannered, curving lines and momentary pose of the Perseus; and the sculptor's manipulation of the marble to counterfeit the softness of flesh — all imply a date in the last quarter of the sixteenth century.

With this tentative date, reached on grounds of style, the documentary evidence is in complete accord. The figure is listed by Borghini among

1. This fountain originally stood in the Palazzo Salviati, later known as the Palazzo Cepparello, now owned by the Banca del Credito Toscano. After its acquisition by the municipality in 1881, it was for a time set up in the convent of San Salvi.

works by Battista Lorenzi: "Later he made the Perseus of marble, four and a third *braccia* high, which is to be seen in the house of Jacopo Salviati, to his great honor." The origin of our figure in the Palazzo Salviati, and the close agreement of the height of the actual statue, 256 centimeters, with that given by Borghini, four and a third *braccia*, or about 252 centimeters, make the identification complete. As Vasari does not mention the figure in his brief account of the young Battista Lorenzi's works in his second edition of 1568, it was probably executed after that year; while a *terminus ante quem* is established by Borghini's mention of the statue in *Il Riposo*, published in 1584.

The same curving lines and pagan delight in counterfeiting soft flesh appear in Battista Lorenzi's figure of Painting, at the left of Michelangelo's tomb in Santa Croce (Fig. 68), long believed to represent the art of Sculpture, because of the *bozzetto* which the figure holds, and therefore wrongly given to Valerio Cioli.[1]

## II. The More Elaborate Types

The wall fountain seems to have been comparatively rare in Florence, where the freestanding form with rich sculptural decoration was always more popular. For the more elaborate development of this type we must turn to Rome, where the addorsed fountain, because of its architectonic character, always enjoyed a particular vogue. Yet, strangely enough, the earliest Roman wall fountains of the more elaborate sort to be constructed during the sixteenth century were designed by two Florentine sculptors, Michelangelo and Ammannati.

In 1536 Michelangelo designed the present arrangement of the Campidoglio at Rome, with the façade of the Palazzo Senatorio (Fig. 69). According to his plan, as known from Dupérac's copy of 1569, the triangles formed by the stairs on either side were to be decorated with two ancient statues of river gods recently excavated, while a colossal figure of Jupiter was to fill the central niche. That his plans specified a fountain, we know from three jets which appear on Dupérac's engraving. Michelangelo's

---

1. The brushes and palette which the figure also holds prove beyond question that the art represented is painting. A passage in *Borghini* (p. 108) shows that this was clearly understood in the sixteenth century.

*Photo Alinari*

FIGURE 67. BATTISTA LORENZI, FOUNTAIN OF PERSEUS
PALAZZO NONFINITO, FLORENCE

*Photo Alinari*

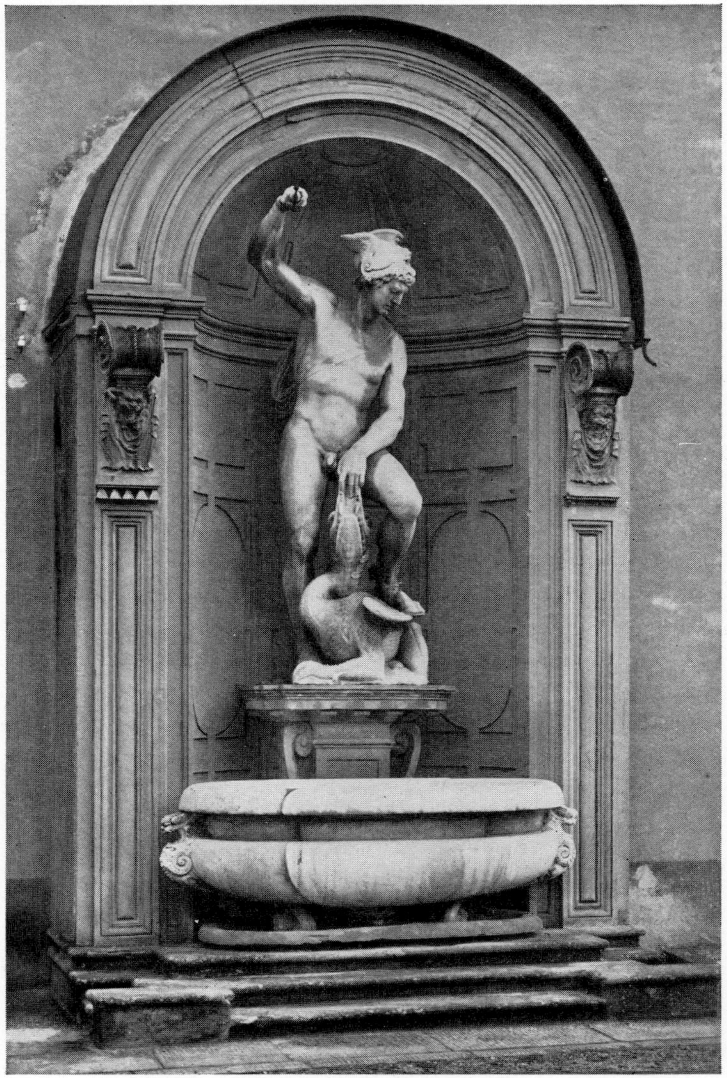

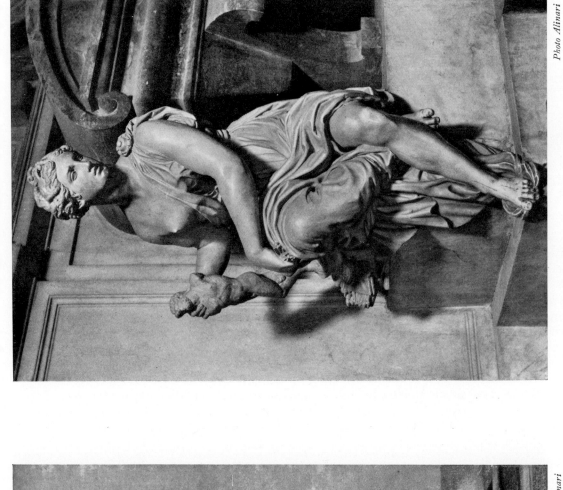

FIGURE 68. BATTISTA LORENZI, ALLEGORY OF PAINTING ON MICHELANGELO'S TOMB
S. CROCE, FLORENCE

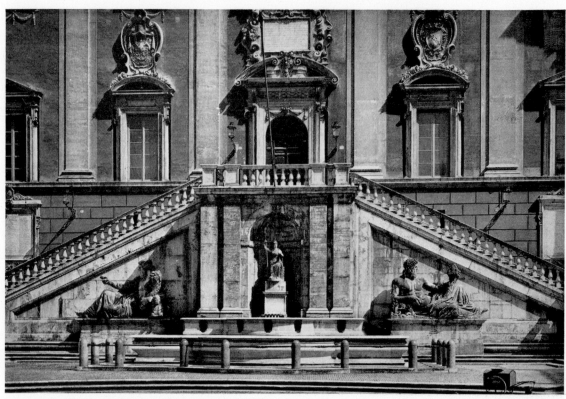

FIGURE 69.  MICHELANGELO, FAÇADE OF THE PALAZZO DEI SENATORI, WITH FOUNTAIN

CAPITOLINE HILL, ROME

FIGURE 70.  MARFORIO

CAPITOLINE MUSEUM, ROME

design was only gradually executed, however; and in 1579 a colossal
Minerva was placed in the central niche instead of the Jupiter. This figure
was replaced in turn, in 1593, by the present small porphyry statue of a
seated goddess restored as Roma. In 1587, a conduit from the Acqua
Felice was brought to the Capitol, making possible a much richer water
effect than Michelangelo had planned and necessitating a larger basin, in
the style of the late Cinquecento. Did the idea of a wall fountain in the
space between converging flights of stairs originate with Michelangelo?
At least the placing of the river gods in the angles seems to have been his
idea. Certainly the authority of his example did much to establish this
type of fountain in Italy. Interesting later instances of this type of composition are the Fountain of the River Gods at the Villa Lante, Bagnaia,[1]
and the Fountain of the Mugnone, set between flights of stairs on the chief
axis of the Villa of Pratolino (Fig. 150).

Michelangelo seemed fated to combine classical fragments into fountains, in the Roman manner, rather than to design fountains which would
afford scope for his own plastic genius. When Julius III (1550–1555)
planned to erect a fountain at the head of the corridor of the Belvedere in
the Vatican, the Florentine master designed a wall fountain which was to
be decorated with a marble figure of his own carving, a Moses striking the
rock, from which the water was to flow. The sculptor doubtless supposed
that the substitution of a Biblical *motif* for the inevitable classical one
would appeal to the Pope; but Julius III rejected the design on the ground
that it would take too much time to execute it in marble. Instead, the
pagan Pope decided to use the ancient figure of "Cleopatra," today known
as the Ariadne of the Vatican, in a grotto of stucco work, giving the commission to Daniele da Volterra. Thus the inexhaustible supply of classical
statuary at Rome tended to discourage the production of original sculpture in that city during the Cinquecento. It was so much easier to erect
an ancient figure over a fountain than to order a new work of a contemporary artist! Besides, the classical figures had the added prestige that
always accompanies the antique, never more potent than in sixteenth century Rome. However, Michelangelo's idea bore fruit later in the figure
of Moses by Prospero Bresciano in the Mostra of the Acqua Felice at

1. Illustrated in Plate CXVII of *Dami*.

Rome (Fig. 74), and again in a fountain in a courtyard of the Archiepisco-
pal Palace at Pisa, by Flaminio Vacca.[1]

Early in his pontificate, Julius III had diverted a part of the water of
the Acqua Vergine, the first of the ancient aqueducts to be restored at
Rome, for use in his Vigna on the Via Flaminia. As there was some protest against this extravagance, he sought to allay the outcries by erecting
nearby a public fountain, dedicated in 1552, which still stands at the corner of the Via Flaminia and the Via di Villa Giulia. This structure was
designed by Ammannati, as both his letter to Marco Benavides at Padua
and a document describing its model prove.[2] We are fortunate in having,
in addition to the detailed description given in Ammannati's letter, two
contemporary representations of this fountain. The one, a rather fanciful
fresco by Taddeo Zucchero in the Villa Giulia, is particularly interesting
for the setting (Fig. 71); the other, an anonymous drawing in Vienna
(Fig. 73), is at once clearer and more accurate in its proportions.

The classical structure shown in the two reproductions might almost be
the façade of an ancient temple. Ammannati describes in detail the Corinthian columns and pilasters and the great inscription in the center, with
the name of the Pope and the year of dedication, and names the statues:
in the rectangular niches to left and right, Felicity and Abundance; above,
as acroteria, figures of Rome and Minerva; at the summit of the pediment,
between the two obelisks, the figure of Neptune, with an attribute that
was probably a trident; over the granite basin, a great head of Apollo,
spouting forth the water. All of the mythological figures were ancient;
perhaps the Felicity and Abundance were carved by Ammannati. None
of the sculpture remains today (Fig. 72); the inscription of Julius III has
been replaced by others, celebrating various owners of the casino into
which the fountain was later incorporated; and a second story has been
added above the original façade. Even the mask and dolphins over the
basin are an addition of the baroque period.

The first of a series of monumental Roman wall fountains, this structure was the prototype of the great *mostre* of modern Rome — façades
marking the outlets of the aqueducts. Ammannati's departure from the

---

1. For other evidence for Michelangelo's concern with the design of fountains, see p. 115.
2. There is no basis for the attribution of this fountain to Jacopo Sansovino.

*Photo Architto Fotografico Nazionale, Rome*

FIGURE 72.   AMMANNATI, PUBLIC FOUNTAIN OF JULIUS III

VIA FLAMINIA, ROME

*Photo D. Anderson, Rome*

FIGURE 71.   TADDEO ZUCCHERO, FRESCO OF THE
PUBLIC FOUNTAIN OF JULIUS III

VILLA GIULIA, ROME

*Photo Brogi*

FIGURE 74. DOMENICO FONTANA, FOUNTAIN OF THE ACQUA FELICE

ROME

FIGURE 73. ANONYMOUS DRAWING OF THE CINQUECENTO,
PUBLIC FOUNTAIN OF JULIUS III

From Egger's *Römische Veduten*

single niche type in favor of a triple division, his accent on the central portion of the façade, and his revival of the classical inscription [1] were followed in the Acqua Felice, a *mostra* in the Piazza di S. Bernardo, Rome, designed by the papal architect Domenico Fontana to mark the outlet of the new aqueduct opened by Sixtus V in 1587 (Fig. 74). As Mrs. MacVeagh has pointed out in her work on the fountains of papal Rome, even the obelisks at the top recall Ammannati's design.

The tapping of the Acqua Vergine on the Via Flaminia also made possible one of the loveliest fountains of the Renaissance, the *nymphaeum* or formal grotto built in 1550–1555 beneath the second courtyard of the Villa Giulia (Fig. 75), not far from the public fountain just discussed. Vasari tells us that the original design was his own, but that Ammannati carried it to completion; and in fact it has been traditionally known as the "Fonte di Ammannati." The low level of the Acqua Vergine at this point necessitated a sunken fountain; hence Vasari's name for it, "Fonte Bassa," or "low fountain."

It is impossible to consider this fountain apart from its setting, since, unlike the usual Florentine fountain, it forms part of a great architectural scheme, serving as the culminating *motif* in an ensemble rather than as a distinct entity.[2] A seventeenth century engraving conveys something of the original effect (Fig. 76). The great court is in two stories, membered with pilasters, separated by arched niches of varying sizes. These were once filled with ancient statues, described in Ammannati's letter to his former patron Marco Benavides, but now long since removed to the papal museums. In the center of the upper courtyard is a mistilinear opening surrounded by a balustrade, from which one looks down upon a sunken court containing the Fonte Bassa. Here all the niches contained minor fountains with figures set against backgrounds of artificial rockwork and maidenhair ferns, their jets feeding the bathing pool that surrounds the rich pavement, inlaid with variegated marbles. The farther end of this lower court extends in the center to form a semicircular exedra, repeating in ground plan the combination of straight and curving lines which the

1. The classical inscription had already been used in the simple wall fountain marking the outlet of the Acqua Vergine as restored in 1453 for Nicholas V by Bernardo Rossellino, under the direction of Alberti; see *Mastrigli*, II, 31.
2. This larger unity is of course due to Vignola's design of the whole villa.

Palladian *motif* of the loggia above gives in elevation (Fig. 75). Four lovely caryatids of white marble support the balustrade above, which takes up the mistilinear *motif* once more.

These marble statues (Fig. 77) personify the source, the Acqua Vergine. Their figures, conventionalized to suit their architectural function, stand at the entrance to the deeply recessed *nymphaeum* of three niches, whose cool darkness is a pleasant foil to the brilliant white of their marble. On the wall behind each caryatid is a similar figure in *mezzo rilievo*. The arched niches within the grotto are covered with stucco *rocaille* and maidenhair fern. Two of them were originally decorated with figures of putti, pouring the water from urns held on their shoulders; the swan of the central niche still remains. The engraving also shows, in the niches on either side of the grotto, groups of three little boys, the central ones emptying urns. These putti, carved by Ammannati himself, were particularly admired. Perhaps the little figures which he carved for the balustrades of two chapels in San Pietro in Montorio during the same period, though naturally more sedate, reveal something of their charm.

Another example of the formal grotto, marking the rear axis of the Medicean Villa of Poggio a Caiano, is commonly attributed to the architect of that villa, Giuliano da Sangallo. The grotto stands between two converging flights of stairs, and is prefaced by four pagan *sileni*, two of which appear in the view shown in Figure 78. Perhaps the interior originally contained other Bacchic figures; but today the three niches stand stripped of all decoration. Only the remains of pipes for surprise jets in the pebbled pavement indicate that the recess once served as a grotto. The style of the *sileni* seems much too free for a Quattrocentist; surely they date from the second half of the Cinquecento. May not Ammannati, who executed other caryatids on a chimney piece within the villa, also have been responsible for these figures?

Soon after the death of Julius III in 1555, Ammannati returned to Florence, where he received the commission from Cosimo I for the façade at one end of the Sala del Gran Consiglio of the Palazzo Vecchio, opposite the one Bandinelli had already constructed. In the center there was to be a great wall fountain decorated with marble figures. Ammannati at once prepared the design and began to execute the statues; but the fountain was

FIGURE 75. AMMANNATI, THE LOGGIA AND
THE FONTE BASSA
VILLA GIULIA, ROME

FIGURE 76. LUDOVICUS ROUHIER, ENGRAVING OF AMMANNATI'S
LOGGIA IN THE VILLA GIULIA
From Falda's *Fontane di Roma*

*Photo Alinari*

FIGURE 77.  AMMANNATI, THE FONTE BASSA
VILLA GIULIA, ROME

*Photo Alinari*

FIGURE 78.  AMMANNATI (?), DETAIL OF THE GROTTO
ROYAL VILLA, POGGIO A CAIANO

never installed in the Palazzo Vecchio. In its stead Cosimo set at that end of the great hall the Victory of Michelangelo, bequeathed to him shortly after that sculptor's death in 1564. About 1579 we find the next duke, Francesco dei Medici, inquiring about the statues, which he later installed in his favorite villa at Pratolino over a freestanding fountain! Francesco's successor in 1587, Ferdinando, seems also to have taken a fancy to the fountain, for he had it transferred to the Pitti Palace. In 1588 the workmen were busy preparing the statues for their new location, the terrace above the grotto of the great courtyard, looking toward the amphitheater of the Boboli Garden. There they were installed about 1590, again over an isolated fountain, which stood until 1639, when it was replaced by Francesco Susini's Fountain of the Artichokes.[1] Once it was dismantled, the statues became scattered, and at length their connection with the fountain was completely forgotten. Indeed, it remained but a series of vague references in the literature until, a few years ago, Dr. Giovanni Poggi identified the five surviving statues, and Dr. Friedrich Kriegbaum, in a brilliant monograph on the fountain, traced its checkered career, and published its scattered members.

The reconstructions at Pratolino and Boboli need not detain us, since they have nothing to do with Ammannati's original design. From Vasari's description we know that it was a wall fountain decorated with columns and sculpture. A letter written by Tanai de' Medici when Ammannati was too ill to see Duke Francesco concerning the figures is more specific. There were six marble statues in all, two of which were to be placed in niches on either side of a "door":[2] the Florence with flowers in her girdle, holding arrows aloft, now in the Boboli Garden (Fig. 79), and a male figure of Prudence, with an anchor and a dolphin, in the courtyard of the Bargello (Fig. 81). Within the central arch reclined the river god Arno and a female figure personifying Hippocrene, the fount of the Muses, both now in the Boboli Garden (Figs. 82 and 83); and between them stood a figure of Ceres pressing her breast, now in the courtyard of the Bargello (Fig. 80). Above the arch sat a statue — now lost — of Juno, flanked by her peacocks. Perhaps the latter were the bronze statues mentioned by Vasari. Borghini

---

1. See p. 31 and Figures 59 and 61.
2. "Porta": does this mean simply the more deeply accented, arched niche in the center?

adds the fact that the six statues were of more than life size, and explains the elaborate allegory of earth, air, and water even more fully. In brief, the whole signified that from the earth (Ceres), aided by the air (Juno), arose the rivers and the springs. We are reminded of the allegory in the Garden of the Labyrinth at Castello,[1] or of the contemporary murals in the Sala degli Elementi in the Palazzo Vecchio. The iconography of the Arno is the traditional one, and the attributes of the Hippocrene are similar to those of the figure of Hippocrene upon Francesco Camilliani's fountain in the Piazza della Pretoria at Palermo (Fig. 136). The placing of the urns between the legs recalls Tribolo's earlier river god at the Villa Corsini at Castello.

Apparently this fountain belonged to the elaborate, triple niche type with which Ammannati had already experimented in his public fountain for Julius III, but it is difficult to reconstruct the arrangement of the four figures within the arch or rainbow containing the river gods and the figure of Ceres in a rectangular division of a classical façade. The portion of the arch which still adheres to the statues of the river gods is certainly not part of a perfect circle. Perhaps it belonged to a lyre-shaped figure, resembling in general contour the bronze knockers with standing figures in the center, which are common in collections of Venetian bronzes. One of these, in the collection of the Schlossmuseum in Berlin, is illustrated in Figure 84. This conjecture seems to me to agree with the silhouette of the fountain as set up on the terrace, seen in a detail from the Boboli lunette of 1599 (Fig. 85).

Another problem is the treatment of the water. The nostrils of the dolphin and the breasts of the Ceres both show borings for pipes; but the urns of the river gods are not pierced, although Ammannati had probably originally so designed them. Did the artist plan to have the water conveyed from the level of one of the central figures to the others in some way, thus paralleling the allegory, as Tribolo had done at Castello?[2] Such ponderings as to the general design lead nowhere; and meanwhile we have before us the five statues. Of these the Ceres is the most pleasing, and certainly one of Ammannati's more attractive works. A strong classical influence is patent, but also something of the fresh Florentine charm with

1. See p. 35.
2. See p. 35.

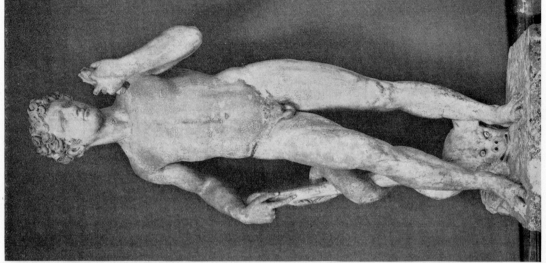

FIGURE 81. AMMANNATI, PRUDENCE

Museo Nazionale, Florence

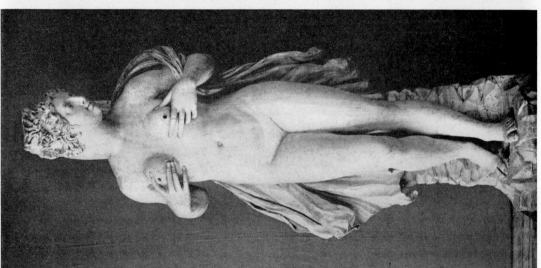
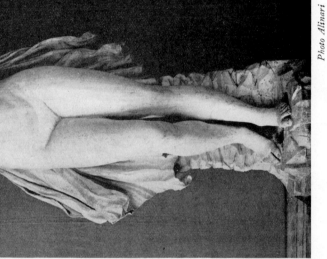

FIGURE 80. AMMANNATI, CERES

Museo Nazionale, Florence

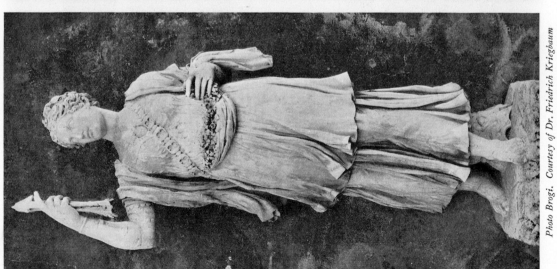

FIGURE 79. AMMANNATI, FLORENCE

Boboli Garden, Florence

FIGURE 83. AMMANNATI, HIPPOCRENE

BOBOLI GARDEN, FLORENCE

FIGURE 82. AMMANNATI, THE ARNO

BOBOLI GARDEN, FLORENCE

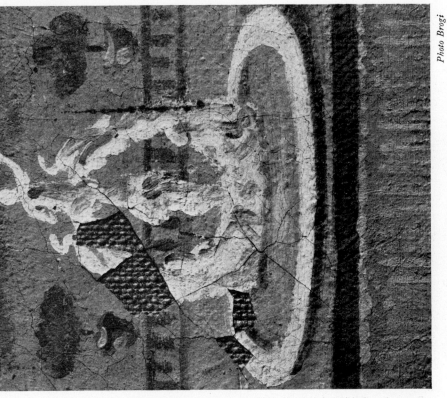

FIGURE 85. DETAIL OF THE BOBOLI LUNETTE, SHOWING THE
FOUNTAIN OF JUNO

MUSEO TOPOGRAFICO, FLORENCE

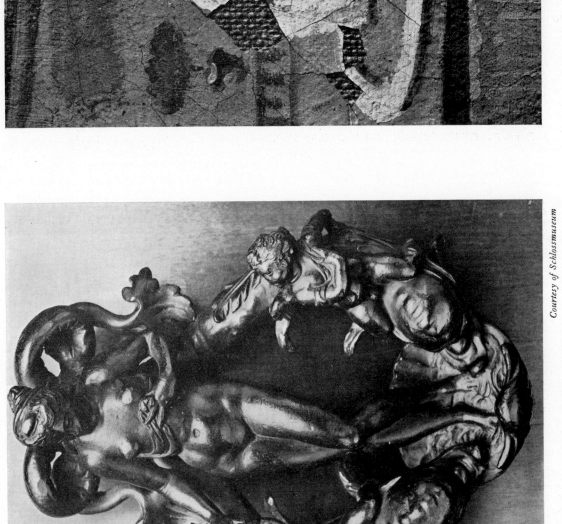

FIGURE 84. TIZIANO ASPETTI, BRONZE KNOCKER

SCHLOSSMUSEUM, BERLIN

FIGURE 86.   PIETRO BERNINI AND MICHELANGELO NACCHERINO, FOUNTAIN OF THE GIANTS
NAPLES

FIGURE 87.   MICHELANGELO NACCHERINO AND TOMMASO MONTANI, FOUNTAIN OF S. LUCIA
VILLA NAZIONALE, NAPLES

which he imbued the classicizing figures of the Virgins of the Fonte Bassa at the Villa Giulia. The poses of the two streams of course reflect those of Michelangelo's reclining figures in the Medici Chapel. In the Hippocrene, this influence is particularly strong.

The date of these statues is established as after 1556, by letters of that year in which the request of Ammannati for four pieces of marble with which to carve the last four figures for the fountain was presented to Cosimo, and granted; while Tanai dei Medici's letter of 1579 affords a *terminus ante quem*. The first design for the fountain was evidently completed before the letters of 1556. In 1560 a model was shown to Michelangelo, who in a letter to Cosimo I praised it highly:". . . and the model of the great hall with the design of the fountain of Messer Bartolommeo that goes in that place. . . . As for the fountain, it seems to me a beautiful fancy and that it will work out admirably." The reuse of the figures at Pratolino and Boboli indicates that Michelangelo's enthusiasm was shared by his contemporaries.

At Rome, as we have seen, the *mostra* designed by Domenico Fontana to mark the outlet of the new aqueduct constructed under Sixtus V was strongly influenced by the triple niche fountain which Ammannati had constructed for Julius III. In the Acqua Felice, however (Fig. 74), the three niches are deepened and the inscription raised to the attic, until the whole approaches the form of an ancient triumphal arch. Other examples of the triumphal arch type of wall fountain, which enjoyed a special vogue at Rome and in its environs, are the Acqua Paola and certain fountains at the Villa d'Este, Tivoli, and at the Villa Aldobrandini, Frascati.[1] In all these Roman examples the fountains are addorsed.

In a version of this type evolved at Naples, the resemblance to the ancient triumphal arch is carried still further; the fountain stands completely free. Two Neapolitan fountains of this type, which date from the early baroque period, must be considered here because they were executed by Florentine sculptors. However florid the detail of the Fontana dei Giganti, now situated on the Via Nazario Sauri (Fig. 86), the fine marble of which it is constructed and its happy silhouette against the unsurpassable setting of the Neapolitan harbor disarm criticism. This fountain,

1. See *Dami*, Pls. LXXXIV, LXXXIX, CLVIII and CLIX.

decorated with figures by the Florentine sculptors Pietro Bernini and Michelangelo Naccherino, was completed in 1601. Save for the great caryatids, usually attributed to Naccherino, the sculptural decoration is completely in the round.

In the even more profusely decorated Fontana di Santa Lucia in the Villa Nazionale (Fig. 87) the triple division is retained, but only the central arch is left open. The additional surface thus gained is covered closely with reliefs depicting the fruits of the sea. In place of the present basin supported by dolphins, the central arch was originally decorated by figures of sirens, spouting from their mouths and breasts. Although the inscription indicates that this fountain was dedicated in 1606, documents prove that the Florentine sculptor Michelangelo Naccherino and a certain Tommaso Montani, of whom little is known, were employed in its decoration as late as 1607.

# CHAPTER V

## THE TYPE WITH A RAISED CENTRAL FIGURE

THE second half of the Cinquecento saw the development of a new form of freestanding fountain, which we may designate as the type with a raised central figure. In this form, the central shaft and minor basins of the candelabrum type are replaced by a large statue elevated upon a pedestal and dominating the subsidiary figures placed on a lower level by its higher position and greater size. A comparison of Montorsoli's two fountains at Messina (Figs. 50 and 88) will illustrate the difference between the two *genres*. The first, with its vertical silhouette and applied sculpture, typifies the graceful, decorative tendency in Florentine sculpture of the Cinquecento. The second, with its more massive and pyramidal contour, and its emphasis upon the great central statue, expresses the rival trend of the century, toward the colossal.[1] The affinity of this form with the pyramidal, freestanding monuments so popular in Europe in the early seventeenth century is obvious: its contour and the disposition of its sculpture recall the monument to Ferdinand I at Livorno, or Andreas Schlüter's monument to the Great Elector. Like them, it seems designed primarily for the public piazza.

This type was particularly favorable to the independent development of sculpture in the round, since there was no need to subordinate the lines of the statues to a shaft or overshadowing basins. It is therefore the sculptor's fountain par excellence. As a result, the water, always a secondary element in the Florentine fountain, becomes still more subsidiary. The fountain function was expressed in the earlier type by the shaft and upper basins; here, by the receiving basin only. The jets that spout from the pedestal and its ornaments seem adventitious, inorganic.

Apparently the first instance of this type was Benvenuto Cellini's design for a fountain of Mars for Fontainebleau. Unfortunately, we know this

---

1. On these rival tendencies in Florentine sculpture of the Cinquecento, see *Reymond*, S. F., IV, 103, and *Post*, I, 223 and 225.

only from Cellini's description, in his autobiography, of the small model which he showed to the French king in 1543. Square in ground plan, it was surrounded by intersecting steps. In the center stood a figure of Mars, raised by a pedestal above the level of the basin, at the corners of which sat figures personifying Literature, Design, Music, and that virtue indispensable to the flourishing of the arts — Liberality. The figure of Mars typified his royal patron, Francis I. This allegory was at once flattering to the king, and, considering the figure of Liberality, suggestive. Cellini executed only the colossal model of the central figure, which towered to the height of fifty-four feet! Indeed, the head of this model for a time served as a hiding place for a girl whom one of Cellini's workmen smuggled into the château; her movements, visible through the eyes of the figure, lent credence to an old rumor that the château was haunted.

Two innovations in fountain design appear in Cellini's description: first, the placing of seated figures on the edge of the basin, so as to form a transition to the central figure; second, the complication of the ground plan by intersecting steps. Provisions for the water are — characteristically — not mentioned. To Cellini's sorrow, the commission for the fountain was later given to Primaticcio; nevertheless, Cellini completed the colossal model of the central figure, displaying it to the king in the same year. In 1544 he departed for Italy, leaving the work unfinished.

The earliest actual example of this type that I have found is Montorsoli's Fountain of Neptune, completed in 1557, situated beside the harbor of Messina. Figure 88 shows it as it stood before the earthquake, silhouetted against the background of Messina's harbor.[1] The scene represented is that of Neptune calming the straits of Messina, typified by the statues of Scylla and Charybdis below. The reader will feel at once the new spirit that animates the whole. This is no decorative group, but a tableau in which the figures are united in a dramatic action. Here we have in the fountain the same transformation which Bernini, a century later, effected in the development of the tomb.[2] However, there is as yet no attempt at a naturalistic setting — the sea-horses and the bases worked to represent rocks and waves are merely symbolical.

1. The fountain is now sunk below the level of the street, where it appears to poor advantage.
2. See Muñoz in Rassegna d'Arte, v (1918), 78–104.

FIGURE 88. MONTORSOLI, FOUNTAIN OF NEPTUNE, MESSINA

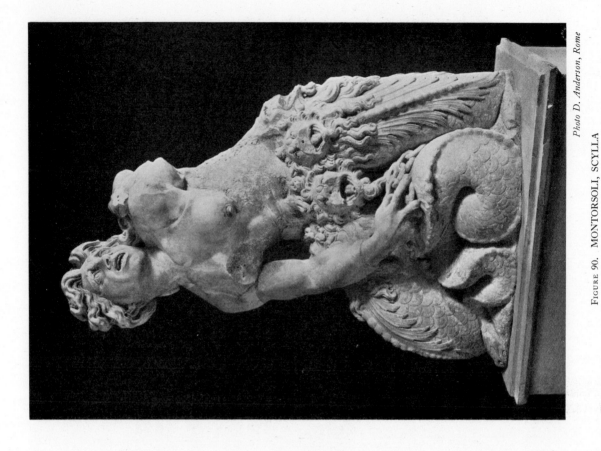

FIGURE 90.  MONTORSOLI, SCYLLA

MUSEO NAZIONALE, MESSINA

FIGURE 89.  MONTORSOLI, NEPTUNE

MUSEO NAZIONALE, MESSINA

The startling contrast between the style of the Neptune and that of his minions, best studied in the original figures of Neptune and Scylla, now in the local museum (Figs. 89 and 90), cannot be altogether explained by their divergent rôles in this marine drama. The two reveal the influence of ancient statues of different periods and styles. The Neptune, which combines a hard, mechanical execution with a Polyclitan conception of form, was evidently based upon some late Roman work; while the agitated, momentary pose of the Scylla is essentially baroque, revealing at once the influence of such "baroque" ancient statues as the Laocoon,[1] and that of Montorsoli's master Michelangelo, with his passion for motion and *contrapposto*. Montorsoli was probably also influenced in his general conception of this fountain by Mantegna's engraving, the so-called "Battle of the Sea Gods," in which we find a similar contrast between a rigid statue of Neptune and the excited motion of sea creatures.

The novel ground plan of this fountain merits special study. The mistilinear contour given to the otherwise rectangular steps by the use of rounded corners (Fig. 91) is repeated within by means of the oval *pile* applied at the four corners of the basin. This interplay of straight and curved lines, introduced for the sake of variety, was later transferred to the ground plans of the basins themselves, resulting in the mistilinear types in which the makers of Roman fountains in the last quarter of the Cinquecento particularly rejoiced, and which they transmitted to the baroque period. This breaking up of the lines of a ground plan in order to produce an effect of movement or variety is another symptom of the baroque to appear particularly early in the development of the fountain. In this point, too, Montorsoli seems to have been the innovator.

Figure 91 reproduces a sixteenth century drawing of the fountain in the Uffizi, which shows the part which the water plays in the design. To the eight falling jets which spout from masks in the sides of the great pedestal Montorsoli opposed, for the sake of variety, four rising ones, struck from the hoofs of the sea-horses at its corners. Twin jets also gush from the outer angles of the receiving basin into the minor receptacles below. Still, the fountain function of this structure remains incidental; it tells primarily as a sculptural ensemble. In this it set the precedent for a long series of

1. Montorsoli had been employed to restore this statue in 1523–1524.

fountains of Neptune, for which the Cinquecento had a particular penchant.

The most famous Neptune fountain of the century was that of the
Piazza della Signoria at Florence, which has a long story.[1] When, about
1551, the Grand Duke first conceived the idea of erecting a public fountain in the chief piazza of Florence, he gave the commission to Bandinelli.
Baccio, after studying the designs for Montorsoli's fountains in Messina,
then the most elaborate in Italy, swore that he would erect a fountain that
should surpass anything in the world; but at the time of his death in 1560[2]
he had got no farther than elaborate plans on paper, and a preliminary
blocking out of the great marble for the central figure, while both Benvenuto Cellini and Bartolommeo Ammannati constantly besought the
Duke to permit them to submit models of their own. On Bandinelli's
death Cosimo opened a competition; and Cellini, Ammannati, Vincenzo
Danti, and the young Giovanni Bologna submitted models for a gigantic
Neptune. Ammannati at last received the commission, doubtless because
of his considerable experience in erecting fountains and colossal marble
figures.[3] It is a pity that neither the designs of the other competing sculptors nor their models for the central figure have been preserved. Their loss
leaves a wide *lacuna* in the history of the Florentine fountain. So far as we
know, none of them made use of their designs or models later with the
possible exception of Giovanni Bologna, who may have utilized his model
for the Neptune in two later fountains, at Bologna and in the Boboli
Garden.[4]

According to his letter to Michelangelo, Ammannati commenced work
on the colossal Neptune in 1561. In 1565 the Marzocco was moved aside
to make room for the fountain, the water brought from the Fonte alla

1. See the detailed account of the competition for this fountain given in Appendix A, pp. 117–
119.

2. The date of February, 1559, in the Florentine style of the Annunciation, quoted by Vasari
from Bandinelli's epitaph, equals 1560, new style.

3. According to Vasari, in the life of Jacopo Sansovino, Ammannati had made a heroic
Neptune of Istrian stone for the Piazza di San Marco at Venice. His colossal statue of Hercules,
made for Marco Benavides of Padua, still survives. For his fountains at Rome, made between the
years 1550 and 1555, see pp. 37, 40–42.

4. Dr. Friedrich Kriegbaum has suggested that the model in the Museo Civico at Bologna may
be the one made for this competition (Fig. 97). Certainly it formed the basis for his Neptune
(Fig. 98) at Bologna and the Oceanus (Fig. 99) of the Boboli Isolotto; *Kriegbaum*, M. D. C.,
pp. 139–140.

FIGURE 91. DRAWING OF THE FOUNTAIN OF NEPTUNE AT MESSINA

GABINETTO DEI DISEGNI, THE UFFIZI, FLORENCE

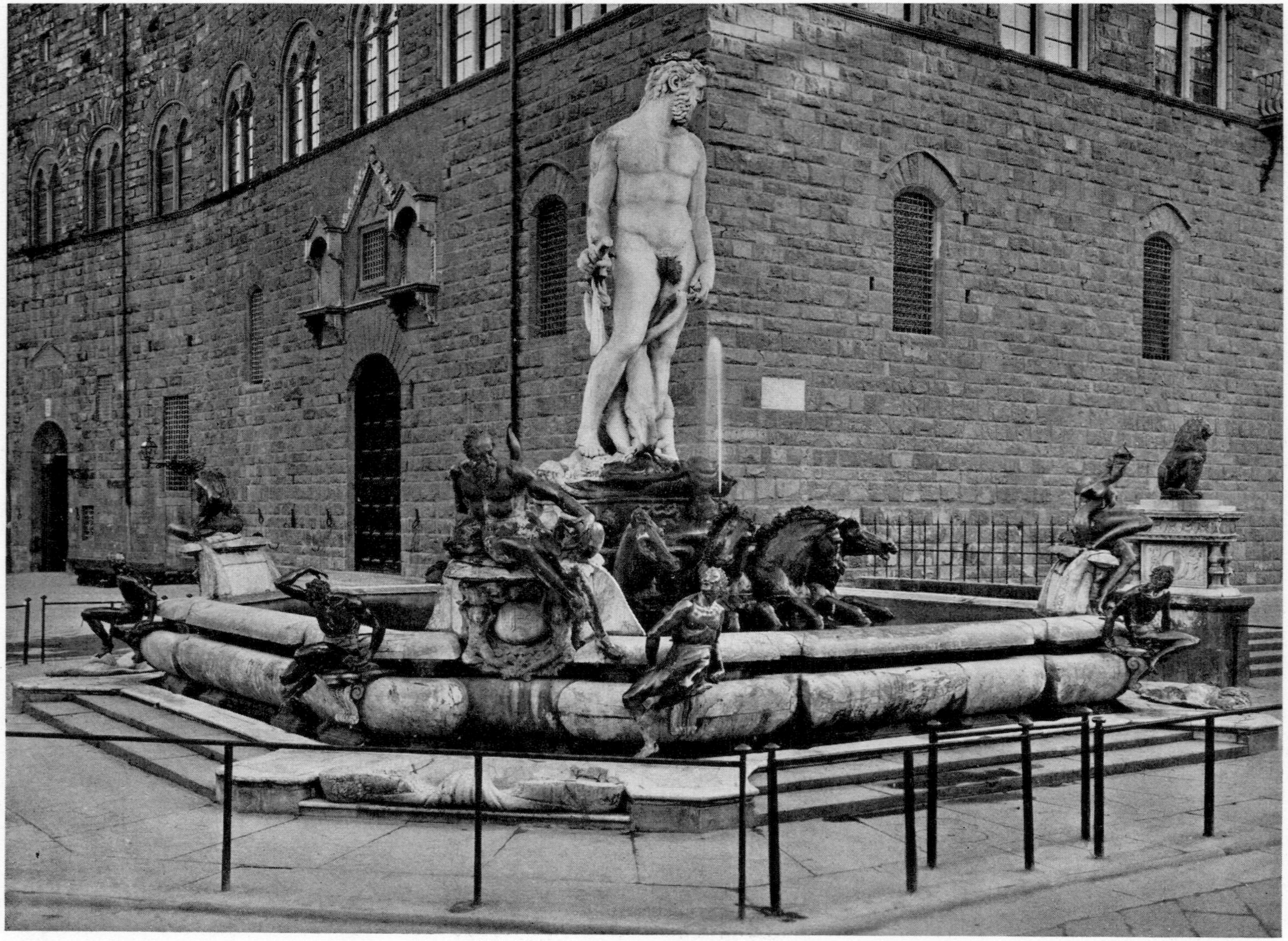

FIGURE 92. AMMANNATI AND OTHERS, FOUNTAIN OF NEPTUNE

PIAZZA DELLA SIGNORIA, FLORENCE

Ginevra, and the central statue completed and exhibited, surrounded by temporary figures of painted stucco, as part of the decoration for the wedding of Joanna of Austria and Prince Francesco.[1] The corner stone of the permanent fountain was, however, not laid until 1571, and the whole unveiled and dedicated only in 1575.

One's first impression of the fountain, on approaching it from the center of the piazza (Fig. 38), is one of confusion. This is due to its unfortunate and cramped position against a corner of the Palazzo Vecchio (Fig. 92). An isolated fountain of such heroic size should stand free in the center of an ample square or garden. Moreover, there is no proper transition between the centrifugal lines and free poses of the bronze figures and the severe walls of the surrounding palaces. Again we see the architectonic world of the piazza invaded by pictorial tendencies that had their origin in the free air of the villa.

Baldinucci's detailed description makes an excellent introduction to the study of the fountain: "In the midst of a great basin full of the most limpid water, gushing from many jets (which basin represents the sea), rises the great Colossus of Neptune, ten *braccia* high, standing on a chariot drawn by four sea-horses, two of white marble and two of variegated, very beautiful and vivacious. The Neptune has between his legs three figures of Tritons, which stand with him upon a great sea shell which serves as a chariot; the basin of variegated marble has eight sides, four smaller and four larger. The four smaller are charmingly decorated with figures of boys and other subjects in bronze, such as sea shells, cornucopias, and the like. From the same level rise certain pedestals, on each of which is placed a statue of metal of more than life-size, four in all — two female, which represent Thetis and Doris, and two male, for two sea gods; at either side of each of these four smaller faces are two satyrs of metal in varied and most beautiful attitudes. The four greater sides are low enough to permit every one to enjoy the limpidity of the water, which, gushing forth, is received by some beautiful shells, and in the great basin; in fine, everything is so well planned, and arranged with so much grandeur, that it is truly a marvel."

1. The reverse of a medal dated 1567, decorated with an aqueduct and a Neptune fountain, commemorates Cosimo's addition to the water supply of Florence, which made possible the elaborate water effects of this fountain as completed in 1575. See p. 16, n. 1.

Baldinucci was particularly impressed by Ammannati's arrangement of the water, which is still subdivided, after the Renaissance fashion, into numerous small jets (seventy, according to Borghini!), which rise from the conch shells held by the tritons round the central figure (Fig. 38), from the dolphins held by the reclining naiads and marine deities, and from the many minor sea creatures that decorate the fountain everywhere. The jets about the figure of Neptune (Fig. 95), being far more concentrated than is usual in the Florentine fountains of this period, play an important part in the general design, softening the contrasts between the great mass of white marble which the Florentines aptly call "Il Biancone" and the outer bronzes, and focussing our attention upon the center of the fountain. It is most unfortunate that, due to the present dearth of water in Tuscany, the full resources of this fountain are today available only on state occasions, so that the fountain usually appears without these unifying jets (Fig. 92).

It is interesting to note the departures from the original type as illustrated by Montorsoli's Fountain of Neptune at Messina. The most striking is the substitution, for the architectural base supporting the central figure, of a naturalistic one — the chariot in the form of a shell drawn by sea-horses (Figs. 92 and 94). Here the subordinate figures are not placed within the basin, as at Messina, but seated at the angles, recalling the position of the four allegorical figures in Cellini's design for the Fountain of Mars. As at Messina, there are smaller receptacles at the four chief corners of the basin, which is octagonal in ground plan; but for the little "tubs" of the earlier fountain, Ammannati substituted a more naturalistic form, flat shells, sunken so that they scarcely project above the compact, horizontal lines of the low steps (Fig. 93). Finally, the great basin, which belongs to the type with a mistilinear profile which we have already studied in Tribolo's two fountains at Castello (Figs. 39 and 40), is compressed into exceedingly low, horizontal lines so that the pool of water, as Baldinucci remarked, is visible even from a distance (Fig. 94). This is the earliest instance I have found, in a fountain designed for a public piazza, of this effect, which was particularly cultivated in the later fountains of the piazzas at Rome.[1] Montorsoli, in adapting the fountain types of Tribolo to the city square,

1. The earliest fountains of this type at Rome date from the latter part of the pontificate of Gregory XIII (1572–1585). The fountain of the Piazza Colonna is a good example.

FIGURE 93.   AMMANNATI AND OTHERS, DETAIL OF THE FOUNTAIN OF NEPTUNE

PIAZZA DELLA SIGNORIA, FLORENCE

FIGURE 94.  AMMANNATI AND OTHERS, FOUNTAIN OF NEPTUNE

PIAZZA DELLA SIGNORIA, FLORENCE

*Photo Giusti and Figli*

FIGURE 95.  DETAIL, SHOWING THE FOUNTAIN OF NEPTUNE PLAYING

PIAZZA DELLA SIGNORIA, FLORENCE

had purposely used higher basins and raised them upon monumental steps. By the use of the low basin and almost negligible steps, Ammannati dissolved the architectural line which separated the fountain from its surroundings. The result was that interplay of sculpture, water, and space, which is usually considered the very essence of the baroque (Fig. 95).

This fountain, like Montorsoli's, was conceived as an aquatic tableau — Neptune riding over the waves, surrounded by the creatures of his domain. According to Vasari, Bandinelli had already so planned the central figure: "Neptune on his chariot drawn by sea-horses." The use of a sea shell for a chariot was evidently suggested by a passage from Statius: "Besides he [Neptune] was represented nude with trident in hand, standing erect in a great sea shell instead of a chariot, drawn by horses whose bodies ended in fish tails." [1] Ammannati's marine tableau was even given a naturalistic setting — the seashell chariot and the spirited sea-horses; while the almost negligible height of the basin enhanced the realistic effect, suggesting a veritable sea. Like Montorsoli, Ammannati has contrasted the calm pose of the lord of the waves (Fig. 92) and the restless attitude of his subjects (Figs. 93 and 95); but he has not achieved the dramatic unity of the earlier fountain. This is due partly to the great discrepancy in size between the colossal "Biancone" and his bronze subjects, which makes the fountain seem top-heavy; partly to the striking color contrasts afforded by the use of such different materials as bronze and marble; and partly to the less compact composition, for there is too great a gap between the outer figures and the Neptune. Here the motion is downward and outward instead of inward and upward, as at Messina.

But the fundamental reason for the lack of unity in this fountain is the great disparity of style that all writers have noted. Ammannati's "Biancone" (Figs. 38 and 92) is in the heavy, classicizing style of the early Cinquecento, while the bronze figures have the slim, elegant lines and involved, excited poses of the Mannerists (Figs. 93 and 95). This discrepancy in style is due not only to the fact that the Neptune was commenced in 1561 and completed by 1565, while the bronzes were executed between 1571 and 1575; the later figures were modelled and cast by a number of assist-

1. The various ways of representing Neptune, according to the ancient authors, are cited by *Lomazzo*, bk. VII, chap. XV.

ants, obviously under the influence of Giovanni Bologna. As Professor Chandler Post has remarked, the *contrapposto* of the satyrs (Figs. 93 and 95), as well as the brackets on which they perch, betray their prototypes, the Ignudi of the Sistine ceiling; but the tempo of Michelangelo's figures has been accelerated to a syncopated rhythm that verges upon that of the baroque.

Ammannati's Neptune is scarcely to our modern taste, and did not altogether escape criticism even in his own day. It lacks the monumental quality which alone could justify its colossal size. Considered as the central figure in an isolated fountain, it is singularly rigid; the torsion which makes a freestanding figure equally interesting from every side appears only in the turn of the head and in a slight curve of the lower limbs; the torso is absolutely frontal. The fact that the majority of Ammannati's previous commissions had been for statues applied to an architectural framework doubtless predisposed him to a frontal treatment. This may also be due in part to the narrowness of the block as prepared by Bandinelli, which, according to Borghini, prevented the sculptor from representing the figure with arms raised. Certainly this statue, commenced in 1561, seems antiquated when compared with the bronze Neptune on the fountain at Bologna (Fig. 98), begun only two years later by Giovanni Bologna.

This young Flemish artist, whose model had been highly praised in the competition of 1560, had been in the employ of the Medici for two years when, in 1563, he was offered the commission for the sculpture of the great fountain of Neptune at Bologna, ordered by Pope Pius IV. Prince Francesco reluctantly consented to release him for this work, with which he was occupied till 1567. The fountain (Fig. 96) was designed by Tommaso Laureti, a painter from Palermo, and the sculpture modelled by Giovanni Bologna. The casting of the bronzes was at first entrusted to Zanobi Portigiani, but after a misunderstanding a new contract was made, and Giovanni Bologna undertook this work also. Save for the receiving basin of variegated stone and the steps of red marble, the structure is entirely of bronze. As a whole, it conforms to the Florentine type with the raised central figure, although here some of the secondary figures and small basins are incorporated into the high pedestal, which is divided into three stages. There is no attempt at a tableau, since the subsidiary figures, with the ex-

*Photo Alinari*

FIGURE 96. TOMMASO LAURETI AND GIOVANNI BOLOGNA, FOUNTAIN OF NEPTUNE, BOLOGNA

FIGURE 99. GIOVANNI BOLOGNA, OCEANUS

MUSEO NAZIONALE, FLORENCE

FIGURE 98. GIOVANNI BOLOGNA, NEPTUNE

DETAIL OF THE PUBLIC FOUNTAIN, BOLOGNA

FIGURE 97. GIOVANNI BOLOGNA, BRONZE
STATUETTE OF NEPTUNE

MUSEO CIVICO, BOLOGNA

ception of the putti at the top, form part of the pedestal; neither is there any suggestion of a naturalistic setting.

The ground plan is roughly square, save for indentations at the corners. The low steps follow the lines of the basin, except at the angles, where they are slightly rounded out, forming a mistilinear figure as at Messina, though with more subtle transitions. Basin and steps are both considerably higher than in the great fountain at Florence, so that the water therein is not visible except at close range, or from a higher point. In this, as in the more conventionalized treatment of the subsidiary figures, this fountain is adapted to its position in a public piazza.

There are numerous water jets, issuing from the dolphin on which the Neptune's foot rests, from the heads of the four winds round the base on which he stands, from the dolphins held aloft by the putti, from the grotesque winged heads about the minor basins, from the breasts of the naiads, and finally from the dolphins on which they ride. To the falling streams, which produce a continuous rhythmic effect, are opposed several rising jets, particularly about the feet of Neptune. These serve to bind his figure more closely to the structure.

At first glance this fountain, with its formal pedestal, seems characteristic of the Renaissance; but there are numerous signs of the transition to the baroque: the sweeping curves of the pedestal, from stage to stage; the swollen forms of the basins and cartouches; and the centrifugal treatment of the upper figures. The sirens at the angles (Fig. 100), for all their naturalism, are made to conform to the architectural lines so as to serve chiefly as a transition to the upper level of the pedestal; but the putti above, with their dangling legs, their *contrapposto*, and the upward lines of their raised dolphins, are given more centrifugal lines; while the colossal figure at the summit of the fountain stands completely free (Fig. 96). Contrast the easy, almost momentary pose and the torsion which makes this figure satisfactory from every side (Fig. 98) with the stiff frontality of Ammannati's Neptune, only a few years earlier (Fig. 92); the advance is astonishing. The contrast becomes even greater if we turn to the small bronze model in the Museo Civico at Bologna (Fig. 97), which may be the one which Giovanni Bologna took to Rome for the Pope's inspection in 1564. Although the form of this model is close to the colossal Neptune of the fountain, the S curve of the body is far more pronounced. The figure, which is conceived as sailing over the surface of the sea, is thrown backward in complete abandon. The reproduction by no means does justice to the original; one must see the model itself to feel its lightness and the astonishing illusion of movement in which it rivals the Flying Mercury of the Bargello. In the final figure, Giovanni Bologna decided upon a more monumental treatment, making the statue more erect and compact, with a gain in dignity but a loss in freshness. Did the Pope, seeing the model, suggest this change, or did the artist himself feel it more suitable for a colossal figure? Or does the change simply represent the development toward the academic, classicizing manner that was to mark this sculptor's more mature style? The same tendency appears in the bronze putti with the fish (Fig. 96) as compared with his earlier figures represented in similar positions (Figs. 177 and 178) but executed in a fresher, more naturalistic vein.[1]

Certainly the great Neptune (Fig. 98) has the dignity that accords with its colossal size, so lacking in the Biancone of Ammannati; indeed, the sculpture of this fountain as a whole is marked by a unity of style lacking in its Florentine contemporary. Although the *motif* of the sirens is not to our modern taste, the figures themselves are superb both as studies of form and in their adaptation to their architectonic function (Fig. 100). Gurlitt has admirably expressed the plastic character of this fountain and its ornament, stressing Giovanni Bologna's ability to fill the classical *motifs* with a new life: "The grotesques of antiquity here receive plastic life and individual pulse-beat; throughout there is a striving to constrain the ancient, outworn forms to new ways of expression." It is significant that this contribution was made by a Northern artist.[2]

For the later history of the fountain with a raised central figure one must turn to the North, where the type continued to flourish even in the seventeenth century. Two Dutch pupils of Giovanni Bologna — Hubert Gerhard and Adrian de Vries — carried the type into Germany, with

1. One difficulty with this theory of a naturalistic early style and a later, classicizing vein in the work of Giovanni Bologna, enunciated by Dr. Friedrich Kriegbaum in pp. 139–140 of the article cited in note 4, p. 50, is that the dates of some of the "early" works of this master have not been completely established. See p. 87 and p. 88, n. 1.

2. A terracotta model related to this fountain in some way, now in the Metropolitan Museum, New York, is illustrated in Figure 101.

FIGURE 101. SCHOOL OF GIOVANNI BOLOGNA, MODEL FOR A FOUNTAIN

METROPOLITAN MUSEUM, NEW YORK

FIGURE 100. GIOVANNI BOLOGNA, SIREN

DETAIL OF THE FOUNTAIN OF NEPTUNE, BOLOGNA

*Photo Kutscher and Gehr*

FIGURE 102. HUBERT GERHARD, DETAIL OF

*Photo Höfle*

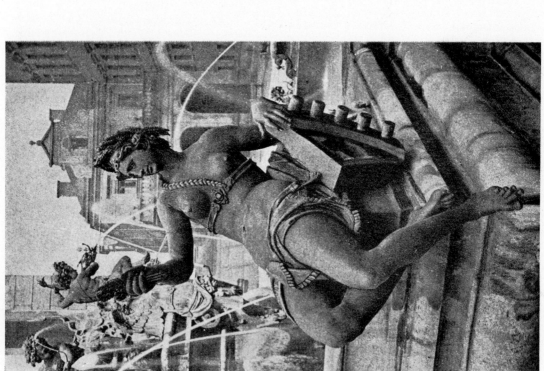

FIGURE 103. ADRIAN DE VRIES, FOUNTAIN OF HERCULES

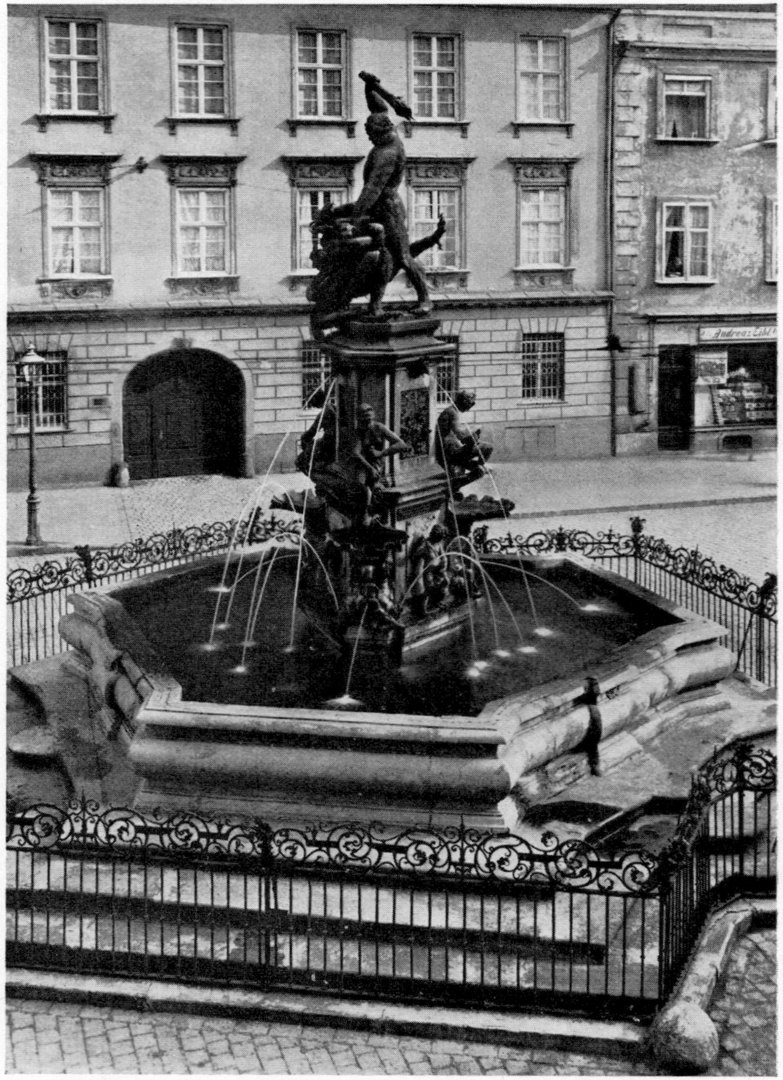

their famous fountains at Augsburg. These show striking similarities to their Florentine prototypes in the subject matter and figure style, in their general composition, and in the use of the water in slender, crossing jets (Figs. 102 and 103). The receiving basins are usually of the elaborate variety with mistilinear ground plan that flourished in Rome in the last quarter of the Cinquecento.

Reminiscences of the Florentine fountains appear everywhere. In the Fountain of Augustus, opposite the Rathaus at Augsburg, erected by Hubert Gerhard in 1589–1594, the bronze recumbent figures (Fig. 102) resemble those on Ammannati's fountain in the Piazza della Signoria at Florence (Fig. 93), as do also the reclining figures on the Wittelsbacher Brunnen in the Residenz at Munich (1590 and later) by the same master.[1] The boys with dolphins at the angles of the pedestal on the fountain of Augustus (Fig. 102) are patterned after those of the fountain of Neptune at Bologna (Fig. 96).

In the works of Adrian de Vries, the influence of his master Giovanni Bologna is always paramount. The division into stages of the pedestal on the Hercules Brunnen (1596–1602) (Fig. 103) in the Maximilienstrasse at Augsburg recalls that of the Neptune fountain at Bologna; while its hexagonal shape, with seated figures between the reliefs on the top stage, is based upon the upper portion of the pedestal of the Fountain of Oceanus at Boboli (Fig. 110). The three *baigneuses* convert the classical *motif* of the Venus Anadyomene, seen in the figure of Florence on the fountain at Petraia (Fig. 44), into Northern genre;[2] and the terminal figure, with its intense motion and raised arm, derives from the group of Samson and the Philistine, which also crowned a fountain (Figs. 120 and 121).

In spite of these similarities in detail, the Northern fountains present quite a different aspect from their Italian prototypes. A fundamental change in contour resulted from the practice of increasing the height of the central pedestal to accord with the vertical lines of the Northern buildings. Thus the massive, horizontal forms of the Florentine type were lost; and the resulting verticality has affinities rather with the candelabrum type (Fig. 103). The fountain erected by Adrian de Vries in 1616–

1. Illustrated in *Brinckmann*, S. D. B., pls. 17–20.
2. But see Chapter X, pp. 98–99, on Florentine genre sculpture, and particularly p. 99.

1623 at the Castle of Fredriksborg in Denmark, a copy of which is shown in Figure 104, illustrates the change.[1] The apparent size of the terminal figure is greatly reduced by the height of the pedestal, so that its domination over the subsidiary figures, so fundamental a characteristic of the Florentine type, is less marked. In the Wittelsbacher Brunnen, the emphasis on the terminal figure is further reduced by the addition of four standing figures. At Fredriksborg, the vertical effect is reinforced by the lines of the tritons, straining upward, and by the raised arm of the Neptune.

The Neptune, signed and dated 1623, is plainly influenced by the figure of Neptune on the fountain at Bologna; but the tempo has been heightened, and the momentary pose made still more unstable. Adrian de Vries' last fountain (1624–1627) was originally erected in the garden of the Palace of Wallenstein at Prague. The surviving figures in the Park at Drottningholm show an advance toward the baroque in the more pictorial modelling of the surfaces, in which this master, as Professor Albert Brinckmann has shown, was far in advance of his time.[2] From these statues, coupled with the basin still at Prague and references in de Vries' letters, we can reconstruct the general form of the ensemble, in which four reclining figures — river gods and nymphs — surrounded a standing figure of Neptune upon a pedestal decorated with grotesque heads as spouts. This fountain, too, plainly conformed to the Florentine type with the raised central figure, carrying its development well into the seventeenth century.

1. The original figures are now at Drottningholm.
2. See *Brinckmann*, B. S., p. 144.

Courtesy of Miss Esther Seaver

FIGURE 104. COPY OF ADRIAN DE VRIES' FOUNTAIN OF NEPTUNE, FREDRIKSBORG

*Photo Istituto Fotografico Italiano, Rome*

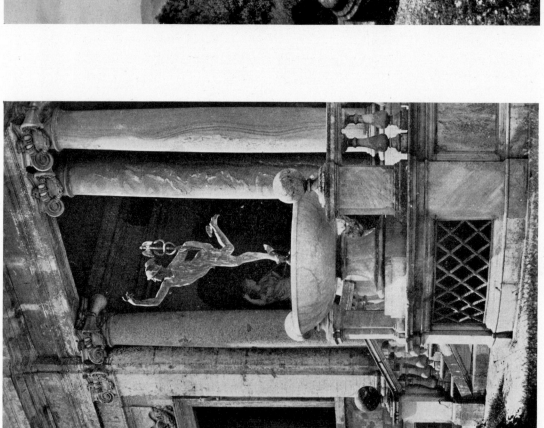

FIGURE 105. FOUNTAIN OF MERCURY, VILLA MEDICI, ROME
(Original bronze by Giovanni Bologna now in the Bargello)

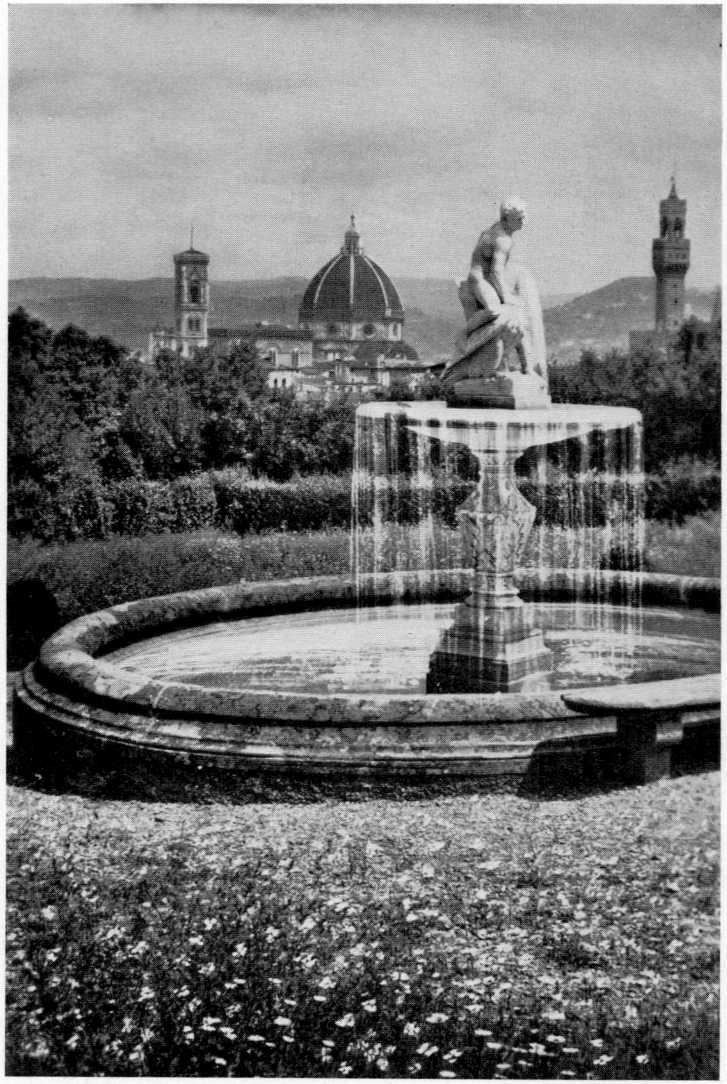

FIGURE 106. FOUNTAIN OF GANYMEDE, BOBOLI GARDEN, FLORENCE

# CHAPTER VI

## THE CYLIX TYPE

THE sculptors of cylix fountains in the Quattrocento devoted much attention to the lavish decoration of the basins in low relief. The Cinquecento masters, with the greater interest in sculpture in the round characteristic of their period, concentrated rather upon the terminal figures, often leaving the basin severely plain, as in the classic fountain at the Villa Medici, Rome, crowned with Giovanni Bologna's famous bronze statue of the Flying Mercury (Fig. 105).[1] Another pleasing example of the type, by an anonymous Florentine sculptor, is the Fountain of Ganymede, situated below the Coffee House in the Boboli Garden (Fig. 106). Cylix fountains of this simple sort, suitable for the decoration of small courts and gardens, were undoubtedly constructed throughout the century; but there was a strong tendency toward the elaboration of the type by the addition of subsidiary figures. The Boboli Garden alone contained three examples of this more complex variety, all carved in the second half of the century.

The earliest of these, Stoldo Lorenzi's Fountain of Neptune, constructed between the years 1565 and 1568,[2] has been dismantled, and the figures which decorated it are now incorporated into a rustic fountain of much later date, which stands in the center of the *vivaio* or fishpond above the Boboli Amphitheater (Fig. 107). In the lunette of the Boboli Garden painted in 1599 this *vivaio* is empty, while the Neptune appears instead over a formal fountain in a garden to the left of the amphitheater (Figs. 35 and 35a). A detail from the lunette (Fig. 108) shows an elaborate cylix fountain, crowned by the bronze Neptune with his trident, raised on a rather baroque pedestal. Additional figures appear below the basin, two marble sea creatures crouching in poses similar to those of the figures on the cliff today. Borghini mentions these subsidiary statues in his life of

---

1. The original bronze (Fig. 180), now in the Bargello at Florence, is replaced on the fountain by a copy.

2. The *terminus post quem* of 1565 is given by the fact that the fountain was suggested by a float in the pageant in celebration of the wedding of Prince Francesco with Joanna of Austria, in that year; and a *terminus ante quem* of 1568 by Vasari's reference to this fountain in his second edition.

Stoldo Lorenzi, published in 1584: "When he later returned to Florence, he was given the commission by Grand Duke Cosimo to make the fountain of the bronze Neptune in the Pitti garden, which statue stands above certain sea monsters of marble." There were probably four of these figures, corresponding to the two naiads and the two tritons on the rustic fountain of today, although only two show in the view of the fountain given on the lunette. Below the "sea monsters" on the lunette appear either steps or a low receiving basin — more probably the latter. The water *motifs* were probably the same as today (Fig. 164), slender jets spouting from the prongs of Neptune's trident, and dripping down from the shells which the tritons and naiads held above their heads.

Even without the present naturalistic setting, the conception of the fountain would remain that of an aquatic tableau — Neptune approaching with lowered trident, while below his subjects crouch in characteristic poses. It has been said that the form of this fountain was inspired by the float depicting the triumph of Neptune in the pageant celebrating the marriage of Francesco dei Medici and Joanna of Austria in 1565, which was so much admired by Duke Cosimo that he asked Stoldo Lorenzi to perpetuate its form in a fountain. However, according to a detailed contemporary description of an eye witness of the pageant, this float had little in common with the actual fountain as shown on the lunette. Evidently it merely supplied the general subject of the "triumph of Neptune," and suggested a dramatic treatment.[1]

Stoldo Lorenzi's Neptune is the most original of the long series of representations of this deity on sixteenth century fountains. He chose to portray the god of waters in his more threatening aspect,[2] and the resulting momentary pose is very different from the monumental attitudes of the calmer Neptunes of Montorsoli, Ammannati, and Giovanni Bologna. The centrifugal lines of this figure, more apparent in a side view of the rustic fountain (Fig. 107), approach the baroque.

1. Both in the Quattrocento and in the Cinquecento there seems to have been a close relation between the forms of such triumphs or floats and the forms of actual fountains; and it may be that the growing freedom of the tableaux upon floats in the Cinquecento had much to do with the frequent appearance of the "aquatic tableau" in sculptors' fountains.

2. *Lomazzo*, bk. VII, chap. XV, p. 584, distinguishes Neptune's calm and threatening aspects; "Nettuno Dio del mare, fu formato in diversi modi, hora tranquillo, quieto e pacifico, e hora tutto turbato come si legge appresso Homero, o Vergilio."

*Courtesy of Dr. Friedrich Kriegbaum*

FIGURE 107.  STOLDO LORENZI, FOUNTAIN OF NEPTUNE

BOBOLI GARDEN, FLORENCE

FIGURE 108. DETAIL OF THE BOBOLI LUNETTE OF 1599

STOLDO LORENZI'S FOUNTAIN OF NEPTUNE IN ITS ORIGINAL STATE. MUSEO TOPOGRAFICO, FLORENCE

FIGURE 109. GIOVANNI BOLOGNA, DESIGN FOR THE FOUNTAIN OF OCEANUS

COLLECTION OF HENRY OPPENHEIMER, LONDON

In 1567 a round granite basin measuring some twenty-three feet in diameter was brought to Florence from the island of Elba, its unusual size making necessary a breach in the city gate. This great bowl formed the nucleus of Giovanni Bologna's Fountain of Oceanus, now in the center of the Boboli Isolotto, but originally erected in the center of the amphitheater, where it appears on the Boboli lunette of 1599 (Figs. 35 and 35a). According to Baldinucci, Francesco dei Medici showed the mammoth *tazza* to Giovanni Bologna, and bade him design a fountain worthy of it. The sculptor's original conception has apparently been preserved in a drawing by his hand in the collection of the late Henry Oppenheimer in London, published by Miss Anny Popp (Fig. 109); but only the central portion of this design was executed, and set up in the amphitheater at Boboli in 1576 (Figs. 35 and 35a).

In its actual form the fountain is merely a colossal example of the cylix type, with subsidiary marble figures clustered about the pedestal which elevates the terminal figure (Fig. 110). This hexagonal pedestal is decorated on three sides with marble bas-reliefs depicting episodes drawn from the mythology of the sea — the rape of Europa, the triumph of Neptune, the bath of Diana (Figs. 111 to 113)—, while the alternate sides are marked by consoles bearing the crouching figures of three river gods (Figs. 114 to 116) — the Nile, Ganges, and the Euphrates, typifying the rivers of three great continents tributary to the ocean —, which serve as a transition to the colossal statue of Oceanus at the summit of the fountain. Round the top of the bas-reliefs runs an inscription giving the date on which the basin was set up in the center of the Isolotto — July 18, 1618; see particularly Figure 111.

Seen at a distance, as the central accent of the Isolotto, with its base hidden by the balustrade and plants (Fig. 142), this fountain is very effective; but at close range (Fig. 110) it seems top-heavy. The hexagonal receiving basin of the original design would have tended to balance the whole by providing a broad base, and the figures of tritons at the angles would have served as a transition to the statues above. The heavy proportions and great size of the terminal figure and its satellites would seem better adapted to the monumental type with the raised central figure than to the graceful cylix type. Indeed, the original marble Oceanus in the

Bargello (Fig. 99)[1] is strikingly similar in pose to the bronze Neptune of the great fountain at Bologna, just completed by the same sculptor (Fig. 98); while its curving lines show even closer affinities to those of the small bronze model in the Museo Civico (Fig. 97).

A photograph of this fountain playing (Fig. 37) shows that the water still follows the original design (Fig. 109). As in the fountain at Bologna, there are both rising and falling jets, those about the pedestal playing upward, round the terminal figure, while others fall from the urns of the three river gods, to collect in the cylix and brim over its sides. In the drawing the effect is further complicated by the streams which the tritons spout inward into the hexagonal basin. Today, a sunken, circular receiving basin catches the water, and likewise serves as an outlet; but of this there is no indication in the sketchy representation of the fountain as erected in 1576 upon the Boboli lunette (Fig. 35).

Whether we study the fountain in its final form or in the original design, the predominance of the sculpture over the structural parts — basin and pedestal — is equally striking. This is felt particularly in the massive figures of the river gods, perched precariously on their inadequate brackets, high above the basin. Contrast these figures with statues placed in a similar position on the earlier Great Fountain at Castello (Fig. 46). There, in spite of the centrifugal poses of the putti, the vertical lines of the central shaft are still preserved; here, the pedestal and even the great basin seem completely overshadowed by these huge, restive forms. As the ceiling painters of the baroque period, with their representations of clouds and of floating figures, painted away the architecture, so in the Florentine Cinquecento sculptors asserted more and more the free plastic representation of their figures in space, slighting the architectonic portions of their fountains.

By the same sculptor, but in a lighter vein, is the charming Fountain of Venus in the Grotticella, as the last chamber of Buontalenti's grotto of Boboli is called. Again, several figures are united in a marine tableau (Fig. 117). Above a rather elaborate cylix of variegated dark green stone a nude *baigneuse* of snowy marble recoils from the gaze of four leering fauns, who clamber over the edge of the vase, blowing water. The theme

1. Now replaced on the fountain by a copy.

FIGURE 110.  GIOVANNI BOLOGNA, FOUNTAIN OF OCEANUS

BOBOLI GARDEN, FLORENCE

*Photo R. Soprintendenza.*

FIGURE 111. GIOVANNI BOLOGNA,
THE RAPE OF EUROPA

RELIEF ON THE FOUNTAIN OF OCEANUS, BOBOLI GARDEN

*Photo R. Soprintendenza*

FIGURE 112. GIOVANNI BOLOGNA,
THE TRIUMPH OF NEPTUNE

RELIEF ON THE FOUNTAIN OF OCEANUS, BOBOLI GARDEN

*Photo R. Soprintendenza*

FIGURE 113. GIOVANNI BOLOGNA,
THE BATH OF DIANA

RELIEF ON THE FOUNTAIN OF OCEANUS, BOBOLI GARDEN

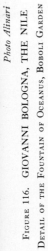

FIGURE 114.  GIOVANNI BOLOGNA, THE EUPHRATES

DETAIL OF THE FOUNTAIN OF OCEANUS, BOBOLI GARDEN

FIGURE 115.  GIOVANNI BOLOGNA, THE GANGES

DETAIL OF THE FOUNTAIN OF OCEANUS, BOBOLI GARDEN

FIGURE 116.  GIOVANNI BOLOGNA, THE NILE

DETAIL OF THE FOUNTAIN OF OCEANUS, BOBOLI GARDEN

Figure 118. FOUNTAIN OF BACCHUS

Victoria and Albert Museum, London

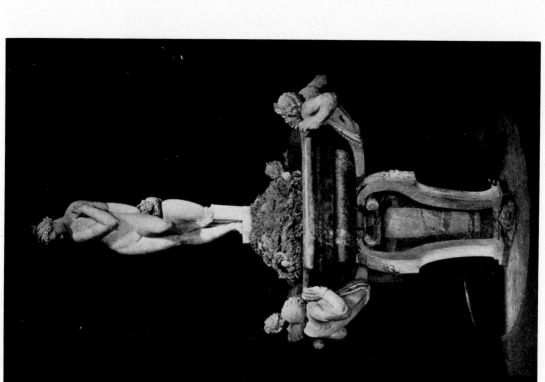

Figure 117. GIOVANNI BOLOGNA, FOUNTAIN OF VENUS

Grotto of Buontalenti, Boboli Garden

is a playful extension of the *motif* of the Venus dei Medici, characteristic
of sixteenth century paganism; but the mythology is here perilously near
to genre. The formal cylix, the conventionalized, termlike satyrs, and the
symbolical representation of the sea by means of wavy lines in the *tondo*
below the fountain contrast oddly with the naturalistic hillock on which
the nymph stands, a mass of rocks and shells cemented with stucco, doubtless suggested by the *rocaille* of the grotto in which the fountain has its
setting.

In addition to the streams which the fauns spout inward and upward,
Signor Vannucci, the genial *fontaniere* of the Boboli Garden, has recently
discovered and restored several slender jets which rise from this hillock to
play about the limbs of the *baigneuse* (Fig. 119) — again the upward jets
which Giovanni Bologna utilizes so often in his fountains, to bind together
basin and terminal figure. Water also trickles from the heads of the four
winds at the foot of the cylix into the wavy *tondo* symbolizing the sea,
which serves as outlet to the fountain.

The figure of the Venus was evidently begun about 1583, for in September of that year Bernardo Vecchietti,[1] in a letter to Antonio Serguidi, secretary of the Duke, asked that a proposed marble statue of St. Mark, ordered
of Stoldo Lorenzi for a niche in Or San Michele, might, owing to the
death of that sculptor before the execution of the work, be replaced by a
bronze statue by Giovanni Bologna — incidentally begging that his protégé
be allowed to use the untouched block of marble in question "for the grotto
at Pitti." The Venus is undoubtedly the figure carved from that marble.

From the Palazzo della Stufa in Florence comes the graceful Fountain
of Bacchus in the Victoria and Albert Museum; but date and sculptor are
unknown (Fig. 118). Certainly it is by a master of the Florentine school,
and dates from the latter half of the Cinquecento. The classicizing style
and backward curve of the terminal statue indicate the influence of some
ancient figure of the Praxitelean school. However, the statue is no literal
translation of the antique, but a version flavored by the sculptor's own
personality. The artist is plainly one who delights in the medium of marble, enhancing its whiteness by the use of black both in the pedestal which

1. The first Florentine patron of Giovanni Bologna, and his lifelong friend. At his villa, Il
Riposo, the scene of Raffaello Borghini's dialogues, Giovanni Bologna spent his last days.

bears the figure and in the four supports for the basin. As the profile of the bowl recalls that of the basin in Giovanni Bologna's Fountain of Venus (Fig. 117), and the grotesque decorations of the cylix are in a similar fantastic vein, the fountain has been attributed to a follower of Giovanni Bologna. The water rose from the cup held by Bacchus, falling into the cylix below, whence it dropped through the mouths of the monsters carved on its exterior, and from the pouting lips of the conventionalized cherubs at the corner of the quadrangular base, into the lost receiving basin.[1]

Two drawings in the Uffizi preserve the design of Giovanni Bologna's famous Fountain of Samson and the Philistine, which was erected in Francesco dei Medici's garden at the Casino di San Marco in Florence between the years 1568 and 1584 (Figs. 120 and 122). The various parts of this fountain, which was sent to Valladolid in the opening years of the seventeenth century, have since been widely scattered; but in 1907 Signor P. N. Ferri discovered the terminal group, a marble statue of Samson belaboring a Philistine with the jawbone of an ass, in the collection of Sir William Worsley at Hovingham Hall, Yorkshire (Fig. 121); and Mr. Randall Davies has recently identified it beyond question with the original group by Giovanni Bologna. In 1929 I had the good fortune to discover the basin in the Jardin de la Isla of the formal royal gardens at Aranjuez, now crowned by a later bronze figure which has no connection with the original fountain (Fig. 123). Even the obscure little figures which decorate the niches of the lower pedestal in the wash drawing (Fig. 120) have been identified by the keen eye of Dr. Friedrich Kriegbaum as bronze monkeys, three of which, traditionally ascribed to Giovanni Bologna, have survived upon the Fontana delle Scimmie in the Boboli Garden (Fig. 124).

As shown in the wash drawing, the fountain seems a curious medley of formal and naturalistic elements. The Biblical subject of the terminal statue, an almost unique phenomenon in the iconography of the Florentine fountain,[2] obviously suggested by Michelangelo's designs for a group of Samson and the Philistine, has not prevented a treatment in the usual pagan vein of the Cinquecento. The exotic form of the basin, conceived

---

1. An interesting drawing of this fountain by *Triggs* shows the water *motifs*; F. G. E., pl. 119, in pt. III.

2. Donatello's Judith and Holofernes and Michelangelo's design for a Moses fountain which was never executed are the only other exceptions; see pp. 12 and 39.

FIGURE 119. GIOVANNI BOLOGNA, DETAIL OF THE FOUNTAIN OF VENUS

GROTTO OF BUONTALENTI, BOBOLI GARDEN

FIGURE 121. GIOVANNI BOLOGNA, SAMSON AND THE PHILISTINE

HOVINGHAM HALL, YORKSHIRE

FIGURE 120. DRAWING OF GIOVANNI BOLOGNA'S FOUNTAIN OF
SAMSON AND THE PHILISTINE

GABINETTO DEI DISEGNI, THE UFFIZI

as a great sea shell with curving lip and deep indentations, and its curious
supports, half consoles and half grotesque sea creatures, contrast oddly
with the formal quadrangular base of the whole. This apparent incon-
gruity between the Biblical subject of the terminal group and the marine
character of the basin and its supports, which would be more in harmony
with a figure of Neptune, raises the question whether the basin, as well as
the figure, can be the work of Giovanni Bologna. I do not believe that
such a combination would have troubled a sixteenth century mind. Certainly in the Great Fountain at the Villa of Castello, entirely designed by
Tribolo, the group of Hercules and Antaeus has no apparent connection
with the playful putti that swarm over basins and shaft.

The design of this fountain, as presented in the more spirited and pictorial wash drawing (Fig. 120), seems to me to possess the unity that comes
only from conception by a single mind. The smaller upper pedestal makes
a nice transition between the larger base and the pyramidal mass of the
group of Samson and the Philistine; and the downward lines of the water
dripping from the indentations of the shell continue the downward lines of
the group. The effect of intense movement produced in the figures by a
skilful use of diagonal lines is continued by the broken curves of the basin,
and reinforced by the actually moving water. Baldinucci's statement that
Giovanni Bologna himself carved the sea monster consoles tends to support the view that he designed the whole. Moreover, both sea monsters
and basin are in the same fantastic vein as his known work, the "Diavo-
lino" or "Satirino," which once decorated the façade of the Palazzo Vecchietti, now in the Palazzo Vecchio; and the naturalism of the vivacious
monkeys is paralleled by that of the series of bronze birds which he made
for the grotto at the Villa of Castello. The arrangement of the water, too,
is characteristic of Giovanni Bologna; upward jets like those indicated at
the corners of the pedestal in the careful architect's drawing of the elevation (Fig. 122) appear in practically all of his fountains. The water dropping from these jets gathered in the basin, to overflow through the indentations and fall into the square receiving basin, which has not come down
to us (Fig. 120).

Interest in this work has hitherto been confined to the terminal group
and its place in the *oeuvre* of Giovanni Bologna. For the history of the

fountain, however, the strange basin with its fantastic supports is of greater importance; for with it commenced the transition from the formal cylix fountain of the Renaissance to the naturalistic type of the baroque period. The substitution of naturalistic elements, usually drawn from the life of the sea, for the architectonic type of basin and pedestal was at first confined to a part of the cylix only. Thus in the Fountain of Samson and the Philistine (Fig. 120), the bowl of the formal cylix was replaced by a naturalistic shell, with curved lips and curious indentations; but the pedestal beneath remained partly architectonic (in the formal base decorated by four niches), partly naturalistic (in the fantastic sea monsters which form consoles supporting the cylix).

In the years 1618 to 1620, when Giulio Parigi gave the Isolotto of the Boboli Garden its present form, he designed four identical cylix fountains to decorate its edge, crowned by four variant figures of cupids, carved by Domenico Pieratti and Cosimo Salvestrini. The basins of these fountains are completely naturalistic (Fig. 126). Again the cylix is formed by a shell, here supported by a pedestal composed entirely of intertwined dolphins. The only vestiges of the formal cylix type are to be found in the base, resembling a capital, which bears the terminal figure, and in the use of the ideal medium of white marble, characteristic of the formal fountains of the Renaissance.

The dependence of these fountains upon the earlier Fountain of Samson and the Philistine (Fig. 120) is obvious. The swelling forms of the shells are similar, and the jets of water issue from the corners of the bases bearing the statues, and from indentations in the shells, in the same manner. Even the pose of Pieratti's Amorino (Fig. 125, right), represented as breaking a heart with a hammer, is humorously reminiscent of the intensity of the Samson and the Philistine.

In 1626 Pietro Tacca commenced the bizarre twin fountains which now decorate the Piazza della SS. Annunziata, Florence, one of which is reproduced in Figure 127.[1] Here the bowl of the cylix, formed of a curious bivalve, is completely naturalistic; but its pedestal, laden with fruits of the sea, still retains its formal character. The crossing jets of water are char-

1. These fountains were originally designed for the piazza at Livorno, as adjuncts to the monument to Ferdinand I; but Ferdinand II decided to erect them in their present site, where they were installed in 1641.

FIGURE 123.   DETAIL OF THE FOUNTAIN OF BACCHUS

ROYAL GARDENS, ARANJUEZ

FIGURE 124.   FOUNTAIN OF THE MONKEYS

BOBOLI GARDEN, FLORENCE.   MONKEYS BY GIOVANNI BOLOGNA

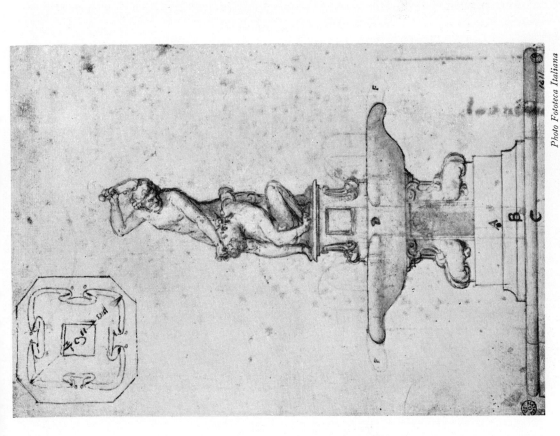

FIGURE 122.   DRAWING OF GIOVANNI BOLOGNA'S FOUNTAIN OF

SAMSON AND THE PHILISTINE

GABINETTO DEI DISEGNI, THE UFFIZI

FIGURE 125. FOUNTAINS OF THE AMORINI

THE ISOLOTTO, BOBOLI GARDEN. DESIGN BY GIULIO PARIGI; FIGURES BY DOMENICO PIERATTI

FIGURE 126. GIULIO PARIGI, BASIN OF THE FOUNTAIN OF THE AMORINO

THE ISOLOTTO, BOBOLI GARDEN

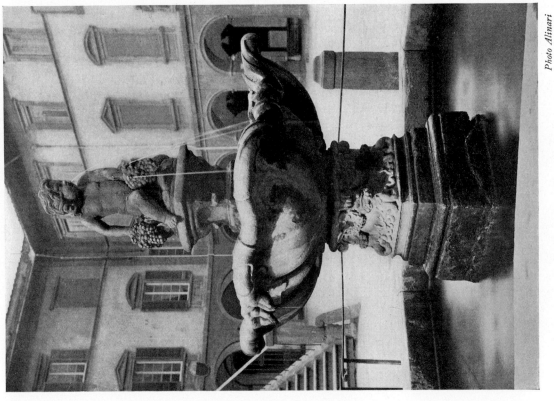

FIGURE 128. FERDINANDO TACCA, FOUNTAIN

PIAZZA DEL MUNICIPIO, PRATO

FIGURE 127. PIETRO TACCA, GROTESQUE FOUNTAIN

PIAZZA DELLA SS. ANNUNZIATA, FLORENCE

FIGURE 129. FERDINANDO TACCA, IL BACCHINO

GALLERIA COMMUNALE, PRATO

acteristic of the baroque period.  Both in the mistilinear receiving basins
and in the indentations at the side of the bivalves through which the water
issues, these fountains recall Giovanni Bologna's fountain of Samson and
the Philistine; but the pupil has here far surpassed his master in the unity
and originality of his design.  Tacca's use of the pictorial bronze, which dissolves into its surroundings, instead of the more sculptural white marble,
which stands out in sharp relief from its setting, is especially happy.

Likewise of bronze is the amusing Fountain of the Bacchino, now in the
Galleria Communale at Prato, the work of Tacca's son Ferdinando, said to
date from 1659 to 1665.  In its original setting, in the Piazza del Commune,
streams of water fell from the clusters of grapes which the child clutches,
and from his full mouth, into the shell-like basin (Fig. 128).[1]  Here both
the upper and lower pedestals remain formal.  Shell and upper pedestal
alike recall the Boboli Fountains of the Amorini.  The chief interest of this
fountain, however, lies in the fascinating bronze putto (Fig. 129), one of
the most pleasing studies of the child form in Italian art.  By the use of a
slight *contrapposto* and by the disposition of the arms and legs in radial
lines, the sculptor has produced a figure that remains interesting, from
whatever angle it may be viewed.

From these transitional forms of the cylix fountain it was but a step to
the completely naturalistic examples of the baroque period.  Here we must
consider two Florentine fountains which, strictly speaking, do not conform
to the cylix type.  One is the utterly fantastic little fountain in marble,
entirely composed of shells and strange sea creatures, which another pupil
of Giovanni Bologna, Pietro Francavilla, added as a sort of excrescence to
Cosimo I's monument in the Piazza dei Cavalieri at Pisa in the year 1594
(Fig. 131), where the Grand Duke stands with one foot on a dolphin, in
the attitude of a Neptune!  The other is the grotesque marble fountain of
a triton, spouting into a shell, one of a series of four designed by Giulio
Parigi (1618–1620) to decorate the edge of the Boboli Isolotto (Fig. 130).[2]
Here there is no thought of formal pedestal or basin; indeed, the conception of the fountain is so completely naturalistic that it is difficult to say
where figure ends and basin begins.

1. A copy now decorates the piazza.
2. These fountains, originally carved in common stone, being in a ruinous condition, were replaced in the eighteenth century by marble copies; see *Inghirami*, p. 129.

# CHAPTER VII

## THE FORMAL ISLAND [1]

THE largest and most elaborate Florentine fountains belonged to the type known as the "isoletta," in which a central island, decorated by a formal freestanding fountain, is surrounded by a moat and approached by a bridge. The earliest extant example is Francesco Camilliani's mammoth fountain in the Piazza della Pretoria at Palermo (1550–1575), where four flights of marble steps lead from an outer marble platform of circular ground plan to a central fountain of the candelabrum type (Fig. 132). The overwhelming effect of this enormous structure, with its profuse decoration of figure sculpture, was summed up by Vasari in one word, "stupendissima."

In many ways this fountain recalls Montorsoli's Fountain of Orion at Messina, particularly in the four river gods with their basins and the smaller urns on each side of the inner flights of steps. The effect of excited motion which we noted in the sculpture of Montorsoli's fountain is even heightened. There, the sculpture on the outer portion of the fountain conformed on the whole to the horizontal lines of steps and basin, centrifugal poses and effects of motion being confined to the figures upon the central shaft; here, the agitation commences in the host of standing figures that adorn the balustrades of the stairs and converse with the river gods; all are cast in contorted, centrifugal poses. The fountain seems alive with turning, gesturing figures.

Perhaps the most startling feature of this curious fountain is the menagerie that peers forth from the arches round the central core of the structure (Fig. 133), perpetuating in monumental form the *serraglio*, or private zoo, so popular among Renaissance princes.[2] A bit of naturalism is introduced in the railing immediately above these exotic creatures, the

---

1. The adjective "formal" is intended to distinguish this type from the "rustic" island, discussed in the following chapter.

2. An actual *serraglio* in the Boboli Garden, in which each animal looked out of a window of his own, as in our fountain, is described by *Cambiagi*.

Figure 131. PIETRO FRANCAVILLA, MONUMENT TO COSIMO I,
WITH GROTESQUE FOUNTAIN

Piazza dei Cavalieri, Pisa

Figure 130. FOUNTAIN OF THE TRITON

The Isolotto, Boboli Garden. Designed by Giulio Parigi

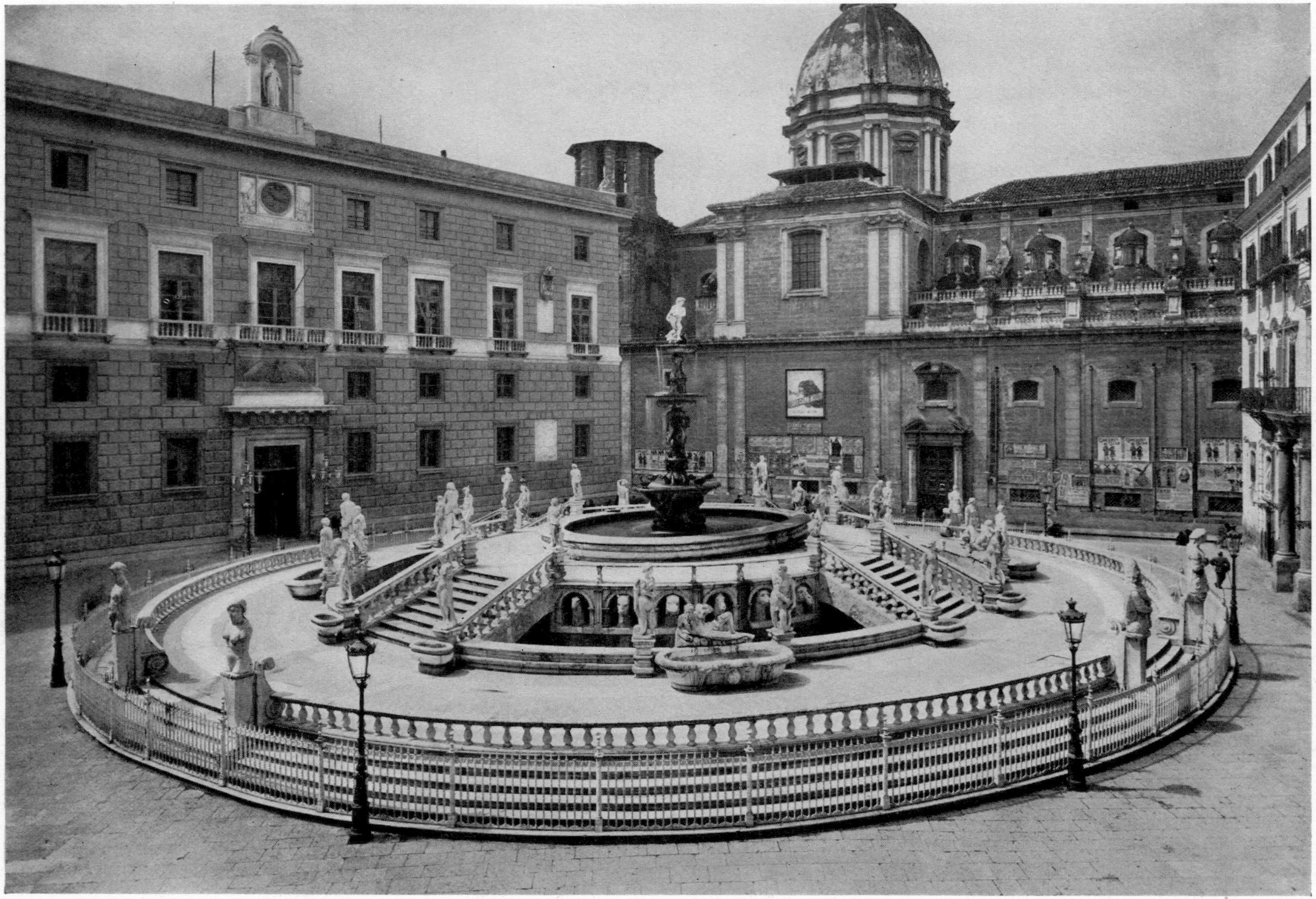

FIGURE 132. FRANCESCO CAMILLIANI AND MICHELANGELO NACCHERINO, FOUNTAIN, PIAZZA PRETORIA, PALERMO

Figure 133. DETAIL OF THE FOUNTAIN IN THE PIAZZA PRETORIA, PALERMO

FIGURE 134. SHAFT OF THE CENTRAL PORTION OF THE FOUNTAIN IN THE
PIAZZA PRETORIA, PALERMO

balusters being composed of two dolphins addorsed, instead of the usual architectural forms! These barely show in the photograph. Another naturalistic note appears in the lifelike fowls perched on the edge of the first basin of the inner fountain, raising their beaks after drinking (Fig. 134).

By far the most pleasing part of the fountain is this central portion, a perfect example of the candelabrum type. Unfortunately its discoloration by water sets it off from the outer figures of glistening white marble, preventing the continuous effect of motion inward and upward which the artist undoubtedly planned (Fig. 133). The strange winged creatures that support the first basin, barely visible at the bottom of Figure 134, are not addorsed against the stem, but placed under the outer portion of the basin, giving the effect of a broad base, which lends stability to the lines of the whole (Fig. 133). The raised hoofs of the sea-horses round the stem above make a transition to the shaft. From this point the eye travels upward through two stages adorned with youths and wineskins and putti on dolphins to the summit, where a running boy pours out a cornucopia, the swift motion and *contrapposto* of his figure (Fig. 134) repeating the dynamic note struck by the restive figures that adorn the balustrades.

This fountain, with its teeming swarm of pagan figures, is ill suited to a city piazza. Such an ensemble demands a spacious garden setting, where the play of light and shade, the background of grass and foliage, would soften the dazzling effect of the plethora of white marble. Indeed, this fountain was originally intended for a garden — the villa in Florence to which Don Pedro di Toledo, Viceroy of Naples and father-in-law of Cosimo I, retired in 1550. The commission for the numerous fountains planned for this villa was given to the Florentine sculptor, Francesco Camilliani; and signatures upon two of the figures at Palermo show that in this fountain at least he was assisted by Michelangelo Naccherino. After the death of Don Pedro in 1552 work on the fountain was discontinued, and the unfinished pieces stored in magazines for many years.

When in 1570 the senators of Palermo decided to erect a great fountain, Don Garzia di Toledo, then viceroy of Naples, recalled the unfinished one in his father's garden, and negotiations were commenced for its purchase, completed in 1573. In the following year, six hundred and forty-four pieces were shipped to Palermo; and in 1575 other parts, carved by Camilliani and Naccherino at Florence on the order of Don Garzia, arrived. Naturally, the piazza had to be enlarged in order to accommodate a structure of such dimensions; and the river gods were duly rechristened with the names of local Sicilian streams, although their attributes still proclaim their classical and Florentine origin. We recognize the Arno with his inevitable lion, the Mugnone with his urn (Fig. 135), the restless Nile,[1] and Hippocrene, accompanied by Pegasus and bearing scrolls and the tragic mask (Fig. 136).[2] In 1576 Camillo Camilliani, Florentine engineer and son of Francesco, came down to set up the structure, which was finally dedicated in 1580, to the great delight of the citizens of Palermo.

This joy was not shared by the monks of the adjoining convent of Santa Caterina, who objected so violently to the nudity of the statues that the most objectionable of those facing the church had to be replaced by less pagan figures — a statue of St. Agatha, in one instance! Yet in spite of such minor concessions to the Counter Reformation, this fountain, with its elaborate mythological repertoire, remains a striking monument to the paganism of the late Renaissance.

Vasari, writing in 1568, tells us that Francesco Camilliani had devoted fifteen years to the making of fountains, and speaks of many others made for the villa of Don Luigi,[3] the fountains of which far outnumbered those of any other villa in Florence, "perhaps in Italy." Of them all, only the one has survived; but as Vasari lauds this above all the others we need not greatly regret our loss. [4] The empty style and superficial modelling of this master do not justify Vasari's praise. Camilliani began as a pupil of the classicizing Bandinelli; but from the sculpture of this fountain it is evident that he later became addicted to the "forma serpentinata" of the Mannerists, who exaggerated the tendency to throw the human figure into curving, calligraphic lines, found in such ancient statues as the Venus dei Medici.

*Isolette* were undoubtedly common in Florentine gardens during the

1. This figure, signed by Michelangelo Naccherino, is thrown into a most excited and unstable position.
2. See also Ammannati's Hippocrene, illustrated in Figure 83.
3. Don Luigi inherited Don Pedro's villa at Florence.
4. Francesco Camilliani also made fountains for the garden of the Duke of Alba at Lagunilla, Spain; *Gothein*, I, 388.

FIGURE 135.  FRANCESCO CAMILLIANI, THE MUGNONE

DETAIL OF THE FOUNTAIN IN THE PIAZZA PRETORIA, PALERMO

FIGURE 136.  FRANCESCO CAMILLIANI, HIPPOCRENE

DETAIL OF THE FOUNTAIN IN THE PIAZZA PRETORIA, PALERMO

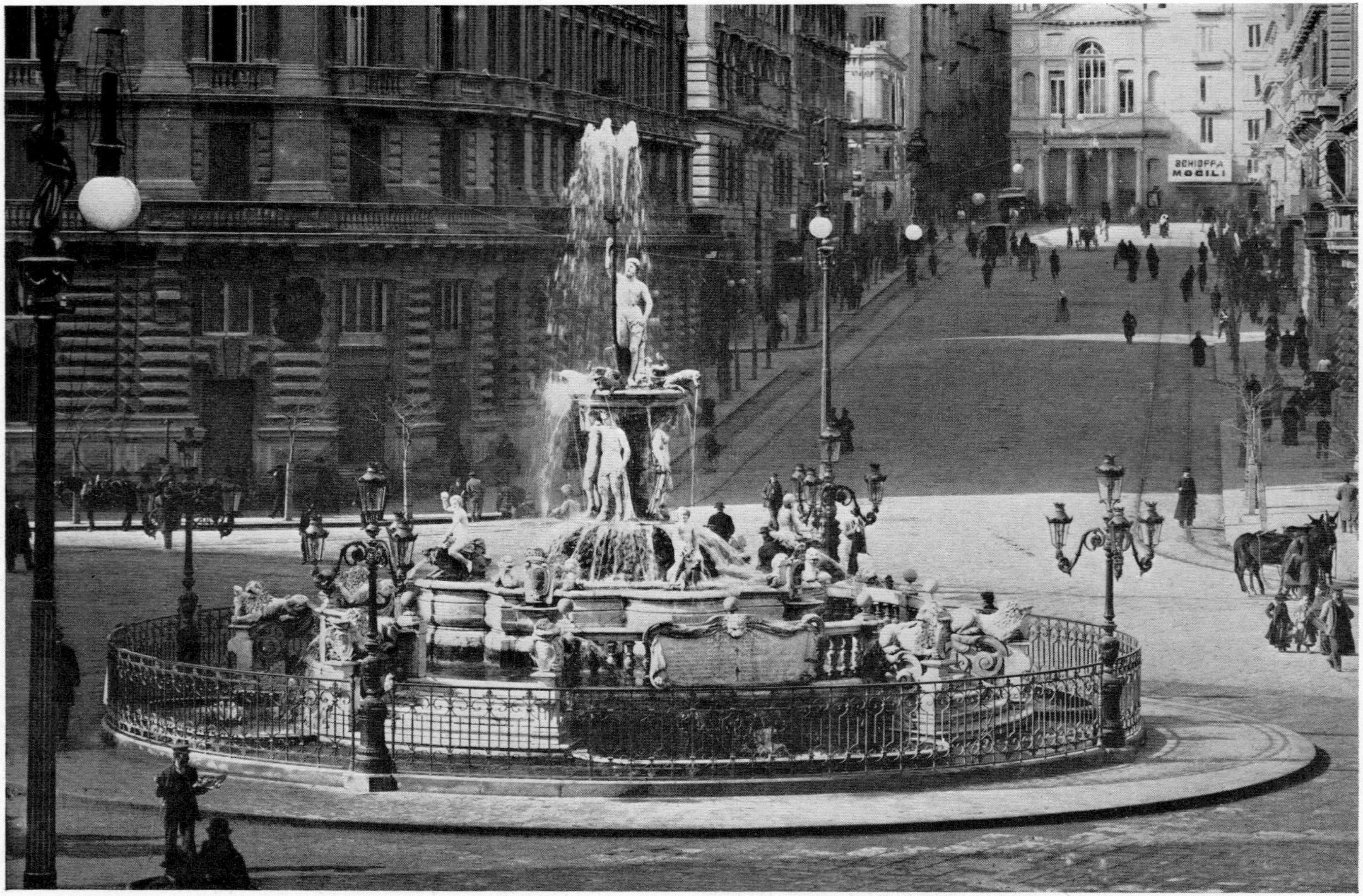


*Photo Alinari*

FIGURE 137. THE FONTANA MEDINA, NAPLES

DESIGN BY DOMENICO FONTANA; SCULPTURE BY PIETRO BERNINI AND MICHELANGELO NACCHERINO

Cinquecento. We have definite references to a fountain of this type at the center of the botanical garden (Giardino dei Semplici) which Cosimo I founded about 1545, adjoining the Medici stables. From the corners of the square garden four covered paths led to the octagonal island in the center, set in the midst of a great *vivaio* or living pool, fed by a canal from the river Mugnone, and approached by bridges lined with surprise jets to trick the unwary. While descriptions of this island give no details concerning the central fountain or its sculptured ornament, it is evidently to be identified with the "fontana isolata" at the Giardino delle Stalle, which Vasari mentions as decorated by Antonio Lorenzi "with many aquatic animals made of marble and of the most beautiful variegated stones." This fountain was probably commenced soon after the opening of the gardens in 1545, and was obviously completed before Vasari's second edition of 1568, in which the reference quoted occurs.

The Fontana Medina of the Piazza della Borsa in Naples (1599–1601) (Fig. 137),[1] although designed by a Roman architect, is obviously influenced by Florentine prototypes, particularly by Francesco Camilliani's island at Palermo. The figure sculpture was entrusted to two Florentines, Michelangelo Naccherino and Pietro Bernini. Four flights of marble steps cross a small, circular moat to the central island, decorated by a fountain of the candelabrum type. The mistilinear ground plan of the great basin and the freedom and grandeur of the water effects are due to the Roman architect and engineer, Domenico Fontana, who designed the whole, although the *motif* of the spouting trident was undoubtedly derived from the Neptune of Stoldo Lorenzi (Fig. 164). The curving consoles, surmounted by shield-bearing lions, and the great inscription are seventeenth century additions, in the baroque style characteristic of southern Italy.

The most famous of the island fountains is the only one preserved in its original garden setting, the "Isolotto" or Great Island at Boboli. This was evidently not commenced until the seventeenth century, since it does not appear upon the lunette of 1599.[2] It received the present decoration during the years 1618 to 1620, under the architect Giulio Parigi. An earlier

1. The Fontana Medina was originally in the Piazza del Municipio, near the Palazzo Sirignano; Muñoz, in Vita d'Arte (October, 1909), plate opp. p. 436.

2. It is of course possible that the island then existed in a part of the garden not shown in the lunette.

and simpler form is, however, indicated by the description of a German traveller, who saw the island decorated by a "tempietto" of greenery, in place of Giovanni Bologna's Fountain of Oceanus, which since 1618 has formed its central accent.

The great *vivaio* is oval in plan, and crossed by two opposite bridges, placed on the axis of the Stradone. These lead to the central, oval island, on which Giovanni Bologna's Fountain of Oceanus towers, surrounded by formal flower beds.[1] The entrance to each of the bridges is barred by an ornamental iron gateway, framed by tall, paired pillars of *pietra serena*, surmounted by the capricorns of Cosimo dei Medici,[2] and flanked by two fountains fed by grotesque marble tritons (Figs. 138 and 130). The center of each half of the pool's circumference is marked by twin fountains of the naturalistic cylix type, surmounted by mischievous cupids.[3] In the pair carved by Domenico Pieratti, one putto is opening a heart with a key, while his companion smashes another with a hammer (Fig. 125); and the two attributed to Cosimo Salvestrini are represented as shooting and drawing arrows. Within the pool are two anonymous statues of indifferent style. On one side of the island sits Andromeda, chained to the rock (Fig. 139); at a corresponding point on the opposite side Perseus, mounted on a sea horse, gallops to her rescue (Fig. 140). The island itself is enclosed by a monumental balustrade which, in spite of its baroque lines, suggests the influence of an earlier island in the more architectonic Roman style, the Fontana dei Mori at the Villa Lante, Bagnaia (Fig. 141). In the center of the vast Isolotto Giovanni Bologna's great Fountain of Oceanus at length found its proper setting (Fig. 142).

1. See Figure 110 and pp. 61–62.
2. Perhaps the capricorns, insignia of Cosimo I, indicate a date within his reign (1537–1574).
3. See p. 66.

FIGURE 138.  GIULIO PARIGI, FOUNTAINS

ENTRANCE TO THE ISOLOTTO, BOBOLI GARDEN

FIGURE 139.  ANDROMEDA

DETAIL OF THE ISOLOTTO, BOBOLI GARDEN

FIGURE 140.  PERSEUS

DETAIL OF THE ISOLOTTO, BOBOLI GARDEN

*Photo Moscioni*

FIGURE 141.  VIGNOLA (?), THE ISOLETTA, WITH THE FONTANA DEI MORI

VILLA LANTE, BAGNAIA

*Photo Mannelli*

FIGURE 142.   GIOVANNI BOLOGNA, FOUNTAIN OF OCEANUS

THE ISOLOTTO, BOBOLI GARDEN

# CHAPTER VIII

## RUSTIC FOUNTAINS

IN THE formal fountains the sculpture, however elaborate or fantastic, was always given an architectonic setting. The designers of rustic fountains, on the other hand, sought to dissolve the line separating the statues from their natural surroundings by placing them in the midst of mossy grottoes or upon rugged cliffs, composed entirely of *rocaille* and simulating as closely as possible the rocky forms found in nature. With this addition of a naturalistic setting the transition toward the aquatic tableau which we have observed in certain formal fountains is completed.

It seems logical to suppose that such fountains first arose in Italy as a reaction against the formal, classicizing types, in the direction of naturalism; yet the evidence indicates that the earliest examples were made in conscious imitation of ancient prototypes. Thus in the fifteenth century Alberti speaks of the ancients' use of "living pumice," often mixed with green wax to simulate moss, in covering the walls of grottoes. Ancient niches with rustic treatment remain today in the Canopus at Hadrian's villa; and such survivals undoubtedly served as the prototypes of the first rustic fountains of the Renaissance. There is evidence for the actual construction of such fountains in Italy in the late Quattrocento; for descriptions of Poggio Reale mention grottoes, and Bembo, writing at the close of the century, speaks of a room hollowed out of the living rock.

One of the rustic fountains of the early Cinquecento has survived in a ruined state, the Fountain of the Valley, built by Giovanni da Udine at the Villa Madama near Rome in the time of Cardinal Giuliano dei Medici (1519–1523). This was a hemicycle made of large stones overgrown by greenery. The water issued "naturally" from the stones into long channels; besides, there was a lion's head spout of pumice stone, which has since vanished. Obviously the painter intended a perfect reproduction of a natural cave. Elaborate and equally naturalistic grottoes are described by

Annibal Caro in a letter of 1538, some of them covered with the pumice stone mentioned by Alberti, others with stalactites. In 1546, Antonio da San Gallo wrote to Cosimo I recommending a particular type of natural stalactite, popular at Rome, for certain rustic fountains planned at the Villa of Castello. The letter makes it clear that the use of these stalactites at Rome was suggested by some found at an ancient villa.

In his section on fountains and grottoes in the introduction to the *Lives*, Vasari lists four types of *rocaille*: first, the natural stalactites, applied to "Tuscan work" (as in the wall fountains of the Arno and Mugnone at Castello); second, a combination of rocks heaped up in imitation of nature, and overgrown with plants (as in the Fountain of the Valley, described in the preceding paragraph); third, stucco inlaid with shells of various sorts; and fourth, a rustic mosaic of many colors, made of bits of overheated bricks and broken glass, set into stucco. Entire figures of men and animals were constructed in this way. Of these four types, if we may judge from the examples of rustic work still extant, stalactites were by far the most popular in Florentine villas of the Cinquecento.

## The Grotto

A type of rustic fountain common in Tuscan villas is the grotto — a concealed room or cave, in which the walls are covered with stalactites. The one at Castello is a perfect example of this *genre* (Fig. 143), consisting of a vaulted room entirely covered by stalactites, in which the ceiling is inlaid with a mosaic of shells and colored stones. Three barrel-vaulted niches contain naturalistic groups of animals, carved from marbles of various hues, which spout water into long, tub-like basins. Water issues from the stalactites, which are fitted with minute lead pipes, and from the mouths of the animals, and even rises on occasion from the pavement itself, which still conceals a series of surprise jets released by the turning of a key. The menageries above the basins (see also Figure 145) reflect the Renaissance delight in exotic animals. Among the many species included are the elephant, camel, giraffe, monkey, bear, and rhinoceros — even a unicorn. No one who has seen the Sala degli Animali at the Vatican, full of sculptured animals from ancient Roman gardens, will doubt that this piece of naturalism, too, was partly inspired by ancient precedent. The

FIGURE 143. THE GROTTO, ROYAL VILLA, CASTELLO. DESIGN BY TRIBOLO

FIGURE 144. GIOVANNI BOLOGNA, BRONZE BIRDS IN THE GROTTO AT CASTELLO

FIGURE 145. DETAIL OF THE GROTTO AT CASTELLO

FIGURE 146.  BANDINELLI AND GIOVANNI FANCELLI, THE GROTTICINA

BOBOLI GARDEN

FIGURE 147. GIOVANNI FANCELLI, BASIN FROM THE BOBOLI GROTTICINA

FAÇADE OF THE PITTI PALACE, FLORENCE

FIGURE 148. VAULT OF THE GROTTICINA

BOBOLI GARDEN, FLORENCE

great basins, modelled after the tubs from Roman baths, are decorated with naturalistic *motifs* drawn from the life of the sea — crabs, fish, lobsters, and a profusion of shells. Even the supporting feet are formed of fish. The sculptors of both animals and basins are unknown; perhaps they are the handiwork of one of the *animaliers* mentioned by Vasari as working in the Medicean villas — Antonio Lorenzi or Giovanni Fancelli. In the same naturalistic vein are the amusing bronze fowls by Giovanni Bologna, perched at the springing of the vaults, shown in Figure 144. His spirited turkey and eagle, now in the Bargello, also belong to this series, which can be dated about 1567 by a letter to Prince Francesco, in which the sculptor writes that he is taking advantage of the hot May weather to hasten the drying of some clay birds, obviously the models from which these works were cast. This letter furnishes a *terminus ante quem*, May 4, 1567, for the completion of the grotto; for the birds would hardly have been prepared before the walls of the grotto were ready to receive them. Tribolo's plan for the grotto must, of course, be dated before 1550, the year of his death.[1]

This early date for the design of the grotto at Castello is supported by the documented date, between September, 1553 and September, 1554, of a similar, though smaller, one at Boboli, which I shall call the "Grotticina" to distinguish it from the later and larger grotto of Buontalenti in the same garden. The entrance to the Grotticina appears on the Boboli lunette of 1599 (Figs. 35 and 35a). As at Castello, the walls of the interior are covered with stalactites. Before the niche at the end stands a small basin, surmounted by an exceedingly naturalistic marble she-goat, which once spouted water (Fig. 146). Water also issued from the head of a ram placed high above, in the center of the niche; while on either side two goats stand in characteristic poses upon branches carved of *pietra bigia*, raising their heads as though nibbling. The original oval basin, decorated with two tiny putti and capricorns in low relief, is now installed beneath a window on the façade of the Pitti Palace, where it serves as a fountain, fed by a spouting lion's head (Fig. 147); it is replaced in the grotto by a cheap copy. The formal, coffered divisions of the stucco vault are decorated with frescoed putti and grotesques, outlined by bands of stalactites to harmonize with the walls of the grotto (Fig. 148).

1. Vasari describes it among Tribolo's plans for Castello.

The sculptured goats and basin, and in all probability the grotto as a whole, were designed for the Duchess Eleonora by Baccio Bandinelli, who himself carved the she-goat over the basin. The execution, with this one exception, was entrusted to Bandinelli's pupil, Giovanni Fancelli. As the attractive putti who hold spouting fish over the basin are out of scale with the other figures in the niche, and are not mentioned in the minute description of this grotto in the Medici account book, it seems unlikely that they formed part of the original design. However, their style proves them to be contemporary works, carved by some follower of Tribolo.

The Villa of Pratolino, acquired in 1569 by Francesco dei Medici and designed by Bernardo Buontalenti, was famous for its elaborate grottoes. These were certainly complete by 1580, when Montaigne visited the spot. Although scarcely a trace of the original villa remains today, we are fortunate in having, in addition to Montaigne's brief description, a detailed account of the villa published in 1586 by Francesco de Vieri, another written by Bernardo Sgrilli in 1742, and some seventeenth century etchings executed by Stefano della Bella. Two of the latter, showing portions of the Grotto of Fame, are reproduced in Figure 149 as typical of the series of grottoes which extended under terraces round the front of the great "Casino." As at Castello, the walls were covered with stalactites, and the vaults decorated by bands of colored shells and stones. In the niches, which were adorned with a bewildering variety of fountain figures, Buontalenti sought still more illusionistic effects, adding painted backgrounds and even enlivening the previously static tableau by the introduction of automata—figures which were made to move or to produce music by means of mechanical devices, operated by water power. There were, for example, a shepherdess who walked to a well, filled her pail, and returned to her niche, and a satyr who played the bagpipe. In addition to the usual water *motifs* in connection with the figures, the walls dripped water; and the inevitable "trick" fountains, already noted in the grotto at Castello, were employed on a large scale. In the Grotto of the Deluge concealed surprise jets might be released at any moment, flooding the entire grotto and blocking the escape of the victim.

All this savors of the amusement park, of mechanics rather than art; yet these grottoes often contained works of some artistic importance. Such

FIGURE 149.  STEFANO DELLA BELLA, ETCHING SHOWING THE ENTRANCE TO BUONTALENTI'S
GROTTOES AT PRATOLINO

THE RIVER GOD MUGNONE BY GIOVANNI BOLOGNA

FIGURE 150.  STEFANO DELLA BELLA, ETCHING OF THE FAÇADE OF THE CASINO AT PRATOLINO,
WITH THE MUGNONE

FIGURE 152.   VINCENZO DEI ROSSI, THESEUS AND HELENA
GROTTO OF BUONTALENTI, BOBOLI GARDEN

FIGURE 151.   GIOVANNI BOLOGNA(?), BRONZE SATYR FROM A GROTTO
AT PRATOLINO

MUSEO NAZIONALE, FLORENCE

was the fountain of the local river Mugnone, placed at the entrance to the grottoes, on the main axis of the villa (Figs. 149 and 150). From the close resemblance of the figure shown in the etching to the statue of the Euphrates upon the Fountain of Oceanus in the Boboli Isolotto (Fig. 114), it seems probable that the Mugnone was carved by Giovanni Bologna. Further support for this attribution is given by the Duke of Württemberg's mention of a "Neptune" by Giovanni Bologna, which he saw at Pratolino about 1599, in a fountain between these stairs.[1] The sitting posture and placing of the urn between the legs recall Tribolo's river god at the Villa Corsini. Fragments of this figure, which was carved in a greenish gray stone called *macigno*, have been discovered *in situ* by Dr. Friedrich Kriegbaum.

Giovanni Bologna's little bronze satyr in the loggia of the Bargello (Fig. 151) once sat astride a cask in a small grotto on the grounds of Pratolino, pouring water from a Tuscan flask in lieu of wine. The *motif* recalls ancient figures of satyrs with wineskins; but the contemporary touch of the flask, the realism with which the body is treated, and the grotesque expression of the face, place the statue with the master's more naturalistic works — a group too often forgotten in estimates of his style. The elaborate *contrapposto* and nervous movement are characteristic of the Flemish master. The emphasis upon diagonal lines and the centrifugal character of the pose verge upon the baroque.

In the three grottoes which we have studied, the statues were executed in the sculptural medium of stone and bronze, their definite forms contrasting sharply with their pictorial setting. In Buontalenti's grotto in the Boboli Garden, however (Fig. 153), this distinction is no longer maintained; the human figures and animals in the pastoral and mythological scenes that adorn the walls are likewise composed of stalactites,[2] so that they merge into their surroundings. Even Michelangelo's gigantic figures of slaves,[3] placed at the angles to bear the vaults, were undoubtedly felt, in their unfinished state, to accord with the picturesque, formless effect of the whole. Instead of the stalactite vaults of the earlier grottoes, banded with mosaic strips which emphasized the architectural divisions, the upper edges of the walls dissolve into painted landscapes, and the center of the

1. On this figure see p. 128.
2. Mixed with bits of colored glass or pottery, Vasari's fourth type of *rocaille*; see p. 74.
3. The originals, now in the Academy, are replaced in the grotto by casts.

vault is left open to the sky. The water oozed from tiny pipes concealed in the *rocaille* down the walls into the channels at either side.

In this grotto we see the culmination of the tendency to imitate natural forms — the exact antithesis to the idealization of the formal Tuscan fountains. Yet even here the more sculptural types made their way, as in Vincenzo dei Rossi's marble group of Theseus and Helena, erected over a fountain basin in the second chamber of the grotto (Fig. 152),[1] and in Giovanni Bologna's Fountain of Venus, which decorates the Grotticella or rear room (Fig. 119).

As we should expect, this grotto was the latest of the four; for payments in the Medici account books show that it was commenced in August, 1583, and the first room was probably completed in 1585, since the four slaves by Michelangelo were set in place by April of that year. Work upon the rear rooms was still going on as late as 1593. The architectonic façade is considerably earlier, having been designed by Vasari to precede a *vivaio* or fishpond, and constructed in the late fifties (Fig. 154). The marble figures of Apollo and Ceres are by Bandinelli, and were originally planned for an altar, where they were to represent Adam and Eve. The upper portion of the exterior is obviously a later addition necessitated by the height of the grotto and intended to harmonize with its more rustic character.

The formal grotto or *nymphaeum* at the end of the court of the Pitti Palace was undoubtedly built in the sixteenth century, under Ammannati; but it received its present decoration in the seventeenth century (Fig. 155). Here the *rocaille* is largely confined to the background of the arched niches, separated by paired Doric columns, which line its walls. Of the seven niches that surround the central, oval *vivaio*, only two contain fountains, one of which is illustrated in Figure 156. Above an oblong trough of variegated marble, festooned with garlands, rises a fantastic, shell-like cylix of the same stone. This is surmounted by a bizarre monster of bronze, who performs the double function of feeding the fountain by a stream that falls from his mouth, and supporting upon his shoulders a bronze oak tree, symbol of Vittoria della Rovere, whom Ferdinand II had married in 1634. The lunette above is filled by a curving shell adorned with terracotta putti

1. In 1560 Vincenzo dei Rossi presented this group to the Duke in the hope that he would be permitted to enter the contest for the fountain of Neptune; *Gaye*, III, 24.

FIGURE 153. BERNARDO BUONTALENTI INTERIOR OF THE GREAT GROTTO, BOBOLI GARDEN

FIGURE 154. VASARI, FAÇADE OF THE GROTTO OF BUONTALENTI, BOBOLI GARDEN

MARBLE STATUES BY BANDINELLI

FIGURE 155. GROTTO IN THE COURTYARD OF THE PITTI PALACE

FIGURE 156.  FOUNTAIN WITH THE ARMS OF VITTORIA DELLA ROVERE
GROTTO OF THE COURTYARD, PITTI PALACE.  PUTTI AND BRONZE MONSTER BY LUDOVICO SALVETTI

FIGURE 157.  ANTONIO NOVELLI, GROTTO OF POLYPHEMUS, ORTI ORICELLARI, FLORENCE

From Luigi Dami's *The Italian Garden*

FIGURE 158.  MONTORSOLI, ISLAND OF THE TRITON

GARDEN OF THE PALAZZO DORIA, GENOA

bearing a bronze crown. The companion fountain on the other side is almost identical, save that a bay tree is substituted for the oak. Both putti
and monsters are by Ludovico Salvetti, who also carved the amusing marble putti in the *vivaio* below — the one at the left swimming, and the pair
at the right struggling in an attempt to duck each other. In strange contrast to these mischievous little figures and to the bizarre twin fountains
are the classicizing allegorical figures in the remaining niches — the central
porphyry figure of Moses (an adaptation from a fragmentary ancient torso
commenced by Raffaello Curradi and completed by Cosimo Salvestrini),
the figure of Legislation, at the left, by Antonio Novelli, and that of Religious Zeal, at the right, by Giovanni Battista Pieratti.

In his Grotto of Polyphemus, constructed in the Orti Oricellari about
1640, Antonio Novelli returned to the completely naturalistic type of
Buontalenti's grotto (Fig. 157). The figures, composed of *rocaille* like their
rustic setting, show the diagonal lines and excited movement of the developed baroque.

### The Rustic Island

While the Florentine grottoes were apparently modelled upon Roman
prototypes, the Tuscan villas of the Cinquecento saw the development of a
kind of fountain which seems peculiarly Florentine — the rustic island.
This had its origin in the *vivaio* or fishpond, a pool commonly of rectangular ground plan, of which several examples appear upon the lunette at
Castello (Figs. 36 and 36a). Within the *vivaio* was set a central hillock or
island of *rocaille* surmounted by a large figure or group, from which the
water issued. As the chief interest lay in the central statue, this type made
a strong appeal to the Florentine sculptor.

Perhaps the earliest example of this *genre* is Montorsoli's Fountain of
the Triton, in the garden of the Doria Palace at Genoa, constructed about
1547 (Fig. 158). In a general view, the rockwork of the island is concealed
from the spectator by an elaborate balustrade, undoubtedly added because
the rustic type seemed out of harmony with the formal character of the adjoining palace. The *vivaio* itself is of the usual rectangular form; but the
rounded corners of the balustrade produce the mistilinear ground plan of
which Montorsoli was so fond.[1] Closer views (Figs. 159 and 160) reveal the

1. See his fountain of Neptune at Messina, Figures 88 and 91.

rocky mound, but do not show its complete form — a hillock pierced by openings on four sides. The central figure rides triumphantly upon a huge, spouting sea monster. Vasari, accustomed to the slender jets of the usual Florentine fountain, particularly mentions the copious stream which gushed from the mouth of this monster.

On the authority of a note by Milanesi, the present triton is commonly believed to be a copy by Gian Giacomo da Valsoldo, made in 1581; but Alizeri has shown that the document in question referred to a statue of a satyr, not a triton; so that there is no need to doubt that the figure is Montorsoli's own. In its diagonal lines and powerful suggestion of movement (Fig. 160) it resembles his statues of Scylla and Charybdis on the fountain of Neptune at Messina (Figs. 88 and 90). The position of the left arm and the turn of the head (Fig. 159) were probably suggested by the raised arm and *contrapposto* of the Laocoon, which he had restored for Clement VII. The statue is admirably adapted to its place over an isolated fountain by means of skilful *contrapposto*, cleverly combined with the convolutions of the monster's tail, so as to carry the eye round the figure and render it interesting from every angle (Fig. 160).

The great *vivaio* in the upper garden of the Villa at Castello was included in Tribolo's plans, although Vasari makes no mention of the crowning statue in this context. The model for Ammannati's colossal figure of the Apennine was ready in November, 1563, and the bronze itself was set in place upon the island of stalactites in the spring of 1565. The whole fountain appears upon the lunette of Castello (Figs. 36 and 36a). Ammannati has represented the mountain god as a broad-shouldered, bearded old man, crouching low above a cliff, and hugging himself as though shivering (Fig. 161). The reason for this gesture is apparent when the water plays.[1] From a sprinkler upon the top of his head the water oozes slowly over his body and down the rocks into the pool. The effect of the dripping water is vividly suggested in Montaigne's description: "There is a large pond, among others, in the center of which you see a natural-looking artificial rock, which looks all frozen over, by means of that same material (i. e. stalactites) with which the Duke has covered his grottoes at Pratolino; and above this rock is a large statue in bronze, representing a very old grey-

1. The conception is that of a mountain in the rain.

*Photo Archivio Fotografico Nazionale, Rome*

FIGURE 159. MONTORSOLI, TRITON

DETAIL OF THE ISLAND, GARDEN OF THE PALAZZO DORIA, GENOA

*Photo Archivio Fotografico Nazionale, Rome*

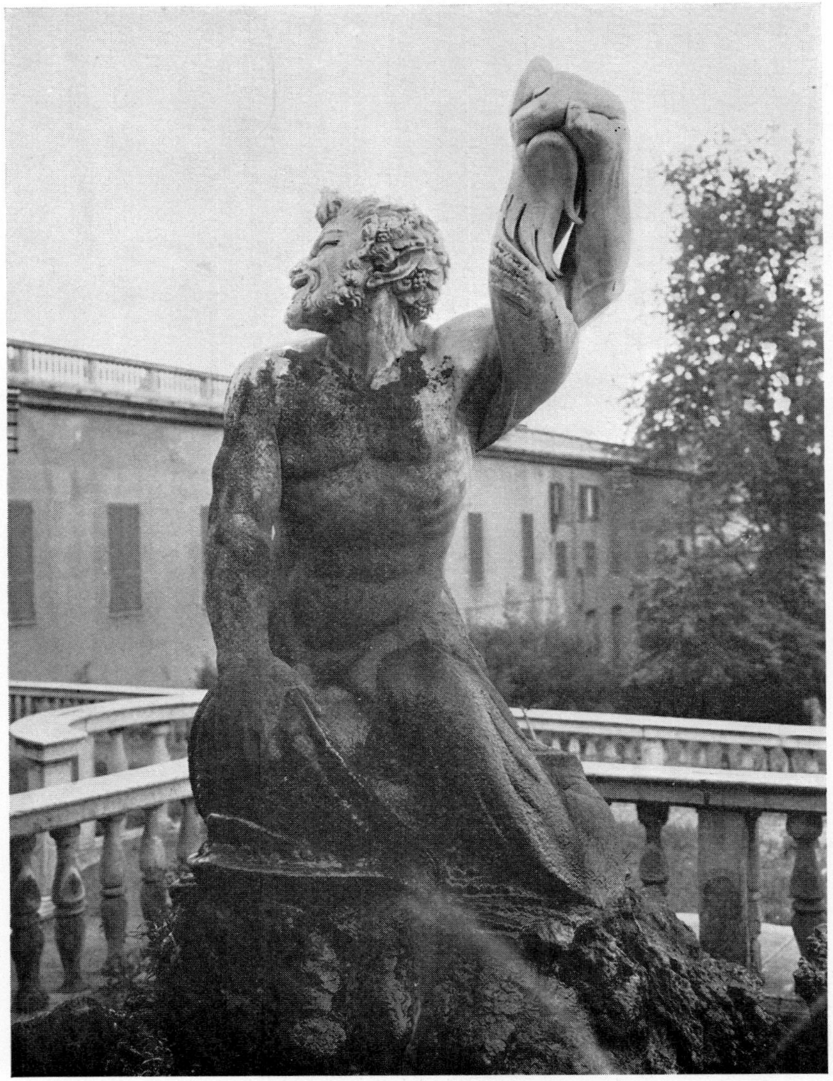

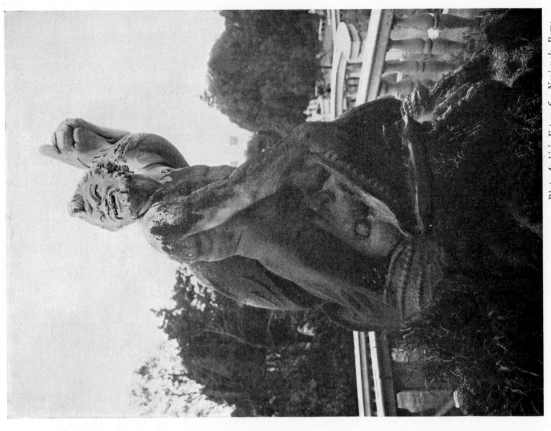

FIGURE 160. MONTORSOLI, TRITON

DETAIL OF THE ISLAND, GARDEN OF THE PALAZZO DORIA, GENOA

FIGURE 161. AMMANNATI, FOUNTAIN OF THE APENNINE

UPPER GARDEN, ROYAL VILLA, CASTELLO

FIGURE 163.  PERSEUS AND THE DRAGON
GROUP FROM A FOUNTAIN AT PRATOLINO.  BOBOLI GARDEN

FIGURE 162.  ESCULAPIUS.  FIGURE FROM A FOUNTAIN AT PRATOLINO
BOBOLI GARDEN

FIGURE 164. STOLDO LORENZI, FOUNTAIN OF THE TRIUMPH OF NEPTUNE

BOBOLI GARDEN

haired man, seated with folded arms, from whose beard, forehead, and hair water is incessantly flowing, drop by drop, so as to represent sweat and tears; and the fountain has no other outlet but that."

From Francesco de Vieri's description of Pratolino we know that the villa contained several rustic islands, two of them crowned by statues still preserved in the Boboli Garden. The fountain function of the marble Esculapius is no longer apparent in its present position over a formal pedestal (Fig. 162); but originally it stood upon a mound of *rocaille*, while water issued from the mouth of the serpent into a pool below. Both in pose and expression this statue is modelled upon the Moses of Michelangelo. In the curious marble group of Perseus with the dragon (Fig. 163), the monster of reddish stone supplied the water to the *vivaio*.

Stoldo Lorenzi's Fountain of Neptune, in its present form over the fishpond above the amphitheater at Boboli (Fig. 164), is a particularly striking example of the island type, in which several figures unite in a marine tableau. As the fountain appears in its original cylix form upon the Boboli lunette of 1599, the present rustic arrangement must date from the seventeenth century.[1] Another Seicento example was Antonio Novelli's great Island of Polyphemus, constructed in the Orti Oricellari for the Cardinal Gian Carlo dei Medici about 1640. In the center of the vast basin stood the island, upon which towered the giant Polyphemus — a colossal nude figure with feet spread far apart, raising a wineskin high above his head, and catching in his mouth the water that fell from it in lieu of wine — a reversal of the usual water *motif*! The great figure, composed of bricks with a coating of stucco, still remains in a damaged state, but pond and island are no more.

In its original form, the colossal rustic fountain of the Apennine at Pratolino, designed by Giovanni Bologna and executed by his pupils in the fifteen eighties,[2] partakes of the character of both *vivaio* and grotto; for both in Stefano della Bella's etching (Fig. 165) and in a wall painting at Villa La Quiete the figure is set beneath a cavern of stalactites. Today, however, it stands alone, an isolated but impressive relic of Pratolino's original grandeur (Fig. 166). The pose of the crouching mountain god re-

1. See pp. 59–60 and Figure 108.
2. In the fall of 1580 it was still in the process of construction; *Montaigne*, p. 107.

calls that of the river god Mugnone at the entrance to the grottoes of Pratolino (Fig. 149); but here the water flows from the head of a monstrous fish, pressed by the arm of the god. Indeed, Professor Albert Brinckmann has shown that the sculptor in his early models for this figure began with the *motif* of the crouching river god, and only slowly evolved the present conception. It is interesting to contrast Giovanni Bologna's personification of the Apennine with that of Ammannati, completed about fifteen years before (Fig. 161).[1] In the earlier figure, aside from the water *motif*, only the great size and adjoining cliff suggest the mountain-character; here, in addition to the truly "mountainous" dimensions of the pile, the rocky character of the Apennines is indicated by the combination of stalactites with the sculptured form.

The colossal size of this statue, which towers some twenty-five feet into the air, can scarcely be realized from a photograph. It contains a series of small rooms in three stories, entered from the rear. One can stand erect in the head; and there the Grand Duke is said to have fished, casting his line through the eyes. There is surely no more striking instance of the love of the colossal in the Cinquecento.

The most curious feature of this most fantastic of fountains is of course the use of stalactites in a colossal human figure.[2] Here the sculptural and rustic types meet — a paradox that is essentially baroque. It would seem that the striving for bizarre effects could go no further.

1. Tribolo had also planned figures personifying mountains, for the Villa at Castello; see p. 35 of the present work. Vasari does not describe these designs fully; perhaps they influenced the conceptions of Ammannati and Giovanni Bologna.

2. This technique had of course been used earlier in figures of ordinary size, in Buontalenti's Grotto at Boboli, Figure 153.

*Photo Fototeca Italiana*

FIGURE 165. STEFANO DELLA BELLA, ETCHING OF GIOVANNI BOLOGNA'S FOUNTAIN OF THE APENNINE
PRATOLINO

*Photo Alinari*

FIGURE 166. GIOVANNI BOLOGNA, FOUNTAIN OF THE APENNINE
VILLA DEMIDOFF, PRATOLINO

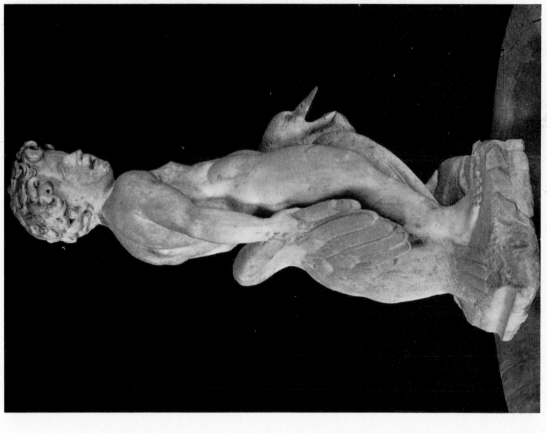

FIGURE 168.  SCHOOL OF TRIBOLO, BOY WITH A GOOSE

DETAIL OF A FOUNTAIN IN THE PITTI PALACE, FLORENCE

FIGURE 167.  TRIBOLO, NATURE GODDESS FROM A FOUNTAIN

THE LOUVRE, PARIS

# CHAPTER IX

## CLASSICIZING FOUNTAIN FIGURES

NUMEROUS fountain figures in the style of the Florentine Cinquecento have come down to us. The majority of these, if one may judge from their small size and from their conception in the round, originally decorated simple freestanding fountains of the cylix type. One of the earliest examples is the so-called "Mercury" in the collection of Mr. Henry Harris of London (Fig. 17), a bronze statuette poised on one foot upon a ball. This has been identified by its owner as a figure executed about 1515 by Gian Francesco Rustici for a fountain of the great court of the Medici Palace, described in detail by Vasari. The upraised hand originally held a "butterfly" or "windmill," which was made to revolve by a stream of water which issued from the mouth. The expansion of the chest and cheeks and the contraction of the waist, the position of thumb and forefinger, in fact, the concentration of the entire figure upward, can be explained only by the *motif* given by Vasari. The exact correspondence with Vasari's detailed account proves beyond a doubt that this is the original figure by Rustici; but in the absence of the usual attributes of helmet, winged sandals, and *caduceus*, I question Vasari's interpretation of the figure as Mercury. The puffed out cheeks would be more suitable to a Wind; compare the figures of winds in Botticelli's Venus Anadyomene and Primavera, or the heads at the base of Cellini's famous salt cellar.

This statue was certainly intended for a freestanding rather than a wall fountain, for the extension of the left leg backward would be impossible in the latter; yet the frontality of the torso belies the centrifugal character of the pose. The figure is thus half-way between the completely frontal treatment of the Quattrocento and the plurifacial handling common in freestanding figures of the later Cinquecento.[1] The most satisfactory views are from the side and front. The treatment of the nude, with its exaggerated

1. See pp. 7 and 8 for a statement of this technical problem. Verrocchio had already achieved a successful solution in his putti (Figs. 15 and 16).

sinews and muscles, recalls the bronzes of Antonio Pollaiuolo, while the stiffness of the pose is reminiscent of the works of Bertoldo.

The classicizing Nature Goddess of the Louvre (Fig. 167) was carved by Tribolo in 1528 to bear an ancient granite basin for the Gardens of Fontainebleau. The head is rigidly frontal, and the body is swathed in a stalk-like sheath, as in the ancient figures of Diana of the Ephesians which served as its prototype. Tribolo however substituted for the usual flat form of the ancient image a cylindrical one, thus adapting the figure to its isolated position and to its function as shaft and pedestal of the fountain. Round the many breasts, which are treated naturalistically rather than conventionalized as in the ancient images, swarm tiny nude putti holding garlands, bewilderingly intermixed with swans — elements drawn from the repertoire of Roman ornament, and handled with an obvious delight in rich decorative detail.

From some sculptor of Tribolo's school, if not by his own hand, comes the marble boy with a goose, set over a basin of Quattrocento style in the upper vestibule of the Pitti Palace (Fig. 168);[1] for it is related in style as well as in *motif* to the putti on the shaft of the Great Fountain at Castello (Fig. 49). Indeed, until recently this fountain stood in the grotto of that villa (Fig. 23). The *contrapposto* by which the sculptor sought to make the figure interesting from various angles is of the simplest sort; head and right leg are turned in a different direction from the torso. The water of course fell from the opened mouth of the harassed fowl.

To the same period and school belongs the seated putto abusing two geese in the great court of the Detroit Museum (Fig. 169).[2] By the extension of the legs of the putto and the neck of the goose in centrifugal lines the sculptor has cleverly adapted the figure to a triangular base, which probably repeats the form of a triangular foot of a lost cylix; and by the skilful use of *contrapposto* he has given it interesting profiles from various points of view.

1. This putto was at first attributed, with the basin, to Donatello, and then to Antonio Rossellino. Recently it has been given to Pierino da Vinci: *Gramberg*, p. 225.

2. Dr. Valentiner's recent ascription of this figure to Pierino da Vinci (Bulletin of the Detroit Institute of Arts, May, 1932) is certainly to be preferred to the old attribution to Domenico Poggini. Obviously the figure is to be associated with the putti decorating the Great Fountain at Castello. There is still much work to be done, however, in distinguishing the styles of the various sculptors who worked under Tribolo upon this fountain; and "School of Tribolo" seems to me sufficiently definite for the present.

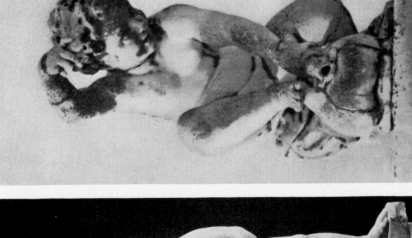

FIGURE 170. PIERINO DA VINCI (?),
PUTTO PISSATORE
MUSEO CIVICO, AREZZO

FIGURE 169. SCHOOL OF TRIBOLO, BOY WITH A GOOSE
DETROIT INSTITUTE OF ARTS

FIGURE 171. PIERINO DA VINCI (?),
BOY WITH A FISH
FOUNTAIN OF THE MONKEYS, BOBOLI GARDEN

*Courtesy of Victoria and Albert Museum*

FIGURE 172. PIERINO DA VINCI (?), TWO PUTTI WITH A FISH
VICTORIA AND ALBERT MUSEUM, LONDON

*Courtesy of Victoria and Albert Museum*

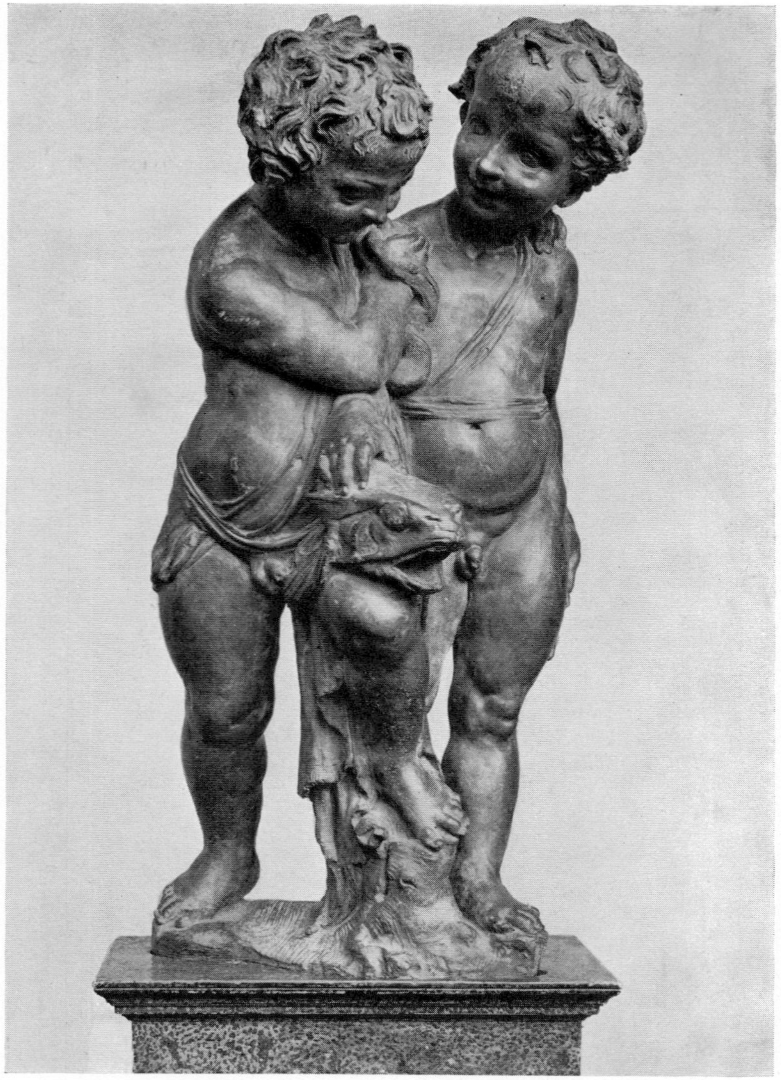

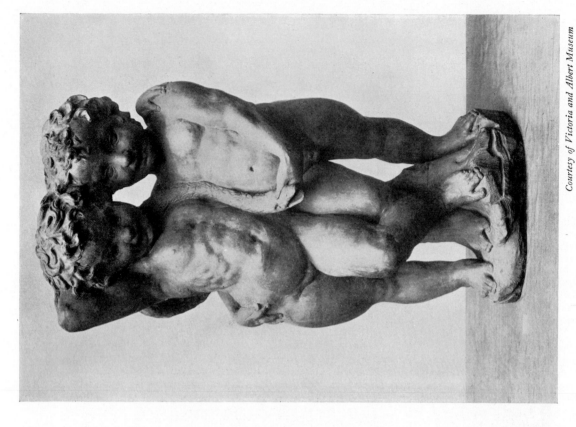

FIGURE 173. SCHOOL OF TRIBOLO, BOY AND GIRL WITH A SWAN
VICTORIA AND ALBERT MUSEUM, LONDON

From the atelier of Tribolo also comes the amusing *putto pissatore* in the museum at Arezzo (Fig. 170), the frontality of which indicates that it was designed to stand in the niche of a wall fountain or at the head of a *vivaio*—probably the latter, to judge from the use of the drapery at the back.  Dr. Ulrich Middeldorf sees in this figure the earliest extant work of Pierino da Vinci, carved for a fountain at the villa of Cristofano Rinieri at Castello, which Vasari describes as follows: "Dette a Piero un pezzetto di marmo, del quale egli facesse un fanciullo per quell' acquaio, che gettasse acqua dal membro virile."  Both the *motif* and the style of the putto support this attribution.

Pierino da Vinci seems to have specialized in the representation of the child form.  Of the two other fountains which he constructed at Castello, one was a marble figure of a little boy pressing down a fish which spouted water.  Is this by chance preserved in the vivacious little marble figure of the same school which now adorns the cylix of the Fontana delle Scimmie in the Boboli Garden (Fig. 171)?  At first glance, the lively movement of the legs and arms seem rather to suggest a date in the second half of the Cinquecento; but a comparison with the putti at the base of the Great Fountain at Castello (Figs. 3 and 48) reveals close parallels both in style and in pose.

Pierino's other fountain for Castello is thus described by Vasari: "And Tribolo having given him a larger piece of marble, Piero carved from it two putti embracing each other, and squeezing fish, so as to make them spout water.  These putti were so charming in both head and person, and their legs, arms, and hair were so beautifully done that even then one could see that he was competent to bring the most difficult work to completion."  It seems possible that a model for this work has been preserved in the fascinating clay model for a fountain at the Victoria and Albert Museum (Fig. 172), although there is a discrepancy in the single fish; for Vasari uses the plural form of this word, "pesci."  The work is somehow reminiscent of the Quattrocento and of the putti of Verrocchio; but this is understandable in an early work by the nephew of Leonardo.  The unusual subtlety of modelling characteristic of Pierino's work, which imparted a quivering life to the marble, would be particularly apparent in the malleable medium of clay.  The preparation of a careful clay model for a work to be executed in

marble was common in the Cinquecento.[1] The heads of the little boys recall those of children in an authentic work by this master, the marble relief
of Cosimo I Resuscitating Pisa, in the Vatican. A second terracotta model
of a group for a fountain from the Victoria and Albert Museum (Fig. 173),
in which a little boy and girl stand arm in arm, squeezing the neck of a
spouting swan, is somewhat later than the group just discussed, showing
the softer and looser modelling of the child form characteristic of the
developed Cinquecento. It is certainly to be attributed to the school of
Tribolo.[2]

The graceful young river god in the Schlichting Collection of the Louvre
(Fig. 174) has been ascribed both to Tribolo and to his pupil Pierino da
Vinci; but the latter attribution is unquestionably the correct one. It is
the river god described by Vasari, made for Luca Martini after he became
*proveditore* of Pisa, and therefore dating from 1548 or later. Dr. Middeldorf has pointed out the same soft, yielding curves and many other similarities in the contemporary relief in the Vatican. The fact that the original
group was sent to Naples, and that the Louvre figure comes from the palace
of the Duke of Balzo in that city, strengthens his case.

The pose of this figure seems to me strongly influenced by that of the
ancient marble youth in the Bargello (Fig. 175), which Cellini had restored
in 1546 as a Ganymede. Pierino has nevertheless given the work a grace
and delicacy of his own, and has intensified the serpentining curve of the
figure, bending the torso backward as well as sideways (Fig. 176). This
penetration of the statue both backward and forward in space, and the
addition of a third putto,[3] who could not be seen from the front, as well as
the round base of the group, prove that this work was constructed for
an isolated rather than a wall fountain. Although unfortunately set in a
corner in the Louvre, the statue is happily provided with a revolving base,
so that its changing aspects may still be enjoyed.

If the fountain figures which we have discussed so far, dating from the
first half of the Cinquecento, could be ranged in a row and those from the

---

1. Tribolo, for instance, made large clay models for the figure of Earth which he was to execute
in marble for the Medici Chapel; *Vasari*, vi, 65.

2. This group has recently been attributed to Pierino da Vinci; *Gramberg*, pp. 224-225.

3. Vasari gives the correct number (three) of these putti, but Middeldorf in his article on
Pierino da Vinci mentions only the two which appear in the front and side views.

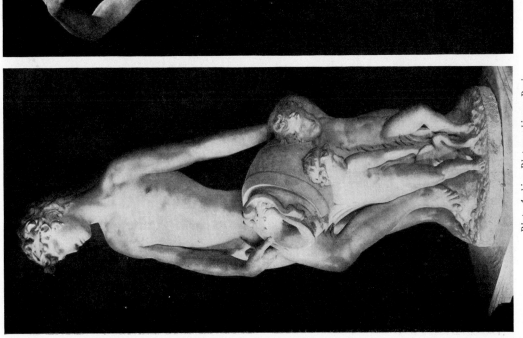

FIGURE 174. PIERINO DA VINCI
YOUNG RIVER GOD

SCHLICHTING COLLECTION, THE LOUVRE

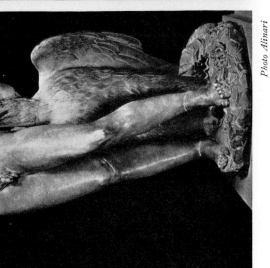

FIGURE 175. GANYMEDE, ANCIENT STATUE
RESTORED BY BENVENUTO CELLINI

MUSEO NAZIONALE, FLORENCE

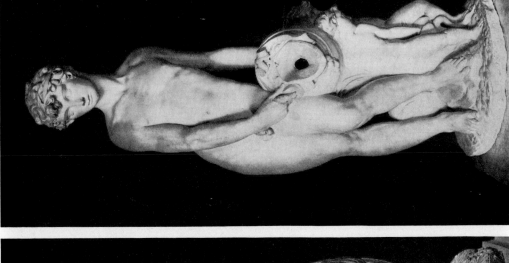

FIGURE 176. PIERINO DA VINCI
YOUNG RIVER GOD

SCHLICHTING COLLECTION, THE LOUVRE

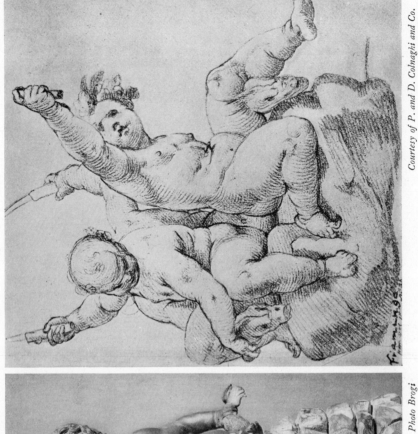

FIGURE 179. DRAWING OF GIOVANNI BOLOGNA'S FOUNTAIN OF
THE FISHING BOYS

From Arthur Strong's Reproductions in Facsimile of Drawings by the Old Masters,
in the Collection of the Earl of Pembroke and Montgomery at Wilton House

FIGURE 177. GIOVANNI BOLOGNA,
FISHING BOY

MUSEO NAZIONALE, FLORENCE

FIGURE 178. GIOVANNI BOLOGNA,
FISHING BOY

MUSEO NAZIONALE, FLORENCE

latter part of the century could be placed opposite, we should at once note certain broad distinctions between the two groups. The earlier figures, in spite of their elaborate *contrapposto*, would appear almost static beside many from the later group, with their centrifugal lines and momentary poses. While the earlier statues would be almost exclusively of marble, among the later ones we should find many instances of the use of the more pictorial medium of bronze. The style of Niccolò Tribolo would dominate the earlier group, while in the later one we should feel the pervasive influence of the Flemish sculptor Giovanni Bologna.

Among his earliest fountain figures are two fishing boys of bronze, preserved in the Bargello. At first glance, the pose of the one reproduced in Figure 177 appears almost identical with that of the marble putto over the Fontana delle Scimmie (Fig. 171), by which it was probably influenced; but Giovanni Bologna has made his figure less compact, turning the body more sharply upon its axis and extending the legs and the upper arm in more centrifugal lines. The second putto is caught in a still more momentary and unstable position (Fig. 178). Dr. Friedrich Kriegbaum has called my attention to a drawing in the collection of the Earl of Pembroke which reproduces the lost fountain in the Casino di San Marco, once decorated by these bronzes (Fig. 179). This shows that the fountain contained a third, lost putto, represented in a pose similar to that of his companions, holding a fishing rod in his raised arm.[1] The triangular composition is one to which this artist returned in his later Fountain of Oceanus, in the figures of the three river gods. The basin is unfortunately omitted in the sketch, since the artist (probably a sculptor) was interested only in the figures; so that it is impossible to reconstruct the fountain as a whole. However, it is apparent that it belonged to one of the isolated types; and the radial lines of the arms and legs of the statues imply a circular ground plan. The hillock on which the trio sits suggests a rustic island. The water issued from the mouths of the struggling fish.

This fountain is commonly dated about 1559 after Desjardins, who was evidently influenced by the fact that Borghini mentions these figures immediately after works executed in that year; but so early a date seems un-

1. This drawing proves that Borghini's description of the fountain with three putti is correct; Baldinucci mentions only two. I question the ascription of the drawing — to François Duquesnoy.

likely. Were these bronzes executed before this artist's departure for Bologna in 1563, or do they belong to the unfinished works which made Prince Francesco importune him to return,[1] but which he did not take up until 1567, after his sojourn in Bologna was ended?

The famous Flying Mercury in the Bargello originally decorated a cylix fountain in the loggia of the Villa Medici at Rome, where it is now replaced by a copy (Fig. 105). A comparison of this statue (Fig. 180), usually dated about 1564, with a bronze figure in a similar pose, Rustici's Mercury, cast about 1515 (Fig. 17), shows an astonishing technical advance. No longer is there any question of lingering frontality; the sculptor has attained to complete representation in the round. Poised on one foot, over the head of a puffing wind, whence the water originally flowed, with the arms and one leg extended in the most centrifugal lines, the statue defies all the rules for compact monumentality commonly laid down for sculpture. The sculptor has here succeeded in representing in a freestanding statue the effect of a figure moving freely in space, achieved in the realm of painting in the early Cinquecento by Raphael and Correggio, and in the field of relief by Benvenuto Cellini, in the Perseus Coming to the Rescue of Andromeda, on the base of his famous bronze in the Loggia dei Lanzi (1548–1551).[2] While the Mercury is already in the hard, generalizing classical style of Giovanni Bologna's later period,[3] which makes little appeal to modern taste, no one can deny its perfect balance, or its miraculous effect of potential motion. By a gradual torsion in the upper part of the body, and by the extension of arms and leg in centrifugal lines, the sculptor has thrown the figure into spiral, serpentining lines, which carry the eye around it and lend it interest from whatever angle it is approached.

A similar predilection for *la forma serpentinata* appears in a figure in the Thiers Collection in the Louvre, which was probably intended for a small table fountain. This fascinating bronze statuette of a triton seated upon three intertwined dolphins and spouting upward through a long conch shell (Fig. 181) is one of three bronzes upon this theme attributed by

---

1. *Gaye*, III, 230, transcribes a letter from Prince Francesco to Giovanni Bologna, dated January 9, 1567: "Vi commettiamo che vi spediate subito di costà, et ritorniate da noi per dar fine a quel che lassasto imperfetto."

2. Both painting and relief undoubtedly influenced Giovanni Bologna, but particularly Cellini's treatment of the torso of Perseus.

3. According to Dr. Kriegbaum's division of his periods and styles; see p. 56, n. 1.

*Photo Mannelli*

FIGURE 180.  GIOVANNI BOLOGNA,
FLYING MERCURY
MUSEO NAZIONALE, FLORENCE

*Photo Giraudon*

FIGURE 181.  GIOVANNI BOLOGNA (?), TRITON
SUPPORTED BY DOLPHINS
THIERS COLLECTION, THE LOUVRE

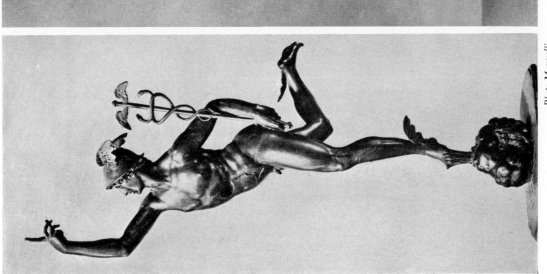

*Photo D. Anderson, Rome*

FIGURE 182.  TADDEO LANDINI, BRONZE YOUTH
DETAIL FROM THE FOUNTAIN OF THE TORTOISES,
PIAZZA MATTEI ROME

FIGURE 185. DETAIL OF A CEILING FROM A FLORENTINE PALACE
MUSEO BARDINI, FLORENCE

Photo Alinari

FIGURE 184. FLORENTINE SCULPTOR C. 1575,
TRITON SUPPORTED BY DOLPHINS
MUSEO NAZIONALE, PALERMO

Photo by Mr. Clarence Kennedy
Courtesy of Frick Collection

FIGURE 183. GIOVANNI BOLOGNA (?),
TRITON SUPPORTED BY DOLPHINS
FRICK COLLECTION, NEW YORK

Bode to Benvenuto Cellini.[1] A comparison of this figure with the Flying Mercury (Fig. 180), however, proves it to be close to the style of Giovanni Bologna, although certainly later than the Mercury. There is the same serpentining line in the torso, the same extension of arms and legs in centrifugal lines, the same repetition of angular forms, by which the Flemish sculptor conveyed the impression of potential motion; compare also the crouching form of the Philistine in his marble group in Hovingham Hall (Fig. 121). The intense concentration upward expressed by every line of the figure is paralleled by the long lines of the triton's horn, and originally culminated in the upward surge of the jet of water. If this statuette be indeed by Giovanni Bologna, it supplies another instance of the influence of this master upon his pupil Adrian de Vries; for the latter repeated this *motif* with slight variations in four figures of tritons which decorate the basin of his fountain at Fredriksborg (Fig. 104). The natural objection to the suggested attribution to Giovanni Bologna or his school, that there is no mention of a triton in any of the lists of this master's works given by the standard biographers, is removed by Müntz's citation of a record in the Medici archives of a bronze triton by Giovanni Bologna which was sent to France in 1598.

The same *motif*, though handled with less freedom, appears in a large marble fountain figure from the garden of the royal palace at Palermo, now set up over a fountain in the court of the local museum, which is probably by the hand of some Florentine sculptor (Fig. 184), and has been tentatively ascribed to Camillo Camilliani.[2] A comparison of this statue with a front view of the Frick statuette (Fig. 183) certainly indicates a common source. The exact *motif* of the two bronzes is again reproduced in a coffered panel in an ornamental ceiling from some Florentine palace preserved in the Museo Bardini (Fig. 185), which contains other panels decorated with well known Florentine bronzes of the Cinquecento.[3]

1. The other two tritons are in the Frick Collection in New York (Fig. 183) and in the Benda Collection in Vienna. The latter I have never seen, nor can I secure a photograph of it. Bode discusses them in his Catalogue of the Morgan Bronzes, I, xxviii, xxix, and II, 5, and Pl. LXXXIV. The resemblance between the Frick and Louvre tritons is much closer than the varying views shown in Figures 183 and 181 indicate; but the dolphins in the former are decorated with scales, and their mouths contain tiny tubes or pipes from which the water spouted.

2. See p. 131, also p. 137 under "Lorenzi, Battista."

3. The Ganymede on an eagle, attributed to Cellini, and a Samson and Philistine, both now in the Bargello.

The exuberant bronze figures of youths sporting with dolphins on the Fountain of the Tortoises in the Piazza Mattei in Rome (Figs. 4 and 182) were executed by Taddeo Landini, a Florentine sculptor and pupil of Giovanni Bologna, between the years 1581 and 1588,[1] while the fountain was designed by the Roman architect Giacomo della Porta. The centrifugal lines of the four raised arms must have been even more striking in the first state of this fountain; for the tortoises which have given it its name are additions of the late seventeenth century. Originally, the figures stood almost entirely free of basin and shaft, quite independent of architectural restraint. The sculptors of the baroque period could go no further than this in the representation of motion; they could only add the paradox of colossal figures in excited poses.

Two figures of spouting tritons by Giovanni Bandini have survived upon a fountain in the garden of the palace of Monsignore Altopascio, now the Palazzo Grifoni (Fig. 186). The composition of the original fountain, which included a Jason in place of the present Venus, was probably based upon Montorsoli's Fountain of Neptune at Messina (Fig. 88), with its contrast of calm central figure and excited satellites. A bust of Monsignore Altopascio which once formed part of the fountain has disappeared. It probably decorated the entablature above the recess; for from the frontal conception of the tritons it seems likely that the fountain, mentioned by Borghini as standing "at the head of the garden," was always, as now, of the engaged type. I have not reproduced the present enframement, as it obviously dates from the baroque period.

The marble group of a Venus and Cupid in the Kaiser Friedrich Museum (Fig. 187), commonly dated about 1570, is certainly by the hand of some Florentine Mannerist. The elongated lines and peculiarly shaped head of the Venus recall the style of a reclining female figure on Ammannati's fountain in the Piazza della Signoria, attributed by Dr. Albert Brinckmann to Andrea Calamec of Carrara, one of Ammannati's assistants upon the great fountain. I believe that the Berlin group is by the same hand. The water originally fell from the mouth of the dolphin on which the putto mounts in his attempt to reach the hand of the goddess.

1. The traditional attribution of these figures to Raphael, who died in 1520, is of course without ground; it is probably based on their resemblance to the Jonah of the Chigi Chapel in Santa Maria del Popolo, which he is said to have designed.

FIGURE 187. ANDREA CALAMEC (?), VENUS AND CUPID

KAISER FRIEDRICH MUSEUM, BERLIN

FIGURE 186. GIOVANNI BANDINI, TWO TRITONS ON A FOUNTAIN

GARDEN OF THE PALAZZO GRIFONI, FLORENCE

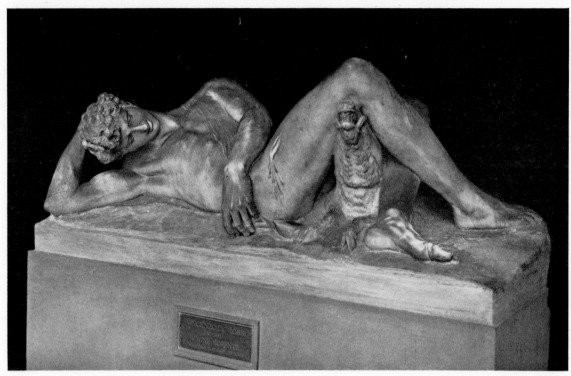

FIGURE 188    VINCENZO DEI ROSSI, WOUNDED ADONIS
MUSEO NAZIONALE, FLORENCE

FIGURE 189.  FLORENTINE SCULPTOR OF THE LATE
CINQUECENTO, GANYMEDE

DETAIL OF FOUNTAIN IN THE BOBOLI GARDEN

FIGURE 190.  FLORENTINE SCULPTOR C. 1550,
VENUS AND CUPID

CASINO DI S. MARCO, FLORENCE

A similar *motif* occurs in the little marble group of Venus and a Cupid in the Casino di San Marco (Fig. 190). The crude basin on which the figure stands can scarcely be the original one. The anonymous sculptor has resorted to elaborate *contrapposto* in an attempt to make this figure interesting from every side, but he has not been altogether successful with the transitions between the various parts of the contorted body. This, together with the rather stocky form, suggests a date shortly after 1550.

From the hand of Vincenzo dei Rossi comes the wounded Adonis, formerly attributed to Michelangelo, ordered by Isabella dei Medici for a fountain in a grotto at the Villa Baroncelli, and therefore to be dated before her death in 1576 (Fig. 188). From its location in the grotto, it seems probable that it was given a rustic background in a wall fountain of the single niche type, with an oblong basin below. As the figure is not pierced, the water undoubtedly issued from the *rocaille*.

An anonymous marble figure of Ganymede, riding upon a spouting eagle (Fig. 189), is set over a cylix fountain in a portion of the Boboli Garden that commands a fascinating panorama of Florence (Fig. 106). The sculptor's chief interest has lain in the plurifacial treatment of the seated figure. By the use of *contrapposto* and by the manipulation of the arms and legs he has sought to vary its profiles as seen from different angles.

Giovanni Bologna's chief pupil, Pietro Francavilla, executed the heroic marble group of Venus attended by a small satyr and a nymph (Fig. 191), lent by Durlacher Brothers to the Fogg Museum. This work is signed and dated 1600, but was probably commenced considerably earlier; for it belongs to a series of thirteen statues ordered about 1585 for the garden of Antonio Bracci's villa at Rovezzano, although this group, when completed, was actually installed in the courtyard of his town house. In spite of the serpentining line in the body of the Venus, her torso remains practically frontal. The two tiny figures personifying Pleasure and Generation which cling to her drapery and arms on either side increase this broad, frontal effect in spite of their contortions; for both the lines of their bodies and the direction of their gaze converge upon the central figure. Probably the group was placed at the end of the courtyard of the Bracci palace, as the culminating accent in a long vista; but it must also have been visible from the rear, since the back of the statue is meticulously finished. The goddess, represented as sailing over the sea upon her dolphins, doubtless stood at the head of a large pool fed by the streams that issued from the dolphins' mouths.

The same sculptor's colossal marble statue of Orpheus charming the beasts, now in the Louvre (Fig. 192), was carved in 1598 for a fountain in Girolamo Gondi's garden in Paris. From its conception in the round it is obvious that it served as the chief ornament of a freestanding fountain of the type with a raised central figure. The listening (and also spouting!) beasts on the lower level were carved by the Florentine animalist Romolo del Tadda. The sculptor has indulged in the most extreme *contrapposto* in order to make the Orpheus plurifacial. This statue, to modern taste the least pleasing of Francavilla's works, so impressed Henry IV that he summoned its author to France.

It is no wonder that the marble group of a river god pursuing a nymph, till recently in the collection of the Marquis Niccolini (Fig. 193), has been dated in the seventeenth century; for in its bold attempt to represent two running figures, in the intense expression in the face of the male figure, and in the free poses of the individual statues, it approaches Bernini's Apollo and Daphne, which it almost certainly inspired. A description of this work in Borghini's *Il Riposo*,[1] however, proves that it cannot be later than 1584, and gives us the name of its author, Battista Lorenzi. The subject of the group is of course Alpheus' pursuit of Arethusa. I quote Borghini's words in the life of Battista Lorenzi: "By his hand we see the two graceful figures of marble, the one made to represent the river Alpheus, the other the fountain [i. e. the fountain Arethusa] in the beautiful garden of Messer Alamanno Bandini Knight of Malta, in his villa called the Villa of Paradise."[2] The pierced urn of the river god indicates that the group decorated a fountain.

Again we note the passion for counterfeiting the soft texture of flesh, another point in which this master anticipates the effects of the baroque, as we have already observed in his Perseus now in the Palazzo Nonfinito

1. I am indebted to Dr. Ulrich Middeldorf for the identification of this group with the one mentioned by Borghini.

2. This villa, in Pian di Ripoli, passed into the possession of the Marchese Niccolini. While still in the possession of this family, the group was shown at the Museo Nazionale. This branch of the Niccolini is now extinct, and the present location of the statue is unknown.

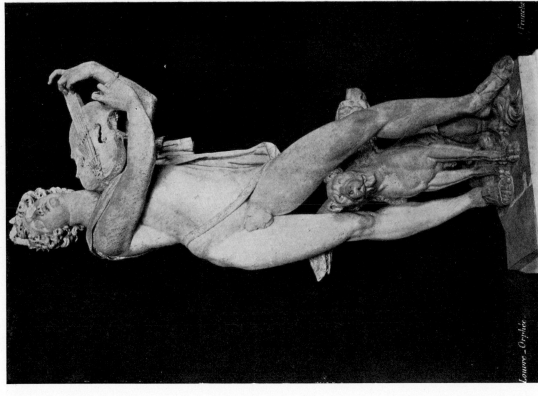

FIGURE 192. PIETRO FRANCAVILLA, ORPHEUS

THE LOUVRE

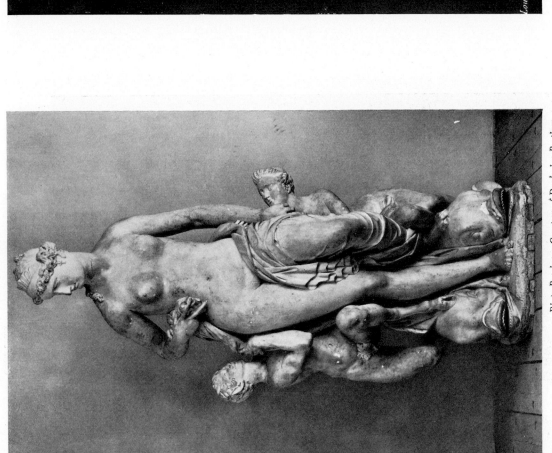

FIGURE 191. PIETRO FRANCAVILLA, VENUS WITH ATTENDANTS

GROUP ON LOAN AT THE FOGG ART MUSEUM, CAMBRIDGE, MASS.

FIGURE 194. FLORENTINE SCULPTOR AFTER 1550, PYTHIAN APOLLO
THE LOUVRE

FIGURE 193. BATTISTA LORENZI, ALPHEUS AND ARETHUSA
COLLECTION OF THE MARCHESE NICCOLINI
now Metropolitan Museum

(Fig. 67), and in his allegory of Painting upon the tomb of Michelangelo (Fig. 68). The facial type of the latter is very similar to that of the Arethusa.

The marble fountain group of Silenus squeezing grapes into the mouth of a panther in the Kaiser Friedrich Museum (Fig. 196), ascribed to Stoldo Lorenzi or some follower of Giovanni Bologna, seems to me definitely of the early Seicento, because of its completely naturalistic form. The basin is formed of a shell, from which the figure rises directly, without the formal pedestal characteristic of the Cinquecento.[1] The complexity of the water *motif*, in which water falling from the grapes disappears into the panther's mouth, is paralleled only in fountains of the seventeenth century, such as Cosimo Lotti's Fountain of the Triton at Aranjuez (Figs. 57 and 58) and Antonio Novelli's Island of Polyphemus.[2] The surplus water that escapes the panther's mouth gathers in the shell and falls through the grotesque mask upon its under side. With these considerations the asymmetrical yet cleverly centralized composition is in complete accord. The upward lines of the body of the panther, the spread legs and raised arm of the satyr, the downward line of the falling water, all alike converge upon a central point. This "occult" balance is certainly the baroque, rather than the Renaissance, way of composition.

Did the charming bronze statuette in the Pitti Palace, known as the Genius of the Medici (Fig. 195), originally decorate a fountain? In a drawing by Mr. H. Inigo Triggs, it stands over a fountain in the Boboli Garden, with water issuing from the raised ball; and the aperture at the top of this globe seems to indicate that it was pierced for a jet of water. Perhaps this is the figure of a boy holding aloft a globe ("un mappamondo") which spouted water, described by Sgrilli in one of the grottoes at Pratolino. Besides the Medici *palla*, this figure carries a capricorn, the device of Duke Cosimo, and hence is probably to be dated before the end of his reign in 1574. It is commonly attributed to Giovanni Bologna, and certainly reveals his influence in its torsion and centrifugal lines.

The attribution of an heroic bronze figure of the Pythian Apollo in the Louvre (Fig. 194) has long baffled scholars. It seems to me obviously the

1. See pp. 66–67 on the transitional forms of naturalistic cylix fountains in the late Cinquecento and early Seicento.

2. For a description of the *motif* of this figure see p. 81.

work of a Florentine Mannerist in the second half of the Cinquecento, for the Mannerists' love of serpentining line is apparent both in the contour of the figure and in the calligraphic treatment of the monster at his feet. The statue evidently served as the decoration of a fountain, with water spurting, in lieu of blood, from a wound in the body of the expiring monster; for an opening in the side of the dragon is fitted with a threaded metal cylinder that can be explained only as a connection with water pipes. The frontal conception of this figure indicates that it was intended for the decoration of an addorsed fountain.

The famous marble Cupid (or Apollo?) in the Victoria and Albert Museum (Fig. 197), long ascribed to Michelangelo, was first considered as a fountain figure by the late Herbert Horne, who saw in it a Narcissus gazing at his reflection in the pool below. Perhaps the "vaso" mentioned by Aldovrandi at the feet of Michelangelo's "Apollo" in Jacopo Galli's collection was a basin. The *motif* of the restored statue remains uncertain. The ardent Cinquecentist, Dr. Friedrich Kriegbaum, also believes that the figure adorned a fountain; but he rejects the Narcissus interpretation, attributing the statue to Vincenzo Danti and relating it to the seated and crouching fountain figures in which the late Cinquecento abounded. He points out that its treatment in the round and its changing aspects when seen from various angles are far more characteristic of the second half of that century than of the late Quattrocento, when Michelangelo is commonly supposed to have executed the figure for Jacopo Galli. In dealing with an attribution to any sculptor except a great innovator like Michelangelo, his argument would be absolutely conclusive.

With no new evidence to present, I shall not attempt to settle a controversy that has engaged so many scholars; but I venture to reproduce beside this statue an ancient fountain figure in a similar pose, which may have inspired its *motif* — the faun riding upon a dolphin in the Borghese Gallery at Rome (Fig. 198). As this work is generally conceded to have influenced Raphael both in his paintings and in his model for the figure of Jonah in the Chigi Chapel at Santa Maria del Popolo, it must have been excavated before his death in 1520, and it is possible that it was known to the young Michelangelo in the late Quattrocento.

*Photo Alinari*

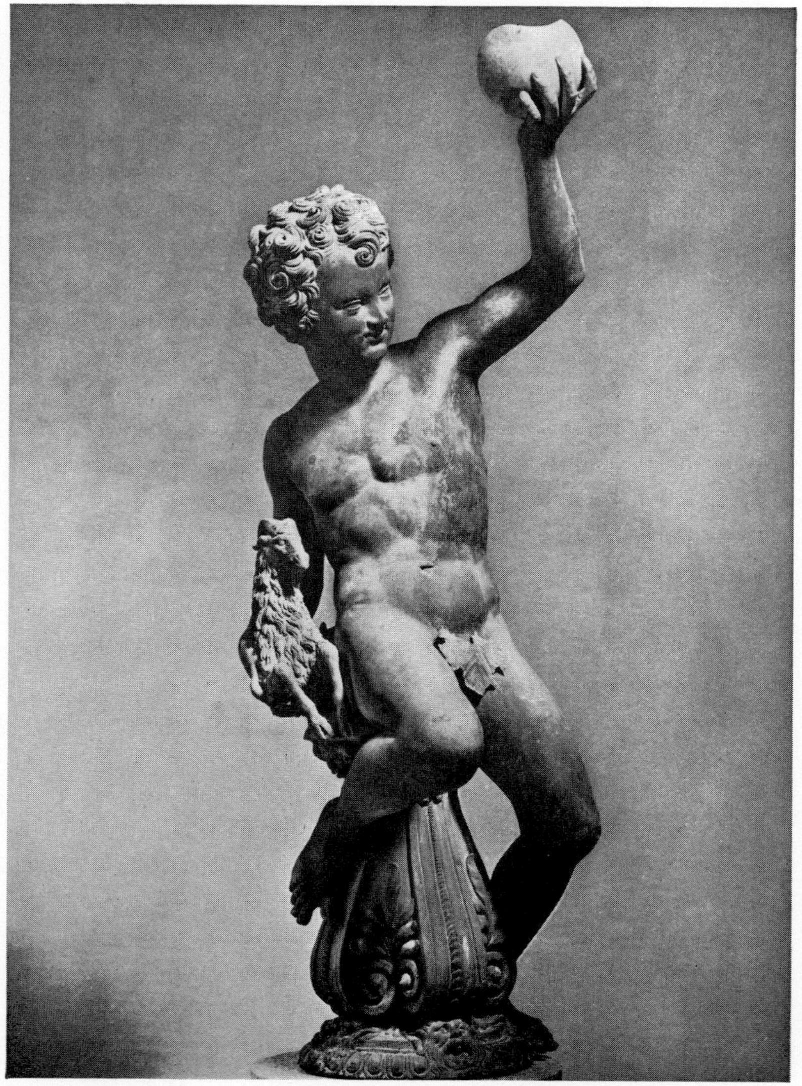

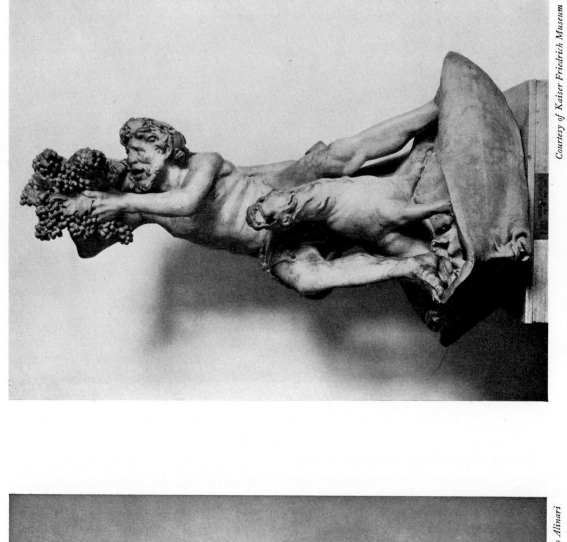

FIGURE 195. SCHOOL OF GIOVANNI BOLOGNA, GENIUS OF THE MEDICI
PITTI PALACE, FLORENCE

*Courtesy of Kaiser Friedrich Museum*

FIGURE 196. FLORENTINE SCULPTOR C. 1600, SILENUS AND A PANTHER
KAISER FRIEDRICH MUSEUM

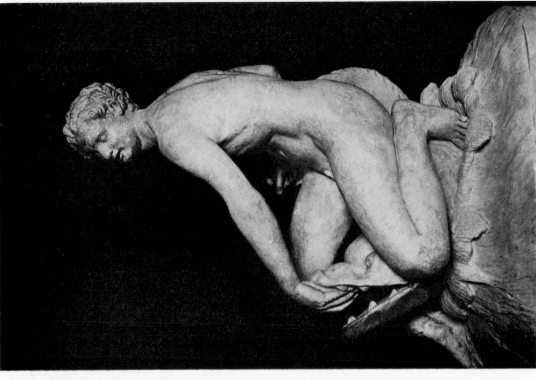

FIGURE 198. FAUN ON A DOLPHIN

ANCIENT FOUNTAIN FIGURE IN THE BORGHESE GALLERY, ROME

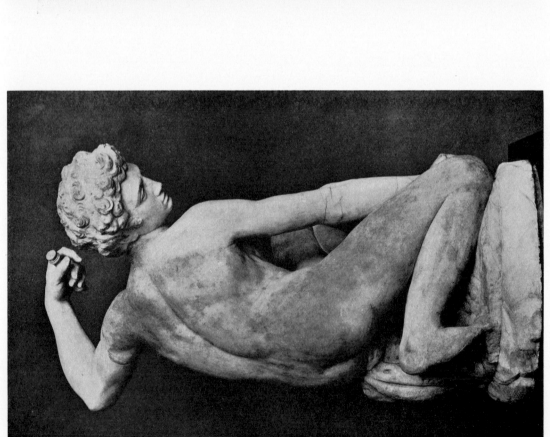

FIGURE 197. MICHELANGELO (?), CUPID

VICTORIA AND ALBERT MUSEUM, LONDON

So great was the passion of the Florentine masters of the Cinquecento for sculpture in the round, that I can find only one example of a bas-relief used as the chief decoration of a Florentine fountain, from this period [1] — the marble relief in the Bargello, by some master of the late Cinquecento, which depicts the union of the river Alpheus with the spring of Arethusa (Fig. 199). The pierced urns indicate the outlet of the water. Was Francesco Mosca's marble plaque of Diana and Actaeon in the same museum (Fig. 200) intended for a similar use? [2] A circular opening in the center of this relief may be interpreted as a preparation for a water spout, while the subject is particularly appropriate to a fountain.

1. Of course reliefs were frequently used as minor decorations on large fountains, as in Montorsoli's Fountain of Orion (Fig. 53) and Giovanni Bologna's Fountain of Oceanus (Figs. 111–113).

2. Several references to lost fountains by this master occur in letters quoted by Gaye; see Appendix B, p. 138.

# CHAPTER X

## FOUNTAIN FIGURES ON GENRE THEMES

AS WE have seen in the preceding chapters, it was the custom of Renaissance sculptors to combine the jets of their fountains with attributes
held by the figures, or even with the human body itself. In the unparal-
leled vogue for fountain sculpture which dominated sixteenth century
Florence, the sculptors carved river gods and nymphs with gushing urns,
satyrs squeezing wineskins, *putti pissatori*, innumerable sea deities with
spouting dolphins or conch shells or tridents, Venuses wringing out their
locks, naiads pressing their breasts, animals and birds of every description
spouting. In the search for unusual exits for the water, the resources of
classical mythology were soon exhausted; yet new villas were continually
built, and the owners demanded novel fountains. The addition of genre
figures in contemporary costume afforded a new range of water *motifs*, and
served as a comic relief to the surfeit of mythological statues. Thus the
gods and nymphs of mythology, clad in the ideal garb of classical antiquity,
changed to homely folk in contemporary costume. The Venus Anadyomene, twisting her streaming locks, became a laundress wringing out
clothes; and the river god with his urn was replaced by a peasant emptying
a cask. The earliest example of this tendency mentioned in contemporary
literature occurs in Vasari's life of Bandinelli — a marble statue of a peasant emptying a barrel, carved by Giovanni Fancelli after a model by
Bandinelli, for a fishpond in the Boboli Garden. This work must have been
carved in the fifteen-fifties, since the work on the Boboli Garden was commenced only in 1550, and Bandinelli died early in 1560. This was surely
the "vivaio del villano" between the Grotto and the Grotticina mentioned
in the Medici account books of the sixteenth century. It is possible that
this very figure is preserved in a marble statue of a peasant emptying a
cask, still in the Boboli Garden (Fig. 205), commonly ascribed to Valerio
Cioli.[1]

1. This figure was at Pratolino in the late sixteenth to eighteenth centuries; but it may nevertheless have originated at Boboli. Compare the migration of Ammannati's Fountain of Juno from
Florence to Pratolino to Boboli (pp. 42–45).

FIGURE 199.  FLORENTINE SCULPTOR OF THE LATE
CINQUECENTO, ALPHEUS AND ARETHUSA

RELIEF FROM A FOUNTAIN, MUSEO NAZIONALE, FLORENCE

FIGURE 200.  FRANCESCO MOSCA, DIANA AND ACTAEON

MUSEO NAZIONALE, FLORENCE

FIGURE 201. VALERIO CIOLI, FOUNTAIN OF
THE DWARF MORGANTE

BOBOLI GARDEN

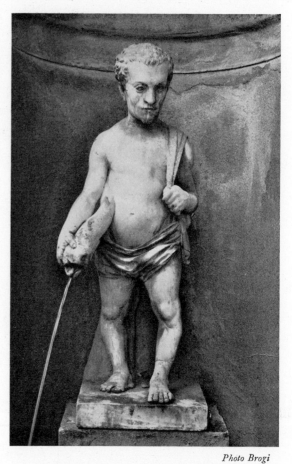

FIGURE 202. VALERIO CIOLI, FOUNTAIN OF THE
DWARF PIETRO BARBINO

BOBOLI GARDEN

FIGURE 203. VALERIO CIOLI (?), FOUNTAIN OF THE DWARF

MUSEO NAZIONALE, FLORENCE

Indeed, the extant works in this vein of Cinquecento date are largely by the hand of this sculptor, to whose genre figures we have many references in the contemporary literature. His earliest works of this sort were the portrait statues of two dwarfs of Cosimo dei Medici's court, Morgante and Pietro Barbino, executed for the Boboli Garden shortly after 1560, when Cioli returned from Rome. The extremely naturalistic figure of Morgante, whose monstrous and paunchy form was the talk of all Florence, is represented as riding over a spouting turtle (Fig. 201). A little bandy-legged dwarf holding a spouting dolphin, also in marble, which stands in a niche in the north wall of the terrace which supports the Fountain of the Artichokes at the rear of the Pitti Palace, facing a little garden closed to the public (Fig. 202), is almost certainly the Barbino; for the sensitive, intelligent expression and dignified carriage of this figure are in keeping with Vasari's characterization: "Clever, learned, and very kind."

The taste for this type of fountain figure continued under Francesco dei Medici, and was indulged to the limit at Pratolino. For this villa Cioli carved four figures, described by Borghini: in *macigno*, a colossal figure of a laundress wringing out clothes, set at the main entrance to the villa; another of a peasant mowing in a marsh where a salamander spouted; and a small *putto pissatore*; in marble, a more classical figure of a satyress milking a ewe from which water issued instead of milk. These figures are to be dated between 1569, when the villa was commenced, and 1584, the date of publication of Borghini's *Il Riposo*; and they probably were completed by 1580, for in that year Montaigne saw the laundress in place on the main axis of the villa, and admired the realistic soap suds that fell from the cloth she was wringing! On the lunette of this villa painted in 1599 (Figs. 204 and 204a) we can make out the lost figures of the laundress, the *putto pissatore*, and the mower;[1] while the satyress milking the ewe is apparently reproduced in one of Stefano della Bella's etchings of this villa (Fig. 206).

In 1595 to 1597 Cioli carved for the Grand Duke Ferdinand, for the Boboli Garden, a colossal marble figure of a woman washing a boy's head, which once decorated the rear edge of the Vivaio of Neptune, above the amphitheater, now preserved in a ruined state in a part of the garden closed to the general public (Fig. 208). In this group, known as the "Lavacapo,"

1. All near the entrance to the villa.

the water fell from the boy's head into the pool below. It is hard to believe that this work, with its superficial modelling, can have been executed by the able craftsman who produced the central figure of Sculpture upon Michelangelo's tomb,[1] or the extremely lifelike portrait statues of the two dwarfs; but the documents leave no room for doubt. If the lost figures done for Pratolino were upon this level, we need not greatly regret their loss.

The vogue for such statues continued, and in 1599 Cioli went to Carrara to obtain the marbles for four others: two dwarfs (a Morgante and a Margutte),[2] and two peasants (a digger and a vintager). As the sculptor unfortunately died before the year was over, the figures were continued after his models by his nephew Simone Cioli, and finally completed in 1606 and 1608. The two dwarfs have been lost; and the statue of the digger, still in the Boboli Garden, apparently had no connection with a fountain. The group of the Vintage still stands in the Boboli Garden, at the end of a path leading from the chief axis of the Isolotto. It consists of a peasant emptying a bucket of grapes into a vat, and a balancing statue of a watching boy (Fig. 209). These figures, released from all architectural restraint, stand free in the surrounding space in the fashion of baroque sculpture. Indeed, this group, with its composition by dynamic thrusts, the momentary poses of its figures, and its conception as a tableau, is undoubtedly the most baroque of Cioli's works; yet its hard, classicizing style is still reminiscent of the Cinquecento. Valerio Cioli's genre figures are the prototypes of the humorous and fantastic garden sculpture of later centuries; but their humor lies chiefly in their *motifs*. He lacked the grotesque style which makes such subjects artistically acceptable.

Other figures of peasants in contemporary costume were executed at Pratolino in the sixteenth century, for in the lunette of 1599, upon a fountain erected on the site originally decorated by Ammannati's Fountain of Juno (Figs. 207 and 204) and therefore still known as the "Fountain of Ammannati," appear several figures clad in contemporary costume, and represented in comic poses.

This group of genre figures, though of little aesthetic interest, are of

1. This figure was long attributed to Battista Lorenzi, and interpreted as Painting, through a confusion discussed on p. 38, n. 1.

2. These names of giants, humorously used for dwarfs in the Renaissance, of course originated in Pulci's poem, "Il Morgante Maggiore."

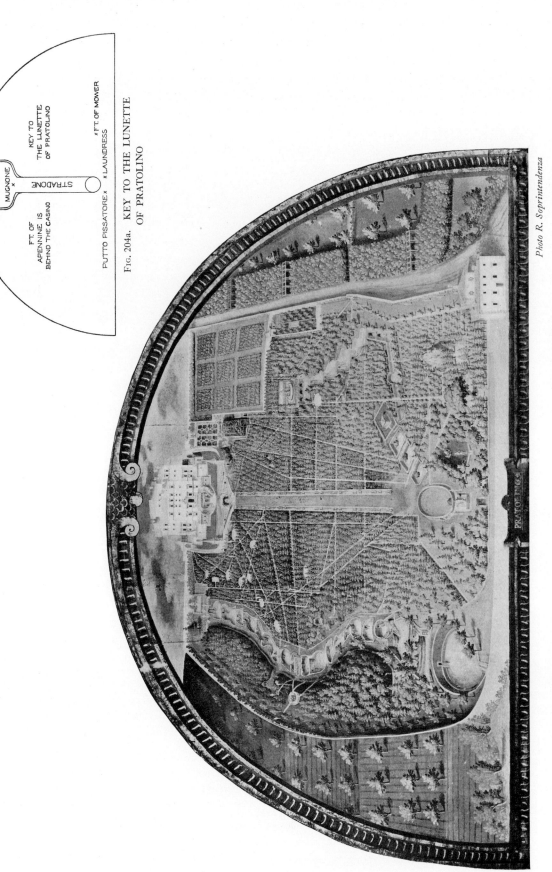

*Photo R. Soprintendenza*

FIGURE 204.   GIUSTO UTENS, LUNETTE OF THE VILLA OF PRATOLINO IN 1599

MUSEO TOPOGRAFICO, FLORENCE

FIGURE 207. GENRE FIGURES ON A FOUNTAIN
AT PRATOLINO

DETAIL FROM THE LUNETTE OF 1599.
MUSEO TOPOGRAFICO, FLORENCE

FIGURE 206. VALERIO CIOLI, SATYRESS, PRATOLINO

DETAIL OF AN ETCHING BY STEFANO DELLA BELLA.

FIGURE 205. GIOVANNI FANCELLI AFTER
BANDINELLI'S DESIGN (?), PEASANT
EMPTYING A CASK

BOBOLI GARDEN

*Photo Brogi*

FIGURE 208.   VALERIO CIOLI, LA LAVACAPO

BOBOLI GARDEN

*Photo Alinari*

FIGURE 209.   VALERIO AND SIMONE CIOLI, FOUNTAIN OF THE VINTAGE

BOBOLI GARDEN

FIGURE 210.  PIETRO TACCA, FOUNTAIN OF THE BOAR

LOGGIA DEL MERCATO NUOVO, FLORENCE

FIGURE 211.  MARBLE BOAR, HELLENISTIC STATUE

THE UFFIZI, FLORENCE

considerable historical importance; for they reveal a tendency to naturalism in Florentine sculpture of the Cinquecento, a school and period noted
for its slavish classicism. How are we to interpret this secondary vein in
the sculpture of the Cinquecento? Are we to see in it a deliberate and conscious reaction against the classicism of the age, a foretaste, in sculpture,
of the attitude of Caravaggio and his followers in painting? I find it difficult to accept this explanation; for, with the exception of the statues of the
dwarfs Morgante and Barbino, which were commissioned as portraits, the
naturalism of subject is not matched by realistic treatment of detail. It is
only in the faithful rendition of the contemporary costume that these figures differ from the classicizing statues of the period. Nor do I believe that
these works reflect a literary interest in pastoral subjects, for it seems to me
obvious that such groups as those of the Vintage and the Lavacapo were
conceived in a comic, rather than a romantic, vein.[1] The most natural explanation of this sudden interest in genre is probably that given at the
opening of the chapter — that the sculptors first carved such figures in an
attempt to enlarge their repertory of fountain *motifs*.

Did this addition of genre subjects to the iconography of the fountain
originate at Florence, or had these figures prototypes in the genre figures
on Northern fountains, like that of the *Gänsemännchen* at Nuremberg? So
far as we know, this figure and others by the same anonymous sculptor do
not antedate the earliest Italian examples. The early prevalence of genre
subjects in small bronzes suggests another possible source of inspiration;
but I cannot find any evidence of direct influence.

It seems to me significant that Valerio Cioli, the chief exponent of genre
sculpture at Florence, had made his reputation at Rome in the restoration
of ancient statues, an occupation which he continued at Florence while in
the employ of the Medici. At Rome he must have seen ancient statues on
genre themes, for the Hellenistic period abounded in sculpture of this type,
now vaguely assigned to the Alexandrian school. Certainly he knew the
figure of the Arrotino in the Uffizi which Cosimo I, ignorant of the fact that
this statue once formed part of a mythological group depicting the punish-
ment of Marsyas, called simply "a peasant sharpening a knife." From
such classical prototypes it was but a step to peasants emptying buckets,

1. It is of course possible that such figures reflect humorous proverbs in the folk lore.

or digging, in contemporary costume. Even the most realistic of Cioli's figures, the portraits of the two dwarfs, show classical influence, both in the use of the nude and in the *motifs*; for the Morgante is obviously conceived as a Silenus, and the Barbino, with his fish and bit of classical drapery, was evidently intended as a travesty on the statues of Neptune in which the fountains of the century abounded. In the satyress of Pratolino we have a completely mythological subject.

Classical inspiration would also explain Cioli's unfortunate use of the ideal medium of marble in his genre figures. The more pictorial bronze is better adapted to such subjects; compare the tiny fountain of a dwarf in the Bargello (Fig. 203), often attributed to Cioli, with his marble figure of Morgante (Fig. 201). The *Gänsemännchen* at Nuremberg and the small bronzes by Giovanni Bologna and his school, depicting peasants catching birds and playing bagpipes, are other cases in point. The rough gray stones whose neutral tones blend with the natural surroundings are also to be preferred to marble for garden sculpture of this sort.

Another instance of apparent naturalism actually founded upon classical precedent, although not a genre figure, may be included here — Pietro Tacca's fascinating bronze Fountain of the Boar, in the Loggia of the Mercato Nuovo at Florence (*c.* 1612); for the *Porcellino* (Fig. 210) is simply a bronze cast made from a Hellenistic marble in the Uffizi (Fig. 211). The delightful, naturalistic setting, with its fascinating studies of small flora and fauna, and the realistic puddle which serves as receiving basin and outlet to the fountain are of course Tacca's own contribution.[1]

1. The original, in a badly worn condition, now in the Museo di S. Marco, is here replaced by a copy.

*Photo D. Anderson, Rome*

FIGURE 212. CARLO MADERNA, FOUNTAIN
PIAZZA DI S. PIETRO, ROME

*Photo D. Anderson, Rome*

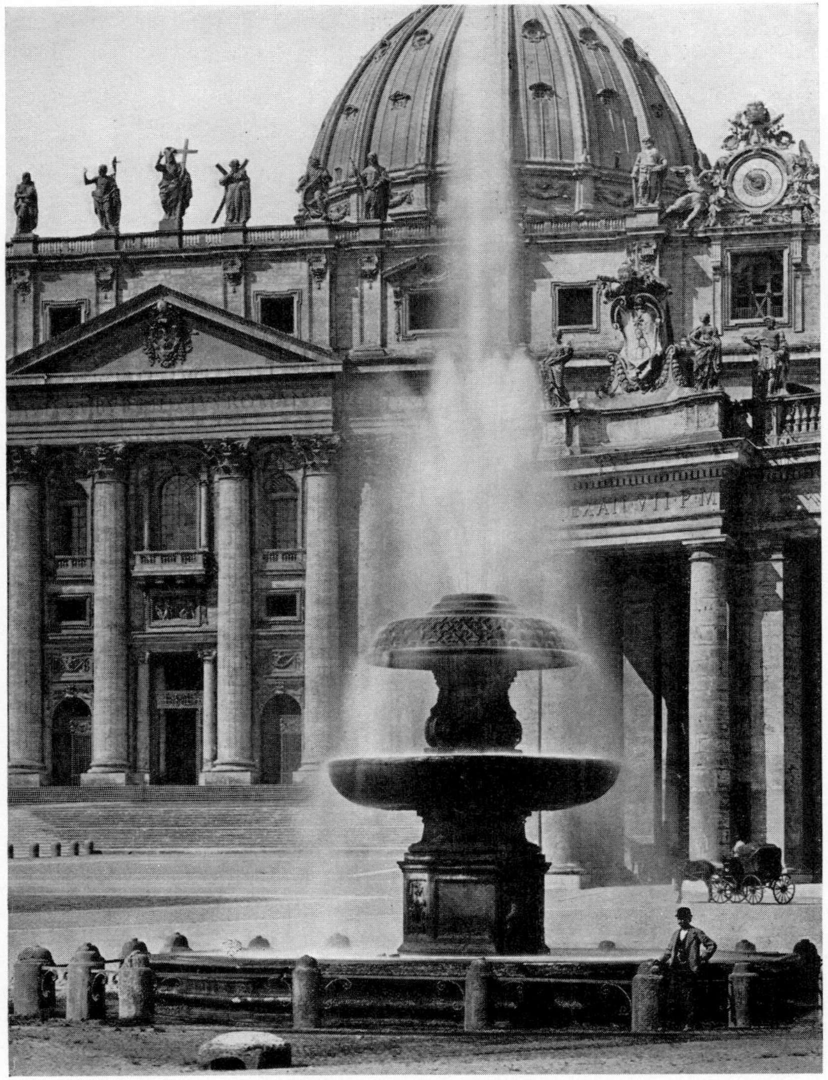

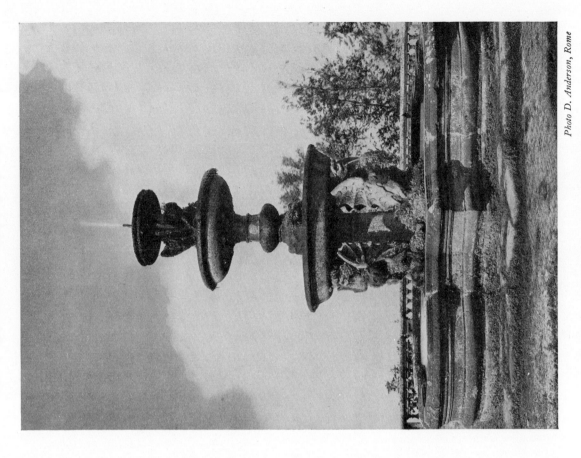

FIGURE 213. GIOVANNI FONTANA, FOUNTAIN
VILLA MONDRAGONE, Frascati

*Courtesy of Lord Yarborough*

FIGURE 214. GIOVANNI LORENZO BERNINI, NEPTUNE AND GLAUCUS
BROCKLESBY PARK, ENGLAND

*Photo Alinari*

FIGURE 215. STOLDO LORENZI, NEPTUNE
DETAIL OF THE FOUNTAIN OF NEPTUNE, BOBOLI GARDEN

# CHAPTER XI

## BERNINI'S DEBT TO FLORENTINE FOUNTAINS

IT IS a commonplace in the history of art that Rome produced no sculptors during the sixteenth century. The popes of the early Cinquecento imported Tuscan artists, such as Michelangelo and Ammannati; but in the latter part of the century, as the Counter Reformation set in, they turned from the Florentine school, with its sensuality and predilection for the nude, summoning Lombard and Flemish sculptors to carve the reliefs upon the tombs in the Sistine and Borghese chapels at Santa Maria Maggiore. The young Bernini, who was forming his style in the early years of the seventeenth century, could learn little from these sterile works. He turned instead to the sensual, classicizing statues of the Florentine sculptors of the late Cinquecento, such as Giovanni Bologna, Battista Lorenzi, and Vincenzo dei Rossi. Both Bernini's pagan temperament and his heritage from his Florentine father [1] inclined him toward Tuscany. Reymond, in his monograph on Bernini, stresses this point: "The Berninis come not from Naples, but from Florence. By blood, by education, by influence, they are Florentines, sons of the city of marble, the city which gives these sculptors to all Italy." [2]

In his fountains, particularly, Bernini looked to Florence for inspiration. Offhand, such a statement seems absurd, for in the late sixteenth and early seventeenth century the number and variety of the Roman fountains, made possible by the restoration of the ancient aqueducts, were the talk of all Europe. What need had a Roman artist to seek elsewhere for models?

We must remember, however, that Bernini's important commissions for fountains [3] were all for centrally composed examples, decorated with figure

1. Pietro Bernini had worked on fountains at Naples (see Figs. 86 and 137), and at Rome was the author of the Fontana della Barcaccia, in the Piazza di Spagna.

2. A free translation from *Reymond*, B., p. 20.

3. His wall fountains are less commonly known: the Fontana delle Api of the Vatican, 1627; the Fontana delle Api, at the corner of the Via Sistina and the Piazza Barberini, 1644; the Fontana dell' Aquila, at the Villa Mattei, 1629; the Fontana del Palazzo Antamaro, 1669, are all minor fountains; while the Mostra dell' Acqua Acetosa, 1661, is an architectural façade without figure sculpture.

sculpture; while the severely architectonic type of freestanding fountain
developed by the Roman architects from Giacomo della Porta to Carlo
Maderna, illustrated in Figures 212 and 213,[1] offered no scope for his plastic genius. It was inevitable, then, that he should turn to Florence, which
was the center for freestanding fountains with figure sculpture during the
sixteenth century and the early portion of the seventeenth century.[2]

Bernini's debt to the Florentine fountains is most obvious in his fountain figures, which frequently recall their Tuscan prototypes in style as well
as in *motif*. The impassioned movement that pervades his baroque figures
was already present in germ in many of the statues of Montorsoli, Giovanni
Bologna, and their followers; he had only to heighten the tempo. This is
patent in his earliest figure for a fountain — the marble Neptune and
Glaucus, carved about 1623 to decorate a fishpond at the Villa Montalto.
One of Falda's etchings shows the group in its original site, at the end of
a pool decorated with ancient statues. It is now at Brocklesby Park, in the
collection of Lord Yarborough, to whose courtesy I owe the photograph
reproduced in Figure 214. Bernini's Neptune plainly belongs to the long
line of Florentine representations of the lord of the sea. The pose and
threatening look are so close to those of Stoldo Lorenzi's Neptune in the
Boboli Garden (Fig. 215) as to indicate a direct influence.[3] Bernini has
heightened the effect of momentary motion already present in the earlier
work by his skilful use of flying drapery and by stressing the diagonal lines
in the composition, and has given his figures more robust forms, which approach the "grand style" of the full baroque. His modelling, although
broader and freer than that of the Tuscan sculptor, is still far from the ease
of his later style. Like his early works in the Borghese Gallery, with which
it is roughly contemporary, this group betrays unmistakably its Florentine
descent.[4]

1. *Guidi* (p. 21 ff.) lists sixteen freestanding fountains of the architectonic type from the
Cinquecento, and only two with figure sculpture. Of these, the figures on the Tartarughe fountain
were executed by the Florentine sculptor Taddeo Landini, who also carved one of the four tritons
added at the end of the sixteenth century to a fountain at one end of the Piazza Navona, now known
as the Fontana del Moro from the central figure added by Bernini (Fig. 216).

2. Her preëminence in this field during this period is proved by the constant importation of
Florentine fountains and their sculptors to other cities of Italy, and even to distant lands.

3. This influence was first noted by *Voss*, p. 122.

4. The Florentine influence is of course apparent in other sculpture by Bernini. The Apollo
and Daphne seems based upon Battista Lorenzi's Alpheus and Arethusa (Fig. 193); the Pluto and

FIGURE 216.  FONTANA DEL MORO

PIAZZA NAVONA, ROME.  FOUNTAIN ERECTED IN THE CINQUECENTO; CENTRAL FIGURE ADDED BY BERNINI

FIGURE 217.  VENTURINI, ETCHING OF BERNINI'S FOUNTAIN OF THE TRITON IN THE VILLA MATTEI, ROME

From Falda's *Fontane di Roma*

FIGURE 218.  GIOVANNI LORENZO BERNINI AND GIOVANNI ANTONIO MARI, TRITON
DETAIL OF THE FONTANA DEL MORO, PIAZZA NAVONA, ROME

For the Villa Barberini in the Borgo (*c.* 1626), Bernini made a fountain surmounted by a marble statue of a woman wringing out her hair, choosing this *motif*, as his Florentine predecessor had, for its adaptability to a limited supply of water; for Professor Antonio Muñoz' conclusion that the sculptor had in mind Giovanni Bologna's similar figure at Petraia (Fig. 44) seems to me inevitable. The marble figure, sold into England in the eighteenth century, has disappeared. It is a pity that no engraving or description of this fountain has come down to us.

The same quickening of tempo which we observed in the Montalto Neptune appears in the figures of the four river gods, on the fountain in the center of the Piazza Navona (Fig. 220), when compared with Giovanni Bologna's figures on the Fountain of Oceanus in the Boboli Garden (Figs. 110 and 114). In Tribolo's river god at the Villa Corsini (Fig. 64) Bernini had an even closer possible prototype for his sprawling figures, representing the four continents of the world, thrown into attitudes of wonder at beholding the obelisk erected by the munificence of Innocent X (Fig. 220). In this instance the figures are of white marble, contrasting with their rocky setting, as in Montorsoli's rustic fountain of the triton at Genoa (Fig. 159). The very allegory of the four river gods follows a long Florentine tradition, which apparently commenced in 1536 with the temporary figures erected at the Ponte Santa Trinità in honor of Charles V, and was continued by Montorsoli and Francesco Camilliani.[1]

For the triton which he modelled in 1633 for the center of a fountain erected in the late sixteenth century at one end of the great Piazza Navona (Fig. 216),[2] Bernini chose the old *motif* of a figure with a spouting dolphin. The standing central figure dominating lesser creatures of the sea, which we have studied in so many Tuscan fountains, is here brought to perfection (Fig. 218), not only in the naturalism and impetuous motion of the statue, but also in its fitness, through the torsion of the body, to be viewed from every side, as the central ornament to a freestanding fountain. The

Proserpina is reminiscent of Giovanni Bologna's Rape of the Sabines, and Vincenzo dei Rossi's Theseus and Helena (Fig. 152); and the David in its intensity recalls the latter's Samson and the Philistine (Fig. 121).

1. See pp. 28, 33, and 70.

2. The figure was executed in travertine after his model by Giovanni Antonio Mari. One of the tritons for this fountain was executed in the late sixteenth century by the Florentine sculptor Taddeo Landini. The original tritons, much worn, are now in the Borghese Garden, near the Giardino del Lago; those on the fountain are modern copies.

skilful use of *contrapposto*, the intensity of the facial expression, and the tossing of the tousled locks reinforce the impression of impassioned movement. The pathos and agitation of baroque sculpture, like that of Scopas in antiquity, seem particularly adapted to the representation of the restless creatures of the sea. At first glance, it may seem a far cry from the Neptunes of Ammannati and Giovanni Bologna (Figs. 92, 98, 99), with their hard modelling, to the freedom and verve of this figure; but Bernini's triumph would have been impossible without the long and arduous research of the Florentine sculptors of the previous century in the problems presented by a figure placed at the center of a freestanding fountain.

Two of Bernini's isolated fountains are decorated with central figures of tritons spouting upward through a conch shell — the lost fountain of the Villa Mattei, constructed about 1629, known only from an etching in *Falda* (Fig. 217), and the famous Fontana del Tritone, erected in the Piazza Barberini in 1640 (Fig. 219). As we have seen in an earlier chapter, the *motif* of the triton spouting upward was known to Florentine sculptors in the Cinquecento (Figs. 181 and 183), and was even utilized as the central *motif* over freestanding fountains (Fig. 184). Dr. Hermann Voss, in his brilliant article upon Bernini's fountains, remarks upon the plurifacial treatment of the triton of the Villa Mattei (Fig. 217), which gave the figure varied aspects, according to the different angles from which it was approached. This treatment he considers an innovation in Italian art, introduced by Bernini; actually, it is but another instance of the Roman master's close dependence, in his early works, upon Florentine fountain sculpture of the Cinquecento. In his later and more monumental triton fountain (Fig. 219) Bernini rejected the plurifacial treatment of his Tuscan prototypes for a simpler frontal conception more in keeping with the colossal proportions of his figure. His use of travertine as a medium is particularly happy. Darkened by the water, and overgrown with moss till it seems a part of nature, this stone dissolves into the surrounding atmosphere more readily than the white marble commonly used at Florence.

In his book on the baroque fountains of Rome, Dr. Massimiliano Guidi says of this fountain: "There was thus introduced into Rome a new type of fountain, which substituted for the architectonic shaft, the figure; for the basin, the shell." This type of fountain was undoubtedly new to Rome;

FIGURE 219.  GIOVANNI LORENZO BERNINI, FOUNTAIN OF THE TRITON
PIAZZA BARBERINI, ROME

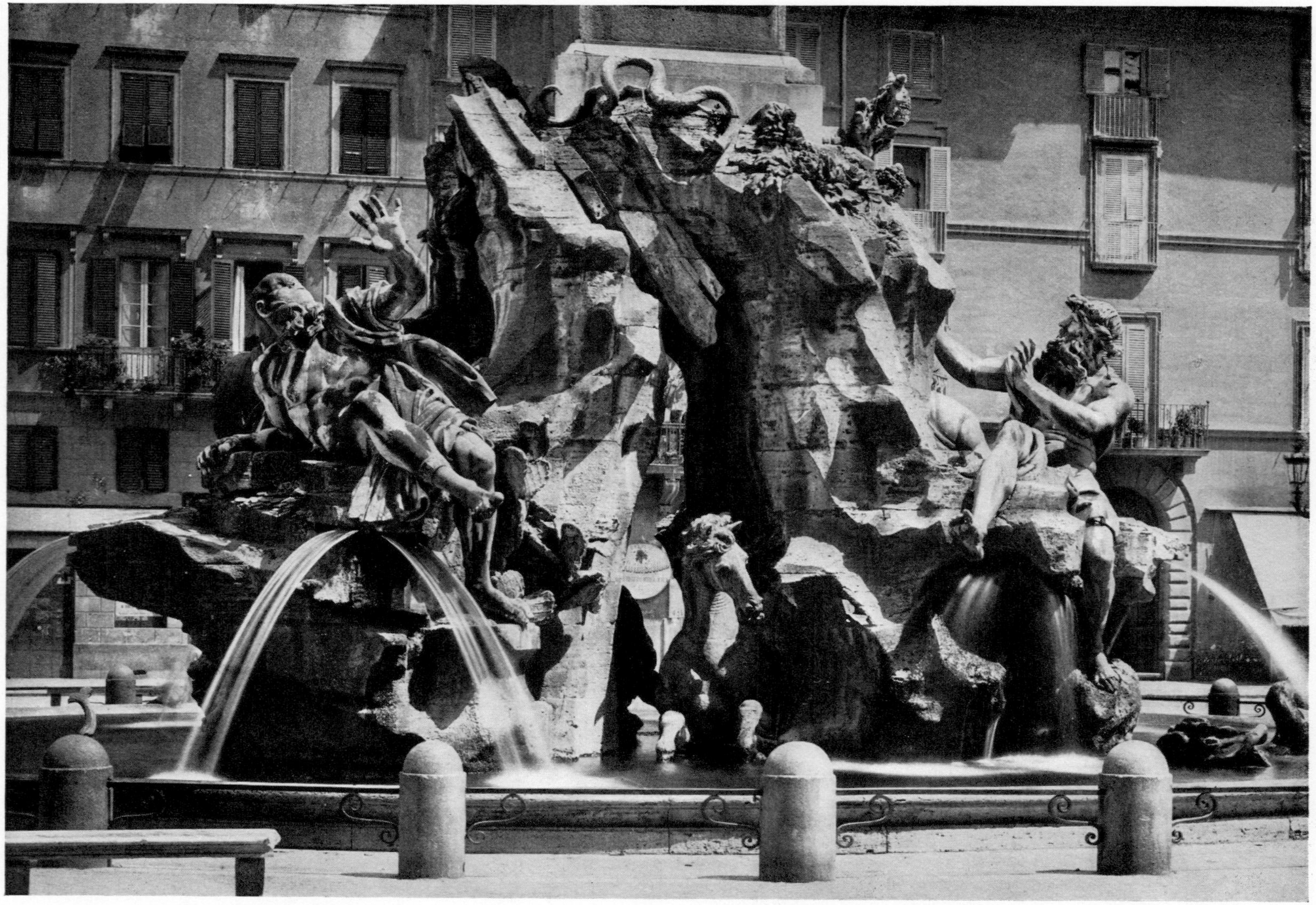

FIGURE 220. GIOVANNI LORENZI BERNINI, FOUNTAIN OF THE FOUR RIVERS

PIAZZA NAVONA, ROME

but the reader who has followed the development of the cylix fountain in Florentine villas will recall that the transition toward this completely naturalistic form commenced at Florence in the sixteenth century, in Giovanni Bologna's Fountain of Samson and the Philistine (Fig. 120), and had been further developed in the fountains of Giulio Parigi (Fig. 125) and of Pietro Tacca (Fig. 127), which antedate Bernini's fountain by several years.[1] In the naturalistic cylix fountains (Figs. 125 and 126) which Giulio Parigi constructed in 1618 to 1620 for the rim of the Boboli Isolotto, only the pedestal beneath the terminal figure remains formal. Bernini discarded this last vestige of the formal cylix; his figure rises directly from the shell.[2] No structural elements remain; the fountain is completely naturalistic, organic.

Dr. Guidi also notes a change in Roman fountains, about 1630, from the severely architectonic type of isolated fountain to a more plastic and naturalistic form, in which figure sculpture and *rocaille* are freely combined.[3] Bernini had a particular penchant for this rustic type of fountain,[4] which is merely a continuation of the "rustic island" of the Florentine villa. In his lost Fountain of the Triton in the Villa Mattei (Fig. 217) we see a rocky island surmounted by a statue, as in Montorsoli's fountain at Genoa or Ammannati's Apennine at Castello (Figs. 159 and 161). His only departure from the Florentine type is his choice of a circular form of basin, as contrasted with the rectangular form which the Florentine sculptors had retained from the old *vivaio*. Bernini's use of a naturalistic rocky rim at the edge of the pool further enhances the effect of an aquatic tableau.

In the Fountain of the Four Rivers in the Piazza Navona (Fig. 220) Bernini even transplanted the rustic island from the villa to the city square. Not that he left the rustic type of the Tuscan Renaissance unchanged. For the somewhat intricate style of the Florentine Cinquecento, with its love of

1. See pp. 66–67. *Guidi* (p. 43) recognized in the fountains of Parigi on the Isolotto and in the twin fountains of Tacca in the Piazza della S. Annunziata prototypes of Bernini's naturalistic cylix; but he did not know Giovanni Bologna's Fountain of Samson and the Philistine. Actual contact between Bernini and Pietro Tacca is proved by a reference in *Baldinucci* (XII, 178–179) to their meeting in Rome in 1625. Later Tacca sent his assistant, Bartolommeo Cennini, to Rome to instruct Bernini's workmen in the art of bronze casting.

2. However, the same stage had already been attained in the fountains of tritons around the Boboli Isolotto, carved in 1618–1620; see Figure 130 and p. 67, n. 2.

3. *Guidi*, p. 41.

4. *Voss*, p. 105: "Bernini nimmt die Fontana rustica gerade zu als Ausgangspunkt."

rich detail, he substituted the new breadth and grandeur of the Roman baroque. This change is apparent in the rockwork; contrast the broad style of these great travertine cliffs, built in courses, with the conglomeration of stucco and stalactites of Ammannati's island (Fig. 161). But above all we feel the new freedom in the handling of the water. Bernini replaced the petty, artificial jets of the Florentine fountains with the naturalistic yet monumental water effects that had been evolved at Rome in the last quarter of the Cinquecento and the opening years of the Seicento. A veritable waterfall gushes from the rocks.

Thus the types of the Florentine Renaissance were translated into the freer idiom of the Roman baroque.

# APPENDICES

# APPENDIX A

## SOURCES AND BIBLIOGRAPHY

### CHAPTER I

*Page 6*. Several lavabos of the Quattrocento are illustrated and discussed by Hilda Weigelt in "Minor Fountains of Florence," International Studio (December, 1929), pp. 87 ff. On the lavabo in S. Maria Novella see *Marquand*, G. D. R., p. 3. For Florentine *acquai* see A. Schiaparelli, La Casa Fiorentina e i Suoi Arredi Nei Secoli XIV e XV (Florence, 1908), I, 80–88. For information concerning the wall fountain no. 5950–1859 in the Victoria and Albert Museum I am indebted to Miss Margaret Longhurst of that museum. It comes from the Casa dei Girolami in the Via degli Archibusieri, Florence, was acquired in 1859, and has been attributed both to Benedetto da Rovezzano and Benedetto da Maiano. Neither attribution seems to me conclusive.

*Page 7*. The Uffizi drawing is no. 8945, Categ. VI; see p. 239 in Disegni Antichi e Moderni Posseduti dalla R. Galleria di Firenze (Rome, 1890). On the Zoan Andrea engraving see Arthur Hind, Catalogue of Early Italian Engravings in the British Museum, Text (London, 1910), p. 386.

*Pages 7–8*. Cupid with a Fish, Victoria and Albert Museum: *Schubring*, D., Pl. 32 and p. 195; *Bode*, I. B. S., vol. I, Pl. VIII and *Colasanti*, D., p. 57, give this figure to Donatello's workshop. On the *putto pissatore*, Museo Bardini, see Lensi, Dedalo, VI (1925–26), 762, 766. On the *putto pissatore* in the Kaiser Friedrich Museum see *Schottmüller*, I. S. B., Abb. 101, p. 44, no. I.151; *Marquand*, A. D. R., vol. II, no. 335.

*Page 8*. Boy with Dolphin, Hoyt Collection: *Marquand*, A. D. R., II, 182, no. 331, fig. 252; D. R. A., pp. 89–90, fig. 38.

Boy with Dolphin, Palazzo Vecchio: *Vasari*, III, 364, "Fece anco a Lorenzo de' Medici, per la fonte della Villa a Careggi, un putto di bronzo che strozza un pesce; il quale ha fatto porre, come oggi si vede, il Signor Duca Cosimo alla fonte che è nel cortile del suo palazzo; il qual putto è veramente maraviglioso"; *Cruttwell*, pp. 68–69, 243; *Mackowsky*, pp. 34–37; *Bode*, F. B. R., p. 226; *Reymond*, V., 46 ff. This figure was moved to the first court of the Palazzo Vecchio about 1555, water was brought from the Pitti Palace, and a new porphyry basin was made by Francesco del Tadda; see *Vasari*, VIII, 323–325; I, 112; also *Gaye*, II, 419–420. See *A. S. F.*, Fabbriche, II, 124 verso, 125, for payments made to "Francesco Giovanni del Dada" on April 20, 1555, and August 31, 1556, for his work on "un pilo di porfido datoli a fare da maestro Gorgo [*sic*] Vasari." For the mechanical device see W. Bombe, Monatshefte für Kunstwissenschaft, v (1912), 220, n. 1. Putto with hammer: *Vasari*, III, 375.

*Page 9.* Putto from the Dreyfus Collection: Catalogue of the Dreyfus Collection (Florence, 1930), Pls. 48–50; *Cruttwell*, p. 70; *Mackowsky*, p. 38; *Reymond*, V., 50, n. 1; *Bode*, Denk., p. 142; P. Vitry, Les Arts (1907), p. 24. This figure is apparently reproduced in a drawing in the Louvre, by some follower of Verrocchio. Unfortunately this sketch, done on the corner of the sheet, shows the raised arm but not the hand, so that the *motif* remains in question. Rustici is listed as a pupil of Verrocchio by *Vasari* (VI, 599).

*Page 10.* The medal by Matteo di Pasti, dated *c.* 1446, is reproduced from Pl. 29, no. 158, of G. F. Hill's Corpus of the Italian Medals of the Renaissance before Cellini (London, 1930); see also p. 38 in that work. On the *acquasantiera* in the Duomo at Lucca see *Yriarte*, pp. 93–95. The mate to this basin bears the lamb.

The Pazzi Cylix: *Albertini*, p. 7, "Nel giardino de' Medici sono assai cose antique venute da Roma; et in quello de' Pazi; et la fonte e per mano del Rossello excepto lo Hercole di bronzo antico." It is possible that the "Rossello" referred to was Bernardo Rossellino, who executed two well-heads at Pienza, and designed fountains for the Vatican garden of Nicholas V. *Vasari*, II, 407: "Fece [Donatello] di granito un bellissimo vaso che gettava acqua [from the context, plainly in the Medici Palace], e al giardino de Pazzi un altro simile ne lavorò, che medesimamente getta acqua," depends upon the Anonimi, cited by Fabriczy on pp. 320 and 365 of his article, "Il Libro di Antonio Billi e le Sue Copie nella Biblioteca Nazionale di Firenze," Archivio Storico Italiano, ser. v, t. VII (1891), the Codice Petrei reading: "Fecie [Donatello] uno vaso di granito con lineamenti di marmo, posto nella casa de' Medici, che gitta acqua; uno altro vaso con simili ornamenti, che fa fonte, molto bello, nello orto de' Pazzi," and the Codice Strozziano, "Un vaso di granito con ornamenti di marmo, nella casa o vero palazo de' Medici, gittante aqua. Uno altro vaso consimile nel' orto de' Pazi, molto bello, che fanno [*sic*] fonte." According to Bode (Jahrbuch der Königlichen Preussischen Kunstsammlungen, XXII [1901], 18, n. 1) the missing part of the stem of this basin was acquired by the painter Tricca about 1870. I can find no photograph of this portion of the fountain, nor do I know its present whereabouts. *Bode*, F. B. R., 2nd ed., p. 37, n. 1, returns to the old attribution to Donatello or his workshop; see also *Schubring*, D., Pl. 190 and p. 203, and Stella Rubinstein Bloch's Catalogue of the Collection of George and Florence Blumenthal (New York, 1926), vol. II, Pl. LXVIII and adjoining text. An illustration in Augusta Patterson's article, "The Residence of George Blumenthal," Town and Country (March, 1930), shows the fountain playing.

*Page 11.* Lost Cylix of the Medici Palace. See the references to the Pazzi Cylix quoted above. Giovanni Battista Gelli's description of this basin, roughly contemporary with the Anonimi already quoted (i. e., dating from the first half of the Cinquecento), is given by Mancini in Archivio Storico Italiano, ser. v, vol. XVII

(1896), p. 59: "Un vaso con molti ornamenti et figure nella Casa de' Medici et uno altro simile nell' orto de' Pazi, che fanno fonte, cosa bella." On the position of this basin in the Medici Palace see p. 219 of Bombe's article, cited on p. 110 of the present work.

*Page 12.* Donatello's Judith and Holofernes. All the necessary references on this group as the decoration of a fountain are given in De Nicola's convincing article "La Giuditta di Donatello," etc., Rassegna d'Arte (1917), pp. 153–159. See also *Colasanti*, D., pp. 81–82; *Bertaux*, pp. 174–177; *Meyer*, pp. 106–109; Venturi, Storia dell' Arte Italiana, vol. VIII, pt. I, pp. 262–263. On the transfer of the group in 1495 see E. Müntz, Les Collections des Médicis au XVe Siècle (Paris, 1888), p. 103.

*Page 13.* Donatello's bronze David. Bode believed that the David originally stood on the column which now bears the Judith and Holofernes: *Bode*, F. B. R., p. 30, n. 1, and K. F. R., p. 26. So *Schubring*, D., pp. xxviii–xxix. According to Schubring, water issued from the head of Goliath and from spouts which originally decorated this column.

The Medici Fountain in the Pitti Palace. For the date of the reduction of the Medici *palle* to six see *Marquand*, D. R. H., pp. 3–4.

*Page 14.* On the attribution of the Medici fountain to Donatello see *Vasari*, II, 407, note; to Rossellino, *Vasari*, III, 93–94, n. 1. Schottmüller is wary as to this attribution; see *Bode*, Denk., p. 338; so *Vasari*, G. G., II, 270, n. 5. Heinz Gottschalk, in a Ph.D. dissertation on Antonio Rossellino (Liegnitz, 1930), p. 93 ff., rejects this attribution, and assigns the basin as well as the putto to the Cinquecento. *Gramberg* (p. 225) places the entire cylix in the second quarter of the sixteenth century; but I know of no Cinquecento basins with carving in this crisp style.

*Page 14.* Fountain from the Louvre Sketchbook attributed to Jacopo Bellini, reproduced from Corrado Ricci's Jacopo Bellini e i Suoi Libri di Disegni (Florence, 1908), II, 24. Other fountains appear in the British Museum Sketchbook, I, 97a, 66b.

*Page 15.* The Cassone in the Schlossmuseum, Berlin. Schubring dates the actual cassone in 1512, but considers the painting from the late Quattrocento: *Schubring*, Cassoni, pp. 173, 399, no. 795, and K. H. R., Pl. 555 and p. 100.

Public Fountain at Asciano. Dated in the Quattrocento by *Voss* (p. 99).

*Page 16.* Bernardo Rossellino's plans for fountains in the Vatican garden were checked by the death of Nicholas V: *Vasari*, III, 100–101; but see *Dami*, p. 32, n. 5.

*Page 16.* Villa of Poggio Reale at Naples. *Müntz*, R. I. F., pp. 434–435; *Dami*, p. 32; *Gothein*, I, 231; A. Colombo in Napoli Nobilissima (1892), pp. 117–120, 136–138, 166–168.

## CHAPTER II

*Page 20.* For the various marbles and stones used in the figures and basins of fountains see *Vasari*, I, 107–127, *passim*, particularly the sections on Carrara marble, "*mischio*," porphyry, granite, *pietra bigia*, and *macigno*. The porphyry *tazza* carved in 1555 by Francesco del Tadda, when the bronze putto of Verrocchio was moved to the Palazzo Vecchio, was considered a marvel, as the art of working porphyry was only then rediscovered. For this Vasari (I, 112) gives the credit to Cosimo I. On Cosimo's plans for Castello upon his succession see *Vasari*, VI, 70–72.

*Page 21.* For Tribolo's plans for Castello see *Vasari*, VI, 72–85.

## CHAPTER III

*Page 22.* Tribolo and his models are identified in the Ragionamenti of Vasari (VIII, 192).

Fountain of the Labyrinth. For a general description see *Vasari*, VI, 79, 123. Terminal figure: *Baldinucci*, VII, 106, "Gettò [Giovanni Bologna] dipoi a Firenze una femmina in atto di pettinarsi le chiome, per l'altre volte nominate Villa di Castello de' Serenissima."

*Page 23.* Fountain of Cardinal d'Amboise at Gaillon: *Justi*, I, 134–135.

*Page 24.* The Great Fountain at Castello. General description, *Vasari*, VI, 74–81, *passim*. Terminal group: Montorsoli's marble group, *Vasari*, VI, 168–169, 639–640; *Gaye*, II, 422–424; Vincenzo Danti's model for a bronze group, *Vasari*, VII, 631; Ammannati's actual group, *A. S. F.*, Archivio de' Nove, 3700, pp. 5 verso, 7 verso. The references cited cover the dates from December 20, 1559, to February 17, 1560, and include payments for materials used in making the mould for the bronze figures.

*Pages 25–27.* The putti on the Great Fountain: *Vasari*, VI, 123–124, VII, 636; *Borghini*, p. 474; *Middeldorf*, A. W. P., p. 305. Were there originally nine putti at the base of the fountain? One of the nine claws on which these putti sit is empty; yet even the Cinquecento writers (Vasari, Borghini) mention only eight.

Payments for work at the Villa of Castello during the years 1549–66 are recorded in the Medici account books: *A. S. F.*, Fabbriche, vols. I, II, XIX. I quote portions relating to the Great Fountain.

I, 237 verso, November 19, 1552: "Per opere 27 di dua schultori, 1 scarpellino, 1 legnaiuolo, et 1 manouale, a piu pregi tenuti da di 24 a questo di a lavorare a Castello per meter su le due fontane del Giardino." The two sculptors mentioned are almost certainly Antonio and Stoldo Lorenzi, for the following documents show that they worked together at Castello, and the next excerpt proves that Antonio (di Gino) Lorenzi was already so employed in the spring of 1550.

I, 238, February 11, 1552 (1553, new style): "E addi detto lire venti dua soldi VIII piccioli si fanno buoni a maestro antonio di gino schultore da Settigniano per opere 16 a lire 1.8 — opera stato a lavorare i marmi dele fontane che non se li sono pagati e sono rimasti indreto da la listra de di primo di marzo 1549 [1550, new style] a la listra di 20 di Settembre 1550," etc.

II, 46 verso, March 1, 1552: "Per opere 38 fra di scultori scarpellini muratori et manouali, serviti a fare il resto del Condotto per laqua de la petraia al secondo giardino; e per meter su il resto de la fontana grande."

II, 73 verso, January 13, 1553 (1554, new style): "E addi 13 di gennaio lire undici piccioli pagati a Antonio di Gino et a Stoldo suo fratello schultori per opere stati a lavorare marmi per la fontana grande del gardino [sic] di Castello et a finire la statua di Schulapio da di 2 a di 5 detto."

II, 108: "E addi 28 detto [February, 1555] pagati a maestro Antonio sopra detto per opere 6 stato a Castello a lavorare su la statua di schulapio [Esculapius] et su la fine del fuso della fontana grande del gardino [sic] di Castello."

*Page 27.* Fountain of Orion at Messina. *Vasari* (VI, 647–649) gives a detailed description. Raffaello da Montelupo was first chosen, but fell ill. Montorsoli was then given the commission, arriving in Messina in September, 1547, with his assistant Martino Montanini. Marble for the fountain was brought from Carrara, the water from the river Cumano. The ground plan is reproduced from *Hittorff*, Pl. 26. On the river gods for the Ponte S. Trinità at Florence see *Vasari*, VI, 637, VIII, 258 ff. Montorsoli's works at Messina are fully discussed in Stefano Bottari's article "Giovanni Agnolo Montorsoli a Messina," L'Arte, XXXI (September–December, 1928), 235 ff., and in G. di Marzo's "Di Un Aneddoto del Montorsoli nel Suo Soggiorno in Messina," Archivio Storico Siciliano, XXIX (1904), 91–102. See also E. Mauceri, Rassegna d'Arte (1917), p. 212, and two articles in the Vita d'Arte, III, 1909 (N. Tarchiani, pp. 89–91, and F. Guardione, pp. 138–147). *Lomazzo* mentions this fountain as the outstanding example of the candelabrum type: bk. VI, chap. XLIX, p. 429.

*Page 29.* Fountain by Loggia in the Palazzo Doria, Genoa. Montorsoli was in charge of the garden works at this palace: *Vasari*, VI, 645–646, "Finita la detta chiesa [S. Matteo] il medesimo principe Doria fece mettere mano al suo palazzo, e fargli nuove aggiunte di fabriche e giardini bellissimi, che furono fatti con ordine del frate." The attributions are as follows:

To Montorsoli: Carlo Patti, Istruzio di Genova, 2nd ed. (Genoa, 1780), I, 358.

To Perino del Vaga: L. T. Belgrano, Il Palazzo del Principe d'Oria a Fassolò a Genova (Genoa, 1874), p. 36.

To Silvio Cosini: Carlo Gamba, Dedalo (September, 1929), p. 241; Orlando Grosso, Genova nell' Arte e nella Storia, p. 83.

To Cosini on the design of Perino del Vaga: Raffaello Soprani, Vite de' Scultori ed Architetti Genovesi (Genoa, 1768), p. 82. Cosini, strongly influenced by Tribolo, is a sort of plastic Giovanni da Udine, famous for his stucco grotesques.

*Page 30.* For actual German fountains of the candelabrum type see *Lindner*, Abb. 135, 156, and for the Stockbrunnen *ibid.*, pp. 65–68. On the Tugendbrunnen of Benedikt Wurzelbauer see *Brinckmann*, S. D. B., p. 1, and *Lindner*, Abb. 165.

*Page 31.* Fountain of the Tritons at Madrid: *Baldinucci*, XVI, 118, on Lotti's departure for Spain in 1628, and *Gothein*, I, 390, attributing the design of the gardens and fountains of Aranjuez, in their first state, to this artist.

*Page 31.* Fountain of the Artichokes. *Baldinucci*, XII, 205–206; *Soldini*, pp. 13–15. This fountain replaced Ammannati's Fountain of Juno; see pages 42–45 of this work.

## CHAPTER IV

*Page 32.* On the wall fountains in the Belvedere Garden see Michaelis, Jahrbuch der Archaeologischen Institut (1890), v, 24.

*Page 32.* The fountain of the Tigris is reproduced from Christian Hülsen's Die Römischen Skizzenbücher im Königlichen Kupferstichkabinett zu Berlin (Berlin, 1913–16), Pl. 63. *Vasari* (I, 114) thus describes the fountain: "Di questa pietra [cippollaccio] è una fonte in Roma in Belvedere cioè una nicchia in un canto del giardino, dove sono le statue del Nilo e del Tevere; la qual nicchia fece far papa Clemente VII [1527–34] col disegno di Michelagnolo per ornamento d'un fiume antico, accio in questo campo fatto a guisa di scogli apparisca, come veramente fa, molto bello." See also *Maclehose*, pp. 115–116.

*Page 33.* On the temporary fountains of 1536 see *Vasari*, VI, 637, VIII, 258. The fountains of the Arno and Mugnone at Castello are dated *c.* 1547 (1546, old style) by a reference in *Varchi*, p. 33; see *Wiles*, T. M. V., p. 68 and n. 31. For the design of the Garden of the Labyrinth as a whole see *Vasari*, VI, 83–84. For a description of the Arno and Mugnone and plans for the adjoining fountains of Monti Asinaio and Falterone see *Vasari*, VI, 77–78.

*Page 35.* On Tuscan work covered with stalactites see *Vasari*, I, 141 ff., "E di questa sorte [i. e., the type of stalactites found at Mt. Morello] ha fatto fare il duca Cosimo del suo giardino dell' Olmo a Castello [a common name of that villa] gli ornamenti rustici delle fontane." See also p. 74 of the present work. On the relief of the Fiesole, from the rear of the niche, see *Wiles*, T. M. V., pp. 64 ff.

*Page 35.* Corsini River God: *Vasari*, VI, 91–92; *Vasari*, G. G., vol. VII, pt. I, p. 263, n. 55; *Triggs*, A. G. I., p. 82; *Wiles*, T. M. V., p. 60 ff. On the treatment of the river god in the Cinquecento as contrasted with that of the Seicento see Muñoz, Rassegna d'Arte, III (1916), 162.

*Page 37.* Fountains of the Tiber and Arno in the Villa Giulia, Rome: *Biagi*, p. 66; *Dami*, p. 36, n. 16; *Vasari*, VII, 594.

*Page 37.* Fountain of Perseus in the Palazzo Nonfinito. Payments by the municipality for this statue are recorded in the Archivio della Soprintendenza dell' Arte Medioevale e Moderna di Firenze, in the records for the years 1881 and following, among acquisitions from the Palazzo Cepparello, as the Palazzo Salviati is now called:

> Indice degli Affari 1881, Inserto 139, Protocollo 628, Posizione 2;
> Indice degli Affari 1884, Inserto 49, Protocollo 1977, Posizione 9, etc.

See also *Borghini*, p. 599, and *Baldinucci*, x, 149.

*Page 38.* On the correct interpretation of the three figures on Michelangelo's tomb in S. Croce see *Borghini*, p. 108. The confusion of these two statues has led to a confusion of the styles of Valerio Cioli and Battista Lorenzi.

Fountain of the Palazzo Senatorio at Rome. Charles V's visit to Rome in 1536 made necessary the embellishment of the Campidoglio, and called forth Michelangelo's design: *Vasari*, VII, 222 ff. See also A. Michaelis, Zeitschrift für Bildende Kunst, N. F., II (1890–91), 184–194; Henry Thode, Michelangelo und das Ende der Renaissance (Berlin, 1912), vol. III, pt. II, pp. 643–646. Another example of this type of composition is found in the Fonte della Torre della Pallata, 1596, Brescia, illustrated in *Colasanti*, Pl. 155.

*Page 39.* Michelangelo's design for the Moses fountain: *Vasari*, VII, 58. Vacca's Moses fountain is illustrated by *Colasanti*, Pl. 159. Other evidence for Michelangelo's connection with the design of fountains must be mentioned here. Heinrich Geymüller interprets Battista da Sangallo's drawing of a façade bearing a note, "Questo in Chastello di Roma di mano di Michelagnolo di Traverti," in the Livre de Michelange, Musée Wicar, Lille, as a wall fountain (Geymüller, Michelangelo als Architekt [Munich, 1904], p. 38); but the actual façade in Castel S. Angelo, from the time of Leo X (1513–22), in the Cortile delle Palle, was apparently never connected with water, and photographs taken before the recent restoration show no basin. As there was no figure sculpture, I have not taken it up in the text. See also Biblioteca d'Arte Illustrata (1923), ser. II, fasc. 19, Pl. XIX, by D. Frey. Michelangelo also drew plans, now lost, for the Villa of Marmirolo, which may have included fountains (*Vasari*, VII, 364); and he planned to install the ancient group of the Farnese Bull in the courtyard of the Farnese Palace as a fountain (*Vasari*, VII, 224–225). A marble Hercules by Michelangelo, once in the Strozzi Palace, was set up over a fountain at Fontainebleau, designed by Primaticcio (perhaps taking the place of the fountain which Cellini had planned; see p. 47 of this work): *Vasari*, VII, 145; Dimier, Le Primatice (Paris, 1900), pp. 64–68, 375–376.

*Page 40.* Julius III's Public Fountain. A complete description and the text of the letter to Marco Benavides are given by Giacomo Balestra in La Fontana Pubblica di Giulio III e il Palazzo di Pio IV sulla Via Flaminia (Rome, 1911), pp. 65–76. A document showing that a model for the fountain was ready on Easter, 1552, and that work was commenced in May, 1552, is given by *Biagi*, p. 65; and the casino into which the fountain is incorporated is treated by the present owner, Ugo Iandolo, Il Palazzo di Pio IV sulla Via Flaminia (Rome, 1928). See also *Mac Veagh*, p. 87. The drawing in the Hof Bibliothek at Vienna is reproduced from Egger, Römische Veduten (Vienna, 1911), taf. I.

*Page 41.* Fonte Bassa in the Villa Giulia: *Vasari*, VII, 81, "Avendo il Vasari fatto sotto il palazzo nuovo, primo di di [*sic*] tutti gli altri, il disegno del cortile e della fonte, che poi fu seguitata dal Vignola e dall' Ammannato, e murata da Baronino." Later (VII, 694) he seems to deny Vignola any part in the fountain: "Jacopo Barozzi da Vignola finì con molti suoi disegni le stanze, sale, ed altri molti ornamenti di quel luogo; ma la fonte bassa fu l' ordine mio e dell' Ammannato, che poi vi resto, e fece la loggia che è sopra la fonte." With this last agrees a document quoted by *Biagi* (p. 66), in which Ammannati speaks of thirty-four months "che io lavorai e disegniai e messi inanzi e le dette fabrice più cose come si vede, la fontana, la logga di detta vigna, il cortile dinanzi a detta logga," etc. See also *Mac Veagh*, pp. 97 ff. On the putti see *Borghini*, p. 592, and *Baldinucci*, VI, 21.

*Page 42.* Ammannati's Fountain of Juno: *Kriegbaum*, E. V. B., gives a complete bibliography for this fountain, but as the publications of the Kunsthistorisches Institut are not everywhere available, I repeat: *Vasari*, IV, 453, VI, 185; *Borghini*, p. 592; *Gaye*, II, 414, 416, III, 35, 579; *De Vieri*, p. 48; *A. S. F.*, Fabbriche, LIII, 90, 94 verso, 101 verso, 117 verso, 154 verso. I do not find in Kriegbaum's article the reference to Tanai dei Medici's letter: *Gaye*, III, 423-424.

*Page 45.* Mostra dell' Acqua Felice: *Guidi*, pp. 24, 67-68; *Tani*, pp. 49-51; *Mac Veagh*, pp. 145-152; *Mastrigli*, I, 131-136, II, 19-23; *Colasanti*, pp. xxxi-xxxii.

*Page 45.* Fontana dei Giganti at Naples. On p. 103 of an article by G. Ceci in Napoli Nobilissima (1896) is an engraving showing this fountain in its original site. See also *Muñoz*, P. B., p. 433.

*Page 46.* Fontana di Santa Lucia, Villa Nazionale: *Sobotka*, P. B., p. 406; G. Ceci, Napoli Nobilissima, vol. XI, fasc. X (1902), pp. 145-147.

## CHAPTER V

*Page 47.* Cellini's design for a Fountain of Mars, described in the autobiography: *Cellini*, II, 91-93. For the argument with Primaticcio see *ibid.*, II, 102, 122; on the colossal model for the central figure see II, 143, 154-156, also a passage in chap. V of the Trattati, for which see *ibid.*, III, 203 ff. In 1546 the model of wooden framework and plaster still existed, for in that year Francis I gave orders to protect it from the weather; see Cust's second edition of the Autobiography (1927), p. 217, and *Plon*, p. 55. Plon (p. 212 and n. 1) assumes that the "intersecting steps" were like those of the well of St. Patrick at Orvieto. But they were spiral stairs constructed within a deep cylinder, and were connected only at the bottom, by means of a bridge; see Gustave Clausse, Les San Gallo (Paris, 1902), II, 256, and accompanying illustration. Cellini's text reads: "Questo modello era grande più di due braccia nel quale avevo fatto una fontana in forma d'un quadro perfetto, con bellissimi iscalie intorno quali s' intrasegavano l'una nell' altra, cosa che mai s'era vista in quelle parti, e rarissima in queste." How could intersecting steps surrounding a square fountain resemble the spiral staircases inclosed in a cylinder? On Primaticcio's fountain see Dimier, Le Primatice (Paris, 1900), pp. 64–66, with note 1, 375–376, also p. 115 of the present work.

*Page 48.* Fountain of Neptune at Messina: *Vasari* (VI, 649–650) is the chief source. See also *Hittorff*, Pls. 24, 25; *Brinckmann*, B. S., p. 70; *Reymond*, S. F., IV, 131. The copies of Neptune and Scylla were made by Gregorio Zappalà: Enrico Mauceri, Rassegna d'Arte (1917), p. 212. The drawing, no. 943 in the Uffizi, is usually attributed to Montorsoli. I do not believe that the large terracotta model of a woman in the Kaiser Friedrich Museum, Berlin, published by Schottmüller (Amtliche Berichte aus den Preussischen Kunstsammlungen [April, 1914], pp. 223–227), illustrated by *Brinckmann* (B. B., I, 46–47, Pls. 11, 12), is by Montorsoli or in any way related to this fountain. The style seems to me absolutely unlike the Frate's. I also question the ascription of the Uffizi drawing.

*Page 50.* Fountain of Neptune, Florence. Story of the Competition: *Vasari*, VI, 186–192, is the fullest source. The idea of decorating the Piazza della Signoria with a monumental fountain was conceived by Cosimo I about 1551, when Baccio Bandinelli was asked to submit a design for the work (*Bottari-Ticozzi*, I, 91 ff., especially 93). In preparing his design, he considered particularly the fountains at Messina, as the most magnificent known at that time, and promised to erect a fountain that would surpass all others. The plans, however, languished until Bandinelli, hearing of a great piece of marble that had been excavated some years before at Carrara, hastened to that quarry and paid a deposit to hold the block. (This was probably in 1558, for, according to Milanesi [*Vasari*, VI, 186, n. 3], Baccio visited Carrara in that year.) He determined to use the marble for a colossal Neptune to decorate his fountain, and importuned the Duke and Duchess to permit him to commence the work at once. The central figure as he conceived it was to represent Neptune on a chariot drawn by sea-horses, probably in a position similar to Ammannati's figure. Baccio proceeded to make several models for the work, from which the Duke might choose; but nothing was actually executed when in 1559 the owner of the quarry came to demand that the balance be paid, threatening to sell the block to others. The Duke then ordered Vasari to pay for the marble, but as he had not yet definitely given the block to Bandinelli Benvenuto Cellini and Ammannati besought him to arrange a competition, in which they also might submit models, the winning sculptor to be given the marble. According to Vasari, the Duke felt sure that Baccio Bandinelli was best fitted to produce this monumental work, but, knowing his customary vacillation, agreed to the competition in the hope that it would spur him to accomplishment.

Baccio redoubled his efforts, making models and plying the Duchess with requests to use her influence in his behalf. At length he received permission to bring the marble to Florence. Once at Carrara, according to Vasari, he cut into the stone so as to render it useless to the others.

On Bandinelli's return to Florence the excitement began once more, for Cellini proclaimed that Baccio had ruined the marble. Meanwhile Bandinelli walled off an arch in the Loggia dei Lanzi as a studio, and (through the Duchess' intercession) at length received permission to begin the great model of the Neptune. He sent at once for his pupil Vincenzo de' Rossi to assist him in the work. One might suppose that the contest was now over, but the death of Bandinelli early in 1560 (the date is given in the epitaph in *Vasari* [VI, 190] as 1559, but that is the old reckoning) reopened the competition. His design is unfortunately lost to us.

Benvenuto Cellini now constantly besought the Duke to see a small model in wax that he had made, while Ammannati contended that his greater experience in the working of marble and in the designing of fountains particularly fitted him for the commission; for he had erected two wall fountains for Julius III in Rome and had designed another for the Palazzo Vecchio in Florence during 1556–60 (see pp. 40–45 of this work), and during his stay in the North had carved a Neptune in Istrian stone for the Piazza di S. Marco at Venice, and a colossal statue of Hercules for the courtyard of Marco Benavides in Padua. At length he sent his model to Rome for Michelangelo's criticism, hoping to secure the work on the latter's recommendation. As a result, he was permitted to wall up an arch in the Loggia dei Lanzi as Bandinelli had done, and to commence a great model. Benvenuto soon demanded and received the same privilege. The two sculptors now worked side by side, although neither could watch the other's progress.

At this point, two younger sculptors entered the lists — Giovanni Bologna, a young Flemish sculptor, who had studied at Rome before his arrival in Florence a few years before, and Vincenzo Danti of Perugia —, though according to Vasari they scarcely expected to be given the commission, wishing merely to show their powers. Each commenced a large model, Giovanni Bologna working in the convent of Santa Croce through arrangements made by Prince Francesco, and Danti in the house of Ottaviano dei Medici. There is even evidence that Vincenzo de' Rossi sought to enter the competition after his master's death: *Gaye*, vol. III, p. 24, no. XXVIII, dated February 24, 1560.

According to Vasari, Cosimo considered only the models of Benvenuto Cellini and Ammannati, and decided upon the latter's. Giovanni Bologna's he refused to see, knowing of no marble statue by this sculptor, and considering him too young to be entrusted with such a great work. According to *Borghini*, however (p. 586), Giovanni Bologna would have won the competition if the Neptune had not already been promised to Ammannati. *Baldinucci* (VII, 90) combines the two sources, saying that Giovanni Bologna's design was preferred by all, but the Duke did not wish to give the work to a sculptor inexperienced in the working of marble.

References in the Archives at Florence, showing dates of the work, are as follows: payments connected with the models of Ammannati, Cellini, and Giovanni Bologna are recorded in *A. S. F.*, Fabbriche, XXI, 69 verso; III, 47 verso; IX, 43. These cover the period from March to June, 1560. In Settimanni's Diario Fiorentino, preserved in the same archive, are to be found the following references to the progress of the work:

> Marble for the Neptune brought to Florence June 22, 1560 . .III, 174
> Marble for the Neptune taken to the Loggia where Ammannati
>     worked on October 17, 1560 . . . . . . . . . . . . . . . . . . . . . . . . .III, 180 verso
>     (According to a letter to Michelangelo in *Gualandi*, I, p. 57,
>     no. 19, Ammannati commenced work on this marble in
>     April, 1561.) The Marzocco moved, March 5, 1564 . . . . . .III, 310 verso
> Foundations for the fountain begun, May 4, 1565 . . . . . . . . .III, 320
> The "Giant" set up among the temporary figures, October 3,
>     1565 . . . . . . . . . . . . . . . . . . . . . . . . . . . . . . . . . . . . . . . . . .III, 328 verso
> The beginning of the execution in marble and bronze of the
>     other figures of the fountain, previously of stucco, in
>     March, 1571 . . . . . . . . . . . . . . . . . . . . . . . . . . . . . . . . . . . .III, 562 verso
>     (The only change in the design was in the basin, which was
>     made lower, so that the water was more readily visible.)
> The fountain unveiled in June, 1575 . . . . . . . . . . . . . . . . . . . . . .IV, 35

The following assistants of Ammannati in the work upon this fountain are listed by A. Lensi (Palazzo Vecchio [Milan, 1929], pp. 200–202), with a reference to documents in the State Archives in n. 81 on pp. 271–272: Andrea Calamec of Carrara, Michele Fiammingo, Girolamo dei Noferi da Sassoferrato. Other helpers whose names appear in the documents are Battista di Benedetto Fiammeri, Donato Berti, and Raffaello Fortini, of whom only Battista is known as a sculptor (see the article on this artist in *Thieme-Becker*). Two drawings of fountains of the candelabrum type, attributed to this sculptor, are preserved in the Uffizi.

The fountain as it was erected temporarily in 1565 is described in great detail in *Vasari*, VIII, 565. The torso of a river god in the Academy, Florence, long attributed to Michelangelo, has been identified as the remains of Ammannati's figures that formed part of the temporary decoration of 1565, by A. E. Popp (Die Medici Kapelle Michelangelos [Munich, 1922], p. 150 and taf. 79). See also *Baldinucci*, VI, 31–32, 100; *Borghini*, pp. 593–594; *Reymond*, S. F., IV, 159; *Brinckmann*, B. S., p. 74; *Post*, I, 229–230.

*Page 54.* Fountain of Neptune at Bologna. Giovanni Bologna was employed by Francesco dei Medici in 1561: *Desjardins*, pp. 115–118. General discussion of this fountain is to be found in the section "Alcuni Schiarimenti Intorno a Giovanni Bologna" appended to Vasari's Lives in 1846: *Vasari*, VII, 644–646. See also *Vasari*, VII, 629. A letter by Zanobi Portigiani relating to the disagreement about the bronze casting is given by I. B. Supino in Arte e Storia (Florence, March 5, 1911). The fountain was dedicated in 1563, for the inscription round the basin reads: "Fori ornamento populi commodo aere publico MDLXIII." I am indebted to Miss Agnes Mongan for calling to my attention a drawing showing rough preliminary sketches for this fountain, ascribed to Tommaso Laureti, preserved at Darmstadt: Zeichnungen aus den Kupferstichkabinett des Hessischen Landes Museums zu Darmstadt, vols. IX–X (Darmstadt 229). On the terracotta model of a fountain see Metropolitan Museum, Catalogue of Romanesque, Gothic, and Renaissance Sculpture (New York, 1913), pp. 77–78, no. 78 and ill. on p. 79. Quotation from C. Gurlitt, Geschichte des Barockstiles in Italien (Stuttgart, 1887), p. 252.

*Page 57*. The German fountains of the type with the raised central figure: Augsburg, Fountain of Augustus, *Brinckmann*, S. D. B., pp. 7, 23 and Pls. 13–16; Munich, Wittelsbacher Brunnen, *ibid.*, pp. 7–8, 24–25, and Pls. 17–20; Augsburg, Fountain of Hercules and Hydra, *ibid.*, pp. 16–17, 33–34, and Pls. 64–70.

*Page 58*. Fountain at Fredriksborg: *ibid.*, pp. 19, 38.

Figures from Prague, at Drottningholm: *ibid.*, pp. 19, 39 and Pls. 95–96; Conrad Buchwald, Adrian de Vries (Leipzig, 1899), pp. 85–89, p. 102; John Boettiger, Bronsarbeten af Adrian de Fries i Sverge Särskildt a Drottningholm (Stockholm, 1884). All of de Vries' figures at Drottningholm, both from the fountain at Fredriksborg and from the one at Prague, are illustrated in the last book.

## CHAPTER VI

*Page 59*. Fountain of the Flying Mercury. In 1598 this figure was still over the cylix at the Villa Medici: *Desjardins*, p. 63, n. 1. It was brought to Florence in the time of Pietro Leopoldo (1769–83): *ibid.*, p. 65 and n. 1. The Flying Mercury which was presented to Emperor Maximilian at Vienna was almost certainly sent on the occasion of the negotiations, in 1564, for the marriage of Prince Francesco and Joanna of Austria. It is known that the first casting of this figure went awry, so that a second one was dispatched to the Emperor. The crack in the torso of the figure in the Bargello tends to identify it with the figure cast first in 1564. See *Vasari*, VII, 647. Desjardins cautiously dates this statue before 1574 because Vasari, who mentions it in this second edition, died in that year (*Desjardins*, p. 61, n. 1); but, as Dr. Friedrich Kriegbaum has pointed out (D. M. P., p. 139, n. 3), it obviously must have antedated 1568, when the second edition was published. *Borghini* (p. 587) makes the figure sent to the Emperor contemporary with the fountain of Bologna, which again would agree with our date of 1564. See *Baldinucci*, VII, 92; *Brinckmann*, B. S., p. 90, and for the Perseus relief by Cellini, p. 83 and Abb. 87. See also p. 88 of the present work.

Stoldo Lorenzi's Fountain of Neptune: *Vasari*, VII, p. 637, "Gli ha poi fatto fare il medesimo signore [Duke Cosimo] per lo suo giardino de' Pitti, una fontana simile al bellissimo trionfo di Nettuno, che si vide nella superbissima mascherata che fece sua Eccellenza nelle dette nozze del Signor Principe illustrissimo"; *Borghini*, p. 608, "Tornato poi in Firenze gli fu dato à fare dal Gran Duca la Fonte del Nettunno di bronzo nel giardino de' Pitti, la quale statua posa sopra certi mostri marini di marmo, e quest' opera da quei, che intendono e stata molto lodata"; *Bocchi*, p. 68 (after speaking of Cioli's Morgante and Barbino, which stood near the entrance at the beginning of the Stradone), "Ed in luogo alto in un vivaio, un Nettuno di bronzo sopra alcuni mostri marini, che sono di marmo, di mano di Stoldo Lorenzi, scultore Fiorentino, di tanta bellezza, che senza fine da tutti gli artefici è lodato." With this see *Gaye*, III, 266 (October 21, 1568): "Il piede di marmo per la fonte del vivaio de' Pitti, che ha da lavorare Stoldo Lorenzi, secondo il modello mandatovi." From this mention of a marble pedestal it is evident that this *vivaio* contained a formal fountain rather than a rustic one such as that which the Neptune now adorns.

A letter from Cosimo to Matteo Inghirami, overseer of the quarries at Seravezza (*Gaye*, III, 204), dated March 22, 1566 (1565 in the letter, old reckoning), ordering four blocks of white marble and a round one of variegated stone prepared for Stoldo Lorenzi, probably relates to this fountain, since the date 1566 is soon after the celebration of the wedding. The phrase "tondo of mischio" is used repeatedly in such letters of the prepared round blocks from which fountain basins were carved. The four pieces of white marble would provide for the four sea creatures.

The description of the Triumph of Neptune as represented on the actual float is given by *Vasari*, VIII, 606: "Ma capriccioso e bizzarro e bello sopra tutti gli altri apparse poi il tredicesimo carro di Nettunno, essendo di un grandissimo granchio, che grancevalo sogliono i Veneziani chiamare, e che su quattro gran delfini si posava, composto, ed avendo intorno alla base, che un scoglio naturale e vero sembrava, una infinità di marine conche e di spugne e di coralli, che ornatissimo e vaghissimo lo rendevano, ed essendo da due marini cavalli tirato; sopra cui Nettunno, nel modo solito e col solito tridente stando, si vedeva, in forma di bianchissima e tutta spumosa ninfa, la moglie Salacia a' piedi e come per compagna avere." I have omitted the account of the train which attended the float on foot. From the above description it seems clear that the actual fountain, as its form is shown upon the lunette, can have resembled the float only in the pose of the Neptune.

*Page 61*. Fountain of Oceanus. On the great basin see *Lapini*, p. 157: "A di 17 di Luglio [1567], in giovedi, si messe in Firenze la bella tazza di granito, che e nel bel palazzo de' Pitti. E per metterle in Firenze bisognò rompere et allargare la Porta al Prato di qua e di la, perche era tanto larga che non vi entrava; venne dall' Elba. La qual tazza gira braccia 35." This block had already been quarried at Elba by Tribolo before his death in 1550 according to *Vasari*, VI, 97: "Dopo queste cose fu mandato il Tribolo da sua Eccellenza nell' isola dell' Elba — perche desse ordine di condurre un pezzo di granito tondo di dodici braccia per diametro, del quale si aveva a fare una tazza per lo prato grande de' Pitti, la quale recevesse l'acqua pella fonte principale. Andato dunque colà il Tribolo, e fatto fare una scafa a posta per condurre questa tazza, ed ordinato agli scarpellini il modo di condurla, se ne tornò a Fiorenza."

Desjardins' dates for this fountain (*Desjardins*, p. 92) in general agree with those given here, although he does not cite the documents upon which his chronology is based. From the numerous references to this fountain which I have found in the Medici account books I cite the following as of special interest:

Giovanni Bologna's two assistants in making the statues were Jacopo di Zanobi, from March 6, 1573 (1574, new style) and Andrea di Jacopo, from October 16, 1574. *A. S. F.*, Fabbriche, XXX, vi verso, vii.

On June 25, 1575 a porter was paid for moving the figures of the fountain to their place ("per opere che anno aiutato condurre le fiure della fontana di sul prato di nostro giardino"). *A. S. F.*, Fabbriche, LI, 124.

From October 31 to November 5, 1575 men were hired to raise the great basin. *A. S. F.*, Fabbriche, LXXXV, 94 verso.

On November 29, 1575 bronze pipes for the fountain were bought. *A. S. F.*, Fabbriche, XC, 8 verso.

On March 21, 1575 (1576, new style) bronze spikes and rivets ("perni e spranghe") for attaching the figures and reliefs ("le fiure e cartelle") were purchased. *A. S. F.*, Fabbriche, LXXXV, p. ciii.

On May 15, 1576 the great pipe for the granite basin and on October 30, 1576 a bronze spike and two rivets to fasten the figure of Oceanus were purchased ("per fermare Oceano sopra le tre fiure"). *A. S. F.*, Fabbriche, LIX, 23 verso. See also *A. S. F.*, Fabbriche, XLII, 9 verso, and Fabbriche, LI, 108; likewise *Gaye*, III, 405.

On April 16, 1575 (*A. S. F.*, Fabbriche, XXX, cxiii verso; LI, 123), a porter was paid for carrying from the Pitti Palace to Giovanni Bologna's studio at the Palazzo Vecchio the three great models for the river gods and eight bundles ("fasci") of small models. Among the latter were probably the two terracotta models of river gods in the Kaiser Friedrich Museum (I 270, I 269) ascribed to Giovanni Bologna and to Tribolo respectively, and two similar *bozzetti* in the Bargello at Florence, long given to Tribolo. In the ascription of all four models to Giovanni Bologna I follow A. E. Popp, Die Medici Kapelle Michelangelos (Munich, 1922), pp. 148–150, and *Brinckmann*, B. B., I, 70–73 and Pls. 25, 26. On the attribution of these models to Tribolo see Umberto Rossi, in Archivio Storico dell' Arte, VI (1893), 13; E. Steinmann, Zeitschrift für Bildende Kunst, N.F. XVII (1905–06), 39–42; A. Gottschewski, Zeitschrift für Bildende Kunst, N.F. XVII, 189–193; and G. Poggi, Rivista d'Arte, IV (1906), 104–106, for the models in the Bargello; and for the *bozzetti* in Berlin see F. Goldschmidt,

Amtliche Berichte aus den Königlichen Kunstsammlungen, xxiv (February, 1913), 87, Abb. 47, 48; and *Schottmüller*, I. S. B., p. 150, Abb. 357, and p. 155, Abb. 369. No. I 270 in Berlin is closely related to the Euphrates upon the Boboli fountain, as Dr. Fritz Goldschmidt pointed out in his article (p. 90 and Abb. 47, 49); but the more dynamic pose seems to me even closer to della Bella's etchings of Giovanni Bologna's lost figure of the Mugnone at Pratolino (Figs. 149, 150 and pp. 103, 104, 177). This group of models indicates a continued study of the problems presented by the crouching figure of a river god, which this master carried still further in his early *bozzetti* for the colossal figure of the Apennine for Pratolino, preserved in the Bargello and in the Victoria and Albert Museum; see *Brinckmann*, B. B., vol. I, Pls. 28, 29 and pp. 76–78. The model in the Victoria and Albert Museum seems to me merely a further development of the *motif* of no. I 269 at Berlin (compare Pls. 28, 26, I in Brinckmann, *op. cit.*). This resemblance strengthens the case for the attribution of the latter to Giovanni Bologna.

*Brinckmann*, B. B., 1, 74–75 and Pl. 27, publishes a terracotta *bozzetto* of a torso in the Horne Collection, Florence as a model for the Euphrates. I doubt if it is even a river god. Count Carlo Gamba's interpretation of this figure as an athlete (Dedalo, 1920, p. 174) seems more satisfactory.

The attribution of the design to Tribolo is based on the passage cited above (*Vasari*, vi, 97), which also states that Tribolo laid out the general design for the Boboli Garden, accommodating everything to its place: "Fece il Tribolo tutto lo spartimento del monte che egli sta, accommodando tutte le cose con bel giudizio ai luoghi loro, *se ben poi alcune cose sono state mutate in molte parti del giardino*." Whether or not Tribolo had prepared a specific design for this fountain, Baldinucci's text seems to imply that Prince Francesco invited Giovanni Bologna to make his own design, adapted to the great basin: "Io ho fatto cavar questo fasso come tu vedi, per fare una bella fonte per lo Giardino: siadunque tuo pensiero il fare essa fonte in modo, che la tazza faccia honore a te, e l'opere tue alla tazza." (*Baldinucci*, vii, 92–93.) The existence of the drawing, with notations in Giovanni Bologna's handwriting, is further evidence in support of his design: Anny E. Popp, Old Master Drawings, vol. ii, no. 6 (September, 1927), p. 23 and Pl. 27. For my knowledge of this drawing I am indebted to Mr. Arthur Hind, who first called my attention to this article; the photograph of the drawing I owe to the courtesy of the late Henry Oppenheimer. The fountain was set up in the Isolotto in 1618 according to the inscription; see *Cambiagi*, p. 52, and *Soldini*, p. 70, note. On the restoration of the figure of Oceanus, in the Bargello, see Edoardo Marchionni, Rivista d'Arte (1909), vi, 161.

*Page 62*. Fountain of Venus in the Grotticella: *Baldinucci*, vii, 106, "E per la grotticina ch' è dopo la grotta grande di Bernardo Buontalenti nel Giardino di Boboli a Pitti, fece [Giovanni Bologna] una bella femmina, che fu posta sopra la tazza d'una fonte; figura attitudinata per modo, che osservata da quante vedute si vogliano, apparisce in atto maravigliosamente grazioso"; *Desjardins*, p. 93; *Gaye*, iii, 460, no. cccxc; *Brinckmann*, B. S., p. 95.

*Page 63.* Fountain of Bacchus, Victoria and Albert Museum. Usually dated about 1600, and attributed to some follower of Giovanni Bologna, according to Mr. Eric Maclagan. The water *motifs* of this fountain are indicated in a drawing by Mr. H. Inigo Triggs: *Triggs*, F. G. E., pt. III, Pl. 119.

*Page 64.* Fountain of Samson and the Philistine. The pen drawing, no. 1411 in the Uffizi collection, has been attributed both to Giovanni Bologna and to Giulio Parigi. The style seems that of the sixteenth century. The wash drawing, touched in color, no. 1416 in the same collection, generally attributed to Pietro Tacca, is certainly by a seventeenth century hand. P. N. Ferri, who first published both the wash drawing and the group in England, gave the latter to Tacca on the basis of the attribution of the drawing: Rivista d'Arte, v (1907), 55–58. Randall Davies, in the Burlington Magazine (January, 1929, p. 27 ff.), traces the movements of the terminal group, but does not reproduce the original. Sir William Worsley writes me that it was exhibited in the Burlington Exhibition of Italian Art, 1930, although not listed in the catalogue. Drawing no. 1411 was shown at that exhibition: I, 263, and no. 844 in A Commemorative Catalogue of the Exhibition of Italian Art (Burlington House, London, 1931); *Desjardins*, pp. 149–150, on the two drawings of this "lost" fountain; *Borghini*, p. 586, "Poi lavorò nel Casino del Gran Duca Francesco la bellissima figura del marmo rappresentante Sansone, che ha sotto un Filisteo, che e sopra la Fontana nel Cortile, dove sono i semplici"; *Baldinucci*, VII, 91–92, "Ebbe Gio. Bologna per lo Casino del Granduca Francesco a scolpire il gruppo del Sansone, che ha sotto un Filisteo, al quale fu dato luogo sopra la fontana del Cortile de' Semplici, ove fece ancora bellissime bizzarrie di mostri marini, che reggevano la tazza. In questo statua del Sansone parve che Gio. Bologna superasse se stesso, conciofosseco sachè gli riuscisse il tenerla alquanto più lontano da un certo ammannierato che hanno alcune delle cose sue, e per conseguenza assai più simile al naturale, e vero." Baldinucci (VII, 92) also records its passage to Spain: "Quella fonte poi fu dal Granduca Ferdinando mandata in dono al Duca di Lelma in Ispagna insieme con un' altra, ov' era Sansone, che sbarra la bocca al Leone, fatta da Cristofano Stati da Bracciano." (On this companion fountain see Appendix B, p. 138, of the present work.) See also *Vasari*, VII, 646–647, in the section "Alcuni Schiaramenti," already referred to: "Nel 1601 tanto il gruppo, quanto la tazza e gli altri ornamenti furono mandati dal Granduca Ferdinando in Ispagna a donare al conte di Lerma, primo ministro di Filippo III"; C. Justi, II, 248: "Im Jahre 1602 erhielt Lerma die Fontana, welche Gian Bologna 1559 für das Casino des Erzherzogs Franz gearbeitet hatte, mit der Gruppe Simsons und des Philisters, die Schale von Meerwesen getragen; und als Gegenstücke Simson mit dem Löwen von Cristofano Stati; er brachte sie in seinem Garten zu Valladolid." By 1623 the fountain had passed into the hands of King Philip IV, for in that year he presented the terminal group of Samson and the Philistine to the Prince of Wales, then visiting at Valladolid: Don José Martí y Monsó, Estudios Histórico-Artístico Relativos Principalmente a Valladolid, p. 616 and n. 3. After Philip III, many works of art were removed from Valladolid, which was no longer a center for the court, so that its passage to Aranjuez can easily be accounted for. It is of course possible that the extant basin is the one of the companion fountain, crowned by Stati's figure; if so, it must have been an exact copy of the original. On the traditional ascription of the monkeys to Giovanni Bologna see *Desjardins*, p. 137. Was the monkey a favorite device of Francesco, or of Bianca Cappello? One appears just below the shell-like lunette over the portal of the Casino di San Marco, in the garden of which this fountain stood. *Desjardins* (p. 22) dates the fountain 1559, evidently because Borghini mentions it immediately after works of that date; but this is impossible, since Vasari speaks of the group as "almost finished" in his second edition, published in January, 1568 (1569, new style). Probably the fountain is to be dated about 1570, the date usually given to the Casino di San Marco. *Vasari*'s text (VII, 629) reads: "E quasi condotto a fine al Signor Principe un Sansone, grande quanto il vivo, il quale combatte a piedi con *due* Filistei." The discrepancy in number naturally raises the question whether Vasari referred to the same group as Borghini and Baldinucci; but as both state that the work was made for Prince Francesco, they evidently had the same statue in mind. Vasari is notoriously inaccurate in such details.

*Page 66*. Fountains on the rim of the Boboli Isolotto, designed by Giulio Parigi, with figures by Domenico Pieratti and Cosimo Salvestrini: *Grünwald*, pp. 33 ff., with illustrations of Pieratti's figures, Abb. 25–26, 28–29, 31; *Cambiagi*, p. 54 ff.; *Soldini*, p. 67 and Pls. XXXIV, XL; *Guidi*, p. 44 and n. 1.

*Page 66*. Tacca's Fountains in the Piazza della SS. Annunziata: *Guidi*, pp. 43–44; *Baldinucci*, XII, 162, "Le due fonti di mettallo destinate situarsi in sul molo di Livorno presso alli soprannotati Colossi, per far' acqua alle galere; al che essendosi per ragioni, che a noi non sono note, forte apposto, e contro il gusto del Tacca Andrea Arrighetti Proveditore delle Fortezze, e soprintendente delle Fabbriche, fu poi dato loro luogo in Firenze, in sulla Piazza della Santissima Nonziata." Again, on p. 178, in discussing Tacca's skill in casting separate parts in bronze: "Usò si fatte diligenze, ed artefizi in ogni sua opera, ma particolarmente nel sopraddetto Cavallo per Ispagna, e nell' Arpie delle Fonti della Nonziata, nelle quali le ritorte code son gettate di per se, e poi attaccate." Documents which place the date of these fountains between their commission, *c.* 1626, and their instalment in the Piazza della SS. Annunziata on June 14, 1641, are quoted by *Vullo Bianchi*, pp. 161–162, 202–204, 210–212.

*Page 67*. Fountain by Francavilla at Pisa: *Baldinucci*, VIII, 79–80, "Il Granduca Ferdinando diede gli [Pietro Francavilla] a fare la fontana di Pisa in sulla Piazza de' Cavalieri colla grande statua di Cosimo I, fondatore di quella Religione di S. Stefano." See also *Desjardins*, p. 108.

## CHAPTER VII

*Page 68.* Fontana della Piazza Pretoria at Palermo. See Walter Biehl's articles on Francesco and Camillo Camilliani in *Thieme-Becker*, vol. v; Gerolamo de Fonzo Ardizzono's article on the fountain in Le Vie d'Italia (Oct., 1924), xxx, no. 10, pp. 1128 ff.; *Maresca*, pp. 15–18. *Vasari* (vii, 628) speaks of the fountain while it was still at Florence, mentioning particularly the statues of the Arno and Mugnone, and praising the latter extravagantly: "Il Mugnone . . . può stare al paragone di qualsi voglia statua di maestro eccellente." Milanesi, in n. 2 on the page cited, reports the signature of "Angelus Vagherinus Florentinus" on one of the figures. This is of course a misreading for "M. Angelus Nacherinus," which appears on the Nile and one of the standing female figures: *Maresca*, p. 15. See also G. Ceci's article on Michelangelo Naccherino in *Thieme-Becker*, vol. xxv.

*Page 71.* The Isoletta in the Giardino dei Semplici: Descrizione di Firenze nell' Anno 1598 in A. von Reumont, Memorie Varie, i (Florence, 1859), 16; Ferdinando del Migliore, Firenze Illustrata (Florence, 1684), p. 239; *Vasari*, vii, 636. The plan of the garden showing the central octagonal island, in the Istituto Botanico at Florence, is reproduced on p. 8 of Guglielmo Volpi's article, "Intorno All' Origine del Giardino dei Semplici di Firenze," Archivio Storico Italiano, ser. vii, vol. ix, 1 (1928).

Fontana Medina at Naples: A. Colombo, Napoli Nobilissima (1897), pp. 65–70; *Sobotka*, P. B., p. 408; *Muñoz*, P. B., pp. 433–435. An illustration in the latter article shows the fountain in its previous site. See also *Maresca*, pp. 51–52.

*Page 71.* Boboli Isolotto: *Cambiagi*, pp. 52 ff.; *Soldini*, pp. 67 ff.; *Grünwald*, p. 33 and *passim*.

## CHAPTER VIII

*Page 73.* Alberti, De Re Aedificatoria, vol. ix, chap. iv.
On Poggio Reale, *Gothein*, i, 231; on Bembo, *ibid.*, i, 231–232.

*Pages 73–74.* Fountain of the Valley, Villa Madama: *Vasari*, vi, 556.
Annibal Caro's letter: *Bottari-Ticozzi*, v, 268 ff., no. xci.
Antonio da San Gallo to Cosimo I: *Gaye*, ii, 344, no. ccxxxix.
*Vasari* on stalactites: i, 140–143.

*Page 74.* Grotto at Castello: *Vasari*, vi, 77, "Comminciò il Tribolo a murare la detta grotta per farla con tre nicchie e con bel disegno d' architettura"; on p. 75, speaking of Tribolo's plans, "E nel muro dirimpetto alla porta che sostiene la terra del monte, aveva a essere nel mezzo una grotta con tre pile, nella quale piovesse artifiziosamente acqua"; and on p. 78, "Seguitando poi il Tribolo l'opera del condotto, fece venire l' acqua della grotta"; *Montaigne*, p. 112, "There is also a handsome grotto, in which are to be seen all sorts of animals, copied to the life, spouting out the water of these fountains, some by the beak, others by the wings, some by the nail, or the ears, or the nostril." Dr. Ernst Kris' brilliant article "Der Stil Rustique" is indispensable to any student of rustic fountains: Jahrbuch der Kunsthistorischen Sammlungen in Wien (1926), pp. 137–208. On p. 200 he dates this grotto *c.* 1580. The letter for the dating of the birds is given by *Gaye*, III, 246, CCXXI, dated May 4, 1567, "Et così io potrò avanzare spesa et molto tempo, quale meterò nela fine di questo [*sic*] uccelli, che adesse a le stagion calda, seccando assai la tera [*sic*], si avanseranno molto"; *Borghini*, p. 588, "Ne ho fatto mentione . . . di molti ritratti di bronzo fatti dal naturale, che sono nella Grotta di Castello"; *Baldinucci*, VII, 106, "Per la grotta della medesima [the villa of Castello] gettò alcuni uccelli pure di bronzo."

*Pages 75–76.* Boboli Grotticina: *Vasari*, VI, 188, "Servivasi ancora la duchessa assai di Baccio [Bandinelli] nel Giardino de' Pitti, dove ella aveva fatto fare una grotta piena di tartari e di spugne congelate dall' acqua, dentrovi una fontana, dove Baccio aveva fatto condurre di marmo a Giovanni Fancelli suo creato un pilo grande, et alcune capre quanto il vivo, che gettano acqua." The date in the fifties implied by this passage (Bandinelli died at the opening of the year 1560) is confirmed by detailed documents in the State Archives:

*A. S. F.*, Fabbriche, LXVIII, 68 verso: payment on April 14, 1554, to twelve porters for carrying "la capra di marmo del Bandinello" from the Opera del Duomo to Pitti for the grotto. *Ibid.*, p. 74: a series of payments on September 15, 1554 to Giovanni Fancelli, sculptor, for the following works in this grotto: the oval basin, with its paws and the reliefs of two putti with capricorns; two heads of goats with necks; ram's head to spout water; eight paws for the goats; marble doorway, with cornice; arms of "Their Excellences" over the door, of *pietra forte*; two branches of *pietra bigia* at the head of the grotto, where the two goats go; two torsos of goats, of marble; and payments for joining the heads and paws of the goats to the torsos with pivots; etc. (It was originally planned to have the bodies of the goats made of stalactites instead of marble, but the Duchess changed her mind!)

According to *Soldini* (p. 30, n. 1) the basin was moved to the Pitti façade in 1696. See also *Cambiagi*, pp. 26–27.

*Page 76.* Grottoes at Pratolino: *De Vieri*, pp. 33–40, 42–44; *Sgrilli*, pp. 18, 21; *Montaigne*, p. 106, "There is a marvel of a grotto with many niches and rooms; this part exceeds anything we ever saw elsewhere. It is formed and all crusted over with a certain material which they say is brought from some particular mountains, and they have joined it together with invisible nails. There is not only music and harmony produced, by the movement of the water, but also the movement of statues and doors with different actions, which the water sets going, numerous animals that dive and drink, and like things. . . . By a single movement the whole grotto is filled with water, and all the seats squirt water up to your back side; and if you fly from the grotto and run up the castle stairs, if any one takes a pleasure in that sort of thing, he may let loose a thousand jets of water from every two steps of that staircase, which will drench you till you reach the top of the house!"

*Page 77.* The Mugnone is named by *De Vieri* (p. 42) and by *Sgrilli* (p. 21). This figure is mentioned by the Duke of Württemberg in his records of his Italian journey of 1599: "Bratelino — Unter einer gewölbten Stiegen an vorgen dachtem Palatio, ist ein schöner Neptunus von Stein gehauen, welchen der Kunstreiche Meister Iohan da Bolonia zu Florenz gemacht hat. Zu hinderst unter diser Stiegen ist ein Engel mit einer Posaunen" (*Württemberg*, p. 51). A comparison of this passage with Stefano della Bella's etching of the interior of this grotto (Fig. 168) proves that the Mugnone is the statue referred to. For a terracotta *bozzetto* by Giovanni Bologna in the Kaiser Friedrich Museum, Berlin (no. I 270), which may have served as a model for this figure, see the references cited on pp. 122–123.

On the grotto containing the bronze satyr see *Sgrilli*, p. 23: "Dall' altra parte della lavandaia verso ponente, vi sono altri vivai, ed una grotticella con un sorgente d' acqua freschissima, detta la fonte di Calciuoli, che esce da un fiasco, che tiene in mano un satirino di bronzo e da una piccola botte di marmo [this last evidently the cask on which the satyr sat]." According to the Catalogue of the Bargello (*Supino*, p. 390, no. 30), this figure came from Castello; but that would not prevent its origin at Pratolino, for most of the statues and fountains of this villa were removed to other Medicean villas in the latter years of the eighteenth century; see *Da Prato*, p. 271, n. 1.

*Page 77.* Grotto of Buontalenti at Boboli. The formless effect of this grotto is admirably conveyed by Kris, *op. cit.*, p. 201. See also *Soldini*, pp. 30–34; *Baldinucci*, VII, 14–15; *Cambiagi*, pp. 19 ff. In 1591 the group by Vincenzo de' Rossi was already in place; see *Bocchi*, pp. 68–70. Documents in the State Archives give the dates of this grotto as follows:

*A. S. F.*, Fabbriche, LXI, 24 verso, mentions August 29, 1583, as the day when the grotto was commenced; Fabbriche, LXII, 137 verso, lists payments on April 27, 1585, for raising in place "le 4 fiure abozzate di marmo de' canti di detta." Fabbriche, LIII, 131, records a payment, on August 12, 1589, for finishing the three niches of the last room of the grotto (where Giovanni Bologna's Venus is). Other works and decoration continued till about 1593.

*Page 78.* On the façade of the grotto see *A. S. F.*, Fabbriche, III, 47, XX, 6 verso. The latter, dated 1557, mentions Vasari's design for the façade. See also *Vasari*, VI, 180 (speaking of the Apollo of Bandinelli), "E sua Eccellenza lo fece mettere nella facciata del vivaio che è nel giardino de' Pitti, col disegno ed architettura di Giorgio Vasari."

On the grotto at the end of the Pitti courtyard see *Grünwald*, pp. 39 ff.; *Soldini*, pp. 11–13; *Cambiagi*, pp. 11 ff.; *Baldinucci*, XIV, 68, 199, 200, XVI, 202. *Baldinucci* (XII, 167–168) gives the marble putti to Giampetroni, pupil of Pietro

Tacca, after wax models by Tacca; *Vullo Bianchi* (p. 183) returns them to Ludovico Salvetti. So the Archives: *A. S. F.*, Fabbriche, xxxiv, 116, June 13, 1636, records a payment for mending the road over which were to be brought "i marmi . . . a Lodovico Salvetti scultore, che servano per fare puttini per la grotta del cortile"; and in *A. S. F.*, Fabbriche, cxl, 32, we learn that the Duke gave an order in 1635 "che le dua nichie della medesima grotta dove si devono fare le dua fontane si dieno a Lodovico Salvetti scultore."

*Page 79.* Grotto of Polyphemus: *Baldinucci*, xvi, 207–208.

*Page 79.* Fountain of the Triton at Genoa: *Vasari*, vi, 645–646, "Finita la detta chiesa [San Matteo], il medesimo principe Doria fece mettere mano al suo palazzo e far gli nuove aggiunte di fabriche e giardini bellissimi, che furono fatti con ordine del frato; il quale, avendo in ultimo fatto dalle parte dinanzi di detto palazzo un vivaio, fece di marmo un mostro marino di tondo rilievo, che versa in gran copia acqua nella detta peschiera"; and "Simile al qual mostro ne fece un altro a que' signori, che fu mandato in Ispagna al Granvela." For the attribution of the present figure to Valsoldo see Milanesi, n. 1 to the passage cited above, and in protest Alizeri, Notizie dei Professori del Disegno in Liguria (Genoa, 1877), v, 347; also *Vasari*, G. G., vol. vii, pt. 1, p. 415, n. 30 a. See also the article on Montorsoli in *Thieme-Becker*, vol. xxv.

*Page 80.* Ammannati's Apennine at Castello: *Vasari*, viii, 340; *Gaye*, iii, 90; letter from Ammannati to Duke Cosimo, dated February 3, 1563, "Io ho fornito la figura dell' Apennino di cera, che va a Castello, e per cagione de' tempi cattivi del verno non ho fatto la forma, ma hora la seguiterò e farolla." According to the Medici account books, on March 3, 1564 (1565, new style), a payment was made to a truckman for moving the Apennine to Castello (*A. S. F.*, Fabbriche, l, 20), and on April 28, 1565, a payment was made for bringing to Castello "legni," used to raise the figure in place (*A. S. F.*, Fabbriche, l, 27). See also *Montaigne*, p. 111.

*Page 81.* On the Esculapius and Perseus at Pratolino see *De Vieri*, p. 32, and *Sgrilli*, p. 11. On Novelli's Island of Polyphemus see *Baldinucci*, xvi, 208. On the Apennine at Pratolino see *Montaigne*, p. 107; *Sgrilli*, pp. 9–11; *De Vieri*, pp. 27 ff.; *Baldinucci*, vii, 103–104 (there interpreted as Jupiter Pluvius!). See *Brinckmann*, B. B., i, 76–79 and Pls. 28, 29, for two terracotta *bozzetti* which served as preparatory studies for this fountain; also page 123, above.

## CHAPTER IX

*Page 83.* Rustici's "Mercury": *Vasari*, vi, 602; and the posthumous article by C. Loeser, Burlington Magazine, lii (June, 1928), 266 and Pl. i.

*Page 84.* Tribolo's "Nature": Paul Vitry, Musée National de Louvre, Catalogue des Sculptures du Moyen Age et Renaissance (Paris, 1922), p. 99, no. 813; *Vasari*, vi, 61. After describing this figure, which Tribolo made at the order of Giovanbattista della Palla for Francis I, Vasari continues, "In the next year, 1529"; therefore the date must be 1528. Vasari describes the figure as raising only one arm.

*Page 84.* Boy with a Goose in the Pitti Palace: *Reymond*, IV, 144, n. 2; p. 10, n. 2 of this work; *Gramberg*, p. 225. On the boy with the geese see Valentiner, Bulletin of the Detroit Institute of Art (May, 1932), where it is attributed to Pierino da Vinci.

*Page 85.* Putto at Arezzo. This was formerly incorrectly attributed to Giovanni Bologna; *Desjardins* (pp. 136–137) illustrates a similar figure in the Museum at Douai. See also *Middeldorf*, A. W. P. V., p. 305; *Vasari*, VI, 121; *Gramberg*, p. 224.

*Page 85.* Putto on the Fontana delle Scimmie at Boboli: *Vasari*, VI, 122, "Lavorò, dopo questo, un fanciullo che stringe un pesce che getti acqua per bocca, per le fonti di Castello."

Terracotta group of putti squeezing a fish, Victoria and Albert Museum, no. A 72. 1910: *Vasari*, VI, 122, "Ed avendogli dato il Tribolo un pezzo di marmo maggiore, ne cavò Piero due putti che s'abbracciano l'un l'altro, e strignendo pesci, gli fanno schizzare acqua per bocca. Furono questi putti sì graziosi nelle teste e nella persona, e con sì bella maniera condotti di gambe, di braccia, e di capelli che già si potette vedere che egli arebbe condotto ogni difficile lavoro a perfezione." Heinz Gottschalk, *op. cit.*, p. 93, rejects them from Rossellino's *oeuvre*.

*Page 86.* Group of Boy and Girl, Victoria and Albert Museum, no. 8527. 1863.

River God, Louvre, dated 1548–1549 by A. M. Vandelli, Rivista d'Arte, ser. II, XV, no. I, (January–March, 1933), 109–113; no. 680, Musée National du Louvre: Catalogue des Sculptures du Moyen Age et Renaissance, p. 83, "Attribué autrefois à Andrea Sansovino. Provenant du palais des ducs de Balzo, à Naples. Legs. Schlichting 1915." See *Vasari*, VI, 126, and *Middeldorf*, A. W. P. V., p. 300; Carlo Gamba (Dedalo, September, 1929, p. 236 ff.) attributes this figure to Tribolo. On the restoration of the Ganymede by Cellini see *Plon*, pp. 215, 216, n. 1. Cellini restored the head, arms, and feet, and added the eagle. The work was done for Cosimo I in 1546 and 1547 and placed over a door in the Pitti Palace. As Pierino was then working for the Duke at Castello, he was undoubtedly familiar with the original statue.

*Page 87.* Fishing Boys, Bargello: *Borghini*, p. 586, "E per un' altra fonte [Giovanni Bologna] gittò tre fanciulli di bronzo," following a mention of another fountain in the court of the Casino di San Marco; *Baldinucci*, VII, 92, "Per un' altra fonte pure nel casino di S. Marco gettò due fanciulli di bronzo in atto di pescare all' amo"; *Desjardins* (p. 153) lists the two under "Lost Works." The drawing is reproduced after a plate from Reproductions in Facsimile of Drawings of the Old Masters in the Collection of the Earl of Pembroke and Montgomery at Wilton House, by Mr. Arthur Strong (London, 1900), pt. III, no. 30. I am indebted to Dr. Giovanni Poggi for a reference to this fountain in an inventory of the seventeenth century: *A. S. F.*, Guardaroba, MDCLXVI, 249, 1667, "Tre putti di bronzo sedenti sopra pesci di bronzo, quali stavano su a una Tazza di Marmo nel Giardino del Casino di S. Marco in atto di pescare al' Amo," etc.; also a notation on the opposite page of the inventory.

*Page 88.* Flying Mercury, Bargello: see p. 120 of this work.

*Pages 88–89.* Tritons attributed to Cellini: Bode, Collection of J. Pierpont Morgan, Bronzes of the Renaissance and Subsequent Periods (Paris, 1910), vol. II, Pl. LXXXIV, no. 121, p. 5, pp. xxviii and xxix in vol. I on the one now in the Frick Collection, New York; references to the Thiers bronze and the one in the Benda Collection, which I have never seen, in *Bode*, I. B. S., vol. II, Pl. CLXIX and p. 41. *Desjardins*, Appendix O, p. 129, on the triton by Giovanni Bologna, sent to France.

*Page 89.* Marble triton at Palermo: W. Biehl in *Thieme-Becker* (V, 440) attributes this to Camillo Camilliani. In Don Vincenzo di Giovanni's Del Palermo Restaurato in vol. I, ser. II, p. 155, of Biblioteca Storica e Letteraria di Sicilia, this figure is described in its original site: "Nel giardino vi è una fonte con un Glauco di marmo, che sona la sua buccina, di tal manifattura, che disse il signor Don Marco Antonio un giorno, che se quella fosse in Roma, si pagherebbe dieci mila ducati." The reference to Marc Antonio Colonna dates it before 1584, when he left Sicily. See also p. 137 of this work.

*Page 90.* Taddeo Landini, Figures on the Tortoise Fountain. The fountain was designed by Giacomo della Porta (1581) and the figures executed by Landini in 1585–88. See *Guidi*, pp. 23, 61–63; *Colasanti*, pp. xxvii–xxviii. An engraving by *Parasacchi* of c. 1647 does not show the turtles, which were undoubtedly added during the pontificate of Alexander VII (1665–67), since an inscription of his time mentions additions to the fountain. See also p. 90, n. 1 of this work.

*Page 90.* Bandini, Tritons: Middeldorf, Rivista d'Arte, VII (October–December, 1929), 506–508. Maclagan, Burlington Magazine, XXXVI (1920), 239, has proposed to identify with the lost central figure a marble Jason in the Victoria and Albert Museum. It seems to me that our knowledge of Bandini's style is not as yet sufficiently complete to enable us either to accept this figure outright, or to reject it as Dr. Middeldorf does. See *Borghini*, pp. 637–638, and *Baldinucci*, x, 183.

*Page 90.* Venus and Cupid, Kaiser Friedrich Museum: *Schottmüller* (I. S. B., p. 153, Abb. 364, no. I 1964) gives this simply to the Florentine school, c. 1570; *Brinckmann* (B. S., p. 75 and Abb. 84) assigns it to the School of Ammannati.

*Page 91.* Vincenzo dei Rossi's Adonis: *Borghini*, p. 597; *Baldinucci*, x, 140; *Grünwald*, p. 22 ff.

*Page 91.* Venus by Pietro Francavilla, loan to Fogg Museum: *Wiles*, F. P. F., pp. 68–72; *Baldinucci*, VIII, 74–75. See also the brochure on this figure privately printed by Durlacher Brothers (London, 1924), pp. 1–2.

*Page 92.* Orpheus, Louvre: *Baldinucci*, VIII, 82; no. 1296 in the Louvre catalogue. Signed and dated 1598. From the Hôtel de Gondi (later Condé) at Paris it found its way to the gardens of Versailles.

*Page 92.* Battista Lorenzi, Group of Alpheus and Arethusa: *Borghini*, p. 598; *Baldinucci*, x, 149. This work is dated in the seventeenth century by *Colasanti* (Pl. 259).

*Page 93.* Silenus with Panther, attributed to Stoldo Lorenzi: *Schottmüller*, I. S. B., pp. 156–157, Abb. 373, no. I 292.

*Page 93.* Genius of the Medici: Young, The Medici, II, 364, 3rd ed. (London, 1928), gives no authority for his statement that the figure was executed for Ferdinand; *Triggs*, A. G. I., p. 74; *Sgrilli*, p. 15, "Dall' altra parte per lo lungo della grotta [Grotta Grande] vi è un fanciullo, che ha una grossa palla somigliante a una mappamondo, girato dall' acqua, e ne getta assai fuori."

*Page 93.* Louvre, Pythian Apollo, no. 682 in the Louvre catalogue, where it is entitled "Hercules fighting with the Hydra!" According to the catalogue it adorned at different times the Château de Rueil, the Gardens of Marly, and those at St. Cloud. The various attributions and numerous articles on this figure are indicated in the recent article on Michelangelo in vol. XXIV of *Thieme-Becker*, by Panofsky and Tolnai.

*Page 94.* Cupid attributed to Michelangelo, Victoria and Albert Museum. Mr. Eric Maclagan reviews all the previous literature in Art Studies (1928), pp. 3 ff., and draws interesting parallels with models by Michelangelo; see also Kriegbaum in Jahrbuch den Kunsthistorischen Sammlungen in Wien, N. F. III (1929), 247–257.

## CHAPTER X

*Page 96.* Peasant emptying a cask, by Bandinelli-Fancelli: *Vasari*, VI, 188, "Nel giardino de' Pitti . . . Baccio aveva fatto condurre di marmo a Giovanni Fancelli suo creato un pilo grande . . . e parimente col modello fatto da se stesso per un vivaio, un villano che vota un barile pieno d'acqua."

*Page 96.* Actual figure of peasant, Boboli. *Soldini* (Pl. XLI and p. 74) ascribes this figure to Cioli; but the earlier writers on Pratolino do not: *De Vieri*, p. 53; *Sgrilli*, p. 25.

*Page 97.* Fountains of Morgante and Pietro Barbino: *Baldinucci* (x, 152), and after him *Cambiagi* (p. 19) and *Soldini* (p. 35), wrongly identify the dwarf on the tortoise with Barbino; but see *Vasari*, VII, 639, "Ed il simile [Valerio Cioli] ha fatto poi nel palazzo de' Pitti a molte statue che ha condotto per ornamento d' una gran sala il Duca, il quale ha fatto fare al medesimo, di marmo, la statua di Morgante nano, ignuda; la quale è tanto bella, e così simile al vero riuscita, che forse non e mai stato veduto altro mostro così ben fatto, nè condotto con tanta diligenza simile al naturale e proprio; e parimente gli ha fatto condurre la statua di Pietro detto Barbino, nano, ingegnoso, letterato e molto gentile, favorito dal Duca nostro; per le quali, dico, tutte cagioni ha meritato Valerio che gli sia stata allogata da sua Eccellenza la detta statua che va alla sepoltura del Buonarroto." See also *Borghini*, p. 600, and *Gaye*, III, 163. Dr. Kurt Busse's article on Valerio Cioli in VII, 4, of *Thieme-Becker* confuses the earlier and later dwarfs.

*Bocchi*, p. 68. *A. S. F.*, Fabbriche, LXII, 92 verso records the mending of the conduit of Morgante and Barbino on June 2, 1584; LXIII, 10, mentions a payment made May 24, 1585, for a pipe used for "la fighura di marmo di Barbino che gietta aqqua." Therefore both dwarfs were utilized as fountain figures.

*Page 97.* The figures for Pratolino: *Borghini*, p. 600, "Ha poi fatto al Gran Duca Francesco una Satira di marmo, che mugne una pecora, e dalle poppe esce l'acqua in cambio di latte; e di macigno una donna maggiore del naturale, che premendo un panno di marmo, finto bagnato, ne fa cader l'acqua fuori, e à canto le è un fanciullino, che alzatasi la camicia dinanzi, quasi scherzando, piscia; e ha sculpito ancora un contadino, che miete, maggiore del vivo, le quei figure sono nella meravigliosa Villa di Pratolino." Laundress: *Montaigne*, p. 106; *De Vieri*, p. 45; *Sgrilli*, p. 22. Mower: *De Vieri*, p. 51; *Baccini*, p. 13. Satyress: *De Vieri*, p. 53; *Baccini*, p. 13.

*Page 97.* The Lavacapo at Boboli. Busse confuses this with the laundress at Pratolino, which was of *macigno*. Luisa Becherucci (x, 384, Enciclopedia Italiana) attributes this figure to Cioli. It is described in its original location by *Cambiagi* (p. 34): see also *Soldini*, note to pp. 20–21. I have found a specific reference to this group which shows that it was completed by 1599: *A. S. F.*, Fabbriche, CXXII, 25, 25 verso. There Valerio Cioli asks permission to go to Carrara to obtain marble to make two dwarfs and two peasants to accompany this figure, already completed: "Per accompagnare la lavacapo, che e di gia fatta." A letter quoted by *Gaye* (III, 520–521) gives the *terminus post quem* of 1597.

*Page 98.* The four figures commenced in 1599: *Baldinucci*, x, 151–152; *A. S. F.*, Fabbriche, CXXII, 25, 25 verso, 28 verso, 29. Death of Cioli, recorded in *A. S. F.*, Archivio della Grascia, Libro dei Morti del 1581–1601, "Valerio di Simone Ciolli Scultore sepolto nell' Annunziata a 25 Dicembre 1599." Work by Simone Cioli: *A. S. F.*, Fabbriche, CXXII, 101 verso; Fabbriche, CXXIII, 31, 31 verso, 32; *Baldinucci*, XI, 162; *Soldini*, pp. 65–66 and Pl. XXXIII; *Inghirami*, p. 135.

*Page 98.* "Fountain of Ammannati": see *Sgrilli*, p. 25 and his map of the villa.

*Page 99.* Genre figures by the Master of the Gänsemännchen: Simon Meller, Die Deutsche Bronzestatuetten der Renaissance (Munich, 1926), pp. 31 ff. and Pls. 42–45. These figures were formerly attributed to Pankraz Labenwolf; see the article by D. Stern on that artist in *Thieme-Becker*, vol. XXII.

Letter on the Arrotino: *Gaye*, III, 240–241, no. ccxvi.

*Page 100.* A small bronze of a dwarf (Morgante?) is preserved in the Kaiser Friedrich Museum: no. I 7107, *Goldschmidt*, p. 34 and Abb. 158; while a clay model for the latter, with a tortoise, is preserved in the same collection: *Schottmüller*, I. S. B., p. 151, no. I 2434, Abb. 360. These do not seem to me to be in the style of Valerio Cioli, in so far as we know it from his marble works and from the bronze candelabrum in the Bargello.

Tacca's Porcellino: *Vullo Bianchi*, p. 187, for the date of 1612; documents given on pp. 209–213; *Baldinucci*, XII, 163, "Nel getto del cignale di Mercato Nuovo sopra l'Antico della R. Galleria."

## CHAPTER XI

*Page 101.* On sculpture in Rome at the end of the sixteenth century see *Reymond*, B., p. 17: *Brinckmann*, B. S., pp. 177 ff.

*Page 102.* Neptune and Glaucus: Maclagan, Burlington Magazine, XL (March 10, 1922), 115, "The death of Cardinal Montalto in June, 1623 gives the earliest possible date." See also Muñoz, L'Arte, XIX (1916), 107–109, XX (1917), 49–50; Fraschetti (pp. 36–37, 439) dates it 1629. He knew only the engraving of Dorigny: Maffei's Raccolta di Statue (Rome, 1704), Pl. LXXI. The Venturini etching of the pool at the Villa Montalto is no. 17 in vol. III of *Falda*.

*Page 103.* Lost statue of Venus Anadyomene: *Baldinucci*, XX, 142, "Mentre avendo pochissima acqua e quella con zampilli sottilissimi, figurò una femmina, che dopo essersi lavata la testa, spreme i capelli dai quali appunto esce tanta acqua, quanta ne può dar la fonte, ed abbisogna all'azione della figura." *Fraschetti*, pp. 119, 440; Muñoz, L'Arte, XIX (August, 1916), 157; *Dami*, p. 43, n. 30, for date of 1626, based upon that of the villa.

*Page 103.* The statues of the four river gods compared with Florentine prototypes of the sixteenth century: *Muñoz*, R. B., p. 178, "Pensiamo ad altre statue di fiumi da cui il Bernini si ispirò. Quelle nella fontana dell' Isolotto a Firenze [1576], le tre figure di uomini dai nudi vigorosi prenunziano le statue del Bernini, ma stanno sedute compostamente."

*Page 103.* Fontana del Moro in the Piazza Navona: *Guidi*, pp. 23, 46, 78–80; *Voss*, pp. 124–126; *Fraschetti*, pp. 201–205. The statue was executed in travertine after Bernini's model by Giovanni Antonio Mari. To the basin, carved in the time of Gregory XIII (1572–1585), were added, in the closing years of the Cinquecento or opening years of the Seicento, four tritons, the work of Taddeo Landini and others. An engraving showing the tritons only is included in *Parasacchi*.

*Page 104.* Villa Mattei, lost Fountain of the Triton: *Falda*, vol. III, no. 19, for the etching by Venturini; *Guidi*, pp. 31, 32, 42; *Voss*, pp. 105–107; *Fraschetti*, p. 119.

Fountain of the Triton in the Piazza Barberini: *Guidi*, pp. 43, 71–72; *Voss*, pp. 107–109; *Fraschetti*, pp. 123–124.

*Page 105.* Fountain of the Four Rivers: *Guidi*, pp. 45, 73–78; *Voss*, pp. 109–114; *Fraschetti*, pp. 179–195.

# APPENDIX B

## LOST FOUNTAINS

BERNINI, GIOVANNI LORENZO
Fountain of Venus Anadyomene: see pp. 103, 134.

BOLOGNA, GIOVANNI
Fountain with a bronze statue in the Casa Antella, Florence: *Cinelli*, p. 309, "E in questa un bel giardinetto con una fonte nel mezzo sopra la quale e collocata una statua di bronzo di Giovanni Bologna bellissima." According to *Desjardins*, p. 154, the basin still remained *in situ* in 1883; as I have never succeeded in gaining access to the Casa Antella, I do not know whether or not it is still there.

The Fata Morgana, a marble statue which stood in a *nymphaeum* or grotto at Il Riposo, the villa of Bernardo Vecchietti: *Borghini*, p. 250, "Esce in larga vena quest' acqua christallina à piè del colle, sopra cui è posta a l'uccellare dalla parte d'Oriente, in una grotta fatta con grande artificio, e tutta per entro vagamente dipinta, e cadendo in una gran pila ovata con dillettevol suono si fa sentire; sopra il vaso, che l'acqua riceve, e una bellissima donzella ignuda di marmo fatta dal Giambologna, in atto d'uscir d'un antro, & una mano si pone al dilicato petto, e l'altra sostiene una conca marina da cui inalzando ricade nel vaso l' acqua, che ariento vivo sembra, e questa bella donna per la Fata Morgana (da cui anticamente fu appellata questa fonte) è figurata." In 1773 the marble statue was acquired by Thomas Patch, who sold it to some collector in England: *Desjardins*, p. 154.

CACCINI, GIOVANNI
An unidentified fountain, probably for Francesco de' Medici, since it is recorded in the Medici account books: *Gaye*, III, 405: on June 23, 1573, there was delivered to Mo. Giovanni Caccini "una tazza tonda di mistio."

CAMICIA, CHIMENTI
This sculptor designed fountains in Hungary for Matthias Corvinus, *c.* 1480; no details are given. Baccio Cellini completed many of his works in Hungary (*Vasari*, II, 651).

CAMILLIANI, FRANCESCO
Many fountains for the garden of Don Luigi di Toledo, of which only the one now at Palermo is preserved. See *Vasari*, VII, 628, and p. 70 of this work.

Other fountains in Spain for the gardens of the Duke of Alba at Lagunilla: Schubert, Barock in Spanien (1906), p. 293; also p. 70, n. 4, above.

DANTI, VINCENZO

Ornaments for fountains in the garden of Signor Sforza Almeni at Fiesole: *Vasari*, VII, 631, "A Fiesole, per lo medesimo signore Sforza, fece molti ornamenti in un suo giardino ed intorno a certe fontane."

FANCELLI, GIOVANNI

Figure of a peasant emptying a cask, for the Boboli Garden: see pp. 96, 132 of this work.

Fountain consisting of a spouting horse's head of *pietra bigia*, evidently for a wall fountain in the garden adjoining the Medici stables in Florence; *A. S. F.*, Fabbriche, II, 139: on February 29, 1555 (1556, new style), a payment was recorded to Fancelli for work done in September "per la monta duna testa di cavallo fatta di pietra bigia per gitare laqua per a beverare i cavalli."

FERRUCCI, ANDREA

A marble fountain, sent to the King of Hungary: *Vasari*, IV, 479 and n. 5, "Fece anco una fonte di marmo, che fu mandata al re d'Ungheria, la quale gli acquistò grande onore." *Gaye* (II, 494) records evidence that work on this fountain was commenced in 1517. See also Fabriczy, L'Arte (1909), XII, 302.

LORENZI, ANTONIO

On his island fountain for the Giardino dei Semplici see pp. 71, 126.

*Vasari* (VII, 636) tells us that he completed the statue of Esculapius, intended for a fountain in the Villa of Castello, and designed and commenced in marble by Tribolo: see p. 139, under *Tribolo*; and *A. S. F.*, Fabbriche, II, 73 verso, quoted on p. 113 of this work.

He also made ornaments placed round the "new *vivaio*" of Castello (the Fountain of the Apennine); see p. 80 of the present work; *Vasari*, VII, 636, "È poi ha fatto alcune teste ed ornamenti, che sono d'intorno al nuovo vivaio di Castello, che è lassu alto in perpetua verzura."

LORENZI, BATTISTA

Fountain of a triton, presented to some Spanish friend of Cosimo I: *Borghini*, p. 598, "Fece poi a richiesta del Gran Duca Cosimo una fontana di marmo, che da Sua Altezza fu mandata a donare a un Signore Spagnuolo; e questa fu una tazza di marmo col piede di mistio in mezo, a cui sedeva sopra tre Delfini un Tritone maggiore del naturale." I venture to suggest that this may be the marble triton from the royal palace at Palermo, now in the courtyard of the National Museum in that city; see p. 131 and Fig. 184 of the present work. If the "Spanish gentleman" mentioned by Borghini was the viceroy of the kingdom of Naples, or some member of his family, its presence in the royal palace at Palermo could easily be explained. As Cosimo married the daughter of Don Pedro di Toledo, a viceroy of that kingdom, such a gift would be natural. For example the Duchess, Eleonora di Toledo, had sent a fountain figure (the young river god by Pierino da Vinci, now in the Louvre) to her brother Don Garzia di Toledo at Naples (*Vasari*, vi, 126, and pp. 86 and 130 of the present work). I expect to do further research upon this hypothesis, and publish my conclusions.

Fountain of a river god in *macigno* — for the Palazzo Salviati, or for some villa of the Salviati? *Borghini*, p. 599, "Per lo qual gentiluomo [Jacopo Salviati] ha etiandio sculpito in macigno un fiume a giacere, il doppio maggiore del naturale."

### MONTORSOLI, GIOVANNI ANGELO

Fountains at Messina: *Vasari*, vi, 651, "Fece anco condurre per lo muro di Santo Agnolo acqua per una fontana, e vi fece di sua mano un putto di marmo grande, che versa acqua in un vaso molto adorno e benissimo accomodato; che fu tenuta bel opera. Ed al muro della Vergine fece un' altra fontana con una vergine di sua mano, che versa acqua in un pilo; e per quella che è posta al palazzo del Signor Don Filippo Laroca fece un putto maggiore del naturale, d'una certa pietra che s'usa in Messina; il qual putto, che e in mezzo a certi mostri ed altre cose marittime, getta acqua in un vaso."

### MOSCA, FRANCESCO ("Il Moschino")

This sculptor made two fountains for the queen of France, concerning which few details are given (*Gaye*, iii, 196, 232, 248, 277, 284–285); and he was also consulted concerning a fountain at Parma (iii, 395).

### ROSSELLINO, ANTONIO

Fountain with putti in the Palazzo Medici, Florence: *Vasari*, iii, 93, "Fece nel palazzo de' Medici la fontana di marmo che è nel secondo cortile; nella quale sono alcuni fanciulli che sbarrano delfini che gettano acqua; ed è finita con somma grazia e con maniera diligentissima." On attempts to identify the basin of the fountain now in the Pitti Palace (Fig. 23) with the work by Rossellino, see the note on this passage by Milanesi; and on the attempt to see in the terracotta group of two putti in the Victoria and Albert Museum (Fig. 172) a model for these figures, see p. 130.

### RUSTICI, FRANCESCO

Was his bronze figure of a "grace pressing her breast" perhaps a fountain figure? *Vasari*, vi, 608, "Fece il medesimo una bellissima femina di bronzo, alta due braccia, finta per una Grazia, che si premeva una poppa; ma questa non si sa dove capitasse, nè in mano di cui si truovi."

### STATI, CRISTOFANO DA BRACCIANO

A fountain of Samson intended as a companion fountain to Giovanni Bologna's in the Duke of Lerma's garden at Valladolid, executed in the opening years of the Seicento. See page 64, and Baldinucci and Justi as quoted on p. 124. I believe I have found the marble terminal figure of Samson opening the lion's mouth in the Gardens of Aranjuez, and hope to publish it later.

The dates of this figure are given in records in the Medici account books. According to these it was executed between March 12, 1604, and October 20,

1607 (*A. S. F.*, Fabbriche, cxxiii, 72 verso), and crated for shipping to Spain on November 24 of that year (Fabbriche, cxxiii, 75).

TRIBOLO, NICCOLÒ

A group of putti in marble, for the Villa of Matteo Strozzi at San Casciano: *Vasari*, vi, p. 59, "Gli diede a far certi putti di pietra, e poco poi, essendogli quelli molto piacuti, due di marmo, i quali tengono un delfino che versa acqua in un vivaio, che oggi si vede a San Casciano, luogo lontano da Firenze otto miglia, nella villa del detto messer Matteo."

A wall fountain of Esculapius for the Villa at Castello; the marble figure was completed by Antonio Lorenzi: *Vasari*, vi, 82, "Al sommo di quest' acqua nel detto giardino di semplici, nel nicchio della fontana dietro a un pilo di marmo, arebbe a essere una statua d'Esculapio. . . . Poi il Tribolo, fatto il modello della detta statua d'Esculapio, cominciò a lavorare il marmo, ma impedito da altre cose, lasciò imperfetto quella figura, che poi fu finita da Antonio di Gino scultore, e suo discepolo." See also p. 137.

VERROCCHIO, ANDREA

A marble fountain figure, listed in Tommaso Verrocchio's inventory, quoted by Cruttwell, p. 243, item 4: "Una fighura di marmo che gietta acqua."

A marble fountain for King Matthias Corvinus, of Hungary? As the marble for this fountain was brought from Carrara, in 1488, when Verrocchio was busy with the equestrian statue of Colleoni, and as he died in that year, it was probably never executed. See *Vasari*, iii, 361, n. 3; *Cruttwell*, pp. 36, 214; C. Carnesecchi, *Miscellanea d'Arte*, i (August–September, 1903), 143; Fabriczy, L'Arte (1909), xii, 302–307.

VINCI, PIERINO DA

On tentative identifications with lost fountain figures by this artist see pp. 85–86, and p. 130.

# KEY TO ABBREVIATIONS

ALBERTINI . . . . . . . . . . . . . Francesco Albertini, Memoriale di Molte Statue e Pitture della Città di Firenze. First printed in 1510; reprinted, Florence, 1863.

A. S. F. . . . . . . . . . . . . . . Archivio di Stato, Firenze.

BACCINI . . . . . . . . . . . . . . Giuseppe Baccini, Pratolino, Capitolo d'Anonimo. Published with Palla Rucellai's Egloga e Canto Pastorale, Florence, 1885.

BALDINUCCI . . . . . . . . . . . . Filippo Baldinucci, Delle Notizie de' Professori del Disegno. Second edition with annotations by Domenico Maria Manni, 21 vols., Florence, 1764.

BERTAUX . . . . . . . . . . . . . . E. Bertaux, Donatello. Paris, 1910.

BIAGI . . . . . . . . . . . . . . . Luigi Biagi, Di Bartolommeo Ammannati e di Alcune di Sue Opere, L'Arte, XXVI (1923), 50–66.

BOCCHI . . . . . . . . . . . . . . Francesco Bocchi, Le Bellezze della Città di Firenze. Florence, 1591.

BODE, DENK. . . . . . . . . . . Wilhelm Bode, Denkmäler der Renaissance — Sculptur Toscanas. Munich, 1892–1905.

BODE, F. B. R. . . . . . . . . Wilhelm Bode, Florentiner Bildhauer der Renaissance. Second edition, Berlin, 1910.

BODE, I. B. R. . . . . . . . . Wilhelm Bode, Die Italienischen Bronzestatuetten der Renaissance. 3 vols., Berlin, 1907–12.

BODE, K. F. R. . . . . . . . . Wilhelm Bode, Die Kunst der Früh Renaissance. Berlin, 1923; in the Propylaean Kunst Geschichte series.

BORGHINI . . . . . . . . . . . . . Raffaello Borghini, Il Riposo. Florence, 1584.

BOTTARI-TICOZZI . . . . . . . . G. Bottari and S. Ticozzi, Raccolta di Lettere sulla Pittura, etc. Milan, 1822–25.

BRINCKMANN, B. B. . . . . . Albert E. Brinckmann, Barock Bozzetti. 4 vols., Frankfurt, 1923.

BRINCKMANN, B. S. . . . . . Albert E. Brinckmann, Barock Skulptur. Third edition, Berlin, 1932.

BRINCKMANN, S. D. B. . . Albert E. Brinckmann, Süddeutsche Bronzebildhauer des Früh Barocks. Munich, 1923.

CAMBIAGI . . . . . . . . . . . . . . Gaetano Cambiagi, Descrizione dell' Imperiale Giardino di Boboli. Florence, 1757.

CELLINI . . . . . . . . . . . . . . Benvenuto Cellini, Opere. 3 vols., edited by G. P. Carpani, in the Classici Italiani series, Milan, 1811.

CINELLI . . . . . . . . . . . . . . Giovanni Cinelli, Le Bellezze della Città di Firenze. Florence, 1677. Revised, enlarged edition of *Bocchi*.

COLASANTI . . . . . . . . . . . . . Arduino Colasanti, Fontane d'Italia. Rome, 1926.

COLASANTI, D. . . . . . . . . . Arduino Colasanti, Donatello. Rome, 1930.

CRUTTWELL . . . . . . . . . . . . Maud Cruttwell, Verrocchio. London, 1904.

DAMI . . . . . . . . . . . . . . . . Luigi Dami, The Italian Garden. Milan, 1925.

DA PRATO . . . . . . . . . . . . Cesare da Prato, Firenze ai Demidoff. Florence, 1886.

DELLA BELLA . . . . . . . . . . Stefano della Bella, etchings of Pratolino — usually incorporated in *Sgrilli*.

DESJARDINS . . . . . . . . . . . . Abel Desjardins, La Vie et l'Oeuvre de Jean Bologne. Paris, 1883.

DE VIERI . . . . . . . . . . . . . Francesco de Vieri, Delle Meravigliose Opere di Pratolino. Florence, 1586.

DI MARZO . . . . . . . . . . . . G. di Marzo, I Gagini e la Scultura in Sicilia. Palermo, 1880–83.

DU CERCEAU . . . . . . . . . . Androuet du Cerceau, Les Plus Excellents Bâtiments de France. 2 vols., Paris, 1576.

DUPERAC, V. D. E. . . . . . Étienne Duperac, Il Sontuosissimo ed Amenissimo Palazzo et Giardino di Tivoli (engraving of the grounds of the Villa d'Este). Rome, 1573.

FALDA . . . . . . . . . . . . . . . G. B. Falda and G. F. Venturini, Le Fontane di Roma. 4 vols., Rome (1691?) (etchings).

FRASCHETTI . . . . . . . . . . . . Stanislao Fraschetti, Il Bernini. Milan, 1900.

GAYE . . . . . . . . . . . . . . . . Giovanni Gaye, Carteggio Inedito d'artisti. 3 vols., Florence, 1839–40.

GOLDSCHMIDT . . . . . . . . . . Fritz Goldschmidt, Die Italienischen Bronzen der Renaissance und des Barock, Königliche Museen zu Berlin. Berlin, 1914.

GOTHEIN . . . . . . . . . . . . . Marie Luise Gothein, Geschichte der Gartenkunst. 2 vols., second edition, Jena, 1926.

GRAMBERG . . . . . . . . . . . . W. Gramberg, Beiträge zum Werk und Leben Pierino da Vinci, Jahrbuch der Preussischen Kunstsammlungen, LII, 1931, pp. 223 ff.

GRÜNWALD . . . . . . . . . . . . . .Alois Grünwald, Über Einige Unechte Werke Michelangelos, Münchner Jahrbuch der Bildenden Kunst, v (1910), 11 ff.

GUALANDI . . . . . . . . . . . . .M. Gualandi, Nuova Raccolta di Lettere. Bologna, 1844–56.

GUIDI. . . . . . . . . . . . . . . .Massimiliano Guidi, Le Fontane Barocche di Roma. Zurich, 1917.

HITTORFF . . . . . . . . . . . . . .J. J. Hittorff and L. Zanth, Architecture Moderne de la Sicile. Paris, 1835.

INGHIRAMI . . . . . . . . . . . . . .F. Inghirami, Description de l'I. et R. Palais de Pitti et du Jardin de Boboli. Florence, 1832.

JUSTI . . . . . . . . . . . . . . . .Carl Justi, Miscellaneen aus Drei Jahrhunderten Spanischen Kunstlebens. 2 vols., Berlin, 1908.

KRIEGBAUM, E. V. B. . . .Friedrich Kriegbaum, Ein Verschollenes Brunnenwerk des Bartolommeo Ammanati, Mitteilungen des Kunsthistorisches Institut zu Florenz, 1929.

KRIEGBAUM, M. D. C. . . .Friedrich Kriegbaum, Der Meister des Centauro, Jahrbuch der Preussischen Kunstsammlungen. Berlin, 1928.

LAPINI . . . . . . . . . . . . . .Agostino Lapini, Diario Fiorentino, ed. by G. O. Corazzini Florence, 1900.

LINDNER . . . . . . . . . . . . . .Werner Lindner, Schöne Brunnen in Deutschland. Berlin, 1920.

LOMAZZO . . . . . . . . . . . . . .Giovanni Paolo Lomazzo, Trattato dell' Arte della Pittura, etc. Milan, 1585.

MACKOWSKY. . . . . . . . . . . .Hans Mackowsky, Verrocchio. Leipzig, 1901.

MACLEHOSE . . . . . . . . . . . .Louisa Maclehose (Baldwin Brown, editor), Vasari on Technique. London, 1907.

MAC VEAGH . . . . . . . . . . .Mrs. Charles Mac Veagh, Fountains of Papal Rome. New York, 1915.

MARESCA . . . . . . . . . . . . . .Antonino Maresca, Sulla Vita e Sulle Opere di Michelangelo Naccherino. Naples, 1890.

MARQUAND, A. D. R. . . .Allan Marquand, Andrea della Robbia and his Atelier. 2 vols., Princeton, 1922.

MARQUAND, D. R. A. . . .Allan Marquand, Della Robbias in America. Princeton, 1912.

MARQUAND, G. D. R. . . .Allan Marquand, Giovanni della Robbia. Princeton, 1920.

MARQUAND, R. H. . . . . . .Allan Marquand, Robbia Heraldry. Princeton, 1919.

MASTRIGLI . . . . . . . . . . . . .Federico Mastrigli, Acque Acquedotti e Fontane di Roma. 2 vols., Rome (1928?).

MEYER ................A. G. Meyer, Donatello. Leipzig, 1903.

MIDDELDORF, A. W. P. ..Ulrich Middeldorf, Additions to the Work of Pierino da
Vinci, Burlington Magazine, LIII (December, 1928), 299–
306.

MONTAIGNE ............The Diary of Montaigne's Journey to Italy, in 1580 and
1581. Edited and translated by E. J. Trechman, Lon-
don, 1929.

MÜNTZ, R. I. F. ........Eugène Müntz, La Renaissance en Italie et en France à
l'époque de Charles VIII. Paris, 1885.

MUÑOZ, P. B. ..........Antonio Muñoz, Pietro Bernini, Vita d'Arte, IV (October,
1909), 425–462.

MUÑOZ, R. B. .........Antonio Muñoz, Roma Barocca. Rome, 1928.

PARASACCHI ............Domenico Parasacchi, Raccolta delle Principali Fontane dell'
Inclitta Città di Roma. Rome, 1647 (engravings).

PERCIER ..............C. Percier and P. Fontaine, Choix des Plus Célèbres Maisons
de Plaisance de Rome et des Environs. Paris, 1809.

PLON .................Eugène Plon, Benvenuto Cellini. Paris, 1883.

POST .................Chandler Rathfon Post, A History of European and American
Sculpture. 2 vols., Cambridge, Mass., 1921.

REYMOND, B. ..........Marcel Reymond, Le Bernin. Paris, 1911.

REYMOND, S. F. ........Marcel Reymond, La Sculpture Florentine. 4 vols., Florence.
1897–1900.

REYMOND, V. ..........Marcel Reymond, Verrocchio. Paris, 1906.

SCHOTTMÜLLER, D. ......Frida Schottmüller, Donatello. Munich, 1904.

SCHOTTMÜLLER, I. S. B. ..Frida Schottmüller, Königliche Museen zu Berlin, Die Italienischen und Spanischen Bildwerke der Renaissance
und des Barocks, Band V. Second edition, Berlin, 1913.

SCHUBRING, C. .........Paul Schubring, Cassoni. Leipzig, 1915.

SCHUBRING, D. .........Paul Schubring, Donatello. Stuttgart, 1907 (Klassiker der
Kunst series).

SCHUBRING, K. H. R. ...Paul Schubring, Die Kunst der Hoch Renaissance in Italien.
Berlin, 1926.

SGRILLI ..............Bernardo Sansone Sgrilli, Descrizione della R. Villa, Fontane, e Fabbriche di Pratolino. Florence, 1742.

SOBOTKA, P. B. ........G. Sobotka, Pietro Bernini, L'Arte, XII (1909), 401–422.

SOLDINI ..............F. M. Soldini, Il Reale Giardino di Boboli. Florence, 1789.

SUPINO . . . . . . . . . . . . . . . . I. B. Supino, Catalogo del R. Museo Nazionale di Firenze. Rome, 1898.

TANI . . . . . . . . . . . . . . . . . . A. D. Tani, Le Acque e Le Fontane di Roma. Turin, 1926.

THIEME-BECKER . . . . . . . . U. Thieme and F. Becker, Allgemeines Lexikon der Bildenden Künstler. Leipzig, 1907 (separate articles cited under the individual artists' names).

TRIGGS, A. G. I. . . . . . . . . H. Inigo Triggs, The Art of Garden Design in Italy. London, 1906.

TRIGGS, F. G. E. . . . . . . . H. Inigo Triggs, Formal Gardens in England and Scotland. London, 1902.

VARCHI . . . . . . . . . . . . . . . . Due Lezzioni di Benedetto Varchi. Florence, 1549.

VASARI . . . . . . . . . . . . . . . . Giorgio Vasari, Le Opere. Edited by Gaetano Milanesi, 9 vols., Florence, 1876–1906.

VASARI, G. G. . . . . . . . . . Vasari, Le Vite. Edited by Adolf Gottschewski and Georg Gronau. Strassburg, 1910.

VENTURINI . . . . . . . . . . . . . *See* FALDA.

VOSS . . . . . . . . . . . . . . . . . . Hermann Voss, Berninis Fontänen, Jahrbuch der Königlichen Preussischen Kunstsammlungen (1910), vol. 31.

VULLO-BIANCHI . . . . . . . . Simonetta lo Vullo Bianchi, Note e Documenti su Pietro e Ferdinando Tacca, Pt. I, Rivista d'Arte, XIII (1931), 131–213.

WILES, F. P. F. . . . . . . . . Bertha Wiles, A Fountain Figure by Pietro Francavilla, Bulletin of the Fogg Museum (May, 1932), pp. 68–72.

WILES, T. M. V. . . . . . . . Bertha Wiles, Tribolo in his Michelangelesque Vein, Art Bulletin (March, 1932), pp. 59–70.

WÜRTTEMBERG . . . . . . . . . Beschreibung Einer Raiss Welche der Herr Friderich Hertzog zu Württemberg im Jahre 1599 in Italien gethan. Tübingen, 1603.

YRIARTE . . . . . . . . . . . . . . Charles Yriarte, Matteo Civitali, Sa Vie et Son Oeuvre. Paris, 1886.

# INDEX

# INDEX

* Also numerous references to his *Notizie* in the Appendices.

* Also numerous references to *Il Riposo* in the Appendices.

* Also many references to his monograph on Giovanni Bologna in the Appendices.

* Also innumerable references to his writings in the Appendices.

# Selection
# Interviewing

# SELECTION INTERVIEWING

## A Management Psychologist's Recommended Approach

**Bradford D. Smart**

*Smart & Associates, Inc.*
*Chicago, Illinois*

**John Wiley & Sons**

**New York   Chichester   Brisbane   Toronto   Singapore**

**Library of Congress Cataloging in Publication Data:**
Smart, Bradford D., 1944–
  Selection interviewing.

  Includes index.
  1. Employment interviewing.   2. Recruiting of
employees.   I. Title.

HF5549.5.I6S6      1983        658.3'1124        82–23887
ISBN 0–471–87351–9

Printed in the United States of America

10   9   8   7   6

...for my wife Mary, inspiring,
encouraging, and wonderfully
tolerant of "when I'm working,
pretend I'm not at home"

...for my daughter Katy, whose
capacity for love at seven years
of age is a marvel

...and for my ten-year-old son
Geoff, my tireless playmate as
he strives to be the world's
greatest athlete and video game
player

# Preface

*Selection Interviewing: A Management Psychologist's Recommended Approach* is a practical, somewhat revolutionary handbook to be used by managers and human resource professionals in hiring managers (at all levels), salespeople, technical specialists, and staff professionals. The intent is to help *you,* the manager,

hire people who are more productive.

hire people whose personalities mesh more favorably with your work environment.

hire people whose needs and motivations blend more favorably with the organization.

know more about candidates' strengths, so that if a person is hired you will be better equipped to maximize those assets and enhance the person's growth, success, contributions, and fulfillment.

know more about a candidate's weaker points, so that you will be more apt to reject people who will not succeed. For those who are hired, you will be better equipped to take appropriate steps to minimize the impact of shortcomings, by structuring the job differently or instituting training and coaching to help, or both.

know better how to manage the person's transition into the organization.

reduce unwanted turnover.

devote less time, money and effort to correcting subordinate deficiencies in motivation, time management, and communications, since hirees are generally self-motivated, efficient, organized, and effective in communications.

enhance your reputation as a capable manager.

This book emphasizes the most crucial step in a selection system—the in-depth selection interview and it deals with some of the closely related processes in hiring, such as how application forms are interpreted and how record checks are conducted. These steps directly affect how the in-depth selection interview is carried out and consequently the quality of the hiring decision.

Some commonly accepted principles are mentioned briefly, but most of the book either adds "new twists" or directly challenges conventional wisdom.

The vast majority of managers exhibit bad habits in selection interviewing, resulting in unnecessary shallowness of insights into candidates. This in turn leads to a lower hiring "batting average" than is attainable through a more comprehensive and efficient approach. That's what this book is all about—a recommended approach that is a little more time-consuming "where it counts" and less time-consuming in other areas, because less-productive steps are eliminated or at least minimized. Most of the examples in this book deal with interviewing candidates for positions above entry level, although from time to time suggestions are made for adapting the principles to factory, clerical, or other hourly paid personnel.

Although selection interviewing is ordinarily thought of as pertaining to *external* selection (hiring from outside the company), it is every bit as important for *internal* selection (promoting someone from a different department or division, for example). A great many managers I have researched regret not having interviewed internal candidates thoroughly; they learned about subordinates' abilities and needs the hard way, after the person was on the job. So, hereafter in this book "selection" refers to both external selection and internal promotion, transfer, or placement.

The recommended approach has built-in flexibility; there are mechanical variations that might fit one organization better than another. The principles put forth will not reduce cholesterol in your blood, make your kids more mature, reduce waxy build-up on your floors, or improve your car's mileage. The intent is not even to remake your interviewing personality, but to suggest some guidelines within which your style can achieve greater effectiveness.

BRADFORD D. SMART, PH.D.

*Chicago, Illinois*
*February 1983*

# Acknowledgments

I wish to express my gratitude to the professors who instilled dedication to scientific objectivity, to Elaine M. Bagby and Lillian Karlov for excellence in organizing and preparing this manuscript, and to the dozens of clients and thousands of interviewees who have taught me which interviewing approaches best reveal and permit prediction of "real world" behaviors. Special thanks also to Dr. Price Pritchett for his instructive review of the manuscript, to Dennis Silverstein for photographing me for the book jacket, and to Peter Economos and Ann Hagan, for their advice regarding legal considerations in interviewing.

B.D.S

# Contents

# Selection
# Interviewing

# Introduction

*Successful selection is like a successful marriage—it is planned, not made in heaven.*

Managers frequently use the language of courtship and marriage, and sometimes divorce, when discussing relationships with subordinates. Recruitment entails "wooing" and "seducing" candidates, with considerable attention to what "turns them on" or "turns them off." Courtship proceeds until a golden moment occurs when a "formal proposal" is made, and the candidate either says "I will" or rejects the offer.

Exhilaration by both parties follows an acceptance and, as the starting date approaches, there is often a little anxiety, with both parties wondering if something, anything, could still prevent the "marriage." When a candidate does show up for the first day of work, the relationship is "consummated," and the "honeymoon period" begins.

Employment relationships sometimes result in pink slips—the counterpart to divorce papers being filed. Sometimes the rejected party seeks to "stick it to" the rejecting party, and the full power of the law is brought to bear on the situation. Palimony suits even have their counterpart in industry, with disgruntled employees successfully suing companies for financial benefits even though there was no employment contract! Both parties agree on one thing—the relationship was regrettable.

Asked why the regrettable relationship occurred, managers like to blame the search firm or the business necessity of hiring someone quickly (a "shotgun wedding") or point the finger at "bad luck." Although marriages and hiring decisions are supposed to involve some rationality, mismatches are sometimes attributed to too much trust placed in the "heart" (for marriage) or to "gut feeling" (for hiring). When executives bypass thorough, professional selection systems and hire an unsatisfactory performer, I have heard them groan, "This marriage wasn't made in heaven!"

After a decision to remove a subordinate, managers experience all sorts of feelings, perhaps similar to those of someone initiating a divorce. They sometimes recall the particular moment during the selection interview when they just"knew"the match was right. Now they feel stupid, resentful, disappointed, and embarrassed. Like divorcees who know that their failure is a part of their permanent record, managers sometimes are fearful of the career consequences of having made a "mis-hire."

This book does not seek to eliminate the intuitive moments in which the decision to make an offer occurs. However, it makes a strong case for a much more accurate approach to selection decisions by infusing the in-depth interview with greater planning, thoroughness, and rationality. The subjective elements of rapport, chemistry, and hitting it off with candidates are truly important, but only within the context of a valid, balanced, thoughtfully planned approach.

Successful manager–subordinate relationships are planned, not made in heaven. Let me warn you that this book advocates a considerably more planned approach to in-depth selection interviewing than that used by 95 percent of the managers I have surveyed.

## What Are the Costs of Making a Wrong Selection Decision?

Think of a job that requires an individual to be in it for a year in order to cost-justify the selection. Suppose the individual leaves six months after being hired—either quits or is fired because of lack of ability, abrasive personality, dishonesty, lack of motivation, or for any reason at all. Assume that the person was only 50 percent productive during the six months. What do you think the costs are to replace that individual? Three examples in Figure 1 represent the costs of "mis-hires" estimated by three different organizations.

A major consulting firm I work with places the missed opportunity figure of mis-hiring a principal at well over $250,000. If you would like to see some pathetically enormous mis-hire numbers, I should include a fourth column representing the mis-hire of a president for a grand old multibillion-dollar company. The president was to achieve a dramatic turnaround of this faltering giant, but quickly proved to be far, far over his head. The wasted salary, benefits, and other costs for the incompetent president were substantial, but one executive later estimated the missed opportunities to be in the billions of dollars, since instead of effecting the company's turnaround, its new president seemed to hasten its demise.

I know improper hiring methods were used when I hear "It was a mistake; I shouldn't have hired him. But I guess I just didn't ask if he would be willing to relocate." Or "It was a mistake, and I feel bad for her and me, but I didn't take the time to check out her technical abilities." Or "It cost this company a fortune—I should have known about his poor attention to detail before hiring him. Now we've lost our best customer."

Perhaps you have the economic expertise to calculate what the costs of mis-hires are to the United States. What would be the financial and human advantages if people were simply recruited, selected, and placed better—not over their heads, not below their capacities? Two researchers calculated that improved hiring procedures in the United States would increase the gross national product $80–$100 billion!*

## Are Interviewees Honest?

Of 1,000 selection interviews conducted in the United States today, how many interviewees behaved with total candor? How many, do you suppose, said to themselves, "The selection interview is an opportunity for me to disclose what I am truly like. If there is not a good match, it would be better to determine that in the interview rather than by my failing on the job. Thus, it is in the best interests of the interviewer, the employer organization and for me to be totally straightforward and sincere." What's your guess—150 in 1,000? 20?

---

*Hunter, J. E., and Schmidt, F. L. Fitting People to Jobs: The Impact of Personnel Selection on National Productivity. In Marvin D. Dunnette and Edwin A. Fleishman (Eds.), *Human Performance and Productivity: Human Capability Assessment*, Hillsdale, N.J.: Lawrence Erlbaum Associates, 1982. Chapter 7, pp. 233–284.

|  | Cost per Job Classification | | |
| Source of Cost | $20,000–per–Year Factory Supervisor | $50,000–per–Year Sales Person | $100,000–per–Year Technical Manager |
| --- | --- | --- | --- |
| Wasted salary of that person (assume the person was only 50% productive) | $ 5,000 | $ 12,500 | $ 25,000 |
| Wasted benefits of that person | 6,000 | 10,000 | 20,000 |
| Severance pay | 500 | 4,000 | 10,000 |
| Placement/search-firm fees | — | 15,000 | 30,000 |
| Other recruitment/training costs (salaries of personnel people, training programs, air fares, motels, etc.) | 1,000 | 10,000 | 25,000 |
| Time of nonpersonnel people (other than hiring manager) in the selection process | 1,000 | 4,500 | 10,000 |
| Time wasted by hiring manager in the selection process and in training and managing the individual | 3,000 | 10,000 | 20,000 |
| Relocation costs | — | 15,000 | 35,000 |
| Reduced morale in the work group, disruption in the office | 10,000 | 40,000 | 55,000 |
| Wasted business opportunities for the organization | 10,000 | 50,000 | 150,000 |
| Total | $36,500 | $171,500 | $380,000 |

**Figure 1. Estimated costs of "mis-hires" who leave in 6 months.**

How many do you think left the interview feeling that they had not held back a little truth? As I review my files, the number of interviewees who seemed to be extremely open and honest is 94 out of 1,000.

It seemed that 23 out of those 94 either had jobs they liked very much and did not particularly want to leave or else had other jobs in mind that were far more attractive to them than the positions for which they were interviewing. In other words, they could afford to be very open, because they had nothing to lose. Seventy-one out of the last 1,000 individuals I have interviewed seemed to be willing to disclose almost anything, without hesitancy, that I asked (and did not think they had a better job elsewhere). That's a 7.1% rate of honesty!

Unfortunately, the vast majority of candidates view the selection process as a game, and society does a pretty good job of encouraging candidates to play by their own rules, not the rules of the employing organization.

Recently, a division of a company in financial trouble was closed, and because there were few opportunities for transfers to other divisions, I was hired to spend a couple of days helping managers, professionals, and executives prepare for their job searches. They are a competent and basically honest bunch, but it took about 12 milliseconds for them to justify deception in job hunting. "Hell, I have three kids in college," lamented one man, as he considered fabricating a college degree for his résumé. These individuals had read books on how to get a job, which often advised that the job seeker try to take control of an interview, admit nothing negative, and generally manipulate the process to self-advantage.

Companies reinforce deception. They don't want hassles after firing people and usually feel a bit guilty about having "done it to old Charley," so there is agreement about what the company will disclose when a former employee's record is checked. Even if Charley was terminated for gross incompetence, the company may claim a "mutual separation," because of something like "a difference in operating philosophy." Some outplacement firms have the integrity to help people find jobs in which they will succeed; other outplacement firms, however, are more interested in fulfilling a contract (they may get part of their fee when Charley gets a job—any job) than in serving the long-term best interests of the person being outplaced. Such firms will encourage Charley to be dishonest. The owner of one such firm crudely bragged to an executive I know, "I can package manure to smell like a rose."

Can we fault the individual job seeker who is not inclined to be very candid? If discharging companies participate in deception, if hiring companies are not smart enough to obtain and fairly weigh negative information about people, if some outplacement firms encourage game playing, if best-selling books advocate "me," "power," intimidation," and "manipulation," and if job seekers are moderately to extremely desperate to find employment, what else can be expected?

Enough groundwork has been laid thus far to make a statement which, if it had been made bluntly at the beginning of this chapter, might have seemed paranoid: I assume that a selection candidate is, during various selection interviews, primarily self-interested, and that there could very well be significant omissions, circumlocutions, and even on rare occasions, blatant deception. I'm willing to become more trusting, but only when the interviewee earns it.

Let's return to the comparison between employee selection and marriage. With the cost of mis-hires (bad marriages) so high and with the interviewer (suitor) realistically suspicious of what the interviewee says, a thoughtful and planned selection interview approach is called for and presented in this book.

# 1 | Overview of the Recommended Hiring Steps

This book is broadly organized around a number of steps in hiring, starting with defining the job to be filled (chapter 2), progressing through prescreening applicants (chapter 3), to the in-depth selection interview, which of course is the major emphasis of the book. The chronological steps in hiring are put on hold for five chapters that elaborate on how best to conduct an in-depth selection interview—how to build and use professional rapport, what are the legal considerations, how to interpret interview data, and how to avoid major interviewing errors. With all of this under the reader's belt, the final step in hiring is to formulate conclusions and decide whether to offer the candidate a job (chapter 9). The book ends with some suggestions for further improving interview skills (chapter 10).

The recommended approach alluded to in the title of this book refers not only to the in-depth selection interview itself but also to recommended steps in the hiring process that occur before and after that interview.

To give you a feel for the chronological steps surrounding the in-depth selection interview, Figure 2 compares the recommended steps

| Recommended Steps | Typical Steps |
|---|---|
| 1. *Job description* | *Same* |
| 2. *Person specifications*—20–40 behaviorally verifiable characteristics considered necessary or desirable in a person for success in the job | Only 4–6 person specifications. Other important characteristics often not thought of until after a person is hired |
| 3. *Recruitment* | *Same* |
| 4. *Application form analysis*—four-page form thoroughly analyzed to screen candidates much more insightfully. Résumés also reviewed | *Résumés* heavily relied on, since the application form is often too short to yield much useful information. Less insightful screening means wasted interview time later |
| 5. *Brief telephone interview*—to further screen applicants and to invite some for personal interview | *Same* |
| 6. *Preliminary interview*—45-minute on-premises interview, to explain job, review highlights of applicants' background and job goals, and then to eliminate some applicants and sell the better ones on you, the job, the company | *Interview* typically lasting 1 hour. This is the substitute for in-depth selection interview. Superficial compared with the combination of preliminary interview and in-depth selection interview recommended |
| 7. *In-depth selection interview*—2½ hours (plus time to "sell" the candidate) to review the candidate's background and goals, to determine if person specifications are met. Using the "In-Depth Selection Interview Guide" virtually insures that basic questions are asked in a nonbiasing way. | *None.* The interview above is shallow substitute. No interview guide is used, so many basic questions are not asked. Since wording of basic questions is not standard, biasing wording is a frequent problem |
| 8. *Understanding negatives*—Mistakes, weaknesses revealed through TORC (threat of record check) methods. Candidates are gradually convinced that the interviewer will learn how their bosses truly felt about them, and to avoid embarrassing surprises, interviewees become more open and honest | *None* |

| | |
|---|---|
| 9. *Short interviews by co-workers*—made more efficient, in-depth, and palatable to the interviewee because topics (goals, technical abilities, etc.) are divvied up for emphasis by different interviewers. Important questions are often asked a second time, permitting a couple of interviewers to discuss most job-relevant aspects of candidate's background, abilities, and goals | **Short interviews by co-workers, but typically not organized for special focus and consequently redundant. Result: Several interviewers have vague, largely unsubstantiated opinions** |
| 10. *Record checks*—conducted with previous supervisors. The *recommended approach* of this book usually extracts honest appraisals of candidates | Often done with so little finesse that the record checks are meaningless. |
| 11. *Thorough review of all notes*—incredibly rich, useful data lurk in notes conscientiously taken by all interviewers. Several passes through the notes give greater depth to insights about the candidate. Each person specification is rated, based upon extensive and relatively objective, verifiable behaviors | *Notes reviewed*, but typically they are few and briefly reviewed. No systematic review of data at all |
| 12. *Hire/no hire decision*—based on rational, logical thought processes. Intuition is a valuable component, but only because the recommended approach for all of the steps provided a solid foundation for the decision | *"Gut-feeling" decision*, made with less confidence and objectivity because it is too often based on superficial data and weak inferences about future behavior from those data |

**Figure 2. Chronological steps in hiring—a comparison.**

| Recommended Steps | | | Typical Method | | |
|---|---|---|---|---|---|
| Hours Spent | Number of Applicants Remaining | Activity | Hours Spent | Number of Applicants Remaining | Activity |
| 2.5 | 30 | 4-page application form, with extensive data, and résumé analysis. Average 5-minute analysis | 1 | 30 | 2-page application form and résumé analysis. Limited data, so, on average, 2-minute analysis |
| 3 | 6 | Preliminary Interview, ½ hour, not including time to "sell" applicants | 8 | 8 | Only interview, one hour average, not including time to "sell" applicants |
| 7.5 | 3 | In-Depth selection interview, 2½ hours, not including time to "sell" applicants | 0 | 8 | None |
| 5 | — | "Sales" time (telephone and all interviews on premises). Less time than "old method" because only the best applicants, more thoroughly screened before the in-depth selection interview, were given much of a sales pitch | 10 | — | "Sales" time (telephone and interview on premises) |
| Total 18 | 1 | | Total 19 | 1 | |

Figure 3.

with the typical steps organizations take in hiring—say, an upper mid-manager.

The recommended steps may appear more time consuming than the typical method companies use. Figure 3 is the result of research showing the recommended steps to be somewhat *less* time-consuming than the typical method. Studying a good (complete, four-page) application form resulted in two fewer applicants called in for interviews. In the typical method some interviews ran two hours, and others were cut as short as 45 minutes (for rejected applicants). In the recommended steps preliminary interviews half an hour and the in-depth selection interviews ranged from two to three hours, so the most interview time was spent with the most viable candidates. In the typical method the hired applicant was interviewed only for 1½ hours, whereas in the recommended steps the hired applicant was interviewed for three hours—twice as much—and yet the total interview time for both approaches was roughly the same. Which approach do you think will result in the better hiring batting average?

If we met on an airplane and you asked me to give you a 30-second course on how to best hire a manager or professional, I'd recite the recommended steps in Figure 2 and hand you the most valuable pages in this book:

"Application Form" (Appendix A)

"Sample Person Specifications" (Appendix B)

"In-Depth Selection Interview Guide" (Appendix C)

That's the book in a nutshell. Follow the recommended steps (Figure 2), use Appendixes A, B, and C, and you will probably improve your hiring batting average.

Lest you think I am fanatically rigid about those recommended steps, a note about flexibility might be helpful. Suppose your organization is not particularly sophisticated in its selection approaches. Chances are you could use many of the dozens of elements of the recommended approach in this book anyway. Write a job description, put together person specifications, supplement your current application form with my more complete version (say, "Mr. Applicant, I'm experimenting with a new application form I might recommend to my company. Would you mind completing it, too?"), and certainly conduct the in-depth selection interview as suggested. If it is not feasible to bring candidates in for both preliminary and later selection interviews, scratch the preliminary interview, spend more time on the phone prescreening applicants, and then conduct in-depth selection interviews in person.

If good personnel managers are available to handle application form/résumé analyses and preliminary interviews—terrific, a lot of your time can be saved. (It could be worthwhile to spot-check their performance from time to time. A personnel manager's accomplishment of these steps will affect your career success and happiness!)

Although hiring the best of 20 or 25 applicants is usually desirable, and the best of 200 applicants rarely necessary, sometimes there is a business need to hire someone right away, and if you can get five applicants you're lucky. OK, you do your best. Be sure to conduct the in-depth selection interview, to know how to best manage the person, if not to confirm the match before hiring.

In short, when you have to bend, bend—realizing of course that there may be some costs in doing so. Note that I don't recommend a group interview in which three or four people sit around a table and ask the candidate questions. If this sort of torture is a realistic part of the job (for a job in public relations at the Tehran embassy, for example), fine. It will show the person's stress tolerance, oral fluency, and perhaps bladder control. However, the group interview should never be used in lieu of a full in-depth selection interview because it is almost impossible to build the rapport and achieve the interview flow that are necessary to yield accurate, comprehensive data.

With an understanding of the nature and purpose of the basic hiring steps in mind, let's begin delving into each component, starting at the beginning.

# 2 | Preliminary Steps

"In the beginning..." a job becomes available. The first thing is to understand that job, and that necessitates a job description (yawn!). Next you must determine exactly what characteristics are necessary or desirable in a successful candidate—"person specifications" (wake up, this might be new). With these steps completed, it's time to drum up candidates—recruitment (usually a frustrating and laborious step). These are the preliminary steps which, if done well, will screen the cream-of-the-crop candidates into your interviews.

## JOB DESCRIPTION—UNDERSTANDING THE JOB

It's easy to be very cynical about job descriptions. The reader has no doubt seen and perhaps written a number of job descriptions and knows full well the theory of what a job description is supposed to be— a comprehensive document outlining title, reporting relationships, responsibilities, accountabilities, authority, key interfaces and some-times such things as promotion opportunities, career paths, salary data, and some pertinent business statistics revealing the scope of operation.

The more experienced reader also knows that job descriptions almost never tell the real or the whole story. Sometimes an incredible amount of creativity is devoted to concealing the truth, because someone wants to build an empire (with much inflated job descriptions), justify salary increases for positions (again, inflating jobs), politically undercut others (by broadening the responsibilities into someone else's pansy patch), or put rigid shackles on incumbents (by carefully narrowing positions). In some organizations the job-description book constitutes an incredible monument to hypocrisy, deception, and runaway egos.

Wouldn't it be fun to write a "real" job description and say such things as

> There is a good chance of massive budget cuts next year, which could make this position expendable.
>
> The job requires working with people in accounting, who are usually uncooperative.
>
> The immediate supervisor of the position is about to be promoted, and the successor still thinks he is a Marine Corps drill instructor.
>
> The job requires a lot more bureaucratic paperwork than most people can stomach.
>
> There has been a lot of turnover in the job because it represents a handy corporate scapegoat.

Writing a totally honest and complete job description could be a hilarious exercise and a fine joke to play on your company—the day after you retire. In order to make job descriptions "compatible with a harmonious organizational climate," there are sometimes a lot of omissions, vague statements, and platitudes.

A written job description is sometimes necessary in order for a manager to obtain authority to fill the job and establish pay levels. It is often useful to circulate such a document in order to achieve a broad consensus on what the job really is all about. A good recruitment firm may want such a document so that candidates can be more accurately found, screened, and sold on the job. Sharper selection candidates may request a complete written job description because they realize that they cannot afford to enter a job that does not work out. They want all the information they can get. Research has confirmed that more thorough and accurate job information improves the relevance of interview questions, not just for inexperienced interviewers but for experienced interviewers as well.*

Too often managers do not thoroughly think through the position. Perhaps it represents a new function reporting to them and they lack technical knowledge. Maybe the job will be in another location and they really do not understand what it is like working there. Or perhaps the organization is dynamic, and the position in question could change, and they don't accurately foresee new job elements.

As a management psychologist, it is not uncommon for me to suggest that a manager think about the position "a bit more" and jot down some of the important elements of the job in order to reduce the vagueness and hype of the description. If nothing else, writing a thorough position description (a classy way to say job description) is apt to help you structure important relationships, to understand advantages and disadvantages in the job, and to figure out how best to sell candidates on it without unrealistically inflating their expectations. Figure 4 is a sample job description. Please at least skim it, since it is the basis of a case study throughout the book.

The job description and person specifications are ideally based on a thorough, scientific job analysis. Some large companies employ human resources specialists who interview incumbents about job components, compare successful and unsuccessful performers, measure tasks with stopwatches, and study published research. Job analysis is the subject for a book in itself; for the purposes of this book, I encourage you to use a job analyst if one is available; if not, at least talk to a few persons who have held the job, ideally including some successes and some failures.

## PERSON SPECIFICATIONS—WHAT IT TAKES TO DO THE JOB

A truly honest and complete job description would state what knowledge, skills, abilities, and personal characteristics the successful candidate should possess, and exactly what objective, measurable behaviors exhibit those characteristics. Few do. Some job descriptions contain educational or experience requirements, but rarely specify what 15 or 30 other important elements are desired. When managers discuss selection candidates, they don't just talk about a job. They also talk about characteristics of the individuals, and they talk about implicit or

*Langdale, J. A., and Weitz, J. Estimating the influence of job information on interviewer agreement. *Journal of Applied Psychology*, 1973, **57**, 23–27.

| | |
|---|---|
| Title | Branch Sales Manager (BSM), New Jersey Division (typically a person hired to become a BSM serves as a sales representative for 6 months) |
| Company description | ACTS is an industry leader in time-sharing and diversified services. It is based in New York City and in 1981 had gross sales of $183 million. Branch sales offices are located throughout the US, Canada, Mexico, Western Europe, and Japan. |
| Organization chart | |

The sales representatives and branch technical manager report to the branch sales manager in Newark, New Jersey, and that individual, and 4 other branch sales managers, report to the area manager for New York City.

Responsibilities — This is a sales and sales-management position. Although the BSM has no personal quota, achieving the branch quota (sum of the quotas for sales representatives) requires most BSMs to do individual selling. BSMs have estimated that they work 65+ hours per week as follows:

*Sales* (20%). The BSM is the sales representative for target accounts—typically high potential accounts lost when ACTS had service problems (1979–1980). Like sales representatives, the BSM participates in an excellent one-month training program (product and selling skills) in New York City. Quotas for sales representatives are established at the beginning of each fiscal year and will derive from calls on data-processing managers, controllers, chief financial officers, and presidents of *"Fortune* 1000" companies (principally manufacturing and retail companies). The BSM typically will do individual sales work with presidents of companies who have canceled contracts with ACTS.

*Management* (60%). The New York area office provides excellent recruitment and training support. The branch sales manager establishes goals (quotas for sales representatives and service/sales support goals for the branch technical manager and technical specialists), using a management-by-objectives (MBO) system. The BSM has a heavy coordination responsibility between sales and technical people, to insure high productivity and to improve the service image damaged in 1979–1980. Most BSMs conduct Monday morning branch meetings, so that everyone in the office has a clear understanding of current priorities (which can rapidly change). A positive, mutually supportive team spirit must be achieved. The BSM is expected to be in the field with sales representatives a minimum of 2½ days per week (with two nights per week out of town) monitoring their performance and, most important, helping them to develop their sales skills. Maintenance of accounts ordinarily consumes 35% of a new sales representative's time, and 65% is spent prospecting. Ten sales calls per week is average for the New Jersey—New York area.

*Administration* (20%). The BSM is required to formulate and present (to New York executives) a comprehensive marketing plan, including analysis of market economic and time-sharing trends, analysis of current and prospective customers, sales and service quotas, budget requests. Following the presentation, final quotas and budgets are established with the area manager. Day-to-day administration is facilitated by an on-line computer system (handled largely by the secretary).

| | |
|---|---|
| Organizational environment | The industry is growing at a rate of 20% per year; ACTS averaged 25% growth from 1975 to 1979. 1979 and 1980 were soft because of an image of deficient service. ACTS began to correct their service image in late 1980, but rebuilding has been difficult. The New York area is extremely competitive, and there are very few easy sales. There are occasional territorial disputes within ACTS, since industry territories (retail, manufacturing) and geographic territories sometimes overlap. |
| Key interfaces | There are constant interactions—with sophisticated clients and ACTS executives, sales representatives, and specialized salespersons and with various technical, management, and clerical persons in the data-processing organizations of client and prospect companies. |
| Career opportunities | After its two soft years (1979–1980), ACTS is rebounding and expected to grow rapidly. Promotions are usually from within. There are 60 branch sales managers and 15 area managers (one in New York City). The New York corporate office has staff and senior executive positions, but the New Jersey branch sales manager would probably have to relocate for promotion to area manager, the usual career step upward. |
| Compensation | The BSM has a base salary of $35,000 and up to a 25% maximum bonus possibility based upon branch sales and budget performance. The BSM has a good chance of earning $45,000 in the first year and $55,000 the second year. |

**Figure 4.  Sample Job Description: Acme Computer Time-Sharing Corporation (ACTS).**

17

stated standards of performance. That's what person specifications are—*characteristics with standards,* or colloquially, what it takes to do the job. No job description I have ever seen, including the sample seen in Figure 4, comes close to indicating the dozens of characteristics that may be essential for success and which, if they are not present to a certain degree, will almost surely result in failure. So, we need a list of person specifications to accompany the job description. Should person specifications be a list of traits? Results achieved? Or observable, measurable behaviors? I believe all should be included, but a short digression is necessary to understand my conclusion.

The expected response in the 1980s is, "Let's forget hiring people for superficial appearances or for such vague qualities as loyalty or friendliness. Let's instead look at what a person has actually done. As long as the job is performed, who cares if Pat doesn't genuflect before the altar of Acme, Inc. every day? So what if a checker has frizzy hair if the customers love her, and she is a terrific sales booster besides?" These trends seem to coincide with some very important voices that are saying, "Who cares if the individual is black, Mexican-American, over 40, partially crippled, or a woman, as long as the job can be performed successfully?"

This reasoning is very appealing and happens to work nicely when writing person specifications for many clerical or factory jobs. But what if I have a new machine—a widget that few selection candidates have run? Or what if we need to hire store managers who can not only succeed in little corner grocery stores but who can grow to run large supermarkets? Is it fair to reject candidates just because they haven't performed some observable, measurable element of the job? Likely candidates often have the desire to grow, and many organizations need people with strong interests and potentials.

If person specifications are to apply to a future position as well as to the entry position, then job analyses should be conducted for both positions. It is also useful to do a human resources forecast (a "manpower plan") so that the person specifications will not be unrealistically high or low and will reflect the real present and future needs of the organization, expected attrition, and anticipated talent availability.

Person specifications directed toward expected future growth might include some traits such as ambition and learning ability. If it is expected that a person will be soon promoted to a sensitive, high security job, then a person specification termed "loyalty" could require discretion and disinclination to chat casually with competitors.

So, we've come full circle, back to rating people's loyalty! What is different in the recommended approach of this book is that ratings of loyalty (as an example) must have a fair and realistic standard, and ratings of the specification must be founded on observable, measurable interview statements and behaviors. An interviewee who cheerfully tells you confidential information about his current employer may fall short of your standard—your person specification—on loyalty!

Another question may have occurred to you. If having clear, accurate, objective, fair, and thorough person specifications is important in the selection process, why do executives so often do a shallow, haphazard job of composing them? Good question, and there are at least four answers. One, it is very time-consuming to try to think of all of the relevant characteristics and to specify the extent to which each one must be exhibited, and managers are usually short on time. Two, in the United States in the 1980s, such thoroughness is not the norm in business, industry, and education. Three, managers typically do not gather enough data in selection interviews or record checks to be able to judge the extent to which person specifications are met. Four, there is often considerable disagreement in the organization over what person specifications are necessary or desired, and clear delineation of the person specifications could be politically disruptive.

But if more thorough, job-relevant data were gleaned from the selection interviews, if you had a more thorough understanding of what person specifications were necessary or desired to meet the job requirements, and if you were able, on the basis of in-depth selection interviews, to make accurate judgments about how people measured up to those specifications, wouldn't you greatly improve the chances of hiring better performers? Of course!

The organization's lack of agreement on the sort of person to be hired is a crucial determinant in the problem of gaining organizational consensus on the job description. If this issue is not resolved before a person is hired, it will surely surface later, and its resolution may leave scars on the back of the person hired (and on you too, God forbid). If you and your company cannot agree that the hired person should be less or more aggressive, have less or greater growth potential, be technically skilled in one or in four areas, you have a political problem, and you must finesse your way out the best you can.

Instead of asking you to create several dozen person specifications for a particular position, Appendix F has more than a hundred, which can be whittled down, reworded, or otherwise modified to suit your needs. Many companies reduce this list to 15 or 20 specifications. To save yourself some labor the next time you hire someone for a mid- to upper-level position, you might simply modify the basic set of person

## Intellectual Characteristics

* 1. Level of intelligence
2. Analytic ability
3. Ability to diagnose client needs
4. Creativity/innovativeness
5. Pragmatism
6. Intellectual flexibility
7. Oral communications skills
8. Written communications skills
9. Education
*10. Experience—technical
*11. Experience—sales
*12. Experience—management

## Personal Makeup

13. Initiative/resourcefulness
14. Self-objectivity
15. Perseverance
16. Independence
*17. Standards of performance
*18. Track record
19. A "doer"
*20. Emotional maturity/stability/resilience
21. Administrative abilities

## Interpersonal Relations

22. First impression
23. Interpersonal flexibility
24. Assertiveness
25. Team player
26. Enthusiasm
27. Empathy
28. Leadership
29. Management—recruitment/selection
30. Management—training/development
31. Management—goal-setting
32. Management—monitoring performance
33. Management—performance feedback
34. Management—removing nonperformers
35. Management—team development

## Motivations and Aspirations

*36. Motivation level
37. Health
38. Ambition
39. Willingness to take risks
*40. Interests compatible with company expectations

**Figure 5. Sample list of person specifications (without definitions). (Asterisk denotes the specifications usually considered most important.)**

specifications in Appendix B. These person specifications apply to a computer services sales representative, promotable to branch sales manager within a year. It sounds like a specialized set of person specifications, but it is used for the ongoing case study in this book because it is so broadly applicable. A successful candidate must have all sorts of intellectual, personal, interpersonal, managerial, and motivational qualities. A number of managers in a variety of organizations have found appendix B to be a useful set of person specifications, needing only a little tailoring to be useful for a number of positions. Figure 5 is a list of these person specifications without the definitions or standards that appear in appendix B.

How many candidates have you interviewed who meet all of the minimum requirements for a given position? Not very many, most likely, because anyone so perfect would not be interested in the job available! Selection candidates always have shortcomings, and the challenge facing you is to weigh the blend of strengths and shortcomings with how hard pressed you are to fill the job quickly and to determine if there is a *good enough* fit of company and candidate.

## The Most Important Person Specifications

The nine starred characteristics in Figure 5 are ones that clients and I usually consider most important, meaning we'd be less apt to forgo requiring these specifications than the others. If a candidate is bright (person specification 1), has sufficient experience (numbers 10, 11, 12), has high standards (number 17), has an excellent record of success (number 18), is emotionally mature, stable, and resilient (number 20), is highly motivated to succeed (number 36), and has interests compatible with the opportunity at hand (number 40), we can sometimes live with shortcomings in other areas. Specifically, the hiring manager might feel it is possible to get creative ideas (number 4) from others and to supervise the person well enough to insure such characteristics as pragmatism (number 5) and decent written communications (number 8). The hiring manager might decide to disregard the candidate's sloppy clothes and scraggly beard (number 22) and meek sales approach (number 24), as long as it works. Or, so what if the candidate tends to be too much a maverick and not enough a team player (number 25) or misses 15 days per year because of colds (number 37), as long as the final sales results are excellent?

Even some of the nine most important person specifications may be absent, and the correct decision is still to hire. For example, the following points should be considered.

**Level of Intelligence.**   Not many successful research chemists fall below the superior level of intelligence, but some do. And I know a few successful presidents of billion-dollar firms who are below average in intelligence, compared with college graduates. They compensate with superb wits, and they know how to select excellent managers whom they can trust. An in-depth selection interview can usually let you know when adequate compensating qualities exist—and when they do not.

**Experience (Technical, Sales, or Management).**   If a candidate for college recruiter is very strong in oral communications (number 7), has a college education (number 9), shows initiative (number 13), makes an excellent first impression (number 22), and displays enthusiasm (number 26) and empathy (number 27), it becomes easy to bend a specification for "three years of recruitment experience" and accept a candidate with one successful year. Several times a year I will strongly recommend for promotion or hiring a candidate without the expected level of experience, because so many compensating characteristics exist.

**Standards of Performance.**   Would you want your neurosurgeon to be lacking in self-discipline, quality standards, or intellectual integrity? No way! However, if a candidate for systems analyst will report to a manager who is superb at injecting professionalism into people, a candidate who is marginal in standards can perhaps be hired.

**Emotional Maturity/Stability/Resilience.**   How much flakiness can you tolerate in your ranks? Although most executives are aware of the "80–20 rule," which (among other things) means that 80% of the successes are generated by 20% of the subordinates, I have found a corollary: 80% of all managerial headaches are created by 20% of the subordinates. Instead of spending 80% of their time helping the best performers become even better, many managers I know find themselves 80% of the time mired in the quagmire caused by the 20% problem employees. These nonperformers usually have ability, but accompanied by garden variety of hang-ups. It may be worth your effort to have a talented screwball around—more power to you if you can channel such a person. However, I am constantly called about such issues, and companies spend a lot of money salvaging talented but difficult persons. My advice is to try to hire people who are basically stable in the work environment. But if you eliminate slightly or moderately neurotic candidates, you might reject fabulous performers and marvelous human beings. Slightly nutty people are sometimes the most exciting, interesting, and stimulating people around.

In the worlds of art, photography, creative writing, social work, adversary law, and (ahem) behavioral sciences, a high level of talent is sometimes accompanied by personal quirks. You must decide on the mix of talent and emotional factors you can accommodate realizing that a fair-rated specification will probably mean an extended depressed mood, an alcoholic bout, an unpredictable explosion of righteous indignation, or a punctuality problem, some or all of which could be unconscious bids for attention.

**Motivation Level.** If you will have to prod a person into performing daily or weekly, the hiring is probably not worth it. I know of several instances, however, in which otherwise poorly motivated people did rise to spectacular heights because of unusual inspiration by the supervisor.* I know a few managers who view this specification as irrelevant, because they create circumstances—organizational climates—in which previously unmotivated people suddenly motivate themselves.

**Interests Compatible with Company Expectations.** Aha, you say, you can't possibly accept someone who expects too high a salary, is unwilling to relocate to the job, or refuses to get to work by your starting time. True, but during recruitment activities the job might be revised in order to accommodate the interests and needs of a particularly attractive candidate. For example, maybe the person would agree to a temporary relocation. Furthermore, what people say they want in compensation and what they would accept are sometimes two different things.

**Track Record.** Hiring someone with a poor recent record of performance takes guts or stupidity, although some exceptions exist. Unconscientious students often become conscientious performers on the job. Occasionally, job-hoppers will perform well when they find the right employers. I work with a couple of firms that are marvelous in turning people with poor previous track records into capable, long-term employees.

---

*"Supervisor" is used throughout this book in place of "superior" or "boss." Thus, the supervisor of a vice president may be the president, the supervisor of a factory worker may be a foreman, and the supervisor of a branch sales manager may be a regional sales manager.

I used to say that there are no hard and fast rules, no set-in-concrete specification except one: If a convicted crook throws up on the interviewer, it's definitely a "no hire" situation. Then I interviewed a convicted crook (15 years in the past he had been an accomplice in a liquor store armed robbery), and the combination of flu and nervousness resulted in his regurgitating all over my desk and me. I later recommended that he be hired by the client, a social service organization that knew about his past. The fellow had been a highly effective minority counselor for the previous decade and has done an excellent job for my client. So the only hard and fast rule about person specifications is: There isn't one. With a job description and person specifications in hand, it's time to find some candidates.

## Recruitment

Most firms have no difficulty running recruitment ads, creating literature with which to sell candidates, and wooing them at lunches and dinners; consequently, this book will not deal with these elements. Where organizations seem lax is in managing search and placement firms. Very important interviews are conducted by these firms, and my comments are intended to help you improve their services on your behalf.

Search firms are typically paid 30% of the estimated first-year compensation regardless of whether the client firm hires a candidate they generate. In contrast, placement, employment, and recruitment firms usually operate on a contingency basis, meaning they are paid only if the client firm hires a candidate they generate; their fees range from 15 to 25%.

As in any profession, search and placement firms have practitioners who are competent and ethical, and some who are less so. Search firms, because they are paid anyway, tend to operate more professionally. Placement firms sometimes indiscriminately push résumés at organizations.

The names of search firms usually represent real people. For example, McFeely Wackerle Associates is run by Clarence McFeely and Fred Wackerle. "Mac" is former president of the Association of Executive-Recruiting Consultants (AERC), the national professional association for search firms. Search firms are typically proud of their names. Recruitment/placement/employment firms usually have fictitious names—Joe Jones Employment Agency probably never had a "Joe Jones" in its employ. The true owners of employment firms are not always proud of their livelihood.

I tend to blame the tainted images of search and placement firms mostly on the organizations that hire them. Search professionals, in my experience, tend to be as ethical, competent, and professional as the average American executive. When things go wrong in searches, at least half the blame belongs with the client organization. Too often, search and placement firms are given vague or inaccurate job descriptions and insufficient consensus regarding person specifications. Even some major corporations (though certainly not my clients!) reject good candidates for the darnedest reasons. Search and placement firms are sometimes accused of inadequate screening interviews, when the problem really rested with the client.

For example, the president of a major construction supply manufacturing company decided during the late 1970s not to hire any hippies, and he believed that anyone who wore a leather wristband must be a hippie. He had somehow not noticed the thin band of rawhide worn by a candidate I interviewed for his company. When I casually asked about it, the candidate said, "It's not comfortable, but my daughter gave it to me for Christmas, and I'll just have to wear it for a while." Informed of the candidate's perspective, the president blurted, "I don't care, I'm not going to hire any damn hippie."

This sort of experience greatly frustrates search firms and actually encourages them to emphasize superficial social graces and image as opposed to substance. However, search and placement consultants can function very professionally, and here are some suggestions for what you can do to ensure that the firm you employ does a topnotch job.

Develop close working relationships with several individuals in search firms (for higher-level searches) and in placement firms (for lower levels). Nurture the relationships so that bonds of mutual trust insure fairness on your part and professionalism on their part. If the professionals with whom you have achieved a good working relationship leave their employing search or placement firm, consider keeping your business with them, instead of remaining with the original firm.

Spend as much time describing the job and outlining person specifications as the search professional requests and arrange for the search professional to meet with other people, so that differences of opinion about the job and person specifications will at least be clear to that consultant. Search consultants are usually very willing to spend such time, but since placement firms operate on a contingency basis, they may not volunteer their own time for such discussions. I recommend that you pay the recruiter (if you are sure the person is capable) to get to know the positions and person specifications.

Ask that search and placement firms have candidates complete a comprehensive application form (like the one in Appendix A) before even a preliminary interview with you or anyone in your organization.

Require search and placement firms to conduct a thorough interview with a prospect and two or three record-check interviews (if at all possible). Let them know that a record check without any negatives looks like a whitewash.

Require search firms to prepare a thorough written report (placement firms cannot be expected to put in the time to do this for lower-level jobs) describing the candidate's background and interests and appraising the strengths, shortcomings, and potentials of the individual. We all have shortcomings—if the search professional can't find any, a harder look is needed.

The recruiters should do all of this work, minimizing your time spent at this stage. If they will not go to these efforts, either they are lazy or you are a crummy client, or both!

Assuming that the search or placement firm has done its job or that you have generated applicants some other way, it's time to prescreen efficiently so that your valuable time is spent interviewing only likely candidates.

# 3 | Prescreening Applicants

## APPLICATION FORM ANALYSIS

A good application form conforms with legal guidelines and yet can provide considerable insight into an individual's strengths, shortcomings, and potentials. As pointed out in chapter 2, when you glean deep insights into applicants before interviews are arranged, you can save yourself an enormous amount of time and money by sorting out the candidates you probably will decide not to interview.

This chapter will suggest guidelines for interpreting application form responses, provide an example of how an application form analysis is done, and end with a test of your application form analysis abilities. A later chapter provides further recommendations for conforming to legal guidelines affecting interviews. Suffice it to say here that an application form is definitely open to scrutiny.

A good application form (Appendix A) looks ordinary, yet contains some unusual but valuable requests for information, such as:

What the person liked most about positions
What the person liked least about positions

Reasons for leaving

Initial and final compensation for each position

Name of immediate supervisor for each position

Request for permission to contact current and previous employers for reference checks

Academic grade-point average and class standing

Complete dates (month and year) for each position and each school attended

A request that the person state qualifications and strengths

Salary goals

Amount of travel acceptable

Plans and goals for the future

As you will soon see, these items can add very revealing depth to what is usually contained in an application form. If you wish your organization's forms could be improved, but getting something closer to the application form in Appendix A would involve fighting too much red tape, perhaps you could obtain permission to put together a supplemental form (like Appendix A) to use with your company's application form. You could refer to the supplement as a "guide to facilitate the interview." This would certainly provide more useful information than a superficial application form and an individual's résumé, which unfortunately is all that many organizations use, even for prescreening high-level professionals and managers.

## Review the Résumé with, Not in Lieu of, a Good Application Form

The more experienced reader realizes full well that résumés can be marvelously creative documents. They are usually designed to conceal weakness and magnify strengths, which they can sometimes accomplish without actually lying.

Résumés should not be totally maligned. When actually created by the candidate (which is not always the case), a résumé can provide more detail regarding accomplishments, scope, and duties than a few lines on the application form and can reveal a few things about taste and judgment that an application form cannot. So, my recommendation is to review the résumé and the application form.

Call (or write) a candidate whose résumé seems promising and say something like, "Your résumé looks interesting, and in order to consider you as a candidate further, would you please complete our application form?" (If a search or placement firm generated the résumé, it will handle this request.)

## An Application Form Is a Test

A superficial application form is a weak test of a person's strengths, limitations, and potentials. Conversely, a well-constructed application form can be an extremely revealing instrument. Before seeing a couple of examples, you need some guidelines for interpretation.

To begin, you do not have to be a psychologist in order to interpret relatively accurately a completed application form. Most experienced business people have seen a great many application forms and with a little practice can perform insightful analyses.

The application form is a "test" in that it includes all sorts of deliberately ambiguous opportunities for an applicant to disclose his or her true characteristics. The Rorschach inkblot test is probably the best-known example of what deliberately ambiguous situations can reveal. The application form appears to be very straightforward, requesting specific information, but if 100 persons with identical backgrounds but diverse personal characteristics complete the same form, it will be remarkably clear who are the extroverts and introverts, the hard-chargers and the passive ones, those who are highly confident and those who are least confident.

Following are interpretive guidelines for a completed application form (Appendix A), starting with general considerations and then progressing through specifics from the first to the last page of the application form:

Look at the form as a whole and judge its neatness. Sloppiness suggests some impatience with detail, maybe a sense of urgency. If the form is extremely neat and complete, a more methodical, patient individual is suggested.

Are there omissions? When a person omits grades earned, class standing, salary information, reasons for leaving a job, or dates of employment, very frequently it is because of some embarrassment—about flunking out, being fired, or something else unfavorable. Sometimes omissions are deliberate, but sometimes the exclusion is unconsciously motivated. Only when a person is both careless and poor at self-promotion are flattering data excluded.

Are there a lot of erasures or cross-outs? If so, there is a chance that a fair amount of concern, frustration, anxiety, or embarrassment is associated with that topic. With this knowledge you can perhaps deduce the specific reasons, which often have job relevance.

Look at the handwriting. Research indicates that graphology is about as valuable as snake oil, when it is used to identify specific personal characteristics. (Graphology is successfully used, however, to detect forgery in handwriting.) Handwriting analysis does not work because the most important influence on handwriting is ordinarily a person's third-grade teacher—Miss Grady taught you to write with a heavy or a slight angle, influenced you to make flowery capitals, and so forth. Just about the only consistent analytic clue is pressure on the writing instrument. You can be pretty sure that a meek individual would not write firm, bold letters, and you can be equally confident that Dick Butkus (former Chicago Bears linebacker) would not write in extremely delicate, fine letters.

Are there many words, or just a few? Filling out a four-page application form is frustrating to a fast-paced, results-oriented individual. Persons who cram this form with a lot of words tend to be extremely thorough, a bit on the slow side, or typically verbose. Crisp, to-the-point, easy-to-read application form data are usually provided by individuals who are crisp, to the point, and easily understood individuals.

Look for recurring themes. If there are two or three instances of blaming others for failures, the chances are very good that the individual does not take full responsibility for his destiny. If there are two or three references to warm, satisfying, harmonious relationships, the chances are reasonably good that the person is people-oriented. Are there several confusing statements? That might indicate something important about the individual—when trapped (in this case, by a form), perhaps the inclination is to control other people by confusing them. Or maybe the person has difficulty organizing and communicating thoughts even when not feeling pressure.

What are the recurring themes in what the individual likes most about jobs, particularly the most recent jobs? Whether it's prestige, money, people, intellectual challenge, travel, or whatever, you would naturally hypothesize that current needs would be similar.

What are the recurrent patterns in what the individual least enjoys? If she says "excessive paperwork," "nit-picking supervisors," or "no growth," you might wonder if the individual is weak at completing paperwork, has problems of her own in dealing with supervisors, or is not worthy of earning new opportunities. Again, a single statement would not cause such an inferential leap, but three or four such instances of the same theme would arouse suspicion.

Is there a pattern in reasons for leaving? The most common response is "opportunity," which tells you nothing. Unusual responses might tell you a lot.

As you step back and look at the entire document, is it generally positive or negative in its statements about life? A lot of negative statements will usually accompany a negative individual or one who is insensitive to the impact on others (in this case, the impact of the application form on a potential employer).

As you review the entire form, with more emphasis on recent career history than early career history, is there a success pattern, a failure pattern, or a failure pattern with excuses? (The latter is sometimes even worse than a failure pattern without excuses, because the individual might be glib.)

Are there many abbreviations? People who write out "street" or "apartment" in addresses are usually more slow and methodical on the job than people who abbreviate. Indeed, almost everyone makes a lot of abbreviations on an application form, so it should probably strike you as quite revealing if an individual does not abbreviate.

Do the work experiences to date suggest the appropriate background for a candidate or, if hired, would the candidate be over or underqualified?

Do responses to "position applied for" and "earnings expected" represent career steps forward? If not, there had better be a good reason, for it suggests that the individual might be desperate (and winners are usually less desperate than losers).

Are the dates of employment and education complete? Are you able to account for every single month and year since the individual began high school? If not, the chances are good that the individual is deliberately concealing something—flunking out of college, an additional job or two that didn't work out, an aborted attempt to start a business, or a stint in the penitentiary.

Does the progress from "initial compensation" to "final total compensation" represent poor progress, average, or above-average progress? How does the applicant stack up in current income level in comparison with others in the field? Watch out for people who only make significant steps forward while changing jobs, but seem to earn few promotions or salary increases while with one employer.

Has there been job-hopping? An average of more than one job every two years is a bad sign. Naturally, in some occupations movement is often necessary for growth (advertising and data processing, for example). However, four jobs in five years for anyone suggests that the individual is not successful, is a bit desperate when switching jobs, is talented but extremely impatient for career progress, or does not show good judgment in investigating new positions.

Are supervisors' actual names provided, as requested? Less formal people, with better relationships with their supervisors usually record "John Smith." More formal, distant relationships are indicated by "Mr. Smith," "Smith," or "J. Smith," (more common in the South). One must suspect a strained relationship if the applicant does not give the supervisor's name. Whether it is unconscious avoidance or deliberate concealment, the omission makes it a little more difficult to conduct a record check.

Is the military experience typical? Are the dates, duties, and highest/terminal rank indicative of above-average, average, or below-average performance?

Is the high school experience in terms of grades, activities, and accomplishments average, unusually successful, or extremely undistinguished? Success during these years is certainly not sufficient for success later on, and failure during these years does not preclude the possibility of success later on. For a candidate for management to have been elected to some offices in school suggests the person was at least able to earn some peer approval—definitely not a negative and usually interpreted as a positive indicator. The correlation between high school academic achievement (class rank, in particular) and later life achievements is not very high, but there is certainly some correlation, so it is worth noting.

Look at college board scores as moderately reliable and valid indicators of intelligence. (These scores are explained in chapter 7.)

Was there a lot of part-time and summer work during school years? If so, the person might have deeper business maturity than peers (at a young age), although there is some risk that the individual did not develop the social flexibility that more peer interaction and less work might have permitted.

Interpretation of college/graduate school data is fairly obvious. You would view A grades at a fine institution and leadership positions held in activities as positives, depending on the position in question. Superstars in school sometimes do bomb out in their careers, however, so unless the school years are in the recent past, both negative and positive data must be taken with a grain of salt, with one exception: a straight-A student at a fine institution (college or graduate school) is almost certainly above average to superior in intelligence.

Applicants who do not complete the section "In the event of an emergency, whom would you wish notified other than spouse?" are usually a bit more independent and less socially oriented than those who do complete it thoroughly.

The only right answer to the question about condition of health is "excellent." "Good" might be an acceptable response, but anything less positive than that tells you something about the person's physical health, but might also reveal a negative self-concept and general lack of sense of well-being. Sometimes people who are preoccupied with health concerns do not have the physical or mental energy levels necessary to be highly productive, to establish very positive working relationships, and to persevere under pressure. On the other hand, people who are physically impaired (blind, loss of limb in a war) often indicate they are in excellent health, truly feel that way, and can be above average in motivation and performance.

The section on activities usually merits very straightforward interpretation. Generally, it is positive if people are at least somewhat active in professional groups in order to maintain skills and keep abreast of trends. However, there are nonperformers who participate heavily in activities because they are ineffective on the job. For them, the approval received at a Jaycee meeting helps to counteract the negative recognition at work. Too many activities is also characteristic of some people who have difficulty focusing their energies—even on the job they might be spread too thin.

What qualifications, abilities, and strong points are listed? This is an opportunity for the individual to sell himself, and should represent a strong, confident, positive perspective. If not, hypothesize that the individual has a weak self-image, lacks empathy, possesses mediocre ambition, or simply lacks interest or concern for the impact of behavior on others.

What ultimate salary does the individual wish to attain? People with astronomically high goals (ten times current salary) are usually very ambitious and high risk takers; depending on the job, that may be good or bad. Conversely, those who ultimately only wish to attain little more than a cost-of-living increase, are usually security conscious and realistic about their career potentials, which are often quite limited. The 35-year-old earning $35,000 and stating a desire to earn $100,000 (at today's dollar value) is typical of capable, aggressive achievers who will one day be executives.

What are plans for the future? Although experienced applicants provide what they think the prospective employer wants to hear ("remain long-term with a fine organization, doing the best possible job in the entry position, and with luck and a lot of work, eventually move up to maximize my potentials and make the best possible contributions to my company"), about 20% of the time there is a very penetrating, revealing comment made.

It frankly makes me a bit queasy to give these guidelines, because there are so many exceptions. But the point is that keen insights can be gleaned from scrutinizing a filled-out, well-designed application form. Let's move on to an example and you'll see what the fuss is all about.

Are you willing to participate in an application form analysis exercise? It can teach you a lot and save you a great deal of time in the steps before preliminary or in-depth interviews. The exercise entails your analyzing the application form of Joseph Fielder—a real person who was in fact hired with assurances that he would be promoted from sales representative to New Jersey branch sales manager in six months. This promotion came about, and one year after he was hired his boss (New York area manager), some subordinates, and others who knew him well spent a day rating him on the 40 person specifications in Figure 5 (and Appendix B) for the job described in Figure 4. Your mission, dedicated reader, should you choose to accept this assignment, is to deduce/guess those ratings, made one year after Joe Fielder joined ACTS. (ACTS is a fictitious name—I've changed names, dates, and certain details to conceal identities and enhance the flow of the exercise, but from an analytic point of view this is a real-life example.)

It may sound like tea-leaf reading, but it is exactly what you have to do as a manager with a stack of application forms, unless you are willing to waste time interviewing people you could have intelligently screened out. Predicting how you and co-workers would rate an applicant after that person has performed on the job, based on application form data, is a skill to be developed, and it is more rational and valid than you might believe.

Here are the steps:

1.  Review the position description (Figure 4) and the person specifications (Figure 5 and Appendix B) for a job a person would enter as a sales representative, learn the company and products for a few months (up to a year), and then move up to

the branch sales manager spot. You may assume that the New York area manager is very good at developing branch managers; that's why the specifications do not require a lot of management experience but do require applicants to be successful in sales and have some management experience.

2.  Study the completed application form (Figure 6). You know that Computer Vistas is a fine company—so if Fielder succeeded there you are impressed.

3.  Record your ratings and rationale for the ratings in Appendix B. Again, these ratings constitute your best guess as to how Fielder's boss and other co-workers rated him one year after ACTS hired him. It is important to note that Fielder only joined ACTS with a guarantee he would be made branch sales manager within six months. This occurred, so your ratings—guesses as to future performance—should take into consideration the fact that Fielder sold for six months and then was New Jersey branch sales manager, in addition to selling, for a full six months before Fielder's supervisor and co-workers convened to rate him. You don't know if Fielder's co-workers concluded that he was great or that he should be fired—that's part of the fun of this exercise, and you'll find out the answers later.

4.  See how well you did. Enter your ratings in the appropriate column in Figure 7 and calculate the sum of the absolute differences between your ratings and those of Fielder's co-workers.

5.  Turn to Figure 8 for the ratings and their rationales given by managers trained in application form analysis.

How did you do? Don't be discouraged if it took you 45 minutes to analyze the application form and write out all of your reasons. In real life, with a little practice, it should only take a minute or so to discard application forms containing several 0 ratings; 15 or 20 minutes is needed for the most viable application forms.

The combined difference scores of the managers I trained in application form analysis were off only 12 points, an average of only 1/3 of a point per person specification. That score comes with practice, but it also helps to have an application form loaded with revealing responses. On top of that, Mr. Fielder obviously has talent, and in this situation it is easy to give a lot of 3 ("good") ratings without risk of being off much. You could accuse me of using a real-life example in which preliminary analysis is unusually valid, and I plead guilty!

# APPLICATION FORM

You are not required to furnish any information which is prohibited by federal, state, or local law.

| | | | |
|---|---|---|---|
| *FIELDER* Last Name | *JOSEPH* First | *A.* Middle | *555-55-5555* Social Security No. |
| *306 E. 76th* Home Address | *N.Y.C.* | | *212-555-1743* Telephone |
| *654 MADISON AVE.* Business Address | *N.Y.C.* | | *212-555-3471* Telephone |

Position applied for *MANAGER, COMPUTER SALES* _____ Earnings Expected $ _____

## I. BUSINESS EXPERIENCE: (Please start with your present position.)

**A.** Firm *SHARING TIME, INC.* Address *654 MADISON AVE.* City *N.Y.C.*

Kind of Business *COMPUTER TIME SHARING* Employed From *3/81* To *PRESENT*
(show months as well as years)

Title *SALES REP./SALES MGR.* Initial Compensation *$30K* Final Total Compensation *$41K* (Base *30K* / Bonus *11K* / Other )

Nature of Work *SELLING COMPUTER TIME SHARING SERVICES TO MAJOR N.Y.C. CO's.*
Supervisory Responsibility *2 SALES REPS.* Name & Title of Immediate Superior *J. RAYMOND, V.P.*

What (do) (did) you like most about your job? *VARIETY OF CUSTOMERS. INDEPENDENCE. VARIETY OF BUSINESS NEEDS (OF CUSTOMERS). TRAINING REPS.*

What (do) (did) you least enjoy? *LIMITED GROWTH + SERVICES OF COMPANY. COMPANY TOO LITTLE. BORED.*

Reasons for leaving or desiring to change *LACK OF GOOD SALES DIRECTION + MANAGEMENT.*

**B.** Firm *COMPUTER VISTAS* Address *747 3RD. AVE.* City *N.Y.C.*

Kind of Business *COMPUTER CONSULTANTS* Employed from *1/77* To *3/81*
(show months as well as years)

Title *SALES REP.* Initial Compensation *$19K* Final Total Compensation *$38K* (Base *32K* / Bonus *6K* / Other )

Nature of Work *SELLING PROGRAMMING SERVICES TO D.P. DEPARTMENTS*
Supervisory Responsibility *COORDINATED/TRAINED 6 SALES REPS,* Name & Title of Immediate Superior *Wm. ANDERSON, V.P.*

What did you like most about your job? *FIRST SALES POSITION + ACHIEVED >100% QUOTA EACH YEAR. PROVED PROMOTABILITY TO MGMT. FAST GROWING COMPANY.*

What did you least enjoy? *PROMISED EQUITY DID NOT COME ABOUT. NO SALES TRAINING.*

Reasons for leaving *RECRUITED.*

**C.** Firm *GRUMMAN CORP.* Address *107 57TH* City *N.Y.C.*

Kind of Business *AEROSPACE* Employed From *5/74* To *1/77*
(show months as well as years)

Title *PROJECT MGR.* Initial Compensation *$17K* Final Total Compensation *$19K* (Base *19K* / Bonus / Other )

Nature of Work *DESIGN OF PARTS OF LUNAR MODULE*
Supervisory Responsibility *2 ENGINEERS* Name & Title of Immediate Superior *T. VITULLI, DIRECTOR*

**Figure 6. Application form.**

What did you like about your job? 2 PATENTS. MANAGEMENT. BACK TO N.Y.C. !

What did you least enjoy? WORK TOO MICROSCOPIC. DISLIKE AMOUNT OF
ADMINISTRATIVE TASKS.

Reasons for leaving PLANNED CHANGE IN CAREER

| Other Positions Held: a. Company b. City | a. Your Title b. Name of Superior | Date (mo./yr.) a. Began b. Left | Compensation a. Initial b. Final | a. Type of Work b. Reason for Leaving |
|---|---|---|---|---|
| D. a. BOEING b. HUNTSVILLE, ALA. | a. ENGINEER b. A. WRIGHT | a. 6/71 b. 5/74 | a. 8/12K b. 8/15K | a. ENGINEERING b. RELOCATE |
| E. | | / | | |
| F. | | / | | |
| G. | | / | | |

Indicate by letter A any of the above employers you do **not** wish contacted.

## II. MILITARY EXPERIENCE:

If in service, indicate: Branch N/A _____ Date (mo./yr.) entered _____ Date (mo./yr.)discharged _____

Nature of duties _____ Overseas _____

Highest rank or grade _____ Terminal rank or grade _____

## III. EDUCATION

(circle highest grade completed)

Elementary 6 7 8    High School 1 2 3 4    College 1 2 3 4 (5) 6 7 8

**A. HIGH SCHOOL**   Name of High School TEACHER'S ACADEMY   Location N.Y.C.

Dates (mo./yr.) attended 8/62 — 6/66 _____ If graduated, month and year 6/66

Approximate number in graduating class 70 _____ Rank from top 21

Final grade point average 92 _____ (A = 90) Scores on ACT ? SAT ?

Extracurricular activities CHESS, TENNIS, STUDENT COUNCIL

Offices, honors/awards _____

Part-time and summer work SUMMER CAMP COUNSELOR

**B. COLLEGE/GRADUATE SCHOOL**

| Name & Location | From | To | Degree | Major | Grade Point Average | Total Credit Hours | Extracurricular Activities, Honors and Awards |
|---|---|---|---|---|---|---|---|
| CITY COLLEGE OF NEW YORK | 9/66 | 6/71 | B.S. | PHYSICS | 3.2 (A = 4) | | |
| COLUMBIA | 8/74 | | | | (A = ___) | | |
| | | | | | (A = ___) | | |

**Figure 6.   (Continued)**

37

What undergraduate courses did you like most _SCIENCES_ Why _INTERESTING_

What undergraduate courses did you like least _SOCIAL SCIENCES_ Why _OBVIOUS_

How was your education financed _SELF (WORK)_

Part-time and summer work _WAITER_

Subsequent courses or studies _GRADUATE ENGINEERING_

## IV. FAMILY

If any personal, financial, or family circumstances might have a bearing on any aspect of job performance, explain in full _NONE._

In the event of an emergency, whom would you wish notified (other than spouse)

Name _MARTHA FIELDER_

Address _N.Y.C._ Telephone _212-555-7787_

## V. PHYSICAL DATA

Condition of Health: _EXCELLENT_ Date of most recent physical exam _8/80_

What physical handicaps or limitations do you have _NONE_

List any serious illnesses, operations, accidents or nervous disorders you may have had with approximate date:
_NONE_

## VI. ACTIVITIES:

Membership in professional or job-relevant organizations (Exclude racial, religious and nationality groups) _NONE._
_INTERESTS IN READING, MOVIES, THEATER + COMPETITIVE TENNIS_

Publications, patents, inventions, professional licenses or special honors or awards _2 PATENTS_

## VII. AIMS:

What qualifications, abilities, and strong points will help you succeed in this job _HIGHLY MOTIVATED, GOOD TRACK RECORD, ANALYTIC ABILITY, HARD WORKING, STRIVE FOR EXCELLENCE, AMBITIOUS, WELL ORGANIZED, PRACTICAL_

What income would you need (in today's dollar value) in order to live the way you would like to live? (Your response will not be taken as dissatisfaction with your present salary, but refers to the salary which you ultimately wish to attain.)

_$150,000_

Willing to relocate? Yes ✓ No____ Any restrictions____

**Figure 6. (Continued)**

Amount of overnight travel acceptable _2 NIGHTS PER WEEK_

What are your plans for the future _(SALES) SALES MGMT. → EXECUTIVE →_
_OWN BUSINESS_

I authorize all schools, credit bureaus and law enforcement agencies to supply information concerning my background. I understand that I have a right to request disclosure of the nature, scope, and results of such an inquiry. I understand that if any statement herein is not true, an offer of employment may be withdrawn.

_Joseph A. Fielder_
Signature

_8/1/82_
Date

**Figure 6.** (Continued)

| Person Specification | Your Rating | Rating by Co-Workers, One Year After Mr. Fielder Was Hired | Absolute Difference (Disregard Pluses and Minuses) |
|---|---|---|---|
| **Intellectual Characteristics** | | | |
| 1. Level of intelligence | | 3 | |
| 2. Analytic ability | | 4 | |
| 3. Ability to diagnose client needs | | 2 | |
| 4. Creativity/innovativeness | | 3 | |
| 5. Pragmatism | | 3 | |
| 6. Intellectual flexibility | | 3 | |
| 7. Oral communications skills | | 2 | |
| 8. Written communications skills | | 3 | |
| 9. Education | | 3 | |
| 10. Experience—technical | | 2 | |
| 11. Experience—sales | | 4 | |
| 12. Experience—management | | 3 | |

## Personal Makeup

| | |
|---|---|
| 13. Initiative/resourcefulness | 4 |
| 14. Self-objectivity | 2 |
| 15. Perseverance | 3 |
| 16. Independence | 3 |
| 17. Standards of performance | 4 |
| 18. Track record | 4 |
| 19. A "doer" | 4 |
| 20. Emotional maturity/stability/resilience | 3 |
| 21. Administrative abilities | 4 |

## Interpersonal Relations

| | |
|---|---|
| 22. First impression | 2 |
| 23. Interpersonal flexibility | 3 |
| 24. Assertiveness | 2 |
| 25. Team player | 2 |

**Figure 7. Comparison of your ratings of Mr. Fielder with ratings by Mr. Fielder's co-workers. Rating Scale: 4 = excellent, 3 = good, 2 = fair, 1 = poor, 0 = very poor.**

41

| Person Specification | Your Rating | Rating by Co-Workers, One Year After Mr. Fielder Was Hired | Absolute Difference (Disregard Pluses and Minuses) |
|---|---|---|---|
| 26. Enthusiasm | | 2 | |
| 27. Empathy | | 2 | |
| 28. Leadership | | 3 | |
| 29. Management—recruitment/selection | | 3 | |
| 30. Management—training/development | | 3 | |
| 31. Management—goal-setting | | 4 | |
| 32. Management—monitoring performance | | 3 | |
| 33. Management—performance feedback | | 2 | |
| 34. Management—removing nonperformers | | 3 | |
| 35. Management—team development | | 3 | |
| **Motivations and Aspirations** | | | |
| 36. Motivation level | | 4 | |
| 37. Health | | 4 | |

| | |
|---|---|
| 38. Ambition | 4 |
| 39. Willingness to take risks | 3 |
| 40. Compatibility of interests | 3 |

$\Sigma$ (Sum of absolute differences) = _____

## Your Performance

Sum of absolute differences ($\Sigma$) = _____

Your average difference: score ($\Sigma$ = _____ $\div$ 40) = _____

| An average difference of | | |
|---|---|---|
| 0.0 — 0.75 | = | super guru |
| 0.75 — 1.00 | = | latent guru |
| 1.0 — 1.5 | = | not bad, but could use more practice |
| 1.5 or higher | = | in the future, don't forget to compare your analyses with those by someone else! |

**Figure 7. (Continued)**

| Person Specification | Rating by Managers, Derived from Application Form Analysis | Rating by Co-Workers | Difference | Positive (+) and Negative (−) Reasons for Ratings Based on Application Form Analysis |
|---|---|---|---|---|
| 1. Level of intelligence | 3 | 3 | 0 | (+) A average in high school; (+) 21/70 in graduating class at private high school; (+) 3.2 GPA in physics in CCNY (good school, though not Harvard). (−) Not straight As at CCNY |
| 2. Analytic ability | 3 | 4 | 1 | (+) Physics major; (+) 6 years of scientific career; (+) says "analytic ability" is strong point; (+) hobby is chess. (−) Flighty (?) career changes (did not analyze job moves thoroughly?) |
| 3. Ability to diagnose client needs | 2 | 2 | 0 | (+) Doubled compensation at Computer Vistas in sales, so can't be too bad. (−) Suffered cut in salary in changing jobs; (−) complains of insufficient sales training (is this because he had major deficiencies?); (−) no mention of people in AIMS (strengths) section (he has not diagnosed prospective employer's "needs" in filling out application form— does not sell himself well for a sales job!) |
| 4. Creativity/ innovativeness | 3 | 3 | 0 | (+) Two patents (?) Limited data |
| 5. Pragmatism | 3 | 3 | 0 | (+) Reasonably successful career; (+) changed careers; (+) considers self "practical." (−) Naive in joining Sharing Time? (is leaving after 1½ years) |

| Item | | | | Rationale |
|---|---|---|---|---|
| 6. Intellectual flexibility | 3 | 3 | 0 | (+) Changed careers; (+) disliked "limited services" at Computer Vistas; (+) likes "variety" at Sharing Time; (+) has taken graduate courses while working |
| 7. Oral communications skills | 3 | 2 | 1 | (+) To succeed he must have communicated well orally. (−) Complained of not having sales training; (−) scientific career probably did not involve speeches |
| 8. Written communications | 2 | 3 | 1 | (+) Application form is completed clearly, precisely, and with good vocabulary and grammar. (−) Too negative application form responses in which he is supposed to "sell" himself |
| 9. Education | 3 | 3 | 0 | (+) B.S. degree in physics from CCNY; (+) graduate courses at Columbia |
| 10. Experience—technical | 2 | 2 | 0 | (+) Five years' computer sales experience. (−) Apparently never a programmer or systems analyst |
| 11. Experience—sales | 4 | 4 | 0 | (+) Five years' computer sales experience |
| 12. Experience—Management | 3 | 3 | 0 | (+) Hard to specify—clearly 1½ years at Sharing Time and perhaps ½ year at Computer Vistas and some time (1 year?) at Grumman. (−) True management experience all with only 2 subordinates at a time |

**Figure 8.** Summary of rationale and ratings based on application form analysis of Joseph Fielder.
**Rating Scale:** 4 = excellent; 3 = good; 2 = fair; 1 = poor; 0 = very poor.

45

| Person Specification | Rating by Managers, Derived from Application Form Analysis | Rating by Co-Workers | Difference | Positive (+) and Negative (−) Reasons for Ratings Based on Application Form Analysis |
|---|---|---|---|---|
| 13. Initiative/ resourcefulness | 3 | 4 | 1 | (+) Worked way through college; (+) changed careers; (+) successful in sales, apparently without sales training; (+) two patents. (−) Could he have done more to make last job more successful? |
| 14. Self-objectivity | 2 | 2 | 0 | (+) Successful career record, so must be able to determine and overcome most shortcomings. (−) Seems to blame others, particularly superiors, for things not working out; (−) naive in accepting job (Sharing Time) that didn't meet his needs? |
| 15. Perseverance | 3 | 3 | 0 | (+) Worked his way through college; (+) graduate courses; (+) 2 patents; (+) succeeded in sales without sales training; (+) has apparently persevered in what he wants. (−) Applying for third job in 7 years; (−) "planned" job change |

| | | | | |
|---|---|---|---|---|
| 16. Independence | 3 | 3 | 0 | (+) Likes independence in current job; (+) apparently taught self to sell and succeeded; (+) eventually wants his own company.<br>(−) Seems to blame others for not training him, for not giving good sales direction, and for not offering good management |
| 17. Standards of performance | 4 | 4 | 0 | (+) Worked way through college and earned B+ grades in physics; (+) scientific career 6 years; (+) successful in sales with fine company (Computer Vistas); (+) complete in filling out application form; (+) says he strives for excellence |
| 18. Track record | 4 | 4 | 0 | (+) Progressed from engineering to project engineering in scientific career; (+) gives "coordinated responsibilities" at Computer Vistas; (+) earning $41,000 at 33 years of age (deduced from high school graduation data); (+) says "proved promotability to management" at Computer Vistas and currently is sales manager.<br>(−) Decline in income from Computer Vistas to Sharing Time |
| 19. A "doer" | 3 | 3 | 0 | (+) Put self through college; (+) successfully changed careers; (+) took graduate courses; (+) completed application form conscientiously.<br>(−) Too much blaming others suggests not the greatest "doer" |

**Figure 8.** (Continued)

| Person Specification | Rating by Managers, Derived from Application Form Analysis | Rating by Co-Workers | Difference | Positive (+) and Negative (−) Reasons for Ratings Based on Application Form Analysis |
|---|---|---|---|---|
| 20. Emotional maturity/stability/ resilience | 2 | 3 | 1 | (+) Overall successful academic and career record; (+) apparently no health problems. (−) Possible problems with superiors suggested in his being promised equity and not getting it; (−) blaming superiors for lack of good sales direction and management; (−) job-hopping? |
| 21. Administrative abilities | 3 | 4 | 1 | (+) Application form complete, neat and well-organized; (+) scientific background requires detail orientation; (+) says he planned his career change; (+) well-enough organized to work his way through college successfully and to succeed in jobs requiring administration. (−) Says disliked amount of administrative tasks at Grumman |
| 22. First impression | 2 | 2 | 0 | (+) Successful sales; (+) bold writing. (−) Scientific early career, so it might have been difficult for him to develop an image that would immediately impress corporate executives; (−) application form is rather cold and shows some insensitivity |

| | | | |
|---|---|---|---|
| 23. Interpersonal flexibility | 2 | 3 | 1 | (+) Has apparently sold successfully to large companies; (+) has had to deal successfully to be promotable to management.<br>(−) A lot of solitary and nonteam activities in school, job situations, and current hobbies; (−) some superiors referred to by first initial, suggesting overly formal and distant relationships; (−) did not "sell" himself on the application form; (−) no activities in high school |
| 24. Assertiveness | 2 | 2 | 0 | (+) Must have closed sales to be successful; (+) has progressed to management.<br>(−) Complains of sales direction and no sales training; (−) was promise regarding equity at Computer Vistas broken because he was viewed as easy to take advantage of? |
| 25. Team player | 2 | 2 | 0 | (−) No mention of people, team efforts, helping subordinates, enjoying camaraderie, or being of service to people, may be out for "number one" only; (−) changing jobs too often |
| 26. Enthusiasm | 2 | 2 | 0 | (+) Successful record in sales so can't be terrible in this regard.<br>(−) Application form responses lack warmth and "humanness" |
| 27. Empathy | 2 | 2 | 0 | (+) Has sold successfully.<br>(−) Application form shows remarkably few insights into the likely feelings and attitudes of whoever is reading it—too much coldness and blaming of others |

**Figure 8. (Continued)**

49

| Person Specification | Rating by Managers, Derived from Application Form Analysis | Rating by Co-Workers | Difference | Positive (+) and Negative (−) Reasons for Ratings Based on Application Form Analysis |
|---|---|---|---|---|
| 28. Leadership | 3 | 3 | 0 | (+) Student council; (+) summer camp counselor; (+) says "proved promotability to management." and "coordinated/trained" six sales representatives at Computer Vistas; (+) management responsibilities—two subordinates at Sharing Time, two subordinates at Grumman. <br><br> (−) Scientific career and solitary interests suggest possible lack in empathy and interpersonal flexibility components of management; (−) no mention of leadership, training, communications, or coordination skills in AIMS (strengths) section of application form; in management jobs, has had only two subordinates at a time |
| 29. Management— recruitment/ selection | 3 | 3 | 0 | (+) Student council; (+) summer camp counselor; (+) says "proved promotability to management" and "coordinated/trained" six sales representatives at Computer Vistas; (+) has two subordinates for management responsibilities at Sharing Time; (+) at least 1½ years of management experience (though none currently). <br><br> (−) Scientific career and solitary interests suggest possible lack in empathy and interpersonal flexibility components of management; (−) no mention of |

leadership, training, communications, or coordination skills in AIMS (strengths) section of application form; (−) only two subordinates at Sharing Time; (−) in management jobs has had only two subordinates at a time

| | | | | |
|---|---|---|---|---|
| 30. Management—training/development | 3 | 3 | 0 | (Same as 29) |
| 31. Management—goal-setting | 3 | 4 | 1 | (Same as 29) |
| 32. Management—monitoring performance | 3 | 3 | 0 | (Same as 29) |
| 33. Management—performance feedback | 3 | 2 | 1 | (Same as 29) |
| 34. Management—removing nonperformers | 3 | 3 | 0 | (Same as 29) |
| 35. Management—team development | 2 | 3 | 1 | (Same as 29) |
| 36. Motivation level | 4 | 4 | 0 | (+) Considers self "highly motivated"; (+) succeeded in academics, succeeded in scientific career, and succeeded in sales |

**Figure 8.** (Continued)

51

| Person Specification | Rating by Managers, Derived from Application Form Analysis | Rating by Co-Workers | Difference | Positive (+) and Negative (−) Reasons for Ratings Based on Application Form Analysis |
|---|---|---|---|---|
| 37. Health | 3 | 4 | 1 | (+) Considers self in "excellent health"; (+) worked way through college; (+) likes "competitive tennis" |
| 38. Ambition | 4 | 4 | 0 | (+) Goal of $150,000 in income; (+) wants to be executive and then run his own company |
| 39. Willingness to take risks | 3 | 3 | 0 | (+) Changed careers; (+) wants management in New York area; (+) willing to be out 2 nights a week; (+) likely $45,000 first year compensation is 10% more than current income. (−) Experienced salary cut and it is not clear if he accepted too much, too little, or in-between risks; (−) Sharing Time apparently not working out—took too big a risk in joining them? |
| 40. Compatibility of interests | 2 | 3 | 1 | (+) Ambitious (and ACME offers opportunity). (−) Seems far too wedded to New York City; (−) too impatient to get ahead? (−) turnover risk? |

**Figure 8.** (Continued)

You might be interested in how the real Mr. Fielder differs from the impression he makes in the application form. First of all, you should know that he is very happy and extremely successful with ACTS. His co-workers (including his supervisor) explained that Mr. Fielder's "written communications" were deficient when the application form was completed, but he was trained at ACTS and improved; they say his "administrative abilities" are superb despite the application form notation, "dislike amount of administrative tasks." They say he is deficient in "diagnosing client needs" (they rate him "fair") because there is "too much of the coldly analytic scientist" in him, he is not a very compelling speaker, and he does not show much empathy in initial client contacts. Once customers get to know him, however, they like and respect him, and thorough, accurate diagnoses are usual. Despite his application form statements showing his strong attachment to New York City, Mr. Fielder has relocated and is happy that he did. He still tends to blame others and is a bit defensive, but these are minor shortcomings—not nearly as bad as the application form suggests. Such is life! The application form is simply not as revealing as an in-depth selection interview; what is remarkable, is how revealing it can be.

A note of caution: It is perfectly appropriate to review an application form and on the basis of these data (and any other available at the time) to determine whom you want to call in for interviews, just as it is perfectly appropriate for scientists to generate hypotheses based upon whatever sparse, limited initial data they have. What is not appropriate is for the scientist to be so intent on confirming initial hypotheses that conflicting data that may emerge in the future are overlooked. It is equally inappropriate for you, during an interview, to be so concerned with confirming your original application form-generated hypotheses that you selectively perceive, or rather misperceive, subsequent interview data. As will be pointed out later in this book, all of us have a natural inclination to bias our perceptions various ways, but most of us, with awareness of this tendency and a determination not to sacrifice intellectual integrity, can control it.

How important is the application form analysis among the various steps recommended? If your organization has a worthless application form and will not permit you to use an extensive one, even on an experimental basis as a supplement, will the recommended approach of this book be lost for you? Only partly. Having well-thought-out person specifications is more important, and allowing enough time to use the "In-Depth Selection Interview Guide" is extremely important. The recommended approach includes hundreds of pointers for how to make the in-depth selection interview more revealing and valid, and that is most important. What the application form analysis does, among the 12 chronological steps in Figure 2, is to insure that a higher percentage of unacceptable candidates will be weeded out at this step, less of your time will be wasted in nonproductive interviews, and more of your time will be available where it counts—with candidates who better meet the person specifications.

If you are doing your own search (running ads, contacting industry associates, among other activities), you might have stacks of completed application forms and résumés on your desk, including perhaps, eight that look sufficiently interesting to pursue. We'll assume that you don't have eight days or eight half-days to spend in interviewing, so you want to narrow the field, but without excluding anyone who might be a good candidate. It's time to conduct very brief interviews over the telephone.

## BRIEF TELEPHONE DISCUSSIONS

In just 5 minutes on the telephone you can clarify a couple of points ("We have IBM machines—how much experience, if any, have you had with them?"), describe the job in a little more detail, and if you both are still interested at that point, invite the person in for a preliminary interview.

The flavor of such an invitation is, "Pat, I'd rather chat in person than over the phone, so if it is convenient I'd like you to stop by for half an hour. We can ask each other a few more questions, and if we are both interested after that, we can plan a more extensive visit.

At this point perhaps you have chopped your list of eight applicants down to six.

## PRELIMINARY INTERVIEWS

Envision yourself with your recruitment efforts well under way, résumés and completed application forms have been analyzed, and after brief telephone discussions with prospects you are ready to start conducting preliminary interviews. These are not the 2½ -hour in-depth selection interviews that are emphasized in this book, but 15–45 minute meetings in which you and the candidate can do further screening.

In medium to large companies, a human resources (personnel)

department might have done recruitment (through ads, search firms, or placement firms) and prescreened candidates through record checks, short preliminary interviews, and maybe even some in-depth selection interviews. If you are an executive, you would then conduct a couple of short preliminary interviews and a couple of in-depth selection interviews and hire the best candidate. Isn't it wonderful to be a high-powered executive and delegate the legwork!

Regardless of who pre-screened candidates, at this step in the hiring process you could waste a lot of time by committing to a full in-depth selection interview, when it could be that in 20 minutes you and/or the applicant would decide that there was not a good fit. Also, as will be explained later in this book, the in-depth selection interview reviews a person's background chronologicaly, so it could be a full hour before you would start asking about the current position or goals. The preliminary interview is the perfect next step, neither too brief nor too long.

In the preliminary interview, after explaining the job and person specifications, and selling the individual on the wonderful opportunity available and the terrific boss you are, it is appropriate for you to:

> Review the application form. Go into most detail about the current or most recent job—responsibilities, accomplishments, high points, low points, reasons for desiring a change—and touch more briefly on education and earlier work history. Take wording from "In-Depth Selection Interview Guide," Appendix C.
>
> Ask the person for a self-assessment—"What are your strong points and any weaker points or areas for improvement?" Add, "What does your current (or most recent) supervisor consider to be your strengths and areas for improvement?"
>
> Conclude the preliminary interview, answer any further questions the person has, say you will be in touch (if you are undecided or negative) or establish a time for an in-depth selection interview (if you are sure you wish to continue).

The application form has been previously analyzed, so a couple of questions that might confirm or disconfirm hypotheses generated from that analysis might be added. That's about all there is to it, although specific wording, the ways of building rapport, using interview probes, ferreting out the negatives, and other techniques are important in all interviews and are thoroughly covered later in this book.

The key question you ask yourself throughout the preliminary interview is, "Is there enough of a match that I would want to grant an in-depth selection interview to this person, with the substantial time commitment that would mean on my part and perhaps [if it is part of the process to include other short interviews during the visit], on the time of others?"

If your organization is in a remote location it may save you time and money to conduct some or all preliminary interviews over the telephone. If you are not unusually skilled at this, though, forget it— you'll cost yourself more in the long run.

Some organizations save time by using this ploy: The individual will be called and told something like, "After reviewing your application form, I am sufficiently interested to ask you to come in for an hour or two to meet with me, review some of the literature on our organization, and take a tour of the offices." If the preliminary interview goes well, the interviewer may extend the talks into a more in-depth interview process. The literature and tour could be put off to another time. But if after 5 minutes the interviewer decides it is a definite "no go," a polite additional 10 minutes might be spent, really just skimming the high points. Then the interviewer might say, "OK, I have briefly covered your background and interests, and I certainly want to provide you an opportunity to get a better feel for our organization. I have asked [administrative assistant] to show you around the offices and give you some literature. We'll be back in touch within three weeks." Lower-level people may think you've been just wonderful, although higher-powered people would immediately sense the brush-off. It is important for you to balance your time needs with the possible adverse effects of seeming to give short shrift to someone—perhaps someone who buys your organization's groceries or wears its manufactured clothes.

## ALTERNATIVE APPROACHES

### Brief Interview Guides for Lower Levels

For factory, retail clerk, warehouse, and comparable levels, a much abbreviated approach is appropriate. A large retailer uses a combination of two interview guides to screen clerks—Appendixes G1 and G2. These guides could easily be tailored for use by virtually any type of organization. The "Quick Screen" interview (Appendix G1) is a 3–7 minute discussion, usually conducted by a receptionist, who should be very perceptive and well trained. The receptionist hands out application forms to be completed on premises and helps the applicant with the form, adding the questions in the "Quick Screen" guide.

Applicants of interest are further interviewed that day or later by a personnel manager or department manager, using the "Retail Store Clerk Interview Guide" (Appendix G2).This requires an interview of 15–30 minutes or more for a candidate with a longer work history. The neat thing about this guide is that responses to all 16 questions about two jobs can be recorded on a single summary sheet—if you can write small enough!

## Interview by a Management Psychologist

Very little is written about management psychologists. The media find us about as interesting as a one-star movie. When management psychologists are used properly, they merely supplement the in-depth selection interviews conducted internally. The assumption in using such an outside professional resource is that impartiality and more interviewing expertise, particularly in evaluating subtle psychological tendencies, justify the costs. Furthermore, some managers feel that since a candidate might be reporting to them in a few weeks, they would prefer not to pressure the person by pointing out inconsistencies or focusing on too many negatives. An outside professional can often deal with negatives more comfortably. Finally, the management psychologist may have developed some clever techniques to finesse disclosures out of candidates who are quite clever and polished in the interview situation.

## Employment Tests

Since the 1960s employments tests, including tests of intelligence and other abilities such as personality, interests, and management styles, have suffered constant controversy. As a result of federal legislation pertaining to test validation and nondiscrimination in impact, many firms decided to abandon testing programs rather than deal with controversy. Nonetheless, a 1975 study by Prentice-Hall and the American Society of Personnel Administration disclosed that 60% of employers with more than 25,000 employees did at least some testing, and 39% of employers with fewer than 100 employees used tests. More than 25% of 2000 companies in the study stated they test only at clerical levels.* The decline in testing is a pity, for psychologists have

*Personnel Management Policies and Practices Report, Englewood Cliffs, New Jersey: Prentice-Hall, 1975.

known for years that a properly developed, validated, administered, and interpreted test battery can greatly outperform all other selection approaches, interviews included. That may sound strange in a book on selection interviewing, but it has repeatedly been proven true. When comparisons have been made between the power of tests and of interviews to predict the job success of persons in factory, clerical, supervisory, sales, and management positions, the tests almost always are superior.

Later in this book I discuss why selection interviewing has such a poor record and what can be done to improve it. For now I'll simply state a belief that the ultimate in predictive value will eventually prove to be a combination of scientifically weighted test scores and interview opinions. Interviewer opinions can be included like any other test score, in a formula that can insure fewer mis-hires and more correct hires than either the tests or interviews alone. The tests and scientific methodology already exist. What is needed now are proven interviewers who have well-developed skills and function within comprehensive selection steps like the ones suggested in this book.

Interviews are used instead of tests at management and professional levels for various reasons, one being fear of discrimination charges. However, research has repeatedly shown tests not to be discriminatory against minorities. Maybe there is hope—a major study by the National Research Council in 1982 should put to rest doubts about ability testing.* The four-year study concluded that ability tests are good predictors of job performance and "predict equally well for all groups of test takers." The study further concluded that ability tests do not "systematically" understate the "performance of minority group members." The "compelling, practical fact" is that employment tests are a source of "valuable information about prospective employees." The research project was conducted by a 19-member committee that claims, "EEOC [Equal Employment Opportunity Commission] is not interested in tests, nor even primarily in merit." Instead, the EEOC's mission has been to ensure that more minorities and women are hired than in the past.

My advice to larger employers has been and will continue to be: Get back into tests and fulfill affirmative action goals through greater recruitment efforts for underrepresented groups.

---

*Ability Testing: Uses, Consequences, and Controversies, Committee on Ability Testing, Assembly of Behavioral and Social Sciences, National Research Council, Alexandra K. Wigdor and Wendell R. Garner (Eds.). Washington, D.C.: National Academy Press, 1982.

# 4 | The In-Depth Selection Interview

As a result of preliminary interviews, validated tests, or interviews by a management psychologist, you have narrowed the field to one or two truly viable candidates. You invite them to come in, "to review your background, interests, and goals in depth and to provide an opportunity for you to ask me a lot more questions." Candidates are asked to allow for 2½–3 hours for this interview, plus additional time to "sell" the candidate, take tours, and have short interviews with co-workers or tours of facilities are to be included. The next five chapters pause in the chronological steps in the hiring sequence and delve deeply into the in-depth selection interview—what to do, why, legal considerations, how to interpret responses, and how to avoid common errors. A discussion of the in-depth selection interview appropriately begins with its superstructure—the "In-Depth Selection Interview Guide."

## RATIONALE UNDERLYING USE OF AN INTERVIEW GUIDE

In surveys of several thousand managers and executives, the vast majority indicated that they do not use a structured interview guide when conducting selection interviews, yet most management psychologists I know do use one. If professionals who specialize in conducting interviews for selection and promotion use guides, why don't business people? Over the past 40 years most publications on selection interviewing have emphasized the value of using such an instrument, and yet the habit of not using one is apparently well ingrained in the American business psyche. Why?

I have asked several hundred business people that question, and most say that they have a vague feeling in their gut that there would be distinct advantages to using a standard format and precise wording of questions, but they simply haven't seen an interview guide they liked. Some have tried structured interview guides, but feel uncomfortable using them, saying:

> I feel boxed in by structured interview guide that tells me exactly what to ask and in which order to ask it.

> Interviews with a structured interview guide lack spontaneity. It seems like a cold question-and-answer session, not a warm, human dialog.

> I feel like a schoolboy reading questions from a paper rather than a seasoned professional who should know what questions to ask and in what order.

> It's too much trouble to memorize questions, and when I read the questions I seem to have the voice of a telephone operator or airline flight attendant. I am sure that turns off the interviewee—it does me.

> It takes too damn much time to ask all those questions!

> Is it not true that clinical psychologists and psychiatrists agree that the most authentic data on an individual are generated through an active listening dialog rather than a standardized question-and-answer format?

> What proof is there that an interview guide is so good?

All of these are legitimate concerns in the sense that people are sincere in expressing them. In the following paragraphs I hope to allay all of these concerns and demonstrate that using an interview guide is "the best game in town."

Over the years I have found that the only truly convincing way for sophisticated businessmen and women to come to believe that a structured interview guide is valuable is to create some circumstances to provide data from which they can evaluate the relative values of different approaches. At the beginning of selection interviewing workshops, the advice is given to stick very close to the interview guide in terms of wording and sequence of questions. But as participants take turns interviewing a volunteer subject, they inevitably wander from the interview guide. It is very handy to have a videotape to play back, so that the manager can readily see how changing just a couple of words in the question severely biased the interviewee's response or how skipping a question resulted in the omission of very important data. After 15 or 20 occurrences like this, managers become convinced that an interview guide is indeed a valuable tool.

Most managers "wing it" in selection interviews. They review the person's résumé and application form in the interview and usually plan to cover work history and career goals, but they obtain nothing close to the comprehensiveness assured by the "In-Depth Selection Interview Guide" (Appendix C). They talk about this and that, meander off on this tangent and that; the topics are job relevant, as a rule, but the nonstructured approach is not comprehensive. If you had 50 hours for such an approach, you might cover all of the very important topics. When a structured interview guide is not used, the spontaneity and depth achieved in some topics is counterbalanced by many significant omissions and shallowness in other important topics.

The overwhelming majority of managers who do not use a thorough, structured interview guide are unable to gain some very important insights into people because they never asked the questions! In a typical individual interviewer training session, after I observe an interview conducted by an executive trainee, we both will pause to sift through our data and write up conclusions. It stands out in neon lights when conclusions are reached regarding Sally's management style and approaches (for example), and yet she was not asked the basic questions on the subject: "Describe your management philosophy and style and guess what subordinates might say are your strengths and shortcomings." "How might you want to modify your management approaches?" "How would you describe key subordinates and their strengths, shortcomings, and overall performance?" "Have you promoted or removed anyone from any of those jobs?"

Most interviewers infer a candidate's management style from interview personality—a risky approach because some managers are docile with interviewers and tough and demanding with subordinates. Executives, managers, and management psychologists all learn to use interview guides by failing to ask a question (or to ask it the right way), realizing later that they blew it and resolving to include the question, asked the right way, the next time. Do that for all relevant questions, and the list of questions becomes an interview guide.

How about the complaint that the in-depth interview, using an extensive interview guide, takes too long? When managers bring this up, my response is, "Fine, let's start eliminating questions—how about the questions about work responsibilities, accomplishments, and failures? No? You say we must keep those? Then how about if we scratch inquiries into plans and goals for the future? No? Then maybe you are not interested in the person's work habits? You are? Then maybe we could scrap that line of questioning about the person's managerial approaches. Oh, you want to keep those questions, too?" You get the message—almost all managers decide that they want responses to almost all of the questions in the "In-Depth Selection Interview Guide," and that's the reason it is long.

What about the concern some people have about looking like a schoolchild reading a list of questions? If a person very awkwardly mumbles through the interview guide, losing one's place, misreading questions and then reading them over, and reading with no eye contact and an artificial-sounding voice, the interview will surely be an abomination. Reviewing the structured interview guide a few minutes before an interview will help the interviewer obtain a smoother delivery.

There is no reason using an interview guide should seem cold or artificial. If you were applying for a job, would you prefer to have an interviewer grope for questions or to have a list of questions which would permit you very thoroughly to describe your successes, accomplishments, goals, and needs? When was the last time you went up to the cockpit of an airplane, demanding that the pilot not use a preflight checklist? Interviewees might be a bit surprised when experienced managers pull out a structured interview guide, but I have yet to hear one complain. Indeed, the thoroughness and precision impress interviewees as evidence of, not lack of, professionalism.

## Scientific Foundations of the In-Depth Selection Interview Guide

Although research pertinent to selection interviewing is incomplete in some respects, I'm pleased to report that when interview approaches are researched, the advantages of using a structured interview guide have consistently been shown.

For example, in some of the most realistic research done on interviewing, Donald Grant and Douglas Bray studied the interview as an important component of assessment centers, which are multiday exercises in which trained managers put candidates for promotion through all sorts of tests, interviews, and simulations of management tasks.* Grant and Bray found interviews using an interview guide to

*Grant, D. L., and Bray, D. W. Contributions of the interview to assessment of management potential. *Journal of Applied Psychology*, 1969, **53**, 24–34.

be both reliable and valid in important respects. These researchers spent years refining the approaches used by managers at AT&T—a marked improvement over most selection interviewing research in which interviewers are college sophomores (very convenient for the academicians but not very realistic) or college recruiters (who conduct 20 brief interviews a day).

More recent research concluded that the structured interview guide is not just desirable, but critical to selection interview reliability.†‡ These scientific findings are supported by my own personal experience that has repeatedly confirmed that managers are much more valid predictors of candidate success when they use guides.

### Time-Out!—To Peruse the In-Depth Selection Interview Guide

Please take a few moments to read Appendix C, the interview guide which forms the basis for this book. Throughout the rest of this book there will be references to certain sections, sequence, and wording of questions. Looking it over now will add to your comprehension of major points.

### Smorgasbord Questions

The "In-Depth Selection Interview Guide" included in this book is not as confining as some interview guides, because it uses a number of "smorgasbord"questions.Atthe beginning of some major sections of the guide is a long "smorgasbord" question including many subparts, and the interviewee is asked to "carry the ball," to respond to all of the subparts. The smorgasbord question regarding work history essentially says, "I don't want to interrupt you constantly with questions about your work history, so let me just tell you all of the things I want to know for each job—employer name, dates, salary progress, responsibilities, high and low points." After asking that long question (in the guide it is even longer), you can proceed with note-taking, maintaining rapport, thinking of useful tangents to pursue, and mentally integrating various responses to questions. More time is available for you to do

---

†Carlson, Schwab, and Heneman (1970) and Schwab and Heneman (1969), reviewed in W. F. Cascio, *Applied Psychology in Personnel Management*, Reston, Vir.: Reston Publishing, 1978, p. 206.

‡Latham, G. P., Saari, L. M., Pursell, E. D., and Campion, M. A. The situational interview. *Journal of Applied Psychology*, 1980, **LS**, 422–426.

these useful and productive things, because less time is devoted to anticipating and asking the obvious questions which essentially have already been asked and which are so clearly outlined in the guide that if the interviewee omits something you will spot it easily.

Essentially the smorgasbord-question format permits a favorable balance between a *totally unstructured interview* with poorly worded questions emerging spontaneously as the interviewer wanders from topic to topic and a *rigidly structured interview* in which the question—answer, question—answer straitjacket seems cold and artificial. Smorgasbord questions do force the interviewee to organize his own experiences and speak with spontaneity, thus revealing a great deal more than the question—answer, question—answer format would permit. At the same time, all bases are covered—something which is practically impossible in the unstructured interview. The structured interview approach, using smorgasbord questions, gently focuses dialog so that the flow can be natural within the parameters of job relevance. On the other hand, the totally unstructured interview tends to elicit nine irrelevant bits of information for every useful one.

In short, what is advocated is actually a semistructured, in-depth interview process, using the guide diligently, but permitting the interviewer to omit questions that are obviously irrelevant, to add questions, to engage in dialog to maintain rapport, and to pursue meaningful tangents whenever it seems worthwhile.

### Write, Write, Write!—The Value of Taking Copious Notes

After years of conducting in-depth interviews, I find that much useful information lurks in my notes, and that only after reviewing those notes several times do important insights—relationships among data, subtle trends in values and behaviors, and the like—become obvious. If I simply trust my memory of the interview, my final conclusions will be much shallower. I also learned early in my career that burying my head in a notepad was bad for rapport—that I must communicate to the interviewee that *he* or *she* is all-important, not my notes.

In an interesting study on note-taking, 40 managers observed a 20-minute taped interview and then gave a 20-item test of simple facts the interviewee had conveyed; the managers were told to perform as if they were conducting the interview.* Those who did not take notes

---

*Carlson et al. (1971) reported in W. F. Cascio, *Applied Psychology in Personnel Management,* Reston, Vir.: Reston Publishing, 1978, pp. 207, 208.

averaged 50% correct on the test, but those who took notes hardly missed any items. The conclusion is to take extensive notes, even though it is a bit of a burden.

Aha! Why not have the best of both worlds—a perfect record of what was said without any note-taking—by using a videotape recorder? Nice thought, and I have tried it a few times, after explaining to interviewees that I was interested in critiquing my own interview style or that of another interviewer I was observing and that the tape would be erased a couple of hours after the interview. But the trouble is, just when Joe is on the verge of admitting that his work habits are crummy, his eyes glance over to the camera, and he clams up. A simple audiotape recorder is almost as inhibiting.

Using videotape recorders for training interviewers, however, has many benefits, one of which is demonstrating the importance of taking notes. Inevitably, some very meaningful responses to questions are not written down by a trainee, and when we go back to look at the tape, the trainee says, "Look at that. I'm staring at the interviewee and just didn't write it down when she said that she never liked to plan too far ahead."

With some practice, interviewers can learn to be very thorough in note-taking while retaining all of the rapport they need. A shorthand course would really be handy, although interviewers quickly develop their own abbreviations, usually intelligible only to them. I use an 8½-by-11 legal pad in a hard-cover notebook, available in any office-supply store. The legal pad is usually inserted on the right side of the notebook, and a flap on the left side can hold documents such as the application form. For the first part of the interview, the interview guide is on the right side, covering the pad of paper, because notes are written directly on the interview guide. Later in the interview, as it progresses to the work history stage, the guide can be inserted under the flap with the application form, and the notepad is used for recording responses.

When writing notes on the pad, I like to keep interview content— what the person is saying—in the main section of the paper. The left-hand margin is used for recording context factors—how the person is saying those things—and any judgments I'm making ("seems sincere—I believe him," "very articulate," "expressive"). Context factors are very important and include voice volume, pace of responses, long pauses, excessive defensiveness, blushing, and humor. Interviews have rhythms, and any changes in the rhythm or context factors should be noted. The importance of these context factors will be discussed in chapter 7.

## Mechanics of the Interview

The mechanics of interviewing are, for the most part, common sense—permit no interruptions, ensure comfortable heating/airconditioning/lighting, provide comfortable chairs, have all paperwork at hand ("In-Depth Selection Interview Guide," application form, and résumé), be sure to have reviewed the application form, and make sure that pens, coffee, and soft drinks are available.

What is not so obvious is the most useful seating arrangement. Almost all interviewing books recommend configuration A or B and criticize configuration C.

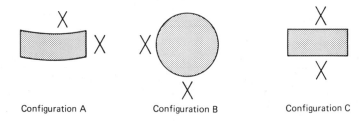

Configuration A          Configuration B          Configuration C

The generally accepted notion is that physical barriers create psychological barriers and that if you are sitting as though you are an equal with the interviewee, more rapport can be generated. Furthermore, if you are physically close, the books say, you can "resonate deeply with one another." Bunk! For most interviewers sitting across a desk does not significantly interfere with rapport (you do it everyday, right?). If your organization happens to be one in which no one would ever conduct an interview from behind a desk—fine. But if you accept configuration A or B, put a minimum of 3½ feet between you and the interviewee.

There is simply no way to do a good job of note-taking if you are snuggled up close to your interviewee. If you constantly write notes on what the interviewee is saying and how, physical closeness will cause the interviewee's eyes to stare at your pen. As soon as you are observed jotting down a negative or two, the person will clam up.

There's another good reason for configuration C over A or B: comfort level for the interviewee. If you were being interviewed, wouldn't you prefer 3½ feet of distance between you and the interviewer—so you could clear your throat or fix your collar less conspicuously or not have to worry about bad breath?

Incidentally, there is nothing inappropriate or sneaky about taking notes. Don't ask permission to take notes as some interview books recommend, unless you are so deferential that you ordinarily ask interviewees for permission to go to the washroom. You are a professional, in charge, and you are documenting the qualifications of the individual. Permission to take notes should be assumed.

So, configuration C is recommended, B is perfectly acceptable if you can be 3½ feet or more from the interviewee, and A is recommended against.

# 5 | Professional Rapport

When the in-depth selection interview begins, everything you say and do either adds to rapport or detracts from it—all with profound consequences for hiring success. If interview words are the lyrics, rapport is the music. This chapter suggests ways to avoid the dullness of Muzak and to create the beauty of Mozart, and makes a case for sometimes choosing to deliberately create harsh dissonance, a la Stravinsky.

Most managers have two basic goals in conducting an in-depth selection interview. The first is to build and maintain enough rapport that the interviewee retains interest in the job available. Although selling the person on the specific advantages of the job should occur before and after the in-depth selection interview, not during it, the behavior of an interviewer during the interview itself can significantly affect the candidate's interest in the job. The manager's second aim is to ascertain the whole job-relevant truth about the candidate—warts, skeletons in the closet, and all. As is repeatedly alluded to in this book, a manager needs to know not only the successes, accomplishments, and goals of the candidate, but also the mistakes, failures, disappointments, and shortcomings, in order to determine accurately the individual's capabilities and interests and how they match with the person specifications for the position available.

Many interviewing publications assume that these two goals are quite compatible, that if the manager generates very positive rapport, it is possible to seduce the interviewee into so liking, respecting, and trusting the interviewer that defenses will be lowered and shortcomings will be admitted. I believe that this is partly true, but that more than positive rapport is necessary to elicit truth from the interviewee. I consider positive interview rapport very important because it might become necessary to risk some good feeling in order to nudge more truth out of the interviewee. But there must be enough positive rapport remaining in order to keep the interviewee interested in the job.

Webster defines rapport as "relation characterized by harmony, conformity, accord, or affinity." The definition suggests a mutuality of interests, a common bond, and a warm, mutually trusting glow. That's fine and dandy, but there seem to be some important elements of rapport building in the in-depth interview other than the interviewer's simply becoming popular with the interviewee.

I prefer the term "professional rapport," which relies on Webster's "rapport," but with an added aura of professional respect. For the interviewer to be buddy-buddy before hiring the individual and then a heavier authority figure afterwards could result in confusion, misunderstanding, disappointment, and lower performance of the individual. Even if the manager prefers a collegial relationship with subordinates on the job, there is almost always some sense of superior power and status. Crass intimidation on the job and during an in-depth interview is ordinarily nonproductive; however, if the interviewee considers the interviewer a pleasant sap, likable but not at all in control, it is very unlikely that the interviewer will elicit valuable negative information about the interviewee. That's why the concept of respect must be added to Webster's definition of rapport.

Professional rapport includes the flavor of the interviewer's being a high-stature, businesslike authority figure who has power and control over the interview. If the likability element far exceeds the power component, the interviewer loses control and may also lose the respect of the interviewee. When the interviewer tries too hard to be liked, the result can be similar to the interchange at an ill-fated sorority or fraternity rush, in which both individuals are so nauseatingly pleasant to one another that each ends up considering the other shallow and phony.

Despite a broad and diverse range of organizations, jobs, and personalities, there remains a remarkable constancy in what professional rapport looks and feels like—with the interviewer keeping the interviewee interested, while eliciting the whole truth. Ordinary business pleasantries gradually evolve into more authentic, spontaneous communications. As the interviewee's work-related and psychological needs and behavioral tendencies are disclosed, the interviewer seems genuinely understanding. There is proper authority exerted gently, so that if and when the interviewee discloses a stupid or immature act, the interviewer might join the interviewee in acknowledging the inappropriateness without seeming condescending; instead of harming rapport, the interviewee will regard the interviewer with more respect. The personal vibrations are positive, yet not saccharine. If the interviewer presses the interviewee, pointing out apparent contradictions or significant omissions, it is for an obviously good reason, or else a legitimizing explanation is given. At all times the interviewer shows respect for the interviewee as a person. In short, professional rapport means there is likability without sticky, mushy sensations, and there is authority without heavy-handedness.

## HOW TO BUILD PROFESSIONAL RAPPORT

After such a build-up about the importance of generating professional rapport, the very experienced interviewer will find many of the professional rapport-building tips to be unoriginal. I hope this section includes a few unique suggestions but, frankly, I have found that people who do a lot of selection interviewing have read about, practiced, and refined rapport-building techniques quite nicely. If you are one of those individuals, you might want to skip ahead.

It can be assumed that communications before the in-depth selection interview have generated at least a moderate level of interest in the job, and that the interviewer has taken care of the usual preparatory and mechanical items—looking over the application form, insuring no interruptions, having coffee or soft drinks available, and setting up the seating arrangement. Following is a catalog, almost a checklist, for building and maintaining both the "liking" and the "respect" components of professional rapport. In order to make the list fairly complete, points made elsewhere are repeated in this section.

1. *Initially, be enthusiastic but don't overdo it.*

Introduce yourself, shake hands (correct for both men and women), and call the person by name. Ordinarily, if it is clear, you would call the individual "Pat," "Dr. Jones," or whatever, but if you are unsure, ask right away, "What may I call you?" If the interviewee does not immediately take a seat in the appropriate place, gesture to the seat and say, "Would you have a seat?" Common business etiquette requires that you offer the person a cup of coffee or something else to drink within the first minute or two. This isn't a little 10-minute conversation coming up—it could very well be 2½ hours long, and the interviewee is going to do almost all of the talking. If much talking does not produce a dry mouth, occasional nervousness will. The combination of these two influences suggests that it would be pretty thoughtless of you not to offer something to drink initially and at least every hour throughout the interview.

Interviewees are usually a bit nervous, and although they appreciate a positive, enthusiastic interviewer attitude, too much excitement and demonstrativeness could be upsetting. Interviewees appreciate calmness and predictability.

During the first couple of minutes, there should be some idle chitchat, to communicate humanness and interest and to help the person get acclimated to your office, settle down in the chair, and be comfortable with you. If you are too clever with your probing in the first moments, you might throw the interviewee, particularly the less experienced in interviewing, for a loop. The author of a recent book on selection interviewing suggests an icebreaker such as, "I see that you attended school in Belgium, Fred. How would you compare European and American educational systems?" Good grief! That might be a nice topic for a Ph.D. dissertation, but something to relax an interviewee—no way!

So, be mundane. If your parking lot is torn up, ask if the visitor had any difficulty in finding a parking space. If the weather is incredibly great or awful, make a brief comment about it. As the interviewer, you so obviously have the upper hand during the opening moments of an in-depth interview, that it would be inelegant and destructive to exert heavy authority or severely test the person's poise—unless (perhaps) the candidate is applying for a sales position where initial poise is crucial.

2. *State the purposes and timing expected.*

The first page of the *"In-Depth Selection Interview Guide"* (Appendix C) gives suggested words.

3. *Be yourself, but try various playacting techniques.*

At times an effective interviewer must pretend to be pleased, disappointed, interested, or perplexed in order to achieve greater insights into the interviewee. The effective interviewer is a pretty good actor. My advice is to strive toward making a skillful, shrewd, perceptive, warm, polished, and manipulative interview style part of the real "you," but don't go so hog-wild trying the techniques that you appear phony. Be gradual. It took years for Laurence Olivier to polish his skills! If you are not ordinarily an exuberant, hail-fellow-well-met type, don't try to adopt that type of personality to conduct an in-depth selection interview.

4. *Be as neutral a stimulus as possible, most of the time.*

Minimize cues as to your interests and biases as much as possible. Your office, the company reputation, your attire, and what you have already told the interviewee in previous discussions have provided a great deal of information, permitting the interviewee to alter responses in ways that might manipulate you. Therefore, don't say much about your alma mater, tennis game, managerial problems, and the like until you have completed the in-depth selection interview.

Later in this chapter, examples are given of times to deliberately not be neutral. But generally in asking questions, it is wise not to bias the responses. The "In-Depth Selection Interview Guide" suggests question wording that is deliberately neutral. It asks, "How would you describe your work habits?" rather than "Do you have pretty good work habits?" Stick with the guide's wording. If there is a useful tangent to pursue, for which you must devise a question, pause for a minute to choose words with no more bias than you want, which is usually no bias.

In response to something the interviewee has said, there are a number of neutral behaviors that serve to keep the interview going in directions you want, without disclosing what you consider a "right" or "wrong" point of view. Here are a few:

### Pregnant Pause

Interviewee:    Let me see if I can think of any other mistakes I made in that job.

You:    (Silence, perhaps with a slight nod, which essentially tells the interviewee that you are interested and patient.)

### Affirmation of Understanding

Interviewee:    Actually, ACME became a division of APEX in July of 1981. That's when my job got interesting!

You:          I see. (A nod, "uh-huh," "I see," or anything of the kind lets the interviewee know you are listening and interested and he should continue.)

**Echo**

Interviewee:  That job was short term because it was just lousy.

You:          Just lousy? (Repeating verbatim the important words of the interviewee's statement invites the interviewee to explain further.)

These neutral behaviors are "neutral" in the sense of being non-biasing responses. They show that you are paying attention, so professional rapport is enhanced.

5.  *Be friendly.*

That's easier said than done. A lot of ordinarily friendly managers I have trained have initially frowned a great deal and communicated a cold attitude, simply because they were concentrating so hard on so many things at once: recording answers to one question, thinking of important tangents to pursue, recalling if there is a contradiction with earlier statements, anticipating the next question, and trying to build and maintain professional rapport.

If you were to go out to lunch with the interviewee and talk business, how much of the time would you be light and friendly and how much would you be serious and purposeful? The ideal interview personality usually shows a similar balance. Most interviewers strive to be friendly professionals, in charge of the situation.

6.  *Speak at the interviewee's level of vocabulary.*

Do this unless you want to test the individual's command of language at some point in the interview.

7.  *Use the applicant's name from time to time.*

However, an interview trainee who had recently taken a Dale Carnegie course said, "John, I'm looking forward to this interview, John, and John, how would you like, John, a cup of coffee?" Using the person's name a couple of times per hour, and not much more than that, is fine.

8.  *Do not write negatives as they are being stated.*

Listen carefully, of course, but raise your pen conspicuously when a juicy negative is given ("I sucker-punched my boss"), so that the individual thinks you are not out to get him. Eventually the individual will say something positive, such as, "My next job was wonderful," and then you should nod understandingly, put your pen back on the paper, and write, "sucker-punched his boss."

9. *Use a broad vocal range, instead of a monotone.*

When interviewers concentrate a lot, it is all too easy to become cold, robot-like, and overly cerebral. A broad, warm, enthusiastic vocal range helps to smooth an interview.

10. *Wear a half-smile.*

A half-smile is the sort of look you have when you are trying to impress someone really important. A selection candidate *is* really important, and it will add to professional rapport if you wear that half-smile at least two or three times an hour, for a couple of minutes.

11. *Talk 10%, listen 90%.*

The "In-Depth Selection Interview Guide" is structured with smorgasbord questions, so that the interviewee can organize thoughts, do almost all of the talking, and let you concentrate on other things— building professional rapport, recording responses, thinking of tangents to pursue, and so forth. Talking too much not only consumes a lot of time, but very frequently results in the interviewer greatly biasing interviewee responses.

Some people think it is important to talk a lot in order to build professional rapport. That's true after you have concluded the in-depth selection interview and begin describing the job in more detail. However, one of the best professional-rapport builders of all is to be quiet and listen—that's what interviewees like and respect.

12. *Show approval and enthusiasm when the interviewee is obviously proud of an unambiguous accomplishment.*

This is one of the exceptions to the "be neutral" rule. You might think it is no big thing for the interviewee to have earned a $5,000-bonus, but if that bonus reflected outstanding performance on the job and the interviewee is obviously ecstatic about it, a neutral reaction on your part would probably seem like an insult, and the professional rapport would be damaged. If you want to be strictly honest and sincere, you might be able to muster an enthusiastic, "Hey, you really felt great about that!" Most of us would say "That's really great!"

13. *Show approval and appreciation of openness and honesty.*

Another exception to the "be neutral" rule. When the interviewee opens up—"Frankly, I just hadn't double-checked the figures. That's why my boss was so critical"—nod understandingly and say something like "I appreciate your telling me that." Then protect the person's ego by saying something complimentary, such as "It's good that you take responsibility for the mistake rather than make excuses." Show approval of the honesty, not approval of the mistake or shortcoming.

14. *Maintain eye contact 25% of the time.*

That might seem like a woefully small percentage, but I have found that most interviewers can build and maintain excellent professional rapport with about that much eye contact. While you take notes it is not difficult to look up every 5 or 10 seconds for a half-second, and when there is nothing to write, it is natural and appropriate to retain eye contact for 10 or 15 seconds before looking away. Something I have never seen in an interviewing publication but believe strongly is this: 30 seconds of nonstop eye contact with an interviewee will make the interviewee feel extremely uncomfortable. It's called staring, and staring is hostile and hostility or apparent hostility is extremely damaging to professional rapport. An interviewee wants and needs a little privacy—to swallow, flick some dust off a sleeve, fix floppy hair, scratch a nose, or take a deep breath, without being conspicuous.

15. *Provide a thorough summary once or twice an hour.*

For example: "Let me see now, there were four reasons for your leaving ACME—they wanted you to move to Des Moines, the pay was not keeping up with inflation, the offices were kept at 80 degrees, and your new boss wanted you to work Saturdays."

An interview that does not include a summary or two like this per hour is probably deficient. If you have missed something important, the summary statement will let the interviewee know and the data can be filled in. If your understanding is complete, the summary will show that you are concerned, fair, a good listener, and professional. It is a very impressive and effective professional rapport builder.

16. *Listen actively.*

Active listening is a very useful skill to learn. It means a lot more than having good eye contact and nodding from time to time. Active listening means reflecting (like holding up a mirror to) the interviewee's unstated feelings. It resembles the thorough summary, which reflects the content of what the interviewee has said, but active listening is deeper. The thorough summary does not require much interpretation; active listening necessitates reading between the lines and making inferences—not about the content ("I was passed over for promotion") but the feelings ("I was hurt and felt rejected"), even if the feelings were not openly expressed. Here are some examples:

*Situation:* Interviewee talks positively about job challenges, but she looks down and her voice becomes quieter as she says that a reorganization made it harder to get things done. The interviewer says: "Although you have talked about the tremendous challenges in that job, it also sounds as though there were some frustrations and disappointments."

*Situation:* Interviewee talks about getting a $1-million budget and goes on to explain that four weeks later the budget was reduced to $500,000. Although the interviewee is emotionless in saying this, the interviewer says: "That must have been a terribly disheartening thing, to have your budget completely approved and then a month later chopped in half."

If the interviewee was truly disheartened (as in the above example) but did not actually use that word, then for the interviewer to use it could contribute to professional rapport, by showing the interviewer to be empathetic, perceptive, and understanding. If the interviewer guesses incorrectly, misperceptions can be corrected.

If you ever sat with an active listener who does not appear to judge you, but who seems to communicate a great deal of regard for you as a person by reflecting back to you what you are saying, paraphrased to show deep understanding of your feelings, you can appreciate what active listening is all about.

Active listening is powerful stuff, and if every now and then you can resonate with what a person is saying and sensitively and empathically describe the feelings being communicated, the professional rapport will soar. Not only is it an excellent technique for getting what you want out of the interview, it is a very satisfying human experience.

17.  *Soften negative statements.*

The next section of this chapter deals with when to challenge the interviewee; as will be pointed out, once in a great while it is worthwhile to confront the interviewee very bluntly. However, even with very confident and tough-skinned interviewees, some efforts to protect the ego and to soften the negative overtones of the subject make it easier for the interviewee to open up.

Use words and phrases like, "I wonder if," "do you suppose," "sometimes," "maybe," "perhaps," "is it possible that," and "could it be that." Protect the person's ego by saying, "We've all made blunders, and recognizing them is certainly an important step toward avoiding them in the future." Say, "Most people have had a boss like that, and it's no fun," instead of, "Why did you have trouble with your superior?"

If you are a direct, lay-it-on-the-line, John Wayne type, these recommended approaches may sound like weasel words. They are weasel words, and they are useful because they permit the interviewer to ask very direct, and possibly deliberately biasing questions, while seeming to nibble around the edges of the subject.

Another example (weasel words are italicized): "*Could it be* that you *might have been a bit* lax with that employee and that's why the deadline slipped *a little?*" The weasel words allow the interviewee to save face by seeming to admit a small shortcoming on the surface, while actually acknowledging a major shortcoming. The weasel words might suggest more empathy and understanding than the interviewer really has, but they greatly help in lowering the interviewee's defenses.

It takes a little time for interviewers to be comfortable with a particular level of softened negatives. Listening to tape recordings of your interviews can be very helpful—it will be obvious when direct wording results in defensiveness on the part of the interviewee. It sometimes takes five or ten seconds to think of wording that would have been more effective. I recommend pausing during the interview—taking the time to try to construct just the right phraseology.

18. *Don't show shock, dismay, or surprise.*

It is not always easy to be neutral, cool, and unflappable, and late in the interview you might even deliberately show an extreme reaction to something. However, if you don't want all subsequent responses to be biased by your reaction, restrict your responses to those that are neutral, and show understanding and minimal bias.

19. *Don't hesitate occasionally to demonstrate genuine superiority.*

A condescending, one-upmanship attitude could detract from professional rapport, but with a little finesse you can show a prospective subordinate that you know your stuff. Honesty is important, however, and overstating your knowledge or competence could backfire.

20. *Acknowledge your deficiencies in a forthright way.*

If you lack some important knowledge or skill, admitting it can build professional rapport—if your demeanor is humble, sincere, and yet confident. The interviewee might regard you as secure enough to show human frailties. Naturally, if your deficiency detracts from the interviewee's interest in learning from you, professional rapport may suffer.

21. *Treat the interviewee with respect.*

There is sometimes a lot of game playing in interviews, by both parties. You must be clever at times. However, don't get so wrapped up in your playacting that you seem more preoccupied with sparring than with relating genuinely with your interviewee. Respect must be the umbrella under which all interview behaviors fall, with only rare exceptions.

## WHEN TO RISK LOSING PROFESSIONAL RAPPORT

The idea of leaning on an interviewee is distasteful to interviewers and interviewees. Yet, to the extent interviewees are less than candid, there are only two basic ways to glean truth—carrots and sticks.

The "carrot" method involves all of the professional rapport-building techniques just enumerated. If the interviewee really likes, trusts, and respects you, defenses might be lowered, and if the interviewee is basically honest and open, the carrot will suffice. For the majority of interviews I have observed and conducted (thousands), at least a little gentle leaning (without showing disrespect) has been helpful. Only rarely has a heavy "stick" been necessary. Indeed, I often find basically honest interviewees relieved to be leaned on slightly, because they realize that deception may not work for them. Otherwise, they would have felt guilty for naively being so honest. Strange world, isn't it, when basically honest people feel guilty being honest!

So, do your interviewee a couple of favors. In a professional, smooth, high-stature way, communicate not only an expectation of honesty but exert your power to demand it if necessary. The second favor is to learn negative information as well as positive, because you are more apt to hire a good candidate you feel you know thoroughly than one who may be even better but who played games with you.

Before discussing specific hows and whens to use the stick, let's briefly explore the concept of psychological leverage, which is a fancy phrase for "stick."

## Psychological Leverage

Psychological leverage is a sort of currency of interpersonal exchange, rather like brownie points gained with another person. Think of it as the amount you can get away with of something offensive or obnoxious to another human being, the degree of offense that will not destroy the relationship.

In an in-depth selection interview you have psychological leverage over the interviewee if the person wants the job and if you have developed professional rapport. If the interviewee is extremely interested in obtaining the job, the interviewer can automatically get away with murder, or in other words, has a lot of psychological leverage. Years ago I interviewed a candidate for an executive with the *Playboy* organization, and one of the "goodies" (not for me—for the successful job candidate) was a weekly invitation to Hugh Hefner's parties at the West Coast mansion. The candidate's level of interest in the job was extremely high. It was simply not necessary to work at building professional rapport in order to obtain more psychological leverage with this candidate.

With substantial psychological leverage, you can feel very comfortable, say, with pointing out an apparent inconsistency in statements made by the interviewee. After leaning on an interviewee this way, perhaps you would lose a few points. (I say "perhaps" because pushing for more truth sometimes does not offend, but actually increases the respect component of professional rapport.) When you feel you need more psychological leverage, strive for a while to build professional rapport by being more responsive, warm, and understanding with the interviewee, and lean less.

Until you feel that you have a lot of psychological leverage, you probably will feel somewhat helpless in interviewing. That is why building professional rapport is so important—to get you more psychological leverage, so that you can take more risks, glean more truth and make better selection decisions.

The most common appropriate and necessary occasions to risk losing professional rapport by exerting psychological leverage are:

1. *When the interviewee tries to dominate the interview.*

Some how-to-get-a-job books suggest that the interviewee try to take charge of the interview, right away. If you witness such an attempt, you must grab control back—right away! Your warm, bubbly personality might have to give way to a serious air, furrows in your brow, and a low, deliberate voice. You might have to sell the interviewee on going through your interview process, by elaborating on the points listed on the front page of the "In-Depth Selection Interview Guide." Convince the candidate that by conducting this interview you will be able to know if there is a good fit, to assure a smooth transition into the job, and to manage the individual for maximum long-term growth, fulfillment, and contributions. If you find yourself in a cat-and-mouse game, it will be important for you to show both finesse and courage.

2.  *If the interviewee appears inconsistent in statements.*

I say "appears" inconsistent, because more than half the time there is no inconsistency, but the words used by the interviewee suggest it. To say harshly, "That's inconsistent," would be crude and inappropriate. You might say, "Excuse me, Chris, you said earlier that you like to delegate a great deal, and just a moment ago you said that your subordinates complain that they don't get to make important decisions. Could you explain?" It might be that the philosophy of substantial delegation is sincere, but that the interviewee's current supervisor demands that certain decisions not be delegated.

3.  *When the individual leaps into an extensive monolog about an irrelevant topic.*

The one best technique for getting a person back on track is to wait for a slight pause in the sentence, smoothly interrupt, say something that ties into what the individual was saying, and rephrase the question so it requires a more succinct response. For example:

Interviewer:   What were any additional high points in that job?

Interviewee:   There were a lot of high points. That reminds me— while I was with ACME, my son's team won the state hockey championship. You should have seen that game! He. . .

Interviewer:   (Interrupting) Exciting, I'll bet, and you certainly sound like a proud father, but let me ask you, since we are running a little short of time, were there any specific job-relevant high points that we have not yet discussed?

Be persistent! Don't permit intentional or unintentional avoidance. Don't leave a pertinent topic until you have recorded all you need to know in order to be able to fully reconstruct later what was said and how it was said.

4. *When the interviewee avoids responding to your question by answering a related question.*

Say, "It's interesting that your division had a great sales year, but I'm really asking about new business that you personally generated."

5. *When the interviewee gives vague responses.*

Experienced businessmen and women are marvelous circumlocutionists. We all criticize politicians for being glib, and yet we all conscientiously develop skills in saying words without communicating true meaning.

If you ask an interviewee how many data-processing projects were completed on time and within budget last year, and the interviewee says, "We did pretty well in that regard," you have learned nothing. Repeat the question until you get the specific, concrete answer necessary for you to make some sort of judgment about the interviewee's performance.

6. *(Sometimes) when the interviewee cries, "Confidential!"*

There are certainly facts and figures that are none of your business as an interviewer, and if the interviewee were to disclose them, there would be a serious question regarding the person's integrity, loyalty, and trustworthiness. That's OK—you don't need to know the actual retail-store locations the real estate manager investigated, but you can certainly ask if the goals for site location were realized last year. You do not need to know what the exact profit figures were for a division, but you can ask if the profit goals were achieved. An interviewee who does not want to disclose current salary is probably naive, young, and excessively influenced by the job-search books that say not to give out that information. You say, "Jan, that is a rather private matter, but frankly, compensation information is something I need to know in order to determine what sort of value employers have placed on your services. Maybe there have been unfair compensation practices or situations beyond your control, but I hope you would consider me sufficiently mature, responsible, and fair in my judgments to put the information in proper perspective."

If the interviewee does not want to tell you what other positions are being considered, you have no business pressing the issue. However, with a little finesse, you can ask for important specifics of prospective jobs—the sizes of the organizations, responsibilities, compensation ranges, and other factors. What you can legitimately inquire about are the interests and need patterns of the individual and how your job opportunity stacks up against other possible opportunities.

7. *When you have repeatedly failed to get sufficient information about a particular person specification.*

It's 4:45 p.m., and you have been interviewing Ralph for 3 long hours. Ralph is slow and vague in some responses, although in most respects you are impressed with his abilities. Lacking is a sense of how well organized he is. It may be time for an eyeball-to-eyeball, direct, firm, and highly loaded question: "Ralph, you've said that three out of four of your most recent supervisors considered you a bit disorganized, and yet when I've asked for clarification I've become confused. Help me out. You're not as well organized as you would like, but I would like to know exactly how you are disorganized."

An example of going to the extreme to control an interview is provided in an interview of former Chief of Naval Operations Elmo Zumwalt (when he was a commander), applying for a position under Admiral Hyman Rickover, "father of the nuclear navy." The interview occurred in 1959 (reported in *Washington Post Magazine*, November 15, 1981):

Rickover:   Aside from summers, did you work or did your family support you?

Zumwalt:   I worked in the summers...

Rickover:   Listen to my questions, goddam it. You've been an aide too long. You're too used to asking the questions. You are trying to conduct this interview again. I said, "Aside from the summers." Now, do you think you can answer the question or do you want to stop the interview right now?

I guess you can operate with a different set of interview approaches if you are an admiral. Maybe not—Rickover's interviewing approach (including lopsided chairs, name-calling, and banishing interviewees to hours in solitary confinement) is said to have caused unwanted turnover in the navy.

Interviewing is hard work, but it can also be fascinating. The in-depth selection interview brings two people together who usually have a great deal at stake. Until the day comes that you pop a truth pill in someone's mouth, you may need to challenge an interviewee from time to time. You need psychological leverage to do that, and once the in-depth interview has begun, the more you can do to build professional rapport with the interviewee, the more psychological leverage you will acquire.

## THE TORC METHODS

I've saved the best for last—the TORC methods. The acronym stands for "threat of record check" and has produced such admissions as:

My boss fired me—we just didn't get along.

I was...uh...in jail for murder.

I guess they would not have let me stay in that job, even if I had wanted to.

Only the chairman and the president know that I flunked the lie detector test three times.

I really didn't take those kickbacks, but I've decided to resign anyway.

Well...I guess you'd say the IRS is after me.

To tell you the truth, I didn't go to college" (although the application form records him as holding a B.S. degree in business administration from Ohio State University).

His [an immediate supervisor's] biggest criticism was that I kept missing deadlines.

My relationship with a secretary got out of hand, and, uh, I was asked to resign.

My supervisor kept telling me either to get better performance out of my subordinates or remove them, and I guess I was so slow at doing this that he told me to find another job.

It was an embarrassing situation—the company agreed not to mention it—but in my job as farm inspector, I was accused of having relations with a...goat.

Yes, these are all comments reconstructed from actual interviews— even the one about the goat. (The poor guy was humiliated when co-workers asked him, "How are your kids these days?")

Clients frequently ask how I manage to get interviewees to fess up in interviews, and my response is usually "I use the TORC methods." TORC methods are quite simple and straightforward, and 80% of their value can be derived without any special expertise, other than a little finesse.

## The TORC Methods—What They Are

Put simply, TORC methods slowly and subtly tell the interviewee that you are likely to conduct extremely thorough record checks with previous supervisors and perhaps peers and/or subordinates and to do this so conscientiously that you will know what every previous supervisor honestly felt were the candidate's shortcomings as well as strengths.

Most experienced interviewers have at one time or another asked what co-workers have felt about the interviewee, but usually such questions constitute a shallow, feeble flirtation with a technique that can be enormously powerful if utilized properly. The difference in effect is like winking at a brass ring instead of grasping it.

Think of it this way—the last time you were interviewed as a candidate for selection, how much did you really disclose about mistakes, failures, or shortcomings? Not very much, right? And how thoroughly did you think your record would be checked? Chances are, you thought one or two short phone calls would be made, and that your supervisors—if called—would say nice, pleasant, uncritical things about you.

## Your Stated Justification for Soliciting Negative Data

Selling the interviewee on the legitimacy of your conducting elaborate record checks is very important. If you are just a nosy, negative-thinking, nit-picking voyeur, then professional rapport could be destroyed very quickly—the process could be seen as demeaning by the interviewee.

A few interviewers I know justify the TORC methods to interviewees in a very direct manner. They happen to be such warm, honest, delightful people that candidates are not put off by this approach. I'm not recommending that you try such directness unless you can feel natural using it, but it is instructive for you to be aware of it, because it is an accurate representation of important elements of the TORC methods:

> Pat, I'd like to explain something to you. Following our interview today, I promise to answer any question you have as honestly as I can—including possibly negative things about me or the job. And I'd like you to double-check what I say by talking to others—even some people who have left the company. If what I tell you coincides with what others say, you'll not only have fewer surprises if an offer is extended and you join us, but

you'll feel more comfortable with me because you'll know I have accurate insights into the job that's open and into what others think of me.

## Here Comes TORC

Conversely, I'm asking you to disclose not only the positives but the negatives in your background, and with your permission, I'll contact previous supervisors, and maybe some peers and subordinates. It's a routine thing in most companies to check the records of selection candidates, but I do it more conscientiously than most. This can benefit you in several ways. First, if I feel I really know you well, a job offer is more likely. Second, if what you guess that others felt about you is largely correct, I'll be delighted because I'll know that you are interested in knowing others' opinions of you, accurate in your perceptions of those opinions, and trust me enough to be candid in the interview. Finally, with more understanding of new employees, I've found I can smooth the transition for them into the organization and can better help them to grow and achieve their career goals. So, let's get to know each other!

For me, and perhaps for you, too, the TORC methods will work best if they evolve very subtly—a gradual encouragement of the interviewee to open up. It may not be necessary to explain your justification for soliciting negatives at all. Whether justification is necessary depends less on your skill than on the interviewee's defensiveness, competence, and the sheer amount and severity of negatives in the past.

TORC is no false, deceptive, manipulative bluff. You should conduct record checks, and if you follow the guidelines in chapter 9 you will be successful most of the time in getting candid record checks. TORC is a set of legitimate approaches—simply a more conscientious way of doing what is an accepted activity in the world of work.

## The TORC Methods—How They Work

The in-depth interview guide asks that for every full-time job the interviewee has held, a number of questions be answered, including dates of employment, responsibilities, and high and low points. One of those questions—the foundation of the TORC methods, is "What would your best guess be as to what [supervisor's name] really felt were your strengths, weaker points, and overall performance?" This is the basic TORC question, although it is preceded by questions asking the name and title of the supervisor, where that person is now, and what the interviewee felt were that supervisor's strengths and shortcomings.

If the interviewee has had five jobs with three employers, the interviewee is expected to provide five guesses as to what each boss truly felt. If there were seven supervisors in those five positions with three employers, the interviewee should be asked the TORC question seven times.

If the interviewee started a career 15 years ago, it might be difficult to reconstruct what a supervisor might have felt then. In many cases, the responsibilities that long ago were technical, and there simply were no significant shortcomings—which is why the person moved up in the organization and is a candidate for a higher-level position today. So, as an interviewer, you should not squeeze the interviewee very hard to get a response.

However, it is important to get some sort of response to the record-check question. If the response is something like "I was only in my job reading blueprints six months, and my boss complimented me a couple of times, but there were no criticisms," leave it at that. The important thing is to plant the seed of expectation that you are very much interested in what supervisors felt were the candidate's strengths and weaker points.

In six out of ten interviews, interviewees explaining their work histories chronologically skip over the TORC question again and again, and I politely repeat it again and again. By the time we get to the most recent and relevant jobs, they are fully primed to respond to the question and the responses are more thorough than if I had permitted them to ignore or avoid the question for early jobs.

After I have reviewed a candidate's full job history, I usually have several pages of notes in response to the TORC questions, and the pattern of responses reveals a great deal about the individual. When my trainees ask why we ask an interviewee about early job history, I answer, "to learn early behavior and need patterns so we can determine what inertia such patterns have today."

TORC can greatly enrich your understanding of how strengths and weak points have evolved, developed, and been coped with throughout the interviewee's career. Furthermore, in discussing previous jobs, interviewees make comments about their current behavior and needs ("My supervisor criticized me for getting to work late—that's always been a problem—still is.")

The TORC methods also lay excellent groundwork for an appendage technique—asking for the individual's self-appraisal; after producing half a dozen self-appraisals from supervisors' perspectives, individuals when asked to appraise themselves as they are today are usually more comprehensive and revealing.

## What If There Is Resistance?

In approximately 20% of my interviews, I find interviewees at least partially resistant to the TORC methods, particularly in relation to what supervisors might have felt were shortcomings. Some people are simply more defensive than others—they lack the ego strength necessary to face their own limitations. Others have had such negative work experiences that they have partially blocked them out, and it is very difficult for them to dredge up the past. Those who have worked in highly technical positions in which they were clearly successful, perhaps have received and deserved only praise. Finally and most frequently the case, interviewees essentially say to themselves, "If I cite negatives, I'll have less of a chance to get the job." Those individuals have to be persuaded of the advantages of being more open and candid, and over the years I have developed the TORC methods for accomplishing that end.

## Coping with Resistance—Level One (Mild Pressure) TORC Methods

The interview climate is typically warm, friendly, and supportive, despite a little resistance on the part of the interviewee. What is needed is a little gentle prodding and some persuasiveness on your part—to induce the interviewee to be more insightful and to fess up a bit more.

### 1. Repeat the Question

If the interviewee moves ahead from the first to the second job, ignoring the basic TORC question:

Interviewee:    ...and so I joined IBM next and...

You:            (Interrupting) Excuse me, Sam, before we go on to your job with IBM, who was your supervisor at the time you left Control Data?

Interviewee:    Bob Price.

You:            Is he still vice president at Control Data?

Interviewee:    Yes.

You:            What was he like to work for, and what were his strengths and shortcomings from your point of view?

Interviewee:    Well, he was technically competent, but not such a good motivator. You just didn't feel like coming to work sometimes.

You:    What is your best guess as to what he really felt were your strengths, weaker points, and overall performance?

## 2. False Bluff—We Can Track Him Down

You:    What would be your best guess as to what Mary Hudson [interviewee's supervisor at the time] really felt were your strengths, weaker points, and overall performance?

Interviewee:    Golly, I don't know, that was a long time ago.

You:    Is Mary Hudson still in the Denver division of ACME?

Interviewee:    No, she left the company a couple of years ago, and I don't know where she is.

You:    No problem; we can track her down. What would be your best guess as to what she might tell me—you know, if I establish good rapport with her and she is totally candid—were your strengths, weaker points, and overall performance at the time you left ACME?

This is not a bluff, but a simple statement of fact—in your quest to be thorough in evaluating a candidate for selection, you will be contacting previous supervisors, and it is usually quite easy to locate anyone who has stayed in a particular industry.

## 3. Clarifying the Question

You:    What would your best guess be as to what Spence Rutledge [supervisor's name at that time] really felt were your strengths, weaker points, and overall performance?

Interviewee:    Oh, I'm sure he felt I was a hard worker, conscientious, and very punctual. He rated me as exceeding job requirements and eligible for promotion.

You:    That is an impressive list of strengths. What would be your best guess as to what he felt were any of your weaker points or areas for improvement at that time?

Interviewee:    I don't know. He didn't tell me.

You:          Did he ever conduct a formal performance review?

Interviewee:  Yes, but he just said I was doing a good job and that was that.

You:          OK, but what I'm really interested in is what you would guess he might have felt were any shortcomings, weaker points, or areas for improvement.

Interviewee:  I don't know, you would have to ask him.

You:          I'll do that, but actually I'm interested in two things—one is what he will say, which I will find out by asking him, and the other is what your level of insight is—what your level of perceptiveness is regarding a very important relationship. That's why I'd like you to guess what he truly felt.

Words like "best guess" and "really felt" are important. If you said, "What did Mr. Rutledge *say* were your shortcomings at the time?" the interviewee might legitimately and honestly respond, "None," even though the interviewee might know that Mr. Rutledge *felt* there were shortcomings (but simply did not or would not state them openly). If you asked, "What might Mr. Rutledge tell me if I call him?" the interviewee might legitimately say, "No weaker points at all," knowing that in the past when called for record checks, Mr. Rutledge had reported no shortcomings.

## 4. Leverage Through Magnified Positives

Suppose the interviewee, when asked what a supervisor several years ago might have felt were the interviewee's strengths, weaker points, and overall performance, a lot of strengths were listed but not any significant shortcomings. Psychological leverage to nudge out the negatives can sometimes be achieved by magnifying the positives.

You:          What would be your best guess as to what Less Maxwell really felt were your strengths, weaker points, and overall performance?

Interviewee:  Oh, he felt I was technically proficient, anxious to learn all I could, very cooperative, willing to work long hours, and ambitious. He never criticized my performance. In fact, he always rated me above average in overall performance.

You:              That's great, Pat. I'd like to hear more about each one of
                  those strengths, so let's go through the list again, and if
                  you will, elaborate on each one and give as many
                  specifics as possible.
Interviewee:      (Rambles on for five minutes, you nodding understand-
                  ingly and writing down the specifics regarding those
                  wonderful qualities.)
You:              That's great. Now, what would be your best guess as to
                  what he felt were any weaker points or areas for
                  improvement?

It would take a certain amount of audacity for the interviewee, after
spending so much time elaborating on strengths, to claim there were
no weaker points at all. Most interviewees will become a bit embarrassed about bragging so much and will become willing to portray a
more realistic, less infallible image.

### 5. How About a Sardine?

Interviewee:      I really don't think Mel Zahn honestly felt that I had
                  any weaker points.
You:              None of us is perfect, and even if you did not show any
                  major areas for improvement, surely there must have
                  been a couple of small things he considered a little
                  weaker than your very favorable qualities.

In other words, if I can't get poached salmon with dill sauce, at least
throw me a sardine. Don't insult my intelligence by giving me nothing
at all!

### 6. Pause—With Disappointment

Interviewee:      No, I'm pretty sure he didn't think I had any weaker
                  points at all in that job.
You:              Hmmm...(looking down with a look of disappointment
                  and maybe a frown), OK, I don't want to beat that topic
                  to death.

Actually, the message is exactly the opposite—you *do* want to beat
that topic to death. If you are discussing a position held 8 years ago,
you would probably move on to the next job held; but you have sent out

a fairly clear message: This is an important question, and it is only with considerable hesitancy that you will accept an unsatisfactory response.

One of the most common follow-up TORC questions, and one which my interview trainees feel very comfortable asking, is described next.

### 7. Self-Appraisal

You: OK, if you can't think of what your boss might have felt were any shortcomings, how about a self-appraisal—what would *you* say were your weaker points while you were in that job?

Note that this does not ask for a current self-appraisal, unless the position being described is the current one. If the job discussed was held three years ago, you ask what the weaker points were at that time.

### 8. I'm Your Coach

This is similar to TORC method 6, but with a slightly more palatable twist.

You: Hey, I think that one of my most important responsibilities is to train, coach, and develop subordinates, so help me out. Let me know not only your strengths, but also what you and others you have worked with have considered to be possible areas for improvement. Maybe I can be more helpful to you, if you join us.

Don't use that approach unless you are a willing, capable, and available coach to your subordinates.

### 9. Selling the Interviewee

The skilled interviewer will want to include in a repertoire of TORC methods some sort of explanation for why this unusual line of questioning is being pursued.

Interviewee: I've never before been asked what my bosses have thought, and frankly, I haven't thought of possible responses. I wonder if you'd be willing to tell me why it's of such great interest to you?

You: That's a very good question. As we began this interview, I said that I was interested in knowing a great deal about you in order to determine if there is a good fit with the position in question; if there is, to know how to bring you into the organization smoothly; and finally, to know how to manage you in order to maximize your growth, fulfillment, and contributions. I have found that conducting record checks with candidates' previous supervisors, asking for candidates' impressions of their own performance, and asking what they think previous and current supervisors might have thought are all useful sources of job-relevant information.

The wording is intended to sell the interviewee on being more open, and it usually works. Your attitude and demeanor must continue to be friendly and purposeful—you must appear unembarrassed by your own questions and nonthreatening. The general tenor of level one TORC methods is relatively easygoing about this line of questioning, but a bit more serious about wanting a response than the interviewee might have anticipated.

### Coping with Resistance—Level Two (Moderate Pressure) TORC Methods

The TORC methods include somewhat heavier armament, to be used when you are convinced that the interviewee is deliberately stonewalling and when the TORC question refers to a position held recently (within the past five or six years). It is also possible that the interviewee is not deliberately concealing negatives, but truly does not know what they are. Whatever the reason, it is important for the interviewer to try a little harder to determine the negatives along with the positives, or if not, to ascertain if the interviewee is dense, playing games with you, or both.

### 10. Your Responses Are Disappointing

Interviewee:   I really can't think of anything my current supervisor, Burt Kaplan, considers a major liability or even a minor shortcoming.

You:   (Exuding genuine concern, speaking in a calm, somewhat disappointed voice) Jan, we've reviewed your work history starting 10 years ago, and I've asked you what the six supervisors you have had might have felt were your strengths, weaker points, and overall performance.

Although you have guessed at what they might have felt were a number of strengths, you have been continually at a loss as to what they might have felt were areas for your improvement. Now we're talking about your relationship with your current supervisor, and even though that individual, as you say, has done a poor job of giving you performance feedback, there are only three reasons I can think of why you would not be able to tell me what you think your supervisor would consider weaker points. One, you're not very concerned about picking up the vibes Mr. Kaplan is subtly sending out to you. Two, you care, but you are simply not tuned in well enough to comprehend the signals. Three, you just don't trust me enough to be forthcoming. If you were to be reporting to me several weeks from now, it would bother me if you were unconcerned with what I consider to be areas for your improvement, and if you would not be perceptive enough to pick up the signals I would send out.

Nice, friendly, rapport-building interview, right? Hardly! This is a harsh TORC method, and rarely used. The truth of the matter is, however, that if an interviewee cannot come up with some highly credible responses to such a challenge, either the person is unconcerned with the supervisor's true appraisal, is as dense as a two-by-four, or is playing games with you. You would have to be a bit desperate to want to live with a subordinate with one or more of those characteristics. If you are not that desperate, you might lay it on the line in this TORC method, with nothing to lose.

I repeat: Exude charm and sincerity. Emulate Ronald Reagan telling poor people why it might be in their best interests no longer to receive food stamps. His smiles, gestures, and friendly nods may not be a good substitute for food stamps, but it's better than a cold, hard, threatening stare. As in previous TORC methods, you may appear to be disappointed at an inadequate response, but don't appear to be demeaning the interviewee.

### 11. Record Checks Do Disclose Negatives

You:   I've conducted more than a hundred record checks during the past three years, and not once have I talked to a previous supervisor of a candidate who has not been able to come up with at least a couple of shortcomings in the candidate.

This particular TORC method will communicate the point that if the interviewee cannot think of what those shortcomings might be, the interviewee has a problem.

How do you use the TORC methods with respect to the current boss? Remember, you cannot contact the current (or any) supervisor without the approval of the interviewee, and that is usually not granted until there is a firm offer from an alternative employer. No problem, you simply say, "I would not contact Mr. Galassini until receiving your approval to do so, but any job offer would be contingent upon no surprises in record checks." The understanding left with the interviewee is that "If I get a job offer, this interviewer will contact Galassini; I'd better think of all of my shortcomings Galassini might mention, because an offer might be rescinded if I overlook my important negatives."

If you were certain that the IRS would audit your tax return this year, you would be pretty honest and thorough in completing the return. If an interviewee is fairly certain that his work history will be *very* thoroughly checked out, more honest and revealing responses will be made to your questions. That's what the TORC method accomplishes. Interviewees usually get the message and cooperate.

Although record checks are useful, and it is strongly recommended that you actually perform them, most interviewers I have trained have found that they learn a lot more from TORC than they do by actually talking with the previous supervisors. In the first place, the interviewer obviously spends a lot more time talking with the candidate than with previous or current supervisors, and the sheer length of communication gives the interviewer more confidence in conclusions reached. Second, the interviewer is face-to-face with the interviewee, asking for information about strengths and weaker points from many different perspectives, and the interviewer is better able to sense moods, voice inflections, and reactions than he can in telephone conversations with former bosses.

A word of caution: TORC is powerful, but a little risky. Experiment with it gradually, and stay with the level one (mild pressure) methods until you can practice them with ease and with only slight risk of losing professional rapport.

## Using Psychological Leverage in the Comprehensive Self-Appraisal

TORC method number 7 asks the individual for a self-appraisal vis-à-vis one particular job. The comprehensive self-appraisal occurs toward the end of the in-depth selection interview and asks the individual to step back and list current strengths, assets, things liked about one's self, and things one does well, as well as weaker points, liabilities, and possible areas for growth or improvement. Even if TORC self-appraisal has been repeatedly used (which is common), the comprehensive self-appraisal should also be used, because the question is much broader than even TORC method number 7 applied to each individual job. Of course, there is redundancy, but new insights are almost always generated.

You should absolutely require thorough, in-depth responses to the comprehensive self-appraisal questions. The positives usually flow out readily, but if you don't get any negatives, you probably could not feel comfortable hiring the person.

With less-experienced interviewees it is a good idea to ask for the positives first. Get a grocery list of positives, clarifying only a little as they are being generated, in order to show interest but not break up the thought flow. Then go back and obtain elaboration as further clarification, leaving the interviewee feeling a positive glow at being so wonderful and so appreciated and understood by you.

Next ask for a list of negatives and don't interrupt to clarify until you have stimulated the longest possible list. If you interrupted after the statement, "I'm slow to get results," and pursued a 3-minute explanation, the interviewee might decide that too much time has been spent on the negatives and that it would be dumb to give any more. After hearing the *list* of negatives, go back and nail down specifics.

Experienced interviewers know that this is a two-part question, so ask for positives and negatives in the same breath. Again, as positives are spoken clarify a little bit, but don't stifle the interviewee's stream of consciousness generation of the longest possible list of both positives and negatives. And again, don't interrupt the listing of negatives for any clarification—get the brief phrases down ("sometimes I procrastinate," "I'm weak in MIS,") even though you haven't the foggiest idea what they really mean. Obtain as many negatives as you can, and *then* return for enough discussion that you fully comprehend each one. Having said, "I'm sometimes forgetful," your interviewee cannot very well deny you an explanation!

How can you encourage and stimulate admission of negatives, if the interviewee is probably trying to conceal them? Here are some suggestions:

You:    That's only a Polaroid snapshot of you, Chris, and I'd really like a comprehensive oil portrait—you know, maybe 15 strengths and half a dozen shortcomings.

That's a rather gentle prod—nothing too threatening, but it lets the interviewee know that you expect more. It might be followed with:

You:    Why don't you take a couple of minutes just to think about this question. We're not in a rush, and I'm very interested in your self-insights.

Suppose the person seems to be holding back a lot. You might want to increase the pressure to include what might sound like an earnest, puzzled question.

You:    Do you think you know yourself pretty well, Jan?

The question demands a reply such as, "Of course, I know myself very well." An expectant pause after that response will usually generate further, more detailed responses.

You have probably heard tricky responses—negatives that sound a bit negative, but which the interviewee actually intends for you to interpret as strengths.

Interviewee:    I'm impatient to get results; I work too hard, and I'm a little too demanding of my subordinates.
You:    Those sound more like strengths than shortcomings, Jan. Could you explain exactly how these qualities have been shortcomings?

"Working too hard" may be a shortcoming, if the person is burning out, or having severe family problems because of it. So do not leave "working too hard" unclarified in your notes.

You:    None of us is perfect, and only if we recognize areas for improvement are we apt to grow and develop.
You:    In my experience interviewing people, I have found that people with the greatest self-insight have the greatest career potentials. Not only do they recognize their strengths and strive to utilize them to the fullest, but they also recognize their shortcomings and work to overcome them. The most successful individual I have ever interviewed listed 28 strengths and 12 shortcomings.

Or, if you are becoming frustrated and perhaps a bit disgusted with the Pablum your interviewee is feeding you, and you are on the verge of eliminating the individual as a candidate, perhaps you would risk the following:

You:    Frankly, Carlyle, I'm a little concerned with the brevity of your self-appraisal. It has been my experience that unless people have reasonably deep self-insights, they are not receptive to constructive suggestions.

If the person has been deliberately withholding negatives, this last comment might spark more cooperation. Usually the interviewee smiles knowingly, with a little embarrassment, and then comes forth with an acceptably revealing self-appraisal. Sometimes you have to outsmart and out-finesse the interviewee!

Toward the end of the comprehensive self-appraisal, it might be worthwhile to ask what the interviewee thinks good friends or a spouse might term the person's strengths or possible areas for improvement.

As you can see, there are some appropriate times to apply psychological leverage in an interview, and there is certainly no shortage of methods to do it effectively. With a full repertoire of techniques for building professional rapport and for taking calculated, purposeful risks of losing it, it is a good time to consider some things you cannot do without risking a legal battle.

# 6 | An Overview of Legal Considerations

Beginning in the 1960s and continuing through the present, a series of federal, state, and local laws, regulations, executive orders, and interpretive rulings have profoundly affected how organizations deal with employees and prospective employees. The methods used to recruit, select, promote, reassign, or remove people fall right in the midst of these legal considerations. Despite attempts in the early 1980s by the Reagan administration to dilute the area of civil rights (EEOC), the message has largely sunk into the workings of American organizations—there must be equal opportunity for all persons irrespective of race, color, religion, ethnic origin, sex, and age. Through extensive media coverage and public education efforts (see Figure 9), people know their rights.

What has also sunk into the fabric of American organizations is a great deal of confusion and frustration about what equal opportunity means and the sense that even with a staff of Philadelphia lawyers, you are "damned if you do and damned if you don't." Even organizations working to conform to both the letter and spirit of the law have found themselves slapped with reverse discrimination lawsuits.

Answer: True. Due to outdated policies or failure to understand the law, many employers do discriminate in the way they hire, fire, promote or pay.

Take this 30-second test and see where you stand.

*An employer*                                                                True        False

1. can refuse to hire women who have small children at home    _____   _____

2. can generally obtain and use an applicant's arrest record as the basis for non employment    _____   _____

3. can prohibit employees from conversing in their native language on the job    _____   _____

4. whose employees are mostly white or male, can rely solely upon word of mouth to recruit new employees

5. can refuse to hire women to work at night because it wishes to protect them    _____   _____

6. may require all pregnant employees to take leave of absence at a specified time before delivery date    _____   _____

7. may establish different benefits—pension, retirement, insurance and health plans—for male employees than for female employees    _____   _____

8. may hire only males for a job if state law forbids employment of women for that capacity    _____   _____

9. need not attempt to adjust work schedules to permit an employee time off for a religious observance    _____   _____

10. only disobeys the Equal Employment Opportunity laws when it is acting intentionally or with ill motive    _____   _____

> *Answers:* The answers to 1 to 10 above are false. The Equal Employment Opportunity Act makes it against the law for an employer to discriminate on the basis of race, religion, color, sex, or national origin. It's a tough law, with teeth, but most Americans think it is a very fair law. Yet unfair practices continue—in big business and in small. So, if you are in private industry, state or local government, or educational institutions, it is your business to know your rights and obligations. Contact your local EEOC office, listed in the phone book under U.S. Government or write to us in Washington, D.C.

**Figure 9. The Equal Employment Opportunity Commission Discrimination Quiz: Could you be practicing illegal job discrimination—and not even know it?**

Society at large is still wrestling with whether equal opportunity means lowering performance standards by requiring quotas of people in protected groups in order to correct for past restriction of opportunity, or if it means maintaining standards but not discriminating against anyone in applying those standards. If a Mexican American can learn the factory job and perform to standard in three weeks but the Anglo, because of previous work experience, is already qualified, and if the company has a smaller percentage of Mexican-Americans in its employment than exists in the community at large—who should be hired? Should the years of internship for neurosurgeons be shortened in order to achieve greater representation of protected groups within surgical teams? Should a company not promote an otherwise well-qualified woman to an executive position simply because her male peers at that level would feel uncomfortable with a woman?

With varied opinions on such matters in society at large, it is understandable that the laws appear to many to be ambiguous and even contradictory. To say that the courts have provided less than total clarity in their rulings is an understatement.

It is beyond the scope of this book to try to resolve or even discuss major societal implications of the various laws affecting employment of people. What is intended is to provide the manager with a brief, practical overview of the major legal guidelines that affect hiring and particularly the interviewing processes; to review briefly some of the court cases testing the law; and to provide advice for operating within those guidelines. This chapter is an overview, certainly not a complete or definitive treatise, and adherence to any advice offered here will not necessarily provide legal immunity from any charges. Every thoughtful, sensitive, and prudent manager should keep abreast of the legalities and check regularly with an attorney who specializes in such matters.

Having dealt with quite a wide variety of organizations in the years since the equal opportunity thrust began, I've acquired the perspective that the individual manager can rarely eliminate, but can usually greatly minimize, the likelihood of legal problems in these matters. With sincere attempts made to conform with the laws, most managers I know have operated without feeling excessively restricted. A small percentage of organizations will probably continue to be made examples of, and the costs in terms of reputation, money, and psychic pain will be quite substantial. In my experience only a small percentage of managers have had their heads in the sand, choosing to ignore societal demands for change and steadfastly refusing to comply with the law. Their daily invitations to big legal problems are apt to be answered.

So, if you are among the majority of managers who basically want to do the right thing, and you make a little effort to learn and comply with the various equal opportunity laws, life may not be nearly as complex or frustrating as it is for a manager who chooses to ignore the law.

Here is a review of some of the more important laws affecting the selection interviewing system in this book.

## Brief Overview of the Laws

1. *Equal Employment Opportunity Act of 1972 and Title VII of the Civil Rights Act of 1964*

These are the famous acts that prohibit discrimination because of race, color, religion, sex, or national origin in any phase of employment. They pertain to employers with 15 or more employees, employment agencies, educational institutions, labor unions, and state and local governments. The enforcement arm of this legislation is the Equal Employment Opportunity Commission (EEOC). An aggrieved employee can file a complaint with the EEOC, and if not satisfied with its decision, he or she may take the matter to the federal courts.

In 1970 and 1978 EEOC issued interpretive guidelines concerning the use and validation of tests; the selection interview was explicitly included under the rubric of "tests." In order for a selection interview to be judged unfair to a minority, evidence would have to show that minorities were judged more negatively than nonminorities on the basis of the interview and that the judgments resulted in "adverse impact" in actual hiring. Then the employer would be required to prove the interview procedure to be reliable and valid. Thanks to *Griggs* v. *Duke Power Co.* (3 FEP 175,1971), the burden of proof of job-relatedness (validity) rests with the employer.

2. *The Equal Pay Act of 1963 (usually included with amendments to the Fair Labor Standards Act)*

These acts require employers to pay men and women performing substantially similar jobs in the same establishment, the same amount. Other criteria, such as department seniority and length of overall employment, may be used to assign different wages, but sex may not.

American Telephone and Telegraph was the first major organization to be compelled to make sizable back-pay awards to women who, the courts contended, were discriminated against in violation of this act as well as the EEO Act of 1972 and Title VII of the Civil Rights Act of 1964.

3. *The Age Discrimination in Employment Act of 1967 amended in 1978*

This act prohibits an employer from discriminating against persons aged 40 to 70 in any phase of employment and is enforced by EEOC.

## 4. *The Vocational Rehabilitation Act of 1973*

Section 503 of this act requires employers that have contracts of $50,000 or more with the federal government and 50 or more employees, to seek actively, through affirmative action programs, to hire handicapped individuals. The act makes it illegal to discriminate against mentally or physically handicapped persons for jobs they are qualified to do. The act specifies that handicapped individuals must meet reasonable standards for employment that are job-related and consistent with job necessity and safe performance of duties. A company must make efforts to accommodate physical and mental limitations of applicants and employees, unless that organization can show that such accommodation would constitute an "unusual hardship" for it.

## 5. *Vietnam Era Veterans' Readjustment Act of 1974*

Section 402 of this act requires federal contractors having a contract in excess of $10,000 to take affirmative action to employ and advance in employment qualified disabled veterans and veterans of the Vietnam era.

## 6. *Executive orders*

Specific executive orders require employers of more than 50 persons that contract with the federal government in amounts over $50,000 to practice nondiscrimination in all aspects of employment activity and to develop and implement written programs that describe the employer's affirmative action compliance. In other words, these employers are required to list numeric goals, establish timetables, and take other action to remedy the effects of past discrimination. This area is monitored by the Office of Federal Contract Compliance of the Department of Labor.

## 7. *The National Labor Relations Act*

This act requires unions to represent its members without discrimination and warns employers not to participate in the commission of any discriminatory practice by any union.

## 8. *State and local laws*

In general, state laws are not weaker than federal laws and spell out the specifics in various areas, such as age discrimination. An Illinois human rights act, for example, prohibits discrimination on the basis of ancestry, marital status, unfavorable discharges from the military, and as retaliation for having filed charges of discrimination or having assisted in an investigation of discrimination. Some state laws have been overturned by the federal courts (such as the so-called Victorian laws that quaintly protect women from working more than certain hours or lifting more than certain weights). The New York human rights law prohibits discrimination in the usual areas, but even for tiny companies with as few as four employees.

### 9. Uniform guidelines on employee selection procedures

On August 25, 1978, employee selection guidelines were issued jointly by the Equal Employment Opportunity Commission, the Department of Justice, the Civil Service Commission, and the Department of Labor. The guidelines went into effect September 25, 1978, and the widespread hope was that they would result in substantially less ambiguity and confusion.

These new guidelines replaced separate directives on employment practices from the EEOC and Office of Federal Contract Compliance for all employers covered by Title VII of the Civil Rights Act of 1964 or by Executive Orders 11246 and 11375 on affirmative action. The current guidelines cover "any measure, combination of measures or procedures used as a basis for any employment decision...from traditional paper and pencil tests, performance tests, training programs, probationary periods and physical education and work experience required through informal and casual interviews and unscored application forms." Until 1982 determination of "adverse impact" was supposed to operate primarily on the basis of the bottom-line concept, which essentially says it was acceptable for an employer to use a selection procedure that screens out a disproportionate number of a particular protected group without validation, so long as the ultimate hiring resulted in selection rates within the 80% figure.

In the case of Teal vs. Connecticut (29FEP 1) 64SF.ZND133, the United States Supreme Court rejected the bottom line defense, saying that any specific stage of a selection process could be challenged even if the employer could show that the final selection was racially balanced. However, the 80% rule in determining adverse impact is still operative. This becomes a bit technical, but probably worth understanding. The "80%" figure is defined as a situation in which the selection rate for one group for a given job is less than 80% of the selection rate for the group with the highest selection rate.

Wait a minute! I don't know of any organizations that have validated the in-depth selection interview, but what the guidelines seem to be saying is that a company just might have to do this if the 80% criterion is violated.

But what exactly is this 80% criterion? Here's an example: Let's suppose that a company has 10 positions open, there are 60 white and 15 black applicants, and this 4-to-1 ratio is representative of white-to-black ratios in the community. Suppose an in-depth interview is conducted with 30 whites (50% of the white applicants) and 5 blacks (33% of the black applicants). At this point in the selection process, the inclusion rate for blacks is obviously not as high as the rate for whites. If, however, the company fills the 10 spots by selecting 8 whites (13.3% of the original white applicants) and 2 blacks (13.3% of the original black applicants), there is no adverse impact. Indeed, the bottom-line selection rates result in 100% equity between the two groups despite the higher rate of exclusion of blacks from participation in the in-depth interviews. The 80% rule says that 100% equity is not necessary, and in this case 10.8% of the black applicants could have been hired because 10.8% is 80% of the 13.5% selection rate for whites. OK, but can a company be sure to avoid a penalty if the 80% criterion is achieved?

As Schanie and Will Holley stated in (*Personnel Administrator*, 1980) "Clearly, employers are being asked, if not told, to abandon the idea of hiring the best qualified in favor of a minimally qualified.... The 80% rule could have the effect of imposed quotas but presumably all an employer need do to avoid the process of validation is to make sure the selection rates are in order.... Although the 80% rule is offered in one section as a practical means of determining adverse impact in enforcement proceedings, a later section cautions [that] 'smaller differences in selection rates may nevertheless constitute adverse impact, where they are significant in both statistical and practical terms.'" Schanie and Holley conclude, "Thus, the 80% rule, which essentially was devised to provide a numeric standard for enforcement, is rendered essentially impotent, at least in the sense that it provides a firm rule." So the 80% criterion, even if achieved, does not preclude the possibility of your having to prove (if charged) the validity of your selection interview procedures.

## Legal Outcomes Pertinent to Selection Interviewing

A glance at the laws that could affect selection interviewing (and related aspects such as application forms and record checks) indicates a lot of potential areas for litigation. Selection interviews can be subjective—perfect havens for expression of unfair stereotypes and bigotry. Suppose that your organization were called upon to prove that its interviewing procedures were nondiscriminatory. How would your company fare under such scrutiny?

The federal government has not intended to eliminate selection interviews, or tests, or other reasonable selection instruments. In the area of testing, for example, the net effect has been for companies to do what they should have done all along—validate the tests to see if they accurately predict job performance. As stated earlier in this book, a great many testing programs have been found to be both valid and nondiscriminatory. If interview approaches are haphazard and shallow, maybe companies would be better off tightening up their interviewing systems, finding out who are the more valid interviewers, and thus serve a double purpose—reduction of discrimination and improvement of selection effectiveness.

The most often cited case in interviewing (*Rowe* v. *General Motors*) actually had to do with evaluations of candidates selected for promotion, and interviews per se were not part of the process. Blacks felt that the subjective evaluations (performance appraisals) of foremen had an adverse impact on them, and the court agreed: "...the subjective evaluation and favorable recommendation of the immediate foreman are a ready mechanism for the discrimination against blacks, much of which can be covertly concealed." In an article summarizing litigation concerning interviews, Richard Arvey noted only eight important cases (see Figure 10).*

Note that in Figure 10 interview validity was proved in only one case. There are plenty of additional cases pertinent to interviews, but the point is that interview validity per se is rarely attacked, and when it is, it does not hold up well.

The in-depth interviewing system in this book was conceived with its principal focus on hiring the best possible candidates for positions, and it happens that its key elements—well-thought-out job descriptions, person specifications, use of interview guides, thorough documentation of notes, and review of conclusions by several people— would probably be exactly the procedures a company could be called upon to institute for interview validation.

---

*Unfair Discrimination in the Employment Interview: Legal and Psychological Aspects,* *Psychological Bulletin,* 1979, Vol. 86, No. 4, 736–765.

| Case | Alleged discrimination against | Adverse impact shown | Validity of interview shown | Comment |
|---|---|---|---|---|
| Rowe v. General Motors (1972) | Blacks | Yes | No | Subjective standards said to be ready mechanism for discrimination |
| Equal Employment Opportunity Commission Decision No. 72-0703 (1971) | Blacks | Yes | No | Hiring system must permit review |
| Hester v. Southern Railway Company (1974) | Blacks and females | No | No | Interview noted to be subjective |
| United States v. Hazelwood School District (1976)* | Females | Yes | No | |
| Weiner v. County of Oakland (1976) | Females | Yes | No | Interview successfully defended on the basis of content validity |
| Harless v. Duck (1977) | Females | Yes | Yes | |
| King v. New Hampshire Department of Resources and Economic Development (1977) | Females | Yes | No | Questions in interview were indicative of discriminatory intent |
| Bannerman v. Department of Youth (1977) | Females | No | | Adverse impact not shown |

**Figure 10. Litigation concerning interviews. *Later appealed to the Supreme Court, but issues associated with the interview were not a part of this later decision.**

## What to Ask and Not Ask in Selection Interviews

I advise organizations not to include sensitive items in application forms or interviews, at least with protected classes of people. The "In-Depth Selection Interview Guide" is constructed to avoid sensitive areas. The following advice, mostly about what not to ask, is given with respect to topics that could conceivably enter into selection interviews.

1. *Do not ask marital status or questions about names and ages of dependents.*

These questions may violate Title VII if the information is used to exclude women or any subclass of women, such as married women or women with preschool children. [*1*/See, 29 C.F.R. 1604.4 (1979); *Phillips* v. *Martin Marietta Corporation.* 404 U.S. 542 (1971). *Sprogis* v. *United Airlines, Inc.* 444 F. 2d 1194 (Cir) *cert. denied* 404 U.S. 991 (1971).] The thrust is the stereotypical view as to the proper role women are supposed to play with regard to family responsibilities will not justify denial of employment opportunities to women with families. (See EEOC decision number 71-2613, June 22, 1972, CCH EEOC decisions (1973) 6285.)*

Recent statistics show that more blacks are widowed, divorced, or separated than are whites, and that proportionately more women than men in the labor force are widowed, divorced, or separated. Thus, this question has the potential to affect adversely both women and blacks.

2. *Do not ask spouse's name.*

Asking an applicant to list a spouse's name, where the purpose of the question is to require that successful female applicants be listed on the employee's personnel forms under a spouse's name, may violate Title VII if no counterpart rule applies to married males. See *Allen* v. *Lovejoy* 553f 2d522 (6th C. cir. 1977).

It is probably acceptable to ask the names of any relatives of the applicant already employed by the firm, particularly if the reason is to avoid security problems by not having relatives work in the same department or division. However, since a "not hire relatives" policy

---

*Data on such matters as marital status, number and ages of children, and similar topics could be used in a discriminatory manner in making employment decisions, but similar information, which is necessary for tax, insurance, social security, reporting requirements, and other business purposes, can and should be obtained after a person has been employed and not through an application form.

might have a disproportionately negative effect on women or minorities, the company might be called on to prove this is not the case.

An inquiry as to the applicant's acquaintances and relatives employed by the employer may not be used to give preferential treatment to friends and relatives where the work force is predominately made up of one race or ethnic group (as established in *Gibson* v. *ILU, local 40* 13FEP Cases 997 (9th Cir. 1976), *Rock* v. *Norfolk & Western Railroad Company,* 473F.2d 1344 (4th Cir.), *cert. denied,* 412 U.S. 993 (1973); *EEOC Decision* #72-032-0, August 17, 1971, CCH EEOC Decision (1973) 6294).

3.  *Do not ask a woman's maiden name or her father's surname.*

This is not relevant to a person's ability to perform a job and could be used for discriminatory purposes. For example, a woman's maiden name might be used as an indication of her national origin or religion.

4.  *It is legal to ask if an applicant has previously worked for the firm under a different name.*

It is also legal to ask if it will be necessary to use a different name to check on the applicant's employment or educational record.

5.  *Do not attempt to ascertain the lineage, ancestry, or national origin of an applicant.*

After hiring a person, such information may be necessary to record for compliance, but it should not be sought until after the person is hired.

6.  *Do not ask if an applicant is pregnant or if the applicant plans to have children.*

7.  *Don't ask the applicant's race or any questions directly or indirectly indicating race or color.*

Such information may be requested and kept separate and confidential after the person is hired.

8.  *Don't ask the applicant's native tongue.*

It's permissible to ask what languages the applicant reads, speaks, or writes fluently if such skills are job related.

9. *Do not ask an applicant's age (unless you suspect the applicant is a minor).*

The Age Discrimination in Employment Act (29 U.S. Cir. 61-34) prohibits discrimination on the basis of age against individuals who are between ages 40 and 70 inclusive. After hiring a person, you may request age information for record-keeping responsibilities relative to the Age Discrimination in Employment Act. For very young applicants, it would probably be considered reasonable to request proof of age.

10. *Don't ask whether an applicant is a lawfully admitted alien or otherwise has proper working papers.*

It apparently is acceptable to ask if an applicant is a United States citizen, and, "if you are not a citizen, do you have the legal right to remain in the United States?"

If a citizenship inquiry is used to reject noncitizen applicants where the rejection has the purpose or the effect of discriminating on the basis of national origin, Title VII might be violated (*Espinoza* v. *Farah Mfg. Co.*, 414 U.S. 86, 92 (1973). Additionally, to refuse employment to any individual because he or she is married to someone of a particular national origin would be viewed as unlawful (see 29 C.F.R. 1606.1 (1979).

11. *Do not ask questions suggesting selection criteria that are not reasonable.*

Selection criteria, even those based on objective and neutral factors, which operate to exclude a class of persons at substantially higher rates than other persons, and which are not job related may violate Title VII. (See Uniform Guidelines on Employee Selection Procedures, 29C.F.R.160.3 (1979); *Griggs* v. *Duke Power* Company, 401 U.S. at 431-432. The guidelines permit an expansive interpretation of selection criteria. Among other things they include written tests, experience, and height and weight requirements.)

12. *Do not ask about the racial, national, or religious affiliation of a school the applicant attended.*

It is certainly acceptable to ask the applicant to supply information about academic, vocational, or professional education at schools attended, if there is a bona fide occupational qualification (BFOQ). It may be deemed discriminatory if educational requirements have the effect of removing protected groups in disproportionate numbers and the higher educational standard is not important for the position in question.

Similarly, asking if an applicant has had specific experience or abilities, which are not validly related to job performance, might be considered discriminatory. In *King* v. *New Hampshire Dept. of Human Resources,* a court of appeals concluded that an interview question, such as if a female candidate for meter patrol officer could wield a sledgehammer, was irrelevant to the job and proved discriminatory intent. On the other hand, requesting a record of previous work experience is quite acceptable.

13. *Do not ask an applicant any questions about birthplace or birthplace of parents, and do not ask the applicant to submit a birth certificate, unless he or she is a minor.*

If the result of such questions is to remove from consideration a disproportionate number of members of protected groups, the questions could be considered discriminatory.

14. *Do not ask an applicant about foreign addresses that would indicate national origin or inquire about names and relationships of persons with whom the applicant resides. Do not ask whether the applicant owns or rents a residence.*

It is acceptable to ask for an applicant's address and how long the applicant has lived there or at previous addresses.

15. *Do not ask the applicant's height and weight.*

The question requiring an applicant to state his or her weight or height may violate Title VII if the requirement disproportionately excludes minorities or females and is not job related. See *Dothard* v. *Rawlinson* 433 U.S. 321 (1977). In this case a minimum height and weight requirement excluded 40% of all females as candidates for correctional counselor, but only 1% of male candidates were excluded. As a practical matter, candidates for professional or management positions are not ordinarily offended by inquiries about height and weight, and therefore these items are included in the sample application form (Appendix A). Your corporate attorney may suggest eliminating written and oral inquiries about height and weight, however.

It is acceptable to ask about physical limitations, since physically handicapped persons must be able to perform essential duties of the job without endangering the health or safety of themselves or others. However, the Rehabilitation Act requires organizations to make efforts to accommodate the mentally and physically handicapped. Furthermore, companies have been required to hire people previously rejected for health considerations, because it was determined that personnel people were inappropriately making medical conclusions. Perhaps the best advice is to stay away from medical issues altogether and let these matters be handled by physicians.

16.  *Do not ask what the person's hair color or eye color is.*

It would be quite hard to justify these as BFOQs, and such information may serve to indicate an employee's race or religion, which could be grounds for a discrimination suit.

New York City passed a local ordinance prohibiting discrimination in employment against recovered alcoholics who have demonstrated by their conduct over a reasonable period of time that they no longer are employment risks.

Don't arbitrarily reject a candidate who has had cancer who is, at the time of application, in remission, or someone with a disease such as diabetes or epilepsy that is under control, or someone who has had heart attacks or strokes and has recovered.

17.  *Be careful in asking what hours an applicant might be available for work.*

The questions may be unlawful if used arbitrarily to reject applicants who want to observe the Sabbath, as their religion defines it, as part of a religious practice. The EEOC Guidelines on Discrimination because of Religion, 29 C.F.R. 1605.2 (1979), state that an employer has a duty to make reasonable accommodations to the religious needs of employees or prospective employees where such accommodations can be made without undue hardship upon the conduct of the employer's business. (See *TWA* v. *Hardison* 432 U.S. 63 (1977); *Yott* v. *North American Rockwell Corporation,* 602 F2d904, 907 (9th Cir., 1979).)

18.  *It is allowable to inquire as to a person's sex only if gender is a BFOQ of the job.*

19.  *Do not inquire as to an applicant's arrest record.*

The EEOC and courts have held that an arrest-record inquiry would tend disproportionately to deter minority applicants. An arrest is not an indication of guilt, and historically minorities have suffered disproportionately more arrests than others. The Department of Labor has also recognized the potential for discrimination in the consideration of arrest records. (See Sec. 62.24 (d3) of Revised Order #4, establishing standards and guidelines for affirmative action programs required of government contractors.)

If an arrest inquiry is made, the employer might be called upon to justify its use as a "business necessity" and must also demonstrate that the policy or practice is essential to the safe and efficient operation of the business. (See EEOC Decision No. 74-79, January 31, 1974, CCH Employment Practice Guide, 6425; *Gregory* v. *Litton Systems Inc.* 316 F Supp. 401, 403 (C.D. Cal. 1976), *Aff'd as MOD* 475-F. 2d 631 (9th Cir. 1976).)

Because minority applicants are convicted more frequently than whites, a conviction inquiry could be expected to disproportionately exclude minority applicants and would be unlawful under Title VII in the absence of a business necessity. However, both the EEOC and the courts have recognized that for certain positions an applicant's record of criminal convictions may be significant evidence of his or her unsuitability for the position. (See *Richardson* v. *Hotel Corporation of America.* 332 F. Supp. 519 (E.D.L.a 1971), *aff'd* 468. 2d 951 (5th Cir. 1972).) Perhaps the best advice comes from a case (*Green* v. *Missouri Pacific Railroad Company,* 523 F. 2nd 1290—8th Cir. 1975, as clarified in 549 F. 2nd 1158 8th Cir. 1977) in which the court held that the employer is not to be prevented from considering an applicant's prior criminal record as a factor in making individual hiring decisions so long as the employer takes into account the nature and gravity of the offense; the time that has passed since the conviction or completion of sentence; and the nature of the job for which the person has applied.

20.  *Be careful in asking about the applicant's credit rating.*

Rejection of applicants because of poor credit ratings has a disparate impact on minority groups and thus has been found discriminatory by the EEOC, unless business necessity can be shown. (See EEOC decision 72, 0274 August 31, 1971, CCH EEOC Decisions (1973) 6312; EEOC Decision 72-1176 February 28, 1972, CCH EEOC Decisions (1973) 6359.) Similarly, inquiries as to bankruptcy, car ownership, rental or ownership of a house, rental or ownership of furniture, length of residence at an address, past garnishment of wages, or other indexes of economic status may violate Title VII, absent business necessity, and could result in penalties. (See EEOC Decision 74-27 September 27, 1973, CCH Employment Practices Guide 6396; EEOC Decision—34, September 28, 1973, *i.e.,* at 60747; *Johnson v. Pike Corporation of America,* 332 F. Supp. 490 (C.D. Cal. 1971).)

### 21. *Do not ask what type of military discharge the applicant had.*

Where the requirement was not shown to be job related, the EEOC has held that an employer's policy of requiring proof of an honorable discharge from the armed services as a hiring condition violates Title VII because minorities receive proportionately more discharges than whites. (EEOC Decision, 74-25, September 10, 1973, CCH Employment Practices Act Guide 6400.) It is acceptable to ask what education and experience the applicant acquired in the armed services.

### 22. *Do not ask if a fidelity bond has ever been refused.*

This question presumably represents an indirect effort to detect any flaws in an individual's past, but the difficulty is that a fidelity bond may be denied for arbitrary and discriminatory reasons, which the individual did not know about and therefore was unable to challenge. This method of ascertaining an individual's past history should be dropped in favor of methods not so likely to be infected with bias. The Maryland Commission on Human Relations has issued an order prohibiting an employer from asking about bond refusal.

### 23. *Do not ask if wages have been garnished.*

A district court ruled that an employer violated Title VII by discharging a black employee because his wages had been garnished several times. The district court based its conclusions on the Supreme Court's testing ruling and on the district court's findings that minorities suffer wage garnishments substantially more than whites do and that wage garnishments do not affect the worker's ability to work effectively. *Wallace v. Bebron Corporation,* 494 F. 2nd 674 (8th Cir. 1974); *Marshall v. District of Columbia* 10 EBD 10, 349 (DDC 1975).

### 24. *Do not ask how low a salary the person will accept.*

To the extent that women have been relegated to poorer paying jobs than men or have been paid less than men for the same work, there is invitation for a lawsuit.

25.  *Don't ask an applicant to list all memberships in clubs, societies, organizations, and lodges. Don't ask what church he/she attends or the name of his priest, rabbi, or minister.*

It's permissible to ask an applicant to list memberships in organizations relevant to the job in question, such as professional societies. Obviously the intent is to restrict information that would reveal race, religion, and ancestry.

26.  *Do not imply that certain jobs are preferably filled by men.*

A New York law firm lost a suit (by the EEOC and the New York Human Rights Commission) for sex discrimination because it emphasized to female applicants that the firm had only one female attorney and that she was assigned to an area of work traditionally performed by women.

# 7 | Interpreting Interview Data

Interpretation of interview data may at times seem a hopelessly complex and abstruse task. Interviewees have defense mechanisms which may cause their descriptions of past experiences to be smoothed out and whitewashed. Furthermore, the individual may want the job so much that there are deliberate, conscious attempts to shade the truth, omit significant events, and in various ways put only the best foot forward. The interviewer is most interested in the interviewee's own evaluations and interpretations—what the interviewee really feels or felt about situations. Thus the task of the interviewer often becomes an attempt to interpret what are biased interviewee interpretations.

This chapter begins with how the recommended hiring steps facilitate interpretation, progresses to eight psychological principles of interpretation, conducts a tour through the "In-Depth Selection Interview Guide," and ends with a graphic example of the interpretive data for a particular job.

## THE RECOMMENDED HIRING STEPS
## FACILITATE INTERPRETATION

Usually interviewers can improve their ability to interpret interview data simply by following the recommended steps (Figure 2), determining job and person specifications, following the "In-Depth Selection Interview Guide" religiously, taking exhaustive notes, reviewing notes after the interview, and sharing data with at least one other interviewer.

### Accurate Person Specifications Facilitate Interpretation

How would you interpret a candidate who says, "Several times during the past year, I have been a couple of days late with my monthly reports." Does this sound like a major liability to you or just a minor shortcoming? Do you interpret such a statement as an indication of disorganization, an inability to set priorities, laziness, or what? These are all dumb questions, because no interpretation is possible without knowing more specifics—exactly what sort of reports, what is meant by "a couple" of days, what have been the consequences of tardiness—and without knowing the job description and person specifications.

In one client organization, it is perfectly acceptable for a sales representative's call-reports (descriptions of what transpired on sales calls) to be submitted to the sales manager a few days late; in another organization this would be grounds for termination. In many companies it is considered wonderful if a computer system is delivered only a few days late. In most companies I work with, the tax manager's head would roll if certain legally mandated deadlines were missed by even a single day.

If you were hiring a store manager for a large supermarket, how would you interpret this candidate's statement: "I take the initiative— I look for opportunities to vary products, shelf layouts, and shelf displays in order best to meet the merchandising needs of a particular store area." Again, you can't properly interpret such a statement without understanding the job description and person specifications. In one client organization such an aggressive, independent spirit would be applauded because store managers are given a great deal of autonomy. In another client organization, the corporate office makes all merchandising decisions, and such an independent store manager would be considered a maverick who can't take direction, who would soon become frustrated and quit or be fired.

"Bad specifications" are inaccurate, not comprehensive, or possibly illegal. "Good specifications" reflect the true nature of the position, in terms of budgets, size, complexity, leadership style, support services, task-orientation versus people-orientation, opportunities for growth, pressures, stresses, and sources of satisfaction.

We have discussed how important thorough, accurate job descriptions and person specifications are for minimizing organizational confusion and maximizing consensus—so that there can be a smooth transition for the individual into the organization and few surprises later on. One of the most important reasons for determining thorough, accurate specifications is for you, as the interviewer, to interpret properly behaviors, responses, values, and experiences as related by the interviewee vis-à-vis what it will take to succeed.

## The "In-Depth Selection Interview Guide" Facilitates Interpretation through Standardized Questions

The reader has been encouraged to follow the "In-Depth Selection Interview Guide" religiously in order not to bias responses (the questions are carefully unbiased), to assure comprehensiveness (the guide contains all the questions, except follow-up questions, necessary to cover all job-relevant areas thoroughly), and to conform with legalities (a record of responses could be used as evidence in a lawsuit). One of the most important reasons for using the guide is that by asking the same comprehensive questions in the same order, using the same wording, the data-gathering process is standardized and interpretation is facilitated. After hearing 100 responses to the question "How would you describe your work habits?" and relating those responses to reference checks and subsequent performance of people hired, it becomes easier to judge when a person is describing strengths or shortcomings in work habits. A couple of examples will help make this point.

If you were hired to critique 100 McDonald's stores, your analysis of the first one would probably be a long and difficult process. After 30 or 40 evaluations of stores, all of which are supposed to follow the same policies and programs for sanitation, cooking, maintenance of machinery, service, and other measures, it will be a lot easier to spot deviations from the acceptable standards. Following the "In-Depth Selection Interview Guide" for 30 or 50 interviews will permit you to do the same thing—to spot acceptable and unacceptable responses in relation to person specifications more quickly and accurately than you will in the first few interviews.

Several years ago I interviewed a man reputed to be one of Chicago's most famous playboys. Since this individual took the liberty to brag about his conquests, I indulged my curiosity by asking, "What's your approach?" Expecting that his "interview techniques" would involve incredible creativity and diversity, it amused me when this Casanova said, "I almost always use the same old trite, worn, mundane question—"How's it going?" It became apparent then that Casanova was using a one-item structured interview guide. "You ask the same question—'How's it going?'—in the same order (first), and with practice you get so good at sensing the rhythm, style, and pattern of responses that in literally half a minute I have all the interpretative data I need for my little interview." Slightly aghast at the thought of my scientific interviewing techniques being used for such purposes, I decided not to ask how many such interviews had to be conducted in a typical evening before his "person specifications" would be successfully achieved.

Fortunately, in job-related contexts you don't have to make an interpretative leap based upon an interviewee's responses to a single question. The guide has more than 100 questions, and by the time you have used it a number of times, asking the same questions, in the same unbiased wording and order, correct interpretation of the data will be your reward.

## Copious Notes Contain Revealing Patterns

Suppose you took thorough notes on Sarah Jones' conversation and behaviors at a dinner party. During cocktail discussions of sports and business, throughout dinner discussions of politics and international relations, and during brandy discussions of vacation plans, there you were, jotting down what she said and how she said it. The next day you reviewed the notes several times and noticed that no one else brought up the subject of societal demands of modern women, but that she brought it up 14 different times. How would you interpret her statements? Right, you would probably wonder if she feels that society places excessive demands on her.

In selection interviews, even though people may be motivated to make their best impression and to conceal shortcomings, unless they are very clever at this, their essential needs and behavioral patterns will still be revealed in their comments and in your interview notes. As you work your way through a person's career, asking about high points, low points, how decisions were made, accomplishments, disappointments, relationships with people, and so on, people's facades tend to crumble and true forms emerge.

The interviewee who has always had a distaste for reading technical journals might plan to lie intentionally about this shortcoming in an interview. Nonetheless, during the 2½-hour interview, there are literally dozens of mini-opportunities for the true perspective of the individual to be revealed. Perhaps in talking about a position held 10 years ago, the individual said, "I liked the job because it was very practical—I didn't have to mess with academic concepts." Perhaps in reference to a position held five years ago a complaint was "They expected you to read a lot of technical journals, but wouldn't let you do it during the work day." Such statements might not strike you as inappropriate, unusual, or negative vis-à-vis the person specifications as they are said, but in reviewing the notes, a pattern of 8 or 10 such comments might proclaim the truth in neon. The interviewee never said, "I don't like to read technical journals," but your notes would strongly suggest that conclusion.

Even people who do an excellent job of taking responsibility for their own destiny and making things happen have plenty of opportunities over a lifetime to blame circumstances or other people for failures or disappointments. During the interview itself, it may not strike the interviewer that the interviewee is an incessant rationalizer of failures, simply because each specific incident seems plausible enough. However, if the interviewee has had 10 positions during the past 25 years, has had no conspicuous successes, and has had a lot of failures, most of which are "someone else's fault," the interviewer has learned a lot about the interviewee, although the interpretation might not come until the notes are reviewed. Whether the interviewee repeatedly exercises bad judgment in accepting new positions, is insensitive to political factors, or has limited intelligence, the pattern of responses will probably emerge from comprehensive notes.

In scrutinizing each job experience, you as an interviewer may not notice that the interviewee has gradually improved in self-confidence, aggressiveness, and work habits until you gain a broad enough perspective from reviewing your notes. No matter how experienced the interviewer is, there are always deeper insights lurking in comprehensive notes. Even if the interviewer is sharp enough to spot the major trends and patterns during the interview, notes will reveal more subtle relationships and clearer distinctions than could possibly have occurred to the interviewer at the time. Conscientious note-taking will not guarantee accurate interpretation, but it certainly is an essential ingredient.

## Sharing Opinions and Conclusions
## Corrects Misinterpretation

Sharing your notes with other interviewers will enable you to reach deeper, richer insights into the candidate. Three or four heads are better than one, when it comes to interpretation. Even if others interviewed only briefly, their perspectives can help to minimize biases or unfounded stereotypes. There are no guarantees. It is like Monday-morning quarterbacking—two persons discussing the Chicago Bears' latest loss can usually combine their perspectives and come up with more a comprehensive, accurate analysis, but of course they could both be wrong.

## Can Interpretation Be Objective?

Wouldn't it be wonderful if an interview could be like a test, with objective and easy to score responses to each question? If the interviewee says, "I want to be a general manager within five years," you look at the score sheet, check the box corresponding to that level of ambition, and after doing this for 150 or 200 questions, you submit your scores to a computer, which produces a profile that states, to the decimal point, the chances of this candidate's being successful on the job. Very scientific, very objective, but how realistic is this notion?

Actually, not only would such systems be nice, they exist and they *are* quite nice, but only under certain conditions. Where there are a large number of jobs (hundreds) that are virtually identical in job description and person specifications, a scientifically weighted interview guide can be developed. Some insurance companies and brokerage firms have experimented with such systems, and the techniques have proven valid, to a certain extent. A recurring problem is that easily scored interview guides and biographical information blanks have been too easy to fake, and when the word gets out that candidates for selection can get away with lying a little, that's exactly what they do and the ability of the instrument to predict success evaporates. I'm thinking about including the TORC methods in such a process, which would greatly increase the validity of such instruments. The point is, interview interpretation can theoretically be quite objective. Until computer-based interpretation fully arrives, however, interviewers can benefit from using some basic principles in their analyses.

## EIGHT PSYCHOLOGICAL PRINCIPLES FOR INTERPRETATION

1. *People's strengths become overused and at times are shortcomings.*

All of us in a sense are practicing behavioral scientists. We know what knowledge, skills, and abilities have seemed to be effective for us in getting us what we want in life. No one has to tell us to utilize our strengths—verbal adroitness, charm, a probing mind, a good eye for detail, or whatever. What people might not tell us, and which we may not fully realize, is that we sometimes beat our strengths to death, relying on what has worked in the past, even when a new situation requires something different.

I always look for evidence of people's strengths backfiring on them. The talents people have for turning lead into gold are often accompanied by an occasional tendency to turn a Montrachet into grape juice. So I ask myself a few basic questions.

Is this warm, friendly, accommodating person with average intelligence and a very generous nature sometimes vulnerable to very bright, dominating types?

Is this very sincere, direct, forceful person occasionally perceived by co-workers as tactless and blunt?

Is this marvelously thorough detail-person sometimes bogged down in minutiae?

Might this thorough planner be a bit indecisive at times?

Might this suave, verbally adroit, charming sales representative make life a bit difficult for supervisors by glibly talking around issues?

Will this highly controlled, extremely cautious individual who never makes an "error of commission" sometimes miss opportunities that involve a little risk?

Will this brilliant systems analyst with four college degrees and a history of spending most evenings reading technical books look for logical, rational solutions to people problems whose solutions require an emotional component?

It would be inappropriate, the egregious caricature of stereotyping, to assume an affirmative answer to any of these questions. However, it is appropriate to assume that a person's strengths might be overused, particularly in pressure situations.

2. *Recent past behavior is the best predictor of near-future behavior.*

A good selection interview emphasizes job-relevant behaviors—what the person has done, under what circumstances, and with what results. In order to determine if the person's abilities, knowledge, skills, interests, and personality will mesh with the responsibilities, opportunities, personalities, and challenges of the position in question, facts are needed, and more recent facts should be weighted more heavily than facts far in the past.

There is a lot more inertia to recent past behaviors than to behaviors that occurred many years ago. An athlete's likely performance next week is a lot more accurately predicted by performance this week than performance five years ago, unless performance in both cases was identical. (The Chicago Bears' offense stunk five years ago and stunk last week, so there's not much doubt as to what it will be like next Sunday.)

If a person was a goof-off in college but for the past 10 years has been responsible, mature, and self-disciplined, the previous adolescent immaturity can generally be disregarded. If a person was stable and responsible for 20 years and in the past year has undergone a midlife crisis that has resulted in three job changes and two wife changes, watch out! The desperate gambles, shallow self-insights, greed, dishonesty, and whatever else were parts of such volatility in the recent past are apt to continue in the near future.

Successful and unsuccessful life patterns tend to repeat themselves. "Winners" obviously work hard to acquire the knowledge, skills, and abilities to make themselves successful. Winners make mistakes just like anyone else, although they work harder and smarter to prevent failure, are usually quicker to spot a failure coming and strive to transform a loss into a win, and are even able, if that fails, quickly to create new wins. Winners exist at all levels of organizations, not simply at the top. Those I refer to as true winners are not necessarily the highest paid or most powerful people, but they are individuals in tune with themselves, who know their capabilities and tend to grow in ways consistent with realistic goals. A lumberjack need not strive to be president of the paper company, and a salesman need not strive to become a sales manager, in order to be winners.

"Losers" have a lot of regrets in life. They are confused by this, disappointed with that, assumed this incorrectly, hoped futilely for that to occur. In sorting through the words flowing from the interviewee, it is useful for the interviewer to step back and consider what the success pattern has been for the individual and try to determine why. In either case—winning or losing—recent past behavior is the best predictor of near future behavior.

### 3. *Nature and nurture are equally irrelevant and relevant.*

Some managers fret excessively about whether certain characteristics (for example, leadership ability, intelligence) are qualities people are born with (nature) or acquired as a result of life's experiences (nurture). If some characteristics are inborn, they reason, then they are not so amenable to change. If energy level is largely determined genetically, for instance, and if the person specification is for a substantially higher energy level than is apparent in the interviewee, the person should not be hired. On the other hand, if a skill is one which is nurtured as a result of life's experiences—listening skills, for example—a person who is a bit deficient in this area, with some training experiences, could perhaps achieve an acceptable level on the person specifications.

The nature versus nurture question follows only religion, politics, and sex in terms of its likelihood of generating hostile controversy. The question of what influence genetics and environment have on intelligence has been intensely debated beginning in the 1960s and continuing into the 1980s. When it comes to selection interviewing, particularly at the levels addressed in this book, I avoid the controversy by saying "it rarely matters." If you are not hiring entry-level people, then you are concerned with the results people have achieved, regardless of what combination of nature and nurture produced those results. If you want to hire an athlete who pole-vaults 16 feet, it is irrelevant how much nature or nurture contributed, as long as the person can pole-vault 16 feet. If you can only afford to hire a pole-vaulter who can clear the bar at 16 feet, and the specification requires the person to progress quickly to an 18-foot standard, the nature versus nurture question takes on real importance.

If you need a little bit more explanation, consider that some characteristics (eye color, body structure, health and energy factors, among others) seem to be more heavily determined by nature than nurture, and some other characteristics (attitudes, beliefs, self-image, for example) appear to be mostly learned. Most psychologists believe that nature provides certain broad parameters, within which people might nurture capabilities, skills, knowledge, and health factors, but that environmental influences (nurture) are extremely important in determining the ultimate level of utilization of inherent, or latent, potentials.

The "In-Depth Selection Interview Guide" traces a person's development over time, so that you can learn the depth and inertia of both nature and nurture and just what sort of interaction has occurred between the two. If Sally has been a high achiever all her life, if Joe talks like a "doer" but has never been much of a performer, or if Charlie worked extremely hard for 10 years but is now slowing down, it generally doesn't make a big difference if the causes are genetic or environmental. From a selection point of view, the decision would be the same in either case. Since the best predictor of near-future behavior is recent past behavior, the interviewer extrapolates from recent past behavior, and while being sensitive to mitigating circumstances, figures that the near future will probably bring more of the same performance and abilities.

4.  *All behavior is motivated.*

Psychologists get into a lot of trouble and leave themselves vulnerable to a lot of joking when they claim that every word, body movement, car accident, gesture, slip of the tongue, every constructive or destructive action with another human being, every success or failure, is motivated either consciously or unconsciously. Do unresolved childhood needs really manifest themselves in behaviors 45 years later, perhaps without the individual's even being aware of such controlling influences? Did my toilet training make me a better controller or a messy impressionistic painter? Are we all, as some behavioral scientists suggest, merely automatons going through the motions of life, pretending that we have free will and choice but inextricably bound to patterns of behavior acquired early in life?

As a first-year graduate student in psychology, I chuckled at what seemed such blatant absurdity and believed that such tenets were conveniently manufactured by insecure, socially maladjusted psychologists. Since so many psychologists were rejected all of their lives (that's why they went into psychology, right?), it was no doubt comforting for them to think of human beings as predictable and controllable.

In the intervening years I have come to believe that everything an individual says or does has some adaptive or need-fulfillment value, whether or not the person is conscious of it and whether or not it seems rational. Every year I become more in awe of the complexity of the human species and of how nonrandom everything is that we say or do.

I have studied a great many videotaped selection interviews, and I've seen my trainees—businessmen and women—become true believers in the all-behavior-is-motivated tenet. We analyze a tape and summarize our conclusions with substantiating data. We study the tape a second time, a third, and sometimes a fourth, and progressively deeper meanings to words, pauses, and nonverbal behaviors leap off the tape. We peel away surface knowledge like layers of an onion in gaining deeper and deeper insights.

The point, of course, is not to videotape interviews—that should be done only for training purposes—but to take notes conscientiously, not only with regard to what the person is saying but *how* the person is saying it, and to review the notes several times before trying to formulate final conclusions. And in this process we should admit the possibility that all behavior is motivated.

5. *Red flags demand interpretation.*

There are a number of red-flag warning signals by which the interviewer can sense that some strong negative feeling is occurring within the interviewee and that further investigation is important for correct interpretation.

Blushing

Overly involved and complex responses, which usually sound well planned and rehearsed

Sudden loss of what had been good eye contact

Any significant change in pace (speeding up or slowing down)

Suddenly higher or lower voice

Inappropriate use of humor

And sudden change in voice volume (louder or softer)

Sudden twitching, stammering, frowning, drumming fingers

Suddenly more formal (rehearsed?) vocabulary

Inconsistency between words and nonverbal behavior (If the candidate says, "I was happy there," and frowns while shaking his head as if to communicate "No, I wasn't," believe the nonverbal cues, not the words)

Sudden loss of professional rapport, for no apparent reason

Grabbing suddenly for something to drink

Fumbling for a cigarette (whereas previously there had not been fumbling)

Suddenly heavy perspiring

Polite surface behavior, though suddenly a clenched fist

Unusually long pauses (for the individual)

It is important to write down when any of these things occur. For pauses, I simply record a dot every five seconds. At the time I may not have the foggiest idea what is going on—is this person suddenly anxious, nervous, angry, or scared? Is the person trying to conceal some shortcoming or failure? Maybe, and maybe not. Perhaps the person's underwear is simply too tight.

When red flags occur, I go on a fishing expedition, using all sorts of follow-up questions to try to arrive at proper interpretation. Usually the individual is trying to conceal something, and that something is a shortcoming. Early in the interview my fishing expedition is cursory—I don't want to risk destroying professional rapport. I ask a follow-up question or two and might make a note to myself to come back later to explore the issue more aggressively.

A comment about the topic of interpreting nonverbal behavior is appropriate here—don't overdo it! There are a number of books on the subject, and they are generally worth reading, so long as you do not go overboard. Crossing one's arms does not necessarily mean a person is becoming defensive. It may mean that blood has accumulated in the extremities and that crossing the arms lessens physical discomfort in the hands. On the other hand, if the interviewee does not like your line of questioning and punches you in the nose, interpretation of nonverbal behavior is not very difficult.

A year ago I was training an interviewer who had done a lot of reading about pupillary dilation. "When people lie," he explained, "their pupils get smaller. Arabs wear sunglasses not because they're into the Foster Grant image, but because they don't want people to know how truthful they're being," he added. At one point in our training seminar he leaped up at the videotape monitor and exclaimed, "Look at her pupils—she must be lying!" "Wait, wait, wait, wait," I implored, "all she did was look toward the window, and the stronger light accounted for the change."

6. *People may and may not change.*

Throughout this chapter we have touched on a couple of important aspects of change—what boundaries nature places on change potential and the importance of recent past behavior in predicting near-future behavior. Frankly, I feel totally stretched, professionally, when attempting to predict behavioral change that is not totally justified by recent past behavior. It takes quite an interpretative leap to predict that in the following instances an individual will succeed:

In Anchorage, although he has always lived in the South and admits disliking cold weather.

Even though he is an alcoholic and had job-related problems as recently as 2 years ago.

In a 20-person company, although she had previously worked only for *Fortune* 500 companies.

In the deep South, although he is black and has only lived in a racially integrated suburb of Washington, D.C.

In a very loosely structured organization, although the person's sole previous experience was with the military.

Do you buy it when an interviewee says, "I know there was a problem in the past, but from now on I'm going to be better organized," "more in control of my emotions," "a harder worker," "a better listener," a "nicer guy," or "a stronger manager." I generally do not believe any of it. It takes either guts or gullibility to believe that people will be happy and successful in job situations requiring dramatic and immediate improvement in a weak area or a radical shift in values or needs. If a person has been criticized by three employers (including the current one) in six years for missing deadlines, don't bet on the person's suddenly being able to improve priority-setting or organization or whatever accounts for the previous problems. If a person has been a heavy-handed autocrat for years, don't readily accept the congenial interview personality and sincere-sounding commitments to treating people better. An awareness of what to improve is certainly not sufficient for change. Although a new position offers a fresh start for someone to try to improve without co-workers' negative expectations, usually the opposite occurs—people may initially be on good behavior in the new job, but when pressures mount they regress to the old ways.

I believe that it is sometimes possible, in light of a specific person's shortcomings, to design a job that will minimize those shortcomings. Unless you make special efforts, however, don't count on anyone's turning over a new leaf.

When do people change? It sounds facetious to say that people can change when they have changed, but it's true. When people demonstrate good insights into shortcomings, have a realistic plan to implement changes, and show at least some success in implementing their plan, I'm often convinced that they can continue to improve. If an alcoholic has been off the bottle for two years, that's a compelling sign. Six months would probably not be so convincing. Ten years would be almost entirely convincing. If a person was easygoing and lackadaisical for a decade in the working world, but a year ago got married, now has a child to support, and for the past six months has been extremely responsible, dedicated, and hard-working, I might consider the person changed. If a person has generally been successful in life, has good insights into strengths and shortcomings, is bright and success-oriented, and generally has overcome liabilities in the past, the pattern induces me to believe that as new challenges bring out new shortcomings, those too will be recognized and corrected. Growth begets growth—constructive change begets constructive change. In short, I'll bet on a person to turn over a new leaf when the individual has shown a history, particularly a recent history, of turning over the leaves.

## Nasty Joe and Meek Mike

If you had to hire one of two people equal in all respects, except that one is so aggressive, hard-charging, and results-oriented that he is often blunt and tactless (Nasty Joe) and the other is unaggressive, passive, and shy (Meek Mike), and if success for either one would require overcoming the respective shortcoming—tactlessness for Nasty Joe and unassertiveness for Meek Mike—which one would you hire? I'd recommend Nasty Joe and here is why: Meek Mike has not developed the assertiveness muscles to exercise, even if he wanted to, but Nasty Joe already has the ability to be tactful, at least sometimes. Meek Mike probably does not feel that he has psychological permission to be a more assertive individual, so developing assertiveness might take him years. It can be done, but it usually requires extended counseling and training.

Nasty Joe, on the other hand, knows very well how to be diplomatic. In a meeting yesterday with the chairman, he was quite gracious and compliant. At his daughter's wedding he was a paragon of compassion. When he heard that a subordinate had terminal cancer, he was understanding, a good listener, and never again used threats with that person. Nasty Joe merely has to use more of certain behaviors he already has in his repertoire and restrain a few of the more outrageous behaviors, before he can be perceived as a new person by co-workers. He may not actually change his personality, but it may seem that way to others.

Each year I work with 10 or 15 "Nasty Joes," and almost all have improved. I provide feedback on how behaviors are perceived in the work environment, and the Nasty Joes improve themselves. It's preferable if Nasty Joe sincerely wants to improve, but the techniques work even if he is just going through the motions in order to get his boss off of his back.

The technique I use is to survey Joe's co-workers (usually subordinates), getting ratings and comments on what they see as Joe's strengths and possible areas for improvement. Then I sit down with Joe to analyze the data and set goals for improvement. Figure 11 is an example of survey feedback with a real-life Nasty Joe.

Joe might read a couple of books (on interpersonal communications or motivation), attend a seminar (on listening or other management techniques), and then we might talk about some specific occurrences on the job. But the real pay-off comes when Joe stops raising his voice, gives a few more deserved pats on the back, invites a few more suggestions from subordinates, and generally counts to five before

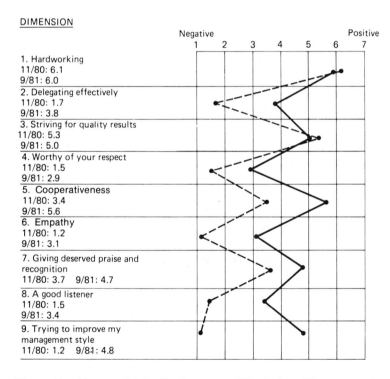

Figure 11.   Managerial feedback survey of Nasty Joe—The means of anonymous ratings by seven subordinates. Ratings in November, 1980: _ _ _ _ _ _; ratings in September, 1981: _____.

reacting to an irritating or frustrating circumstance. Nasty Joe is usually quite pleased with himself when surveys six months and one year later document his great improvement. He usually reports that the new behaviors are no longer playacted, but have become quite sincere. His subordinates stop covering up mistakes and begin to tell him when problems are arising. Finally, turnover is usually down and morale up. These are the sorts of things that register with Nasty Joe, so that the changes actually become permanent. Basically, it is the same old Joe, but he no longer is viewed as nasty, and co-workers really appreciate his efforts to improve, even if those efforts have not been totally successful.

A Meek Mike can want to change, but he is not immediately able to, even if his job is on the line. When Meek Mike tries to become dramatically more assertive, it is usually so awkward, ludicrous, or offensive that the effort is ineffective.

It will probably be smart not to hire anyone if a 5% or greater behavioral change is required to overcome meekness, or if a 15% or greater change in throttling aggressiveness is required. These percentages are not based on scientific research—just my impression that it's easier to file down Nasty Joe's rough edges than it is to build aggressiveness in Meek Mike.

7. *Evaluative judgments and attributions reveal underlying needs.*

Knowing that a person worked 13 hours a day, 7 days a week for a year can be important, but knowing how the person felt about workload can be even more important. If the person felt burned out after one week or "couldn't get enough of this interesting challenge, even after one year" could be essential for accurate interpretation.

The "In-Depth Selection Interview Guide" directs you to ask what the interviewee believes were high points and low points, successes and failures, accomplishments and disappointments, why each employment situation was liked or disliked, what is desired in a new job, and how co-workers would judge various actions. These are rich, meaningful data because they require the interviewee to evaluate—to express feelings and needs.

Although the interview guide guarantees that the interviewer will have evaluative judgments available for interpretation, it obviously does not contain follow-up questions and useful tangents to pursue. My advice for when you meander away from the guide is not just to find out what occurred in the interviewee's life, but constantly to ask what the interviewee thought of this, what was liked, and what was disliked.

To what does the individual attribute success or failure? What motives does the interviewee attribute to subordinates, peers, superiors, and others? Determining attributions provides a rich source of interpretive data. If, in reviewing his own 20-year-career, it seems to the interviewee that his career progress has been consistently hampered because of other people's stupidity, insensitivity, greed, or selfishness, it is likely that some or all of the problem is with the interviewee. If Susan tells you that people have been repeatedly uncooperative with her, the chances are very good that Susan has not developed the interpersonal skills to engender cooperation from others. If a person's successes are real and are repeatedly attributed to the competence and good intentions of subordinates, the chances are pretty good that the interviewee is an effective manager in recruiting, selecting, training, coordinating, developing, and communicating with subordinates. When an interviewee attributes career difficulties to himself—"I'm just too gullible"—the interviewer might correctly wonder if there is not some psychological mechanism which will continue to fuel such gullibility. People who are constantly "let down" by others almost always have a self-fulfilling need for others to let them down.

In short, when things repeatedly happen to people, their explanations often reveal a psychological need to perpetuate those situations.

8. *At higher levels in organizations, people succeed not so much because of their outstanding strengths, but because of their lack of significant liabilities.*

I call this statement the "rowboat theory of career success," the reasons for which will be clear later in this discussion. It may have occurred to the reader that the emphasis of this book has been disproportionately on determining shortcomings, liabilities, and areas for improvement as opposed to strengths and assets. Interpretation of negatives is, to put it simply, more important than interpretation of positives, because success at upper levels of management often is more dependent on absence of conspicuous major shortcomings than on the existence of spectacular strengths.

Bookstores are loaded with books giving career advice, and very often the advice is to think positively, determine your strengths, work hard to maximize those strengths, and don't pay a whole lot of attention to shortcomings. After all, so many of these books say, dwelling on the negatives can only cause you to lose self-confidence.

Actually, that is not bad advice for someone on an assembly line or even a technical professional up to but not including first-level supervision. If a chemist, for example, is very bright, very responsible, dedicated, and knowledgeable, just about all that is necessary for success is to build on those strengths.

Once a person progresses to management, however, the ballgame changes. Others are doing more of the technical work, and although it's important to remain in tune with technical matters, a greater percentage of time is spent planning, organizing, staffing, directing, and controlling. By the time a person becomes an executive, technical matters account for only a minuscule percentage of the workweek, and managerial matters consume almost all of the time.

A person strongly motivated to rise to upper management or executive positions can be compared with someone in a rowboat race. The college graduate or M.B.A. emerges from the hallowed halls fresh, innocent, sporting a Brooks Brothers three-piece suit, and very anxious to jump into the boat and row to success. There are holes all over the bottom of the rowboat, however, and during the race some holes will get bigger and some will be plugged up, depending on how adept the person is at rowing and filling in holes at the same time. For an electrical engineer fresh out of college, there is only a little hole for technical expertise, but if the person does not conscientiously work to fill in the hole, it will get bigger because the expertise of electrical engineers is outdated very quickly. Once the individual gets to a mid-management position, technical expertise might not be so important, and the wood around the hole will swell enough to fill the hole completely. However, technical prowess is ordinarily a major factor contributing to promotion through management, so it can't be ignored at the beginning of the race. There are other holes around—knowledge of time management, salesmanship, how to recruit, how to train people. There are numerous holes having to do with general business knowledge—marketing, finance, operations, personnel, business law. It's not so much the hard rowers who finally win the race to the executive suite—the reasonably hard rowers who do a reasonably good job of plugging most of the holes finally get there.

That chemist we were just discussing might row like mad and have no holes at all in the areas of technical expertise, conscientiousness, and dedication, but on entering the rapid currents of management, leaks gush all over the boat, and the person is in danger of sinking because of hiring the wrong people or applying the wrong motivation techniques.

As I look back over the records of thousands of executives I have evaluated, there is one inescapable conclusion: the only truly distinguishing characteristic of consistently successful executives in large, publicly owned companies is lack of major liabilities. Executives are usually bright (though rarely geniuses), their work habits are good (although commonly a little disorganized), and they are usually effective managers (although some are a little too tough and others a little too soft, and most don't offer sufficient praise and recognition). The successful executives are usually politically aware (although not master gamesmen) and have good appearances (although usually not supercharismatic). Eight times out of ten, however, they are not very dumb, not technically incompetent, not very disorganized, not politically naive, and really not very anything that is negative.

For these reasons, it is very important for you to focus your interpretive sights not only on the positives but particularly keenly on the negatives. Shortcomings and liabilities, even minor ones—will probably contribute disproportionately to any failures that might occur in the position you are filling.

## SAMPLE SPECIFIC INTERPRETIVE DATA

As an additional interpretive aid for you, let's refer to the case study used throughout this book, and look at actual (excellent, good, fair, poor) ratings for specific data that might be generated at various selection steps, from various candidates for the job.

You will recall that our case study deals with candidates for the position of computer sales representative, with the expectation that the individual will be promotable to sales manager within a year. It is a rich, instructive case study because you as the hypothetical interviewer must consider a broad range of dimensions—intellectual, personal, interpersonal, and motivational.

What follows are specific data from a *variety* of candidates collected by psychologists and trained managers. The phrases and statements are so succinct that you will be able to think of a compelling exception to practically all of them! If you would like to know the rationale that experienced interviewers ordinarily come up with for ratings, the following pages will be of interest to you.

| 4 or 3 Rating | 2 or 1 Rating |
|---|---|

### Person Specification 1: Level of Intelligence

| 4 or 3 Rating | 2 or 1 Rating |
|---|---|
| Harvard Phi Beta Kappa (4) | Struggled to achieve passing grades at junior college (2) |
| B+ average at U. of Illinois (3) | |
| 120 IQ, tested on Wechsler Adult Intelligence Scale (3) | Flunked out of mediocre college despite studying hard, carrying only 12 credit hours, and not working (1) |
| Quick to understand all interview questions and very incisive and well organized in responses (3 or 4) | 110 IQ, tested on Wechsler Adult Intelligence Scale (2) |
| Ranked number 1 (of 20) in IBM sales-training class in learning new products (4) | In response to smorgasbord-type questions, answers last parts and forgets earlier parts (2 or 1) |
| Rapid career progress, with global, complex responsibilities (4 or 3) | Very poor grammar and word usage, though graduate of large urban high school (2 or 1) |
| "I enjoy rapid changes" (4 or 3) | |
| Scholastic Aptitude Test scores of 544 (verbal) or 575 (math) (3) | Repeated history of substantial confusion when placed in new situations (2 or 1) |
| 23.9 composite American College Testing (3) | Repeated failures because of not understanding important things (1) |

### Person Specification 2: Analytic Ability

| 4 or 3 Rating | 2 or 1 Rating |
|---|---|
| Consistently earned As in analytically oriented courses (math, logic, statistics, physics) (4) | Gross misinterpretation of application form (1) |
| Successful competitive chess player (4) | Work history of jobs requiring little analytic ability (2 or 1) |
| Well-organized responses to complex interview questions; appropriate sequence of responses; prompting unnecessary (4) | Shallow, off-target responses to questions (2 or 1) |
| Success in dealing with complex projects requiring in-depth analyses (4 or 3) | Repeatedly shocked or dismayed at events; rose-colored glasses (2 or 1) |
| States current supervisor would say, "digs into problems in depth" (4 or 3) | Opinionated; in interview was closed to facts that contradicted his opinions (2 or 1) |
| Asks penetrating questions in interview (4 or 3) | States that supervisor would say, "too often misses important relationships among data" (2 or 1) |
| "I'm very methodical—extremely thorough in acquiring and reviewing all pertinent information (4 or 3)" | Serious mistakes due to shallow thought processes (2 or 1) |

**Figure 12. Sample specific interpretive guidelines—candidates for sales representative promotable to branch sales manager. Rating scale: 4 = excellent, 3 = good, 2 = fair, 1 = poor, 0 = very poor.**

| 4 or 3 Rating | 2 or 1 Rating |
|---|---|

*Person Specification 3: Ability to Diagnose Client Needs*

"Clients would tell you I spend more time with them and have gotten to know their needs more than other salesmen have" (4 or 3)

Outstanding sales record (4)

Sales success very quickly achieved in new territories (4 or 3)

Above average performance in retaining clients (4 or 3)

Asked by sales vice president to conduct a "consultative selling" course (4 or 3)

Several statements showing misperception of interviewer intent (2 or 1)

Says supervisor would criticize listening skills (2 or 1)

"I never get into customers' plants—I guess I'd learn a lot if I did" (1)

"I'm a little intense, so customers don't open up very quickly with me" (1)

Slow growth curve, with poor initial sales performance and good eventual sales performance in a territory (2 or 1)

*Person Specification 4: Creativity/Innovativeness*

Four patents in six years (4)

Often won awards for suggestions (4 or 3)

Success in newly created job, with little direction or supervision (4 or 3)

Preference for low structure jobs, with many "vacuums" to fill (4 or 3)

In discussing accomplishments within jobs, lists several meaningful, original methods or systems devised for each job (4 or 3)

Preference for highly structured, repetitive, routine jobs (1)

"I'm a good implementor—other people can invent wheels" (1)

Canned, trite, pat answers (2 or 1)

Succeeded as McDonald's manager (following the "cookbook") but failed in own restaurant business (2 or 1)

*Person Specification 5: Pragmatism*

High percentage of ideas implemented (4)

No wild ideas that turned out to be costly failures...(4 or 3)

Logical, sensible career moves; few later regrets in terms of job content, co-workers, or the like (4 or 3)

Older, seasoned person with consistently successful career record (4)

Criticized for being repeatedly impractical (1)

Changed jobs four times in past four years, with unrealistic, unfulfilled expectations in each (1)

Unrealistic career goals (1)

Naive, impractical viewpoints about jobs stated in interview (2 or 1)

**Figure 12. (Continued)**

| 4 or 3 Rating | 2 or 1 Rating |
|---|---|
| States supervisors would say, "practical, down-to-earth decision-maker, with lots of savvy and street sense" (4) | Young, inexperienced—not necessarily many failures, but not many career successes (2 or 1) |
| | Berated by several supervisors for "not keeping promises" (2 or 1) |

### Person Specification 6: Intellectual Flexibility

| 4 or 3 Rating | 2 or 1 Rating |
|---|---|
| Full-time work and college—and good performance in both (3) | "I can't stand interruptions of any kind!" (2 or 1) |
| Successful in new, complex positions without much guidance (4 or 3) | Absence of "stretch responsibilities"; repeated dull, mundane jobs (1) |
| Successful management of several projects simultaneously (4 or 3) | Constantly trite, pat, shallow responses to questions (2 or 1) |
| In interview, comfortably able to move from discussing tangible, concrete topics to abstract, conceptual issues (4 or 3) | Preference for doing one thing to completion before beginning another task (2 or 1) |
| "I love to have a lot of balls in the air" (4 or 3) | Unusual difficulty switching from one topic to another in the interview (2 or 1) |

### Person Specification 7: Oral Communications Skills

| 4 or 3 Rating | 2 or 1 Rating |
|---|---|
| Won debate contests in school (4 or 3) | Mumbles, talks too fast or too slowly, too loudly or too softly, in interview (2 or 1) |
| Frequent requests to give speeches (4) | Monotone; drab and expressionless; few gestures during interview (1) |
| Elected president of Toastmasters Club (4 or 3) | |
| Successful in positions requiring formal presentations to groups—public relations, sales, politics, etc. (4 or 3) | Noticeable but not egregious errors in grammar, word usage, or syntax (2) |
| "My subordinates feel the meetings I conduct with the six of them are pretty good—participative, thorough, and even fun, but I do let people get off on tangents too much" (3) | Rambles on and on in interview (1) |
| | Poor listener in interview (1) |
| Extremely clear, crisp, and organized responses in interview (4) | "I'm nervous when making speeches—my voice shakes and I just read my notes" (2 or 1) |
| Fairly good eye contact, gestures, voice volume, modulation, and enunciation in interview (3) | "Somehow I just don't get people to participate in small-group meetings" (1) |
| Flawless grammar, vocabulary, word usage, and syntax in interview (4) | Excessive nervous mannerisms (thumping pencil, drumming fingers) in interview (2 or 1) |
| Charismatic and dynamic in interview (4) | |

**Figure 12. (Continued)**

| 4 or 3 Rating | 2 or 1 Rating |
| --- | --- |

### Person Specification 8: Written Communications Skills

| 4 or 3 Rating | 2 or 1 Rating |
| --- | --- |
| Widely acclaimed master's thesis (4) | Application form incomplete, replete with erasures; it is cold, doesn't sell the applicant as a competent, friendly professional (2 or 1) |
| "The vice president asks me to write his speeches—I'm pretty good at it" (4) | |
| "Here are samples of memos and letters I've written recently (clear, well-organized, proper grammar and word usage, and appropriate friendliness and purposefulness) (4) | "One thing my customers tell me is that the proposals I write are too long" (2) |
| "I've studied letters written by salespeople and developed a number of basic formats for letters. I simply tailor these to the specific needs of a situation" (4 or 3) | "In my sales work I've never had to write many memos, letters, or proposals" (2 or 1) |
| | Deficient grammar in interview (2 or 1) |
| "My spelling stinks, but I've always made sure an excellent secretary has edited my work" (3) | |

### Person Specification 9: Education

| 4 or 3 Rating | 2 or 1 Rating |
| --- | --- |
| B.A. Electrical Engineering—Columbia University (3); M.S. Computer Sciences—UCLA (4) | College degree 15 years ago but has not kept up professionally and is generally out of date (2 or 1) |
| "I read 2 hours every night in technical, trade, and business periodicals and journals" (4) | "I guess if there is something important for me to know, my employer will tell me, so I don't do much reading on my own" (1) |
| No college degree, but work experience, extensive readings, and professional seminars have produced equivalent knowledge (4 or 3) | Associate's Degree from Triton College; insufficient readings, seminars, conferences, work experiences to compensate for lack of formal education" (2 or 1) |

### Person Specifications 10–12: Experience—Technical, Sales, Management

[Interpretation precisely matches the person specifications as written.]

### Person Specification 13: Initiative/Resourcefulness

| 4 or 3 Rating | 2 or 1 Rating |
| --- | --- |
| Consistently has successfully worked under minimum supervision (4 or 3) | Constant excuses for job failures (1) |
| Continued education beyond job requirements (4 or 3) | Has expressed desire for heavy supervision (1) |
| | Content in nondemanding jobs (1) |

**Figure 12.   (Continued)**

| 4 or 3 Rating | 2 or 1 Rating |
|---|---|
| Has volunteered for special projects (4 or 3) | History of failure and nonachievement (1) |
| Has presented many ideas to management (4 or 3) | Key decisions passed on to others (e.g., to change jobs, go to college) (2 or 1) |
| Has developed many subordinates for promotion, and they have succeeded in their new responsibilities (4) | Stated accomplishments, particularly in most recent jobs, amount to doing what required but has missed many opportunities to make a greater contribution (2 or 1) |
| Has started new projects, groups, activities, entrepreneurial ventures (4 or 3) | |
| Has experimented with new management/work techniques, with notable success (4 or 3) | |

### Person Specification 14: Self-Objectivity

| 4 or 3 Rating | 2 or 1 Rating |
|---|---|
| Admits real shortcomings, liabilities, mistakes, failures and disappointments—comprehensively (4) | Blames circumstances, other people, luck, etc., for repeated failures or problems (2 or 1) |
| Willing to disclose negatives without excessive interviewer pressure (4 or 3) | Has not acquired necessary tools (knowledge) and denies their importance (1) |
| Has corrected negatives (classes, seminars, counseling, etc.) (4 or 3) | Has not corrected deficiencies in work habits, management approaches, dealing with people, etc. (2 or 1) |
| Good listener in interview (4 or 3) | Denies valid perceptions of others— "My language ain't so bad" (2 or 1) |
| Actively seeks feedback from subordinates, peers, superiors and family, friends, interviewer (4 or 3) | Sincerely claims no real areas for improvement (2 or 1) |
| | Exaggerates strengths (2 or 1) |
| | Sincerely does not understand why passed over or fired (2 or 1) |

### Person Specification 15: Perseverance

| 4 or 3 Rating | 2 or 1 Rating |
|---|---|
| Worked full-time while attending school full-time (4 or 3) | Many failures along with many excuses (2 or 1) |
| Succeeds despite setbacks (health or personal problems, unpopular boss, difficult new location, market declines) (4 or 3) | Extremely accommodating, unassertive personality style; agrees with interviewer despite interviewer's changing opinions or statements (2 or 1) |
| Sells ideas despite repeated rejections (4 or 3) | "I give up too easily" (1) |
| "Supervisors say I'm like a British bulldog—I just never give up" (4) | Changed job 4 times in 3 years because of "insufficient opportunity" (1) |
| | "I never argue with my boss" (1) |

**Figure 12. (Continued)**

138

| 4 or 3 Rating | 2 or 1 Rating |
| --- | --- |

### Person Specification 16: Independence

| 4 or 3 Rating | 2 or 1 Rating |
| --- | --- |
| Successful performance with minimal supervision (4 or 3) | Inconsistent performance (thus requiring supervision) (2 or 1) |
| Stated preference for minimal supervision (4 or 3) | Stated needs (not wanting overnight travel, e.g.) inconsistent with job requirements (3 nights per week overnight travel) (2 or 1) |
| Having jobs in which supervisors lacked technical proficiency (4 or 3) | |
| Successful performance in charge of remote location (4 or 3) | Excessively slow, overly participative decision making, to the point of irritating supervisors, peers, and subordinates (2 or 1) |
| Challenging supervisors, without being obnoxious (4 or 3) | "My supervisor would say I'm too hesitant to act on my own" (1) |

### Person Specification 17: Standards of Performance

| 4 or 3 Rating | 2 or 1 Rating |
| --- | --- |
| Consistently excellent performance (4) | "Sometimes I procrastinate so much that quality suffers a little" (2 or 1) |
| "I just can't go home at night unless I complete my 'to do' lists" (4 or 3) | "My boss would say I'm too much a softie with my subordinates because some of them just can't cut it" (2 or 1) |
| "Proposals are key to our business, and I'm regarded as the best proposal writer of the 22 of us" (4) | Excessive deadlines missed (2 or 1) |
| Works 60 hours a week because 55 hours would be insufficient to achieve excellence in a new, fast-changing job (4 or 3) | Excessive inaccuracies (2 or 1) |
| Estimates customers would rate professionalism and service as "excellent" (4) | |

### Person Specification 18: Track Record

| 4 or 3 Rating | 2 or 1 Rating |
| --- | --- |
| Seven years of sales experience comparable to position in question; exceeded sales quotas the past 4 years (4) | Job hopper—5 jobs in 12 years (1) |
| Above-average compensation growth within employers (not just as a result of changing jobs) (4 or 3) | Fired for nonperformance in past 3 years (1) |
| | Excellent performance, but in much smaller, much less demanding type of job (2 or 1) |
| Consistently above-average performance ratings (4 or 3) | Inconsistent performance with recurring "good excuses" ("my boss was too demanding," "my kids didn't like the schools," "budgets for promotional materials were cut," etc.) (2 or 1) |
| Academic, athletic, social successes in high school and college (more important for recent college graduate) (4 or 3) | |

**Figure 12. (Continued)**

| 4 or 3 Rating | 2 or 1 Rating |
|---|---|

### *Person Specification 19: A "Doer"*

"I live for goals; that's how I keep score" (4 or 3)

"My pace is fast or very fast—I earn twice my age by getting results and I do that by busting my tail." (4)

"I can't stand it when people don't follow through on commitments" (4 or 3)

"Customers would tell you I do an excellent job of investigating problems and getting back to them" (4 or 3)

"I trust my subordinates too much and should see that they do what they say they're going to do" (2 or 1)

"It's not how many hours you work that's important" (spoken by mediocre performer with a casual attitude) (1)

"My boss feels I could sometimes work a little harder, be more aggressive" (spoken by person with inconsistent performance) (2 or 1)

Long, rambling discourse about insignificant points (2 or 1)

### *Person Specification 20: Emotional Maturity/Stability/Resilience*

Multiple indications of knowing and accepting self; self-confidence without egotism (4 or 3)

Consistently good performance despite stress-inducing events (divorce, relocation, financial disaster, extreme criticism from supervisor, etc.) (4 or 3)

Constantly seeking challenges, problem situations (4 or 3)

Invests more energy/effort in order to cope successfully with new drive by competitor (4 or 3)

Key life decisions have been sensible; few recent foolish risks taken (4 or 3)

Good health, despite heavy work and/or personal pressures (4)

After merger, accepted by new parent company (4 or 3)

Any indication of excessive alcohol use or drug dependency (2 or 1)

Excessive temper outbursts (2 or 1)

Taking a job with expectation of leaving soon (1)

Any indication of kickbacks or other activities showing lack of ethics or a conflict of interests (1)

Taking jobs out of desperation to find work and experiencing substantial failures or disappointments (1)

Family problems repeatedly interfering with work (1)

Frequent, recurring lows (in terms of productivity and moods) (1)

Recent emotional breakdown due to exhaustion (1)

Several job changes representing flight from tough situations (2 or 1)

Excessive defensiveness when challenged by interviewer (2 or 1)

**Figure 12. (Continued)**

| 4 or 3 Rating | 2 or 1 Rating |
| --- | --- |

*Person Specification 21: Administrative Abilities*

| 4 or 3 Rating | 2 or 1 Rating |
| --- | --- |
| Thorough, comprehensive application form (4) | Person admits being spread too thin, with consequent low performance (2 or 1) |
| Thoroughly processes questions in the order asked (4) | Late for interview without good reason (2) |
| Track record of successfully managing large-scale projects or large groups of people (4) | Describes self as procrastinator and misses deadlines by substantial lengths of time (1) |
| Ability to articulate specific plans and goals for self (4 or 3) | Chasing tangents in the interview; cannot seem to stay focused (2 or 1) |
| Keeps weekly/daily plans, makes comprehensive checklists (4 or 3) | Forgetful, yet does not take comprehensive notes (1) |
| Keeps annual time log in order to find ways to improve efficiency and time usage (4) | Forever "fighting fires" and never able to get to important long-range issues (2 or 1) |
| "My supervisor would say I'm very well organized" (4 or 3) | Insufficient knowledge to be able to prioritize properly (2 or 1) |

*Person Specification 22: First Impression*

| 4 or 3 Rating | 2 or 1 Rating |
| --- | --- |
| Appropriate attire (4 or 3) | Applying to job at IBM and wears jeans (1) |
| Good grooming (4 or 3) | Filthy hair (1) |
| Friendly greeting and firm handshake (4 or 3) | Quiet, shy, doesn't carry conversation (1) |
| Good posture (4 or 3) | Weak handshake (1) |
| Good personal hygiene (4 or 3) | Poor eye contact (1) |
| Good oral communications (see specification 7) | Dominates early moments of interview with loud voice, inappropriate joking (1) |
| At ease; friendly yet businesslike demeanor (4 or 3) | Plops down in your chair (1) |
| Good eye contact (4 or 3) | |
| Not too deferent or forceful (4 or 3) | |

*Person Specificiation 23: Interpersonal Flexibility*

| 4 or 3 Rating | 2 or 1 Rating |
| --- | --- |
| Frequently chosen for leadership positions ( 4 or 3) | History of arguments with co-workers (2 or 1) |
| Social presence, engaging manner, poise, ability to carry conversation, sense of humor, proper attire, eye contact, smile, warmth (4 or 3) | Difficult to relate to in interview (2 or 1) |
| | Overly critical of past co-workers (2 or 1) |

**Figure 12. (Continued)**

| 4 or 3 Rating | 2 or 1 Rating |
|---|---|
| People-intensive activities (4 or 3) | Prejudices expressed (2 or 1) |
| Success in sales, politics, public relations (4 or 3) | High turnover among valuable subordinates, due to candidate's style (1) |
| "Supervisors would say I am cooperative but not a yes-man" (4 or 3) | Easily intimidated—obsequious in interview (2 or 1) |
| | In response to questions about what was liked about jobs, no mention of liking supervisors, peers, subordinates, or customers (2 or 1) |
| | In response to questions about accomplishments, no mention of winning approval or respect of co-workers or customers (2 or 1) |
| | In self-appraisal, no mention of people skills as strength; acknowledges lack of interpersonal flexibility as shortcoming (2 or 1) |

### Person Specification 24: Assertiveness

| 4 or 3 Rating | 2 or 1 Rating |
|---|---|
| When challenged in interview, comes back in a confident, articulate, firm manner, yet not apparently hostile (4) | Excessively acquiescent in interview (2 or 1) |
| Cooperative in interview—goes along with TORC methods requirements, yet constantly puts best foot forward (4 or 3) | Supervisors would say, "insufficiently aggressive" (1) |
| Several instances of challenging superiors—and winning the points (4 or 3) | Extremely pushy and obnoxious in the interview (1) |
| As manager, openly confronts nonperformance (4 or 3) | Unable convincingly to describe sales style (2 or 1) |
| | In describing sales style, fails to mention asking for the order (2 or 1) |

### Person Specification 25: Team Player

| 4 or 3 Rating | 2 or 1 Rating |
|---|---|
| Successful in politically complex organization (4 or 3) | Repeatedly finding co-workers at all levels "stupid," "uncooperative," or "incompetent" (1) |
| States what liked about jobs, "spirit of cooperation," "helping others to achieve their goals," "camaraderie" (4 or 3) | Criticized by supervisors for being too independent, self-seeking, or harmfully competitive (2 or 1) |
| "Accomplishments" include some contributions to team effectiveness (4 or 3) | Has left several jobs because of "politics" (2 or 1) |

**Figure 12. (Continued)**

| 4 or 3 Rating | 2 or 1 Rating |
|---|---|
| Does not fight legitimate company policies (3) | Reprimanded for competing harmfully with peers—undercutting their performance (2 or 1) |
| "I'm a team player, but frankly I'm out there primarily to achieve for myself" (3) | Criticized for refusing to participate in special projects to benefit the company (2 or 1) |
| Volunteers to train others (4 or 3) | |

### Person Specification 26: Enthusiasm

| | |
|---|---|
| Expressive, dynamic, enthusiastic in interview (4 or 3) | Bland interview personality (1) |
| Lists "enthusiasm" as an asset (4 or 3) | "Supervisors would say I'm too low-keyed" (2 or 1) |
| "Supervisor would say I'm ebullient and that my spirit is contagious" (4) | Initially slow to succeed in a territory (2 or 1) |
| | "About two days a week I just drag along—can't get the old spark going" (1) |

### Person Specification 27: Empathy

| | |
|---|---|
| Shows sensitivity to interviewer's needs ("Let me help clean up that spilled coffee") (4 or 3) | Moves considerably faster or slower than pace interviewer wants (2 or 1) |
| "Co-workers frequently use me as a sounding board" (4) | Fails to thank secretary for fetching a Coke (1) |
| Total absence of hostile, demeaning remarks about previous co-workers (4) | "Subordinates would say I'm insensitive to their needs" (1) |
| In evaluating subordinates, shows deep insight into any performance problems (4) | Goes around superior in order to get a request approved (1) |
| "Customers would say I'm totally aware of their feelings about things" (4 or 3) | Unable to articulate customers' complaints or concerns (1) |
| "Flows" with interviewer's pace (4 or 3) | |

### Person Specification 28: Leadership

| | |
|---|---|
| Elected to leadership positions in school (4 or 3) | Has held no leadership posts—not even project supervision or high school student council—and is 35 years old (1) |
| Confident, authoritative, inspirational manner exhibited in interview (4) | |

**Figure 12. (Continued)**

143

| 4 or 3 Rating | 2 or 1 Rating |
|---|---|
| Able to retain talented subordinates despite undesirable job elements (4 or 3) | Inconsistent results in leadership positions (2 or 1) |
| "Subordinates would do anything for me because I'm totally involved with them, totally fair, and I really care about them" (4) | Describes subordinates as "uncooperative, unmotivated, or hard to manage" (1) |
| Far exceeded goals as head of United Way campaign (4 or 3) | Has not actively sought leadership positions (2 or 1) |
| Elected to community or sport leadership positions (4 or 3) | Criticized by supervisors for running dull meetings (2 or 1) |

*Person Specification 29: Management—Recruitment/Selection*

| | |
|---|---|
| In past 4 years, recruited and selected 14 people, 12 of whom earned satisfactory or better performance ratings after a year (4) | No experience recruiting or interviewing selection candidates (2) |
| Participated in selection interviewing workshop (4 or 3) | In past 3 years used placement firms to recruit 6 people; 1-hour selection interviews conducted; 4 out of 6 failed within 6 months (1) |
| Asked by co-workers to interview selection candidates, because of proven competence at it (4) | Virtually any violation of the system in this book, combined with less than satisfactory results (2 or 1) |
| Adherence to the various elements of the system presented in this book (4 or 3) | |

*Person Specification 30: Management—Training/Development*

| | |
|---|---|
| In past 5 years, trained 15 persons, all of whom succeeded at initial positions and 4 of whom were subsequently promoted to supervisory positions where they were rated satisfactory or better (4 or 3) | "I don't have the time to train my subordinates" (1) |
| | No training experience (2) |
| Asked by management to train high-talent recruits (4) | Responsibility for training, yet criticized by supervisor for not training people more thoroughly (1) |
| Has career development plans and goals with each subordinate (4) | States that subordinates would say, "doesn't delegate enough" (2 or 1) |
| Earned attitude survey ratings, by subordinates, of "excellent" on "training" (4) | Hated student teaching (2) |
| | Few subordinates promoted, because they were considered "not qualified" (2 or 1) |

**Figure 12. (Continued)**

144

| 4 or 3 Rating | 2 or 1 Rating |
|---|---|

### *Person Specification 31: Management—Goal-Setting*

"I use an MBO system, in which team goals are established as a team and individual goals are established individually with me" (4)

"Each subordinate understands his or her accountabilities perfectly, and when and how performance will be measured" (4 or 3)

"I meet quarterly with subordinates, individually and as a group, to review goals and accountabilities, both of which can be changed in light of new circumstances" (4)

"Subordinates may complain about the goals' being too challenging, but attitude-survey results show they consider the goals very clear and fair" (4 or 3)

"An attitude survey showed that 2 out of 10 of my subordinates were a little confused about exactly what I expect" (2)

"My subordinates complain that I change the goals too often" (2 or 1)

"My boss would say I don't have very difficult goals for my people" (2 or 1)

"I tell my people their goals, and they'd better listen" (2 or 1)

"I don't like performance appraisals, because people always complain that I hold them responsible for some things they didn't consider part of their job" (1)

### *Person Specification 32: Management—Monitoring Performance*

"I require a proposed itinerary for each week for my sales people, and any changes are to be called in. Call reports state purpose, amount of time, what transpired, and what to do next. Each salesperson has a cassette recorder, so these reports can be prepared while driving" (4)

"I ride with each salesperson once a month—less often with highly experienced and successful sales people. Half the time I choose which day of the week and half the time they pick it" (4)

"If I sense call reports are fudged, I spot check—call the customer and chat for a minute, so I can subtly check up on the salesperson" (4 or 3)

"As long as sales people are doing the job, I don't require call reports and I never visit customers with them" (1)

"Monitoring people is like a parent checking on kiddies—it's insulting to a professional sales representative" (1)

"Subordinates complain of inadequate communication" (2 or 1)

"My boss says I ought to get out in the field two days a week with sales people, but I just don't have the time" (1)

**Figure 12. (Continued)**

| 4 or 3 Rating | 2 or 1 Rating |
| --- | --- |

*Person Specification 33: Management—Performance Feedback*

"Subordinates know exactly where they stand with me—I'm very open and give daily performance feedback" (4)

"I've studied positive reinforcement, and I use praise and recognition almost exclusively to shape behaviors of subordinates. I use constructive criticisms but rarely find it helpful to blast someone" (4)

"Subordinates love to have me around. I critique their methods and performance thoroughly, but I truly care about them as people. I use a lot of tact, and frankly we have a hell of a lot of fun together. They walk away feeling they learned a lot. They feel good about themselves, and they feel good about me" (4 + !)

"I let subordinates critique themselves first, before I throw in my two bits. They diagnose problems, evaluate corrective plans, and identify their own strengths and areas for improvement, and then I agree, offer some additional opinions, praise their correct insights, or disagree. I learn more about their strengths and shortcomings and treat them more as adults and professionals if they diagnose and correct problems themselves; it makes them more in charge of their lives—which is what we both want. Frequently I find that they criticize themselves more than I would, so instead of pointing out weaknesses I simply say, 'That shows good self-awareness, Pat. Pre-planning sales calls more sounds very useful for you.' Subordinates have improved a lot with this technique, and they both like and respect me a lot more, too" (4)

"Attitude survey results showed that half of my subordinates don't feel they know where they stand with me" (1)

"I wait until the annual performance appraisal for major criticisms; that way our relationship is more positive the rest of the year" (1)

"Subordinates might feel I emphasize the negative too much" (2)

"I'm a little lax when it comes to telling people what they're doing wrong" (2 or 1)

**Figure 12. (Continued)**

| 4 or 3 Rating | 2 or 1 Rating |
| --- | --- |

*Person Specification 34: Management—Removing Nonperformers*

"If a subordinate fails to meet agreed-upon performance objectives within a very reasonable time frame and after exhaustive efforts by me to train, coach, and counsel the person, I will transfer, demote, or even terminate a person, although I rarely have to initiate such actions because nonperformers receive enough feedback to know when they are failing. They realize that I've been totally fair and helpful, and they usually quit or ask for different responsibilities" (4)

"It's tragic if the wrong people have been hired, but more tragic if they are left in jobs where they will continually fail" (4)

"With the merger I had to combine two sales forces and let half the sales people go. With clear objectives and performance feedback, it quickly became clear who would make it, and the poorest performers quit, one by one" (4)

Description of subordinates shows several extremely weak performers who are not improving, and no plans to remove them (1)

"My superior says I'm tolerant of mediocrity, but I'm friends with my subordinates and feel they deserve more chances" (after two years of chances) (1)

"I don't believe in second chances—if someone isn't cutting it, bam! they're gone, and coddling them won't do any good" (1)

*Person Specification 35: Management—Team Development*

"My greatest asset is being able to create a very positive, productive team atmosphere" (4)

"Our monthly staff meetings are very open and participative. We get everything out on the table, hash issues through, and decide what to do. Conflicts are resolved, not ignored" (4)

"Once a year we have a team development session for three days, during which we build trust, open up communications, improve our decision-making approaches, and generally get ready to tackle the next year" (4)

"The biggest frustration in my job is that subordinates fight and undercut each other all the time" (2 or 1)

"My subordinates say they want staff meetings, but I consider them a waste of time" (2 or 1)

Turnover of capable subordinates who complained of inadequate support from above, lack of coordination among peers, feeling "left in the dark" or unappreciated (2 or 1)

Failures or missed deadlines due to people not functioning as a cohesive, effective team (2 or 1)

**Figure 12.  (Continued)**

| 4 or 3 Rating | 2 or 1 Rating |
| --- | --- |

"I ask every subordinate to critique me several times a year—I learn from it how best to manage, and the process is a useful symbol of how we should all seek to help each other" (4)

"I conduct an annual climate survey—attitude survey—and my team and I analyze the results together and figure out what to do. The survey is a barometer of our team effectiveness, and each year we seek to improve in decision making, listening, resolving differences, etc." (4)

"I'm decisive and will make some decisions without consulting subordinates, but where many inputs and widespread commitment to a course of action are important, I'm very participative" (4)

### Person Specification 36: Motivation Level

"Fifty-hour work weeks are typical, but if the slightest need arises, I'll work a lot more" (4 or 3)

"I love a fast pace. Problems, challenges, pressures—I thrive on them" (4)

"I love my work. I've moved at 90 miles an hour, 60 or 70 hours a week, for years—not because I have to, but because I want to" (4)

"I'm not into long hours, but I sure intend to succeed. I've always exceeded sales quotas, and although a 40-hour work week is average for me, at times it is 80 hours" (4)

Stated ultimate goal of wanting income five times current income (in comparable dollar value) (4 or 3)

"Spotty" success; admits working 45 hours a week at a "moderate" pace (2 or 1)

"I don't have time to take any college courses," yet the person watches TV "12 hours a week" (1)

Slow, lethargic pace in interview (2 or 1)

"My boss says I should be more of a workaholic" (2 or 1)

**Figure 12. (Continued)**

| 4 or 3 Rating | 2 or 1 Rating |
|---|---|

### Person Specification 37: Health

Recent thorough physical examination showed perfect health (4)

Has thorough annual physical examination (4)

Has missed fewer than four days of work in the past year on account of illness (4 or 3)

Exercises four or more times a week at aerobic level, 40 minutes or more at a time (4)

Exercises three times a week, at aerobic level, for 30 minutes at a time (3)

Not overweight; better (lower) than normal cholesterol level (4)

Normal blood pressure (4)

Feels and appears energetic and healthy (4)

Does not have thorough annual physical examination (2 for under 40 years of age, 1 for older than 40)

Missed four to ten days from work in past year on account of illness (2)

Missed more than ten days from work in past year on account of illness (1)

Substantially overweight (2 or 1)

Does not exercise at aerobic level three times a week, minimum (2)

Other health problems (2 or 1)

Weariness toward end of interview (2 or 1)

### Person Specification 38: Ambition

Stated reasons for changing jobs include opportunity to move into management (4)

Well-articulated philosophy of management (4 or 3)

Has made special efforts to acquire management tools (through readings, courses, seminars, coaching through mentor, etc.) (4)

Has been elected to community or special interest leadership posts (4 or 3)

No desire to move into management (2)

Failed as manager in past five years (1)

Unconvincingly states an interest in moving into management (1)

Recent superiors rated the person "not promotable—but suited for individual production" (1)

### Person Specification 39: Willingness to Take Risks

Has left successful jobs for chance to be even more successful (4 or 3)

Has held firm on price with customers, risking loss of orders but generally achieving more profitable sales (4 or 3)

Criticized by supervisors for being excessively cautious (2 or 1)

Criticized by supervisors for seeking approval for decisions too often (2 or 1)

**Figure 12.** (Continued)

| 4 or 3 Rating | 2 or 1 Rating |
|---|---|
| Started own business and was successful (4 or 3) | Criticized by subordinates for being too passive in supporting their needs upward (2 or 1) |
| Went to customer contact's supervisor and won big contract, though risked losing it by offending lower-level customer contact (4 or 3) | "I never argue with my superiors" (2 or 1) |
| | Slow career growth within static, highly structured, noninnovative organizations (2 or 1) |

### Person Specification 40: Interests Compatible with Company Expectations

| 4 or 3 Rating | 2 or 1 Rating |
|---|---|
| History of job changes that resulted in no negative surprises and the person being happy and successful (4) | History of disillusionment in new jobs (2 or 1) |
| Absence of job hopping (average stay of four years or more with a company)(4 or 3) | Job-hopper (perhaps more than one employer change every three years, on the average, during past ten years) (1) |
| Stated needs for money, growth, type of supervisor, type of peer, product line, financial well-being of company, travel requirements, geographic location, type of community, recognition, prestige, autonomy, power, achievement, budgets, affiliation, and spouse approval consistent with opportunities available (4 or 3) | Important considerations in past job changes not able to be met in position in question—unless the need is clearly no longer extant (2 or 1) |
| | Stated needs of candidate not compatible with available opportunities—even if candidate downplays apparent incompatibility (2 or 1) |

**Figure 12. (Continued)**

## A TOUR THROUGH THE INTERVIEW GUIDE
## AND INTERPRETIVE GUIDELINES FOR
## SPECIFIC QUESTIONS

When looking at the "In-Depth Selection Interview Guide" (Appendix C) for the first time, managers wish to know why a question is included, why particular phraseology is used, and what sorts of interpretive insights can be gleaned from responses. This chapter walks you through the guide, explaining the rationale for questions and offering some highly specific guidelines for interpreting responses. Please forgive me for making all sorts of generalizations for which there are many, many exceptions. The specific guidelines I suggest are indicative of trends I have noticed. Anchorage is sometimes warm when Dallas is not; in order to reduce the length of this chapter I say such things as "Anchorage is not as warm as Dallas," but we both recognize that this statement is sometimes incorrect.

### Introductory Comments and Interpretive Guidelines

The opening moments of an in-depth selection interview can be quite revealing, although chapter 8 emphasizes how overweighting the first impression is a common and very serious interviewer error. In the first five minutes you are able to evaluate the interviewee's handshake, eye contact, poise, graciousness, physical appearance (grooming, cleanliness, attire, personal hygiene), and one-to-one communication skills (vocabulary, grammar, word usage, inflections). Chapter 5 suggests how to structure introductory comments in terms of idle chitchat and how to flow into the explanation of purposes; essentially the recommendation is to be friendly and get the interviewee talking.

Candidates for low-level factory or for higher-level positions not requiring people contact might be awkward and less impressive in appearance, and still not fall short of any person specification. A candidate for a high-level sales position which involves a lot of "cold calling" on senior executives of major corporations, however, would desirably look and act like the sort of person who would favorably impress high-powered clients. This candidate is supposed to be selling you on hiring him, and you can justifiably rate the person on this "sales call." If the candidate will be calling on executives who wear $500-conservative suits and $200-shoes, Sears suits and penny loafers might not do. You would expect a firm handshake (and not a clammy hand), a warm smile, being addressed by name, and a relaxed, confident, and perhaps even charismatic personality. The person should fill your deliberate pauses with appropriate conversation—sitting like a bump on a log is a negative indicator. You would probably not reject a candidate based on impressions surrounding the introductory comments, since preliminary interviews would no doubt have established the fact that the candidate has somehow achieved success—perhaps *despite* a lousy first impression. Opening moments can yield job-relevant data, however, and your impressions should be written down.

## Education

You will notice that the first substantive section of the guide is education, and that might strike you as odd. Starting with an individual's high school days might seem a sure way to turn him off and at best a source of hopelessly out-of-date information. The very thought of asking a mature manager or professional about high school might make you frown.

In the short *preliminary* interview, it is appropriate to discuss recent and current career responsibilities; data regarding high school days typically are not important enough to be included. In the in-depth selection interview, however, the goal is to know about the entire iceberg, not just the tip, and there is sometimes great value in seeing how the person developed and blossomed, beginning with adolescent years.

Starting with high school days is not always of crucial importance, and frankly, I encourage managers to include it when interviewing candidates for lower or mid-management positions, but not for senior executive ranks. If you are uncomfortable with the idea of asking any level interviewee (except a recent high school graduate) the questions about high school, scratch the section, and start with college. Having said that, permit me to continue making a case for including this line of inquiry.

In every selection interviewing workshop I have conducted over the years, I have asked trainees to withhold judgments regarding the value of those three minutes of questioning about high school until the workshop is near completion. After two or three days of interviewing a real live guinea pig in depth and after all of the conclusions are arrived at by the trainees, we go back and look at the conclusions generated by those brief questions regarding high school days. Inevitably trainees are amazed at how much job-relevant information was gleaned from the high school questioning, even if the person has changed dramatically.

There is sometimes discomfort in asking and answering questions about high school days, because for some of us they were traumatic times. Ask any teenager when the last crisis was experienced, and chances are that it occurred within the past week. Regardless of whether high school years were happy or sad, fun to talk about or embarrassing, for a lot of people, those years were very important in deciding not so much what specific occupation would be pursued, but what patterns of relationships with people would be experienced later in life and what life experiences would definitely be avoided in the future. They were truly formative years, and it is a shame to bypass them in an interview.

The rationale for questions regarding college is similar to that for high school, although they have more face validity—more transparent job relevance—than do questions regarding high school, and I recommend including questions about college years even for senior executive candidates.

## Interpretive Guidelines—Education

Often the greatest value in discussing high school days is not what occurred back then, nor even the behavioral dies that were cast in the important developmental years, but in the *current* attitudes, behavioral patterns, and characteristics revealed in discussing those high school years. The interviewee is sometimes caught a little off guard when asked about high school, and even polished people sometimes blurt out real truths, such as:

I was an independent SOB then—still am, I guess.

I've never really trusted people since my best friend betrayed me in high school.

After winning the state championship and being elected senior class president, I decided I could do anything I put my mind to; that attitude has stuck with me ever since.

Man! I was really in a shell back then.

Now, let's scrutinize each question in the education section of the guide, as well as certain specific items from the application form (since in conducting the interview the interviewer constantly refers to the application form).

**Highest Grade Completed (stated on application form).** In the 1980s it is fashionable to say that what is important is knowledge and ability, not some piece of paper showing a degree was earned or some number of years was spent in classrooms. And it is always heartwarming to interview a high school drop-out who has the knowledge of a Harvard M.B.A. or UCLA Ph.D. in chemistry. For people who are mobile within corporate America, however, it's kind of silly—needlessly self-hampering—not to obtain those pieces of paper that confirm knowledge.

The College Level Examination Program (CLEP) permits people to acquire college credits by taking tests, and institutions such as the State University of New York offer accredited degrees that can be obtained without setting foot in New York, through credit for CLEP tests, seminars, life experiences, and so forth. The vast majority of upper-management positions are filled by college-educated candidates, and the percentage is continuing to increase.

If the "highest grade completed" falls short of the person specification, then work-history achievements must suggest the equivalent knowledge level, or else the applicant may be appropriately rejected.

**Name of School (high school, college, graduate school), Location, What School Was Like, Class Rank (high school), Grade Point Average (high school, college, graduate school), Dates Attended.** Becoming valedictorian of a tiny rural Kansas high school is apt to be a lot easier than placing first among graduating seniors at a large suburban college-preparatory high school. Twin Cities Tech is not exactly Yale. Carrying 20 credit hours per semester in electrical engineering at a topflight university, earning B+s, working 20 hours a week, and graduating in three years with no summer breaks suggests more motivation, perseverance, and intelligence than carrying 12 credit hours per term, majoring in physical education, goofing around during summers, and graduating in four years. Knowing the social climate—pressures, opportunities to party, and the like—can also be enlightening. Carlton College is a morgue compared to the University of Arizona.

Correct interpretation in relation to person specifications can occur only in considering how long it took to achieve what grade, in how difficult a curriculum, with measurement (grades) against how rigorous a standard.

Candidates should be asked to submit transcripts from college and graduate school. Since the 1981 *Washington Post* scandal (in which a Pulitzer Prize—winning newspaper story turned out to be fictitious and its author a liar about graduating from Columbia University), companies are more apt to verify education data. Speaking of sneaky—since neither the application form nor the interview guide requests age or birthdate, a close estimate of someone's birthdate can be obtained by subtracting 17 from the high school graduation data.

**Curriculum.** For someone to become an executive one day, it is usually advantageous to take a college-preparatory curriculum in high school. It is not unusual for students to change majors in college, but it is worth finding out why. Was the engineering curriculum too difficult? Was general business easier than finance? Or was there a realization that music might make a nice hobby but not provide a career with adequate financial rewards?

**Scores on ACT/SAT.** Younger candidates usually recall their college board scores, and these scores can reveal intellectual caliber. The ACT (American College Testing, Iowa City, Iowa) provides scores for English, math, social sciences, and natural sciences. The range is 1 to 36 for a composite score. The average (mean) was 18.1 in 1979, and the 68th percentile of all those who took the test was 23.9.

The SAT (Scholastic Aptitude Test, Educational Testing Service, Princeton, New Jersey) has two tests, one of verbal and the other of math abilities. A perfect composite score is 800. In 1980 the average (mean) score for males on verbal was 428 (68th percentile was 548) and on math was 491 (68th percentile was 611); for women the 1980 verbal average was 420 (68th percentile was 529) and math was 443 (68th percentile was 552).

Average colleges expect a combined SAT score of 1000, and the finest schools require 1200 or 1300. For those hiring many recent college graduates, the SAT and ACT scores can be particularly helpful in determining intellectual achievement.

**Study Habits.** Even if you know the school's quality and rigorousness of curriculum and the candidate's grades, it is important to determine the amount of academic effort expended. The person who "never cracked a book" may be considerably brighter than a counterpart who studied constantly for the same grades.

**Activities, Class Offices, Social Life, Jobs Held.** It is favorable, though not at all definitive (particularly for people who have been out of school many years), for a candidate to have participated in some extracurricular activities. Sports tend to build discipline, and elected leadership positions suggest at least some peer acceptance. Work experiences can build character and independence and they can so dominate a young person's life that studies are hurt and social skills are underdeveloped.

Generally, it is advantageous if throughout school years there existed a balance of effort in all four areas—studies, activities, social life, and work. Neglect of studies suggests a goof-off attitude at that time. No social life suggests a social isolate, possibly with low self-esteem or a superior attitude. By age 21 if a person has not achieved social acceptance by peers, it is unusual for that person to meet person specifications later on—even years later—for jobs requiring substantial social skills. No work at all during high school or college suggests a possible "spoiled kid." Some students do not participate in activities because of work responsibilities (which are often developmentally valuable). Some students do not participate in sports because of frailty (low self-concept?), rejection by peers, or book-worm inclinations.

**Special Achievements, Honors, Awards.**    National Honor Society status is awarded to good high school students who are also good citizens. They get to compete for college scholarships. Although admission to NHS is easy at some schools, becoming a NHS finalist is very difficult. Only very bright kids who have learned a lot become finalists. The job relevance of honors, awards, and special achievements sometimes requires that the interviewer dig for specifics—how many people received the award, on what was it based, and so on.

**High Points/Low Points.**    These are often the most revealing questions regarding educational experiences, since responses require a current evaluation of previous years. Candidates talk about mentors who taught values retained ever since ("Professor Smith taught me report writing and that's been very useful in my career"); winning track events ("Becoming state champion convinced me I could do just about anything if I worked hard at it"); dating a future spouse ("She's what I live for"); and having fun as a soda jerk ("That's when I learned to be a comic"). For someone 10 years out of school, negative events per se (drug problem, dropping out, conflict with teachers, flunked courses, got pregnant) are not as relevant as the interviewee's attitudes now expressed toward the events. A hostile, defensive attitude suggests that the problems (intellectual, personal, interpersonal, or motivational) might still exist. A calm, mature viewpoint suggests that the person has grown up.

**Strong and Weak Subjects (Courses Most and Least Liked).**    People tend to do well in courses they like and are good at and vice versa.

There are plenty of exceptions, of course, but the interviewer should be highly attuned to course preferences (and why) and performance for courses integral to the person specifications. Naturally, this whole line of inquiry is more relevant for recent students than for those who left school 8 or 18 years ago.

A C in speech for a salesperson only two years out of school should elicit some follow-up questions. It would be strange for someone applying for an engineering or data-processing job to have done poorly in mathematics. If the position in question requires rote memory, then a student who loves courses requiring original thought might become bored quickly. I've done a fair amount of counseling with recent Harvard/Stanford/University of Chicago M.B.A.s whose education so instilled a chief-executive-officer perspective that they have difficulty "lowering themselves" to address issues merely at technical or operating levels.

**How Education Financed.**    Those who fully finance their education were almost always very serious, purposeful, and persevering, at least at that time. Why else would they study and attend classes twelve hours a day, work six hours, survive on five or six hours of sleep—and do this for years!?

The rich kid who toured Europe every summer and never held even a part-time job by college graduation seldom enters the business world with total dedication, willingness to sacrifice, and commitment to work hard (although I've known exceptions). In hiring recent college graduates, you would generally expect that candidates will have had at least a couple of summer jobs and will have performed conscientiously in them.

The distinction between someone who has contributed 100% or 25% to college expense is vague and becomes less relevant each year following graduation.

**Subsequent Courses or Studies (taken from application form).** Since the application form has a section on college/ graduate school, the section "subsequent courses or studies" usually evokes indications of participation in workshops, seminars, or ongoing professional development courses taught in evening classes. Average performers with average potentials for growth and development don't ordinarily do much in terms of "ongoing education." Highly capable people on a fast track to executive suites often do a lot more than learn solely from on-the-job experience—as valuable and essential as that experience is. The fast-trackers and those who would like to be are often willing to supplement work experience and previous education with up-to-date information on finance, law, data processing, motivation tools, time management, or whatever.

Someone who completed a college degree in business education 20 years ago and who had done nothing educationally since may be out of date. Oh, sure, there are people with fantastically rich and diverse careers who can get the equivalent of an M.B.A. every five years on the job; chances are, those folks did a lot of business-related reading at night because they had to. The guide will insure that you learn of such developmental activities. Conversely, there are people who are perennial students, who enjoy studying all sorts of things, love to go to fancy hotels for seminars, and who don't work very hard or very effectively.

Although the absence of seminars and courses may be totally justifiable as well as irrelevant, and the inclusion of many such activities may be indicative of poor performers, a program of ongoing education is important for upwardly mobile people who work in dynamic, fast-changing organizations. Those people don't do the same old job, day after day, and so they achieve more flexibility, more adaptability, and more competence by acquiring business tools before the job absolutely requires it.

The University of Michigan course for newly appointed supervisors does not guarantee success on the job—but participants spend several days thinking through critical issues before they occur on the job. The general manager out of school 15 years and not a superconscientious reader can clear out the cobwebs and learn fresh approaches to business issues as a result of attending one of the Stanford executive programs. The senior executive in a complex, highly competitive industry might need to be abreast of current, progressive approaches in all business areas, and so the Harvard Advanced Management Program (an M.B.A. acquired in two summers) would be just the ticket.

## Transition Questions

The importance of the transition questions cannot be overemphasized. The value is more obvious for discussion of reasons for recent job changes but even a high school to college transition can be revealing:

I wanted the biggest and best college around—my dad always used to say, "shoot for the stars," and that's what I've always done.

I wanted to go away for school. Actually, I felt a bit stifled as an only child, because my parents were always making decisions for me. I matured a great deal in going to a school that required me to make some decisions on my own.

I just picked a school. Any school. I really don't think you can plan your life too much; you just have to take what comes along.

By the time you have thoroughly probed important transitions in life, such as high school to college, college to military, and half a dozen job changes, you will have a very good idea of a candidate's value system, self-image, decision-making processes, and judgment when facing life's major opportunities. If the person is thorough, haphazard, confident, insecure, desperate, impulsive, materialistic, or deceptive, the pattern is often clearly revealed in what the individual now says about those previous decision points.

## Military

Section B of the interview guide, "military service," should be completed in the chronological order of the interviewee's life, usually, but not always, following education.

This section usually tells only a little about the individual, unless the individual was career military. For a great many people who have risen to professional and management levels, the military experience was homogenizing. The vast majority didn't particularly want to go in the service, didn't particularly like the restrictions, didn't learn a heck of a lot of value, did mature a lot, and were damn glad to get out. Chances are, in three or four minutes most of the nine items in this section can be covered, and you can move on to work history.

In one out of ten instances, this pattern does not fit at all, and so a more in-depth discussion is warranted. For the one-in-ten exceptions (including career military people), the military service should be explored in as much depth as any full-time job would be at that time in the person's career.

## Interpretive Guidelines—Military

Specific interpretive guidelines are like those for any other job and are covered in the work history section. There are some unique combat-related circumstances, however.

A year ago I interviewed a prospective plant manager and his application form indicated that he was looking for a "better opportunity" and that his reason was "personality clash." As it turned out, the fellow had lost his temper and had tried to stuff his boss in a giant mixmaster-type of machine used in manufacturing. I might not have learned this had I not explored the candidate's military career in some depth. It went like this:

Interviewer:    What were least enjoyable aspects of your military tour?
Candidate:      Uh, it doesn't sound so good, but I had a personality clash with my CO [commanding officer].
Interviewer:    I guess we've all had problems with bosses at one time or another. Tell me about this one.
Candidate:      Well, I'd been in Cambodia trackin' the goddam gooks, and when I got back my CO criticized my appearance. Said I was dirty and unshaven, for Chrissake!
Interviewer:    So, what did you do?
Candidate:      Almost killed him—pulled out my UZI [illegally concealed Israeli tommygun], started to pull the trigger, and a buddy clobbered me. He got the gun away, but I still punched three teeth out of that SOB CO's face!

Not the sort of guy you'd want your sister to marry, nor have as a plant manager, since he had become violent on the job at least once in recent months. Knowing about his experience with his commanding officer naturally induced me to probe a little deeper into "disagreements" and "personality clashes" in the work history. The greatest interpretive value for the military section usually comes from asking about high and, as in this example, low points.

## Work History

Section C of the interview guide, "work history," begins with an incredible mouthful of a question. Even if you like the idea that smorgasbord questions group a number of items together and force the individual to organize his or her thoughts so as to reveal the true person in how responses are formulated, the work history questions might seem to be "too much." But if you rehearse the question half a dozen times now and once before your first several interviews, you'll do just fine.

There are 16 interview subtopics to be covered for each job. If an individual has had 10 jobs, that's 160 questions to be asked, not counting questions for clarifications and any tangents. Think of the time efficiency in essentially asking the 160 questions right up front, in a mere 45 seconds! If you were simply to ask those 160 questions in the question–answer, question–answer format, not only would you waste a lot of time asking the questions, but the answers might not be particularly revealing. On the other hand, after you have told the interviewee all of the information you would like about the work history, a lot is revealed if the interviewee rushes ahead, or skips over half the questions you wanted answered, or conveniently forgets to identify mistakes or disappointments. As much is revealed about the candidate if there is a very well organized, comprehensive, honest account of the career history.

## Interpretive Guidelines—Work History

**Name and Date of Employer.**    This information is requested on the application form and helps you decide how much time to devote to a particular job. A six-month position held 12 years ago might be probed for why it was so short, and little more. Longer-held and recent positions merit thorough responses to each of the 16 subquestions, in addition to follow-up questions for clarification and accurate interpretation.

The more you know about the world of work, the better equipped you are to interpret responses about it. If through career experiences, reading, and education you happen to have learned a lot about an employer the interviewee worked for, it will be easier for you to comprehend successes, accomplishments, and disappointments. If you do not know much about the organization, ask. Responses will give you an idea if the organization was large, lumbering, and bureaucratic, or small and aggressively growing. Excellent companies (growing, profitable, positioned well in the marketplace) tend to attract higher-talented people, and organizations experiencing difficulty often find their best (most marketable) people bailing out first. Companies in "Chapter 11" (bankrupt but protected from creditors by the courts) sometimes pay heavily for super bright, super aggressive executives who flourish in the crisis mode but often have difficulty in stable organizations.

**Expectations for the Job and the Extent to Which They Were Achieved.**    A person's expectations for the next job say a lot about a person's self-concept, values, and needs. Of equal value is learning the extent to which the person's expectations were actually met in the next job. The pattern of expectations versus how things worked out is in many ways the story of a person's life—what they are all about and what they are going to be all about in the near future.

Favorable responses for a 40-year-old manager are realistic expectations for increased opportunities, challenge, working relationships, and salary, followed by success, for all jobs held in the past eight years. Young people generally can be expected to have such limited insight into the world of work and their own potentials that they overshoot or undershoot and consequently experience more disillusionment and job changes than more experienced people.

An extended pattern of unfulfilled expectations is a very bad sign. By about age 30 a person can reasonably be expected to have sufficient maturity, self-insight, and knowledge of prospective job situations to avoid many gut-wrenching failures. Does the candidate show repeated attempts to "shoot for the moon" with high-risk jobs (entrepreneurial start-ups or turnaround situations, for example), or does he only consider job changes that would be small steps upward? Is there a pattern of broken promises to the candidate? If so, they probably were not definite promises to begin with, and the interviewee is apt to be at fault for being naive. Are factors such as housing costs and spouse's needs carefully considered, or do such factors pop up later and cause job changes? Are important career decisions made thoroughly and systematically or haphazardly and instinctively? Above all, are the most recent years of the pattern characterized by mature, insightful decisions?

**Starting and Final Compensation Levels.** As crass and materialistic as it may sound, current compensation level (tempered with an understanding of the recent past) is often an accurate indicator of current ability. This was not always the case in the United States. In the late 1950s it was not very uncommon to find someone worth $30,000 a year working in a job at $15,000. In the 1980s this can still occur, but it is less likely because professional and management people are more aware of their marketability. *Business Week, Fortune, Forbes, Harvard Business Review, Wall Street Journal, Money,* and any number of additional publications often include articles showing compensation levels, trends for different occupations, geographic discrepancies, and so forth. Thus, informed professionals and managers have taken more advantage of their marketability since the 1960s. For those who did not read current business publications, the proliferation of search firms assured people of knowing their worth. Finally, the "me-generation" books of the 1970s reflected a societal norm supportive of "getting every buck you can."

Exceptions to the "compensation proves job worth" notion should be noted. There are not-for-profit organizations some of whose employees could earn a lot more money in private industry. There are factors which sometimes make it "lucky" for people to be in a certain place at a certain time. There are people so unconcerned with money that organizations take advantage of them. Finally, some people simply emphasize life-style (geographic location, art rather than accounting, four-day workweeks, a wonderful boss in an unsuccessful company) and give money a lower priority. Consequently, if someone's compensation progress is below average, it doesn't necessarily mean that the person is not competent, bright, efficient, or cooperative.

From an interpretation point of view, the interviewer can be well advised to pay attention to those frequent compensation surveys reported in the media and to ask, "How does this interviewee's compensation progress stack up with others of equivalent age, education, and experience?" Whether the answer is below average, average, or above average, the next question is, "Why?" The answer to that question lies in the person's work history.

Not only is compensation often a reasonably accurate standard, it is verifiable, and selection candidates know it. That adds some power and thrust to the TORC methods, which essentially induce the interviewee to do a lot of the tough interpretative work for the interviewer. If the person specification is for an "excellent" track record, the chances are remote that a person with only a "fair" record of compensation progress will qualify, and it's extremely remote that one with "poor" compensation growth will meet all other specifications.

On the other hand, someone moving up extremely rapidly in bucks may be on such a fast career track that your organization would lose the person in a year or two. Another risk in someone whose salary progress has been unusually great is if several big income jumps have occurred not with one employer but by switching employers; it could be a sign of greed or more show than substance.

In sum, income level can be very revealing, but only if you dig into the whys and wherefores, to understand the pattern of abilities and needs.

**Title, Responsibilities, Accountabilities, Results, Challenges, Problems, Luck, Mistakes.**    The intent of these meaty questions is to learn what the candidate did and how the job worked out. Has there been steady progress or backsliding? People often move from technical to supervisory, then to management, and finally to executive responsibilities; if there is a break in this sequence, determine why.

A candidate for controller of a $1.5-billion company had progressed so rapidly he had bypassed some basic accounting, taxation, and data-processing experience and suddenly found himself a chief financial officer of a $50-million company but not marketable at that level to much larger companies. He decided, sensibly, to fill in the gap by going back to a controller's job for a couple of years. My client would have met his needs but wanted a controller in the job for at least five years, and the candidate would have wanted a chief financial officer position within two years. There was a bad fit from the company's standpoint, which was realized only by studying the candidate's work history in depth.

Success does not always speak for itself. Was it due to luck (a great boss who made the major decisions, competition going out of business), initiative, hard work, or independent action (perhaps grabbing responsibility in a way unacceptable to your organization)? To what extent were failures or mistakes due to shortcomings of the person? To what extent does the candidate take responsibility for failures or pass the buck to others? Interviewees want to put their best foot forward and not admit many failures, but with enough probing you will sense if there really is something to own up to or not.

Challenges and problems permit people to show true abilities, strengths, and shortcomings. Again, it is the pattern that is revealing. Repeated problems in retaining employees, getting along with bosses, or meeting deadlines suggest significant interpersonal shortcomings. Repeated surmounting of major obstacles suggests all sorts of favorable characteristics.

**Most and Least Enjoyable Aspects of the Job.**  It is useful to know that a plant-manager candidate set a company record for overall production, met all cost and quality standards, and did all of this by recruiting a top industrial engineer, creating a team decision-making approach among six key managers, and installing an incentive pay system in the plant. Very useful, interesting, and impressive! It's every bit as useful, however, to learn that the candidate "hated the laborious detail work" in devising the compensation program and "just loved getting out and recruiting."

How the pattern of likes and dislikes meshes with the position in question is of critical importance. Perhaps your company would not permit a plant manager to recruit an engineer ("bad fit" indicator) or could provide support for detail work ("good fit" indicator). Perhaps your company frowns on participative decision making but you believe that this candidate is good at it and you would be willing to run interference for him at corporate level. An interviewee may be superbly talented and currently an outstanding performer, but without compatibility of likes and dislikes a disaster could ensue.

Quite often interviewees are well aware of their shortcomings and will either fabricate "likes" to appear to fit the job or will want to like something, but don't. "I like to get out in the field twice a week" may really mean "I haven't gotten out in the field enough, but I should, and I want to like it, and I promise myself I will do better in the future." Usually, such an unconscious double message is accompanied by a frown, loss of eye contact, or some mannerism—it just doesn't sound like a sincere, heartfelt statement. Further probing is called for.

What people like in jobs corresponds fairly well to what they are good at—but that may not correspond to the person specifications. A project manager in data processing is perhaps good at systems programming but should be delegating such responsibilities. A candidate's liking for technical responsibilities that should be passed on to subordinates could be a negative indicator.

Favorable indicators go beyond simple observations that a candidate will like the basic job, geographic location, compensation, and your management style. If the person specifications call for an "excellent" in initiative and perseverance, the sorts of statements reflective of that level would be:

I worked 70-hour weeks for months and loved it—we actually got the contract.

I thrive on challenges—the vice president said the assembly line couldn't produce 50 and we consistently got 58.

Dislikes can often be stated by a candidate in a neutral-sounding manner, and only when specifics are ascertained will it be possible to determine if a shortcoming exists. For example:

Disliking "lack of corporate support in accounting" may turn out to show that the candidate did not have the initiative to take an accounting course. Instead, she expected corporate accountants to teach her the basics, which was not good use of their time.

Disliking "insufficient budgets" may really mean that the person was so disorganized that budgets were exceeded and his bonus was cut on account of it.

Disliking "oversupervision" may mean that the person is independent and self-motivated, but with specifics given, you may learn that the person can't take criticism no matter how tactful.

Disliking a "nit-picking boss" may mean the candidate was lazy, technically incompetent, disorganized, or any number of things.

**Supervisor's Name/Title/Describe Supervisor/Your Best Guess about Supervisor's Evaluation of You.** How properly to ask for and interpret responses to TORC questions is very important and covered thoroughly in chapter 5.

**Why Left/Transition Question.** The most favorable response to these questions is "I was happy and successful in my job, but a company came along with a fabulous opportunity and I accepted it." Anything less than this sort of response suggests something went awry. Perhaps a merger, a change of immediate supervisor, an economic reversal that could not have been foreseen, division relocation to a different part of the country, or a health problem induced the candidate to want a job change. Perhaps the candidate made major business errors, was hostile to co-workers, sexually harassed a secretary, or wouldn't work hard enough to keep up.

Interviewees not proud of reasons for leaving a job often fabricate a more favorable sounding rationale and rehearse it. You should never accept "better opportunity" as a sufficient explanation for a job change. In asking "What were some of the other factors that contributed to your leaving?" you may learn the real reason or reasons.

Early in one's career it is normal for job changes to be made for naive, foolish, illogical, childish reasons. As stated in the section on "expectations, and how they worked out," however, only rarely are there good excuses for bombing out in one job, the next job, and the next job. "The company got into financial trouble"—perhaps the candidate should have investigated it more thoroughly, even if privately owned. "My boss turned out to be a jerk"—the candidate should have talked with subordinates and former subordinates to find out what the boss was really like before accepting an offer.

A confident, competent, successful person can certainly say, "Thank you for the job offer, but before accepting I would like to talk to some more people, inside the company and outside, to see if the match will be excellent for you, the company, and me. How can any hiring manager refuse such a legitimate request from a candidate? It's rare for a manager to say, "No—either accept the offer or not, right this minute, and I want to keep you in the dark about the job until after you're on board."

Everyone in the world of work is responsible for seeing to it that job changes are successful—without major regrets. To the extent regrets occur, there are indications of shortcomings, and the question facing you as a manager is, "To what extent do regrettable career decisions in the past indicate that the person falls short of current person specifications?"

## Plans and Goals for the Future and Interpretive Guidelines

The standard response to questions about plans and goals is, "I seek a position with challenge, an opportunity to make a real contribution and a chance to progress based on performance, blah, blah, et cetera, et cetera." That is exactly what an interviewee once said, including "blah, blah, et cetera, et cetera." In fact, every third or fourth sentence this rather "blah" man uttered ended with "blah, blah, et cetera, et cetera." He was on a very slow career track, spoke in a monotone, if you know what I mean, blah, blah, et cetera, et cetera.

Almost everyone seems to think the right response should show ambition, but not too much, a desire to serve, and an understanding that promotions are earned. (This was discussed in the section on interpreting application form responses.)

In order to sort out people's true goals and motivations, questions are directed at the next job, at five years from now, and at what the candidate would ultimately like to be doing in regard to career and life outside the job. Such an array of questions usually forces platitudes out and thoughtful and sincere responses into the interview, permitting you to judge—is there a good match?

Any apparent discrepancy must be explored. If the person likes delegating technical tasks, would he be frustrated in the job you're hiring for, which requires more "rolling up the sleeves?" If southern California had tremendous allure a year ago, would the candidate be lying (or kidding himself) about wanting to move to Duluth?

If a person has failed three times to start a business and claims to have concluded that a big company is what is really wanted, and if you aren't convinced, you must craft a clever question and perhaps challenge the interviewee. For example, you might smile and say "C'mon, Pat, you're still an entrepreneur at heart, aren't you? You'd still like to run your own show sometime, wouldn't you?" If the interviewee smiles and says, "I guess so," you know there may be a turnover risk.

Is the candidate overshooting—wanting too much of a job too fast for your company to accommodate? Undershooting is more common than many executives suspect; it is typically embodied in a very senior executive's claim of the desire to take a smaller job, to relax and enjoy life more, and to work in a smaller organization "where the frustrations of the large bureaucracy don't exist." Sounds great, but that perspective usually comes from desperation—the Detroit executive without a job and wanting to believe that even a much smaller job will be acceptable, anything to become employed! If you hire this person, inside of six months your new employee may push you for a bigger job, or quietly look elsewhere.

## This Company (and Interpretive Guidelines)

This series of four questions is intended to let the interviewer precisely determine the candidate's understanding of all aspects of the job and what the person feels are the advantages or disadvantages of joining the organization in the position available. Again—is there a fit?

It is a favorable sign when a candidate has researched the company and asks you a lot of probing questions. It suggests an individual who takes responsibility for his life and who does not intend to fail or be disappointed because of lack of foresight or shallow research on possible employers.

It is a negative sign if the individual wants the job without really knowing what it will entail, or if the person wants it, recognizes potentially serious problem areas, but is so desperate that banana peels in the path are disregarded.

A person might reject your job offer twice, but if you remove some concerns (add some responsibilities, reduce travel requirements, or whatever) and that person finally looks you in the eye and sincerely says, "I want this job and I'll give it everything I've got," that's fine. However, if the candidate really dislikes some aspect of the job available—for instance, doesn't really like the reporting relationship or considers the estimated budget too low (and you won't or can't change the job to meet the candidate's needs)—don't extend an offer unless losing that person in six months is acceptable.

## Self-Appraisal (and Interpretive Guidelines)

If you had time only to ask questions in one section of the interview guide, section F (self-appraisal) contains the questions you should ask. Chapter 5 elaborated on how to generate the most useful information from this section.

## Management

Section G (management) contains questions to be asked of people applying for management positions and of those who might be promoted to a management position in the not-too-distant future.

The first question—"How would you describe your management philosophy and style?"—is intended to prime the pump for a more probing inquiry: "What would you suppose subordinates have felt to be your strengths and shortcomings?" Having surveyed thousands of people regarding their attitudes about their supervisors, fewer than 5% rate their bosses perfect. So when interviewees balk, I'm quick to say, "Hey, I'm not perfect as a manager, and I don't know anyone who is, but if we're in tune with our subordinates' perceptions of us, we can manage more effectively."

An unusual question asks the interviewee to describe the strengths and shortcomings of subordinates in current and previous jobs. A most revealing exercise! As the interviewee discusses several subordinates, the interviewee's character, values, attitudes, and managerial approaches are inevitably laid out before you.

Asking a person who has never been a manager to portray what the management style will be in the future is sometimes too hypothetical for young and inexperienced interviewees; however, it is worth asking of more experienced people, particularly those who expect to become managers within the next two or three years. By this time in their careers, they have usually experienced a variety of managers, and they have some fixed notions about what they intend and intend not to do when they become managers.

## Interpretive Guidelines—Management

Time out! If I'm going to suggest how you should interpret selection candidates' responses to specific questions about management approaches, you'd better know what my biases are.

I believe the best management approach is one that succeeds, and in the vast variety of organizations I deal with, what succeeds is flexibility. Many management theorists have suggested that a particular style is appropriate for a particular type of organization. For example, the "benevolent autocrat" may be the prototype for retailers because discipline is needed not creativity (no oblong hamburger ideas for McDonald's!). Government organizations and utilities are often said to need a "bureaucratic" style that is moderately people-oriented (but not so lax as to get the voters mad at waste) and moderately results-oriented (but not so demanding as to necessitate extremely high salaries). Finally, religious organizations are sometimes said to need "people-oriented" managers (nurturing, supportive, and empathetic) and not results-oriented managers (whose stiff requirements would evoke unreligious attitudes).

Having counseled with hundreds of managers in these three types of organizations (and many in-between varieties), I have come to believe that broad flexibility is advantageous in almost all organizations. The tough, hard-nosed retail manager who constantly monitors subordinates, for example, can sometimes be more effective if there is very strong empathy, open, two-way communications, and a lot of sincere interest in people.

Mayor Daley of Chicago (an interesting client in my early consulting days) had some very effective bureaucrats, each of whom sought to appear middle of the road in results-orientation and people-orientation. However, on any given day the most effective ones exhibited a lot of flexibility—leaning very hard on a subordinate who had proven unresponsive to positive motivation techniques, being warm and nurturing with a subordinate whose parent died—and were not rigidly bound to a middle-of-the-road approach.

A bright and capable priest I know certainly wanted to maximize the personal religious experiences of seminarians when he brought 13 religious orders together to form the Catholic Theological Union. However, in order to extablish an accredited institution, he sometimes used a "velvet brick" to ensure cooperation and high academic standards.

The chairman of a large manufacturing client was once quoted as saying, "Leadership is demonstrated when the ability to inflict pain is confirmed." Heart-warming statement, right? But even this man, referenced in a *Fortune* article a couple of years ago on "The Ten Toughest Bosses in America," has had a change of heart. He has become much more flexible in his dealings with people, and his broadened range of management skills has paid off.

I believe that the ideal manager has the flexibility to be extremely tough and results-oriented, or extremely people-oriented, or even both simultaneously, no matter what the organization is like. The very best of the managers I know constantly strive to master a full repertoire of management and technical skills. These managers strive to be equipped to meet virtually any challenge.

The manager you hire had better mesh with your expectations and needs, which may be unique. That's why the person specifications on leadership and management—eight in all—must be shaped, reworded, eliminated, or expanded by you to reflect your ideal as well as the minimum you can live with.

With that digression digested, let's return to interpretation.

**Describe Your Management Philosophy and Style.**    At this point in the interview, you probably have an abundance of data on management approaches used by your candidate. If an interviewee has held seven jobs, there have been seven opportunities to talk about (managerial) accomplishments, (managerial) failures/problems/challenges, (managerial) likes and dislikes in each job, and seven guesses as to what supervisors felt were the candidate's (managerial) strengths and shortcomings. Chances are good that you have already heard some basic managerial values ("I truly believe you can't socialize with subordinates"), but the broad philosophy-and-style question can draw those beliefs together.

Of greatest importance is the extent to which favorable results have been achieved through subordinates and the degree to which specific management skills exist in relation to what will be needed in the position. If there will be a lot of hiring, recruitment and selection interviewing skills will naturally be scrutinized, and a candidate should have more experience and talent in this area than would be expected of a candidate for a managerial position in which there is minimal turnover of subordinates.

For managerial candidates for meaty positions in which subordinates will have to be upgraded—through training, termination, recruitment, improved morale—all of the person specifications for leadership and management should probably be met at an "excellent" or "good" rating level. You might have problems—perhaps surmountable and perhaps not—if you hire a person who has repeatedly and recently:

Not inspired subordinates to want to follow ("leadership" person specification)

Made many hiring errors ("Management—Recruitment/ Selection" person specification)

Delegated far too much or far too little (part of the "Management—Training/Development" person specification)

Asked too much or too little of subordinates or has confused subordinates with goals and expectations ("Management—Goal-Setting" person specification)

Oversupervised so much that good people quit or undersupervised so much that major mistakes occurred ("Management—Monitoring Performance" person specification)

Experienced performance problems among capable subordinates who felt browbeaten or had nonperforming subordinates who were unaware of their own performance deficiencies ("Management—Performance Feedback" person specification)

Lived with hopelessly incompetent people long after they had failed repeatedly to achieve fair, realistic, goals that they agreed should be met ("Management—Removing Nonperformers" person specification)

Experienced substantial dissension, unwanted turnover, or lessened performance among subordinates because of a failure to achieve an open, mutually supportive team atmosphere in which differences of opinion are surfaced and constructively resolved ("Management—Team Player" person specification)

Hiring subordinates with poor abilities in any one of the leadership/ management specifications could mean headaches for you. If you could pay an astronomical salary, you could probably hire a truly exceptional manager in all of these dimensions. If the person must perform at a "good" or "excellent" level in a particular management dimension within one year, perhaps a current rating of "fair" is tolerable—if you have the skill, time, and willingness to work to correct the deficiency and if you believe the candidate is sufficiently trainable and growth oriented to learn the particular skills quickly.

If a person is weak at recruitment/selection, for example, perhaps you or the human resources department can handle the bulk of these responsibilities for your new manager, while that person picks up the skills by attending a seminar, reading a book on the subject, observing capable interviewers, or being observed by other interviewers.

If your candidate's previous subordinates have been confused about goals that were not written down, perhaps you could institute a management-by-objectives (MBO) program for this subordinate, requiring thoroughly documented goals and objectives in writing.

If your new manager is a softy and has historically been reticent about giving subordinates any critical performance feedback, perhaps you could sit in on semiannual performance appraisals to be sure that nonperformers are properly counseled.

Finally, if your new subordinate has deficiencies in understanding his impact on subordinates and often does not communicate thoroughly or positively with them, perhaps you could:

Require the new subordinate to conduct a semiannual survey of the attitudes and opinions of that person's subordinates. A 20-item survey, taking only 10 minutes to conduct, can be a real eye-opener for you and your new subordinate and provide an ongoing yardstick of your new subordinate's managerial effectiveness, particularly in communications.

Require that monthly communications meetings be conducted in which that person's subordinates air their needs and concerns, and perhaps you should sit in on those meetings from time to time.

Ask internal or external organization development consultants to work with your new manager. A little training and a two-day retreat once a year are usually all that are necessary to insure a collaborative and more productive team consisting of your manager and his or her subordinates.

In sum, following the guide will inform you clearly of a candidate's managerial strengths and shortcomings, but ultimately you have to judge if the person specifications must be strictly adhered to or if your candidate's shortcomings can be sufficiently overcome by whatever special efforts you or your organization might make.

**What Subordinates Have Felt Have Been Your Strengths/Shortcomings.**  With the possibility expressed of your actually contacting previous subordinates (part of the TORC methods), interviewees often blurt out all sorts of truths. An "I have no idea what my subordinates have felt are my shortcomings" response is negative, suggesting that two-way communications have not existed, that the interviewee is insensitive or unconcerned with how best to manage, and that the interviewee takes a superior, autocratic stance with subordinates.

**In What Ways Might You Want to Modify Your Approach to Subordinates?**  If your interviewee is perfect (or thinks so) then the response will be, "I want to continue exactly what I've been doing as a manager." Your retort should be, "None of us is perfect—surely there are some ways you can improve a bit as a manager!" Any meaningful response is a plus. No meaningful response suggests the person is dense, unconcerned with improvement, or playing games with you.

**Describe Each Subordinate (in a Paragraph or Two).**  If the interviewee recruited and selected excellent performers with no major, debilitating shortcomings, you probably have a winner on your hands. If subordinates have shortcomings that are being addressed through counseling or training, and improvement is taking place at a reasonable pace, that's fine. For every nonperforming subordinate your interviewee has, however, you must ask why.

It is always enlightening to hear about a candidate's "problem employees" and more important, how they have been dealt with.

Are young, bright employees resented and stifled or nurtured and channeled?

Is the office rumormonger ignored or counseled into more appropriate behaviors?

Does the candidate always have "a bunch of bums" working for him? If so, there are management deficiencies, perhaps even an unwholesome need to have appropriate people around as the focus of complaining.

Is the hopelessly incompetent performer, after extensive training and counseling efforts have failed, simply tolerated, or removed?

What a manager's subordinates have been (and are) like tells you as much about your candidate as a painting tells about the artist.

Any suggestion of blaming subordinates should be scrutinized. Managers are paid to prevent or correct significant deficiencies in subordinates—preferably to prevent major problems by good selection; if that hasn't worked, to correct the problem through active feedback, counseling, and training; and if that fails, to correct the situation through transfer, demotion, or termination. Managers are not paid to moan and groan about subordinates or to kick them fruitlessly.

Doing subordinates' jobs for them is one way to deal with nonperformance, and you must determine if your candidate is temporarily covering the subordinates' deficiencies as the subordinate grows, or indefinitely filling in because the candidate is a poor developer, trainer, delegator, or recruiter/ selector.

**What Will Your Management Style Be?**   What would you guess subordinates in your first managerial job will consider your strengths and shortcomings? (for those without management experience but who expect to become managers). Favorable responses to these two hypothetical questions can reveal some thought and study of the issue, some experimentation (perhaps through community leadership experiences), and some statements consistent with your person specifications. The most negative responses show ignorance of basic management tools or, even worse, a strong commitment to function in a way not acceptable in your organization. People sometimes overreact to deficiencies in supervisors they have had and lock into beliefs that are too extreme in the opposite ("My current boss is wishy-washy; let me tell you, when I'm boss I tell people what to do, when, and how, with no questions asked!").

The section on education, followed by those on the military, work history, plans and goals for the future, and this company, essentially ask everything important from a chronological point of view. If you were very thorough in covering these sections in an interview, you will already have most of your data for the self-appraisal, management, work habits, and technical expertise sections.

Essentially, the next group of sections in the guide ask the individual to take one more pass through the entire career, focusing on the various sub-categories such as management, work habits, and technical expertise. It is rather like studying the history of the world in one semester, and the following semester spending four weeks each on military history, economic history, sociological history, religious history, and communications history. For most interviews, the work history section provides useful, relevant, but not quite complete data with respect to self-appraisal, management approaches, work habits, and technical expertise, and that's why these additional sections are included.

## Work Habits

This section begins with a short and deliberately ambiguous question: "How would you describe your work habits?" Chances are that the individual has already indicated the number of hours worked in a typical week, the pace, how pressures are handled, sources of motivation, and so forth. If the response to that first general question merely confirms what you already strongly suspect, you will not have to press for much elaboration and will probably have to ask only one or two additional questions to complete the section. If not, go ahead and ask each of the sub-questions in the section.

## Interpretive Guidelines—Work Habits

**Typical Workweek.**    Responses to this question permit you to spend a hypothetical typical week with the candidate, and you can infer from the description the hours worked, pace, organization, priorities, and other aspects of the job. Interpretation for specifics follows.

**Hours.**  We all think it is grand and wonderful when people obtain excellent results working 40 hours a week. "What counts," we say, "is achievement, not putting in hours." However, if an organization is under stress (from fast growth or restructuring, for example), an employee may have to work longer. In a turnaround situation, a new manager could legitimately be expected to work 60 or 70 hours a week. I find it unusual for a successful manager to work fewer than 50 hours a week.

**Pace.**  The South and West generally are slower paced than the Midwest, which is slower than the Northeast. Exceptions abound, but I've seen many a non-New Yorker go bananas trying to keep up with Big Apple locals, and New Yorkers exported to other parts of the country drive the laid back good ol' boys up the wall. Any self-report of a pace differing from the expected pace of the position in question should trigger further exploration.

**How Do You Typically Handle Yourself under Stress and Pressures; Describe Emotional Controls, Things That Dominate or Get You Down.**  This is a very direct series of questions, occurring at a point in the interview when rapport should be excellent. Asking the questions with a sincere, nurturing attitude should elicit honest responses. A response indicating anything less than considerable maturity, resilience, and emotional control should be probed for specifics.

**Intelligence.**  Even if an excellent intelligence test is administered, it is useful to ask this question. All you are looking for is a response confirming what all the other data (test performance, academic record, interview behavior) have suggested. If there is a large discrepancy (which rarely occurs, but if it does, is almost always in the direction of overestimated intelligence), ask for supporting data. If the candidate has nothing other than a cocky, unsubstantiated, and obviously erroneous self-opinion, imagine what it would be like to manage such a turkey.

**What Motivates You.**  If you suspect that someone is hungry for power, control, domination, money, or prestige, it could be worthwhile to say so directly, though with an empathetic attitude. These are less socially acceptable sources of motivation than "making a contribution," "providing for my family," or "earning the respect of my colleagues," so it may require some cleverness on your part to induce the interviewee to open up.

The key interpretive point is not so much what motivates a person so long as there is a *lot* of motivation and the sources of motivation as expressed will be acceptable to your organization. The 1980s is seeing more emphasis on collaboration; the 1970s produced the power-through-intimidation types who are now passing out of vogue.

**Troublesome Problems.**  This item constitutes a fishing-trip opportunity for important data.

**Organization/Efficiency.**  For managerial candidates, favorable indicators generally include daily priority selling-and-action plans, tickler files, use of a competent secretary, and involvement of subordinates in annual plans. Negative indicators are missed deadlines, indications of low productivity or inefficiency, and a style that has been criticized by supervisors. Fanatic detail orientation is not always a plus (sometimes punctilious managers nitpick subordinates and stifle creativity).

**Describe Your Decision-Making Style.**  A very modern professional-manager response is: "I'm decisive and intuitive when confronted with familiar decisions that subordinates can't handle or with unimportant mini-decisions, and I'm thorough and systematic when faced with important and unique decisions. For those, I like to get as many opinions as possible, weigh them all carefully, and then act. I act on my own when time is crucial and subordinates do not have the perspective or knowledge to do more than contribute, and in those cases, my style is consultive. For decisions affecting many subordinates, if time permits, I generally prefer a participative approach in which we work toward consensus. This takes time but often results in both the best decision and the broadest support for implementation."

**What You Find the Most Important/Most Difficult Decisions.**  Asked what are the most important or difficult decisions faced, managers' most frequent responses are "changing jobs," "how to play political games in companies," and "decisions to remove people." Asking the interviewee for specifics will give you a good feel for what sorts of things you will be counseling this person on, should an offer be extended and accepted. In talking about "decisions to remove people," for example, you might learn that the candidate just can't bring himself to actually let someone go, even long after the necessity is apparent. You might realistically anticipate some long, arduous counseling sessions if you hire him, particularly if a shake up will be necessary within his subordinate group.

**Describe Your Planning/Budgeting Methods.** Some organizations have quite sophisticated strategic planning models, requiring five- and ten-year perspectives and highly complex financial, computer, and economic expertise. If the job calls for such executive talents, it would be worthwhile for you to request actual samples of planning/budgeting documents the candidate has prepared or worked under. For mid- and lower-level managers, planning and budgeting usually encompasses weekly, monthly, quarterly, or (at the most) annual commitments. Favorable indicators are the same as for questions regarding organization/efficiency—projects completed on time and within budget. If planning and budgeting systems at your organization are different from what the candidate has experienced— if your budgets are a lot tighter, if the political aspects of planning are messy, or if time constraints are much more severe—you have cause for concern.

### Technical Expertise (and Interpretive Guidelines)

The technical expertise section may be omitted altogether if you have done a very thorough job of pinpointing technical strengths while reviewing the work history. It's not a bad idea, however, to have a list of technical areas that you want to have a reading on and simply to ask the individual to rate current expertise (on a scale of excellent, good, fair, and poor) and to give you a paragraph or two summarizing courses, seminars, experiences, and accomplishments in each of the areas. Appendix B gives some sample lists of technical areas for a retail-store manager, personnel executive in a manufacturing company, industrial engineer, and sales manager.

How's this for a cop-out—it would require a library of books to summarize the sorts of responses to technical questions for all 25,000 occupations listed in the *Dictionary of Occupational Titles*. Actually, interpreting technical questions is apt to be no problem for you if you happen to be in a first- or second-level of management and promoted in part because of your technical wizardry.

If you are an executive who is knowledgeable in only one or two of the half dozen or more areas of responsibility, have technical experts (board members, consultants, professors) interview candidates in the areas in which your knowledge is incomplete.

## Final Self-Analysis and Wrap-Up Questions (and Interpretive Guidelines)

The section on final self-analysis contains some interesting supplemental questions, which may already have been answered in the interview, but sometimes are useful. "How do first impressions you make differ from the way you are?" is particularly valuable to ask of younger candidates who might be intimidated by the interview. If the person is serious and purposeful throughout the interview and a fun-loving cutup on the job, responses to these questions might help you to understand how the candidate is able to generate loyalty and productivity among subordinates.

By asking the interviewee for a self-rating on each person specification, any major discrepancy with the interviewer's conclusions might be explored further. If, for example, the candidate gives an "excellent" self-rating on creativity/innovativeness, and you thought a "fair" would have been generous, it's time to ask, "What examples can you give me that would show excellence in creativity/innovativeness?"

The section on wrap-up questions is a final and usually futile attempt to ferret out anything important that somehow has managed to pass through the rather intricate filtering methods of the in-depth selection interview. One time in 25, something really juicy and meaningful pops up—like an employer pressing legal charges, a former secretary with a paternity suit, a very negative employment experience not mentioned because it only lasted three days, or a severe alcohol problem that currently destroys job performance.

## Addendum—Sensitive Questions (and Interpretive Guidelines)

These addendum questions are sensitive because persons in legally protected classifications (minorities, women, handicapped persons, among others) could file charges if they suspect discrimination has taken place. Even if the questions were not intended to discriminate and even if discrimination can be proved *not* to have occurred, the reputation of your organization and legal costs probably make such questioning not worth the risk.

How about asking nonprotected people these questions? That's up to you, but I have some suggestions—only ask such questions if you are a seasoned interviewer and are sure you won't offend, if you believe that they are job related, and if you are sufficiently knowledgeable that you can validly relate responses to person specifications.

## Family Background (Sensitive)

"What circumstances in your early home background have contributed to the way you are today—your interests, motivations, strengths, hopes, or whatever might be pertinent to the job?" "Pertinent to the job" is a phrase intended to lessen offensiveness. When this question is asked with a philosophical, thoughtful, compassionate attitude, it almost always generates responses. If you choose to ask the question, do it this way: "OK, Pete, I think we have pretty well covered your background, interests, and goals for the future, and what I would like to do now is just get away from the job for a few minutes and talk a bit more on a personal level. I am really interested in knowing what circumstances in your early home background...." (You fill in the blank.) Look up when you ask this question, furrow your brow quizzically, gain eye contact, smile warmly, and it is practically impossible for an interviewee to respond, "Nothing."

## Interpretive Guidelines—Family Background

**How Your Background Contributed to the Way You Are.**
Interpretation is usually best at a surface level, and I even encourage psychologists to stay away from trying to glean unconscious motivational patterns. When a person grew up on the wrong side of the tracks, describes how rotten it was, and says, "I vowed I'd make it some day, and although I've crossed the tracks, I haven't begun to satisfy my need for success," you understand all you need, without being concerned about oedipal influences. The candidate reared by a harsh alcoholic father may have difficulties relating to authority figures and can explain what a gut-wrenching feeling it is to be ordered to do anything. Simple, straightforward interpretation is quite sufficient.

**Parents' Main Advice.**   With startling frequency, kids grow up to conform to parental advice. Where parental advice is not followed, it is enlightening to hear how the individual broke away from these influences. Kids repeatedly told "better safe than sorry" and "look before you leap" ordinarily become more security conscious as adults than do children reared on "no pain, no glory" and "you can do anything you put your mind to." Candidates for executive positions are typically highly achievement-oriented, and drummed into their young heads was advice such as "you have to go to an Ivy League school, so keep your grades up," and "the world is full of losers, so pay the price and you'll be a winner."

**Similarities/Dissimilarities—Father and Mother.**    Executives describe their parents in remarkably similar terms. Mom was "just a good mom—always there, always loving." Dad was "rarely around and liked sports, was somewhat strict and a very hard worker." Mom seemed to provide a basically sound identity, and Dad's approval had to be earned through hard work. This pattern substantially fits 60 percent of the last 500 executives I've interviewed—a useful topic for a Ph.D. dissertation!

Executives often say they are similar to their fathers in being dedicated, responsible, hardworking, and a strong leader and are similar to Mom in—"hm, can't think of any ways."

Happy Mother's Day, Mom! You gave your son, the hotshot manager, a terrifically solid ego, and the ingrate considers himself dissimilar to you in almost all respects! Most executives are grateful to dear Mom, but truly consider themselves more like Dad.

As an interviewer, you feel a little more confident in the conclusion that Sandra is exact with details if she says she is similar to parents in that "They were perfectionists and so am I." Or, "My father was an abusive drunk and that's how we're different—I'll never touch a drop of alcohol."

What these questions ask for is a self-appraisal from an unusual, and unusually probing viewpoint. We all carry with us values, attitudes, beliefs, and behavioral tendencies acquired as children and adolescents, and interpretation is facilitated when the inertia of early home influences is discerned in light of how the individual has evolved.

## Home Life (Sensitive)

The phraseology in the guide—"Are there any circumstances centering around your home life—your marriage, children, personal finances, or whatever—which might have a direct bearing on your effectiveness with this company?" is again intended to minimize offensiveness.

## Interpretive Guidelines—Home Life

Problem situations beget problem situations, and if a marriage is collapsing, a teenager is busted for peddling drugs, or a candidate is deeply in debt, job performance might be affected. The younger and lower level the candidate, the more likely job performance would be harmed. Seasoned executives usually have an extraordinary capacity to compartmentalize work life and insulate it from personal life.

When a candidate has experienced considerable life changes, symptoms of excessive stress may occur—depression, overeating, headaches, insomnia, high blood pressure, tics, temper outbursts, fatigue, marital and family disorders, accident proneness, or alcohol or drug excesses. Although the research on stress is not yet complete, many scientists believe that even favorable life events, such as vacation, marriage, or business success can contribute to excessive stress symptoms.

A stress is simply something (favorable or unfavorable) that requires adjustment in one's life—intellectual, emotional, physical, or interpersonal adjustment. Some stress is important for it evokes the stress response, which amounts to an emergency reserve that is sometimes necessary for excellent performance, increased self-esteem, and the capacity to cope successfully with similar stresses in the future. There are tremendous individual differences, with some people seeming to thrive on change and having terrific resiliency in the face of pressures and others crumbling with the slightest disruption of their status quo. It seems fairly clear, however, that for anyone who undergoes an extended, severe stress response, the risks of experiencing the symptoms listed above increase.

Figure 13 is a 43-item stress-indicator quiz—one of many being researched. In this version a score of 300 is supposed to be indicative of high risk of developing stress-related disorders. It could be 15 years before a very reliable, valid diagnostic quiz is developed, but taking this short quiz may alert you to the sorts of life events that may be worth noting as you evaluate a candidate.

I'm not suggesting that you actually give this quiz to a candidate, but simply that you should be aware of responses to the "life circumstances" question in light of all of the other data you have gathered on the person. Then ask yourself (and perhaps the candidate, too), "Is the position in question going to cause excessive stress?"

If personal life is apt to interfere with the job, the chances are you will have heard about it by the time you get to this section of the interview, since you have already scrutinized all sorts of factors contributing to success, failure, likes, and dislikes in each job.

The only right answer to the "life circumstances" question is a quick, apparently sincere "No." Any pauses, loss of eye contact, or other indication of tentativeness should be interpreted as indicating a possible problem.

The same interpretation is appropriate for responses to the question on a spouse's willingness to move. Anything short of "No problem at all—she/he would support it 100%" should be investigated fully.

## Recreations and Avocations, and Interpretive Guidelines (Sensitive)

Asking about reading habits, social activities, hobbies, interests, and TV viewing time can produce some useful information—about how important the career is viewed in relation to other elements of life and what sort of balance the person has in terms of career, family, and other interests. Interviewers find, for example, that if a candidate has no time for reading to keep abreast of his or her field and yet watches TV three hours a night, that person may not have the self-development orientation you expect in the job. Several clients don't want interviewers to ask these questions even of nonprotected groups in the in-depth selection interview. They suggest that only candidates for high-level jobs be asked these questions—over dinner as part of friendly conversation.

## Health (Sensitive)

Unless you are a medical doctor, there might be legal risk in your trying to make diagnoses, so don't! Keep your inquiries simple and job related and require a physical examination for medical judgments.

## Interpretive Guidelines—Health

If you choose to go ahead with the health questions, here are pointers on interpretation, not diagnosis. The point is to know when to require a physical examination.

**Serious illnesses, accidents, operations.**   Unless the response is an unqualified "No," require a thorough physical examination. Of course, people often fully recover from serious illnesses, but some people do not like to admit, even to themselves, any serious health problems.

In discerning the health data requested on the application form, the point has been made that any response to condition of health that is less than "excellent" is possibly an indication of some health issues and/or a self-concept short of being totally positive, aggressive, and confident.

**Handicaps, physical limitations.**   Assuming you do not wish to discriminate against people with physical limitations that are irrelevant to job performance, all you are looking for in this question is an indication of any physical problem that might not have been disclosed in responses to the first question in this section.

| Event Rank | Event Value | Happened (✔) | Your Score | Life Event |
|---|---|---|---|---|
| 1 | 100 | | | Death of Spouse |
| 2 | 73 | | | Divorce |
| 3 | 65 | | | Marital separation |
| 4 | 63 | | | Jail term |
| 5 | 63 | | | Death of close family member |
| 6 | 53 | | | Personal injury or illness |
| 7 | 50 | | | Marriage |
| 8 | 47 | | | Fired from job |
| 9 | 45 | | | Marital reconciliation |
| 10 | 45 | | | Retirement |
| 11 | 44 | | | Change in health of family member |
| 12 | 40 | | | Pregnancy |
| 13 | 39 | | | Sex difficulties |
| 14 | 39 | | | Gain of new family member |
| 15 | 39 | | | Business readjustment |
| 16 | 38 | | | Change in financial state |
| 17 | 37 | | | Death of close friend |
| 18 | 36 | | | Change to different line of work |
| 19 | 35 | | | Change in number of arguments with spouse |
| 20 | 31 | | | Mortgage over $10,000 |
| 21 | 30 | | | Foreclosure of mortgage or loan |

| | | | |
|---|---|---|---|
| 22 | 29 | ___ | Change of responsibilities at work |
| 23 | 29 | ___ | Son or daughter leaving home |
| 24 | 29 | ___ | Trouble with in-laws |
| 25 | 28 | ___ | Outstanding personal achievement |
| 26 | 26 | ___ | Wife begin or stop work |
| 27 | 26 | ___ | Begin or end school |
| 28 | 25 | ___ | Change in living conditions |
| 29 | 24 | ___ | Revision of personal habits |
| 30 | 23 | ___ | Trouble with boss |
| 31 | 20 | ___ | Change in work hours or conditions |
| 32 | 20 | ___ | Change in residence |
| 33 | 20 | ___ | Change in schools |
| 34 | 19 | ___ | Change in recreation |
| 35 | 19 | ___ | Change in church activities |
| 36 | 18 | ___ | Change in social activities |
| 37 | 17 | ___ | Mortgage or loan less than $10,000 |
| 38 | 16 | ___ | Change in sleeping habits |
| 39 | 15 | ___ | Change in number of family get-togethers |
| 40 | 15 | ___ | Change in eating habits |
| 41 | 13 | ___ | Vacation |
| 42 | 12 | ___ | Christmas |
| 43 | 11 | ___ | Minor violations of the law |

Figure 13. Stress indicator quiz: What events have happened to you in the past 12 months? (Reprinted with permission from *Psychology Today*, April 1972.)

**Days missed.**  People who honestly consider themselves in excellent health have admitted being absent 20 days a year, which most of my clients would consider excessive. If hourly workers are allowed 10 sick days a year, I don't interpret 10 days missed yearly as necessarily anything other than taking advantage of a policy. Further probing usually elicits an admission that the person was really ill only three or four days.

If a candidate indicates being absent four or more days because of illness in the previous year, I recommend a thorough physical examination. Super high-powered executives I have interviewed miss one or two days a year, maximum, with the most common response being "No days." Why? They keep themselves in top shape and find a cold or mild flu annoying, but nothing to stay home from work with.

You're finished—the tour of the in-depth selection interview guide is completed. In chapter 1 the contention was made that devoting 2½ hours to interviewing a mid-manager, salesperson, or technical specialist is often necessary—unless you would feel comfortable eliminating some items in the guide. If you retain 90% of the items, including all 16 items for each job, you can easily spend 2½ hours, and I hope it strikes you that you will have acquired a wealth of job-relevant information.

Faithful following of the "In-Depth Selection Interview Guide" will immediately improve many interviewers' effectiveness, although this is not sufficient to guarantee valid hiring decisions. All interviewers make errors, but being alerted to the major pitfalls can help one avoid many of them.

# 8 | Major Interviewer Errors

Conclusions I have reached on what are the major interviewer errors and how they can be corrected have several origins:

1. My own goof-ups. I have worked with most of my clients for many years and typically find out later the accuracy of my analyses of candidates. By doing autopsies on interviews that resulted in a misjudgment, I have learned—the hard way.

2. Reading the research. As incredibly complex, rich, and even scientific as is a lot of research in applied behavioral sciences (perception, physiological psychology, learning theory, statistics, interpersonal communications, motivation), the actual research in selection interviewing is woefully deficient. Still, existing research offers some useful guidance on interviewing pitfalls.

3. Training managers in selection interviewing techniques. I frequently observe trainees conducting interviews, and after noticing a significant error I will interrupt, hold a private coaching session, and advise the trainee how to improve the approach. Frequently videotapes are made of entire interviews,

and in later analyses my trainees can easily see what they did well, and what were errors.

Cataloging major interviewer errors may be disheartening exercise, for even experienced interviewers might say, "My Lord, if all of those things can go wrong, how can I possibly conduct a valid interview?" It's not that hopeless, really.

Selection interviewing is more like Olympic basketball playoffs (lots of games and lots of opportunities to correct errors) than like Olympic skiing (one missed gate and that's it for these Olympics!). In a 2½ hour interview there are many, many opportunities to regain lost professional rapport or to deal with a topic skimmed over too quickly. If Ralph's work habits have been terrible for years, and you didn't learn this in asking about job number one, maybe you'll catch it in asking about jobs two, three, or four, or in the section on work habits, or in the self-appraisal. So, please don't feel overwhelmed by how extensive is the following catalog of interviewer errors.

## Not Adhering to the Basics

Unfortunately, the fact that interviews can be "saved" is an invitation for some interviewers to become a bit sloppy and bypass important elements of the recommended approach in this book. Managers I have trained usually adhere religiously to the basics for a while, then they begin cutting corners, and this sometimes leads to regrettable mistakes. Later, with what is considered "maturity and seasoning," the basics are adhered to once again. I would be very critical of this lapse in judgment if I could honestly say that I did not succumb to these same temptations (naturally, this was many, many years ago).

Here is a sample of some of the problems and the "back to basics" corrections:

| Sample Problems | Corrective Actions |
| --- | --- |
| Misunderstanding the true nature of the job responsibilities | Construct very thorough, written job descriptions |
| Overlooking important person specifications | Prepare written, thorough person specifications, based on a job analysis |

| Sample Problems | Corrective Actions |
|---|---|
| Wasting too much time conducting preliminary interviews with too many unacceptable candidates | Thoroughly review the application form and résumé and conduct brief telephone interviews before inviting people in for face-to-face preliminary interviews |
| Failing to ask important questions regarding work habits and management style | Stick to the "In-Depth Selection Interview Guide" |
| Asking misleading and biasing questions | Stick to the wording in the "In-Depth Selection Interview Guide" (unless pursuing a tangent) |
| Forgetting responses to several important questions | Take comprehensive notes on what the person says in response to questions |
| Forgetting just when the interviewee was nervous, awkward, and uncomfortable | Take comprehensive notes on the context, rhythm, and nonverbal behavior of the interviewee |
| After offering the person a job, noticing several apparent inconsistencies in interview notes | Review notes carefully three times before forming final conclusions and making job offer |
| Learning after the person was hired that there were two important job failures in the past | Personally conduct record checks with previous supervisors |
| Forming biases/prejudices/ stereotypes | Share interview notes and conclusions with other interviewers |

Adhering to these basic steps will make it very unlikely that the interviewer will blow it. The last problem listed—biases, prejudices, and stereotypes—is a complex issue, meriting some special comments.

## Succumbing to Biases, Prejudices, and Stereotypes

We all are aware of the very real harm that can befall individuals, organizations, nations, and the entire world when incorrect stereotypes, deeply felt prejudices, and rigidly held biases creep into the human equation. In the 1980s of course we all know that women frequently have better attendance records than men, that redheads are not more hot-tempered than others as a group, that high foreheads do not correlate with greater intelligence, that some accountants actually are more outgoing than some salespeople, that some New Yorkers are more friendly than some Southerners, and that some football players do appreciate the arts. Actually, unfounded stereotypes are not so obvious to many people. When asked, most business people, including selection interviewers, say they witness all sorts of invalid stereotyping in others. Most of us, however, feel that our particular biases are valid, logical, and reasonable.

The psychological dynamics are basically the same for biases, prejudices, and stereotypes—they all involve extrapolations from previous experience to account for current judgments and feelings. What is so often overlooked in discussions of this topic is that the psychological dynamics—the processes that may lead to inaccurate, unfair, or impractical conclusions—are themselves normal, understandable, and indeed necessary for survival.

Every day of our lives, every normally functioning person in the world makes tens of thousands of mini-assumptions about the world. We assume that the meat in the restaurant is edible, that the shaving-cream can will not explode, that the airplane will fly, and that the chairs will hold us. If we were all to take a fresh, totally unbiased look at everything and every person in the world we face each day, we would have no more capacity to function in the world than does a neonate, who simply has not existed long enough to generalize from experience. Everyday survival is based on the learning process of extrapolatinig from previous experiences and making assumptions about current situations.

Let's discuss racial prejudice—is it normal, logical, or heinous? The Cabrini Green housing project in Chicago has from time to time earned a reputation as number one in crime in the United States. All races are victims. For a person of any race not to be wary of strangers at Cabrini Green is to be naive. For a person walking home alone late at night and seeing six teenagers of any other race, not experiencing a fear response would be unnatural and illogical. Similarly, for someone employed at the World Bank, full of talented professionals of all races, to be fearful of half a dozen people of a different race walking down the hall in their three-piece suits would also be unnatural and illogical. In most real life instances, if you understand what a person has heard, seen, read, or in other ways has experienced, the so-called biases, prejudices, and stereotypes are understandable because the same logical processes have permitted the individual to survive in many other respects.

In a selection interview context, stereotyping involves making judgments about people on the basis of their membership in a particular group (race, sex, age). Thus, stereotyping involves both the formation of trait descriptions of specific categories of people and the assumption that a particular individual is not an exception to those trait descriptions. The key question is whether the assumptions, or prejudices, about this individual are correct. If the stereotype is correct, making a tentative hypothesis about a particular characteristic for an individual while remaining open to disconfirming evidence is fine. If a person specification for a plant manager in Mexico is "must speak fluent Spanish," favoring applications of those with Spanish surnames seems justified (so long as those with non-Spanish surnames who indicate fluency in Spanish are not denied an opportunity to apply).

What perpetuates so much harm in the world, and what is immoral, illegal, and disadvantageous for corporations, are unfounded, invalid generalizations, either about a category of persons or about a specific individual. Many racial, sexual, geographic, and other stereotypes held by people are simply not true, and those that might statistically be true for a category of people are demonstrably not true for many particular members of that category. It is unfortunate when our personal needs, hang-ups, peer influences, and early home life influences happen to conflict with reality. It is particularly unfortunate when biases are not based in fact, yet stick to us like barnacles.

In short, stereotyping is a normal and very useful cognitive function, and when accurate, can save us a lot of time and hassles. So much for a favorable view of stereotyping.

As a consultant, I have been appalled that:

The president of a major building-products corporation refused to hire a brilliant and highly talented advertising executive because "she has blonde hair, so she is probably a dumb blonde."

The chairman of a major railroad refused to hire an extremely well qualified black man as personnel manager (in 1978, incidentally). The candidate looked and acted like a statesman, but the chairman said, "Those types would probably come to work wearing a super-fly hat."

A vice president of sales refused to hire his first female salesperson, despite overwhelming evidence that she was an aggressive "ball of fire," because, he said, "Women just aren't tough enough." She joined a competitor and rose to number one (of 165) sales representatives.

Until we as interviewers become omniscient and Spock-like in our calculations, we will all lack the total wisdom, maturity, and courage to be completely fair to others, ourselves, and our employing organizations.

A major summary of 23 studies on biases, prejudices, and stereotypes in selection interviewing yielded the following conclusions:*

1. *Candidate sex.* Females are generally given lower ratings than males if the candidates have similar or identical qualifications. However, a third of the studies having to do with sex discrimination showed no unfounded discrimination against women.

2. *Candidate race.* Though not thoroughly researched, there is little evidence that interviewers give more unfavorable ratings to black job candidates versus white candidates. What research does exist has generally employed young liberal people as interviewers.

3. *Candidate age.* In two studies cited, age played no role in the ratings of barely competent candidates, but younger, highly competent individuals were preferred over relatively older, also highly competent, candidates.

4. *Candidate handicap.* There is very little research, but one study showed an interviewer bias in favor of the handicapped. (The 132 interviewers—college recruiters—viewed the handicapped candidate "as a courageous figure who had overcome physical adversity rather than as an employment risk because of physical handicaps.")

In short, the good news is that research to date does not show consistently bad evidence of biases, prejudices, and stereotypes in selection interviewing. The bad news is that research on the subject is

*Arvey, R. Unfair discrimination in the employment interview: legal and psychological aspects. *Psychological Bulletin*, 1979, **4**, 736–765.

mostly with college kids pretending to be job interviewers. The real world, in my opinion, suffers from more wide-spread unfounded prejudices, although I'll admit my opinion is not scientifically founded.

## How to Prevent Unfounded Biases, Prejudices, and Stereotypes

If the processes underlying biases are normal and understandable and yet the results can and are sometimes harmful, what is an interviewer to do?

At the risk of being nauseatingly redundant, the best advice is to follow the "In-Depth Selection Interview Guide," asking all of the pertinent questions in the wording given and doing so for all interviewees regardless of race, age, sex, or other stereotypical category. If this candidate from a foreign country just "looks dumb," and I omit the questions on academic performance, perhaps I will miss the opportunity to learn that the individual is an academic wizard. The guide forces facts into the interviewer's awareness. By comparing notes with two or three others who have conducted interviews with the same candidate, all sorts of biases based on invalid information can be squashed. Studies by Wexley and colleagues and Latham and colleagues demonstrate that workshop training of interviewers geared toward minimizing rating errors are effective.*

## Overweighting the First Impression

Several years ago I interviewed Phil Alexander (not his real name) for an important position in the entertainment business. He made a terrific first impression—handsome, cordial, and dressed in an expensive, fashionable business suit. Furthermore, at 37 years of age he was president of one of the three major record companies in the United States. He was confident, poised, gracious, and smart as a whip. He had packaged himself so perfectly that the chairman of my client company—one of the most famous men in the entertainment field—hired him after only an hour interview. I talked with Phil after he was on the payroll, in order to provide my client with some clues as to how

*Wexley, K. M., Sanders, R. E., and Yukl, G. A. Training interviewers to eliminate contrast effects in employment interviews. *Journal of Applied Psychology,* 1973, **57,** 233–236. Latham, G. P., Wexley, K. N., and Pursell, E. D. Training managers to minimize rating errors in the observation of behavior. *Journal of Applied Psychology,* 1975, **60,** 550–555.

best to manage this high-talent fellow. Unfortunately for my client, Phil was all show and very little substance; he had a perfect career record of turning gold into lead, and my client was shocked to learn this. He was great at parties but not at managing businesses, and my client paid dearly for his premature positive assessment.

One of the most oft-cited interviewing studies was part of the decade-long McGill University research on interviewing; it showed interviewers to crystallize their hire/no hire opinions in only four minutes!* Subsequent research showed that just one unfavorable impression was followed by a reject decision 90% of the time and that positive information was given much less weight.† I should point out that these were quickie, 15-minute (on the average) selection interviews—just the sort of shallow approach that forces the interviewer to make haphazard judgments. The research, which has been replicated, is disturbing nonetheless, because it shows a widespread inclination toward inadequate, premature weighing of interview data.

When first meeting an interviewee, the interviewer perceives the individual. This woman reminds me of Aunt Matilda, who is bossy and bitchy, and even if this interviewee is not that way at all, I may even unconsciously look for signs that she is bossy or bitchy. Even if no signs are there, my perceptive tendencies might induce me to conclude that she was simply putting on a good show during the interview—very unfortunate for her, the interviewer, and the organization. Fortunately, there are some effective techniques to prevent or at least to minimize such tendencies.

In the first couple of minutes of an interview, ask yourself, "Whom does this person remind me of?" Write down the name or names of people who seem to be similar in visual appearance, manner, voice qualities, or any way at all. Tell yourself, "One thing is for sure—if I'm inclined to think this person is hardworking, lazy, friendly, or hostile, the chances are that at this point in the interview I have too few data to substantiate such a conclusion and that all I am doing is unfairly extrapolating from my previous experiences."

Compare notes and conclusions with one or two others who have conducted interviews. If your perceptions are from left field, you'll find out!

---

*Springbett (1954, 1958), reported in W. F. Cascio, *Applied Psychology in Personnel Management,* Reston, Vir.: Reston Publishing, 1978, p. 204.
†Springbett (Bolster and Springbett, 1961, also reported in W. F. Cascio, *Applied Psychology in Personnel Management,* Reston, Va.: Reston Publishing, 1978, p. 204.

## Hiring in One's Own Image

Hiring a person like yourself is obviously not all bad and at times might be extremely beneficial, particularly if you happen to be highly successful, bright, enterprising, and generally wonderful as a person. But it is unfortunate when highly capable candidates are rejected in favor of a less capable candidate who happens to have some nonessential similarity—the same alma mater, similar athletic interests, or whatever—with the hiring manager. This sort of prejudice may be legal and quite conscious, but can be very costly in terms of performance or excessive recruitment costs.

A very fine consulting firm, and one that truly hires only the cream-of-the-crop professionals has for years rejected "sophisticated Eastern types." It is widely felt in the Chicago headquarters that someone with an appreciation of the arts, a willingness to spend $600 on a tailored suit, and a preference for Montrachet over Napa Valley wine would seem "too snobbish for us in Chicago." There have been very fine candidates who happened to be from the East and reasonably cultured but not at all arrogant or snotty. These persons might have helped some of the plain Midwesterners to broaden their horizons a bit, but they were rejected, mostly, I believe, because of the insecurities of a few Midwestern executives.

Throughout my career I have advised companies and individuals not to hire so much in a current narrow image. "Enrich the mix— tolerate more individuality," I implore. When they heed this advice, they usually do so gradually and almost always are glad they became more flexible.

Deliberately not hiring people who are smarter, more competent, or higher in potential than oneself is something to watch out for in your subordinates. Some of them may feel, "Why should I bust my tail to hire someone who might grab my job?" In expanding organizations, the higher-talent individuals can afford to hire very talented subordinates, because promotions will be plentiful and having a solid back-up is essential. In fast-growing companies, it is the people of average or lower talent who constitute a ball-and-chain on growth by consciously and unconsciously undercutting the aggressive "doers" who by natural rights should run past them.

In relatively static organizations the problem is worse. Several layers of management avoid hiring people who might seem a threat to their power, influence, control, or even job security. The reason for hiring mediocrity is sometimes stated as "We would not be able to hold onto a very talented individual." That may be very true, because the mediocrities will make life miserable for highly talented individuals.

The solution to this problem must come from the top, from senior executives who will insure the recruitment and selection of high-talent individuals and who will monitor their work experiences sufficiently to make sure they are happy enough to stick around.

Hiring in one's image has been investigated. Researchers have shown that racial similarity between interviewer and interviewee results in higher ratings of competency, but no greater likelihood of recommended employment. Studies show that sex preferences exist, with men favoring men but also women favoring women as candidates for managerial jobs. Though interviewed by nonhandicapped people, physically handicapped applicants do not suffer lower evaluations from "being different."*

### Unwanted Biasing of Responses

Even very bright executives, early in their interview training, will commit the error of biasing a response at least once or twice during an interview. Instead of asking, "How did you like that job?" they will ask, "Did you like that job quite a bit?", a question that almost forces a positive response out of the interviewee. "How many hours per week have you worked during the last year?" might be transformed into, "Would you say you are a pretty hard worker?" Later, while looking at a videotape of the interview, the disadvantages of leading the witness are very apparent, because the interviewee usually hems and haws, conforms with the way the question was phrased, and leaves the interviewer puzzled as to what the responder truly believes.

Asking leading questions is only one source of unwanted bias. A more subtle, but also more lethal source is unwanted, unconscious verbal and nonverbal reinforcement of candidate behaviors or attitudes. Although some nodding, smiling, and agreeing by the interviewer is desirable in building professional rapport, the interviewer must be very careful not to reinforce systematically the attitudes or opinions that are being tested. For example, if I convey a lot of approval every time Meek Mike shows the slightest bit of assertiveness, by the end of the interview he might be grabbing me by the lapels, shouting in my face. Such behavior modification, incidentally, could be unconscious for both the interviewer and the interviewee.

*Baskett, C. D. Interview decisions as determined by competency and attitude similarity. *Journal of Applied Psychology,* 1973, **57,** 343–345. Rose, G. L., and Andiappen, P. Sex effects on managerial hiring decisions. *Academy of Management Journal,* 1978, **21,** 104–112. Rose, G. L., and Brief, A. P. Effects of handicap and job characteristics on selection evaluations. *Personnel Psychology,* 1979, **32,** 385–392.

There are times when you will want to bias the responses, such as to test a hyphothesis. "You really don't like to be supervised closely, do you?" can be a very appropriate question late in an interview if you suspect that a candidate would be very difficult to manage. Unless showing enthusiastic approval is a deliberate ploy by you, don't show shock, dismay, or surprise. If the interviewee says, "I missed the sales goal by $1 million," and you slap your forehead, lean forward, and shout "a million bucks!" the person might be inclined to clam up.

## Halo

The candidate was Phi Beta Kappa at Harvard, and I assume because of her obvious high intelligence that she must be a good planner and show very good judgment in all of her dealings with people. I could be dead wrong. Or, a person inadvertently made a wisecrack about my alma mater and therefore "must be" stupid, insensitive, and incompetent. I could be very wrong again. "Halos" can be positive or negative and put a person in a good or bad light, simply because of a reaction to one characteristic or behavior. The deduction could be correct, but there are simply insufficient data to support it. One important study showed interviewer training to be very effective in reducing halo effects.*

## Succumbing-to-Order Effects

Some interviewers tend to view interviewers more or less favorably depending upon the time of day; some are fresh in the morning and more optimistic in their view of people; others are slower and more negative in the morning. Some interviewers, in their excitement to complete a search early, view initial candidates more favorably. Others are more pessimistic, believing it very unlikely that an excellent candidate would come along early; they tend to view later candidates more favorably, perhaps out of desperation.

Studies have supported the notion that ratings of an interviewee are influenced by the quality of preceding interviewees.† The research shows that when an average applicant was preceded by two poorly

*Latham, G. P., Wexley, K. N., and Pursell, E. D. Training managers to minimize rating errors in observation of behavior. *Journal of Applied Psychology,* 1975, **60,** 550–555.
†(Carlson, 1968, 1970; Hakel, Ohnesorge and Dunnette, 1970; Rowe, 1967; Wexley, Yukl, Kovacs and Sanders, 1972; and Wexley, Sanders, and Yukl, 1973, all reported in Schmitt, N., Social and situational determinants of interview decisions: implications for the employment interview, *Personnel* Psych., 1976, **29,** 79–101)

qualified candidates, the ratings of the average candidate shot up. Conversely, when an average candidate followed two highly qualified candidates, the ratings of the average candidate plummeted. How does an interviewer combat such tendencies? Be aware of them, through training, the research indicates. Untrained managers commit contrast errors, it was found; but none of the trained managers did, even six months following training.*

## Projection

If you really want to know what an interviewer's hang-ups are, ask that person to conduct half a dozen interviews and prepare reports on them. If you see three or four interviewees criticized for having sexual attachments to goldfish, you might wonder about the interviewer who elicited such information, and your hunch would probably be right on target. We all should ask, "Are we projecting our own strengths, our shortcomings, or our needs onto an interviewee who does not have such characteristics?"

A typical pattern for insecure interviewers is to see deep-seated insecurities even in the most robust, confident, resilient candidates. A hostile interviewer might conclude there exists much hostility in interviewees who are wonderful, loving, unabrasive human beings.

The solution (here we go again!) is multiple interviews, with the interviewers able to correct each other. "Come on, Jack, what is this nonsense about the candidate's being insecure—what evidence do you have of that?" That's just the sort of mutual critique that will minimize invalid conclusions stemming from projection.

## Failure to Quantify

Statements like "I was out of work a while" or "I sometimes procrastinate" must be pinned down. Exactly how long was the person out of work—two weeks or a year? "Sometimes procrastinate" is a meaningless phrase since everyone procrastinates sometimes. It is necessary to find out exactly how often the person procrastinates, on what types of things, with what consequences. Maybe there were no negative consequences because the person scrambled to complete things on time despite procrastination. On the other hand, maybe

---

*Latham, G. P., Wexley, K. N., and Pursell, E. D. Training managers to minimize rating errors in the observation of behavior. *Journal of Applied Psychology*, 1975, **60**, 550–555.

there were disasters. Without quantification, you are left with vague gibberish.

When interviewers take their time, follow the "In-Depth Selection Interview Guide," and don't mind a couple of moments of silence while carefully recording what people are saying, "failure to quantify" is a rare error. Too many interviewers, experienced as well as inexperienced, feel obligated to keep the conversation going and consequently don't pause to think, "Do I really understand what she meant by 'a little short of quality standards'?" Later, when notes are reviewed, fuzzy, ambiguous data have the impact of a wet blanket.

The interviewer should use contemplative pauses following responses that are not 100% clear. Interviewees are not going to be the slightest bit disconcerted if you ask for clarification of what they meant by "a lot of improvement"; they will very willingly wait while you record 25% increase in quality, 75% increase in output, 127% decrease in expenses."

## Losing Control of the Interview

I'll admit to losing control of the interview only twice during my career. In both cases I permitted myself to be intimidated. The interviewees were probably smarter and more polished than the interviewer (I don't like to criticize myself in the first person); they were in extremely high demand; and my client firms were desperate to hire them. They very politely and smoothly refused to answer certain questions, pointing out that they were not sufficiently sold on joining my client organizations to disclose such information.

If you find yourself courting an individual not sufficiently sold on your organization to submit to a thorough interview, I would suggest that you put your sales hat back on, abo.·t the in-depth selection interview, and continue only if the individual shows definite interest in your position (which may be 10 minutes or 10 weeks later).If you find yourself losing control in an in-depth selection interview, take a break and reread the chapter 5 recommendations on how to regain control.

The past five chapters have examined the in-depth selection interview in considerable depth. Let's return now to the chronological steps in the hiring process and consider what to do after the in-depth selection interview has been completed; remember that the very first interviewer error was "not adhering to the basics," which include the remaining recommended steps.

# 9 | Formulating Conclusions

After three hours in an in-depth selection interview with a candidate for an executive position with his $1.5-billion manufacturing company, the president emerged from his office, warmly bade the man farewell, promised to get in touch with him very soon, and strutted confidently into the office of his vice president of human resources.

"Hire him, right away!" exclaimed the president.

"He must have made a terrific impression," commented the VPHR. "Of all the candidates we have seen for this job, what impresses you most about this fellow?"

"I'm convinced he's a seasoned, mature executive, who carefully weighs data before making important decisions. He is methodical, precise with details, and doesn't shoot from the hip. He'll be a great corporate planner!"

"OK, what should we offer him in a compensation package?" queried the VPHR.

The above scenario is enacted too many times every day, and only the names, color of carpeting on the floor, and titles differ. Did you grasp the irony, the egregious breach of logic inherent in this dialog? If not, it is probably because it is so common, and yet it is commonly unfortunate. Here is the president of a large corporation, totally committed to systematic decision-making processes in which data are carefully gathered, dissected from different vantage points, and thrown open to careful critique, in the midst of making a very important decision—whether to hire a certain executive—and this president hip-shoots! The president is most impressed with the candidate's "weighing data before making important decisions," and yet in making the hiring decision, the president is not at all careful to weigh the data. The irony would be comical if it weren't so often tragic. At the moment the in-depth selection interview is completed, there are several important steps remaining before making the accept–reject decision:

Short interviews by co-workers
Telephone record checks
Thorough review of all notes

## SHORT INTERVIEWS BY CO-WORKERS

Often in larger organizations when an applicant is called in for a thorough in-depth interview, a full day is set aside and three or four other people in your organization will each have a half-hour to an hour-interview with the candidate. From an interviewee's point of view, it is ghastly if there is not a well-organized plan for such interviews. After the fifth half-hour interview in which an ill-prepared manager says, "Tell me about yourself," interviewees are legitimately disgusted. For many companies it makes sense for major topic areas to be divvied up among three or four interviewers. Naturally, each interview will include some rapport building, but it might also be useful if each interviewer focuses on a different area, such as technical skills, career experience, management style, or immediate and long-term goals, the different parts of the full in-depth selection interview. A later pooling of these multiple perspectives will not be a substitute for an in-depth selection interview, but can produce some rich, meaningful data.

## TELEPHONE RECORD CHECKS

Most organizations make an attempt to contact previous employers of prospective applicants in search of positive or negative indicators to help make the hire/no hire decision. Trouble is, telephone record checks too often are not helpful at all. That is a shame, because some techniques exist for gleaning excellent information from them. This is an important topic, worthy of elaboration.

When managers are asked what problems occur in performing record checks, they cite such things as:

It takes too much time for me to do it personally.

Applicants give only favorable references. Everyone has a few buddies who will say only good things, so why waste time calling them?

Many companies will refer you to the personnel department, and that department will only confirm employment dates, title, and compensation—and only with written authorization of the applicant.

I rely on the search and employment firms to do record checks, even though I recognize the reports might be biased and not include negative opinions.

Even if I get to my candidate's previous superior, how do I know if what that individual tells me is accurate or biased?

When I have terminated someone, I usually feel bad about it. If a prospective employer calls, I'll tell a few white lies and just say the nice things I know about the person I fired. It would be naive of me to assume that others don't do the same.

Maybe the previous supervisor wants to do a hatchet job on the candidate, so what good are his opinions?

No time to do record checks in person, and on the phone you certainly can't build any kind of rapport, so why try?

So usually the personnel department does the record checks, and the 1 in 20 times that they come up with some really useful additional data makes the whole process worth it. After all, it was someone else's time that was wasted!

You should ask yourself a fundamental question: If you were on an airplane, sitting next to a previous boss of an applicant you are interested in, would you want to talk about the applicant? Suppose the applicant reported to your flight companion for four years, ending six months ago. If you would not want the former boss' opinions, skip this record-check section. If you would be interested, read on, because you apparently have sufficient belief in your maturity and judgment to put this supervisor's opinions in proper context. Perhaps after asking this supervisor a number of questions you will conclude, "I can see why the applicant had problems with this jerk." Chances are, however, that you will learn a few valid and useful things about the applicant; perhaps you will become more inclined to reject the applicant and perhaps you will become more inclined to hire. If you hire the applicant, having talked with the previous supervisor will probably give you some hints as to how you can most effectively manage the person.

Before suggesting techniques that permit record checks to yield very useful data, let me ask you how you respond to the typical approach some companies use in performing record checks—that is, when Mildred Lipsnitch, personnel clerk, calls, performing her 750th record check for the year:

> Hello, Mr. Rockefeller [she says to you with that telephone-operator nasality that comes only from feigning interest], I'm a personnel specialist with ACME Corporation and I'm calling to perform a record check on Ms. Smith, who is applying for a job as an industrial engineer with ACME. May I ask you a few questions about her employment with you?

Maybe you fired Ms. Smith, who is the sole support of five children, and you feel guilty enough about it to agree to talk to Mildred Lipsnitch because you might be able to help Ms. Smith get another job. (Dumb. You should refer Mildred to your own personnel department. When Ms. Smith is out of work and has five kids to feed, it may occur to her that there is nothing to lose by raising a legal stink if a poor reference prevents her being hired. Heck, maybe your company would settle for $50,000 out of court.)

Suppose you do foolishly agree to answer some questions. "What were Ms. Smith's responsibilities?" asks Mildred, obviously going through the motions and filling in the blank of some questionnaire. What a turn-off question! It probably did not surprise you to read it here, because it is so, so typical. Although I am a very strong advocate of the use of the guide for the in-depth selection interview, in telephone record checks the use of an interview guide usually sounds too trite, constrained, and bureaucratic. If Mildred Lipsnitch has to ask you what Ms. Smith's responsibilities were when she worked for you, it suggests that she doesn't know much about Ms. Smith. Asking that question could communicate to you that she is bored with the task, uninformed about this recruitment, and really doesn't much care about your response.

In short, the record-checking systems some organizations use all but guarantee shallow and misleading information. A better way exists. Suppose instead of Mildred's calling you, you get a phone call from a former subordinate (Ms. Smith), asking that you talk with someone who might call to perform a record check—Ralph Jones. Ralph calls and immediately gives his title (which usually shows he is at your level, a peer of yours) and company name. He impresses you by seeming friendly and businesslike. In a sincere way he says something like

> I'm really sorry to interrupt your day, but I have a very important decision to make, and you are one of the few people who has some information that could be pertinent. I'm considering hiring Ms. Smith for an important industrial engineering position I have available. I've spent quite a bit of time with her, and I know this is an important decision for her, since she has five kids to feed. At the same time, my division is under a great deal of pressure to make some improvements, and the industrial engineer simply must perform very well or the division and I will be in trouble. Would you be willing to answer just a few questions I have about her?"

You explain to Ralph that your company only permits the personnel department to give out record-check information, and that is limited to dates and titles. Ralph is understanding, and says, "I know—we have the same policy. But I really need a little more information if we are to hire Ms. Smith." So you agree to answer a couple of questions. "Incidentally," Ralph comments, "I will not disclose to Ms. Smith or anyone else what your comments are, and no notes from this conversation will be retained." (These promises must of course be kept!)

Isn't this a better start? Here is a guy slugging through life just as you are; he really needs your help and sounds both capable and trustworthy.

Ralph might go on to say that he has already heard a great deal about her responsibilities, accomplishments, and possible failures when she worked for you, but if you wouldn't mind, would you please just review these topics briefly in order to cover the same ground from a different perspective—your perspective. (Contrast that question with Mildred's inane, "What were her responsibilities?")

As you respond to Ralph, he may ask you to clarify a point or two, or he may relate how he feels about a matter (without biasing your responses), and you might find yourself warming up to him—he is not just going through the motions. In a few minutes he asks you, "What are Ms. Smith's strengths, assets, things you like and respect about her, both personally and professionally?" Sure, you'd be glad to list her strong points. When you run dry he asks you to elaborate on each of the strengths you listed, so that he will have a better understanding of them. This takes several minutes, and then he asks again if you can think of any additional strengths. If not, he might ask if you would include her outstanding language skills and her level of education as assets; these are both obvious and verifiable, and it impresses you that he could add several that you've overlooked.

At this point, you probably would not have regrets about granting this telephone record check, although you probably would feel a twinge of guilt about saying so many positive things about Ms. Smith, portraying her as faultless. So, when Ralph asks, "What were any shortcomings or possible areas for improvement?" you gladly give a couple. This is Ralph's technique. By drawing so many positives out of you he gets you to want to say some negatives! Maybe you say, "She wasted a little too much time chatting over coffee," and "She had a little impatience." Actually, she was extremely impatient with chains of command—she had the unfortunate habit of going around you and complaining to your superiors, which was very embarrassing. At this point, Ralph does not ask for clarification of the word "impatience," and you are relieved. Instead, he asks, "any more shortcomings? If not major ones, then perhaps minor ones?" Egads, you say to yourself, of course everyone has a lot of minor shortcomings.

"Yes," you say to him quietly, "her detail orientation was not as consistent as it should have been, and she did encounter some difficulty working with the controller." Actually, she was repeatedly sloppy with details, and you had to redo her work, and actually she blew up three times at the controller, when he politely asked her to get her reports in on time. You counseled with her repeatedly during the past year and a half, and to no avail, and that's why she was terminated. But, you haven't told Ralph any of this yet.

Yikes! Now Ralph asks you for detailed examples about each of her shortcomings. You comply. There is no choice—you mentioned four of her shortcomings, and Ralph by now knows you would not frivolously disclose negative opinions. This is no coincidence; had he stopped you and asked for clarification when you said, "She wasted a little too much time chatting over coffee," you probably would have done so, but then you would no longer have felt obligated to list further shortcomings. That's part of Ralph's technique: Get a list of negatives and then go back and get elaboration on each.

This fellow, Ralph, next describes the responsibilities, accountabilities, working climate, likely pressures and risks associated with the job, and asks you to envision if Ms. Smith could succeed or what you would recommend that he do in order to train her or in any other way help her to succeed. Even if you very much want her to get a job, if this one is such a bad fit, by the end of this telephone record check you will probably believe that you have done Ms. Smith a service by providing opinions that led to her not being hired.

Next Ralph asks the circumstances under which she left—all her initiative, all yours, or mutual? Chances are you'd tell the truth, and Ralph would listen empathically to how and why you fired her. He would finally thank you for your candor and assistance, reassure you about confidentiality, and say good-bye.

One additional technique might have been used—putting negative words in your mouth. Suppose Ralph had said, "I noticed Ms. Smith's handwriting was very sloppy, and although she said that on the job she makes it a whole lot neater, I kind of doubt it. Is it true that her handwriting is not as neat as it should be?" Suppose her handwriting was crummy; you know it and now you know that this fellow who might hire her knows it too. So you admit it. This is one of the many times in the selection process that the usual rule, "Never phrase a question in a way that might bias a response," is deliberately, meaningfully, appropriately, and necessarily violated.

Contrast Mildred's canned approach to record checking with Ralph Jones' technique of building rapport, communicating professionalism, showing interest in you, and showing sincere interest in Ms. Smith.

This approach is not guaranteed to work, but generally it does, even when there are company policies forbidding managers to say anything in record checks. By the time three or four previous supervisors have been contacted, a pattern will almost certainly occur that will give you a great deal more confidence in the accuracy of your total assessment of the individual. Who knows—perhaps business necessity would induce you to hire Ms. Smith. At least you would have a better idea of how to manage her than if the record checks had not been done the recommended way.

### How to Conduct a Record Check

Figure 14 is a summary of Ralph's techniques, the techniques recommended for you. Because in a telephone situation spontaneity and rapport are so important, I suggest once again that you do not turn this technique into an interview guide, but simply refer to the "noninterview guide" before conducting a telephone record check.

### Record Check—Who, What, and When

If a search firm and personnel department are involved and competent at conducting record checks, you can save a lot of your own time by delegating to them most of these calls. After you conduct an in-depth

1. Introduce self
2. State purpose
3. Apologize for interrupting day
4. Say how important it is for you to make correct selection
5. Ask permission to ask a few questions regarding the candidate
6. Permission granted, or if there is any wavering, make the statement that everything said will be kept in total confidence and no written records of the conversation will be kept
7. State that you have knowledge of what the candidate's responsibilities were, but ask for an explanation of them, along with accomplishments and possible failures, in order to get additional perspective
8. Ask for strengths, assets, things liked and respected about the candidate, personally and professionally. Ask for more, when the list runs out. Add any that you think are assets and have not yet been listed (in order that this person feels that the candidate is getting full credit for all assets). Obtain elaboration on strengths, so much so that the person you are talking with might become embarrassed at saying so many positive things about the candidate and want to say a negative or two to make the assessment seem more balanced
9. What were any shortcomings or possible areas for improvement? Don't interrupt—get the list of shortcomings, and only after this list has been exhausted entirely, go back to clarify and obtain specifics
10. Describe the position and person specifications (if it has not been done earlier in your conversation)
11. Put negative words in the person's mouth, in order to test your hypotheses about particular shortcomings ("Would you say that punctuality was a problem?")
12. Ask the circumstances in which the person left. Was it 100 percent the person's initiative, termination, or mutual? Would you rehire the person?
13. Close the conversation. Ask if there are any further comments, thank the individual once again for being helpful, make assurances once again regarding confidentiality, and say good-bye

**Figure 14. Telephone record check noninterview guide.**

selection interview, if you wish to pursue the candidate further, it is usually advisable for you personally to call a couple of the candidate's previous supervisors. So what if an employment specialist in your firm already called the person—if you have some lingering doubts or questions, do it again!

By conducting some record checks yourself after the in-depth selection interview, you will have an improved chance of:

Building the rapport and trust necessary to induce the previous supervisor to state honest and complete opinions (in the in-depth selection interview you ask the applicant to describe the supervisor and evaluate that supervisor's strengths and shortcomings, so you know something about the person you are calling).

Gauging the validity of the supervisor's judgments (by the time you have heard both the applicant's and previous supervisor's views of each other, you will probably be able to judge if the record-check comments are worthless, highly revealing, or something in between).

Pinpointing the applicant's specific strengths or shortcomings (by discussing certain characteristics and incidents in considerable depth).

If you cannot delegate preliminary record checking, and must do all of it yourself, be flexible! If you personally know a previous supervisor, a two-minute call before even a preliminary interview could save you a lot of time (convincing you to eliminate the candidate or, at the other extreme, to bypass the preliminary interview and conduct an in-depth interview). If you are lukewarm on a candidate after the preliminary interview, a record check or two could help you decide to proceed or not.

Never be so flexible that you fail to obtain permission (preferably in writing) of the applicant to conduct record checks. A slip-up here could land you in litigation—if your call causes the applicant to be fired for taking unauthorized time off for interviews, for example.

Efficient allocation of record-checking time might involve one record check before the preliminary interview (particularly if you personally know a previous supervisor of the applicant), one after the preliminary interview) with a different former supervisor), and two after the in-depth selection interview (including a repeat call to any supervisors you talked with previously.

Incidentally, this section has assumed that record checks would be conducted with supervisors, and the more recent the relationship the better. Occasionally, it is appropriate to contact a peer (particularly if peer relationships are important in the job you have open and you sense some problems in this area with your applicant), a subordinate (particularly if there is a highly talented subordinate who has progressed far since reporting to your applicant), or a customer (sometimes the most revealing record check for a salesperson).

How about all of the problems that managers say exist in performing record checks? Let's go back to the original list and note the appropriate responses to those concerns.

It takes too much time for me to do it in person.

Fine, then instead of conducting record checks in person, do them over the telephone.

> Applicants give only favorable references. Everybody has a few buddies who will say only good things, so why waste time calling them?

You conduct record checks, not reference checks, because what is of interest is not what the applicant's chosen references say, but what really occurred. You decide whom to call—generally immediate supervisors, and occasionally a peer or subordinate.

> Many companies will refer you to the personnel department, and that department will only confirm employment dates, title, and compensation, and only with written authorization of the applicant.

Have the prospective employee call ahead to be sure the person you want to talk with will be receptive. Then build professional rapport with the person. If you don't mind being a little deceptive, do what one client does —pretend you are probably going to hire the person and merely are calling for advice as to how best to manage him. This client claims that it works every time.

> I rely on the search firm to do record checks, even though I recognize they might be a little biased.

Fine, let the search firm do record checks, but also do three or four yourself as you approach the hire/no hire decision.

> Even if I get to my candidate's previous supervisor, how do I know if what that individual tells me is accurate or biased?

Because you've conducted the in-depth-selection interview and the record checks, and you trust your judgment, that's how. During that interview you have learned what the relationship was like from your candidate's point of view, and what that person considers the supervisor's strengths and shortcomings. By your asking a previous supervisor to comment on the same topics, you get both points of view, and you are thereby in a better position to judge what occurred and to make evaluations of the candidate's person specifications.

> When I have terminated someone, I usually feel bad about it, and if a prospective employer calls, I'll tell a few white lies. It would be naive of me to assume that others don't do the same.

Correct. It is often because previous supervisors want to say something nice about previous subordinates that they ignore their organization's record-check prohibitions. Use that to your advantage. Build rapport, and get out all of the pluses, strengths, and assets as perceived by the previous supervisor. Almost invariably the individual will then be willing to acknowledge some of your candidate's shortcomings.

> Maybe the previous supervisor wants to do a hatchet job on the candidate. What good are his opinions?

They are plenty good, in the sense of your learning the full range of perspectives regarding the candidate. Some of those perspectives may be inaccurate or unbiased, but you are smart enough to sort it all out!

> No time to do record checks in person, and on the phone you certainly can't build any kind of rapport, so why try?

It is not difficult to build rapport, following the "Ralph" guidelines described above, including the oft-repeated statement, "Do not let the question-asking sound as though a record-check form is being filled out as you talk."

Some people have had only one employer and will tell you (on the application form and in person) that you do not have permission to contact anyone with that employer. So you don't, but even in this circumstance you are not helpless. Perhaps there are some individuals (former supervisors, preferably) who have left the organization and could be contacted. If nothing else, make it very clear to the candidate that any employment offer would be contingent on "no surprises in record checks," to be done with the current employer, at a time in the selection sequence that would meet the approval of the candidate (which is usually after a formal offer of employment has been made). Making this clear (orally and in a written employment offer) to a candidate will greatly increase his candor regarding his current employment relationship.

## Thorough Review of All Notes

When the in-depth selection interview is completed, and co-workers have had short interviews with the person, and record checks have been performed, there is the tendency to leap to a final conclusion. I suggest a more thorough approach.

It is impossible for me, after thousands of interviews, to formulate a sound conclusion immediately following an in-depth selection interview, aside from what other interviews or record checks have disclosed. Before comparing notes with other interviewers, you should systematically digest your notes of the in-depth selection interview.

I always experience positive, neutral, or negative feelings as the candidate departs my office, but over the years I have come to realize that these feelings can be very misleading. Approximately 1 in 10 times, my immediate postinterview reaction is exactly the opposite of the conclusion I reach after systematically evaluating my notes.

I spend at least half an hour reviewing notes gathered in a 2½-hour interview. Until you are highly experienced at this, devoting an hour to the review might be sensible. All sorts of truths may lurk in your notes, but they may not have emerged into your consciousness during the interview, since at any given moment in time you were:

Recording the content of an interviewee's comments

Recording the context, style, and interview rhythm comments on the margin of a notepad

Anticipating the next question in the *"In-Depth Selection Interview Guide"*

Wondering if what was being said required further elaboration or probing

Trying to maintain a professional demeanor

Wondering if the individual wanted some coffee or needed to take a break

Thinking constantly about the position description and person specifications and how this individual was matching up

The process is unfortunately a bit like that of a reconnaissance pilot zooming over uncharted enemy territory, looking for camouflaged missile silos. What is noted from the cockpit might not be as useful as what is recorded by photographs. In the case of the interview, what is recorded in notes, plus what is marked on the guide, can later add up to well-developed insights.

It doesn't do the pilot much good to have the photographs, or the interviewer to have the notes, if these materials are not very carefully reviewed and analyzed. For these reasons, a number of steps are recommended:

1. *Take one careful pass through your notes, including any record-check notes (if you got permission and took them) in order to refresh yourself about all that has been said and done.*

This will permit you to add some important things that you did not record at the time, to clean up your unintelligible handwriting while you can still remember what the scratchings mean, and to start to observe the forest through the trees. A "tree" might be a job change due to a plausible disagreement with a boss; the "forest" might be a pattern in which four out of four job changes were due to disagreements with superiors. The pattern (not any one job change) suggests that the candidate has bad judgment in accepting jobs destined for problems or has some interpersonal weaknesses, or both. A "tree" might be a candidate's succeeding despite substantial obstacles; the "forest" might be a pattern of impressive successes without a significant failure despite formidable obstacles. The pattern might be far more indicative of resourcefulness, flexibility, or judgment than any single accomplishment.

2.  *Go to Appendix B ("Sample Person Specifications and Data Summary Form"), and while making your second pass through the notes, record the specifics for each person specification.*

Some firms require that this step be done in a very neat, thorough fashion with typewritten reports that will become part of a permanent file. Most business people I work with simply follow this step for their own benefit and quickly scratch out information which only they can read.

3.  *Go back to review all of your original notes again.*

Be sure that nothing important has been overlooked, that apparent inconsistencies have been resolved, and that the picture you now have of the individual is complete and coherent. This step usually takes only five minutes and can often add a little insight or clarity.

4.  *Make your ratings of the interviewee on each person specification.*

Use the "In-Depth Selection Interview Data Summary Form"(Appendix D) to do this. What constitutes 4 (excellent), 3 (good), 2 (fair), or 1 (poor) may seem like the most subjective part of the entire selection process. In reality, organizations develop their own norms and, with a little experience, the norms become very clear and disagreements tend to be about small gradations—whether the person is a 3 or a 3 −. Usually it is while the job description and person specifications were being developed that it was determined what would justify 4,3,2, or 1 ratings.

5. *Summarize your conclusions along with the independent conclusions of others who have conducted interviews on the "In-Depth Selection Interview Rating Summary Form" (Appendix D).*

This form permits you to see at a glance the extent to which here is agreement or differences of opinion regarding each person specification and the ultimate hire/no hire decision. It is worthwhile if steps 1 through 5 have been independently performed by all interviewers, so that you don't bias someone else's independent judgment and vice versa. At this point in the process, however, ordinarily all the data are in—the application form is completed, preliminary interviews have been conducted, record checks have been performed, and one or more in-depth selection interviews have been conducted, and now it is necessary to resolve any differing opinions and to achieve whatever consensus is required in the organization to confirm the judgment as to hire or not hire.

It is very worthwhile for all those who conduct the interviews to get together, if only briefly, to review each of the person specifications. Even if ratings are identical for a person specification, it is instructive to look at supportive data. Inevitably, you will have observed something someone else did not, or an unfounded bias will have crept into your conclusions or another interviewer's evaluation. Not only will the validity and reliability of the ratings improve, but sharing notes is a great way to help each improve interviewing skills.

Perhaps two interviewers feel strongly that their own data are accurate and that the other's data are incorrect. Well, it's time to gather further information—perhaps another record check or even calling the interviewee in once more for a friendly lunch in which the issue or issues can be comfortably raised and, one would hope, resolved.

## Hire/No Hire Decision

Companies ordinarily have well-oiled mechanisms for hiring decision making—who must talk to whom, who has veto power, who merely has advisory power, and so forth.

Steps 1 to 5 may sound time-consuming, but this is true only when a person is hired, and in that case, the time is extremely well spent. Contrast this approach with the scenario portrayed at the beginning of this chapter, with the company president bleating "hire him, right away!" without any of the steps taking place at all, not even superficially.

The advantages to a thorough approach to formulation of conclusions have not come from my having a compulsive nature (my professional associates who edited this book disagree, but what do they know?!) or a great affection for detail work. The conclusions have come from making mistakes—stupid, avoidable, and sometimes mortifying mistakes. It is a sad day when a person does not work out on a job and when a retrospective glance at notes recorded a year ago provide many clues as to what the problem turned out to be. But the notes were simply not reviewed carefully at that time, and such insights were overlooked. When you see where you missed important information that was right there to see, you swallow hard and commit yourself to doing a more thorough job next time.

In short, take several passes through your notes, record the data supporting your ratings, bounce your thoughts off another person who has done an in-depth interview, and you will be a hero!

## How to Tell a Candidate "No Go."

Many "no go" decisions are made at the preliminary interview stage, when nothing close to a deep relationship has been established. At that juncture, aborting the selection sequence is not often very painful for you or the applicant. You simply tell a person that the selection process is just beginning, that a number of others will be interviewed, and that within six weeks (do try to give a specific amount of time) you will contact the individual again if there is an interest in pursuing the matter further. In other words, "Don't call us, we'll call you if we are still interested."

Although I am a great believer in candor and know that feedback can be extremely valuable for a rejected candidate, until the position has actually been filled, don't do it. Even after the position is filled, don't do it unless you really like and are skilled at counseling, don't mind tears, and are willing to hear defensiveness and maybe real threats ("I'll go to your boss, to the EEOC, or to the local Action Line").

You should not explain to an applicant why he was rejected because:

You may change your mind later, after interviewing worse candidates.

The person may be offended and bad-mouth your organization.

You will devote a lot of time and effort to an explanation, and for your efforts you will probably receive only a lot of defensiveness—not constructive attitudes or behaviors.

The person may strike you with a chair (isn't it better if the person simply tears up a rejection letter six weeks later?).

Having cautioned against it, I'll admit to occasionally enjoying talking with rejected candidates after someone else has been hired, because it can be very valuable to them. People can be encouraged to get a college education, to wear more appropriate business attire, to think through their career objectives. The rejected person might be reassured by the thought that after being rejected by the interviewer's company he has nothing further to lose and might as well try to learn something. Frankly, these sorts of conversations are best done by someone outside of your organization.

# 10 | Improving Interview Skills

*We at the Duart Farquart Tennis Camp cannot teach you to play good tennis in four days; all we can do is teach you how to teach yourself gradually to improve, and then it is up to you to practice.*

*In our Playperson Sex Therapy Clinic, we cannot teach you to be a good lover, all we can do is teach you how to teach yourself to become a better lover.*

After reading this book, can you go out and conduct a more insightful selection interview, or will you have to gradually improve your skills after you practice, practice, and practice the principles put forth? Part of the answer has already been given in the introduction and chapter 1. There I suggested that most managers and executives (unlike clients of the tennis camp or sex clinic) can immediately and substantially improve their selection interviewing skills by simply doing such things as creating person specifications, religiously following the "In-Depth Selection Interview Guide," and taking a few passes through their notes after the interview.

This reassurance is only a partial answer, however. Over the years I have had the benefit of working with managers who have not been

216

content merely improving, but have made some effort to continue to refine and polish their techniques and who have become superbly insightful in interviewing. Here are some approaches that have worked well for those who wish to become superb interviewers:

1. *Practice, practice, practice.*

Conduct 100 interviews or, better yet, 500.

2. *Every third or fourth interview, ask an experienced interviewer to sit in and observe you.*

Pilots and surgeons do this, so why not interviewers?

Having a third person present can intimidate an interviewee a bit, although this need not be the case, as long as the interviewee is a relatively confident, successful, talkative individual. This question, of course, can be determined in a preliminary interview, and it would probably be best for you not to have someone observe the interview process if the applicant is very quiet or lacking in self-confidence. If there is any reason to believe that the interview will be awkward (if a very negative record check occurred, for example), it is probably advisable not to have an observer present.

Having an observer can be a very useful learning tool for all interviewers, from the completely inexperienced to the highly experienced and professional. Inexperienced interviewers usually hear comments such as, "I noticed one seven-minute period when you did not look at the interviewee at all"; "you forgot to ask the interviewee if she would like to take a break after 1½ hours"; and "you demanded clarification of the first shortcoming the interviewee mentioned in her self-appraisal, and she didn't mention any more." Biasing interview responses is a serious fault, and an observer can be very specific in noting exactly when and how this is done.

When an observer sits in with a more experienced and professional interviewer, rarely are there significant suggestions for improvement in overall style, wording of questions, follow-up on leads. However, the later discussions between the interviewer and observer focus on interpretation, and myriad subtleties in verbal and nonverbal communications are discussed.

Use the "Observer Rating Form" (Appendix H) which makes the observer's job quite easy. The observer should have reviewed the application form and have a copy of the "In-Depth Selection Interview Guide," the "Observer Rating Form," and a notebook. Half an hour is usually a minimum amount of time for the observer to be present.

3. *Observe other interviewers.*

Many of the principles in this book were gained through my observations of others. Each of us becomes somewhat enamored of our own style, and it is useful to see how other interviewers show a little bit more humor, use a little different intonation in asking a certain question, or alter the rhythm of an interview. Particularly if you have already interviewed an individual, observing another interviewer who at times seems to obtain more useful data than you did is an extremely helpful and painless way to enhance your repertoire of interview techniques.

4. *Forever continue to broaden your business knowledge and interests.*

Read everything, try everything, and constantly enter into relationships with various people in your industry, in different geographic regions and at different points in their careers. If you can use this advice to convince the IRS that pursuing your wildest fantasies is tax deductible, terrific! The point is not made facetiously, however, for ultimately your insights and conclusions are based on how you weigh interviewee behaviors and responses against all of the attitudes, opinions, impressions, and predilections which are formed from your own life experiences.

5. *Become a pop psychologist.*

Become a student of behavior, for the more you learn why people are the way they are, the more accurately you will be able to assess behavior and predict future behaviors. In the 1980's, there are all sorts of books, seminars, and courses available. Any major bookstore includes a broad range of books in the psychology section (and usually in the business section, too), and a little browsing will help you to select books that will be useful and interesting.

Selecting courses offered at colleges and universities is somewhat more difficult, because the titles are often unclear. Very useful courses have been titled "Business Psychology," "Principles of Human Behavior in Business and Industry," "Motivation Theory in the Work Environment," "Interpersonal Communications," "Organization Theory," "Principles of Supervision," "Modern Management Methods," "Organization Development," "Transactional Analysis for Business," "Minimizing Harmful Conflict in Work Situations," "Nonverbal Behavior," and "Interpreting Human Behavior." It is usually worthwhile to ask a registrar, dean, or head of the psychology or business division what sorts of practical, applied psychology courses are most enthusiastically received by students. Once people have taken a course or two at a college or university, casual discussion with other students will identify the drudge courses as well as the interesting and useful ones.

Finding good seminars to attend is also more of a problem. There are good ones around, but the selection is overwhelmingly tilted toward the impractical or dull. The titles are as varied as they are for psychology courses in colleges and universities. A seminar might be excellent one month and terrible the next because the instructor is changed.

Heads of training and development at major corporations usually have good information about at least a few seminars, and these persons are usually quite willing to spend a few minutes on the telephone with someone who is interested. The next step is to talk to the seminar instructor and to request a roster of people who attended the most recent seminar. If the instructor is unwilling to provide that information, forget it! If the names are produced, either you or your secretary can in just a few minutes on the telephone obtain all of the information you need in order to determine if that seminar would be worth your time and effort.

6. *Observe a professional psychologist conducting an interview.*

After you observe the psychologist's interview, switch places so that you are observed and coached. This is the best (and most expensive) approach to improving selection interviewing skills.

7. *Attend a selection interviewing workshop.*

Training can certainly accelerate the acquisition of effective interviewing skills, as research results suggest. For example, three researchers designed a workshop to minimize common rating errors (for example, bias and halo).* All of the errors dealt with in the workshop were reduced following the training, and improvement was sustained at least six months.

Is training important for all interviewers? No. Many managers can read a book like this one and learn and apply the principles on their

---

*Latham, G. P., Wexley, K. N., and Pursell, E. D. Training managers to minimize in the observation of behavior. *Journal of Applied Psychology*, **51**, 369–382.

own. Others find a dialog with professionals and other participants, videotape feedback, and a structured learning format to be helpful and exciting. But whatever your learning experience is, you should walk away with a powerful tool for increasing your perceptiveness with people, which will surely improve the quality of people you hire.

APPENDIX

Sample
Application
Form

# APPLICATION FORM

You are not required to furnish any information which is prohibited by federal, state, or local law.

| | | | |
|---|---|---|---|
| Last Name | First | Middle | Social Security No. |
| Home Address | | | Telephone |
| Business Address | | | Telephone |

Position applied for_____Earnings Expected $_____

## I. BUSINESS EXPERIENCE: (Please start with your present position.)

**A.** Firm _____ Address _____City_____

Kind of Business_____Employed From_____To_____
(show months as well as years)

Title _____ Initial Compensation _____ Final Total Compensation _____ ( Base _____ Bonus _____ Other _____ )

Nature of Work_____
Supervisory  Name & Title of
Responsibility _____ Immediate Superior_____

What (do) (did) you like most about your job?_____

_____

What (do) (did) you least enjoy?_____

_____

**221**

Reasons for leaving or desiring to change_____

_____

**B.** Firm_____Address_____City_____

Kind of Business_____Employed from_____To_____
(show months as well as years)

| | Initial | Final Total | Base _____ |
| Title _____ | Compensation _____ | Compensation _____ | Bonus _____ ) |
| | | | Other _____ ) |

Nature of Work_____

Supervisory
Responsibility _____

Name & Title of
Immediate Superior_____

What did you like most about your job?_____

_____

What did you least enjoy?_____

_____

Reasons for leaving_____

_____

**C.** Firm _____Address _____City _____

Kind of Business_____Employed From_____To_____
(show months as well as years)

| | Initial | Final Total | Base _____ |
| Title _____ | Compensation _____ | Compensation _____ | Bonus _____ ) |
| | | | Other _____ ) |

Nature of Work_____

Supervisory
Responsibility _____

Name & Title of
Immediate Superior _____

What did you like about your job?_____

_____

What did you least enjoy?_____

_____

Reasons for leaving_____

| Other Positions Held: a. Company b. City | a. Your Title b. Name of Superior | Date (mo./yr.) a. Began b. Left | Compensation a. Initial b. Final | a. Type of Work b. Reason for Leaving |
|---|---|---|---|---|
| D. a._____ | a._____ | a.__/__ | a._____ | a._____ |
| b._____ | b._____ | b.__/__ | b._____ | b._____ |
| E. _____ | _____ | __/__ | _____ | _____ |
| _____ | | __/__ | | |
| F. _____ | _____ | __/__ | _____ | _____ |
| _____ | | __/__ | | |
| G. _____ | _____ | __/__ | _____ | _____ |
| _____ | _____ | __/__ | | |

Indicate by letter_____any of the above employers you do **not** wish contacted.

## II. MILITARY EXPERIENCE:

If in service, indicate: Branch_____Date (mo./yr.) entered_____Date (mo./yr.)discharged_____

Nature of duties_____Overseas_____

Highest rank or grade_____Terminal rank or grade_____

## III. EDUCATION

(circle highest grade completed)

Elementary  6  7  8        High School  1  2  3  4        College  1  2  3  4  5  6  7  8

**A. HIGH SCHOOL**    Name of High School_____Location_____

Dates (mo./yr.) attended_____If graduated, month and year_____

Approximate number in graduating class_____Rank from top_____

Final grade point average_____(A = ____)  Scores on ACT_____SAT_____

Extracurricular activities_____

Offices, honors/awards _____

Part-time and summer work_____

**B. COLLEGE/GRADUATE SCHOOL**

| Name & Location | From | To | Degree | Major | Grade Point Average | Total Credit Hours | Extracurricular Activities, Honors and Awards |
|---|---|---|---|---|---|---|---|
| | | | | | (A = ___) | | |
| | | | | | (A = ___) | | |
| | | | | | (A = ___) | | |

What undergraduate courses did you like most_____Why_____

What undergraduate courses did you like least_____Why_____

How was your education financed_____

Part-time and summer work_____

Subsequent courses or studies_____

## IV. FAMILY

If any personal, financial, or family circumstances might conceivably have bearing on any aspect of job performance, explain in full_____

In the event of an emergency, whom would you wish notified (other than spouse)

Name_____

Address_____Telephone_____

Health of father_____Age_____Health of mother_____Age_____

## V. PHYSICAL DATA

Condition of Health:_____Date of most recent physical exam_____

Weight_____Height._____Vision _____

What physical handicaps or limitations do you have_____

List any serious illnesses, operations, accidents or nervous disorders you may have had with approximate date:

## VI. ACTIVITIES:

Membership in professional or job-relevant organizations (Exclude racial, religious and nationality groups)_____

_____

Publications, patents, inventions, professional licenses or special honors or awards_____

_____

## VII. AIMS:

What qualifications, abilities, and strong points will help you succeed in this job_____

_____

_____

_____

_____

What income would you need (in today's dollar value) in order to live the way you would like to live? (Your response will not be taken as dissatisfaction with your present salary, but refers to the salary which you ultimately wish to attain.)

_____

Willing to relocate? Yes_____ No_____ Any restrictions_____

Amount of overnight travel acceptable_____

What are your plans for the future_____

_____

_____

_____

_____

_____

_____

I authorize all schools, credit bureaus and law enforcement agencies to supply information concerning my background. I understand that I have a right to request disclosure of the nature, scope, and results of such an inquiry. I understand that if any statement herein is not true, an offer of employment may be withdrawn.

_____
Signature

_____
Date

# Sample Person Specifications and Data Summary Form

**Position:** **Computer Services Sales Representative, with promotion to Branch Sales Manager within one year.**

Rating Scale:  4 = Excellent, 3 = Good, 2 = Fair, 1 = Poor, and
0 = Very Poor

## INTELLECTUAL CHARACTERISTICS

Rating

**\*\*_____** **1.** *Level of Intelligence:* Preferably above average intelligence, compared to college graduates. Applicant need not be a genius (4), but must be quite bright (3). Average intelligence compared to people in general (2) is insufficient.

\*\*The most important person specifications

(data explaining rating)

_____

_____

_____

_____

_____ **2.** *Analytic Ability:* Ability to analyze problem situations in depth and make decisions in a methodical, systematic, and decisive manner. Should show solid, rational judgment. Prefer (4) level; (3) is minimum expected. (2) level would include impulsivity, indecisiveness, or shallowness to a significantly negative degree.

_____

_____

_____

_____

_____ **3.** *Ability to Diagnose Client Needs:* Proven experience in quickly and accurately determining client needs and valuable sales opportunities. (3) is minimum expected, *or else* definite potentials to become at least a (3) within one year of being hired.

_____

_____

_____

_____

_____ **4.** *Creativity/Innovativeness:* Ability to generate new ideas and solutions to problems. Prefer (3) level or better.

_____

_____

_____

_____

_____ **5.** *Pragmatism:* Ability to generate practical, sensible, realistic solutions to problems. (3) or better required.

_____

_____

_____

_____

_____ **6.** *Intellectual Flexibility:* Ability to juggle several projects simultaneously, to think both concretely and abstractly, and to deal with complexity and diversity in technical and business matters. (3) or better expected in all subcategories.

_____

_____

_____

_____

_____ **7.** *Oral Communications Skills:* Ability to communicate effectively, one-on-one, in meetings and in public speaking contexts. Fluency, "quickness on one's feet," clarity, organization of thought processes, and command of the language are all important. (3) or better for each subcategory preferred; potential to become at least (3) within one year is required.

_____

_____

_____

_____

_____ **8.** *Written Communications Skills:* Ability to write clear, precise, well-organized memos, letters, and proposals, while using appropriate vocabulary, grammar and word usage, and creating the appropriate "flavor" (desired image). (3) or better preferred, *or else* potential to achieve (3) within one year required.

_____

_____

_____

_____

_____ **9.** *Education:* College graduate with demonstrated orientation toward continued acquisition of new knowledge. (3) level (accredited bachelor's degree) or equivalent in demonstrable knowledge required. (4) Graduate degree from fine school desirable.

_____

_____

_____

_____

\*\*_____ `10.` *Experience—Technical:* (4) level is four or more years of experience as programmer or systems analyst (preferably with data base solutions). (3) level is three years, (2) is two years, (1) is one year, and (0) is less than one year of technical experience. Data processing *sales* experience is considered half as valuable as programming/systems analysis experience on *this* specification, so six years of computer sales with no programming experience would constitute a (3). A (2) level is minimum expected.

_____

_____

_____

_____

\*\*_____ **11.** *Experience—Sales:* Two years of sales experience necessary (computer-related sales strongly preferred, although high level intangible sales considered necessary). (4) is four years of experience, (3) is three years, (2) is two years, (1) is one year, and (0) is less than one year of sales experience.

_____

_____

_____

_____

**\*\*_____**     **12.** *Experience—Management:* One year (1) of management experience minimum expected, although two years (2), three years (3), or four years (4) are desirable.

_____

_____

_____

_____

## PERSONAL MAKEUP

**_____**     **13.** *Initiative/Resourcefulness:* Actively seeks out opportunities to make a contribution, rather than passively accepting situations. (3) is minimum requirement.

_____

_____

_____

_____

**_____**     **14.** *Self-Objectivity:* Awareness of one's strengths and shortcomings. Takes responsibility for shortcomings rather than blame others excessively for failures or show excessive defensiveness. (4) preferred, (3) minimum expected.

_____

_____

_____

_____

_____    **15.** *Perseverance:* Ability and willingness to "hang in there" to successful completion, despite obstacles. (3) level minimum expected.

_____

_____

_____

_____

_____    **16.** *Independence:* Ability to operate successfully without constant supervision. (3) level minimum expected, unless strong trend toward (3) level within one year.

_____

_____

_____

_____

**_____    17.** *Standards of Performance:* Self-discipline; maintenance of realistically high standards in terms of quality; intellectual integrity. (4) level preferred; (3) minimum required.

_____

_____

_____

_____

**_____    18.** *Track Record:* A "winner" with a history of success. History of *repeated* failures with "good excuses" is probably not acceptable. Recent track record is weighed most heavily. (3) level minimum required; (4) level strongly preferred.

_____

_____

_____

_____

_____    **19.** A *"Doer"*: Action- and results-oriented. Does not just talk but follows through. (4) level strongly preferred.

_____

_____

_____

_____

**\*\***_____    **20.** *Emotional Maturity/Stability/Resilience:* Remains emotionally in control, honest, and productive under pressure from competition, time scarcity, personal problems, requirements by supervisors, or other factors, does not make "flighty" decisions or excessively "lose one's cool." Positive self-concept. Able to "take rejection" while maintaining effectiveness. (3) level strongly preferred.

_____

_____

_____

_____    **21.** *Administrative Abilities:* Planful, well-organized, effective in time management, and sufficiently detail-oriented. Schedules, handles budgets, coordinates, keeps priorities in line, and maintains appropriate records so as to complete projects on time. (3) level expected; (2) acceptable only if strong trend toward (3).

_____

_____

_____

## INTERPERSONAL RELATIONS

_____    **22.** *First Impression (Impression made in first 30 seconds of interaction):* Favorable bearing and demeanor. Professional in attire and manner. Demonstrates warmth, outgoing personality, and confident attitude. (4) or (3) strongly preferred, although (2) could be acceptable if compensating qualities exist.

_____

_____

_____

_____

_____ **23.** *Interpersonal Flexibility:* Ability to win the liking and respect of others; cooperative; ability to deal successfully with a broad range (education level, age, experience, etc.) of people; friendly; not petty. (3) level strongly preferred.

_____

_____

_____

_____

_____ **24.** *Assertiveness:* Ability to be strong, take control, and dominate, if necessary and appropriate, without being excessively abrasive or hostile. (3) preferred; (2) minimum required.

_____

_____

_____

_____

_____ **25.** *Team Player:* Willingness to cooperate with superiors without competing harmfully with peers. (3) preferred; (2) minimum required.

_____

_____

_____

_____

_____ **26.** _Enthusiasm:_ Although some sales people and some managers are very successful in a low-keyed manner, the ability to at least sometimes show charisma, energy, and excitement are worthwhile. (3) or (4) strongly preferred.

_____ **27.** _Empathy:_ "Tunes in" accurately to the feelings, needs, and attitudes of others; understands the impact of one's own behavior on others; good listener. (3) or better strongly preferred.

_____ **28.** _Leadership:_ Ability to inspire people to follow. It is expected that the Sales Representative will be promotable to Sales Manager within a year (or so). (3) minimum preferred, but (2) minimum acceptable.

_____ **29.** _Management—Recruitment/Selection:_ Record of success in recruitment; effective selection interviewer and record checker. (3) preferred.

___ **30.** *Management—Training/Development:* Record of successfully training people for current assignments and developing people for promotion to positions in which they succeeded. Delegates enough to stretch people yet not overwhelm them. (3) minimum preferred.

___

___

___

___

___ **31.** *Management—Goal Setting:* Record of setting clear, fair, challenging goals *with* subordinates, using MBO (Management by Objectives) or comparable approach. (3) minimum preferred.

___

___

___

___

___ **32.** *Management—Monitoring Performance:* Record of knowing what subordinates are doing in sufficient depth to "spot" emerging problems early without "oversupervising." (3) minimum preferred.

___

___

___

___

___ **33.** *Management—Performance Feedback:* Record of providing clear, thorough, positive (praise and recognition) performance feedback on a day-to-day basis within the context of high performance standards; thorough, sensitive annual performance appraisals conducted; ability to be demanding when appropriate. (3) minimum preferred.

_____

_____

_____

_____

_____ **34.** *Management—Removing Nonperformers:* Record of removing, through demotion, transfer, or termination, "hopelessly" incompetent performers—those who have repeatedly
failed to meet agreed-upon performance standards after
extensive training/coaching attempts. (3) minimum
preferred.

_____

_____

_____

_____

_____ **35.** *Management—Team Development:* Record of achieving
highly cohesive, effective (in achieving task goals) team of
subordinates. Team "climate" characterized by open, honest,
mutually supportive communications and relationships in
which differences are constructively resolved rather than
ignored, suppressed, or denied. (3) minimum required.

_____

_____

_____

_____

## MOTIVATIONS AND ASPIRATIONS

**\*\***_____ **36.** *Motivation Level:* Demonstrated ability and willingness
to maintain high activity level. Compelling desire to succeed.
Although hours per se are less important than results, most
Branch Sales Managers say the complexity and frequency of
communications require 65 hours or more per week. (4)
desirable, although (3) minimum expected.

---

---

---

---

_____ **37.** *Health:* Does not have health problems that may seriously affect attendance or productivity. (3) level minimum required.

---

---

---

---

_____ **38.** *Ambition:* In addition to showing a high level of motivation for the current job, the individual will preferably show a desire to move upward in management (4 or 3).

---

---

---

---

_____ **39.** *Willingness to Take Risks:* Willingness to "go for the big sale," within the bounds of realism. (2) level (cautious) could be acceptable. (4) corresponds to a bold but successful risk taker rather than an extreme risk taker.

---

---

---

---

**\*\***_____ **40.** *Interests Compatible with Company Expectations:* In order for an individual to succeed, it is important that the individual's needs (for money, recognition, affiliation, achievement, prestige, promotion, power, location, amount and type of travel, family orientation or whatever) are consistent with the opportunities within this company. (3) level minimum requirement.

_____

_____

_____

_____

# In-Depth Selection Interview Guide

**IN-DEPTH SELECTION INTERVIEW GUIDE**

Name of Interviewee:_____(Called_____)

Interviewer:           _____ Date:_____

**Use of the Interview Guide**

1.  Use a hard back binder, with 8½ by 11 pad of paper on the right and a pocket to hold the application form (and other pertinent documents) on the left. The *In-Depth Selection Interview Guide* is usually placed on top of the pad for use. When the Interview Guide does not provide enough space for notes, it is moved to the left side of the binder, to permit reference to the questions, and notes are taken on the pad on the right side.

2.  Arrange the interview area so that notes can be taken inconspicuously. Either sit behind a desk or, if you sit next to the interviewee, allow at least 3½ feet between the two of you.

3.  Prior to the in-depth selection interview, review the application

form once again for supplemental questions you might want to ask. Read this *Guide,* adding or deleting questions (if she was not in the military, obviously skip that section) and modifying any wording to suit this particular interview. This review will also help refresh your memory regarding the sequence and wording of questions, and thus ensure a smoother interview.

4. *Introductory Comments.* Naturally, the introductory comments should be tailored to the specifics of the situation—how many interviews the individual has had, how much time you expect to spend in the interview, and so on. It is usually appropriate to spend several minutes on professional rapport-building "idle chit-chat," before "getting down to business." It is useful to give the individual some idea of the time frame (2 hours, 3 hours, or whatever), and to state the purposes of the interview. You might say something like, "I've asked you to come in for (several hours) today to:

Review your background, interests, and goals, in order to determine if there is a good match with the position and opportunities at (this company), to...

Determine some ways of smoothing the transition from your current job to (this company), should we offer a job and you accept it, to...

Get some ideas regarding what we or you can do in order to maximize your growth and long-range fulfillment and contributions, and to...

Tell you more about (this company) and answer any questions you might have, following this interview.

## A. Education

So that I can get a good feel for your background—your education, work experience, and the like—let's *briefly* go back to your high school days and come forward chronologically, up to your current work situation. Then we'll talk about your plans and goals for the future.

### High School

1. I see from the Application Form that you attended _____(high school), graduating in _____(year). Would you please give me a general rundown on your high school years. I'd be interested in

knowing what the school was like, what you were like back then, the curriculum, what you did with your time, how you did in school, any high and low points, and so forth. (If the answers to this general question are incomplete, ask the remaining questions in this section.)

2. Give me a feel for what kind of school it was. (If necessary, specify large/small, rural/urban, cliquish, etc.).

3. What was your curriculum (general, technical, college preparatory)?

4. What school activities did you take part in?

5. What sort of grades did you receive, and what was your class standing?

6. How would you describe your study habits?

7. Tell me about those subjects you did best in and those most difficult for you. (Follow-up question: What was there about those subjects that appealed to you or were more of a problem?)

8. How would you describe your social life during high school? (Accepted or rejected by peers?)

9. Were there any class offices, awards, honors, or special achievements during your high school days?

10. What were high points during your high school days? (If necessary, clarify what were the most rewarding, happy, or successful occurrences during those years, both in school and out of school.)

11. What were low points, or least enjoyable occurrences, during your high school days?

12. Give me a feel for any jobs you held during high school—the types of jobs, whether they were during the school year or summer, hours worked, and any high or low points associated with them. (If the person did not work during the summer, ask how the summer months were spent.)

13. (TRANSITION QUESTION) What were your career thoughts toward the end of high school, and what did you do?

*Note:* Transition Questions in life that involve choices—what to do, when, how to go about it—are very revealing, not only about the individual at the time those choices were made, but about the person's current attitudes regarding those transition decisions and values. So, probe very thoroughly whenever major life directions were altered.

## College

Now about your college days. Would you give me the same sort of highlights about those years as you did for high school. (Ask the following questions to obtain complete data not included in answers to the general "smorgasbord" question.)

1. What college did you attend, and why was that particular school selected? (If more than one school was attended, ask this and subsequent questions about each one.)
2. What sort of curriculum did you focus on? (Follow-up: Exactly what majors did you have, and why were there any changes in majors?)
3. What sort of campus activities did you get involved in? (Follow-up: What was your level of involvement—passive, leadership, or what?)
4. What was your final grade point average? (Follow-up: Did you earn any academic honors or encounter scholastic problems at any point? If academic performance was rather weak, inquire whether any courses were failed, or if the person was on scholastic probation or suspended at any time.)
5. Tell me about your strong and weak subjects. (Probe for specifics.)
6. How would you describe your study habits during college? (Look for clues as to amount of effort expended.)
7. Please give me a feel for any work experiences you had during college—the types of jobs, whether they were during the school years or summers, hours per week worked, and any high or low points. (If not active in campus activities, and there were no work experiences, determine how spare time during the school year was spent and how summer months were spent.)
8. Have you gotten involved in any subsequent formal education? (Determine specifics of graduate work, correspondence courses, workshops, seminars, etc.)
9. What were high points during your college days?
10. What were low points, or least enjoyable occurrences, during your college days?
11. (TRANSITION QUESTIONS) What were your career thoughts toward the end of college? What did you consider doing and how did it work out (joining such and such company, going on to graduate school, or whatever was the case)?

## B. Military Service

Note from the Application Form if time was spent in the military. If not, and the interviewee is male, ask:

1a. How did it happen that you had no military obligation to fulfill?
     If time was spent in the military, say:
1b. Give me a brief account of your time in the military (Ask subsequent questions in this section in order to determine specifics.)
2.  Where were you trained and later stationed?
3.  Basically what were your duties?
4.  Tell me about your rate of advancement? (Probe for specifics if faster or slower than typical.)
5.  What were your accomplishments during the service? Did you receive any awards, honors, or decorations?
6.  What were any significant failures or mistakes made?
7.  Were there any disciplinary actions, reprimands, or reductions in rank? (If so, ask for details. Don't ask minorities this question.)
8.  What were your thoughts about making the military a career?
9.  (TRANSITION QUESTIONS) What were your thoughts toward the end of your military career? What did you consider doing and how did it work out (joining such and such a company, attending college, or whatever was the case)?

## C. Work History

*Note:* If the work history is extensive, cover the early jobs more quickly (obtaining where the person worked, dates, responsibilities, and high and low points), in order to leave maximum time for discussing more recent positions.

Now I would like for you to tell me about your work history, starting with your first full-time job after your school years and working up to the present. There are a lot of things I would like to know about each position. Let me tell you what these things are now, so I won't have to interrupt you so much. Of course I need to know the employer, dates of employment, your titles, and salary history. I would also be interested in knowing what your expectations were for each job, whether they were met, what major challenges you faced and how they were handled, and what were the most and least enjoyable aspects of the jobs. I also want to know what you feel were your greatest accomplishments and significant mistakes or disappointments, what each supervisor was like and what you would *guess* each supervisor really felt were your strengths and weaker points. Finally, I would like to know the circumstances under which you left each position. Now, will you please go back to your first full-time position and work chronologically to the present?

*Note:* If the person worked for a single employer and had, say, three jobs with that employer, consider each one of those a separate position, for which *all* of the following information must be gathered.

1. What was the name of the employer? (Get a "feel" for the organization by asking about volume sales, number of employees, products or services, and profitability.)
2. What were the dates of employment?
3. What were your expectations for the job, and to what extent were those expectations met?
4. What were the starting and final levels of compensation?
5. What was your job title?
6. What were your responsibilities and accountabilities, and what results were achieved?
7. What were the major challenges and problems facing you in the position, and how were they handled?
8. All jobs seem to have their pluses and minuses; what were the most enjoyable or rewarding aspects of this job?
9. What were the least enjoyable aspects of the job?
10. To what extent did luck—that is, fortunate or unfortunate circumstances beyond your control—enter into your record of performance?
11. We all make mistakes; what would you say were the most significant mistakes or failures that you made on this job?
12. What was your supervisor's name and title? Where is that person now? (Note a subtle threat that you will conduct a record check).
13. What was it like working for (him/her) and what were (his/her) strengths and shortcomings, from your point of view?
14. What would your best guess be as to what (supervisor's name)

really felt were your strengths, weaker points, and overall performance?

15. What were the main reasons for your leaving? People usually have several reasons for making a job change. *What were some of the other factors that contributed to your leaving?* [Try to get beyond planned answers and rationalizations, and determine the *real* reasons. Seek out not only circumstances—a promotion, a company going bankrupt, and so on—but how the interviewee *felt* about the circumstances, what career options were considered, and what the person felt were the advantages and disadvantages of the various options. Also probe for what others (supervisors, spouse, etc.) felt about the various options.]

*Note:* When it is learned what the "next job" was, a useful question is, "Would you please tell me *what you did, how you did,* and *how you liked it?*"

16. (TRANSITION QUESTION) I think we have pretty well covered your work history, so let's talk about the future.


## D. Plans and Goals for the Future

1. What are you looking for in your next job? What is important to you, what do you wish to avoid, what are your various options, and how do you feel about each one?

2. What about five years down the road; where do you expect to be by then?

3. What would you like to be doing ultimately, careerwise?

4. What do you want to do with your life, aside from your career?

## E. (This Company)

1. How did you hear about the position at (this company)?

2. It may be premature to ask this, but at this time what is your best understanding of what the position consists of, and how does it differ from other positions you might be interested in?

3. What do you view as advantages or possible advantages of joining (this company)?

4. What do you view as disadvantages or possible disadvantages of joining (this company)?

## F. Self-Appraisal

1. OK (name), now what I would like you to do is to give me a thorough self-appraisal, beginning with what you consider to be your strengths, assets, things you like about yourself, and things you do well. (Usually it is worthwhile to ask follow-up questions, and to urge the person to continue. For example, you might say such things, as, "Good," "Keep going," and ask supplemental questions such as:

   "What other strengths come to mind?"

   "What are some other things you do well?"

   "What sorts of problems do you seem to handle best?"

   Obtain *lists* of strengths and then go back and ask the person to elaborate on what was meant by each strength listed—"conscientious," "hard working," or whatever.)

2. OK, let's look at the other side of the ledger for a moment. What would you say are shortcomings, weaker points, or areas in which you hope to improve? (Be generous in your use of the pregnant pause here. Urge the person to list more shortcomings by saying such things as, "What else comes to mind?" "Keep going, you are doing fine," or just smile and nod your head and wait. When the person has run out of shortcomings, you might ask supplemental questions such as:

   "What personal characteristics do you have that sometimes interfere with the way you work?"

   "What three things could you do that would most improve your overall effectiveness in the future?"

   Obtain as long a *list* of negatives as you can with minimal interruptions on your part, and *then* request clarification. If you interrupt the individual for clarification of one, there might be so much time spent on that one negative that the individual will be very hesitant to acknowledge another one.)

## G. Management

### Management for People Who Have Had Previous Management Experience

1. How would you describe your management philosophy and style?
2. What would you suppose that subordinates have felt have been

your strengths and shortcomings, from their points of view? (Note: this is another subtle threat that you just might contact some subordinates.)

3.  In what ways might you want to modify your approach to dealing with subordinates?

4.  Could you give me a paragraph or two about each one of your subordinates, indicating their title, how long they have worked for you, what are their strengths, shortcomings, and overall performance? Have you promoted or removed anyone from any of those jobs? (Note: You might want to ask that question for a couple of positions. Before you leave this section, make sure you have a good feel for how many people were recruited and selected, what approaches were used, how the people were trained and developed, how each worked out, and for those who did not work out well, what happened with them.)

### Management for People Who Have Not Had Previous Management Experience, But Who Might Want To in the Future

1.  What do you suppose would be your management style and approach, and how would your managerial behaviors differ from those of other managers?

2.  What would be your best guess as to what subordinates that you may have in your first managerial job will consider your strengths and shortcomings?

### H. Work Habits

1.  How would you describe your work habits? (Fill-in with the following questions in order to complete this section.)

2.  Describe a typical work week, from the time you get up Monday morning to the time you are done for the week. (Look for organization, pace, etc.)

3.  How many hours do you work in a typical week?

4.  How would you describe the pace at which you work—fast, slow, moderate, or if it varies, under what circumstances?

5.  How do you typically handle yourself under stress and pressure? Describe yourself in terms of emotional control. What sort of

things irritate you the most or get you down, and how do you handle such pressure?

6.  How would you size up your intellectual resources? Do you see yourself as below average, average, a genius, or what?

7.  What is it that motivates you?

8.  What sort of problems or work situations are most likely to cause you trouble?

9.  How well organized are you, and in what aspects of your work do you tend to be inefficient or a bit neglectful?

10. How would you describe your decision-making style—systematic, thorough, impulsive, rational, intuitive, or what?

11. Give some examples of the most important decisions you have made during the past three years, and how they have worked out?

12. What do you find to be the most difficult types of decisions to make? Why?

13. How would you describe your planning and budgeting methods, and how have they worked out?

## I. Technical Expertise

*Note:* Since by this point in the interview you have reviewed the individual's complete work history, you may feel that you have an excellent understanding of the person's technical strengths and shortcomings. Most interviewers, however, feel that it is worthwhile to put together a supplemental list of technically oriented questions, the answers to which will add a bit more depth and clarity. Experienced interviewers, with a great deal of technical expertise, sometimes ask the question, "What are your strengths and any areas for improvement in technical areas," and then spend 3 or 30 minutes in free-flowing, unstructured interview. Others prefer to be more systematic, extrapolating from the job description a series of questions which will organize this line of questioning (several examples are given in Appendix E.) Using this approach, the opening comment is:

1.  In order to be sure that I have a thorough understanding of your technical/professional abilities, I'm going to read a list of topic areas and ask that you rate your current level of competence on a scale of Excellent, Good, Fair, or Poor, and then summarize for each area your education, courses, seminars, personal readings, experiences, and what you consider to be major strengths or areas for improvement in each.

## J. Final Self-Analysis Questions

1. How does the first impression made differ from the way you *really* are? How would three or four people who know you well describe you?

2. How do your behaviors, attitudes, and personality differ on the job versus off the job?

3. How would you describe your mood swings; how high or low are they; with what intervals do they occur; what seems to contribute to the highs or lows, what impact has there been on job performance?

4. How often do you become angry, and why? Have you lost your temper on the job during the past year? (If so, get details.)

5. What troubles you most about yourself?

6. What changes in your personality would you like to see come about during the next few years?

7. What sorts of people do you enjoy working with most? (Probe for specifics at the superior, peer, and subordinate level.)

8. [Review each person specification and if there are doubts about your assessment of the candidate, read the specification, ask for a self-rating (on a scale of excellent, good, fair, or poor), and request elaboration/specifics to explain and justify the self rating.]

## K. Wrap-Up Question

1. Are there any questions I have not asked regarding your abilities, goals, strengths, or shortcomings which I should have asked in order to get to know you or your potentials for compatibility and success in the position we are discussing?

## ADDENDUM

These are sensitive questions, to be asked only by highly experienced interviewers and *never* of protected groups (minorities, etc.).

## L. Family Background (Sensitive)

1. Now I would like to get away from the job for a moment and ask you about some other areas briefly. What circumstances in your early home background have contributed to the way you are

today—your interests, motivations, strengths, shortcomings, hopes, values, or whatever might be *pertinent* to the job?

2. What was your parent's main advice to you when you were growing up and to what extent have you followed it?

3. How would you describe your father—perhaps when you were growing up? In what ways would you say that the two of you are similar or dissimilar?

4. How would you describe your mother—perhaps when you were growing up? In what ways would you say that the two of you are similar or dissimilar?

## M. Home Life (Sensitive)

1. Are there any circumstances centering around your home life—your marriage, children, personal finances, or whatever—which might have a direct bearing on your effectiveness with (this company)? (If so, probe.)

## N. Recreations and Avocations (Sensitive)

1. What type of social activities do you (and your spouse) get involved in?

2. What hobbies and interests do you have?

3. Tell me about your reading habits. (Be specific about work-related reading habits—what publications read, how thoroughly, etc.)

4. How many hours of television do you watch during the typical week?

## O. Health (Sensitive)

1. Have you had any major illnesses, accidents, operations, or nervous disorders that might have a direct bearing on your performance with (this company)? (If so, ask for specifics, but be sure to arrange for a medical examination.)

2. Do you have any handicaps or physical limitations that might have a direct bearing on your performance with (this company)? (If so, ask for some specifics, but be sure to arrange for a medical examination.)

3. How many days have you missed from work during the past year because of ill health? (If more than two or three, obtain details.)

# Sample In-Depth Selection Interview Rating Summary Form

# In-Depth Selection Interview Rating Summary Form

Position: Sales Representative

Rating Scale: 4 = Excellent, 3 = Good, 2 = Fair, and 1 = Poor. (Note: pluses and minuses may be used.)

Date of Application: _____

Name of Applicant: _____

| Dimension | Rater #1: | Rater #2: | Rater #3: | Rater #4: | Rater #5: | Rater #6: |
|---|---|---|---|---|---|---|
| **Intellectual Characteristics** | | | | | | |
| 1. Level of intelligence | | | | | | |
| 2. Analytic ability | | | | | | |
| 3. Ability to diagnose client needs | | | | | | |
| 4. Creativity/ innovativeness | | | | | | |
| 5. Pragmatism | | | | | | |
| 6. Intellectual Flexibility | | | | | | |

251

| Dimension | Rater #1: | Rater #2: | Rater #3: | Rater #4: | Rater #5: | Rater #6: |
|---|---|---|---|---|---|---|
| 7. Oral communication skills | | | | | | |
| 8. Written communication skills | | | | | | |
| 9. Education | | | | | | |
| 10. Experience—technical | | | | | | |
| 11. Experience—sales | | | | | | |
| 12. Experience—Management | | | | | | |
| **Personal Makeup** | | | | | | |
| 13. Initiative/ Resourcefulness | | | | | | |
| 14. Self-objectivity | | | | | | |
| 15. Perserverance | | | | | | |
| 16. Independence | | | | | | |
| 17. Standards of Performance | | | | | | |
| 18. Track record | | | | | | |

| | | | | | | | | | | |
|---|---|---|---|---|---|---|---|---|---|---|
| 19. A "doer" | | | | | | | | | | |
| 20. Emotional stability/resilience | | | | | | | | | | |
| 21. Administrative abilities | | | | | | | | | | |
| **Interpersonal Relations** | | | | | | | | | | |
| 22. First impression | | | | | | | | | | |
| 23. Interpersonal flexibility | | | | | | | | | | |
| 24. Assertiveness | | | | | | | | | | |
| 25. Team player | | | | | | | | | | |
| 26. Enthusiasm | | | | | | | | | | |
| 27. Empathy | | | | | | | | | | |
| 28. Leadership | | | | | | | | | | |
| 29. Management—Recruitment/selection | | | | | | | | | | |
| 30. Management—training/development | | | | | | | | | | |

| Dimension | Rater #1: | Rater #2: | Rater #3: | Rater #4: | Rater #5: | Rater #6: |
|---|---|---|---|---|---|---|
| 31. Management—goal setting | | | | | | |
| 32. Management—monitoring performance | | | | | | |
| 33. Management—performance feedback | | | | | | |
| 34. Management—Removing nonperformers | | | | | | |
| 35. Management—team development | | | | | | |
| **Motivations and Aspirations** | | | | | | |
| 36. Motivation | | | | | | |
| 37. Health | | | | | | |
| 38. Ambitious | | | | | | |
| 39. Willingness to take risks | | | | | | |
| 40. Compatibility of interests | | | | | | |

# Supplemental Person Specifications for Technical Specialties

## Bl. SUPPLEMENTAL DIMENSIONS OF TECHNICAL/PROFESSIONAL COMPETENCE FOR RETAIL STORE MANAGER*

In reviewing the technical/professional competence of a candidate for retail store manager, the interviewer might find it worthwhile to ask the interviewee to rate his/her overall competence and knowledge, on a scale of Excellent, Good, Fair, and Poor with respect to some or all of the following dimensions, and to request a thorough explanation of any courses, seminars, and experience in each area:

achieving sales goals
in-stock/out-of-stock conditions
rotation and price marking
creating effective displays
support of sales plans
space allocation (planograms)

*Supplemental interview questions can be devised from these dimensions.

gross profits

shrink control

inventory control

productivity (measured in terms of sales per man-hour and labor percent)

work scheduling

store standards (cleanliness, orderliness, etc.)

customer relations

controllable expenses

store contribution

planning and organization

training and development of subordinates

employee relations

employee turnover

laws/ordinances affecting stores

community involvement

## B2.  SUPPLEMENTAL DIMENSIONS OF TECHNICAL/PROFESSIONAL COMPETENCE FOR HUMAN RESOURCES (PERSONNEL) VICE PRESIDENT*

recruitment (use of advertisements, use of search firms, skill in reviewing application forms, skill in conducting telephone interviews, skill in "selling" the organization to candidates)

selection (skills and techniques in conducting in-depth selection interviews)

training (one-on-one coaching, stand-up training—how many of what sessions conducted with what subjective and objective results)

development (what sorts of career development programs designed and implemented; what has been the record of preparing subordinates for promotion)

compensation (wage and salary administration, compensation surveys, job evaluations, sophisticated reward/incentive programs, executive compensation, how much administrative experience versus actual design experience)

*Supplemental interview questions can be devised from these dimensions.

benefits (knowledge of ERISA, pension/insurance programs, alcohol/credit counseling services; how much design versus administrative experience)

human resources (manpower) planning (what systems designed or administered); computerized personnel systems including performance appraisals, psychological appraisals, attitude survey results; growth situations versus cutbacks in labor force

union avoidance

labor relations (grievances, arbitration, contract negotiation, decertification)

organization development climate (attitude/opinion surveys), team development, intergroup conflict resolution, quality circles

## B3. SUPPLEMENTAL PERSON SPECIFICATIONS OF TECHNICAL/PROFESSIONAL COMPETENCE FOR SALES MANAGER*

general approach to marketing and marketing planning

presales call planning

ability to initially establish rapport

trial closings

ability to close a sale

aggressiveness (soft sell, consultative, pushy, etc.)

closeness with clients

ability to handle conceptual sales

writing skills (letters and formal reports)

verbal abilities (vocabulary, grammar, clarity of expression, fluency, enthusiasm)

technical knowledge of products

telephone solicitation habits and style

formal "stand up" speaking skills

(The interviewer might find it worthwhile to actually "role play" a sales call by having the interviewee "sell" something to the interviewer.)

---

*Supplemental questions can be devised from these dimensions.

## B4. SUPPLEMENTAL PERSON SPECIFICATIONS OF TECHNICAL/PROFESSIONAL COMPETENCE FOR INDUSTRIAL ENGINEER*

organization analysis
work simplification
MTM
other predetermined time systems
time study
ratio delay analysis
quality control
safety eng·neering
business economics
planning/scheduling
methods engineering
production processing
process chart procedures
motion study
materials handling
labor standards
performance rating
maintenance controls
wage-incentive plans
job evaluation
production control systems
inventory control procedures
budget analysis
critical path scheduling
plant layout
location analysis
operations research
office methods and systems
work sampling
statistical analyses

*Supplemental interview questions can be devised from these dimensions.

## B5.  SUPPLEMENTAL PERSON SPECIFICATIONS OF TECHNICAL/PROFESSIONAL COMPETENCE FOR PLANT MANAGER*

manufacturing: direct labor, productivity (assembly time per order), rework (labor to direct hours)

quality: scrap rate, returned goods as percentage of monthly sales, tolerances achieved

inventory: turns, out of stocks, supply on hand, cost of maintaining inventory

production control: percent master schedule achieved, percent machine capacity, percent delivery dates met, actual to forecasted number of products, time to process orders

purchasing: cost for each dollar produced; value of orders in dollars

engineering: number of estimates per month; backlog; stan-dardizations

sales: new orders; backlogs, gross margins

administration expenses: as percent of sales

traffic: average time (hours) to process materials; frieght costs

personnel: turnover rate, labor as percent of sales, amount of overtime

---

*Supplemental interview questions can be devised from these dimensions.

# F | Catalog of Characteristics from Which Person Specifications Can Be Derived

## INTELLECTUAL CHARACTERISTICS

1. *Level of Intelligence.* What level of native intelligence must the individual possess? Is it necessary that the individual be above average in intelligence in comparison with college graduates, average in comparison with the population at large or what?

2. *Functional Intelligence.* Aside from "native intelligence" how adept is the person at making sound business judgments, in combining experience, education, and "native intelligence?"

3. *Ability to Learn Quickly.* In academic situations, or from real life experiences.

4. *Logical Ability.* Ability to form logical judgments, to mentally organize data. Is a mind like a "steel trap" necessary, or are the logical demands so minimal that only "obvious" logical conclusions would be required?

5. *Analytic Ability.* Ability to analyze problem situations in depth; ability to show a probing mind that sorts the "wheat from the chaff." How incisive or probing must the individual be?

6. *Number Facility.* Must the individual be a mathematical wizard, a competent statistician, or a financial analyst, or is it only important that the individual be able to perform basic mathematical calculations?

7. *Literal vs. Abstract Thinking.* Is there an acceptable balance between concrete, literal thinking and the ability to deal in abstract, conceptual terms? What degree of each characteristic is desired or necessary?

8. *Precision with Detail.* How necessary is it that the individual be precise, detail-oriented, and exact? Is it necessary that the person be punctilious or just conscientious in dealing with detail?

9. *Creativity.* Ability to generate truly original ideas or solutions to problems.

10. *Innovativeness.* Ability to borrow from and/or modify accepted or available approaches in order to meet the requirements of the current situation.

11. *Systematic Decision Making.* Ability to make decisions in a methodical, systematic, and orderly fashion.

12. *Foresight.* Ability to stand back, anticipate ramifications, and plan as opposed to acting before thinking.

13. *Pragmatism.* Ability to generate practical, sensible, and realistic solutions to problems.

14. *Decisiveness.* Ability to sort through available data and perhaps incomplete data, and to make a decision quickly, versus procrastinating until all the facts are in, ponderously "chewing on" problem situations excessively, or simply failing to act.

15. *Intuition.* Ability to make "hunchy" intuitive decisions.

16. *Favorable Balance in Decision Making Approaches.* Ability to be decisive, reflective, systematic, foresighted, or intuitive as appropriate.

17. *Intellectual Flexibility.* Ability to juggle several projects simultaneously, to cope successfully with diversity and complexity, to integrate seemingly unrelated data, and to reduce complex notions into relatively simple terms.

18. *Appreciation of Different Points of View.* Ability to see issues from various points of view as opposed to seeing things only one's own way.

19.  *Memory.* Ability to store facts, figures, names, and faces for later use. Lack of absentmindedness or forgetfulness.

20.  *Written Communications Skills.* Ability to write memos, letters, and reports in a clear, concise fashion with appropriate vocabulary, grammar, and word usage.

21.  *One-to-One Communications Skills.* Ability to communicate effectively with superiors, peers, subordinates, and others on a one-to-one basis, using appropriate vocabulary, grammar, and word usage. Clarity, organization of thought processes, and expressiveness are all part of this dimension as is an ability to think quickly "on one's feet." Articulate, fluent.

22.  *Thinking Quickly On One's Feet.* Ability to hold his or her own in conversation.

23.  *Meeting Participation Skills.* Ability to participate effectively as a member of a decision-making or problem-solving group, articulate thoughts clearly, show a good sense of timing (when to say something and when to be quiet), and to contribute to cohesiveness and effectiveness of the group.

24.  *Meeting Conduct Skills.* Ability to actually *run* effective meetings, in which good results are achieved through a well-organized, mutually supportive, efficient group effort.

25.  *Intellectual Honesty.* Ability to regard facts as facts, without self-interests, biases, or prejudices interfering with good judgment. Ability to think independently—to have the courage of one's convictions despite possible political or other consequences.

26.  *Intellectual Curiosity.* Thirst for knowledge, desire to learn new or better approaches; hunger for mastery, quest to see interrelationships among different bodies of knowledge.

27.  *Receptivity to Change.* Ability to cope successfully with change and to welcome fresh approaches, as opposed to being stuck in an intellectual rut.

28.  *Mental Drive.* Level of intellectual vigor; desire to search for new or better solutions rather than passively accepting old ways or waiting for problems to fall in one's lap.

29.  *Educational Background.* Appropriate amount of formal education, specified in terms of credit hours, grade point average, and "quality" of the institutions.

30. *Technical Knowledge.* How complete is mastery of certain knowledge areas? Is a person current and up-to-date in areas of technical knowledge?

31. *Breadth of Knowledge.* Does the individual have the range of knowledge and interests necessary for the position in question?

32. *Specific Experience Requirements.* Years of experience in the function or industry.

33. *Other "Credentials."* Completion of requirements such as CPA, completion of American Institute of Banking Program, or other certifications, registrations, and professional standards.

34. *Methods of Intellectual Mastery.* Aside from intellectual curiosity, what has the person done in terms of formal education, reading habits, seminar participation, and so on in order to stay abreast of one's field and "up-to-date" in related fields.

35. *Rationality.* Ability to control emotions and defense mechanisms so as to make rational, dispassionate judgments.

## PERSONAL MAKEUP

36. *Emotional Maturity/Stability.* Takes responsibility for one's feelings, behaviors, and life occurrences in general. Calm, even-tempered. Continually growing in perspective of life; has a sense of proportion of life and an integrated value system. Not burdened with *excessive* emotional insecurity, anxiety, nervousness, feelings of inferiority, fearfulness, mood swings, helplessness, frustrated needs, rebelliousness, rigidity, irrational hatreds, or ego needs.

37. *Emotional Resilience.* Under pressure from time scarcity, personal problems, requirements by superiors, competition or other factors, remains emotionally in control, honest, and effective on the job. Ability to take rejection and criticism without becoming excessively defensive. Does not overreact to situations. Not too "thin skinned." Emotional flexibility: ability to bend with situations.

38. *Self-Objectivity.* Awareness of one's strengths and shortcomings, potentials, psychological needs, hangups, prejudices, and biases.

39. *Openness to Criticism.* Willingness to actively solicit, comprehend, and take appropriate action to constructive criticism.

40. *Self-Development Orientation.* Proven effort and degree of accomplishment in maximizing strengths and overcoming shortcomings.

41. *Personal Life in Order.* Favorable relationships with family, spouse, neighbors, and friends; personal finances in order; good balance in terms of outside interests.

42. *Competence.* Has the ability to perform the job satisfactorily.

43. *Successful Track Record.* A "winner" with a history of overcoming obstacles to success. Failures with "good excuses" are not ordinarily acceptable. Recent record of performance is weighted most heavily.

44. *Initiative/Resourcefulness.* Actively seeks out opportunities to make a contribution rather than passively accepting situations.

45. *Developmental Potentials.* Has as-yet undeveloped capabilities.

46. *Hard Worker.* Willing to work X number of hours per week, work overtime when needed, and work on weekends as required.

47. *Welcomes Challenges.*

48. *Adaptable to Change.*

49. *Sense of Urgency.*

50. *Self-Discipline.*

51. *Persistence.* Does not give up.

52. *Aggressiveness.* Pushes, though not in a hostile manner, to successful completion of tasks.

53. *Competitiveness.*

54. *Self-Confidence.* Though not excessively egotistical.

55. *Courage.* Willing to take reasonable risks.

56. *Positive Attitude.*

57. *Good Humored.*

58. *Is a "Doer."* Action and results-oriented.

59. *Patient.*

60. *Solid Administrative Abilities.* Constantly plans for the short- and long-term; well-organized; good attention to detail.

Schedules, coordinates, and keeps priorities in line. Keeps appropriate records and has a good filing system.

61. *Professionalism.* High standards of performance, intellectual integrity, and conscientious. Pays attention to details.

62. *Efficient in the Use of Time.*

63. *Productivity.*

64. *Honest/High Integrity.* Behaves ethically and in accordance with accepted moral standards; not deceitful or excessively self-serving.

65. *Reliability.* Can be counted on to follow through to successful completion of tasks.

66. *Absence of Job-Hopping.*

67. *Independence.* Ability and willingness to operate without constant supervision. Absence of passivity and dependency. Not in need of constant reassurance.

## INTERPERSONAL SKILLS

68. *Interpersonal Flexibility.* Ability to deal with varied types of people in a broad range of circumstances; not rigid or stubborn; willing to yield when someone else is "right."

69. *Extroversion.* Warm, outgoing, friendly personality; cordial and amiable.

70. *Self-Confidence.* Positive self-image; not excessively arrogant or cocky; not excessively deferent or obsequious.

71. *Likable.* Able to win the liking of people; easy to talk with.

72. *Respected.* Able to earn the respect of people.

73. *Tolerance of Individuality.* Able to accept and respect people despite differences in values, appearance, or behavior.

74. *Optimally Assertive.* Able to be forceful, strong, aggressive, and dominant without being excessively offensive, hostile, or abrasive. Not readily intimidated; willing to defend one's opinion; not excessively "soft" or vulnerable.

75. *Team Player.* Willingness to work with people at all levels to promote the common interest; cooperative yet not a "yes man."

76. *First Impression.* Able to make a favorable first impression in terms of appropriate attire, physical appearance, bearing, manner, and posture.

77. *Ability to Sell.* Convincing, persuasive, and credible; able to initially impress and also win the long-term confidence and trust of people.

78. *Expressiveness.* Animated, colorful, lively in expression, versus dry and boring.

79. *Dynamic Personality.*

80. *Charismatic.*

81. *Good Sense of Humor.*

82. *Competitiveness.* Strong instinct to win.

83. *"Streetwise."* Shrewd in dealing with people; not naive or gullible.

84. *Empathy.* Ability to "tune in" accurately to the feelings and needs of others; aware of what one's image is among others and what is the impact of one's behavior.

85. *Listening Ability.* Knowing when to talk and when to listen; able to communicate thorough understanding of other people's points of view.

86. *Humility.*

87. *Loyalty.* Able to maintain long-term commitments and loyalty to friends, employers, and co-workers.

88. *Political Ability.* Able to perceive political forces and to deal with them effectively.

89. *Conflict Resolution Skills.* Willingness and ability to surface and resolve differences of opinion.

90. *Personality Depth.* Able to relate with people below surface levels; not shallow or superficial.

91. *Receptivity.* Willingness to accept other's advice, opinions, and criticisms.

92. *"Old Shoe".* Able to wear well with people over time.

93. *Consistent.* Not flighty, "up and down," or harmfully unpredictable with people.

94. *Sincerity.* Openness and directness in dealing with people; not phony or glib; absence of lying or deceit.

95. *Trustworthy.* Able to be trusted and to hold confidences; discreet.

96. *People-Oriented.* Generous, kind, and helpful, with genuine regard for other people.

97. *Social Sensitivity.* Well mannered, polite, gracious; able to carry on "chit-chat" as appropriate.

98. *Acceptance of Authority in Superiors.* Not a rebel who unreasonably fights legitimate authority in others.

99. *Language Ability.* Able to communicate effectively one-on-one, in small groups, and in making formal speeches. Good voice quality, vocabulary, grammar, word usage, eye contact, inflections, volume, and expressiveness.

100. *Aloofness.* Able to maintain "professional distance" from co-workers, clients, and other business associates.

101. *Executive Stature.* A presence suggesting the air of a seasoned diplomat.

102. *Management Skills.* Ability to achieve excellent results through subordinates, ability to successfully recruit, conduct selection interviews, place people, give clear direction, train, coach, develop people for promotion, build cohesive and effective teams, achieve positive and productive "working climates," monitor performance thoroughly, delegate effectively, give constructive on-going performance feedback, conduct effective annual performance appraisals, and invite criticism from subordinates.

    Willing and able to transfer, demote, or terminate subordinates who have failed to achieve reasonable and agreed-upon goals after a fair and reasonable amount of time for training, and after such efforts have failed.

    Ability to inspire cooperation, mold opinion, and influence behavior.

    Low tolerance for mediocrity, high standards of excellence.

    Both people and results-oriented; appropriately participative, consultative, or autocratic, as the situation demands.

    Available when needed.

    Trusted and respected by subordinates.

    Inspirational.

## MOTIVATIONS AND ASPIRATIONS

103. *High Motivation Level.* Must be highly motivated to succeed, short-range and long-range.

104. *Values and Interests Consistent with the Job.* The job content, growth opportunities, geographic location, travel demands, achievement, power, financial rewards, recognition, prestige, and affiliation opportunities within the position in question; not power-hungry, requiring too much money, or having higher needs for satisfaction which are not apt to be filled on the job.

105. *Realistic Goals/Aspirations.*

106. *Clear Goals/Aspirations.*

107. *Well Integrated Goals.* Not ever-changing, knows what is wanted out of life and work.

108. *Willingness to "Roll Up the Sleeves" and Help Out.*

109. *High Aspirations.* Wanting to move beyond the position in question.

110. *Self-Motivated.*

111. *Balanced Personal and Work Lives.*

112. *Social/Community Involvement.*

113. *Family Oriented.*

114. *High Energy Level.*

115. *Sense of Urgency.*

116. *Very Good Health.*

117. *Ability to Manage Stress Well.*

118. *Willingness to Take Risks.*

119. *Appropriate Balance.* Between conservativeness/caution and venturesomeness/boldness.

120. *Ability to Work with Routine Matters.*

121. *Consistency of Motivation.* Not ever-changing or constantly up and down.

122. *Spouse/Family.* Helpful and supportive, rather than blocking or a hindrance.

123. Willing to operate within established corporate policies.

# APPENDIX G1 | Quick Screen Interview Guide for Retail Store Clerk

Overall Rating: _____ Excellent

_____ Good

_____ Fair

_____ Poor

_____ Very Poor

Name _____ / _____ / _____ _____
              last              first            MI          Interviewer

Date _____ Store or area preference _____

First position choice _____ Second position choice _____

Hours available: AM _____ afternoons _____ evenings _____ nights _____ weekends _____

LIMITATIONS _____

What are you looking for in a job? _____

Why are you interested in working for this company? _____

|  | YES | NO |
|---|---|---|
| Age 18 or older | —— | —— |
| Similar work experience | —— | —— |
| Transportation available | —— | —— |
| Returning veteran | —— | —— |
| Previously employed by the company (if so, is person eligible for "rehire") | —— | —— |
| Relative employed by the company (in urban areas, cannot work in same stores as a relative) | —— | —— |
| Wages acceptable (what are your compensation requirements?) ——————— | —— | —— |

Grooming/Appearance —— excellent —— good —— fair —— poor

Comments ————————————————————

Personality —— excellent —— good —— fair —— poor

Comments ————————————————————

Communication skills —— excellent —— good —— fair —— poor

Comments ————————————————————

## Further Comments

_____

_____

_____

_____

_____

_____

_____

## Dispensation

_____ Continue _____ Reject

_____ Credit check _____ Reject

_____ Record check _____ Reject

_____

_____

_____

272

# Retail Store Clerk Interview Guide

Interviewee Name: _____

Interviewer Name: _____     Date: _____

## A. Education—High School

I'd like to get a feel for your work experiences, job interests, and education, starting with your high school days.

I see from your application form that you attend(ed) _____
High School, graduating in _____ (year). I'm interested in knowing about your grades, activities and high and low points.

1. Final grade point average _____

2. Activities (any leadership positions?) _____

_____

3. High points (awards, honors) _____

_____

4. Low points _____

(Note: summer or parttime jobs covered in Section C).

## B. Education—College

I notice on your application form that you attend(ed) _____
(school) from _____ to _____ (dates ) and completed a _____ degree. Please tell me about your college days in terms of grades, activities, and high and low points.

1. Grades (A = 4.0 or what) _____

2. Activities (any leadership positions?) _____

3. High points (awards, honors) _____

4. Low points _____

## Work History

(*Note:* If candidates have held no full-time jobs, the following data sheets can and should be completed for part-time jobs, starting with the present job and moving back in time, covering as many jobs as seems appropriate. Military service can be considerd another "job.")

I have a pretty good feel for your education. Let's talk now about your work history. I'd be interested in knowing about various work experiences, starting with your (current) (most recent) job and working back in time. I'd like to know several things—what were your work responsibilities, accomplishments, any challenges, high and low points, and what your immediate supervisor really felt were your strengths and any weaker points.

275

## WORK HISTORY FORM (CURRENT OR MOST RECENT JOB)

Employer _____ Dates (month/year) _____

Location _____ Type of business _____

_____

Title _____ Dates with Title _____

Salary (Starting) _____ Final _____

Expectations _____

_____

_____

Responsibilities/Accountabilities _____

_____

_____

Successes/Accomplishments _____

_____

_____

Failures/Mistakes _____

_____

_____

Most Enjoyable _____

_____

Least Enjoyable _____

_____

Continued on next page

Work History Form (cont'd)

Luck_____

Reasons for Leaving_____

_____

_____

## TORC

| | |
|---|---|
| Supervisor's name | Title |

| | |
|---|---|
| Where now | Permission to contact? |

Appraisal of Supervisor

   His/Her Strengths_____

_____

   His/Her Shortcomings_____

_____

Best guess as to what he/she really felt at that time were your

| Strengths | Shortcomings |
|---|---|
| | |
| | |
| | |
| | |
| | |
| | |
| | |

Overall Performance_____

_____

Continued on next page

## WORK HISTORY FORM (NEXT MOST RECENT JOB)*

*NOTE:  Add as many forms as jobs held

_____
Employer                    Dates (month/year)

_____
Location                    Type of business

_____


_____
Title                       Dates with Title

_____
Salary (Starting)           Final

Expectations_____

_____

_____

Responsibilities/Accountabilities_____

_____

_____

Successes/Accomplishments_____

_____

_____

Failures/Mistakes_____

_____

_____

Most Enjoyable_____

_____

Least Enjoyable_____

_____

Continued on next page

Work History Form (cont'd)

Luck_____

Reasons for Leaving_____

_____

_____


## TORC

_____
Supervisor's name                    Title

_____
Where now                            Permission to contact?

Appraisal of Supervisor

  His/Her Strengths_____

_____

  His/Her Shortcomings_____

_____


Best guess as to what he/she really felt at that time were
your

| Strengths | Shortcomings |
|---|---|
|  |  |
|  |  |
|  |  |
|  |  |

Overall Performance_____

_____

## D. Plans/Goals

What do you hope or expect to be doing 3, 5, or 10 years from now?

3 years _____
5 years _____
10 years _____

## E. Self-Appraisal

I'd like a comprehensive self-appraisal, starting with what you consider your strengths, assets, things you like about yourself, and things you do well.

What are your weaker points, liabilities, or possible areas for improvement?

Assets                          Liabilities

(Note to reader: Allow full page for Assets and Liabilities)

## F. Job Requirements

(Interviewer describes the job(s) in terms of hours, physical requirements, pay, and so on.)

What do you suppose the advantages or disadvantages of working for HEB might be?

Advantages _____

Disadvantages

## G. Supplemental Questions

1. Have you been late for work during the past year?

2. How would you describe your level of knowledge for the position in question?

Experience

Training

3. Are there any circumstances surrounding your home life, health, interests, finances, or anything we have not talked about that may have a direct bearing on your effectiveness in the job?

# APPENDIX H

# Observer Rating Form

Interviewer _____ Interviewee _____

Observer _____ Date _____

Number of Minutes Observed _____

Rating Scale: 4 = Excellent, 3 = Good, 2 = Needs Improvement, 1 = Good Grief, N/A =
Not observed *and* would not have been appropriate or useful in interview.

## Initial Rapport Building

**Rating**

1. Greeting (warm, friendly, smile, handshake)     _____

   Comments: _____

2. Offered something to drink     _____

   Comments: _____

3. "Idle chit chat" (not too short or too long; got     _____
   interviewee talking comfortably)

   Comments: _____

4. Purposes and timing expected     _____

   Comments: _____

5. Mechanics (appropriate seating, all forms handy, notebook used, private)   |

  Comments: _____

## Throughout the Interview

1. All appropriate questions in Interview Guide asked, without substantially altering the wording   |

  Comments: _____

2. Eye contact (minimum of 20%, but no staring unless purposefully to intimidate)   |

  Comments: _____

3. Friendliness, warmth, enthusiasm   |

  Comments: _____

4. Maintaining control   |

  Comments: _____

5. (Apparent) sincerity   |

  Comments: _____

6. Thoroughness of notes taken on content and context (determined after interview)   |

  Comments: _____

7. Unobtrusiveness of note taking

   Comments: _____

8. Follow-up question (asked and asked with appropriate wording and style; quantification of vague responses)

   Comments: _____

9. Absence of (unintended) biasing of question responses

   Comments: _____

10. Interviewee talks 90% (A), 80% (b), 70% (C), less than 70% (D)

    Comments: _____

11. Appropriate vocabulary level

    Comments: _____

12. Voice clarity

    Comments: _____

13. Vocal range (not monotone)

    Comments: _____

285

14. Expression (interested, friendly, half smile; not blank, not excessive frowning)

Comments:_____

15. Interview pace (not too fast or too slow)

Comments:_____

16. Use of applicant's name (once every half hour minimum, but more than once every quarter hour excessive)

Comments:_____

17. Show approval of openness or when interviewee is obviously proud of an unambiguous accomplishment

Comments:_____

18. Protect interviewee's ego (use of "weasel words" rather than unintended bluntness)

Comments:_____

19. Controlling shock, dismay, or surprise

Comments:_____

286

## Interview Probes

1. Thorough summary (at least one per hour)

   Comments:_____

2. Pregnant pause

   Comments:_____

3. Affirmation of understanding ("I see")

   Comments:_____

4. Echo (repeating all or part of a question)

   Comments:_____

5. Active listening (reflecting interviewee's unstated feelings) so as to deepen understanding and professional rapport

   Comments:_____

6. Direct question (usually used when softer approaches have failed)

   Comments:_____

7. TORC Methods

   Comments:_____

# Index